This fascinating book marks an important step forward in our understanding of the diffusion of Western economics in East Asia since the seventeenth century up until modern times. This is not simply a story about the adoption of Western economic doctrines, but about their adaptation to different cultural habitats and political and economic needs and their confluence with domestic economic and philosophical thought. The attention focuses on China, Japan, Korea and Malaysia and the doctrines of Adam Smith, Friedrich List, Karl Marx, John Maynard Keynes, Friedrich August von Hayek and Joseph Schumpeter. Under the guidance of Malcolm Warner a set of leading international experts succeeded in elaborating a remarkably thorough and highly instructive work. Against the background of the stunning economic growth in recent decades of some of the countries covered, the book touches also upon the intriguing question of whether there is a relationship between economic views held by politicians and economic advisers, on the one hand, and the economic performance of nations, on the other. This book is a must for economists, historians of economic thought, economic historians, political scientists and sociologists interested in the transmigration of economic ideas and concepts.

Heinz D. Kurz, *Emeritus Professor of Economics, University of Graz* and
Graz Schumpeter Centre, Graz, Austria

This edited book by Professor Malcolm Warner, a long-time observer of the Asian scene, is a must read for all who seek to understand *what*, *why* and *how* economic principles and concepts that originated in the West have influenced development and growth in select Asian countries, including China and Japan. The chapters shed important insights on why certain principles have been more readily embraced by the Asian countries under consideration and how they are translated into action in these economies.

Rosalie L. Tung, *Ming and Stella Wong Professor of International Business,*
Simon Fraser University, Canada

The story of how economic analysis as developed and practised in Europe and North America has spread to the rest of the world has not been systematically told. That spread was sometimes gradual with fits and starts and sometimes extremely rapid, but today 'Western economics' dominates the curriculum of universities all over the world but particularly in Asia. Economic policy there is largely analysed and practised using these tools, not always wisely to be sure. *The Diffusion of Western Economics Ideas in East Asia* is a major step forward in explaining how this diffusion of economic ideas occurred. It is a fascinating piece of intellectual history that has had a profound impact on how East Asian societies operate today.

Dwight H. Perkins, *Harold Hitchings Burbank Professor of Political Economy,*
Emeritus in the Faculty of Art ˙ *Sciences, Harvard University,*
Cambridge, MA, USA

T0341158

East Asia comprising China, Japan, South Korea, Taiwan, etc. has been dubbed the world's most dynamic economic region, having sustained high growth for over 50 years. Yet surprisingly, the region has no equivalents to such great Western economists as Adam Smith, Karl Marx or John Maynard Keynes, whose ideas and concepts had profoundly influenced many Asian scholars and leaders. Mao Zedong had once said when he died he would be happily going to meet Karl Marx. China's most distinguished premier, Zhu Rongji, had also likened his 'Macroeconomic control' policy to Keynesian demand management.

Clearly, there is no such thing as Eastern Economics vs Western Economics. It is all about how major Western economic thought and theory had been transmitted to the East and how they were embraced in the academic and political circles.

This book, edited by Malcolm Warner, promises fascinating reading to those who want to follow how many great Western economic ideas have been diffused in East Asian societies under different historical and institutional settings – even more importantly, how they have impacted the modernization and transformation of these societies.

John Wong, *Professorial Fellow and Academic Advisor*
(formerly Director, Research Director) of the East Asian Institute,
National University of Singapore, Singapore

The Diffusion of Western Economic Ideas in East Asia

This book examines the diffusion of economic ideas in East Asia, assessing the impact of external ideas on internal theory and practice. It considers economists from Adam Smith onwards, including Marx, Keynes, Hayek and contemporary economists, and covers the subject historically, as well as including present day and likely future developments. The book covers all the major countries of East Asia, and pays particular attention to specific economists who have had a strong impact in specific countries, and to important developments in economic theory in East Asia, exploring how far these have been driven by Western economic ideas.

This book will be welcomed by students and scholars of East Asia and South-east Asia, politics and political theory, as well as by those interested in economics, economic history and management.

Malcolm Warner is Professor and Fellow Emeritus, Wolfson College, Cambridge and Cambridge Judge Business School, University of Cambridge, UK.

Routledge Studies in the Growth Economies of Asia

The Diffusion of Western Economic Ideas in East Asia

Edited by Malcolm Warner

Routledge
Taylor & Francis Group

LONDON AND NEW YORK

First published 2017 by Routledge

2 Park Square, Milton Park, Abingdon, Oxfordshire OX14 4RN
711 Third Avenue, New York, NY 10017

Routledge is an imprint of the Taylor & Francis Group, an informa business

First issued in paperback 2018

British Library Cataloguing in Publication Data
A catalogue record for this book is available from the British Library

Library of Congress Cataloging in Publication Data
Names: Warner, Malcolm, editor.
Title: The diffusion of Western economics in East Asia / edited by
Malcolm Warner, University of Cambridge.
Description: Abingdon, Oxon ; New York, NY : Routledge, 2017. |
Series: Routledge studies in the growth economies of Asia ; 137 | Includes
bibliographical references and index.
Identifiers: LCCN 2016039030 | ISBN 9781138925243 (hardback) |
ISBN 9781315681290 (ebook)
Subjects: LCSH: Economics–East Asia–History. | Economics–History. |
East Asia–Civilization–Western influences.
Classification: LCC HB126.E18 D54 2017 | DDC 330.1095–dc23
LC record available at https://lccn.loc.gov/2016039030

ISBN: 978-1-138-92524-3 (hbk)
ISBN: 978-0-367-02691-2 (pbk)

Typeset in Times New Roman
by Wearset Ltd, Boldon, Tyne and Wear

Contents

Illustrations

Figures

Tables

Contributors

Bernadette Andreosso-O'Callaghan, Jean Monet Professor of Economics, University of Limerick, Limerick, Ireland and Professor of East Asian Economics, Ruhr-Universität Bochum, Bochum, Germany.

Steve Cohn, Charles W. and Arvilla S. Timme Chair in Economics, Knox College, Galesburg, Illinois, USA.

Dilip K. Das, President, Institute for Research on Global Economy and Business, Toronto, Canada; lately Professor of International Economics and Finance and Director of the Institute of Asian Business, SolBridge [*sic*] International School of Business, Woosong University, South Korea.

Fuqian Fang, Professor of Economics, Renmin University, Beijing, PRC.

Xinyuan Feng, Professor at Graduate School of Chinese Academy of Social Sciences and Cathay Institute for Public Affairs, Beijing, PRC.

Hoon Hong, Professor of Economics, Yonsei University, Seoul, South Korea.

Hongyi Lai, Associate Professor, School of Contemporary Chinese Studies, University of Nottingham, Nottingham, UK.

Weisen Li, Professor of Economics, Fudan University, Shanghai, PRC.

Qunyi Liu, Associate Professor of Economics, Peking University, Beijing, PRC.

Mark Metzler, Professor of History and Asian Studies, University of Texas–Austin, Austin, Texas, USA.

Tadashi Ohtsuki, Lecturer, Gunma University, Maebashi, Japan.

Rajah Rasiah, Professor of International Development, University of Malaya, Kuala Lumpur, Malaysia.

Tatsuya Sakamoto, Professor of the History of Social and Economic Thought, Keio University, Tokyo, Japan.

Richard J. Smethurst, Professor of History Emeritus, University of Pittsburgh, Pittsburgh, Pennsylvania, USA.

Liang Sun, Lecturer, School of International Business, University of Foreign Languages, Dalian, PRC.

Paul B. Trescott, Professor of Economics Emeritus, Southern Illinois University, Carbondale, Illinois, USA.

Malcolm Warner, Professor and Fellow Emeritus, Wolfson College and Cambridge Judge Business School, University of Cambridge, Cambridge, UK.

Michael Webber, Professor Emeritus in Geography, University of Melbourne, Melbourne, Victoria, Australia.

Kiichiro Yagi, President, Setsunan University, Osaka, Japan, formerly Professor of Political Economy, Kyoto University, Kyoto, Japan.

Jin Zhang, Fellow of Wolfson College and University Lecturer in International Business, Cambridge Judge Business School, University of Cambridge, Cambridge, UK.

Ying Zhu, Professor and Director of the Australia Centre for Asian Business, University of South Australia, Adelaide, South Australia, Australia.

Preface

This edited book will critically examine *the diffusion of Western economic ideas in East Asia*, a topic which we believe needs to be more extensively covered by scholars of modernity in this increasingly important part of the global economy. Whilst a limited number of books have dealt with the spread of modern economic concepts worldwide on a broad cultural front, for example, very few have dealt with this theme comparatively vis-à-vis Asia in the main and East Asia in particular.

The main themes of the book will be seen through the eyes of a team of specialists in the field who know the economics of the region – and the selected countries within it – very closely. The authors who know their respective subjects in detail are based in a wide number of campuses, both inside and outside Asia. Many of them are scholars at the Professorial level and a few are Emeritus.

The contributors are mostly economists but others are historians of Economic Thought, Economic Policy or Management; the approach we encouraged them to take would be *interdisciplinary*. Many of the authors have for some years now published widely in their specialist fields in the history of Economic Thought across different countries and cultures, say on China or Japan or elsewhere. Potential contributors were asked to commit themselves to producing a specialized chapter for this particular book, based on their respective expertise and ongoing research.

The collection is intended to be an up-to-date account of the 'state of play' with respect to the impact of exogenous ideas in Economics on indigenous theory and practice. The treatment of the subject matter we hope will be not only *historical* but will also extend to *contemporary* developments. It is hoped that it will fit in with a number of existing Routledge series relating to Asian economics, the history of Economic Thought and other associated fields of study.

The work will concentrate on the spread of Western Economic Ideas over the last three centuries, from Adam Smith (1723–1790) from the eighteenth century onwards, to later theorists such as Karl Marx (1818–1883) and Friedrich List (1789–1846) in the nineteenth century, as well as John Maynard Keynes (1883–1946) and Friedrich Hayek (1899–1992) in the last century, amongst others, then on to contemporary economists and how all these have affected theory and practice in the present day.

The book will start with an introductory chapter by the Editor, setting out a framework for the subject matter to come. The next section deals with long-term issues and themes relating to the diffusion of Western Economic Ideas in East Asia in general, as well as by country, including coverage of China, Japan, Korea, amongst others respectively. After this, the work of specific economists, whose work relates to the countries involved, is introduced. A good example to put forward here is a chapter on Adam Smith and China, as well as that specific author and Japan. After such contributions on individual economists, several further chapters deal with a set of wider issues and themes, relating to the developments at the end of the last century and in the present one, such as China's economic, business and management reforms after 1978.

Although each chapter author was given a specific brief regarding the focus of the contribution, we have allowed them all a reasonable degree of leeway with respect to the content and the approach adopted. In some of the early chapters, there was, for example, a varying degree of emphasis on the respective economic backgrounds, the economic policies adopted and the specific Western economists whose work has been adapted to the national circumstance in question. The choice of specific foreign economists to cover was, also, largely eclectic, and the treatment sometimes idiosyncratic, with allowances made for the preferences of the authors we approached and their willingness to agree to write a chapter. We valued originality, vividness and scholarship above all. The issues and themes chosen for the discussion section were also chosen using the above criteria.

The 'devil is in the details' and this volume has indeed plenty of detail, to say the least. All in all, we hope that the final product will shed light on this fascinating phenomenon of economic ideas diffusing from West to East and how they were adapted in specific contexts of *time* and *place* in the countries concerned.

Acknowledgements

It would be ungrateful not to acknowledge my debt to the 'Cambridge Circus' who taught me Economics in the post-Keynesian years, particularly those with an interest in China, most notably Joan Robinson (1903–1983) who had visited it more than a few times, on six occasions in all. At Cambridge, Iain Macpherson (1924–2011) also influenced me a great deal on Japanese Economic History, and at Stanford, Thomas C. Smith (1917–2004) enhanced my knowledge of this topic. I must, of course, also thank the 'Master' of his field, Joseph Needham, (1900–1995) with whom I was privileged to have a number of discussions on the history of the 'Middle Kingdom'.

A number of academic institutions have been very helpful over many years in assisting my research in this field, involving the Chinese Academy of Social Sciences, Institute of Industrial Economics, the China-Europe International Business School, as well Tsinghua and Zhejiang Universities in China – as well as the Japanese Institute of Labour, Nanjing, Japan Productivity Centre, as well as Chuo, Kobe and Tokyo Universities in Japan, amongst others. The Chinese University of Hong Kong, the City University of Hong Kong and the University of Hong Kong should also be added here. The long-term support of Wolfson College and Cambridge Judge Business School, both in the University of Cambridge, has been invaluable in encouraging my interest in this field. Further, I cannot say how grateful I also am to the fellow-contributors to this volume – who have exceeded the call of duty to pen such scholarly and indeed well-written essays.

I would like to thank, in turn, the following academic colleagues, collaborators and contacts in the fields of economics, business and management for their advice and help in the development of the ideas in this work over the years or in correspondence on the present volume: John Benson, Chris Brewster, William Brown, John Child, Ngan Collins, Daniel Z. Ding, Vincent Edwards, Keith Goodall, Geoff Hodgson, Susan Howson, the late Kwok Leung, Sek Hong Ng, Jane Nolan, Peter Nolan, Riccardo Peccei, Gordon Redding, Chris Rowley, Randall S. Schuler, Robert Skidelsky, Bill Starbuck, Rosalie Tung, Morgen Witzel, John Wong, Cherrie Zhu, Ying Zhu and many others.

I must particularly thank Peter Sowden at Routledge, my in-house Editor over the years, for his encouragement and support.

I must also thank Routledge for permission to reproduce materials incorporated in this book which were originally written by myself.

Part I
Introduction

1 The introduction of Western Economics in East Asia

Malcolm Warner

Introduction

In this introduction, we will discuss the *diffusion* of Western Economics in general and in East Asia in particular. We will deal with a region which has experienced unprecedented changes on the road to *modernity* in the last one and a half centuries (see Woodside, 2006), as well as extraordinary *economic growth* over the last half-decade (see Das, 2015). New ideas, we will argue, were introduced by a process of diffusion which was likely to involve a process of *evolutionary selection*, unrestricted by the *type of innovation* examined, the *adopters involved* and the *place* or *culture* (see Rogers, 1962).

Another more recent work regards the work of Charles Darwin (1809–1882) as a 'guiding light' here (see Hodgson and Knudsen, 2010). But yet another theorist, Nelson (2005) thinks that:

> [E]volutionary theorizing in the social sciences goes back well before Darwin. The writings of Bernard Mandeville [1670–1723] (1724), and Adam Smith [1723–1790] (1776), to name two well-known 18th century authors, [as well as David Hume [1711–1776] (see 1739)] are rich in theorizing about cultural and economic change that has a strong evolutionary flavor. That tradition of empirically oriented evolutionary social science has continued to the present time.
>
> (Nelson, 2005: 4)

The argument by Hodgson and Knudsen (2010) goes on to invoke culture as further complicating the evolutionary process 'by enhancing the role of diffusion alongside selection' (2010: 105). Diffusion is defined by these authors 'in a way that includes the copying of replicators from one entity to another' (2010: 105).

Translation becomes the vehicle for the cultural transfer of 'modernity' (see Xie, 2009). It enacts a 'resignification' for a new audience eager for change; but no Western idea comes un-adapted or un-hybridized (2009: 6–7). Western ideas often spread via new works in the original language or in translation, for example. The translation process, we would argue, is an important intervening variable in any model of such diffusion and we will return to this theme in the final chapter of this work. Many Western books on Economics were to be translated into Japanese in the 1880s and into Chinese after the turn of the century, with their influence spreading into the twentieth century, across East Asia, as we shall later see.

Narrative of diffusion

Many of the Western ideas with which we are dealing diffused across the globe through early trade contacts, such as along the 'Silk Roads' (see Warner, 2014: 27). Links stretched across thousands of miles between East and West, whether by land or by sea (see Frankopan, 2015). An English ship had first landed in Japan for example as early as 1613 but Western traders had closed their factory there by 1623, mainly as the locals refused to allow them to export raw silk. But cultural exchanges with the local population were limited at that time. Some writers, however, go so far as to regard yesterday's State-enabled trading entities, such as East India Companies[1] which had such early trade relations with Asia, as the precursors of today's Multinational Corporations and diffusers of innovation and would even go so far as to see them as the face of imperial expansion (see Robins, 2006).

To start with, Japan begins to open up its ports at the time of the Meiji Restoration of 1868 and to foster new knowledge in order to protect itself from the incursions of the Western Imperial powers (see Macpherson, 1987). This all comes about just after the end of the American Civil War in 1865 and the unification of Germany in 1871 (Kurz *et al.*, 2011: 1). It has a sizeable population of around 35 million or so, comparable with that of the United Kingdom at the time, although the Chinese are then more than ten times as numerous. A 'modern' State in Japan is soon in the making, to educate its citizens in new ways, to create new governmental institutions and to build a new infrastructure. In less than half a century, by 1905, the nation becomes a regional military power, as Korea, Manchuria and Taiwan in their turn fall under Japanese rule (see Gordon, 2003).

China emerges from its centuries of isolation to modernize the 'Middle Kingdom',[2] in order similarly to keep the foreign intruders at bay (see Spence, 1990). It soon overturns the Imperial dynasty, establishes a Republic in 1911 under the leadership of Sun Yat-sen (1866–1925) and sets up a wave of economic, governmental and social reforms. Both countries participate in the First World War on the Allies' side – but Japan does better than China by gaining Shandong Province as a result of the 'Versailles Treaty', triggering the 'May the Fourth' Incident in Beijing in 1919, which galvanizes urban youth. The Chinese Communist Party (CCP) is soon set up in 1921, with Mao Zedong (1893–1976) as a founding member. Nationalists and Communists soon clash in a Civil War. Shortly after, Japan invades China in 1937 but by 1945 it is defeated, undergoing a second wave of 'modernization' with Allied Occupation. Mao takes power in Beijing in 1949 and the People's Republic of China (PRC) is declared. The Korean War in 1950 changes the 'name of the game' in East Asia once again and American funded re-armament helps trigger the rise of the 'Little Dragon' economies (Vogel, 1991). The scene is now set for the rise of the 'developmental state',[3] as well as the era of the 'Big' as well as the 'Little Dragons'. Taiwan takes the lead as the first of the latter dragons to make a breakthrough followed by the Republic of Korea (henceforth, South Korea), Hong Kong SAR and Singapore (see the chapters by Das in this volume). Although having 'family resemblances', the economies and their business systems are respectively distinct in a number of key ways[4] (see Warner, 2014; Nolan *et al.*, 2016).

To our knowledge, we are not aware of previous work on the diffusion of Western Economics dealing with this specific focus on East Asia commensurate with its significance, although there have been a number of books to date which have been more concerned with the broad sweep of the development of economic and management thinking internationally. We now live in a globalized world and this has been accompanied by the phenomenon of *global* economic thought but this was not always the case (see Barnett, 2015). We will first discuss this coverage of what is now understood as the history of economic ideas in the West and beyond, before going on to broaden our discussion of the main East Asian themes concerned.

There are a good number of histories of economic thought as such but they largely cover the field either by criss-crossing by author or by period, rather than by country/nation or by region. Such histories sometimes go back millennia and may cover for instance Ancient China (see Cheng *et al.*, 2014), India (see Chandrasekaran, 2015) or Classical Greece (see Amemiya, 2007) and so on. In China, figures such as the early Chinese economics thinker, Sima Qian[5] (*c.*145–89 BC) in the Western Han dynasty, said to be a pioneer of writing about its economy and who has been compared to Adam Smith (1723–1790), are widely cited in the literature (see Liu, 2013: 49). In India, the thinker, Chankaya Kautilya (350–275 BC), treated economic topics in his writings, particularly in the classic *Arthasasthra* (Chandrasekaran, 2015: 324ff.). Whereas in Greece, Aristotle (384–322 BC) and Plato (424/423–348/347 BC) are mentioned. The Nobel Laureate, Amartya K. Sen (1933–) has noted the contribution of both Aristotle and Kautilya (see Sen, 1998). But Economics as a distinct discipline did not surface until modern times and was subsumed under Philosophy as *Political Economy*, broadly speaking, until the Industrial Revolution. It was later to be spoken of more as a 'scientific' subject in the nineteenth century and is today viewed as a major 'social science'. Although Economics is often seen as a 'Western' intellectual fief, many cultures and nations stake their claim, from past to present, from West to East, looking backwards in time to their own antecedents. China is no exception, evoking 'Chinese learning as the base, Western studies for use' (*zhongxue wei ti, xixue wei yong*) (see Cheng *et al.*, 2014: 2). It became the catchword for the 'Self-Strengthening' (*ziqiang*) movement (1861–1895), a period of institutional reforms at the end of the Qing dynasty after a set of defeats by Western powers, including technological modernization (Spence, 1990: 197).

History of economic thought

Titles in the evolution of the discipline include Eric Roll's *History of Economic Thought* (1938) and others, such as Robert L. Heilbroner's *The Worldly Philosophers* (1953), a 'best-seller' of its genre.[6] A veritable acknowledged classic was Joseph A. Schumpeter's (1954) *History of Economic Analysis*, which covers a wide swathe of the field. Mark Blaug (1962) looked at *Economic Theory in Retrospect* not long after. William Letwin's (1964) *The Origin of Scientific Economics* is another work of interest. Roger Backhouse's *A History of Modern Economic Analysis* (1985) added to the debate. A later work in this area was by Heinz D. Kurz and colleagues (2011) who published *The Dissemination of Economic Ideas*, covering Europe and Japan but not China. Most recently, Vincent Barnett (2015) has edited the *Routledge Handbook of the History of Global Economic Thought*, which encompasses over 30 countries across the world, including the Asian 'Little Dragons' and China – but not Japan.[7] Again, a new work by Heinz D. Kurz (2016), *Economic Thought: A Brief History*, was published last year.

As far as publications on *specific economists* are concerned, the following may be of interest: on Adam Smith (1723–1790), we find namely, Cheng-Chung Lai's edited (2000) *Adam Smith Across Nations: Translations and Receptions of the Wealth of Nations*, which includes both China and Japan. Colin Mackerras and Nick Knight (1986) in another edited book, *Marxism in Asia*, point to the range of Karl Marx's (1818–1883) contribution internationally and especially in the region. The diffusion of Marshall's work is discussed by Raffaelli *et al.* (2010) in *The Impact of Alfred Marshall's Ideas: The Global Diffusion of his Work*. Later, on the reception of John Maynard Keynes' (1883–1946) ideas in the twentieth century, there is an interesting work edited by Peter A. Hall (1989), which portrays their influence as diffused globally, in *The Political Power of Economic Ideas: Keynesianism Across Nations*, which covers many national exemplifications, including Japan, although missing out China.

This spread of economic ideas was to be part and parcel of a narrative of imperial expansion by the Western powers (see Ferguson, 2004). As the Industrial Revolution became a global phenomenon culminating in today's ascendancy of East Asia, the transmission of knowledge, be it in the dominant paradigms of, say, Physics or Economics (see Kuhn, 1962) follows a distinct pattern, encompassing a set of concepts and practices that may help to define a scientific discipline in any one period of time.[8] Economics, in its turn, develops its own pattern over the course of this Darwinian evolutionary trajectory and is soon tagged as a 'science'. Cambridge-based Alfred (1842–1924) and Mary Paley Marshall (1850–1944), for example, use the term 'science' as a substitute for 'political economy', which had been used earlier by Adam Smith[9] (Marshall and Marshall, 1879: 2). However, Smith does note that '*Political oeconomy*' may be considered as 'a branch of the *science* of a statesman or legislator' [italics added] ([1776] 1880, Book Four, Introduction: 1).

Selected background historical events in East Asia

The narrative relating to the diffusion of Western Economic Ideas in East Asia which unfolds in this edited book may be seen as punctuated by a number of key historical events,[10] *a selection of which we set out below (see Table 1.1).*

Structure of the book

This volume, details of which are set out below, is divided into a number of parts. The first one is *introductory*, where we present an *overview* of how economic ideas diffused across the globe as well as the contents of the respective chapters in the volume. We set out a number of generalizations to start with, then offer *summaries* of the respective chapters and, last, offer some conclusions.

The next part deals with the diffusion of Western Economics in *specific country contexts*, such as *East Asia* (as a region), *China, Japan, Korea* and so on (as nations), mainly discussing the period from the mid-nineteenth century to the present day, although this varies from one chapter to the next (see the chapters by Das, Trescott, Yagi, Hong and others respectively). Here, we cover the main nations of East Asia and two in South-East Asia as above, namely *Malaysia* (see the chapter by Rasiah) and *Singapore* (by Das). There is also a chapter on a subset, the 'Newly Industrializing Economies' (NIEs), or 'Little Dragons' (see Vogel, 1991), such as the smaller ones of *Hong Kong, Taiwan* and *Singapore*. We have presented the countries covered here *alphabetically* but the order also covers the difference in size of population, with China preceding Japan, although industrialization and the import of exogenous ideas started earlier in the latter. By contrast, the NIEs are all 'post-war' industrializers, as well as being relatively smaller in size.

We have not, however, dealt with other countries in South-East Asia and South Asia, because of constraints of the East Asia focus we chose, as well as considerations of space. We have thus left out *Vietnam*, for example, in the 'socialist' subset, as well as (except in passing) *North Korea*. We have also not included *Indonesia* here and left *India*, as well as *Pakistan* and *Bangladesh*, to others to deal with. In Barnett's (2015) volume, there is an account of economics in some of these places, for example, *India* (Chandrasekaran, 2015) and *Indonesia* (Lee and Wie, 2015).

After this, we present a number of cases, such as the *influence of specific Western economists in a particular East Asian country*. Here, we cover both classical and more recent economists who have had an impact in China (and Taiwan) and Japan. Adam Smith (1723–1790), for example, is discussed both in the Chinese as well as the Japanese contexts, if perhaps in somewhat different ways (by Lai, as well as by Sakamoto). The same is the case for Friedrich List for instance (1789–1846) who is covered (first, by Liu) and also elsewhere in the volume (by Trescott and by Yagi respectively). There is also an attempt at a kind of *symmetry* as in the cases referred above but we have not

Table 1.1 Timeline of selected historical events vis-à-vis East Asia

1688	Whig Revolution in Britain
1776	American Declaration of Independence
1776	Publication of Smith's *Wealth of Nations*
1789	Onset of the French Revolution
1815	Fall of Napoleon
1841	Publication of List's *National Economy*
1842	First Opium War
1853	Arrival of Perry's 'Black Ships' in Japan
1856	Second Opium War
1859	Publication of Darwin's *Origins*
1861	Britain acquires the Kowloon peninsula
1867	Publication of Marx's *Das Kapital/Capital*
1867	Britain takes over the Straits Settlements
1868	Meiji Restoration in Japan
1877	Tokyo University founded
1885	Foundation of Yonsei University in Seoul
1882	Korea signs treaty with USA, ending isolation
1895	First Sino-Japanese War starts
1895	Japanese takeover of Taiwan
1898	Peking University founded
1899	Boxer Rebellion spreads
1902	Anglo-Japanese Naval Treaty
1910	Japanese Occupation of Korea
1911	Chinese Republican Revolution
1911	Foundation of University of Hong Kong
1914–1918	First World War
1917	Russian Revolution
1919	Treaty of Versailles
1921	Chinese Communist Party founded
1923	Kanto Earthquake
1925	Death of Sun Yat-sen
1926–1989	The Showa period in Japan
1928	Founding of National Taiwan University in Taipei
1929	Wall Street Crash
1933	Adolf Hitler takes power
1936	Publication of Keynes' *General Theory*
1939–1945	Second World War
1944	Publication of Hayek's *Road to Serfdom*
1945	Hiroshima and Nagasaki A-bombs
1945	Taiwan now run by Nationalists
1949	Mao Zedong takes power in Beijing
1949	Foundation of University of Malaysia in Kuala Lumpur
1950–1953	Korean War
1957	Malaysian Independence
1960	Sino-Soviet Split
1965	Singapore's Independence
1966–1976	Chinese Cultural Revolution
1972	Richard Nixon's visit to China
1975	Death of Chiang Kai-Shek
1976	Deaths of Mao Zedong and Zhou Enlai
1978	Deng Xiaoping launches his reforms

Table 1.1 Continued

1980	Foundation of National University of Singapore
1991	Japan's Lost Decade begins
1997	Asian Financial Crisis
1997	Handover of Hong Kong to China
2001	China enters the World Trade Organization (WTO)
2008	Global recession unfolds
2016	Trans-Pacific Partnership (TPP)

Sources: miscellaneous.

managed a totally neat order of famous economists described, with a match between China and Japan for some but not others. The role of the classical British economists is highlighted in the volume, as in the case of Adam Smith, whose influence was vast, as well as his fellow British classical thinkers, David Ricardo (1772–1823) and Thomas Malthus (1776–1834), both of whom were well known, as well as a number of German ones. Here, Friedrich List (1789–1846), Karl Marx (1818–1883) and others are also noted in a number of the chapters on China and on Japan. We also have a chapter on the influence of Friedrich Hayek (1899–1992) in China and Taiwan (by Li *et al.* later in this volume) but not for Japan. In turn, Joseph Schumpeter's (1883–1950) contribution to Japanese economics is well covered (by Metzler). Most of the chapters here, which deal with *specific economists*, may also refer back to the more *generic* surveys of the field by country contexts (by Trescott and Yagi and others respectively).

Following this, we present a number of discursive essays *on wider themes*. Here, we deal with Western 'schools' or 'sets' of authors, such as the Neoclassical, as well as Institutionalist economists, who became *de rigueur* in many Chinese faculties after 1978, or with the revival of interest of Western Economics more broadly (see the specific chapters by Fang, Cohn, Zhu and Webber as well as Zhang, respectively, in this volume). Next, we have a *comparative* section which deals with East Asian exemplifications, with the last of the contributions (by Andreosso-O'Callaghan) covering the philosophical underpinnings of economic thought in East and West and, last, a set of Concluding Remarks by the Editor of this work.

Country contexts

In the chapters which follow, as we noted above, we deal with the diffusion of Western economic ideas in a number of country contexts, across East Asia and South-East Asia, such as China, Japan, Hong Kong, Korea, Malaysia, Singapore and Taiwan.

Each of these aforementioned places is a specific *nation state* but also has overlaps with others. China, for example, has been a dominating force in the region for many centuries and its culture has shaped the values of its neighbours (see Warner, 2012, 2014). Japan, too, had spread its influence in the region after this, particularly in the last century. It had also ruled Korea (1910–1945), Taiwan (1895–1945) and parts of China, such as Manchuria (1904–1945).

Das

The start of these contributions, Chapter 2, represents a broad-brush overview of Asia's economic development, the diffusion of Western economic and management ideas within it and the key exogenous economic thinkers concerned. The author here is *Dilip K. Das*, a noted academic economist now based in Canada, formerly a Professor of Economics in a Korean university, who has long experience in writing about the region, both in books and articles. His chapter attempts to offer a constructive synthesis of outside influences there and the effects these were to have on indigenous developments. He first looks at the source of the range of economic strategies and policy thinking in the dynamic Asian economies covered, which led to their rapid economic development, adopting a broad-brush approach. Although he argues that there are many key Asian economic thinkers and highly effective economic policy concepts that have contributed to the field, he goes on to make the point that Economics or economic policy-making cannot be just seen as an 'Asian' science. He notes that one must stress that – of the economic ideas, concepts and strategies that these Asian economies deployed and benefitted from – most often came from the West. They were then absorbed, adapted and adopted by the Asian policy-makers concerned.

Economic history has few equivalents, Das continues, that can be compared to the record of these high-growth Asian performers in recent times. In his chapter, he paints a miniaturist set of portraits of such national developments since 1945. Each one of these economies was, he suggests, *sui generis* and became a rapidly growing economy at a different point in time (see subsequent chapters in this volume by Trescott, Yagi and Hong, respectively). They were also a heterogeneous and diverse set of economies in terms of their culture, macroeconomic policy, natural resource, population and so on. The economies described also pursued a wide range of macroeconomic policies in this respect. For instance, whilst Hong Kong SAR was known for its market-led, *laissez faire* policies, with a high degree of market liberalization, others such as Japan, Korea and Taiwan pursued highly selective *Statist* policy regimes at different times. The People's Republic of China (PRC, hereinafter China) which initially pursued a 'Marxist' path may be included in this subset of economies, having emphasized state-direction. The respective policy regimes of South-East Asian economies also varied from those of the others noted.

Economic ideas, concepts and strategies that the dynamic Asian economies deployed, and took advantage of, were, the chapter concludes, mainly 'Western', predominantly Anglo-American, as well as German, with a few others in the train. It traces how they came to Asia and how they were diffused across a spread of countries. Das identifies some of the key policies from which the Asian economies benefitted and relates them to theoretical concepts from which they were derived and the leading scholars who propounded them, such as Adam Smith (1723–1790), Friedrich List (1789–1846) and Joseph Schumpeter (1883–1950), as well as Friedrich Augustus Hayek (1899–1992), amongst others. They did not blindly and uncritically copy these rich Western economic and business concepts, mainly because Asian countries were still low-income and underdeveloped economies. In order to apply these concepts and theories, he argues, *pragmatic* adjustment to domestic economic reality was *de rigueur*.

Trescott

The next essay, Chapter 3, which focuses on China is written by *Paul. B. Trescott*, a noted authority on the history of Western Economics in that country, who has taught in US academia and on many Chinese campuses. It deals with the spread of such ideas in the 'Middle Kingdom' (*Zhongguo*) over the last century and a half, in terms of a very detailed treatment of this phenomenon in terms of the introduction of the subject and how it began to be taught there. He starts by stating that China's intellectuals were cut off from the West during a time when Western Economics was taking new shape. By the 1840s, he continues, the 'unequal treaties' arising from the Opium Wars coerced China into admitting Western traders and missionaries and with this emerged new ideas from the outside world. Step by step, a path to 'modernity' was thus pursued.

He relates how the first course in Western Political Economy to be offered in China was by an American missionary, William A. P. Martin (1827–1916) in the 1860s and subsequent decades. Next, Yan Fu's 'iconic' if idiosyncratic translation of Adam Smith's (1776) *Wealth of Nations* appeared in 1902 (see Wang, 2009). Yan's friend, Liang Qichao (1873–1929), a prominent journalist, publisher and reformer, reached a wider audience with his essays entitled *Concise [or Short] History of Economic Thought*, written in the vernacular, which appeared not long after (Liang, 1903). He attempted to praise Smith's ideas but ended up refuting them (see Kurtz, 2012). He believed that: emphasizing that 'translating Western learning is the most important tool to rejuvenate China' (Liang, 1999: 45). He argued for the practice of 'Chinese learning as the fundamental structure for Chinese society, and western learning as a useful tool with significance for practical matters (*zhong xue wei ti, xi xue wei yong*)' (ibid.: 85).

Their contemporary, Sun Yat-sen (1866–1915), soon to become leader and 'father' of the new Chinese Republic in 1911, was greatly influenced by the contemporary ideas of the US economists, Henry George (1839–1897) and Richard T. Ely (1854–1943) and proposed a new Economics agenda. Sun's later vision of a state-dominated platform for economic development was in turn to influence later Chinese leaders, both the Nationalist leader, Chiang Kai-shek (1887–1975), as well as the Communist icon, Mao Zedong (1893–1976).

Western ideas diffused through new institutions which soon appeared on the scene. Modern universities, college and schools, the chapter author recounts, began to be established in China, as the nineteenth century came to an end. By

1910, as Trescott shows, there were 19 missionary colleges in place, with over 1,000 college-level students. Economics as a 'field of study' soon became popular with these initiates. In their early years, many of these bodies offered one or two semesters of elementary Economics. A popular US textbook at hand was Richard T. Ely's *Outlines of Economics*, which was translated into Chinese in 1910. Earlier, in 1898, the Imperial Court had set up Peking University (*Beida*), which went on to become China's 'flagship' university and, many claim, remains so. The United States government had also sponsored the founding in 1911 of the Qinghua College (soon to be University) to prepare Chinese for study overseas. Both of these institutions are today the most high-profile universities in the PRC. By 1917, Qinghua's campus was offering a range of courses in college-level Economics. Between 1914 and 1929, Trescott argues, 1,268 of its preparatory students were to enter American universities. Of these, 187 were Economics students, of whom 144 went on to graduate-level study. At least 48 of these, Trescott continues, came home to teach Economics in China, establishing the foundations of the subject in a Chinese setting.

This overview of Western Economics (*Jingji xue*) goes on to pinpoint the impressive number of Chinese students who went on to study abroad to the West, as well as to Japan. In particular, 1,228 Chinese students undertook graduate-level study of Economics in the US down through 1949. Of these, less than 10 per cent, 149, completed doctorates and another 88 finished all but their dissertation. It identifies 277 Chinese who went from graduate study in America to teach Economics in Chinese colleges and universities, which included just over one-quarter, as many as 64 with PhD degrees. In all, 391 Chinese studied Economics in Britain and Western Europe. Of these, just under one-third, 162 studied in Britain, 92 of them attending the London School of Economics (LSE). By 1940, the typical Chinese university had several Western-educated economists on its faculty. American textbooks were also soon to be commonly used. The Chinese who studied in the West, Trescott goes on to note, were soon immersed in ideas of 'free-market failure' and 'unfair income distribution'. But 'Keynesian economics', he believes, was to draw attention away from the 'Quantity of Money' theory and thus impede understanding of the accelerating inflation which developed after 1937.

At the end of the 1940s, China underwent a historic shift, when Mao Zedong went on to take control of the Mainland and set up the PRC in the capital. But by the end of 1949, many of the Western-educated economists had left China. Most of those economists who remained were to be persecuted in the coming years in the 'Anti-Rightist' campaign of 1957–1958 and even more so in the tumultuous period of 'Cultural Revolution' through 1966–1972, an era during which the universities were closed. Not much emerged in the infertile years in terms of economic scholarship. But not long after, Mao's death in 1976 opened the way for Deng Xiaoping (1904–1997) to adopt his reform policies to promote China's economic development with his 'Four Modernizations' and 'Open Door' policies in 1978. Chinese students again went to study in the West, whilst the Fulbright and Ford Foundation programmes brought in Western visiting professors.

By the end of the millennium, the discipline of Economics in China was thus transformed and Western Economics was again re-established in Chinese universities.

Yagi

The next piece, which is Chapter 4, is by *Kiichiro Yagi*, an eminent Japanese Professor of Economics, now a University President. It deals with the diffusion of Western Economics in Japan, starting with an overview of the new regime and its emergence and search for modernity. Since the Meiji Restoration in 1868, which created the foundations of its modern state, the influence of Western ideas over Japanese intellectual life went on to enjoy a history of over a century and a half. During this period, as he describes, Japanese scholars were to assimilate several successive waves of overseas economic schools of thought, taking on board new approaches by reading Western books and journals and studying abroad, as well as attempting to create their own theories in the field.

The chapter is divided into five phases: 1. Encounter and enlightenment: from the 1850s to the 1880s; 2. Assimilation of German-style economics: from the 1890s to the 1910s; 3. Quest and disarray for Japanese economics: from the 1920s to the war years; 4. Rehabilitation after the War: from 1945 to the 1970s; and 5. Age of globalization: from the 1980s to the present.

However, Yagi argues that it may not be necessary to delve into details of the fifth phase, in which Japanese economics has fully synchronized with that of the international level, as this is better known and is extensively described in the literature. By the end of the 1980s, he continues, the *synchronization* of Japanese economics with that of the international community seems to have been completed. He then describes the 'state of play' in the field up to the present time.

Last but not least, Yagi concludes, Japan has a rich tradition in research regarding the history of economic theory and economic thought. This may be seen as a *by-product* of the reception of Western Economics in Japan, he continues. However, a critical study of past and present classics in economics, he goes on to argue, may be a source for a reconsideration of contemporary economics. In every period of the reception of Western Economics in Japan, he asserts, scholars were to seek new paths of interpretation, examination, criticism, reconstruction and innovation. All of them, he concludes, are worth careful investigation.

Hong

After this, we have Chapter 5, on the diffusion of Western Economics in South Korea by *Hoon Hong*, a Professor of Economics who is based in its capital, Seoul. During the last half a century or so, as he describes, this nation has not only been 'industrialized' but also 'democratized'. Over the years, it had imported economic ideas from the Western world, first via Japan and then directly. Smith, Marx and Keynes, amongst others, were first read in Japanese translations, then later in Korean versions. The Korean War (1950–1953) led to much devastation and then reconstruction, with American aid and influence to the fore. This coincidence, he argues, leads him to note that there may have been significant interactions between its socioeconomic development and its adoption of Western ideas.

Motivated by this historical background, this chapter seeks to examine links between development and Western economic ideas. First, it gives a short history about how Korea absorbed Western economic ideas from the end of the nineteenth century. Second, it focuses on what Hong dubs the 'dualism' in economic thinking in the intellectual history of his country and the 'divergence' between economic theories and reality in the Korean society. Third, it seeks to show how Western economic ideas were to be reshaped, transformed and perhaps even misunderstood. Hong states that *Mercantilism*, the *German Historical School* and the *Austrian School* had not been seriously debated in his country, even although they may have been mentioned from time to time in classes in the history of thought. Among others, lack of interest in the Historical School is noteworthy, even odd, he concludes, since the 'developmental state' of Korea which had pursued export-driven growth during the 1960s and 1970s was to bear a close resemblance to its position.

Rasiah

After this, we have Chapter 6, on the diffusion of Western Economics in Malaysia in South-East, rather than East Asia but with close links to it, by *Rajah Rasiah*, a Professor of Economics in Kuala Lumpur.The influence of outside economic thinking on the Malaysian economy can be traced to 'colonial rule'. Whilst no Western economists were directly involved in defining monetary or fiscal policies in Malaya, the chapter author continues, the currency used in Malaya, British Borneo and Singapore since colonial rule until 1967 was the Malaya and British Borneo dollar with a fixed exchange rate of M$8.57 to a British pound, in a policy framework which he states followed the 'Keynesian' developmental model of that period.

It was not until 1959 that Economics in the *University of Malaya* in the capital, Kuala Lumpur, was established, Rasiah continues. At that time, Professor Ungku Abdul Aziz became the founding Dean when the country's first Faculty of Economics and Administration was launched in 1966. Unlike the early Malaysian economists, who demonstrated a keenness to tread a somewhat neutral line of ideological orientation, most such economists since the 1990s, he argues, were trained in the standard Neoclassical Western framework. Rasiah goes on to note that they researched and published on the Malaysian economy looking at the world through such lenses, albeit with some exceptions like his own work. Economists like Nobel Laureate Milton Friedman (1912–2006) and Anne O. Krueger (1934–) were also influential, in spite of the protectionist regime. Many have since begun to question the merits of Malaysia as a model of successful development since the crisis of 1997, he continues. In his chapter,

Rasiah traces the causes of the boom of the late 1980s and early 1990s, and the later slowdown. The boom, he argues, appears to have been shaped by increased flows of foreign direct investment through a combination of pressures forcing East Asian investment abroad and liberalization of domestic policies, depreciation in exchange rates and introduction of export-oriented incentives.

A major shortcoming of the Malaysian economy, he continues, that slowed down government initiatives to stimulate structural change from low to high value-added activities, was the lack of the 'Schumpeterian' focus on the type of government intervention, although high-technology activities were promoted strongly from 1988, and especially from 1990 when the Action Plan for Industrial Technology Development (APITD) was launched. In sum, the chapter concludes that the Malaysian economy has been well served by a rich vein of Western economic theories but even so, he concedes, government policy has been simultaneously driven by diverging economic arguments.

Das

After this, we have a further contribution, Chapter 7, by *Dilip K. Das*, on the *Newly Industrializing Economies in Asia* (NIEs), such as Hong Kong, Singapore and Taiwan, which have been described as the 'Little Dragons'. In terms of size, he notes, the first two are island city-states, while the third one is a small-island economy. Korea is the fourth Asian NIE one might have considered but it has been excluded as it is the focus of another chapter (see the contribution by Hong in this volume). The four Asian NIEs remained the most admired economies for rapid and sustained growth by theorists and policy-makers for many decades. In terms of economic growth, developing economies in Africa, Latin America, South Asia and West Asia were no match vis-à-vis the NIEs. The dynamic economies of Asia, Das argues, became the principal 'driver' of growth of the global economy, contributing as much as two-fifths of total economic growth.

Until 1960, all the four NIEs were desperately poor and low-income economies that showed little promise of future rapid growth. They were often cited as examples of quite hopeless economic cases. They had all too few natural resources and were believed to be destined to perpetual poverty. But the outward-oriented development strategy in these economies was squarely based on the principle of 'comparative advantage', a theory pioneered by the classical economists such as David Ricardo (1772–1823), amongst others. Their scenario underwent a dramatic transformation. During the 1970s and 1980s, before the PRC took off and became the most rapidly growing large economy globally, the four Asian NIEs were the most lauded economies for their economic dynamism and textbook-perfect economic performance as well as measured and well-thought-out macroeconomic policy frameworks. They are also all extolled for stability in social, political and macroeconomic environment. Adjectives like 'miracle' economies were freely used to describe them.

The pragmatic use of the principles of *Neoclassical* economics was noticed and appreciated by the academic community, Das notes. For the most part, these economies relied on market signals for resource allocation. However, concomitantly governments went beyond the pure Neoclassical prescription of providing public goods, like infrastructure, maintaining law and order and providing legislature. Government, or State, played a crucial role in the economic growth process of these economies, which stood out as something of a contradiction to the Neoclassical economic principles. Hong Kong was, however, perhaps an exception in this regard.

Spectacularly rapid growth in the four NIEs focused attention on the relevant lessons that might be learned for the other developing countries, Das argues. The economic terminology devised for this group of high-growth performers included terms like 'Revisionist', 'Structuralist', 'Heterodox' and the 'New Interventionist' economics, he points out. Approbation of the economic success of the NIEs motivated a huge amount of research and spawned a large literature, enough to fill a library. Several economists, Das cites, such as the late Alice Amsden (1943–2012) and Robert Wade (1944–) in recent times, became well-regarded in the academic literature and are still widely cited in development studies.

Specific economists

In this next section, we deal with specific economists, whose work has been taken up in East Asian countries, particularly focusing on China and Japan.

Lai

The next contribution, Chapter 8, by *Hongyi Lai*, a Chinese scholar now an Associate Professor in a UK university, surveys the introduction of the main works of Adam Smith (1723–1790) and sums up his influence in Mainland China. It starts with the translations of his works there from the late nineteenth century to the early twentieth century, throughout the Republican period, Mao's era and to the post-1978 reforms. The main focus of the chapter is on 1902–1937 and on post-1978. Specifically, it evaluates the impact of Smith's translated works on intellectual and academic circles.

It is suggested that in the first of the two aforementioned periods, Smith's main work, *The Wealth of Nations* (1776) as translated by Yan Fu (1854–1921), in 1902, had a profound influence on the leading scholars of the Intellectual Enlightenment movement in China. Despite the growing assimilation of Western Economics among its leading universities during the 1930s and the 1940s, the 'free market' notion as championed by Smith left little imprint on the governmental policies, however, as many economists at that time favoured government-led industrialization and development, he concludes.

In Mao's China after 1949, Western 'Bourgeois' Economics was largely ignored or even banned, he claims. Smith was noted mainly for his 'labour theory of value', arguably a secondary element in his contribution to the subject but still of interest to Marxists. In the reform era after Deng took office, particularly since the late 1990s, the translated works of Smith were to be increasingly accepted by mainstream economists in China. But to an extent similar to the period of 1928–1949, the governmental policies in the second period did not always favour a 'free market', at least as set out by Smith. The government does recognize, at least rhetorically, the relevance of the 'free market', Lai argues, to the efficiency associated with private ownership, performance-based rewards for employees, and competition.

Moreover, Smith's 'invisible hand' (*kan bu jian de shou*) remains very popular among a good number of economists and, to a lesser extent, liberal academics in contemporary China, he continues. Many intellectuals and scholars today employ Smith's theories to criticize governmental interventions and even in their view distortions and to affirm pro-market governmental policies. This chapter goes on to review some of the main places where Smith's works are frequently discussed in the recent Chinese literature in the reform period (especially since the mid-1990s) and outlines contemporary Chinese Marxist scholars' views on Smith's economic ideas.

Trescott

In the next essay, Chapter 9, we move on to the German influence on Chinese Economics. With the onset of the twentieth century, as *Paul B. Trescott* recounts earlier, Chinese universities began to take root, attracting their faculty from Western countries, as well as sending students abroad for study. Despite superior access to universities in America, Britain and France, Chinese students were particularly attracted to *German* universities, mainly because of their strong reputation for preparing people for *public administration*. German economists, such as Friedrich List (1789–1846), largely disdained abstract theory to emphasize government-directed economic development and national strength and had a strong appeal to intellectuals in China, as was also the case in Japan.

The chapter identifies 134 Chinese candidates who studied Economics in Germany in the period ending in 1950. Many had come through German-language training at Tongji University and Peking University. Quite a few had prior study in Japan, which gave them a good grasp of economic concepts. A high percentage, in fact more than a half, namely 81 of the 134, received doctorates. Most of their dissertations dealt specifically with China. The Chinese students were particularly drawn to the study of 'Public Finance' and 'Land Economics'. Intellectually, German-educated Chinese contributed especially to these subjects. However, the path-breaking innovations in economic theory associated with others, such as Carl Menger (1840–1921), Friedrich von Wieser (1851–1926) and Eugen von Böhm-Bawerk (1851–1914) did not attract Chinese students quite as much, he goes on to argue.

Many of these Chinese students became government officials, explaining why so many migrated to Taiwan when the Communists came to power in 1949 and the Nationalist regime called the 'Kuomintang' (now written as Guomindang) left for that island. There was also considerable German influence in 'FuRen

University' in Beijing. But Chinese Marxism stressed 'revolution' rather than Marx's economic ideas as such. It is worth noting Karl Marx's (1818–1883) ideas were not widely known anyway, nor followed much in China, prior to the Russian revolution in 1917. According to Trescott, by 1900, very few professional economists in the West paid much attention to Marxian economics either. However, many universities offered courses dealing with the history of economic thought or of socialist ideas. Marx's ideas were thus widely disseminated at that time and of course much more at a later date but ultimately contested by Neoclassical and other Western economists.

Liu

The next view, Chapter 10, which deals with the German economist, Friedrich List (1789–1846) best known for his book, *The National System of Political Economy* (1841), is by *Qunyi Liu*, an Associate Professor of Economics in the PRC capital. It examines the diffusion of Western ideas from this thinker, through the works of Kaihua Wang (1894–1976), a noted Chinese economist of his time who acted as translator in 1927 for his main work (List, [1841] 1927), in order to explore List's ideas for their 'Chinese characteristics'. The chapter begins with a brief illustration of List's image in Germany and the United States as a reference point, then introduces Wang's life in its historical context. In this part, Wang's description of List through his dissertation is analysed in detail. The fourth and fifth part focus on Wang's influence and the following reception of List in China. The chapter ends with a set of concluding remarks.

Compared with his image in Germany and in the US, as a proponent of liberal free trade, we find that List demonstrates several different characteristics in China and this is mainly due to the context of his 'anti-Marxism'. His reception by today's Chinese government discloses further information about his practical *Statist* approach towards economic development. The author stresses the 'industrialization process', indeed as an addition to List's theory of commercial policy and productive power, which may remind readers of the Japanese understanding of List during the two world wars. The new element of 'Neo-Listian' thought can be described as 'industrialization' in a 'globalization' era, similar to Wang's assertion of China's economic independence. The re-creation of List in China, the author of the chapter concludes, remains an ongoing affair.

Li et al.

The next piece which is presented here, Chapter 11, by *Weisen Li*, *Xinyuan Feng* and *Liang Sun*, all Professors of Economics in the PRC, is on an important Austrian theorist, Friedrich August von Hayek (1899–1992). This Austrian and British Nobel Prize-winning economist is portrayed as a great thinker who had a significant influence on the understanding of modern societies, not just in Economics. In his nearly 60 years of academic research life from the 1920s to the 1980s, they write, Hayek has left us with nearly 20 works and a cache of academic papers. In the 1920s and 1930s, F. A. Hayek and Ludwig von Mises (1881–1973) had debated with left-leaning Oscar R. Lange (1904–1965), as well as Abba P. Lerner (1903–1982), on the possibility of what was known as 'socialist calculation' regarding the possibility of a rational economic calculation in a socialist economic system.

Hayek had published the book on *Collective Economy Planning* in 1935, then followed this with *The Road to Serfdom* in 1944, and wrote *Individualism and Economic Order* in 1948, in which he analysed the infeasibility of central planned economies in depth, interpreted the rationality of the market economy, and discussed the general rules and principles of modern society, democracy and the 'Rule of Law'. In the 1930s and the 1940s, Hayek went on to debate with John Maynard Keynes (1883–1946), another much-cited economist in the twentieth century (see the later chapter on Keynes and China in this volume), particularly on the issues of monetary theory and business cycles, for more than a decade (see Caldwell, 2004).

In China, the diffusion of Hayek's thought, according to the chapter authors, follows two main lines: one in Taiwan after 1949, and the other somewhat later in Mainland China, because of the specific historical and political circumstances. The introduction and study of Hayek's thought first originated with Taiwanese scholars. What is more, its spread in the Mainland is based on the early work of these writers. The tide of studying Hayek's thoughts flowed from the 1950s, peaked in the 1960s, and then ebbed after the later achievement of a liberal regime and free market in Taiwan. However, in Mainland China, it rose in earnest in the 1980s and went further in the 1990s. A subsequent decline, as was the case in Taiwan, has not yet come to pass. It is Hayek's thought that is said to have contributed to the 'economic miracle' of Taiwan in the late 1960s and affected the formation of its now liberal regime and free markets. As for Mainland China, Hayek's thoughts, Li and associates claim, have definitely influenced the opening-up and reforms of the 1980s. Furthermore, the influence of Hayek, they argue, is now increasingly influential in the shaping of the key direction of economic and political reforms of Mainland China, the world's second largest economy.

Warner

This study that follows, Chapter 12, by the Editor of this volume, an Emeritus Fellow at Cambridge University, examines the British economist, John Maynard Keynes (1883–1946) and his influence on China. It is divided into three sections, respectively covering the early, interim and later periods of this link. The first section deals with his initial interest as a young man in the 'Middle Kingdom'; the next one is concerned with the translation of his main works and the diffusion of his ideas in Republican China; the *General Theory* was translated in 1957 (see Keynes, [1936] 1957) and the last deals with the impact of his thinking in the People's Republic of China, after 1978, up to the present time, vis-à-vis the notion of 'Keynesianism with Chinese characteristics'. First, the influence of Keynes in China is considered in the context of the spread of Western notions of 'modernity' to Asia and China, in particular over the last 150 years. It may be said that Westernization spread with the 'flag' across Asia for good or for ill, depending on your point of view. A concept current at the time, both in general relevance and vis-à-vis economics, was *ti yong*, namely indigenous (Chinese) 'essence' (*ti*) versus exogenous (Western) 'usefulness' (*yong*). These notions may today be also taken up and are clearly of relevance for 'Keynesianism' in its Chinese manifestation.

Second, a growing awareness of Western Economics over the period, the chapter author continues, must be taken into account and specifically Keynes' theories in their diffusion in China both in English and in translation. Western theories are now in play in the PRC in what has been dubbed a synthesis of '*Confucius*, Lenin, Schumpeter and Keynes', called '*Guanxi* Economics'. The terms 'Neo-Keynesian' and 'Post-Keynesian' have also been employed here. In another contemporary contribution, Marx's, Schumpeter's and Keynes' ideas have been seen as used to come to grips with the rapid nature of China's economic growth trajectory. Around 200 books in all, by, or on, 'Keynes' or 'Keynesianism', ranging from 1936 to 2016, appear in the *World Catalogue*, a major online international bibliographical site.

Third, the last consideration is the degree, in the chapter author's view, to which contemporary Chinese economic theory or policy is dubbed 'Keynesian', with or without this or that set of characteristics. The chapter argues 'Keynesianism with Chinese characteristics' is a term which may be useful in the debate but perhaps it is often used in a relatively broad sense, rather than a strict one. Policies adopted by the Chinese leadership may be given labels *post hoc*, whether or not they have read any one given Western economist. Great caution should be employed here, the chapter argues, as it is often the case that economic commentators use adjectives an academic might be cautious to employ.

Sakamoto

In Chapter 13 which follows, *Tatsuya Sakamoto*, a Professor of the History of Social and Economic Thought in Japan, looks at the classical economist, Adam Smith (1723–1790) as an 'icon' in past as well as modern times. He examines his links to the reformer Yukichi Fukuzawa (1835–1901), one of the intellectual builders of Modern Japan at the time of the Meiji Restoration in 1868, who helped to disseminate the new ideas, including Smith's *Theory of Moral Sentiments* (1759), as well as *The Wealth of Nations* (1776). However, he continues, Smith has been seen by many not merely as the 'founder' of Economics but has been regarded also as that of social science itself, and some even ponder as the inventor of everything relevant to modern civilization. He has been read and studied not only as a discoverer of the 'market' mechanism and the father of liberal economics but also as a powerful promoter of the 'fundamental values' of modern civilization and civil society. In particular, Sakamoto recounts, Smith has been regarded by Japanese scholars as a typically 'democratic' thinker and as a model.

After 1945 in particular, Smith's name has also been strongly associated with an ideological contrasting figure, namely Karl Marx (1818–1883) as one of the most influential precursors of modern thought. No matter how 'anachronistic' it was, in order to bridge the gap between Smith's capitalism and Marx's socialism by the idea of democracy, a convenient term 'civil society' was deployed by some 'Marxian-Smithian' scholars during the war in Japan. The term has been employed until recently to pass as the ultimate ideal of 'human civilization', Sakamoto continues, as it combined the 'intellectual legacy' of both Smith and Marx.

The chapter does not, however, attempt to provide a general survey of the historical complexities of the introduction of Smith's thought into modern Japan, the author continues. The task has been already been undertaken to a certain extent by many past studies in the field, he notes; the chapter seeks rather to analyse the various contexts in which Smith's theory of 'sympathy' has been translated and interpreted by Japanese scholars. It rather argues for the fundamental similarity in the ways in which Smith and Fukuzawa have respectively discussed the nature and function of 'sympathy' vis-à-vis such principles as 'justice' and 'prudence'.

In so doing, the chapter author discusses the important sense in which both these writers almost completely agreed, he thinks, about the paramount importance of 'moral autonomy' and 'independence'. Indeed, they both made great efforts to appeal to their respective audiences on the highest moral requirement called for – in the form of a just and proper combination of the non-egoistic and socializing function of 'sympathy' and individualistic and autonomous function of the 'impartial spectator'.

Smethurst

The chapter which follows next is by *Richard J. Smethurst*, a Professor Emeritus in the US, who sets out to study economic policy – rather than economic theory as such – in twentieth century Japan. The subject, Takahashi Korekiyo (1854–1936), served seven times as its Finance Minister between 1913 and 1936, and is known as 'Japan's Keynes', or 'Keynes before Keynes'. Yet, Takahashi had an unpromising beginning for a man who rose to become Prime Minister, seven times Finance Minister and Governor of the Bank of Japan later in his life.

Takahashi was to implement a policy of expanded fiscal spending, using borrowed money to stimulate economic recovery, in the Summer of 1932, three and a half years before the publication of John Maynard Keynes' *The General Theory of Employment, Interest and Money* (1936) and only shortly after Keynes' student Richard F. Kahn (1905–1989) introduced the term 'Multiplier' into economic parlance in 1931. In fact, Takahashi had already written about fiscal spending working 'twenty or thirty times over' in a pre-Kahn 1929 essay in which he invited the nation to go to a 'geisha house' and spend wastefully (morally) and productively (economically). Smethurst thinks we can safely say that Takahashi was *not* a typical mainstream Japanese cabinet minister in the increasingly militaristic years in the 1930s. In 1936, army officers, with the tacit approval of some of their superiors, he notes, brutally murdered this Japanese 'Mr Keynes'.

The US economist, Barry Eichengreen (1952–), has called these economic steps as 'Takahashi's Revenge' since he reversed the actions of his 'contractionist' predecessor as Finance Minister and challenged the fiscal orthodoxy of the times. Although we cannot find a 'smoking gun', Smethurst continues, one may well speculate that there is a direct connection in practice between Keynes' idea of a spending policy to bring economic recovery during the depression and Takahashi's policies. Keynes' ideas, he makes clear, circulated widely among the elite in the interwar period. But even if Takahashi read Keynes or about him, *The General Theory* (1936) was not published nor 'Keynesianism' created in Takahashi's lifetime (see Yagi's chapter on Western Economics and Japan earlier in this volume); in turn, the Japanese translation of the major work came out, later, in 1941 (see Keynes, [1936] 1941). Rather, Smethurst thinks he learned the 'proto-Keynesian' notions for his policies from reading widely and talking with many people interested in such new ideas, who had followed Keynes' writings, as well as from thinking through solutions to problems which he faced as a financial policy-maker.

This Japanese 'doer and thinker', he concludes, was a 'modern' economic statesman who spoke and read English fluently and could easily have learned Keynesian, or more to the point, 'proto-Keynesian' ideas, to which he would have no doubt had access over his formative years.

Metzler

This chapter by *Mark Metzler*, a Professor of Asian History at a US campus, investigates the reception of Austrian-born Joseph Alois Schumpeter's (1883–1950) ideas in Japan, focusing on his ideas of inflationary credit-creation and long economic cycles, developed in their final stages at Harvard. Schumpeter's concept of innovatory 'new combinations' funded by bank credit had a strong resonance in Japan, where it influenced policy thinking during the so-called 'Age of High-Speed Growth' (1955–1973).

Metzler's chapter surveys key moments of the reception of Schumpeter's ideas in Japan, taking his developmental schema as a 'point of reference' and as an object for 'constructive criticism'. For historians, the chapter author believes, Schumpeter's dynamic and dramatic vision of economic development has the advantage of helping bring into a single 'focus' the whole span of Japan's modern history. In this, it is like the unifying historicized vision of Karl Marx (1818–1883), whose *Das Kapital/Capital* (1867) was eventually translated into Japanese in 1924 (see Yagi's chapter in this volume); this is earlier than in China, however, where it came out as late as 1938 (see Marx, [1867] 1938). Schumpeter's work was in many ways a critical response to Marx, and this aspect of it was in people's minds in Japan. Unlike the crisis-focused approaches of many of Marx's later interpreters, Schumpeter's approach, Metzler thinks, engages the 'boom' side of economic life, as fully as the side of 'depression' and 'crisis'.

Schumpeter's conception of development through cycles also blended well with Japanese circumstances, Metzler argues. In this regard, the widening and extension in time of Schumpeter's schema by the econometrician Shinohara Miyohei (1919–2012), he continues, was especially notable. In the spirit of this work, Metzler concludes with an overview of the history of Japanese economic thought, conceptualized as a succession of 'generational moments' that he thinks accords well with a 'Schumpeter-style' chronology.

Ohtsuki

The last chapter in this section is by *Tadashi Ohtsuki*, currently teaching at a Japanese University, who looks at the legacy of Belgium and the Netherlands, in the form of the influence of *'L'Institut Supérieur de Commerce d'Anvers'* (Higher Institute of Commerce of Antwerp) on Japanese business education and economics. Neither the details of higher commercial schools themselves, nor the influence of Belgium and the Netherlands, he argues, have been studied sufficiently in the mainstream history of Japanese economic thought.

His study examines this unrecognized part of the narrative of the development of business education and management training in Japan, overlapping as it did with the evolution of economics. The author argues that the notion of economics, commercial studies and commerce imported from the West was almost alien to most Japanese people at the time of the Meiji Restoration in 1868. In such a situation and after the Restoration, the Japanese government, which was to send many lecturers to the 'West' and also employ foreign ones at home, attempted to establish educational institutions in order to teach these subjects and also to develop those for students who were to be engaged in business with the outside world. In 1862, the Japanese government was to dispatch two scholars, Nishi Amane (1829–1897) and Tsuda Mamichi (1829–1903), to the Netherlands. They undertook private lessons on the subjects of 'natural law', 'international law', 'national law', 'economics' and 'statistics' from Simon Vissering (1818–1888), who was the Professor of Political Economy at Leiden University at the time.

Looking back on the development of economics and business studies in Japan, two higher educational institutions, he recounts, were of significance: One, *Imperial Universities*, the other being *National Higher Commercial Schools (HCS)*. Already in 1877, Tokyo (later Imperial) University had begun to give lectures on Economics – some time before the establishment of the first national higher commercial school in 1884. This was followed by Kyoto Imperial University in 1899. But both these universities had started to give their lectures on Economics as subjects in the faculty of law. In contrast, the roles of what were to be called the 'Higher Commercial Schools' were to be quite different. In Japan, the first of these was attached to the 'Tokyo School of Foreign Languages' in

1884, which was modelled on '*L'Institut*', now part of the University of Antwerp itself as of 2003.

These higher commercial schools went on to play an important part in the diffusion of business education and economics in Japan from the 1880s to the 1940s and indeed to the present day. With the beginning of the reform of the education system in May 1949, 'new universities' were re-organized, comprising not only the former Imperial Universities but also the previous higher level schools which taught social sciences, natural sciences or technology. All the previous HCSs, but one, became a faculty of economics of these universities.

Wider themes

In this section, we present a number of chapters which deal with several wider themes, mainly relating to the re-introduction of Western Economic Ideas in the PRC.

Fang

The next chapter, by *Fuqian Fang*, a Professor at 'People's University' in Beijing, known as 'Renmin Daxie', abbreviated to 'Renda', deals with the way Western Economics was received in China in the post-Second World War period, from the founding of the People's Republic in 1949 up to the beginning of the reforms and the Open Door policy in 1978. His analysis has a wide historical sweep, taking in the challenges of the 1950s, as well as the tumultuous years of the 1960s and the accommodation of the 1970s. He observes that Chinese economists' attitude towards Western Economics was almost 'one-sided', believing that Western Economics was 'bourgeois vulgar economics' and 'bourgeois ideology', which they alleged was harmful and useless to China and should be boycotted and criticized.

Since around the mid- and late-1980s, the attitudes of Chinese economists to Western Economics have been changing, he argues, turning from an almost *unanimously negative* attitude gradually into four kinds of attitudes: the first attitude is the completely negative attitude; the second attitude is completely positive, implying that Western Economics is a 'universal truth' that applies to China; economists with the third attitude believe that some schools of Western Economics theories and policies are suitable for China, while others are not; economists with the fourth attitude think that learning and applying Western Economics require a combination of it and China's actual practice.

We can see from the mainstream of China's economic trends and policy practice that there are more and more economists holding the fourth attitude currently. The transformation of Chinese scholars' attitudes towards Western Economics is thus linked to China's reforms and opening-up, with many exemplifications, by the chapter author.

Cohn

This chapter by *Steve Cohn*, a Professor of Economics at Knox College, explores the state of economic paradigms in China since Mao. He finds that Neoclassical economics 'with American characteristics' currently dominates the work of Chinese economics departments. This influence, he claims, orients discussion towards Neoliberal economic theories and policy recommendations. Despite some new initiatives in Chinese Marxism and a modest increase in academic attention to Heterodox Economics, interest in Marxist theory, he argues, remains low in Chinese economics departments. If there is to be an effective challenge to Neoclassical theory's dominance of academic economic discussions in China, he asserts that it would be helpful for Heterodox and Marxist economists to carve out a common set of criticisms, even if they are unable to agree on a common alternative.

Economic reform, Cohn continues, has brought with it a deep rooting of Neoclassical Economic Theory (with a well-developed branch of Chicago School Economics) in Chinese Economics departments. Polemical government attacks on 'Western ideas', such as those recently made by Yuan Guiren, the Minister of Education in 2015, he believes, are unlikely to mobilize wide academic support but have been persistent. Far more effective in expanding the realm of economic discourse in China would be to free up Marxist theory from political oversight and expand support for Heterodox Economics research and course offerings. Cross-pollination among Marxist and Heterodox Economists, Cohn believes, might produce a genuine alternative ('with Chinese characteristics') to the so-called 'Washington Consensus' (light and strong versions) as currently anchored in Neoclassical economics.

Zhu and Webber

The next chapter, by *Ying Zhu and Michael Webber*, who teach in Adelaide and Melbourne respectively, looks at the impact of Western Economic Theories on Chinese economic reforms from the late 1970s to the present. Over the last 40 years, they argue, China has embarked on an unprecedented economic reform journey, which they characterize as a departure from traditional communist thought and ideology towards a *hybrid* philosophical and economic thought that combines multiple sources and influences predominately from the West.

This chapter sets out to identify the different stages of economic reform in China from the late 1970s to nowadays, and then analyses the impact of the Western economic theoretical ideas on the formation of the government's economic reform policy and agenda and on the debates among different economists' groups within China about the development of a 'Socialist market economy with Chinese characteristics' (*zhongguo tese shehuizhuyi shichang jingji*). The general observation they make is that China is not blindly following the West either economically (to a fully market-oriented economy) or politically (to multi-party democracy and freedom of speech, press and association). What China is seeking to develop, they argue, could be very different from the existing Western market economies and democracy, as well as from the 'Dependency Approach' on the economic front and the former Nationalist/Socialist authoritarianism on the political front.

The dilemma for the Chinese government and its people, the authors believe, is to develop something *unique* that combines elements from different economic schools in order to lead the 'Dragon Boat' towards the realization of 'China's Dream' and the elements needed to reach it. These all need further illustration and clarification by both the regime and people in China during their new 'Long March' journey.

Zhang

The next contribution, by *Jin Zhang*, who teaches Economics at Cambridge, examines the dissemination of the Western economic ideas of 'Corporate Governance' among Chinese economists and policy-makers and their influence on China's gradualist reform of its largest state-owned enterprises (SOEs). It is divided into four sections. The first discusses the dissemination of the theories of corporate governance since the 1980s, focusing on the 'principal-agent' problem and mechanisms of board of directors; the second examines the influence of these Western ideas on the policy measures of restructuring China's largest SOEs in the strategic industries in the late 1990s and the establishment of the 'modern industrial enterprise' in the 2000s; the third looks into the key issues involved in the current reform of ownership of the central SOEs, namely the 'principal-agent' problem and the role of the Chinese Communist Party (CPC) pertinent to the further reform of China's largest SOEs.

Here, Zhang argues that the diffusion of Western economic ideas on Corporate Governance has produced a profound impact on its reform in China's central SOEs. The PRC has come a long way in corporate governance reform regarding identifying principal and agent and the function of board of directors. The current round of mixed ownership reform will, she relates, continue tackling the core issues of the principal-agent problem and the board of directors. It is yet to be seen to what extent these issues will be resolved. But one can be sure that it will involve a great deal of experimentation and evolution based on what has already been achieved. China will keep learning from the Western Economic Theory and practice on corporate governance and continue finding a way that is suitable for China on such governance.

Comparisons

In Part V, we look at comparisons across East Asia in terms of an East–West perspective in the last two chapters of the book.

Andreosso-O'Callaghan

The penultimate contribution, namely Chapter 21, in this edited book is written by *Bernadette Andreosso-O'Callaghan*, a Professor of Economics in Ireland and Germany, on the philosophical basis of contemporary economic policy-making in Asia and Europe, respectively. She argues that it can be traced back to a number of well-known philosophers born around the same time in history: Plato and Aristotle, as well as Confucius and Laozi. Yet, the contemporary literature on the conceptual and philosophical roots of economic policy-making in the case of East Asia, she continues, is still replete with references to Confucianism, whereas the Platonic and Aristotelian heritages have been ignored.

This chapter therefore has two main objectives: first, to explain why the legacy of Plato and Aristotle has been overshadowed in the case of Europe ('the West'); second, to analyse the similarities and differences existing in these early East/West philosophical schools and their mutual interaction; the influence of the dominant Western Neoclassical economic paradigm on economic policy-making in Asia will be studied using the 'role of the state' as the leading thread in the analysis.

The essay concludes that economic policy-making in Europe and Asia has been intimately delineated by dominant economic schools that have been deeply fashioned by philosophers as well as by theologians in the case of Europe. The author has noted that European (i.e. Greek) and Asian (mostly Chinese) classical philosophies have had a number of features and concepts in common between them, notably their ethical basis and the notion of the 'virtuous' person who acts for the common good. But, the author also goes on to argue, Asia's opening to the outside world since the nineteenth century helped the Western-born dominant 'Neoclassical paradigm' to increasingly influence policy-making in the case of Asian countries.

Warner

In a final chapter, the 22nd, the Editor of this volume offers a set of concluding remarks about the emerging 'academic plurality' (Ma and Trautwein, 2013: 10) in East Asia with respect to Western Economics.

Conclusions

To sum up, in this volume, we set the scene in Part I, namely this introduction. In the respective chapters, we next deal in Part II with the diffusion of Western economic ideas in a given region such as Asia, followed by a number of countries, across East Asia and South-East Asia, such as China, Japan, Hong Kong, Malaysia, South Korea, Singapore and Taiwan. In Part III, we cover the contribution of specific Western economists, such as Adam Smith, Karl Marx, Friedrich List, John Maynard Keynes and others. In Part IV, we look at selected wider themes. We end last, in Part V, with a set of comparisons.

The reader must now turn to the individual contributions to the volume in the chapters which follow, which we hope will exemplify the foci we have set out above.

Notes

1 There was not only a British East India Company which received its royal charter in 1600 but also a Dutch counterpart, as well as French and Danish rivals.
2 The description 'Middle Kingdom' (*Zhongghuo*) is often used to refer to China.
3 The term 'developmental state' is said to have been coined by Chalmers A. Johnson (1931–2010) whose book on MITI was published in in the early 1980s (Johnson, 1982).
4 Nolan *et al.* (2016) on business systems in Asia covers China, Japan and Korea, as well as developments in South-East Asia including the Straits region (comprising Singapore and parts of Malaysia and Indonesia), Thailand, Myanmar and Vietnam, a rather broader remit than the present edited volume.
5 Sima Qian was a famous Chinese historian who lived in the time of the Han dynasty; the dates of his birth (*c.* 145 BC) and death (*c.* 89 BC) remain somewhat approximate.
6 The book had gone into seven editions by the year 1999.
7 The Editor of the work informed me that the prospective Japanese chapter author did not deliver the ms on time.
8 The concept of 'paradigms' was extensively explored by US physicist, historian and philosopher of science, Thomas Samuel Kuhn (1922–1996) in his 1962 book.
9 Smith uses the term 'political economy' only 3 times but notes 'political oeconomy' 13 times in the text of *The Wealth of Nations*.
10 We have selected the events we consider 'key' to the narrative of modernity we illustrate in this edited volume.

References

Amemiya, T. (2007). *Economy and Economics of Ancient Greece*, London: Routledge.

Backhouse, R. (1985). *A History of Modern Economic Analysis*, Oxford: Basil Blackwell.

Barnett, V. (ed.) (2015). *The Routledge Handbook of the History of Global Economic Thought*, London and New York, NY: Routledge.

Blaug, M. (1962). *Economic Theory in Retrospect*, Cambridge: Cambridge University Press.

Caldwell, B. (2004). *Hayek's Challenge: An Intellectual Biography of F. A. Hayek*, Chicago, IL: University of Chicago Press.

Chandrasekaran, B. (2015). 'India', in V. Barnett (ed.), *The Routledge Handbook of the History of Global Economic Thought*, London and New York, NY: Routledge, 323–336.

Cheng, L., Peach, T. and Wang, F. (eds) (2014). *The History of Ancient Chinese Economic Thought*, London and New York, NY: Routledge.

Das, D. K. (2015). *An Enquiry into the Asian Growth Model*, Basingstoke: Palgrave Macmillan.

Ely, R. T. (1893). *Outlines of Economics*, New York, NY: Hunt and Eaton, translated into Chinese in 1910.

Ferguson, N. (2004). *Empire: How Britain Made the Modern World*, London: Penguin Books.

Frankopan, P. (2015). *The Silk Roads: A New History of the World*, London: Bloomsbury.

Gordon, A. (2003). *A Modern History of Japan: From Tokugawa Times to the Present*, New York, NY: Oxford University Press.

Hall, P. A. (ed.) (1989). *The Political Power of Economic Ideas: Keynesianism across Nations*, Princeton, NJ: Princeton University Press.

Hayek, F. (ed.) (1935). *Collective Economy Planning*, London: Routledge.

Hayek, F. (1944). *The Road to Serfdom*, London: Routledge.

Hayek, F. (1948). *Individualism and Economic Order*, Chicago, IL: University of Chicago Press.

Heilbroner, R. L. (1953). *The Worldly Philosophers: The Lives, Times and Ideas of the Great Economic Thinkers*, New York, NY: Simon and Schuster.

Hodgson, G. M. and Knudsen, T. (2010). *Darwin's Conjecture: The Search for General Principles of Social and Economic Evolution*, Chicago, IL and London: University of Chicago Press.

Hume, D. [1739] (1962). *A Treatise on Human Nature*, New York, NY: Macnabb.

Johnson, C. A. (1982). *MITI and the Japanese Miracle: The Growth of Industrial Policy, 1925–1975*, Stanford, CA: Stanford University Press.

Keynes, J. M. (1936). *The General Theory of Employment, Interest and Money*, London: Macmillan.

Keynes, J. M. [1936] (1941). *The General Theory of Employment, Interest and Money* [Koyo, Rishi oyobi Kahei no Ippan Riron], translated into Japanese by T. Shionoya, Tokyo: Toyo Keizai Shimpo-sha.

Keynes, J. M. [1936] (1957). *The General Theory of Employment, Interest and Money* [Jiu ye, li xi he huo bi tong lun], translated into Chinese by Y. Xu, Beijing: China SDX Joint Publishing Company.

Kuhn, T. S. (1962). *The Structure of Scientific Revolutions*, Chicago, IL: Chicago University Press.

Kurtz, J. (2012). 'Translating the Vocation of Man: Liang Qichao (1873–1929), J. G. Fichte, and the Body Politic in Early Republican China', in M. J. Burke and M. Richter (eds), *Why Concepts Matter: Translating Political and Social Thought*, Leiden and Boston: Brill, 153–176.

Kurz, H-D. (2016). *Economic Thought: A Brief History*, New York, NY: Columbia University Press, translated from the German by J. Reimer.

Kurz, H.-D., Nishizawa, T. and Tribe, K. (eds) (2011). *The Dissemination of Economic Ideas*, Cheltenham: Elgar.

Lai, C.-C. (ed.) (2000). *Adam Smith Across Nations: Translations and Receptions of the Wealth of Nations*, Oxford: Oxford University Press.

Lee, C. and Wie, T. K. (2015). 'Indonesia and Malaysia', in V. Barnett (ed.), *The Routledge Handbook of the History of Global Economic Thought*, London and New York, NY: Routledge, 306–314.

Letwin, W. (1964). *The Origin of Scientific Economics*, London: Routledge.

Liang, Q. (1903). *Concise History of Economic Thought* [Yin-pin-shih Wen-chi] in Chinese, serialized in the bi-weekly *Xinmin congbao* [New Citizen], from seventh issue onwards, Yokohama: New Citizen.

Liang, Q. (1996). 'On the Relationship Between Fiction and the Government of the People'. trans. K.-M. Wong and K. A. Denton (eds), *Modern Chinese Literary Thought: Writings on Literature, 1893–1945*, Stanford, CA: Stanford University Press, 74–81.

List, F. [1841] (1927). *The National System of Political Economy* [Guojia Jingjixue], Beijing: Commercial Press, translated into Chinese by K. Wang.

List, F. [1841] (1966). *The National System of Political Economy*, New York, NY: Kelly.

Liu, Q. (2013). 'The Reception of Adam Smith in East Asia', in Y. Ma and H.-M. Trautwein (eds), *Thoughts on Economic Development in Asia*, London and New York, NY: Routledge, 35–55.

Ma, Y. and Trautwein, H.-M. (eds) (2013). 'Introduction', *Thoughts on Economic Development in Asia*, London and New York, NY: Routledge, 1–11.

Mackerras, C. and Knight, N. (eds) (1986). *Marxism in Asia*, London: Croom Helm.

Macpherson, W. J. (1987). *The Economic Development of Japan, 1868–1941*, Cambridge: Cambridge University Press.

Mandeville, B. [1724] (1970). *The Fable of the Bees*, London: Penguin.

Marshall, A. and Marshall, M. P. (1879). *The Economics of Industry*, London: Macmillan.

Marx, K. [1867] (1938). *Capital*, translated into Chinese in a complete version by Y.-N. Wang and T.-L. Kuo, Beijing: Foreign Languages Publisher.

Marx, K. [1867] (1954). *Capital*, Moscow: Progress Publishers.

Nelson, R. R. (2005). 'Evolutionary Theories of Cultural Change: An Empirical Perspective', Working Paper, http://et.ss.net/files/Nelson_Cultural_Change.pdf (accessed 4 June 2016).

Nolan, J., Rowley, C. and Warner, M. (eds) (2016). *Business Networks in East Asian Capitalisms: Enduring Trends, Emerging Patterns*, London: Elsevier.

Raffaelli, T., Becattini, G., Caldari, K. and Dardi, M. (eds) (2010). *The Impact of Alfred Marshall's Ideas: The Global Diffusion of his Work*, Cheltenham: Edward Elgar.

Robins, N. (2006). *The Corporation That Changed the World: How the East India Company Shaped the Modern Multinational*, London: Pluto Press.

Rogers, E. M. (1962). *The Diffusion of Innovations*, New York, NY: Free Press.

Roll, E. (1938). *History of Economic Thought*, London: Faber and Faber.

Schumpeter, J. A. (1954). *A History of Economic Analysis*, London: Allen and Unwin.

Sen, A. K. (1998). 'The Possibility of Social Choice', Nobel Lecture, 8 December.

Smith, A. [1776] (1880). *An Inquiry into the Nature and Causes of the Wealth of Nations*, edited by James E. Thorold Rogers, 2nd edn, Oxford: Clarendon Press, 2 vols.

Smith, A. [1759] (1882). *The Theory of Moral Sentiments*, edited by D. D. Raphael and A. L. Macfie, New York: Liberty Fund.

Smith, A. [1776] (1902). *An Inquiry into the Nature and Causes of the Wealth of Nations*, translated into Chinese by F. Yan, Shanghai: Nanyang Translation Institute.

Spence, J. (1990). *The Search for Modern China* (1st edn, 1990; 2nd edn, 1999; 3rd edn, 2013), New York, NY: W. W. Norton.

Vogel, E. F. (1991). *The Four Little Dragons: The Spread of Industrialization in East Asia*, Cambridge, MA: Harvard University Press.

Wang, F. (2009). 'The Relationship between Chinese Learning and Western Learning According to Yan Fu (1854–1921)', *Knowledge and Society Today*, Lyon: Multiple Modernity Project.

Warner, M. (ed.) (2012). *Managing Across Diverse Cultures in East Asia: Issues and Challenges in a Changing Globalized World*, London and New York, NY: Routledge.

Warner, M. (2014). *Understanding Chinese Management: Past, Present and Future*, London and New York, NY: Routledge.

Woodside, A. (2006). *Lost Modernities: China, Vietnam, Korea, and the Hazards of World History*, Cambridge, MA: Harvard University Press.

Xie, S. (2009). 'Translating Modernity Towards Translating China', in X. Luo and Y. He (eds), *Translating China*, Bristol, Buffalo, NY and Toronto: Multilingual Matters, 135–156.

Part II

Country contexts

2 The diffusion of Western economic ideas and policy concepts in the dynamic Asian economies

An overview

Dilip K. Das

Introduction

What was the source of the sound strategies and policy-thinking in Economics in the dynamic Asian economies over the last century and a half, which were to lead them to their rapid economic rise in such a record time-span? This is the most salient question to ask in pursuing this important issue, as we shall soon see, in the chapters that follow in this edited volume.

Although there are numerous notable Asian thinkers in the field and efficacious policy concepts that yielded positive results here, Economics, we argue, cannot be regarded as an essentially 'Asian' science, as such. We go on to posit that the Economic Ideas, Concepts and Strategies that the dynamic Asian economies deployed, and benefitted from, were essentially *Western*, principally Anglo-American in origin in recent years, if with associated European influences. They were then successfully *gleaned, adapted* and *adopted* by the Asian policy-makers (see the Introductory chapter to this volume).

An distinct attempt has been made in this chapter to identify the principal policies from which the Asian economies benefitted, then relate them to theoretical Economics concepts from which they were derived and to the scholars who propounded them. Our objective here is to examine these productive, constructive, innovative, growth-spawning concepts and strategies and explore how they reached the dynamic Asian economies. The theory-driven and policy-relevant overview of the field in this chapter explores the track they were to take.

The end of the Second World War, we would argue, is the appropriate point in historical time for this exposition to start and we will work *back* to the foundations of these developments in the mid-nineteenth century. First, the Japanese economy recovered at a breathtaking pace in 1945 and after a time-lag, a number of dynamic economies of East Asia and South-East Asia grew at a prodigious pace. One Asian economy took off after another from economic stagnancy – to achieve an annual growth rate of 8–10 per cent, or even higher. Sustained and rapid growth with equity, or shared growth, was to be their remarkable achievement. The pace and scale of economic transformation of the dynamic Asian economies were unprecedented (see Das, 2015).

There is indeed a great deal of academic interest in the Economic and Institutional factors, as well as ideas that may help explain this precipitous GDP growth path and industrial competitiveness, as well as in their sources of pragmatic economic policies, as we shall soon explore. Economic history over recent time has few equivalents that can be compared to these high-growth Asian performers. Each one of these economies may be seen as *sui generis* and became a rapidly growing economy at a different point in time from its neighbours (see Nolan *et al.*, 2016), as subsequent chapters will reveal. These were a heterogeneous and diverse group of economies in terms of natural resources, population, culture and macroeconomic policy frameworks. They followed a range of macroeconomic policies. For instance, whilst Hong Kong SAR was known for its market-led, *laissez faire* policies, with a high degree of market liberalization, others – Japan, Republic of Korea in the South (hereinafter Korea) and last, Taiwan – pursued highly selective *Statist* policy regimes. The People's Republic of China (PRC, hereinafter China) may also be included in this sub-group of economies. The macroeconomic policy regime of the South-East Asian economies also varied from those of others.

The performance of several Asian economies was referred to as 'miracle' growth in the academic Economics literature and policy conclaves (World Bank (WB), 1993; Page, 1994; Easterly, 1995; Campos and Root, 1996; Lee and Hong, 2012). Not long ago, Ben Bernanke (1953–) of the Brookings Institution, former Chair of the US 'Federal Reserve' termed it (2009: 1) 'one of the great success stories in the history of economic development'; later, Ross (2015) echoed the same sentiment. The ascent of the dynamic Asian economies is, arguably, the most distinguished event in Economic History since the Industrial Revolution (1760–1850). A Canadian consultant, Dominic Barton (1962–), Global Managing Director of McKinsey & Co, has termed it the 're-rise of Asia' (Christensen, 2014: 3).

Moribund and backward Asian economies

In stark contrast to the present, in the early and mid-twentieth century, much of Asia was an impoverished and underdeveloped part of the global economy. Asia had, in effect, missed out on the 'Industrial Revolution'. In the 1960s, expressions like 'backward' or 'basket-case' were freely bandied about when discussing Asia. Erstwhilst developing economies regarded it as a hopeless and hapless case. Eminent development scholars were at first pessimistic about the future of Asian economies (see Gerschenkron, 1962; Kuznets, 1973). They hypothesized that these societies were incapable of rapid economic growth and developing a modern economic framework because they did not possess the same innovative and entrepreneurial characteristics that European societies did. It was believed, following the view of German sociologist Max Weber (1864–1920), that philosophies like Confucianism that gripped the Asian mind were too esoteric and complicated and not conducive to 'rational' Economic thinking (see Warner, 2014: 34). If anything, such philosophies obstructed, he continued, espousing ideas and concepts that might lead to rapid growth.

Largely because of the uneven performance of the Asian economies during the early stages of their growth, the Western Economics profession was not convinced of the possibility of an Asian 'Economic Miracle' for quite some time. The probability of Asian economies emerging from economic stagnation was not considered seriously until the late 1980s or early 1990s (see Hicks, 1989). Not many believed that they would turn in a 'stellar' economic performance, comparable to Japan's post-War recovery. It was not irrational to think this as some of them had performed well and seemed to catch up for a short time in the 1950s and then slackened. Indonesia was a good example of this phenomenon. Also, of the four newly industrialized economies (NIEs)[1] of Asia, only Taiwan performed noticeably well in the initial stages and stayed the course, whilst the other three NIEs were unsteady (see the chapter by Das on these economies later in this volume).

When per capita incomes in the dynamic Asian economies did start growing rapidly, for some time, it was regarded as a mere 'chance' occurrence (Fogel, 2009). Again, Krugman (1994, 1998) had been prominently sceptical regarding the Asian 'miracle' and waited for the marginal productivity of capital in the dynamic Asian economies to decline, causing a downfall of these economies. According to Krugman (1994), the Asian 'miracle' was premised on investment in physical and human capital, or mere capital accumulation. It was not based on efficiency of growth, or on 'total factor productivity' (TFP) improvements. This became known in Economics as the 'Krugman–Young' hypothesis (see Das, 2015). It stated that TFP and technology advancement played a merely subsidiary role in the dynamic Asian economies.

An alternative view was that if TFP in the Asian economies was not remarkable, their unprecedented growth performance based on trade, investment, foreign direct investment (FDI) and institutional development was. No doubt significance of capital accumulation cannot be denigrated in the above process. However, numerous researchers were critical of the factor-accumulation explanation of Asia's rapid growth. A clearer and more logical view has now emerged. Recent research extended the growth-accounting framework to prove that factor accumulation was the driving force in the early stages of growth in the dynamic group of Asian economies, whilst TFP became the 'prime mover' during the later stages (see Aghion and Howitt, 2007; Hsieh and Klenow, 2010; Lu, 2012; Madsen and Ang, 2013).

'Miracle' growth in Asia

The Asian 'Economic Miracle' has been characterized by the 'Flying Geese' paradigm of growth; in this scheme of things, Japan was the 'leading Goose'. It achieved high GDP growth in the mid-1950s, which was sustained until the first oil-shock of 1973. The economy surpassed its pre-War potential trend in the 1960s. By the mid-1960s, it began to be perceived as an industrial 'behemoth', with a diversified set of complex and heavy industries. By 1968, Japan became the second largest economic power in the world, after the United States (US)

– but is now third, as China has now taken its place. Growing at 10 per cent per annum, or higher, during the 1955–1973 period, Japan was able to quadruple its GDP in real terms. As the yen was appreciating in real terms, per capita GDP in Japan denominated in US dollars at the market exchange rate overtook that of the US by the late 1980s (see Ito, 1996) (see the chapter by Yagi later in this volume).

Half a century ago Asian economies were abjectly poor, but several of them industrialized fast and Asia positioned itself as the 'factory of the world'. They developed numerous export-oriented competitive industrial sectors, which subsequently spurred autonomous domestic demand. The precipitous ascent of a group of Asian economies turned Asia into the most dynamic region of the global economy. Asia not only propelled global economic growth but also structurally influenced global economic and international business landscape (Bernanke, 2009; Arora and Vamvakidis, 2010). Rapid growth in a sub-group of Asian economies appreciably reshaped the global economy and international business. After 1990, Asia saw an efflorescence of regionally based economic initiatives. Since the turn of the millennium, this trend accelerated further. During and after the global financial crisis (2007–2009), the impact of the Asian economies on and their contribution to the global economy discernibly increased (Das, 2011). Between the global financial crisis and the present, the global average annual growth rate has been 4 per cent, with Asia contributing 2.3 percentage points, or almost 60 per cent (Asian Development Bank (ADB), 2015). The centre of gravity of global economic activity has, in turn, been rapidly shifting from the US and Western Europe to Asia (see Quah, 2011; McKinsey Global Institute (MGI), 2012).

The dynamic Asian economies, that are now acclaimed as 'miracle' economies as noted above, were woefully underdeveloped only a few decades ago. For instance, South Korea is geographically relatively small (38,691 square miles), has a mountainous terrain and little in the name of natural resources. Its per capita income was a measly US$61 in 1961. However, in two generations it grew into the fourth largest economy of Asia and the seventh largest trader in the world (WB, 2015). In 2015, its per capita income was US$27,195 and its exports were larger than those of the United Kingdom (UK). Korea's success here can be attributed to sound economic fundamentals, high savings rates, upgrading in quality of physical and human capital, technological upgrading, strong institutions, prudent fiscal and monetary management and an open-economy framework (see the chapter by Hong on Korea later in this volume).

In terms of macroeconomic policy structure, Korea became something of an exemplar economy for the developing countries to replicate (Das, 1991; Chung, 2007). Adopting a similar growth model, Taiwan also performed exceedingly well (Kim and Nelson, 2000; Gill and Kharas, 2007). Likewise, the 'Little Dragon' economies, the former city states of Hong Kong SAR and Singapore grew briskly and emerged as globally significant centres of finance and trade and now enjoy high living standards (see the further chapter by Das later in this volume).

At the time of independence in 1965, Singapore was a poor economy, in places without even paved roads, let alone any industrial infrastructure. At US$511, its per capita income was low and illiteracy – as well as unemployment – was menacingly high. Economic uncertainty worsened when the Royal Navy abandoned Singapore's port in 1971. Under the leadership of Lee Kwan Yew (1923–2015), Singapore adopted pragmatic economic policies. According to the World Bank data published in 2015, Singapore's per capita income (US$54,040) was higher than that of the UK (US$41,680), Canada (US$52,200) and the US (US$53,474) (WB, 2015). Singapore's per capita income is now higher than that of the US, both in terms of purchasing-power-parity (PPP) and at market prices and exchange rates. At present, Singapore is a flourishing, trade-oriented, open-market economy. It has several well-developed high-technology industrial and service sectors. Due to its status as one of the freest, most competitive and business-friendly economies in the world, it is also a leading FDI recipient and a favourite location for the transnational corporations to make their regional head-quarters (see the later chapter by Das in this volume). The ASEAN-4 economies (Indonesia, Malaysia, the Philippines and Thailand) were relatively homogeneous, fairly identical and now integrated. Chronologically, they were the next to become a group of rapidly growing economies (International Monetary Fund (IMF), 2006; Hussain and Saidin, 2012; Chia, 2013). But a caveat is necessary here – there was no *common* 'Asian growth model' that was put to use by the dynamic Asian economies (see Das, 2015).

China made an unprecedented journey in transforming itself from a closed, agrarian, non-market, autarkic, marginal economy to a powerful force in the 'geo-economic' arena. Its economic 'miracle' surpassed those of the other Asian economies. In 1978, China was a low-income economy with a large number (250 million) of rural poor living below the national poverty line. The real per capita GDP in China at this juncture was one-fortieth of the US and one-tenth that of Brazil (Zhu, 2012). The pace and scale of China's economic transformation was overwhelming. It is now the world's largest manufacturing powerhouse (see Warner, 2014). It displaced the US as the world's largest manufacturing country in 2010. China overtook Germany in 2009 to become the world's largest exporter, albeit it was almost an 'autarky' in 1978. In 2013, it became the largest trading economy in the world, with goods trade surpassing the US$4 trillion mark. In 2015, China became the world's largest recipient of FDI (US$128 billion). With FDI inflows of US$86 billion, the US fell to the third largest host-country (United Nations Conference on Trade and Development (UNCTAD), 2015). In 2000, China's GDP was one-third that of the US (Das, 2008; Wen, 2015). However, in the last quarter of 2014, on the basis of PPP, China overtook the US to become the largest global economy. At this point, China's GDP was US$17.61 trillion compared to US$17.48 trillion for the US. Its GDP per head in current prices was US$7990 (but US$14,107 in PPP). Since 1872, the US had been the global economic leader. It was now to be pushed to the 'second perch' on the ladder. Yet this historic transformation did not surprise anyone. It merely was evidence of the rising role of Asia on the global stage in what began to be referred to as the 'Asian century'. Given the large size of the Chinese economy, its rapid growth affected the regional economy favourably. It also strengthened regional economic integration significantly (see Das, 2014).

Macro-prudential policy measures were extensively used by the dynamic Asian economies during the global financial crisis. For instance, policies related to restraining housing-market excesses helped lower credit-growth. Such policy measures worked well for Asia and it spearheaded the global economic recovery of 2010 (see Das, 2011). In general, Asian economies strengthened their resilience to global-risks and are likely to 'continue to be a source of global economic dynamism' (IMF, 2014: ix). Notwithstanding the sub-par growth in the Eurozone, as well as in the US, Asia remained the world's growth leader both in 2014 and in 2015 (IMF, 2015: 53). Despite a slowdown in China, Japan and Indonesia, Asia continued to be the most dynamic part of the global economy. According to the IMF (2015) the region is projected to outperform the rest of the world over the medium term. As the fastest growing region of the global economy, Asia makes a significant contribution to global growth. It is today a net capital exporter of significant proportion. Excess savings of the dynamic Asian economies can be readily deployed to finance domestic investment and consumption.

Japan's role as the strategy frontrunner

Japan's rise from the devastation of the Second World War was as rapid as it was remarkable. During 1950–1968, Japan increased its per capita income ten times. Leaders of the 'Industrial Revolution' took almost a century and a half to achieve this feat (see Kuznets, 1971). As considered below, Japan's swift-paced recovery had a decisive 'demonstration effect' on the neighbouring Asian economies. They learned from Japan's experiments and experiences and after a time-lag applied many of these policies in a *mutatis mutandis* manner to their own economies. Other than application of a sound and pragmatic economic policy framework, developing proper institutions and export-led industrialization, Japan's growth strategy is known for the market-guiding role of the state, or the developmental state concept, and 'market-friendly' policies. Many of Japan's richly beneficial and practicable policy concepts (Das, 2015) emanated from Classical and Neoclassical Economics (see the chapter by Yagi later in this volume).

The four NIEs were the first to pick up the baton from Japan and make use of the Japanese Economic prototype. They took a leaf from its book and made a successful attempt to break out of their economic stagnation. No doubt each NIE made its own modifications of Japan's prototype according to its own predilections and circumstances and also adopted its own unique concepts and strategies. Their economic experiences were as diverse as their approaches to growth. It is well known that Hong Kong SAR was very different from the other three NIEs. In addition, the four Asian NIEs are also known for making large investments in education. They methodically learned from the Western world and invigorated their education systems. They succeeded in creating a university education system comparable to the Western world.

It is less well known that during their 'take-off' period the NIEs had forged close economic ties with Japan, as well as among themselves. At this juncture, the Japanese economy had picked up growth momentum and it was technologically far more advanced than the NIEs. Therefore, it was capable of working as a 'growth-pole' for the NIEs. They managed to grow at an average rate of 8 per cent over 1960–1997. This economic performance was comparable to that of post-War Japan. It enabled them to advance in a self-assured manner on their 'convergence' path. This success was much admired in the academic and policy conclaves and a good deal of theoretical and empirical research was addressed to their noteworthy success.

However, following Japan's lead in economic policies and strategies was not all that the NIEs, the ASEAN-4 and China economies did. For these economies, the post-1960 period was also characterized by the acceleration of absorption of knowledge and productive Economic Concepts from the advanced Western countries. This was their own period of renaissance, or intellectual discovery, which brought novel ideas and concepts in Western Economics to them. As the NIEs, ASEAN-4 and China were relatively late 'bloomers', Information Technology was more helpful in the dissemination of new knowledge than it was in Japan. It soon facilitated them in becoming high-skill, technologically advanced, regionally and globally integrated economies.

Initiation of diffusion: trail-blazing role of Japan

Japanese culture is widely regarded as 'porous' within limits and it is apt at absorbing beneficial ideas. During the early decades of the Meiji Restoration period (1868–1912), Japan found, studied and successfully selected concepts in Economics, as well as technology from the Western world and absorbed them, as subsequent chapters will show (see the chapters by Yagi, Sakamoto, Smethurst, Metzler and Ohtsuki respectively in this volume). The early decades are known for the development of private-sector enterprises supported by official assistance (see Ohno, 2006). The Meiji leaders were eager to establish an education system to catch up with the West. Therefore, an ambitious educational development plan was launched in 1872. This was when teaching of Economics and Law began in Japan. Some scholars put this date at the 1900s when Economics and Law were introduced widely in the education system (Taniguchi, 2011), others earlier.

The University of Tokyo had already been established in 1877. At this time, an Education Order was promulgated to introduce a democratic education system similar to that of the US (Duke, 2009). During the early twentieth century, primary education in Japan was egalitarian and universal. Conversely, tertiary education was multi-tracked, highly selective and elitist. It was largely limited to a small number of Imperial universities. Educational reforms in Japan continued and exhibited a strong influence of American, British and German and other educational reforms (Okada, 2012), as well as those of Belgium, France and the Netherlands (see also the chapter by Ohtsuki later in this volume).

The foremost objective of the *Meiji Restoration* was to propel Japan of the Tokugawa Shogunate (1603–1867) period into a modern and fast industrializing society based on rapid technological advancement. To this end, the Meiji government introduced a series of economic, financial and technological reforms. It was sincerely committed to achieving its broad objectives. Japan readily began drawing on Western systems, particularly the technology and education system 'whilst retaining national identity' (Ohno, 2006: 43). To the credit of Japanese society, particularly the elite, who were eager for a social and economic transformation, the reform process continued in an efficacious and earnest manner as well as at a steady pace. Western Economics was not introduced in its original form but with modifications to fit the Japanese environment and needs (see the chapter by Yagi and other subsequent contributions on Japan in this volume).

Official efforts were fervently made to replicate Western institutions, employ highly skilled Western advisers, build Western-style industrial infrastructure, create research centres and establish state-owned enterprises (SOEs). Large *zaibatsu* conglomerates were also created during the Meiji period. By 1915, Japan succeeded in building a modern financial superstructure comparable to those in the West (Huff, 2003). Judged by the norms of the period, pre-Second World War Japan was a modern and economically resourceful society. It had successfully created institutions necessary for a modern economic and financial life and had become technologically modern. The pre-War Japanese economy was contemporary and comparable to the leading countries of North America and Western Europe in a number of ways (see Goldsmith, 1983).

Conduit of diffusion: from Japan to Asia

Japan's post-War boom was *inter alia* accelerated by pursuing sensible economic policies, like balanced budgets, market liberalization, market-friendly policies for the private sector, as well as emphasis on upgrading of technology and honing human capital. In pursuing many of these strategies, Japan relied on Western economic concepts and countries. Basic economic reforms, like private-sector ownership and liberalizing the economy and opening up to foreign markets, which were adopted by Japan, were essentially based on application of Neoclassical Economics.

Scientific knowledge and Macro- and Microeconomic theories in the important economic policy and business-related areas like price, interest, currency, competition, growth, trade and foreign exchange, enterprise behaviour, corporate strategy, from which Japan and the other 'miracle' economies of Asia benefitted had originated in the Western academic world. This is not to deny the contribution made by Asian scholars in these fields, however. The Asian economies learned from these invaluable theoretical concepts and adapted them in a practical and realistic manner, so that they fit the Asian reality. They did not blindly and uncritically imitate these rich Western Economic, Business and

Management principles and concepts because Asian countries were still low-income and underdeveloped economies. In order to apply these concepts and theories, *pragmatic adjustment* to domestic economic reality was mandatory. Major Western economic concepts that were directly adopted by the dynamic Asian economies are discussed below (and in further detail in the later chapters of this volume).

Japan's post-war recovery and pragmatic economic policies

The Second World War ravaged Japanese factories and infrastructure. Large parts of Osaka, Nagoya and Tokyo were destroyed and standards of living plummeted sharply. There were severe food shortages, particularly in urban areas. Besides, Japan had few natural resources; however, Japan did have an educated population and labour-force, many with training in science and technology. When the War ended, Japan had to plan its economic recovery and implement reconstruction efforts. This was a new starting-point for the economy from a low level.

Japan's post-War Economic Strategy was functional, pragmatic, knowledgeable and result-oriented. It can serve even now as a prototype for any developing economy that is trying to fast-track its GDP growth. An analysis of the economic ascent of Asia would be incomplete without an understanding of how post-War Japan achieved technological advancement and productivity growth necessary to reach industrial-country status in such a remarkably short time span. Japan's miraculous recovery is often attributed to its success in redeveloping a robust and competitive manufacturing sector. Many of its manufacturing product lines proved to be competitive in the international marketplace. Its growth was supported by technology imports and innovation, as well as by mild repression in the financial and banking system.

Economic ideas imparted by the occupying powers

Several economic reform measures were initiated in Japan by the occupying Allied Powers in 1947 and this was the first dose of Western Economic Ideas during the post-War period. It included three major steps: breakup of the *zaibatsu*, land reform and labour democratization. The *zaibatsus* were the powerful business conglomerates that were treated preferably by the government. They paid lower taxes and received huge government financial support. Breakup of these giants started intra-industry competition, which marked the beginning of rapid economic growth. The control of businesses by *zaibatsu* was eliminated by breaking up the holding companies that were the principal source of their power. Running of the businesses was further made democratic by enacting the Anti-monopoly Law and Decentralization Law of 1974.

Another initial dosage of new Economic Ideas came to Japan through the 'Dodge Plan' of 1948. Inflation in post-War Japan was exceedingly high. The three policies initiated to quell it under the Dodge Plan were: emphasis on a balanced budget, suspension of new loans from the Reconstruction Finance Bank so that currency growth in the economy could be truncated and sharp reduction or elimination of subsidies. Japanese policy-makers took the balanced budget policy seriously and continued to follow it until the mid-1960s. It became a source of economic stability. The virtue of a balanced budget was a fiscal lesson that the other Asian economies learned from this case.

Japan's efforts to economize and accumulate capital assisted in its recovery. The Korean War, which started in 1950, led to a significant boom in the Japanese economy because Japan was used as a logistical base for it. An important benefit of the Korean War to Japan was a dramatic rise in much needed foreign currency earnings. There was, *pari passu*, an increase in investment in plant and equipment in the Japanese economy.

Concept of the 'Developmental State'

The concept of the 'Developmental State' is a descendant of the economic ideologies postulated by Friedrich List (1789–1846) and Joseph Schumpeter (1883–1950) respectively, amongst others (see subsequent chapters by Trescott, Yagi and others in this volume). The term is said to have been coined by Johnson (1982) and subsequently elucidated by economists such as Amsden (1989) and Wade (2004).[2] There is, however, no consensus definition of a 'developmental state'. A broad definition could be as follows: When a state gives overriding priority to the objective of rapid economic growth and actively pursues policies which are instrumental in achieving this all-important objective, it is called a 'developmental state'. 'Statism' is a concept embodying the notion that the state should administer the economy and deliver rapid growth and prosperity for its denizens. It is often referred to as 'government-directed capitalism'.

In Japan the source of the concept of synergetic collaboration between political and government institutions and business firms dated back to the Meiji Restoration period. In the 1870s and 1880s, the early Meiji period, the state played an active role in development and catch-up with the industrialized economies. During that period, various economic models were studied by the Japanese mandarins and the Prussian-style government-directed capitalism was considered most suitable for Japan and therefore deliberately chosen. Listian, as well as Marxian and Keynesian Economics amongst others were taught in Japanese universities. Such capitalism directed by the State was not an exclusively Asian phenomenon. It was used in other countries as well. For instance, Bismarck's Germany had adopted it in the 1870s and the US much earlier after the 1780s, soon after its independence.

An important contribution to post-War Economic Recovery and Growth in Japan was made by a *virtual consensus* between the ruling political party, government bureaucracy and leaders in industry on the primacy of economic objectives and the means of achieving those objectives. Since 1950, Japanese politicians and bureaucrats worked in tandem with corporate leaders and business executives to achieve the all-important objective of economic recovery and rapid industrialization. *This approach is the 'cultural' or 'institutional' explanation that is often given for Japan's 'miracle' economic recovery and reconstruction.*

In a developmental state, the *government*, not market forces, plays a vital role in determining how the productive resources are allocated and what the Economic System produces. The government intervenes in the economy so that efficient policies are pursued and policy coordination can be done properly. For allocating capital the government also controls the financial system. In contrast, in the Anglo-American system capital is allocated by banks, stock markets and business firms. This mode of capital allocation was considered as ungainly, unreliable and wasteful, therefore rejected by the Japanese policy mandarins. For them, the economic growth objective was of the highest importance. Even the legal framework is made subservient to it. This objective is regarded as basic and viewed as serving the nation, not business firms or individuals (see Ellington, 2004).

Many Asian economies concurred with the developmental state role played by government in Japan. Impressed by this concept, they adopted it as a template for their own economic strategy. In the 1970s and 1980s, the 'developmental state paradigm' was, in turn, adopted in one form or the other by Korea, Singapore and Taiwan. No doubt, however, the success of this strategy in the Asian economies was not uniform and varied from country to country.

In a developmental state, the government has a compelling market-guiding role (Beeson, 2004). It is also the main actor promoting socio-economic development. The concept of developmental state is based on the assumption that the role of the State is to facilitate the structural transformation of an agrarian economy to a modern, high-productivity, manufacturing economy (see Kasahara, 2013). Interventionist policies were applied to industrial development as well as to trade and the financial sector. The Japanese bureaucracy was indeed 'export-friendly' and the government rewarded successful exporting firms. Thus, the outward orientation of the economy was carefully nurtured by the State. Subsequently, the NIEs and other Asian economies utilized this strategy.

The Japanese model followed a model of State-directed capitalism. The State selectively targeted individual sectors and industries for promotion and for regulating the pace of their global integration. During the post-War period, the Ministry of International Trade and Industry (MITI) and the Ministry of Finance (MoF) played a uniquely *proactive* role in this regard. The MITI was an instrument of formulating economic policy in Japan and devising industrial structure which made catch-up with the erstwhilst advanced economies attainable. The MITI was both revered and feared by the industries it espoused and nurtured. It intervened both at the firm level and at the level of macroeconomic policy to promote export-driven growth. The elite bureaucrats who ran it were generally top quality. The MITI successfully promoted Japan's industry, exports and productivity improvement efforts. This was in accord with the developmental state role of the government. Together, the MITI and MoF were instrumental in Japan's rapid recovery and catch-up. Like Japan, the 'catch-up' effects in several

Asian economies were significant and were found to be the principal source of TFP growth in them (see Johnson, 1982; Park, 2012).

Early during the post-War period Japan suffered a shortage of savings. The household saving rate was paltry, at 10 per cent (Otsubo, 2007). A low saving rate was a serious obstacle to increasing the investment rate. The apprehension regarding Japan falling into the savings-shortage trap and stagnation was real. In its developmental state role, the government intervened in the financial markets. It created a system of mobilizing and directing capital to crucial industries so that the investment rate could be increased and the economy could recover rapidly. Financial intermediaries and fiscal investment and loan programmes were developed and used to mobilize and channel savings to the key industries, selected by the MITI. These financial institutions played an important role in Japan's post-War recovery and catch-up.

Similarly, the Japan Development Bank, a newly established institution, and small-loan corporations were helpful in channelling savings and investment in the direction chosen by the government. Japan's main-bank system was also helpful in this regard. The capital adequacy ratio for banks was kept low and they were encouraged to provide long-term credit to industries and businesses that were competitive, or had a possibility of becoming competitive. This frequently resulted in over-lending and some banks faced financial difficulties. To avoid bankruptcies, weak banks were merged with the healthy ones. These policies and institutions were devised to cope with the specific issues that Japan faced. It cannot be justly said that they were borrowed from the West. Many Asian Economies, particularly the NIEs, followed these financial models and also created comparable institutions. To sustain and reinforce rapid growth and industrialization a developmental state intervenes in the economy unreservedly. Directed credit-programmes, selected promotion of industries and of exports were the three interrelated interventionist policies that were pursued by Japan first and the other Asian economies later.

Among the NIEs, the economic achievements of Singapore are outstanding. It followed the developmental state principle and is often called an 'authoritarian democracy'. There are timely elections, but it maintains a de facto one-party state. The government has controls over social and economic life. Likewise Taiwan is also regarded as an 'authoritarian democracy' but pursued the ideas of Friedrich Hayek (1899–1992) amongst other Western liberal economists, alongside political constraints (see the chapter by Li *et al.* later in this volume). The Ministry of National Development (MND) and the Economic Development Board (EDB) in Singapore played a vital role in meticulously planning economic strategy and the so-called 'Singapore model'. They were squarely and calculatingly based on the distinctive characteristics of the Singaporean economy. Developing high value-added industries and services was given high priority by the MND and EDB. Growth relied heavily on trade and development of services. To promote these sectors, government paid a lot of attention to long-run productivity improvements and short-run competition. Importing the best technologies was a part of the Singapore model. The government devised tax incentives and attempted various methods to attract FDI and persuade foreign firms and MNEs to operate in Singapore. Investment was directed to high-productivity sectors. The political–economic model followed by Singapore attracted the neighbouring Association of Southeast Asian Nations (ASEAN) countries because of its economic successes and lack of social conflict. Indonesia, Malaysia and Thailand find Singapore's model attractive and have tried partially to emulate it.

Technology upgrading and innovation

When the Allied occupation ended in 1951, Japan was a technology 'laggard' and needed Western technical aid badly. It could nonetheless afford to import technology because of its increasing foreign exchange earnings from the Korean War. The technology imports continued in a significant manner, even after the Korean War and Japan imported virtually all of the technology for its basic and high-growth industries from the West. The principal source-country for this purpose was the US (see Johnson, 1982). Foreign technology was actively absorbed in essential industries like strip mills in steelmaking, electric welding in shipbuilding, chemical fertilizers and heavy electrical machinery. Other industries that benefitted significantly from technology imports were automobiles, textiles, synthetic fibre and consumer electric machinery.

In his ground-breaking and celebrated article, US Nobel laureate, Robert M. Solow (1957) applied a 'Cobb–Douglas' production function in Economics to prove that technological advancement, or exogenous technological change, is the largest source of growth.[3] Similar models also were proposed by Trevor Swan (1956) and James Meade (1961), another Nobel Prize-winner. Their principal contribution was to make TFP a more important variable for growth than labour- and capital-productivity. TFP became the principal measure of technological change or economic efficiency.

Subsequently, other theorists of this period regarded *endogenous* technical change as a source of improvement in the quality and quantity of labour and physical capital. This group included leading US economists, Moses Abramowitz (1912–2000), Simon Kuznets (1901–1985), Douglass C. North (1920–2015) (again, a Nobel achiever) and Theodore W. Schultz (1902–1998). Japanese, and subsequently other Asian policy-makers, were constantly devoted to technological upgrading in their respective economies. They were cognizant of the fact that their factories can neither produce modern products nor be highly productive without moving up the technology ladder.

Technological advancement in any economy is a function of the import of new technology as well as domestic innovation and imitation of the technology produced in other places and available on the shelf. Technology imports from the West made a great deal of contribution to productivity growth, or TFP improvements, and to Japan becoming an industrial power in a short time span. Likewise the other dynamic Asian economies also benefitted from the import of advanced technology and innovation. Along with that Japan and the other dynamic Asian economies gave high priority to upgrading their educational sector, particularly physical sciences and technological education and engineering. They incessantly improved enrolments in primary, secondary and tertiary education and determinedly modernized their domestic education systems. Several Asian countries now have universities and research institutions that are becoming comparable to the best in the world.[4] They also sent a large number of students to universities in Europe and North America for graduate education. This helped in developing human capital, indispensable for rapid and sustained growth (see Schultz, 1962 and 1971).

First, Japan and then the other dynamic Asian economies paid a great deal of attention to and deployed resources in technological upgrading and developing human capital, two complementary strategies. These countries were convinced about the synergy created by following these two strategies together. When they followed in tandem, they ensured that the marginal product of increasing capital investment does not decline sharply or plateau. Intangible capital can retard the decline in marginal productivity of capital. Marginal productivity of labour has risen significantly in Asia, whilst marginal productivity of capital was low initially but high in the recent periods (see Ichimura, 2013). After 1995, the return on investment in the dynamic economies of Asia was the highest in the world (Ohanian and Wright, 2014).

A continuously narrowing technology gap with the advanced economies of the West was a key driver of rapid economic growth in Japan and the dynamic Asian economies (Hu, 2015). Technology imports prepared Japan and the other Asian economies for domestic technological innovations, which have a direct bearing on the competitiveness of the business firms. They also are crucial for sustained economic growth. Efforts to raise GDP growth rates were propped up by the ability of Japanese people to learn skills quickly, improve them and apply them to their own system. They improved imported Western technologies and made practical use of them. They were also good at combining new imported technologies and creating something entirely new and more effective than the original imported technology. Besides, *Kaizen* is regarded as a uniquely Japanese principle with its philosophy of 'continuous improvement' and it served the Japanese economy for centuries. This applies to the dynamic Asian economies as well. These countries, particularly the NIEs, had a notable penchant for innovation and for *Kaizen*. Technological innovation is here the elixir of economic progress (see Das, 2015).

Japanese firms were able to turn imported technologies into industrial strengths only because they were supported by domestic innovations. This factor made an immense contribution to what became known as the 'Japanese economic miracle'. The global success of Japan's steel, automobile, shipbuilding and electronics industries is a good example of this phenomenon. By the 2010s, Japan, Korea, Hong Kong SAR and Singapore had come close to the global technology frontier. Taiwan and some of the ASEAN members were also doing well in technology catch-up (Hu, 2015).

Although China has made tremendous progress, it is still far from the global technology frontier. However, in the 2000s China began to produce and employ an increasingly large labour-force of trained scientists and engineers at relatively high earning levels. China's research and development (R&D) expenditure has been rising steadily. After 2002, R&D output also rose sharply. There have been significant qualitative improvements in technological research (Yu *et al.*, 2014). Government supported the expansion in the size of science and engineering cadres. Therefore, recent growth in China's labour-force in these areas has been exceedingly fast. There is also recent evidence that China is catching up fast in terms of technological innovation. Most of these innovations are of an incremental variety, rather than substantive new technologies. These incremental innovations are not trite, but constructive and valuable. They may account in large part for China's successful growth (see Breznitz and Murphree, 2011).

Japan's assertive dispersion drive

Contented with the success of the developmental state and other strategies, a confident government of Japan tried to make them a part of the mainstream international development strategy in the mid-1980s. By 1984, Japan had become the second largest shareholder of the World Bank. As the Japanese government was convinced about the superiority of the developmental state and other strategies noted above, it encouraged the World Bank to accommodate them in its development philosophy as well as promote it among the developing countries that received multilateral assistance from the World Bank. By 1989, Japan had the largest bilateral aid programme in the world. When Japan disbursed bilateral loans, they were frequently in the form of directed loans. Whilst disbursing bilateral loans and other economic assistance to the neighbouring Asian economies, the Japanese government insisted on disseminating market-friendly strategies and directed credit concepts to these countries.

Japan and then the dynamic economies of Asia were trying to catch up with the advanced economies. An economy that is catching up generally benefits from latecomers' advantages. The latecomers can advantageously target short-cycle technology sectors and specialize in them. This enables a latecomer to disrupt the dominance of the incumbent (Lee, 2013). Besides, in order to achieve the goal of rapid catch-up Japan often followed competition-restricting practices. They were helpful in permitting the Japanese economy to achieve high GDP growth in the mid-1950s and beyond.

The principle of 'Comparative Advantage'

The seeds of the Classical Economics notion of 'Comparative Advantage' can be traced to the British, in fact Scottish economist, Adam Smith (1723–1790) whose impact on both China and Japan will be discussed in later chapters in this volume (see the chapters by Trescott, as well as that by Lai on China and Sakamoto on Japan respectively later in this volume). It was subsequently embellished by his successors, David Ricardo (1772–1823), Robert Torrens (1780–1864), James Mill (1773–1836) and John Stuart Mill (1806–1873) in the first half of the nineteenth century. This principle was proactively and advantageously used by the Japanese policy-makers. Japanese experience shows that trade can play an imperious role in rapid growth and industrialization of a country. Trade or exports became an 'engine of growth' for Japan and subsequently for the dynamic Asian economies (see Stiglitz and Yusuf, 2001; Irwin and Tervio, 2002). By the 1990s, trade became the economic lifeblood of the dynamic Asian economies and buttressed their dramatic growth. During the preparation for WTO accession China's reforms and liberalization advanced to a new stage and its export expansion took off after WTO accession in 2002.

The outward-oriented or export-led growth strategy was posited by Krueger (1978) and Balassa (1978) and developed by several other scholars of this period. Notable among them were: Bhagwati (1978, 1988), Grossman and Helpman (1991), Frankel and Romer (1999), Rodriguez and Rodrik (2001) and Rodriguez (2006). The advocates of the export-led growth hypothesis postulated that GDP growth can be achieved by expanding exports and that export can become a veritable 'engine of growth'. The association between export and growth can be created by positive externalities for the developing economies resulting from participation in the global markets. It can lead to efficient reallocation of productive resources, exploitation of scale economies, training of domestic labour as well as improved competitiveness stemming from innovation and technological advancement. No country in the post-War period succeeded in achieving a sustained high level of GDP growth and increased per capita incomes significantly without trade expansion. Economic openness and export-led growth have distinctively resulted in major benefits for the dynamic economies of Asia. For the most part Asian exports grew in sectors with increasing returns to scale (Gill and Kharas, 2007).

Trade has a quantitatively large and robust positive effect on growth and income, although it was found to be moderately statistically significant (see Frankel and Romer, 1999). A large body of literature demonstrates that trade and growth have a high correlation, albeit causation remained under dispute (Frankel *et al.*, 1996). These empirical studies had, however, methodological shortcomings. Rodriguez and Rodrik (1999) criticized these flaws and argued that most of the explanatory power of measures supposedly of trade or openness came from factors other than trade, like institutions and governance. A large body of research is available that shows that there is a positive link between trade and growth and income, with causality assumed to be running from trade to growth and income (see Dollar, 1992; Sachs and Warner, 1995; Edwards, 1998). Findings from panel instrumental variable regression confirm that trade caused growth and income to rise on an average across the successfully trading economies (Farrarini, 2010).

As the Asian economies grew and wages increased, comparative advantage in labour-intensive manufacturing dissipated. It shifted to capital- and technology-intensive products. The reason was that increases in wages were offset by healthy productivity gains. Examples of this can be seen in Japan and Asia. Another factor supporting exports as an engine of growth has been improvements in transportation infrastructure in Asia. Asian firms took advantage of low-cost shipping hubs, like Hong Kong SAR, Shanghai, Singapore and Tanjung.

To carry out an export-promotion strategy, openness of the economy to trade and FDI were essential factors. The dynamic Asian economies voluntarily liberalized their trade and FDI regimes within the frameworks of the 'General Agreement on Tariffs and Trade' (GATT) and the World Trade Organization (WTO). The resulting expansion of trade and FDI became a growth driver for this group of economies. Liberalization also enabled Asia to become the largest recipient of FDI in the world. Convincing evidence is available that shows that firms in more open sectors tend to be more productive, and record faster productivity growth (Pavcnik, 2002). Openness of the policy regime indisputably stimulated GDP growth in the dynamic economies of Asia (Jiang, 2014). Additionally, by stimulating innovation and productivity growth microeconomic factors positively played a role in making exports an engine of growth.

Growing trade and FDI flows were responsible for creating a new form of industrial organization called 'vertical production networks'. Production fragmentation or slicing up the value-added chain into different locations made it feasible. It entails importing industrial raw materials, parts, components and sub-assemblies and then producing products at the most cost-effective locations. It leads to agglomeration benefits arising from a new form of specialization. Vertical production networks and supply chains were successful in Asia because of inter-country wage and skill differentials, lower trade and freight costs and specialization in products that exhibit increasing returns to scale. This amounts to taking the principle of comparative advantage one step further, or refining the principle of comparative advantage. Production networks and supply chains transformed the structure of global trade and turned Asia into the 'factory of the world'. Factory Asia is not only transforming the global economy but also making Asian economies prosperous. To trim their cost-structures, large firms and multinational corporations (MNCs) are now slicing up their value-chains and are dispersing their production across multiple countries.

'Heckscher–Ohlin' theory

The beginning of Asian economies' export-led industrialization paradigm can again be traced back to Japan's post-War recovery. A well-known policy that Japan adopted early during the post-War recovery period was export of labour-intensive goods. It was rationally premised on the fact that Japan had a well-trained and disciplined labour-force, placid workplace relations and a well-established tradition of long-term employment.[5] Japan also suffered from scarcity of capital and was a technological laggard. Production and exports of labour-intensive goods, like textiles, were, in turn, in accordance with Neoclassical Economics principles and 'Heckscher–Ohlin' theory (see Das, 2015).

Early in the recovery stages, Japan exported labour-intensive manufactured products to earn much-needed foreign exchange, which was utilized to import capital goods, which included capital- and technology-intensive manufactured products. Japan also needed to import technology and industrial raw materials. Japan protected its tradable goods sector in the early stages so that it was strengthened and grew competitive. Government controlled imports, inflows of FDI and foreign exchange transactions. However, protectionist policies could not be applied forever, particularly for a country that was trying to create a niche as a multilateral trader. As Japan became a successful exporter in several product lines in the late 1950s, importing Western economies pressurized Japan to dismantle its protectionist barriers. In 1960, the government initiated the market-opening process in a methodical manner. Also, a comprehensive plan to liberalize trade was adopted and the yen became a convertible currency. As the yen was on a fixed exchange rate, the new genre of capital- and technology-intensive products remained price-competitive in the world markets. By the end of the 1970s, Japan was so successful that it repeatedly began having current account surpluses. Its burgeoning trade surplus became a global issue by 1977. Its continuing success in exports of medium- and high-technology products, particularly autos, electronics and other products, exposed Japan to accusation of following mercantilist policies.

Subsequently, this strategy was replicated by the NIEs and the other dynamic Asian economies. With the passage of time as capital accumulated and technology was upgraded, exports from Japan and the other Asian economies became technology- and capital-intensive. It is widely believed that if one growth strategy of the dynamic Asian economies is directly associated with their so-called 'miraculous' success, it is their export-led growth. They are regarded as export-oriented economies. The hypothesis is that their exports, or net exports, or trade surplus, or current account surplus was the causal factor behind their ebullient growth performance. This seems to be a narrow argument. Rodrik (2009) corrected it by stating that Asian growth successes were based on broader *tradable sector growth* rather than merely on exports.

The export-led growth of Japan and several Asian economies was admired by other developing economies. How exporting firms from this group of countries approached the development of their technological capabilities and organizational competence to create competitive product lines is an issue of serious academic research and policy interest. Manufactured exports destined for advanced economies tend to have a robust association with GDP growth (Razmi and Hernandez, 2011). The countries that followed an export-led growth strategy in Asia were generally open economies. Estimates of growth equations demonstrate that openness had a role in the rapid growth of Asian economies (Frankel *et al.*, 1996). Competitive pressures and potential learning from foreign rivals proved to be important mechanisms of growth for them. As export industries advance and converge with those of the market leaders, the importance of these mechanisms for growth enhances.

Market-friendly policies

The popular term 'market-friendly' is somewhat vague and can be mere tautology. That Japan cautiously followed market-friendly policies is often misunderstood as Western-style market liberalization or *laissez faire* policies; it is neither. The term market-friendly implies creating an enabling environment for nurturing and rapid growth of private-sector industries and services. Market-friendly environments encourage investment by domestic entrepreneurs, large foreign firms and MNCs. This step entails engendering a combination of a range of policies and institutions. The principal ones are: developing a legal and economic infrastructure, ensuring macroeconomic stability, adherence to free trade principles, creating an educated labour-force, having an efficacious, steadfast, conscientious and non-obstructive bureaucracy and a regulatory framework that does not obstruct but favours private-sector investment and stimulates market competition. Policies that can stimulate and nurture such an operational environment are collectively called 'market-friendly'. The 'market-friendly' approach is also in line with the Neoliberal Economics which prevailed, it may be noted. That this is an effective and operational approach to development was clear from the experiences of post-War Japan and subsequently other Asian economies. Many developing countries failed to industrialize because of the weakness of their enabling environment for private-sector growth.

As the Japanese government was committed to recovering from the ravages of the War, creating a market-friendly environment for industrialization and accelerating GDP growth, government thoughtfully and meticulously took initiatives to create a market-friendly environment. These efforts were born of Japan's needs of the hour. Being a developmental state, Japan took the market-friendly strategy further. To make it more effective, Japan and subsequently other Asian economies added the strategy of directed credit. It implied subsidized and earmarked credit to support private-sector industrialization in designated sectors. This was a policy concept that is natural to a developmental state. A regulated financial sector was another analogous strategy. It helps in delivering concessional credit to priority sectors, like economic and industrial infrastructure, and potentially high performing industries, particularly in the tradable goods sectors.

Japan was known to have followed, and subsequently advocated for the other developing countries-directed credit as a pragmatic growth strategy. Whilst this was a controversial proposition and fell under the category of financial repression, the saving grace was that it was financial repression of only a moderate order. Although the strategy of directed credit went counter to the grain of the Neoclassical Economics espoused by the IMF and World Bank, Japan insisted on the superiority and efficacy of this strategy. The Japanese government was convinced that whilst development strategies require a healthy respect for market mechanisms, the role of the government in development cannot be disregarded.

Economic reforms and macroeconomic restructuring

The term 'Economic Reforms' implies altering, modifying and adjusting existing policies, institutions, regulations and even legislation. This is not an easy exercise because they are governed by political, economic and cultural factors. There are no general 'rules of thumb' about them. They are regarded as challenging because they are country-specific and situation-specific. The policy areas that can potentially benefit from reforms vary from economy to economy. For instance, in 2014–2015 China was undertaking reforms in the following areas: fiscal, monetary, financial system, deregulation of SOEs, private sector participation, pricing policies, *hukou*[6] and urbanization and labour productivity (IMF, 2014). Of these, financial sector reforms are at the top of the policy agenda. Besides, economics as a discipline has not provided any clear direction regarding how and why economic policy reforms are needed and what kind of institutional mechanism is necessary for developing and adopting reforms that eventually lead to an efficacious economic policy regime. It is an area that falls at the intersection of economics and politics (Lee and Hong, 2012). Therefore, political obstacles frequently come in the way of economic reforms (see the chapters by Trescott, Cohn, as well as Zhu and Webber, respectively in this volume).

Japan and the dynamic Asian economies are known to have followed fairly conservative macroeconomic policies, which was unlike the other developing economies. Macroeconomic policies and reforms were aimed at a 'balanced budget', or even an occasional surplus. For the most part, real interest rates in this group of economies were positive and rates of inflation low or very low. They did not allow overvaluation of their currencies and generally promoted domestic competition in manufacturing. Market forces were allowed to make the industrial sector domestically and internationally competitive. Prudent fiscal policies also led to low public debt, or virtual absence of public debt. In addition, labour-market deregulation was an important area of reforms. Although industrial sectors and business firms were supported by government, as the resources were limited only a few selected ones were promoted. This became known as 'picking winners' or 'making winners' (see Haggard, 2004; Wade, 2004; Haggard and Huang, 2008; Huang, 2008). As the bureaucracies in Japan and many of the dynamic Asian economies were not overblown and generally competent, the incidence of rent seeking remained low. Like other developing countries, 'graft' at all levels of the government system was not prevalent in this group of economies.

Pragmatic economic reforms and restructuring played a key role in the achievement of rapid GDP growth in dynamic Asia. Reform policies were highly effective and yielded laudable outcomes in this group of economies. They were essentially based, as we have argued, on Neoclassical Economics or Open-Economy Macroeconomics.

Institutional development concepts

The last quarter century witnessed the rise of Orthodox, Neoclassical, Institutional and numerous Heterodox Economics theories in East Asia. According to them, institutional development or 'development reform' plays a distinct role in promoting economic growth. It is logical to stress that a country's institutions and economic policies make a decisive contribution to its long-term economic growth performance. If a low-income, developing economy adopts sound macroeconomic policies and creates effective institutions and therefore is able to implement them efficiently, it will characteristically enjoy rapid growth and catch-up. Theory based on institutions developed and the 'New Institutional Economics' integrated institutional development into mainstream Neoclassical Economics. The writings of Nobel Laureate Ronald Coase (1910–2013) are regarded as pioneering in this area. He had introduced the concept of *transaction costs* into economic analysis (see Coase, 1937).

The role of institutions and governance in economic development was theoretically developed by other Neoclassical Economics scholars. Two of the noted names in this regard are US economist, Douglass North (1920–2015) (1981), another Nobel Prize-winner, as well as Mancur Olson (1932–1998) (1981). Their seminal research inspired researchers and policy-makers to investigate empirically the impact of institutions on economic growth and development. Following their lead, several analysts concluded in empirical cross-national studies that there is *a positive association between institutional development and governance and GDP growth* (see Knack and Keefer, 1995; Barro, 1996; Kaufmann et al., 2000; Feng, 2003; Knack, 2003; Kaufmann and Kraay, 2008). After these theoretical developments and empirical researches, steady and intensive institutional development and good governance began to be seen as a necessary pre-condition of sustained long-term growth. The dynamic Asian economies benefitted from steady institutional development. However, as regards how institutions affect growth, or which institutions are necessary in what form, or what is the *causal* channel of effects remained uncertain and vague (Helpman, 2004; Chang, 2007; Rodrik, 2008).

There is thus now a growing literature that stresses the role of *Institutions* and *Governance* in promoting rapid growth in Asia. Some even talk of an 'institution/governance-growth nexus'; high economic performance was held logically to be a function of both policy framework and institutions that implement it (Rodrik et al., 2004; Acemoglu et al., 2005). Many studies regard institutional development and adaptation and superior governance a rationale behind the economic success of the Asian economies (Radelet et al., 1997; Milo, 2007; Lee and Hong, 2012). A study of institutional development in developing economies found that *seven* of the 11 developing countries that made satisfactory advances in institutional development were from Asia. They were *Hong Kong, Japan, Korea, Malaysia, Singapore, Taiwan* and *Thailand* (Knack, 2003).

Using the Neoclassical growth framework augmented with institutional controls and the latest estimation techniques in panel data analysis, Hall and Ahmed

(2014) found evidence of a positive institutional effect on the growth of the Asian economies. The dynamic Asian economies were christened the 'catch-up' countries, that is, those that were likely to rapidly catch up with the advanced economies of the West. Efficient political and other institutions supported rapid economic growth in this group of Asian economies (Feng, 2003; Nawaz, 2015). Governments in many dynamic Asian economies, particularly in Korea, Taiwan, Singapore and China were widely considered autocratic but they did create conditions for growth by providing political order and social stability necessary for sustained economic growth.

According to a ranking of institutional development by Zhuang *et al.* (2010), the dynamic Asian economies were ranked at the top in terms of political stability, government effectiveness and control over bureaucratic corruption, but somewhat surprisingly they were ranked second in regulatory quality and rule of law. They were not ranked high in terms of voice of the people, or freedom of expression. Regulatory quality was found relatively higher in the South-East Asian economies than in the East Asian economies.

Diffusion of Western Economics and policy concepts in China

The Opium Wars of 1839–1841 were an epochal time for China, when 'unequal treaties' were foisted on it by the Western powers. The objective of these series of treaties was to open China's lucrative markets to Western trade. The British forced the issue by attacking the Chinese port cities of Guangzhou and Tianjin in the Second Opium War (1856–1860). These treaties granted a number of rights and privileges to Western powers. Until this time, China was intellectually and politically remote and isolated from the West. Businessmen and missionaries could enter China after this point. This was the period when China 'entered a turbulent and painful process of modernization' (Trescott, 2007: 1).

This also marked the gradual beginning of teaching of political economy by the American missionaries in China. In 1902, Adam Smith's *Wealth of Nations* was translated in Mandarin by Yan Fu (1854–1921) and a more accessible *Concise History of Economic Thought* was published by Liang Qichao (1873–1929) a year later in 1903 (see Liang, 1903; Trescott, 2007; Borokh, 2012). These were two important first steps in China's Economics education. A noted Chinese contributor to the Economics debates of this period was Sun Yat-sen (1866–1925), the founding-father of Republican China, who was highly influenced by the writings of Henry George (1839–1897) and Richard T. Ely (1854–1943). Both the Chinese leaders Chiang Kai-shek (1887–1975) and Mao Zedong (1893–1976) were highly swayed by Sun's thesis of a *State-guided* programme of economic development, as will be noted in later chapters.

The introduction of Western Economic ideas into China began in the late nineteenth century, and discernibly accelerated in its last decade (see the chapters by Trescott later in this volume). Towards the end of that century, modern universities were set up in China. The prestigious Peking University (*Beida*) was established in 1898 by the Imperial regime. There also were about 20 colleges run by missionaries. They offered elementary courses in Economics. A small trickle of the Chinese students started attending US universities to study Economics at graduate level. By the mid-twentieth century, there were close to 150 students with US PhDs and nearly 400 who did their PhD in mainland Europe or the UK. Most returned to teach in the Chinese universities. When the Civil War ended and the Communist regime took over political power in 1949, many Western-trained economists left China. The ideas of Karl Marx (1818–1883) were taught in the universities mainly as ideology, although the Economics literature imposed was by Joseph Stalin (1878–1953). This trend reversed in 1977, however, when Deng Xiaoping (1904–1997) came to power. As the Chinese culture values education highly, Chinese students again started going to Western universities in an ever-increasing number (Trescott, 2007). A path to a form of *academic pluralism* had been initiated.

'Sinicizing' economics before absorbing

China no doubt benefitted from the Classical and Neoclassical macro- and microeconomic principles and tools of analyses, but there was a subtle ideological difference in Chinese applications of these universally applicable concepts, as subsequent chapters in this volume show in greater detail. Whilst China rapidly absorbed the modern economic concepts, it was not without 'Sinicizing' them. The Western capitalist system is oriented toward the success of an individual entrepreneur, whilst the Chinese ideology emphasizes the importance of the nation or society. In the same vein, it favours government intervention over free-market triumphalism. Where free markets operate, they are mutated and moderated by the government. This is a characteristic feature of a developmental state. Although this goes counter to what the 'Washington Consensus' is said to propose, it would be wrong to say that Chinese policy-makers ignored a 'Smithian' genre of economic growth (Arrighi, 2007) (see the chapters by Trescott, Li *et al.*, Fang, Zhu and Webber and others respectively in this volume).

There is a justification for government control of markets. Whilst the concepts and tools provided by Economics are intellectually appealing, many of them often have limited applicability for the developing and transition economies, particularly when they are at an *early* stage of Economic Growth. The latter group of economies is necessarily different from the mature ones of the West. The State has a duty to regulate the key areas of the economy (see Stiglitz, 2003). In his book *Freefall* (2010), Nobel Laureate Joseph Stiglitz (1943–) persuasively defended government's necessary role in free markets, even for the advanced economies. He has laid bare how free-market ideologists at the US Treasury and the IMF botched the Asian crisis of 1997–1998 and drove the crisis-ridden economies – particularly Indonesia, Korea and Thailand – deeper and longer into recessions. The IMF *post hoc* publicly admitted this mistake. The Asian crisis, it would seem, was a mere 'warm-up act' for the global financial crisis of 2007–2009.

A successful developmental state

The Chinese Cultural Revolution (1966–1976) was a period of grave political disorder, which had a serious destructive impact on the economy. Therefore, when it ended, the Economic Reforms became the *top priority* of the Communist Party of China. Continuing as usual with central planning was difficult because it had weakened during the chaos of the Cultural Revolution. Also, at this point, China was more cognizant of the prosperous Western countries and the economic success of Japan and other neighbouring Asian economies. It was reasonable for the Chinese leadership to ignore the ideology and look for a realistic path of economic growth, or an economic model that can deliver (see the chapters by Cohn, Fang, as well as Zhu and Webber respectively later in this volume). To attain this objective, the Chinese leaders considered applying a similar set of developmental strategies as the fast-growing Asian neighbours. China's basic growth model resembles the core features of the prototype followed by the NIEs. It also conforms to many of the principal characteristics of the models followed by Japan and the dynamic Asian economies.

That the authoritarian government of China, in turn, adopted a 'developmental state' model will not come as a surprise to anybody, albeit its institutional experiences were different from the other developmental states. It assigned the highest priority to deep-seated economic reforms to achieve the objective of rapid GDP growth.

In 1978, China thus unfolded a 'pragmatic' developmental model with the State still playing a transformative role in the economy. What followed was in effect a State-directed economic miracle. It promoted economic growth by providing incentives to the bureaucracy, which turned bureaucrats into entrepreneurs and reformers, encouraging a 'socialist market economy' with 'Chinese characteristics'. The bureaucracy followed development-oriented policies. Fiscal decentralization and patronage relationships helped in providing further incentives for economic growth (Knight, 2014).

China's rapid expansion represents the traditional state-guided development and resembles the American system of the early nineteenth century, with 'Listian' and 'Schumpeterian' concepts of Political Economy (see the chapters by Liu, as well as by Metzler, respectively later in this volume). It also benefitted from the experiences of the successful developmental states of Asia (Bolesta, 2012). The Chinese policy-makers have begun clairvoyantly chalking out their own reform frameworks. For instance, during the Third Party Plenum (November, 2013) and the Fourth Party Plenum (October, 2014), critical policy areas were chosen for reform. They covered financial sector reforms, central-local fiscal relations, competition policy, SOE reforms, rural land policy, foreign trade and foreign investment. The newest area of reform was legal reforms, so that the 'rule of law' could be strengthened. It has dawned on the Chinese policy-makers that for 'good' governance, the rule of law is indispensable. Implementation of financial sector reforms and central-local fiscal relations was the first to take off.

Proactive role of the multilateral institutions

After 1978, the two Bretton Woods institutions and the Government of Singapore became significant sources of expedient and valuable economic concepts and advice. They helped transform the 'non-market' Maoist China towards becoming a 'market economy' (see Vogel, 2013). By the end of the 1990s, before joining the WTO in 2001, China had made a good deal of progress in adopting such principles, without becoming a market economy (see Coase and Wang, 2013). An 'amber signal' is necessary here as modern China is *not* yet a market economy but a 'mixed economy'.

The two Bretton Woods institutions moved their representative offices from Taipei to Beijing in 1980. A proactive relationship with multilateral agencies facilitated China's reform policies and transformation processes. These two supranational institutions provided China with unique opportunities to learn from the experiences of the other transition economies 'in a professional and politically neutral international setting' (see Bottelier, 2006: 2). The World Bank offered policy advice in the late 1970s and played a significant role in purveying practical and wholesome Economic Concepts. Soon a cooperative relationship developed and China made good use of policy advice from this source. On its part, the World Bank remained sensitive and responsive to China's explicit needs. For instance, it did not aggressively assert comprehensive market liberalization or privatization. Some of the important areas which benefitted from its counselling are: fiscal reforms, SOE reforms and privatization, exchange-rate reforms and banking reforms (Bottelier, 2006).

Deng Xiaoping's admiration for Singapore's rapid economic rise led him to accepting advice from its founder, Lee Kuan Yew (1923–2015), and the government of Singapore (Herrmann-Pillath, 2012; Vogel, 2013). Deng not only liberated China's economy from the shackles of its ludicrous dogmatic ideology but also engineered China's embrace of rich concepts like globalization, promoting Western education and encouraging mass urbanization. The strategy of launching market-oriented Special Economic Zones (SEZs) first as an experiment and then as a major development strategy was learned from Singapore and Taiwan. When Deng launched his celebrated 'Open Door' policy in 1978, the Chinese economy was moribund. He was aware that China urgently needed Japanese and US technology, investment and knowledge for economic development because China was extremely deficient in all three. Hindsight reveals that the US and other foreign firms and transnational corporations played a crucial role in China's Economic Growth and Modernization as well as becoming a manufacturing juggernaut (see Vogel, 2013).

Neighbouring Asian economies: learning by observing

Learning from its dynamic neighbours, China liberalized its economy with regard to trade and FDI. It deliberately created welcoming incentives and regulatory environment for mobilizing FDI. During the initial period, FDI served for domestic entrepreneurship. China's large and wealthy 'Diaspora' was eager to invest in China. Attracted by China's investment opportunities, large volumes of FDI began flowing in. FDI policies evolved continuously alongside economic development and strengthened industrial capacity.

China adopted an outward-oriented, export-led growth strategy in the 1980s. Inbound FDI played a vital role in China's economic development and export success. Indeed, export-led growth has been more significant for China than for other Asian countries (see Tingvall and Ljungwall, 2010). In the Seventh Five Year Plan (1986–1990), such growth was assigned a regional order of priority. The Eastern provinces of China were to adopt this strategy first, followed by the Central provinces and Western provinces. At the same time processing trade was adopted as a long-term growth strategy. The term processing trade implies importing intermediate inputs and raw materials, assembling or processing them into final value-added products and exporting them.

As China suffered a deficit in capital and technology, the processing trade suited China well. It learned about the concept of processing trade from the surrounding Asian economies, which had had a successful run in this area. It became immensely popular in China. Essentially due to China's post-1978 'Open Door' policy and establishment of export-promotion zones (EPZs), processing trade grew fast. This regime went on becoming increasingly important throughout the reform period. Soon, processing trade became more than half of China's total trade. It peaked in 1990 at 60 per cent of total trade. Thereafter, it stabilized at above 50 per cent. An important driver of China's export growth was the success of its processing-trade regime (Dean *et al.*, 2009). By definition, processing trade creates trade surpluses. Since 1990, an increasing amount of China's trade surpluses originated from this source.

Largely because of its proximity to Hong Kong SAR, Guangdong Province had become successful in processing trade in the 1980s. The other Eastern provinces followed suit. China's accession to the WTO in 2002 was a *defining moment* for its trade. Both exports and imports grew after 2001, but their rate of growth was not remarkable. However, after 2004 their pace of growth was much more impressive, with exports growing at a relatively faster pace leading to increasing current account surpluses. Rapid growth in trade increased China's trade dependency. Around this period, trade was 65 per cent of GDP and continued to hover at that level (Yao, 2011).

Since the mid-1980s, China was active in international production sharing with Hong Kong SAR, Japan, Korea, Taiwan, Thailand and the other Asian economies. China actively participated in the vertical production-networks and supply-chains. As China's economic integration with the regional and global economies enhanced, it became deeply integrated into the Asian production-networks (see Das, 2014). Although China was a latecomer to fragmented production and the international division of labour, Asian production-networks are now largely hinged on China. China is an integral part of these networks. They have made a significant contribution to growth in the dynamic Asian economies.

China is regarded as 'special' in exporting sophisticated products, not comparable with a country of its income level. The product-range that China exports, however, seems to repudiate *prima facie* the 'Heckscher–Ohlin' principle in Western Economics. In an influential paper, Rodrik (2006) argued that China's success in trade cannot be explained simply by specialization according to comparative advantage. The sophisticated products that are exported from China are comparable to those from a country having per capita income three times higher than China. It is partly the result of a large number of foreign firm, MNCs and their affiliates operating from China and partly that of the industrial policy. The total number of MNCs and their affiliates in China at the end of 2014 was 458,000. China's exports to the US show a large overlap with the exports from the OECD countries. However, Chinese products and varieties are priced lower than the OECD counterparts. In several products, Chinese relative prices have a falling trend (Schott, 2008).

Continuous updating of education

A 'University of International Business and Economics' had already been set up in Beijing, as early as 1951. It was given the status of a 'key' university under the Ministry of Education. But being 'red' rather than 'expert' soon prevailed as the guiding policy. Cognizant that China's education infrastructure ended up in a state of complete disarray at the end of Mao's reign, Deng Xiaoping made a strategic decision in 1978 to send 3,000 students and scholars annually to overseas universities for higher education. This number went on rising and between 1978 and 2006, 1.06 million Chinese students went overseas for higher education (Ryan, 2011). In the process of higher education reforms and internationalization of education China substantially borrowed from the Western models, particularly from the American higher education system. Often this resulted in tensions and contradictions in the Chinese universities. Since 2000, China's education reforms grew more wide-ranging than ever, pushing all levels and every aspect of education. This brought about a 'sea change' in China's higher education system. As the reforms progressed, importance and popularity of Economics and Business education rose. In 1984, MBA education was initiated in China in Dalian and has flourished, with China having several highly rated Business Schools today (see Warner 2014: 125).

During the 2000s, Economics and Business education in the Chinese universities incorporated many standard courses that were taught in the US universities, although Marxist courses still lingered on in many places mostly at undergraduate level (see the chapters by Fang, Cohn as well as Zhu and Webber respectively later in this volume). They were to use the same textbooks as in the US, but translated into Mandarin. Courses in International Microeconomics, International Macroeconomics and Econometrics were compulsory for students working for degrees in Economics. High-scoring high school graduates selected Economics or Business Administration as their major in the universities. Even when they choose other subjects – say, Engineering – as their major, Chinese students often prefer Economics and Business Administration as a minor (see Qian, 2014). Colleges and universities in the US have become the most popular among Chinese students. According to the Institute of International Education, there were 274,000 Chinese foreign students studying in the US in 2014 (IIE, 2014). By 2016, over half a million went abroad for study, with over four million in total having been overseas since the reforms (see Ministry of Education, 2016); many are yet to return. China now has a large middle class and families can afford to send their offspring for tertiary education to the US, as well as Australia, Canada, the UK and so on. The popular subjects that particularly attract Chinese students are science, technology and engineering degree courses, as well as business and economic ones.

Conclusions

To sum up, several Asian economies followed essentially logical, sound and synergetic economic policies over the preceding half century, which were instrumental in their extraordinary growth performance. This chapter addresses the question: *What was the source of economic ideas and policy thinking in the dynamic Asian economies, which led to their brisk economic ascent in a record time span?* This remains an important one because Economics, or Economic Policy-making, was not an 'Asian' science as such in its origins. Economic ideas, concepts and strategies that the dynamic Asian economies deployed, and benefitted from, were we have argued essentially *Western*, at times predominantly Anglo-American in recent times. This chapter traces how they came to Asia and how they were disseminated across a range of countries. We identify some of the principal policies from which the Asian economies benefitted, relate them to theoretical concepts from which they were derived and the leading scholars who propounded them. We examine these productive, constructive, innovative, growth-spawning concepts and strategies and explore how they reached the dynamic Asian economies. Other chapters will amplify these remarks and spell them out in greater detail vis-à-vis their country contexts and in terms of the specific Western economists involved.

The post-Second World War period is the optimal time frame chosen for such a study. The Asian economic 'miracle' is characterized by the 'Flying Geese' paradigm of growth. In this paradigm, Japan was the 'leading Goose'. Pre-War Japan enjoyed economic maturity and a standard of living comparable to that of the mature industrialized economies of the West. By 1968, Japan had become the second largest economic power in the world, after the US, although now overtaken by China.

Japan was the first to absorb the Western economic concepts and benefit from them (as several further chapters in this edited volume will attest). Japanese culture is widely regarded as porous and is apt at absorbing beneficial economic ideas. During the early decades of the *Meiji Restoration* period (1868–1912), Japan found, studied and successfully selected economic concepts and theories as well as technology from the Western world and absorbed them. The *Meiji* leaders were also eager to establish an education system which was good enough to catch up with the West. Therefore, an ambitious education development plan was launched at an early stage, which in turn helped in disseminating the Western economic concepts.

Japan's swift-paced post-War recovery had a decisive *demonstration effect* on its neighbours. Japan became the principal conduit of Economic Concepts for the dynamic Asian economies, spreading to South Korea, Singapore, Taiwan and so on. They learned from Japan's experiments and experiences and after a time lag applied many of these policies in a *mutatis mutandis* manner to their own economies. Besides the application of a sound and pragmatic economic policy framework, developing proper institutions and export-led industrialization, Japan's growth strategy is known for the 'market-guiding' role of the State, or the 'developmental state' concept, and 'market-friendly' policies. Many of Japan's richly beneficial and practicable policy concepts emanated from Classical and Neoclassical economic principles. The four Asian NIEs took a leaf from Japan's book and made a successful attempt to break out of their economic stagnation. No doubt each NIE made its own modifications to Japan's prototype according to its own predilections and circumstances and also adopted its own unique concepts and strategies (see the later chapter by Das in this volume). However, following Japan's lead in Economic Policies and Strategies was not all that the NIEs, the ASEAN-4 and China economies did. For these economies the post-1960 period was also characterized by the acceleration of absorption of knowledge and productive economic concepts from the advanced Western countries. This was their own period of Renaissance, or intellectual discovery, that brought novel ideas in Economics to them.

Japan's post-War boom was *inter alia* accelerated by pursuing sensible economic policies like balanced budgets, market liberalization, market-friendly policies for the private sector as well as emphasis on upgrading technology and honing human capital. In pursuing many of these strategies, Japan relied on Western Economics for its concepts. Basic economic reforms, like private sector ownership and liberalizing the economy and opening up to foreign markets, which were adopted by Japan, were essentially based on the application of Neoclassical Economics. Scientific knowledge and macro- and microeconomic theories in the important economic policy and business-related areas like price, interest, currency, competition, growth, trade and foreign exchange, enterprise behaviour and corporate strategy, from which Japan and other 'miracle' economies of Asia benefitted had originated in the Western academic world. This is not to downplay the contribution of individual Asian economies in absorbing and disseminating the Western economic concepts and applying them *pragmatically* to their own economies, as well as revamping and refurbishing their education systems and universities.

To sum up, this chapter, in turn, has traced the Western origins of the concept of the 'developmental state' and how it was disseminated in Asia to the NIEs, as well as later to China. Similarly, the roots of some of the characteristically Asian strategies and economic concepts, like emphasis on liberalization of the economy, export-led industrialization, macroeconomic reforms and restructuring, and institutional development, as well as technological upgrading, have been tracked down.

Notes

1 The four NIEs are Hong Kong SAR, Korea, Singapore and Taiwan.
2 Three noted country-specific analyses of the 'developmental state' are Johnson (1982) for Japan, Amsden (1989) for Korea and Wade (2004) for Taiwan.
3 See also Solow (1956, 1958).
4 The National University of Singapore is voted top in the rankings.
5 These can be dubbed three pillars of Japanese success in this regard.
6 The 'hukou' is a system of household registration in the PRC.

References

Acemoglu, D., S. Johnson and J. Robinson. (2005). 'Institutions as a Fundamental Cause of Long Run Growth', in P. Aghion and S. Durlauf (eds), *Handbook of Economic Growth.* Amsterdam: Elsevier, 218–240.

Aghion, P. and P. Howitt. (2007). 'Capital, Innovation and Growth Accounting'. *Oxford Review of Economic Policy.* 23: 79–93.

Amsden, A. (1989). *Asia's Next Giant: South Korea and Late Industrialization.* New York, NY and Oxford: Oxford University Press.

Arora, V. and V. Vamvakidis. (2010). 'China's Economic Growth and International Spillover'. Washington, DC: International Monetary Fund. Working Paper, No. WP/10/165. July.

Arrighi, G. (2007). *Adam Smith in Beijing: Lineage of the Twenty First Century.* London: Verso.

Asian Development Bank (ADB). (2015). *Asian Development Outlook 2015.* Manila: ADB.

Balassa, B. (1978). 'Export and Economic Growth: Further Evidence'. *Journal of Development Economics.* 5: 181–189.

Barro, R. J. (1996). 'Democracy and Growth'. *The Journal of Economics Growth.* 1: 1–27.

Beeson, M. (2004). 'The Rise and Fall (?) of the Developmental State', in L. Low (ed.), *Developmental State: Relevancy, Redundancy or Reconfiguration?* New York, NY: Nova Science Publishers, 29–40.

Bernanke, B. S. (2009). 'Asia and the Global Financial Crisis'. Paper presented at the conference on *Asia and the Global Financial Crisis*, organized by the Federal Reserve Bank of San Francisco, NY, at Santa Barbara, CA, on 19 October.

Bhagwati, J. N. (1978). *Foreign Trade Regime and Economic Development.* Cambridge, MA: Ballinger Publishing Co.

Bhagwati, J. N. (1988). 'Export Promoting Trade Strategies: Issues and Evidence'. *The World Bank Research Observer.* 3: 27–57.

Bolesta, A. (2012). *China as a Post-Socialist Developmental State.* London: London School of Economics and Political Science [LSE], Unpublished Doctoral Dissertation.

Borokh, O. (2012). 'Adam Smith in Imperial China: Translation and Cultural Adaptation', *Œconomia [sic].* 2–4: 411–441.

Bottelier, P. (2006). 'China and the World Bank: How a Partnership was Built'. Stanford, CA: Stanford Center for International Development, Working Paper, No. 277, April.

Breznitz, D. and M. Murphree. (2011). *Run the Red Queen.* New Haven, CT: Yale University Press.

Campos, J. E. and H. R. Root. (1996). *The Key to the Asian Miracle: Making Shared Growth Credible.* Washington, DC: The Brookings Institution.

Chang, H. J. (2007). *Institutional Change and Economic Development.* Tokyo: United Nations University Press.

Chia, S. Y. (2013). 'The ASEAN Economic Community: Progress, Challenges and Prospects'. Tokyo: Asian Development Bank Institute. Working Paper, No. 440, October.

Christensen, K. (2014). 'Thought Leader Interview: Dominic Barton'. Toronto: Rotman School of Management. Spring. Available at www.rotman.utoronto.ca/-/media/Files/Programs-and-Areas/Rotman%20Magazine/Thought%20Leader%20Articles/Barton.pdf (accessed 19 October 2015).

Chung, Y.L. (2007). *South Korea in the Fast Lane: Economic Development and Capital Formation.* Oxford: Oxford University Press.

Coase, R. (1937). 'The Nature of Firm'. *Economica.* 4: 386–405.

Coase, R. and N. Wang. (2013). 'How China Became Capitalist'. *CATO Policy Report.* 35: 1–12.

Das, D. K. (1991). *Korean Economic Dynamism.* London: Macmillan.

Das, D. K. (2008). *The Chinese Economic Renaissance: Apocalypse or Cornucopia.* Basingstoke: Palgrave Macmillan.

Das, D. K. (2011). *The Asian Economy: Spearheading the Recovery from the Global Financial Crisis.* London and New York, NY: Routledge.

Das, D. K. (2014). *China and the Asian Economies: Interactive Dynamics, Synergy and Symbiotic Growth.* London and New York, NY: Routledge.

Das, D. K. (2015). *An Enquiry into the Asian Growth Model.* Basingstoke: Palgrave Macmillan.

Dean, J., M. Lovely and J. Mora. (2009). 'Decomposing China–Japan–US Trade: Vertical Special Specialization, Ownership and Organizational Form'. *Journal of Asian Economics.* 20: 596–610.

Dollar, D. (1992). 'Outward-Oriented Developing Economies Really Do Grow More Rapidly'. *Economic Development and Cultural Change.* 40: 523–544.

Duke, B. 2009. *History of Modern Japanese Education.* New Brunswick, NJ: Rutgers University Press.

Easterly, W. (1995). 'Explaining Miracles: Growth Regressions Meet the Gang of Four', in T. Ito and A. O. Krueger (eds), *Growth Theories in the Light of the East Asian Experience.* Chicago, IL: University of Chicago Press, 133–163.

Edwards, S. (1998). 'Openness, Productivity and Growth: What Do We Really Know?' *Economic Journal.* 108: 383–398.

Ellington, L. (2004). 'Learning from the Japanese Economy'. *Japan Digest.* Stanford Program on International and Cross-Cultural Education. Available at http://spice.fsi.stanford.edu/docs/learning_from_the_japanese_economy (accessed 19 October 2015).

Farrarini, B. (2010). 'Trade and Income in Asia: Panel Data Evidence from Instrumental Variable Regression'. Manila. Asian Development Bank. Working Paper Series, No. 234. November.

Feng, Y. (2003). *Democracy, Governance and Economic Performance: Theory and Evidence.* Cambridge, MA: The MIT Press.

Fogel, R. W. (2009). 'The Impact of Asian Miracle on the Theory of Economic Growth'. Cambridge, MA: National Bureau of Economic Research. Working Paper, No. 14967. May.

Frankel, J. A. and D. H. Romer. (1999). 'Does Trade Cause Growth?' *American Economic Review.* 89: 379–399.

Frankel, J. A., D. H. Romer and T. Cyrus. (1996). 'Trade and Growth in East Asian Countries: Cause and Effect'. Cambridge, MA: National Bureau of Economic Research. NBER Working Paper, No. 5732, August.

Gerschenkron, A. (1962). 'Economic Backwardness in Historical Perspective', in A. Gerschenkron (ed.), *Economic Backwardness in Historical Perspective.* New York, NY: Praeger, 26–52.

Gill, I. and H. J. Kharas. (2007). *An East Asian Renaissance.* Washington, DC: The World Bank.

Goldsmith, R. W. (1983). *The Financial Development of India, Japan and the United States.* New Haven, CT: Yale University Press.

Grossman, G. M. and E. Helpman. (1991). *Innovation and Growth in the World Economy.* Cambridge, MA: MIT Press.

Haggard, S. (2004). 'Institutions and Growth in East Asia'. *Studies in Comparative International Development.* 38: 53–81.

Haggard, S. and Y. Huang. (2008). 'Political Economy of Private Sector Development', in L. Brandt and T. G. Rawski (eds), *China's Great Economic Transformation.* New York, NY: Cambridge University Press, 337–374.

Hall, S. G. and M. Ahmed. (2014). 'Revisiting the Institutions-Growth Nexus in Developing Countries: The New Evidence'. *New Zealand Economic Papers.* 48: 301–312.

Helpman, E. (2004). *The Mystery of Economic Growth.* Cambridge, MA: Harvard University Press.

Herrmann-Pillath, C. (2012). 'A "Third Culture" in Economics? An Essay on Smith. Confucius and the Rise of China'. Frankfurt, Germany. Frankfurt School of Finance and Management. Working Paper, No. 159.

Hicks, G. (1989). 'The Four Little Dragons: An Enthusiast's Guide'. *Asian-Pacific Economic Literature.* 3: 35–49.

Hill, H. (2013). 'The Political Economy of Policy Reforms'. *Asian Development Review.* 30: 108–130.

Hsieh, C. T. and P. J. Klenow. (2010). 'Development Accounting'. *American Economic Journal: Macroeconomics.* 2: 207–223.

Hu, A. G. (2015). 'Innovation and Economic Growth in East Asia: An Overview'. *Asian Economic Policy Review.* 10: 19–37.

Huang, Y. (2008). *Capitalism with Chinese Characteristics.* Cambridge and New York, NY: Cambridge University Press.

Huff, G. (2003). 'Financial Transition in Pre-World War II Japan and Southeast Asia'. Paper presented at the *Economic History Association Annual Meeting* in Nashville, TN, on 20–23 July.

Hussain, F. and N. Saidin. (2012). 'Economic Growth in ASEAN Countries: A Panel Data Analysis'. *International Journal of Economics and Finance.* 4: 32–61.

Ichimura, S. (2013). *Political Economy of Japanese and Asian Development.* Tokyo: Springer.

Institute of International Education (IIE). (2014). 'Open Doors Report on International Education Exchange'. New York. Available at www.iie.org/Research-and-Publications/Open-Doors (accessed 27 October 2015).

International Monetary Fund (IMF). (2006). *World Economic Outlook.* Washington, DC: IMF, September.

International Monetary Fund (IMF). (2014). *Regional Economic Outlook: Asia and Pacific.* Washington, DC: IMF, April.

International Monetary Fund (IMF). (2015). *World Economic Outlook.* Washington, DC: IMF, April.

Irwin, D. A. and M. Tervio. (2002). 'Does Trade Raise Income? Evidence from the Twentieth Century'. *Journal of International Economics.* 58: 1–18.

Ito, T. (1996). 'Japan and the Asian Economies: A "Miracle" in Transition'. *Brookings Paper on Economic Activity.* 2: 205–272.

Jiang, Y. (2014). *Openness, Economic Growth and Regional Disparities.* New York, NY: Springer.

Johnson, C. (1982). *MITI and the Japanese Miracle.* Stanford, CA: Stanford University Press.

Kasahara, S. (2013). 'The Asian Developmental State and the Flying Geese Paradigm'. Geneva: United Nations Conference on Trade and Development. Discussion Paper, No. 213, November.

Kaufmann, D. and A. Kraay. (2008). 'Governance Indicators: Where Are We?' Washington, DC: World Bank, Research Working Paper, No. 4370, April.

Kaufmann, D., A. Kraay and P. Zoido-Lobaton. (2000). 'Governance Matters: From Measurement to Action'. *Finance and Development.* 37: 18–22.

Kim, L. and R. Nelson. (eds) (2000). *Experiences of the Newly Industrializing Countries.* Cambridge: Cambridge University Press.

Knack, S. (2003). *Democracy, Governance and Growth.* Ann Arbor, MI: University of Michigan Press.

Knack, S. and P. Keefer. (1995). 'Institutions and Economic Performance: Cross-Country Tests Using Alternative Institutional Measures'. *The Journal of Economics and Politics.* 7: 207–227.

Knight, J. (2014). 'China as a Developmental State'. *The World Economy.* 37: 1335–1347.

Krueger, A. O. (1978). *Foreign Trade Regimes and Economic Development: Liberalization Attempts and Consequences.* Cambridge, MA: Ballinger Publishing Co.

Krugman, P. (1994). 'The Myth of Asian Miracle'. *Foreign Affairs.* 736: 2–78.

Krugman, P. (1998). 'What Happened to Asia?' Cambridge, MA: Department of Economics, Massachusetts Institute of Technology. Available at http://web.mit.edu/krugman/www/DISINTER.html (accessed 19 October 2015).

Kuznets, S. (1971). *Economic Growth of Nations: Total Output and Production Structure.* Chicago, IL: University of Chicago Press.

Kuznets, S. (1973). 'Modern Economic Growth: Findings and Reflections'. *American Economic Review.* 63: 247–258.

Lee, J.W. and K. Hong. (2012). 'Economic Growth in Asia: Determinants and Prospects'. *Japan and the World Economy.* 24: 101–113.

Lee, K. (2013). *Schumpeterian Analysis of Economic Catch-Up.* Cambridge: Cambridge University Press.

Liang, Q. (1903). *Concise History of Economic Thought* [*Yin-pin-shih Wen-chi*] in Chinese, serialized in the bi-weekly *Xinmin congbao* [*New Citizen*] from seventh issue onwards. Yokohama [*sic*]: New Citizen.

Lu, S. S. (2012). 'East Asian Growth Experience Revisited from the Perspective of a Neoclassical Model'. *Review of Economic Dynamics.* 15: 359–376.

Madsen, J. B. and J. B. Ang. (2013). 'The Asian Growth Miracle: Factor Accumulation'. Melbourne: Monash University. Department of Economics. Discussion Paper, No. 23/13.

McKinsey Global Institute (MGI). (2012). 'Urban World: Cities and the Rise of the Consuming Class'. *Insights and Publications*. June. Available at www.mckinsey.com/insights/urbanization/urban_world_cities_and_the_rise_of_the_consuming_class (accessed 1 October 2015).

Meade, J. E. (1961). *A Neo-Classical Theory of Economic Growth*. New York, NY: Oxford University Press.

Milo, M. S. (2007). 'Integrated Financial Supervision: An Institutional Perspective for the Philippines'. Tokyo: Asian Development Bank Institute. Discussion Paper, No. 81. October.

Ministry of Education (2016). *Blue Book: Report on Education*, 25 March. Beijing: Chinese Ministry of Education.

Nawaz, S. (2015). 'The Institution-Growth Nexus: Stages of Growth'. Munich: MPRA Archive. Paper No. 36961. Posted on 26 February 2015. Available at http://mpra.ub.uni-muenchen.de/36961/1/MPRA_paper_36961.pdf (accessed 19 October 2015).

Nolan, J., C. Rowley and M. Warner. (eds) (2016). *Business Networks in East Asian Capitalisms: Enduring Trends, Emerging Patterns*. London: Elsevier.

North, D. C. (1981). *Structure and Change in Economic History*. New York, NY: W. W. Norton & Co.

Ohanian, L. E. and M. L. J. Wright. (2014). 'Bad Investments and Missed Opportunities: Capital Flows to Asia and Latin America'. St Louis, MO: Federal Reserve Bank of St Louis, Working Paper, No. 2014–038A. October.

Ohno, K. (2006). *The Economic Development of Japan*. Tokyo: GRIPS Development Forum.

Okada, A. (2012). *Education Policy and Equal Opportunity in Japan*. New York, NY: Berghahn Books.

Olson, M. (1981). *The Rise and Decline of Nations: Economic Growth, Stagflation, and Social Rigidities*. New Haven, CT: Yale University Press.

Otsubo, S. T. (2007). *Post-War Development of the Japanese Economy:* Nagoya: Nagoya University.

Page, J. (1994). 'The East Asian Miracle: Four Lessons for Development Policy', in S. Fischer and J. J. Rotemberg (eds), *NBER Macroeconomic Annual 1994*, Vol. 9, Boston, MA: MIT Press, 219–282.

Park, J. (2012). 'Total Factor Productivity Growth in 12 Asian Economies: The Past and the Future'. *Japan and the World Economy*. 24: 114–127.

Pavcnik, N. (2002). 'Trade Liberalization, Exit, and Productivity Improvement: Evidence from Chile'. *Review of Economic Studies*. 69: 245–276.

Qian, Y. (2014). 'Economics and Business Education in China', in S. Fan (ed.), *Oxford Companion to the Economics of China*. Oxford: Oxford University Press, 488–499.

Quah, D. (2011). 'The Global Economy's Shifting Center of Gravity'. *Global Policy*. 2: 3–10.

Radelet, S., J. D. Sachs and J. W. Lee. (1997). 'Economic Growth in Asia'. Harvard University. Harvard Institute of International Development, Cambridge, MA, Discussion Paper, No. 609. November.

Razmi, A. and G. Hernandez. (2011). 'Can Asia Sustain an Export-Led Growth Strategy?' Tokyo: Asian Development Bank Institute. Working Paper, No. 329. December.

Rodriguez, F. (2006). 'Openness and Growth: What Have We Learned?' New York: United Nations University. Department of Economics and Social Affairs. Working Paper, No. 51.

Rodriguez, F. and D. Rodrik. (1999). 'Trade Policy and Economic Growth: A Skeptic's Guide to Cross-National Evidence'. Cambridge, MA: National Bureau of Economic Research. Working Paper, No. 7081.

Rodriguez, F. and D. Rodrik. (2001). 'Trade Policy and Economic Growth: A Skeptic's Guide to Cross-National Evidence', in B. S. Bernanke and K. Rogoff (eds), *NBER Macroeconomic Annual 2000.* Cambridge, MA: National Bureau of Economic Research, 261–338.

Rodrik, D. (2006). 'What's So Special about China's Exports?' Cambridge, MA: National Bureau of Economic Research. NBER Working Paper, No. 11947.

Rodrik, D. (2008). 'Thinking About Governance', in World Bank, *Governance, Growth and Development Decision-Making.* Washington, DC: World Bank.

Rodrik, D. (2009). 'Growth After the Crisis'. Washington, DC. Commission on Growth and Development. Working Paper, No. 65.

Rodrik, D., A. Subramanian and F. Trebbi. (2004). 'Institutions Rule: The Primacy of Institutions over Geography and Integration in Economic Development'. *Journal of Economic Growth.* 9: 131–165.

Ross, J. (2015). 'How Singapore Achieved Higher Per Capita GDP than the US'. *Key Trends in Globalization.* 1 April. Available at http://ablog.typepad.com/keytrendsin-globalisation/economic-theory/ (accessed 1 October 2015).

Ryan, J. (2011). *China's Higher Education Reforms and Internationalization.* London and New York, NY: Routledge.

Sachs, J. D. and A. Warner. (1995). 'Economic Reform and the Process of Global Inte-gration'. *Brookings Papers on Economic Activity.* 26: 1–118.

Schott, P. K. (2008). 'The Relative Sophistication of Chinese Exports'. *Economic Policy.* 53: 5–49.

Schultz, T. W. (1962). *Investment in Human Beings.* Chicago, IL: University of Chicago Press.

Schultz, T. W. (1971). *Investment in Human Capital: The Role of Education and Research.* New York, NY: The Free Press.

Solow, R. M. (1956). 'A Contribution to the Theory of Economic Growth'. *The Quarterly Journal of Economics.* 70: 65–94.

Solow, R. M. (1957). 'Technical Change and the Aggregate Production Function'. *Review of Economics and Statistics.* 39: 312–320.

Solow, R. M. (1958). 'A Skeptical Note on the Constancy of Relatives'. *American Economic Review.* 48: 618–621.

Stiglitz, J. E. (2003). *Globalization and its Discontents.* New York, NY: W. W. Norton & Co.

Stiglitz, J. E. (2010). *Freefall: America, Free Markets and the Sinking of the Global Economy.* New York, NY: W. W. Norton & Co.

Stiglitz, J. E. and S. Yusuf. (eds) (2001). *Rethinking the Asian Miracle.* Washington, DC: World Bank.

Swan, T. W. (1956). 'Economic Growth and Capital Accumulation'. *Economic Record.* 32: 334–361.

Taniguchi, K. (2011). 'History of the Idea of Citizenship and its Teaching in Japan', in N. Ikeno (ed.), *Citizenship Education in Japan.* London and New York, NY: Continuum International Publishing Group, 1–3.

Tingvall, P. G. and C. Ljungwall. (2010). 'Is China Different?: A Meta-Analysis of Export-Led Growth'. Stockholm: Stockholm School of Economics. Working Paper, No. 15. April.

Trescott, P. B. (2007). *Jingji Xue: History of the Introduction of Western Economic Ideas into China.* Hong Kong: Chinese University Press.

United Nations Conference on Trade and Development (UNCTAD). (2015). *Global Investment Monitor.* Geneva and New York: UNCTAD. 29 January.

Vogel, E. F. (2013). *Deng Xiaoping and Transformation of China.* Cambridge, MA. Harvard University Press.

Wade, R. (2004). *Governing the Markets.* 2nd Edition. Princeton, NJ: Princeton University Press.

Warner, M. (2014). *Understanding Chinese Management: Past Present and Future,* London and New York, NY: Routledge.

Wen, Y. (2015). 'Making of an Economic Superpower'. St Louis, MO: Federal Reserve Bank of St Louis. Working Paper, No. 006A. March.

World Bank (WB). (1993). *The East Asian Miracle: Economic Growth and Public Policy.* Oxford: Oxford University Press.

World Bank (WB). (2015). *World Economic Indicator Database.* Washington, DC. Available at http://data.worldbank.org/indicator/NY.GNP.PCAP.CD (accessed 29 October 2015).

Yao, Y. (2011). 'The Relationship between China's Export-led Growth and China's Double Transition'. *Asian Economic Papers.* 10: 52–76.

Yu, X., C. Zhang and Q. Lai. (2014). 'China's Rise as a Major Contributor to Science and Technology'. *Proceedings of the National Academy of Sciences.* 111: 9437–9442.

Zhu, X. (2012). 'Understanding China's Growth: Past, Present and Future'. *Journal of Economic Perspectives.* 27: 103–124.

Zhuang, J., E. de Deos and A. Legman-Martin. (2010). 'Governance and Institutional Quality'. Manila: Asian Development Bank. Working Paper Series, No. 139. February.

3 The diffusion of Western Economics in China[1]

Paul B. Trescott

Introduction

Although China has had a long and distinguished intellectual tradition in the past, the country's scholars were long isolated from the West during the seventeenth and eighteenth centuries, at the very time Economics (*jingji xue*) was evolving in the West (see Trescott, 2007). Whilst China's economy had been prosperous by world standards down to roughly 1500, isolation, dysfunctional government and a powerful Malthusian process brought China's per-capita income levels to a very low level by 1900.

As early as 200 BC, some Chinese intellectuals envisioned the self-adjusting processes of market economy (notably the historian, Sima Qian, *c.*145 or 135–86 BC). But by the nineteenth century, China's government appeared to lack both vigour and an awareness of policy. The country's intellectual tradition had neglected the new science and technology, its written language lacked an 'alphabet', and there were no modern universities (see Spence, 1990).

China's isolation began to crumble, however, in the 1840s, when 'unequal treaties' generated by the 'Opium Wars' forced China to admit Western traders and missionaries. Japan, which experienced similar Western pressures, reacted by aggressive modernization (see the chapter by Yagi on Japan later in this volume). China, however, suffered major setbacks in this period. The first of these was the 'Taiping Rebellion' (1851–1864), which inflicted as many as 30 million deaths and devastated a substantial area of central China. The second was the 'obstructionist' position of Li Hongzhang (1803–1901), an influential adviser to the dowager Empress.

The Empress (Cixi Taihu, 1835–1908) herself was initially receptive to modernizing efforts. In 1861, another adviser Zeng Geofan (1811–1872) established China's first modern arsenal in Anqing. Soon after, the creation of the huge Jiangnan Arsenal became a centre for translations of Western works. The same impulse underlay the decision in 1870 to send 120 young men to America for study. This scheme was abruptly terminated in 1881, a decision no doubt symbolizing antagonism toward Westernization. The reluctance of the Chinese government to study Japan's modernization set the stage for China's military defeat in 1894–1895 – one which brought a turn toward reform.

Conservatism was also manifest in the Imperial Examinations, success in which opened the path to becoming an official and achieving power, prestige, comfort and wealth. The examinations tested familiarity with classic Chinese writings and traditional literary styles. They were, however, abolished in 1905. Many Chinese intellectuals were distressed for years by the unequal treaties and by China's economic backwardness. Wei Yuan (1794–1857) and Wang Tao (1828–1897) were among many who wrote about Western economic institutions and stressed the importance of trade, commerce and transportation as means to economic prosperity and national strength. Ma Jianzhong (1845–1900) was probably the first Chinese person to study Economics in the West, as part of his Law studies in Paris in 1876–1877.

In 1861, the Chinese government opened a school to prepare diplomatic interpreters. They engaged an American missionary, William A. P. Martin, (1827–1916) as Director. He introduced a course in 'Richer Nations' Policy' (Political Economy), for which he and Wan Fengzhao translated (in 1880) Henry Fawcett's *Manual of Political Economy* (1863). Another Language School was opened in 1863 and a Translation Bureau was added in 1868, headed by John Fryer (1839–1928), an English missionary. He and his Chinese colleagues produced a wide variety of translations, including *Money* by James Platt (new in 1880), Thomas Farrer's *The State in Its Relation to Trade* (originally 1883) and a compilation of works on mints and coinage. The most influential of Fryer's translations involved *Political Economy for Use in Schools and for Private Instruction by* John Hill Burton (1809–1881) (translated in 1885, originally published in Edinburgh in 1852). Of its 154 pages, about 50 were devoted to a broad survey of the evolution of social institutions. These sections attracted wide attention from intellectuals in both Japan and China. Burton had spoken enthusiastically about Britain's free-trade policy but in the translation, the repeal of the 'Corn Laws' in 1847 was ignored. The translation failed to convey Burton's faith in the beneficial workings of free competitive markets and ignored his clear statement that the reward to labour must reflect workers' productivity.

Westernizing Chinese

A landmark in the introduction of Western Economics came with the 1902 translation of Adam Smith's (1723–1790) classic, *An Inquiry into the Nature and Causes of the Wealth of Nations*, abbreviated as the *Wealth of Nations (WN)*, first published in 1776 (see Trescott, 2007: 7). The translator, Yan Fu (1854–1921), had studied in England and had experienced Western prosperity and institutions at first hand. But his translation, which he called *Origins of Wealth (Yuan fu)* did not have a major impact, for several reasons.

Smith's work was written as a critique of economic interventionism, particularly controls on international trade associated with English mercantilism. China had already been forced to adopt 'free trade' and Chinese intellectuals resented this, believing the policy held back China's own industrialization. Second, Smith's book was very lengthy and wordy. Its organization was idiosyncratic – major topics like factor-pricing were developed in sections ostensibly devoted to other topics. Yan wrote in a rather convoluted traditional style, which was not easy for many Chinese to follow. Smith's enthusiasm for commerce, trade and competition contravened strong Chinese prejudices against merchants and for agriculture. Smith's tribute to the optimizing potential of free competitive markets was poorly rendered by Yan (see Liu, 2013) (see the chapter by Lai later in this volume).

But Smith's book was above all a tribute to the importance and analytics of the process of economic growth. His view stressed the central role of capital, generated by saving and investment, aided by technological innovation and Yan Fu handled this very well. He endorsed Smith's conviction that growth of capital would raise the demand for labour and thus increase real wages. Higher family incomes would reduce infant mortality and lead to population growth. Smith did not share the impending fear that diminishing returns would prevent increase in per-capita real incomes.

The priority of capital investment in promoting economic growth became a standard feature of Chinese discourse down to the present day, involving such authorities as Sun Yat-sen (1866–1925) and Mao Zedong (1893–1976). But it took a long time before people appreciated the importance of an 'optimizing' framework to use capital efficiently. Smith's sections on colonies presented a brilliant analysis of how the relative supplies of the different factors of production would impact the distribution of income. The analysis clearly explained why China displayed very low wage rates and high costs for land and capital. Yan rendered this analysis clearly. But it received little attention in China, where people preferred the politically popular denunciations of landlords, merchants, moneylenders, foreign imperialists and so on.

Smith had much to say about China (see Lai, 2000). China was a very poor country and was not displaying economic improvement. Much of the country's poverty could be attributed to defective government policies and cultural attitudes:

> In China commerce and business are considered as mean professions. Sailing on the sea is prohibited. Trading with foreign countries is a shameful business, such that Western ships are allowed in only one or two ports. In this kind of country, commerce is seldom developed, and many commodities are not fully circulated. Moreover, politics is another problem. The leading houses [families] having political and economic powers, tend to take over others' properties; the middle-level businessmen are exploited by the general administration. Contracts are not reliable...[2]

Adam Smith's ideas reached a much wider audience through the writings of Liang Qichao (1873–1929). Although he never learnt to read a Western language, he took on the role of an intellectual 'intermediary', drawing extensively on Japanese translations of Western commentaries on social and economic topics and writing in a vernacular style for a wide Chinese audience (see Liu, 2013) (see the chapters by Lai and by Sakamoto respectively later in this volume).

In 1902, Liang wrote a series of newspaper articles subsequently published as a *Concise History of Economic Thought*. The survey did not extend beyond Smith. It was drawn mainly from Japanese translations of surveys, such as by Luigi Cossa (1831–1926) and John Kells Ingram (1823–1907). However, Liang's discussions of Smith drew chiefly on his friend Yan Fu. Liang expressed very clearly Smith's praise for the guidance given by competitive market prices to the division of labour. But the former strongly advocated 'Mercantilist' policies for China.

Economic development was also a preoccupation for Sun Yat-sen. He had studied in Hawaii and Hong Kong, became fluent in English, mastered Western medicine and professed a belief in Christianity. As the end of the nineteenth century approached, he became committed to promoting the overthrow of China's Qing monarchy. Unlike traditionally educated Chinese like Liang and Yan, Sun was mainly influenced by current economic writings, notably by the US economists, Henry George (1839–1897) and Richard T. Ely (1854–1943). As a rebel, Sun chose to live in Japan for a decade, connecting with the Japanese fervour for economic development, functional government and eagerness to learn from the West.

Henry George published his best-known work, *Progress and Poverty*, in 1879, and it soon became quite influential. According to George, private property in land caused much of the benefit of economic progress to go to landowners, whose mere ownership was not in itself a productive act. He advocated taxing away the 'unearned increment' in land values. George's book contained many references to China. He denied the validity of the 'Malthusian' interpretation of China's poverty, blaming it instead on unequal land ownership, bad domestic government and imperialism. Sun began to advocate 'equalization of land rights', using a phrase taken directly from *Progress and Poverty*.

Sun spent several years in America and Britain, and was painfully aware that many people, including Chinese immigrants, lived in poverty. He and Liang Qichao became Japan-based rivals in trying to organize overseas Chinese to bring about the overthrow of China's monarchy. Liang challenged many of Sun's pronouncements, arguing that China should give priority to increased production rather than focusing on relieving inequality. Off and on from 1899, Sun advocated 'All land to the tillers', a slogan which ultimately influenced land-policy both in Taiwan, as well as in the People's Republic.

Sun did not participate personally in the Revolution which overthrew the Chinese monarchy in 1911–1912 but he served for a year as Provisional President of the new Republic. The real power was held by Yuan Shikai (1859–1916), a 'strong man', who had the support of the armed forces. He appointed Sun as the Director of National Railways, a position he held for about a year, and which stimulated him to propose plans for national economic development. Until his death in 1925, Sun wrote prolifically on economic and political topics, trying in vain to gain more power in the national government. He watched closely the developments in the new-formed Soviet Union, especially Lenin's New Economic Policy (NEP), which combined national ownership and control of leading sectors – with reliance on private markets for much of the economy. In 1922, Sun published his book entitled *The International Development of China* in an English version. He hoped to persuade the victorious Western powers to provide capital and expertise to create in China a vast network of state-owned and state-dominated enterprises. This vision was largely carried out in the 1950s, with the aid of the Soviet Union, until Mao Zedong broke off relations at the beginning of the 1960s.

By the 1920s, Sun was a thoroughgoing 'Socialist' we can say – but not a Communist. His 'collectivist' approach to economic development was taken over when his protégé Chiang Kai-shek (1887–1975) became head of the Chinese government, after a military coup in 1927–1928. Outbreak of war with Japan in 1937 provided the rationalization for government domination of industry, transportation and finance. Sun, like Henry George, was bitterly opposed to viewing China as a victim of a Malthusian process, and the government reflected his prejudice into the 1940s.

The Japanese channel

Despite the rivalry which led to war in 1894–1895, many Chinese admired and desired to imitate Japan (see Liu, 2013). That nation had been confronted by potential Western incursion in the 1840s, as had China. But Japan turned this into an advantage, studying Western institutions and learning from them. Many Western economic writings were translated into Japanese, as in the case of *The Wealth of Nations* in the 1880s (see the chapter by Sakamoto on Smith and Japan later in this volume), as we saw with Burton's book and with Liang's history of Western thought. Japanese written language contained many Chinese characters, and educated Chinese, such as Liang and Sun Yat-sen, could read Japanese fairly easily. Between 1898 and 1911, some 25,000 Chinese studied in Japan, although far fewer achieved the equivalent of a university education.

One of the most distinguished Chinese economists was S. C. Tsiang (Jiang Shuojie) (1918–1993), who studied in Keio University in Japan before completing a doctorate at the London School of Economics. Zhao Lanping also graduated from Keio in 1922 and held teaching positions at several Chinese universities. He published widely used textbooks transmitting mainstream Western Economics, including an elementary text which went through 20 editions between 1932 and 1947. Many of the earliest recorded Chinese economics textbooks were adapted from Japanese sources.

The development of Chinese universities

Modern universities in China appeared in the waning years of the nineteenth century – some sponsored by government, some by private individuals and some by Western missionaries (see Spence, 1990). A stimulus was China's military defeat by Japan in 1894–1895. Most started as secondary schools, which then evolved to higher levels. University-level enrolment in missionary colleges was estimated at 164 in 1900 (Lutz, 1971: 78). By 1910, there were 18 Protestant colleges with 1,000 college-level students. Christian colleges accounted for more than 40 per cent of all Chinese university students in 1900–1910, about one third in the next decade, and one fourth in the 1920s. The Protestant colleges were overwhelmingly American in curriculum and many of their courses were taught in English. In early years, most offered one or two semesters of elementary Economics using American textbooks, especially works by the US economist, Richard T. Ely (1854–1943). His *Outlines of Economics* (originally published 1893) was translated into Chinese in 1910. Ely had studied in Germany and was a strong devotee of the 'Social Gospel'.

The first non-missionary university was Beiyang ('North Sea') University, which opened in Tianjin, China's third-largest city, in 1895. A sister-institution in Shanghai, Nanyang ('South Sea') University, opened its doors in 1896. Early Economics instruction at Nanyang was directed by an American, Clement Moore Lacey Sites (1865–1958), who had completed a PhD in Political Science at Columbia in 1899. He published an English-language mini-textbook in 1904 for the course.

Peking University ('Beida') was officially established by the Emperor in 1898; it absorbed the translators' college, and William A. P. Martin became a dean. The earliest reported course in Economics was taught by a Japanese tutor, Sugi Eizaburo. In 1912, Economics became a separate department. Initially undistinguished, *Beida* upgraded itself dramatically after Cai Yuanpei (1868–1940) became President in 1916. The early Economics programme was led by Gu Mengyu, who, like Cai, had studied in Germany. From that time on, *Beida* has been one of China's top universities and still is.

Qinghua University originated from the indemnity imposed on China following the Boxer Rebellion in 1900. In 1908, the United States government agreed to devote a portion of its share to support China's educational development. Scholarships were provided for Chinese to study in the US. Qinghua College was also established in Beijing (beginning 1911) to prepare Chinese to study in the US. It had begun as a secondary school, however by 1917, courses equivalent to college freshmen and sophomores were in place. The first Economics teacher was Clarence Dittmer (1885–1960), a doctoral student at Wisconsin, who wrote his dissertation on living standards in China. His textbook for his courses was Ely's *Outlines*. Another early Qinghua teacher was Liu Dajun (D. K. Lieu), a graduate of Michigan. He left in 1919 – to begin a distinguished career carrying out economic research in China.

Between 1914 and 1929, 1,268 Qinghua preparatory students entered American universities. Of these, 187 were Economics students, of whom 144 continued into graduate-level study. Of these, 18 completed doctorates and another 11 were ABD (all but dissertation). We know the subsequent occupations of 115, of whom 48 returned to China to teach Economics, 11 of them at Qinghua. A scholar, Chen Daisun went from there to complete a doctorate at Harvard in 1926. He returned to become chair of Economics at Qinghua and Dean of the Law School. After 1929, it became a regular university. It continued to send many students to the US and hired many Chinese with American degrees. Under the Communist regime, it was restricted to science and technology. Chen and other economists were transferred to *Beida*. By 1983, Chen was appointed to be chair of Economics at *Beida* and served as a mentor to the present author. Qinghua returned to comprehensive status in the 1980s.

Chinese in US graduate Economics programmes

Chinese began to enter American graduate programmes in Economics early in the twentieth century. My book, *Jingji Xue* (Trescott, 2007), identified 1,228 Chinese who studied graduate-level Economics in the US down through 1949. Of these, 149 completed verified doctorates, and another 88 were ABD. Of the ABDs, 16 received Economics doctorates in 1950 or after. A total of 572 received masters' degrees as their highest degree; in addition, many other Chinese completed Master of Business Administration (MBA) degrees. Finally, 419 Chinese attended graduate Economics courses but did not receive a graduate degree – some completed degrees in 1950 and after. The largest number of Chinese students studied at Columbia University in New York City – 273, including 29 doctorates. Harvard ranked second, with 130, including 28 doctorates. The universities of Michigan, Pennsylvania and Wisconsin each accounted for about 100 Chinese graduate students in Economics.

The first reported Chinese Economics doctorate went to Chen Jintao (Chin-tao) at Yale in 1906. His dissertation on 'Societary Circulation' [*sic*] was inspired by the noted US economist Irving Fisher (1867–1947). Chen returned to China for a career mainly in government positions. The first Columbia doctorate went to Chen Huanzhang (Huan-chang) in 1911 for a comprehensive study of the economic ideas of Confucius, reviewed in fact by no other than Keynes (see the chapter on Keynes later in this volume). One of Columbia's most distinguished Chinese doctorates went to Ma Yinchu in 1914. Ma returned to China to become professor at *Beida* and one of China's most prominent and outspoken economists. Besides university positions, he served nearly 20 years in the national government's Legislative Yuan (legislature). He became an outspoken critic of Chiang Kai-shek and the Kuomintang/Guomindang government and was placed under house arrest for two years. He used this time to compose a textbook in economic principles which became a bestseller. After 1949, he became president of *Beida*, but was removed for his criticism of government actions which seemed to encourage rapid population growth.

China's Christian colleges also sent a large number of Economics students to the US – these colleges developed English-language fluency and attracted students from wealthy families. Of the 1,228 Chinese identified, 652 students reported undergraduate degrees in China. Of these, 42 per cent were from Christian colleges.

Study in Europe

The earlier study, *Jingji Xue* (Trescott, 2007), looked at 391 Chinese who studied Economics in Europe; 12 more have been added (see the chapter by Trescott later in this volume). The distinction between graduate and undergraduate levels was not as clear-cut as in the US, so we tabulated all reported students. The largest number went to Great Britain, which recorded 162, of whom 92 attended the London School of Economics (LSE). Cambridge accounted for 33 and Oxford only 12. The doctoral degree was not an important part of British higher education prior to 1940. Only 18 British Economics doctorates were awarded to Chinese in our time-period, of which 12 were at LSE. One of these doctorates went to S. C. Tsiang (Jiang Shuojie), whose 1945 dissertation on business cycles was directed by Friedrich Hayek (1899–1992). Tsiang published influential critiques of the Keynesian theory of interest rates. He returned to China briefly to teach at *Beida* as civil war and hyperinflation were raging. He urged the government to offer price-indexed savings certificates to assure savers a positive return on their savings. Chiang's government ignored the recommendation, but it was successfully adopted by the Communists in 1949. Beginning in 1954, Tsiang became an important advisor to the government of Taiwan, becoming head of the Chung-hua Institute for Economic Research. He and Liu Dazhong (T. C. Liu, PhD, Cornell, 1940) collaborated to guide Taiwan to policies which achieved an outstanding record of rapid economic growth with widely distributed benefits. Hu Jichuang (1903–1993), who completed a Master's degree at LSE in 1939, returned to become China's most distinguished historian of Chinese economic thought.

Of the 391 students recorded, 184 came in the 1930s, the peak decade for all three major countries. This was the case even for Germany, reflecting momentary Sino-German rapprochement and relative indifference by Chinese toward Hitler. Of the 162 students who studied in Britain, a total of 68 returned to teach Economics in China. Of these, 44 had studied at LSE. Cambridge was, after 1930, the site of the revolutionary developments in macroeconomics associated with John Maynard Keynes (1883–1946). In both France and Germany, most university students were candidates for a 'doctorate', which required a thesis. The standards were less demanding than in America or Britain. French and German governments published lists of all doctoral theses, and individual theses were normally published. They were roughly equivalent to an American Master's thesis. In both countries, Economics was often taught in schools of law. The continental universities gave less attention to economic theory than did the Anglo-schools.

A distinguished Chinese student in Berlin (1932) was Xiao Zheng (Hsiao Cheng). He returned to become a professor at the Central Political Institute and Dean of the Graduate School of Land Economics. A strong advocate of the Sun Yat-sen doctrine of equalization of land rights, he ultimately moved to Taiwan and became Vice-Minister of Economic Affairs, playing an important role in Taiwan's successful land reform.

In 1925, a Franco-Chinese University was established in Peking, based on funds from France's 'Boxer Indemnity'. It was linked with the 'Institut Franco-Chinois' in the French city of Lyon, which offered tutorial programmes and other assistance for Chinese students coming to France. Lou Tongsun studied under Charles Gide (1847–1932) in Paris in the mid-1920s. He held a number of academic positions in China and served as Secretary-General of the National Economic Council in 1936–1937. He translated several of Gide's books into Chinese and wrote biographies of both Gide and Robert Owen (1771–1858). Subsequently, he headed the China Cooperatives Association.

Jingji Xue had pin-pointed 21 Chinese who had studied Economics in other European countries, chiefly Belgium, Italy and Switzerland. Xue Guangqian (Paul Sih) completed a dissertation at the University of Rome in 1936 on China's banking system. Returning to China, he participated in a diplomatic mission in 1937–1938 which attempted to prevent the German-Japanese rapprochement. He became Ambassador to Italy. After 1949, he moved to Taiwan in diplomatic service but relocated to the United States in 1959. He joined the faculty of St John's University and edited several books dealing with China.

Returned students in Chinese universities

In all, there were 942 Chinese who taught Economics in Chinese universities (including missionary colleges) prior to 1950. Of these, 544 studied abroad. The largest proportion was the 277 who studied graduate-level Economics in America, including 64 with PhD degrees. They were equally represented in Christian colleges and indigenous Chinese universities. In all, Britain and Western Europe contributed 153. Of these 69 studied in Britain, 46 in Germany and 41 in France. Another 55 of the total had studied in Japan. The Christian colleges engaged significantly fewer European and Japanese-educated economists.

In the 1920s and 1930s, a total of 590 Chinese came to the US for graduate-level Economics study. Of those, 173 returned to teaching positions in China, representing 29 per cent. In contrast, of the 474 who came in the troubled 1940s, only 47 returned to mainland teaching positions. Of the students returned from study in Europe, the proportions who taught Economics were relatively uniform, ranging from 43 per cent for British to 36 per cent for French.

Qinghua was virtually a transplanted American university. The curriculum and course requirements for Economics imitated American models, as did practices for examinations and grading. The *Jingji Xue* study identified 47 persons who taught Economics at Qinghua 1926–1947. Two of these were Americans. Besides Clarence Dittmer, in the early 1930s, John K. Fairbank (1907–1991), on his way to becoming a leading sinologist at Harvard, taught Economic History for two years. All told, 27 of the 47 had studied in the US, including nine PhDs. Only seven came from Britain or Western Europe.

Nankai University in Tianjin also displayed a large American influence. Although it did not begin work until 1919, by the 1930s it became a leader in

Economics. Its upgrade began with the appointment of He Lian (Franklin Ho) in 1926. He had completed a doctorate at Yale and worked with Irving Fisher for several years helping develop index-numbers, a topic he pursued extensively at *Nankai*. He recruited his Yale class-mate Fang Xianting (H. D. Fong) to join him there. To prepare for his teaching, he visited a dozen major Chinese universities and reported 'I did not find any college which offered a course on the economic development and organization of China or on rural economics in China' (Ho, 1967: 72). Under He Lian, *Nankai* became strongly oriented to research and publication and developed impressive skill in obtaining grant funding from such sources as the Rockefeller Foundation and the Institute of Pacific Relations which both had a significant interest in China.[3]

Peking University had a much more diverse curriculum and faculty than its rivals. Nineteen of the earliest 23 Economics faculty studied abroad, including 11 in either Germany or Japan. *Jingji Xue* identified 76 Economics faculty at *Beida*, of whom 44 had studied abroad. Twenty-two studied in American graduate programmes, including seven with doctorates. Sixteen had studied in Britain and Western Europe and ten in Japan. Further, economics topics were covered by a number of distinguished people who did not have formal training in Economics, notably Li Dazhao, Liang Shuming, Chen Hansheng and L. K. Tao. Of all the prominent Chinese universities, *Beida* probably demonstrated the largest share of Marxist influence in Economics, beginning with Li and Chen. Karl Marx's (1818–1883) *Das Kapital* (Capital/Marx,1954) originally published in 1867, had been translated into Chinese in a complete version but only in 1938, which was later than the 1924 version in Japanese (see the chapter by Yagi on Japan and by Trescott respectively later in this volume).

Missionary colleges

In their early years, China's Christian colleges engaged a significant number of Westerners, primarily Americans. The *Jingji Xue* study noted that there were nearly 500 persons who taught Economics in Christian colleges. Of these, 89 were Westerners, and 206 of the Chinese had studied in the West. Four Western economists stand out for their length of service, their efforts to present China-relevant material, and efforts to break down the typical Chinese social distance between faculty and students. These were Kenneth Duncan (Lingnan), Carl Remer (St John's), and especially John Lossing Buck at Nanjing and John Bernard Tayler at Yanjing.

Tayler (1878–1951) was an English missionary, trained as a chemist, who initially came to China in 1906. After several years directing a boys' secondary school, he agreed in 1917 to head the Economics Department at newly forming Yanjing University in Peking. He spent a year preparing by attending LSE. Tayler was an excellent promoter and administrator and during the 1920s built up one of the largest Economics departments of any Chinese university. He went beyond the classroom in two important dimensions. First, he was committed to aiding the formation of cooperatives, especially for China's rural residents.

Second, he was a pioneer in promoting what we would now call 'appropriate technology', seeking simple but effective devices that would improve productivity especially for rural China. His assistant, Lu Guangmien, helped to organize a very successful cooperative among cotton growers. This evolved into the Hubei Cotton Improvement Commission, which (according to Douglas Reynolds) had by 1937 'a staff of 240 persons working in 52 counties ... with an annual budget of CNC $500,000 and marketing some CNC $10 million worth of cotton annually' (Reynolds, 1975: 459). In the mid-1930s, Tayler's ideas and personality were at the heart of an ambitious programme for rural development sponsored by the Rockefeller Foundation. He also pioneered the idea of industrial cooperatives, an idea which took off during the War through the efforts of Lu Guangmien, Rewi Alley and numerous Yanjing staff. His daughter, Gladys Tayler Yang (1919–1999), became a distinguished translator (with her husband) of Chinese literature into English.

John Lossing Buck (1890–1975) was raised on a farm in New York State and studied agriculture at Cornell. Inspired by the Social Gospel, he came to China in 1916 as an agricultural missionary. There he met and married Pearl Sydenstricker Buck (1892–1973), daughter of long-time China missionaries. She had spent her childhood in China and was fluent in the Chinese language. The couple often visited rural homes as a team, John talking with the men and Pearl with the ladies. In 1920, John joined the faculty of missionary Nanjing University, assigned to develop courses in agricultural economics, farm management and rural sociology. He found the available teaching materials had little relevance to Chinese conditions. He began sending students out to interview farmers and collect data on their farming operations. This survey programme pioneered in getting students to visit real farms and meet real farmers. Ultimately, Buck assembled much of the survey material as his doctoral dissertation, published in 1930 with the title, *Chinese Farm Economy*. It was rich in descriptive detail about farm life in China. Analytically, Buck clearly recognized that rural overpopulation and low productivity were at the root of rural poverty. He saw that increased opportunities for non-farm employment, rather than land redistribution or collectivization, were the most appropriate remedies. This perspective was vindicated by developments after 1949.

Buck was very successful in attracting grant funding and bringing in visiting scholars from the West. The Nanjing programme became a major producer and publisher of research on Chinese agriculture. Buck, like Tayler, assembled a large and dedicated faculty, many of whom took graduate work at Cornell. Like Tayler, Buck was influential in promoting cooperatives. By 1934, Nanjing staff members had promoted the formation of 50 cooperative societies with membership of over 1,200 persons. Pearl published her novel, *The Good Earth*, in 1931; it helped her to win both Nobel and Pulitzer prizes for Literature (see Spurling, 2010). But she was a 'sophisticate' and John was not; she divorced him in 1935. During the War, John Buck and John Tayler both moved to West China and assisted with a network of industrial cooperatives, which by 1941 had on board 1,737 of them, with about 23,000 members.

Western advisers

Several Western economists came to China as advisors under the sponsorship of the League of Nations (Trescott, 2010a). Sir Arthur Salter (1881–1975), head of the Economic, Financial and Transit Section of the League, visited several times. Salter was an Oxford graduate who had held high positions in economic administration in the British government during the First World War. He first visited China in 1931. In that year, the Chinese government created a National Economic Council to work with the League toward economic development. But Chiang Kai-shek was already preoccupied with trying to suppress the Communist insurgency. Since 1927, the Guomindang had been struggling to defeat Communist rebels occupying the 'red' base-areas in West China.

Salter returned in 1933 to participate in formulating a development strategy for Zhejiang Province, working with He Lian and Fang Xianting. Their proposal emphasized infrastructure, chiefly transport and schooling, as well as institutions for testing and grading commodities, programmes already in place for cotton and silk. Salter consistently cautioned against overly grandiose government involvement. A former League staff member, Jean Monnet (1888–1979) came to China in November 1933 and helped organize the China Development Finance Corporation, designed to float bond issues overseas to finance development projects. The Corporation was making a promising start, particularly in aiding railroad construction, when the outbreak of war in 1937 brought its operations to a halt. Monnet went on to achieve outstanding success as one of the architects of European economic unification after the Second World War.

What did they learn?

The economic wisdom which was most relevant for China in the early twentieth century in my estimation had been developed by the British Classical economists, Adam Smith (1723–1790) and Thomas R. Malthus (1766–1834) (see Trescott, 2007). China desperately needed economic growth and population restraint. However, Western Economics had now moved on. Economic theory had become captivated by 'marginal utility' and by the opportunity to apply differential calculus. At the same time, Institutional Economics in the United States shifted emphasis away from theory to descriptive analysis of real-world conditions, incorporating history, law, psychology and sociology. Many Western economists were convinced there existed serious 'market failures'. There was much concern with monopoly, and the economic theory of 'imperfect competition' became *de rigueur*. Many perceived the distribution of income as 'unjust' and were particularly distressed by unemployment, 'mass joblessness', especially in the 1930s. Extensive government regulations were proposed and imposed to deal with these supposed imperfections.

Chinese economists displayed a moving commitment to becoming familiar with the latest developments in Western Economics, as we observed in our studies of the Marshallian, Institutional and Keynesian genres (Trescott, 1992,

2010b, 2012). However, they were not given much exposure to the work of Friedrich Hayek (1899–1992) at that time in my view, which had emphasized the fallacies of Marxian economics and the disastrous performance of the Soviet Union (see the later chapter by Li *et al.* in this volume). The American introductory textbook by Fairchild, Furniss and Buck was widely used in Chinese universities, both in English and in a Chinese adaptation.

American monetary economics had been preoccupied by issues of the monetary standard. The gold standard was celebrated for promoting stable exchange rates and convertible currencies, facilitating efficient international trade and investment. One of the leading proponents of the gold standard was Princeton professor Edwin Kemmerer (1873–1945), who led a Commission of Financial Experts to China in 1929. China's monetary standard was 'silver'. The Kemmerer Commission recommended that China create a 'gold-exchange standard'. Fortunately for China, this proposal was not adopted. After 1929, the Gold Standard dragged down every country which adhered to it, especially the United States. Several Commission members remained in China to work with various ministries, notably Arthur Young, a Princeton PhD who served as a principal economic advisor to Chiang Kai-shek until 1947.

The economic disasters of the 1930s inspired the macroeconomic innovations of John Maynard Keynes (see the chapter on Keynes later in this volume). Although his analysis was explicitly designed to deal with industrialized countries with labour markets that did not readily equilibrate, it found numerous adherents in China. Regrettably, the Keynesian analysis eclipsed the traditional quantity theory of money and weakened the ability of Chinese economists to resist the hyperinflation which arose during the War. After 1949, the Communists recognized the source of the problem and quickly brought an end to the currency expansion and rapid price increases.

The Chinese who studied Economics in the West did become conversant with a number of useful research techniques. One was survey research, which we encountered in the work of Dittmer and Buck. One estimate found over 9,000 surveys in China between 1927 and 1935. Most did not provide calculations of sampling error, so readers could not readily evaluate their results. Many projects lacked computational facility to handle large amounts of data. Another prominent research focus was index-numbers. Price indices became very relevant as China entered escalating inflation after 1937. Many of the university Economics departments calculated price indexes for their locality. National-income estimation, which was still in its infancy in the West, was pioneered in China by Wu Baosan (Ou Paosan, PhD, Harvard 1949) as well as by Liu Dazhong.

Research organizations dealing with China's economy developed after the Chinese government created its Bureau of Economic Information in 1921. By then, a number of government agencies were producing statistical data – the Customs Service, the Ministry of Finance, the National Railway System. The Chinese Economic Association was itself formed in 1923. Later, the China Foundation for the Promotion of Education and Culture was created in 1924 to administer the American Boxer Indemnity funds. In 1926, they created a

Department (later Institute) of Social Research. Two years later, the newly formed Guomindang government established the *Academia Sinica* in 1928 to conduct and promote scientific research. They soon established their own Institute of Social Sciences and the two institutes merged in 1934. Many young scholars worked for these organizations for a time and then went overseas for graduate study; this was indeed the case with Wu Baosan. There was a steady increase in professional journals publishing economic research, including journals sponsored by Nankai, Yanjing and Nanjing universities. The research department of the Bank of China formed in the 1930s and was very well regarded. In its prime, it was headed by the first prominent female economist in China, Zhang Xiaomei (Chang Hsiao-mei). She had studied at NYU, Chicago and LSE. In the 1940s, research leadership passed to the Central Bank of China which had, by 1947, a staff of 120. The Director was Ji Chaoding (Chi Chaoting) who had received a doctorate from Columbia and worked for several years for the Institute of Pacific Relations.

By the 1930s, there was a large output of Chinese publications dealing with China's economy. *Nankai* identified about 1,300 such books and pamphlets published by Chinese authors in 1930–1935. By 1935, there were at least 61 Chinese periodicals dealing with China's economy. Earlier research has analysed ten different database collections of publications on China's economy by Chinese authors (see Trescott, 2007). They were quite consistent in showing a rather small representation by Western-trained economists – in the order of 15 per cent. Many of the publications represented journalism rather than research, and many of the authors worked in business or government.

The experience of *Nankai* professor, Fang Xianting, demonstrates the difficulties faced by Chinese economists in trying to apply Western Economics to China's problems. In the late 1920s and early 1930s, he relied on radical empiricism, accumulating a vast amount of information on China's industrialization. Next, the influence of the Rockefeller Foundation led him to study and promote grass-roots rural development. An ambitious programme was destroyed by the outbreak of war in 1937. He shared in the 1931 study by Sir Arthur Salter (above). However, in contrast to Salter's scepticism, Fang next became enthusiastic about government-driven industrialization along the lines suggested by Sun Yat-sen, stressing the role of capital formation. In 1942, he recommended creating a China Reconstruction Finance Corporation to direct such a scheme. He also attempted to incorporate Keynesian analysis. In 1944, Fang was persuaded by his mentor, He Lian, to head the research department of the government's Central Planning Board, which produced an extensive draft plan in December 1945. In the post-war chaos, it could not be implemented. Fang left China to join the research staff of the UN Economic Commission for Asia and the Far East.

By 1940, China was producing international-class economists, publishing in the leading Western professional journals. Prominent among them were Li Zhuomin, Jiang Shuojie, Wu Baosan, Zhang Zijun, Pu Shan and Liu Dazhong (see Trescott, 2007).

War with Japan, 1937–1945

Japan had been encroaching into Chinese mainland territory since 1931, when they established a presence in Manchuria. When full-scale war erupted in 1937, the Japanese soon controlled Chinese coastal cities. Many Chinese universities migrated to locations further inland. Here, *Beida, Qinghua* and *Nankai* formed the Southwest Associated Universities which operated in Kunming. Yanjing and other missionary colleges relocated to Chengdu. Economists in Tianjin, who did not leave, formed the Adam Smith Institute around 1939, headed by Professor Yuen Wenpu (Yuen Xianneng, PhD, NYU). It was primarily a teaching institution directed to the study of Western economic ideas, including those of Keynes. Nankai created a Master's programme in 1939 in the wartime capital of Chongqing. Its graduate theory course dealt primarily with the works of Alfred Marshall (1842–1924), Edward Chamberlin (1899–1967), John R. Hicks (1904–1989), J. M. Keynes (1883–1946) and Joan Robinson (1903–1983).

Fang Xianting had learned about Keynes and Keynsianism from its proponent, Alvin Hansen, (1887–1985) whilst visiting Harvard in 1941. He shipped Keynesian literature to Nankai and subsequently taught the graduate theory course along with Li Zuoming (Choh-Ming, PhD, Berkeley). The 1940s witnessed a large increase in Chinese studying Economics in the West. Of our 1,228 Chinese studying graduate-level Economics in the United States, 431 came in 1945–1950.

John Buck, John Tayler and many of their students played a leading role in developing industrial cooperatives, which significantly augmented China's industrial production. However, after a promising beginning, the programme was largely taken over by the Chinese government. This undermined its effectiveness, except for the Communist-dominated areas where it thrived. Most of the Westerners who had been teaching in Chinese universities left China. An exception was Michael Lindsay, who joined the Yanjing faculty in 1938. Lindsay had studied with Keynes at Cambridge and offered a tutorial on Keynes at Yanjing (see Warner, 2015). He became involved in the anti-Japanese underground, furnishing supplies to the Communists who held some rural areas near Peking. In 1941, he married one of his Chinese students. After Pearl Harbour, he and his wife made their way to Yanan and worked for the Communists there. After the War (the later Lord) Lindsay became disillusioned and strongly criticized abusive actions by the Communists.

Monetary affairs

Monetary management in China was thrown into disarray by the 1933–1934 policy of the US government to raise the market value of silver. This increased the international value of Chinese currency, reducing export sales, and causing a large outflow of silver from China which reduced the Chinese monetary base. Whilst Chinese diplomats tried in vain to dissuade American authorities, China's Ministry of Industry appointed a Committee for the Study of Silver Values and

Commodity Prices. It included three members of the agriculture faculty from Nanjing University – John Buck, Ardron Lewis and Chang Lulwan. Lewis was a disciple of the monetary views of his Cornell professors George Warren and Frank Pearson, who were supporting the US increase in the price of gold as a measure to raise farm prices.

The Silver Committee and the former Kemmerer Commission members helped develop an agenda which, in November 1935, took China off the silver standard. Banknote currency was established as legal tender. Chinese currency was to be stabilized in relation to the dollar and pound. The Chinese were able to sell some of their monetary silver to the United States on favourable terms, to build up their monetary reserves. These arrangements were quite successful in the short run, and China's economy entered two years of prosperity and progress. But the new arrangements facilitated issuing more paper money to finance government deficits. Inflation accelerated from 40 per cent per year in 1937–1939 to 300 per cent in 1945–1948.

Monetary topics generated a large amount of publication by Chinese economists in universities, government and business and were widely pursued as thesis topics by Chinese students in Western universities. Only a small proportion of Chinese economists accurately diagnosed the sources of inflation in the government deficits and currency expansion. The popularity of Keynesian ideas in China (see the chapter on Keynes later in this volume) contributed to this neglect. The inflation was demoralizing and undermined support for Chiang Kaishek and the Guomindang.

By the 1940s, the typical Chinese university Economics department had several senior faculty with Western training. However, there were numerous junior faculty and instructors with only undergraduate degrees from Chinese universities. But Western textbooks, chiefly American, were widely used. American influence was especially predominant in the missionary colleges, in *Qinghua* and in *Nankai*.

By the 1940s, it is likely that the majority of Chinese economists supported the kind of collectivism associated with Sun Yat-sen. Institutional Economics, possibly the consensus view in American Graduate Economics, stressed varieties of 'market failure' (as did Keynesianism), and viewed income distribution as unfair. There were, in turn, a few outright Communists.

In the 1940s, Harvard awarded PhD degrees to three Chinese brothers named Pu. All of these persons were Communists and returned to prominent positions in the Chinese government after 1949. Chen Hansheng and Ji Zhaoding have been described as 'closet' Communists – while working for the Institute of Pacific Relations in the 1930s. There were also a few Chinese economists who became forthright defenders of free markets. Li Zhuomin praised the conditions in China's Treaty Ports (of which there were 50 by 1915). With Western standards of law and order and urban infrastructure, they grew rapidly in the first half of the twentieth century. Jiang Shuojie and Wu Yuanli had studied with Friedrich Hayek at LSE and imbibed his free-market enthusiasm. In 1956, Wu perceptively wrote:

Because the [Chinese] government had played an increasingly important role in the actual allocation and use of resources both before and after the war, and because inadequate attention had been given to the development of the economy through individual initiative within a well-ordered economy and established rule of law, there was not a broad and vigorous capitalistic economy in China at the time the communists took over.

(Wu, 1956: 42–43)

The reign of Mao Zedong

In October 1949, the Chinese Communists emerged victorious from the prolonged civil war, whilst Chiang Kai-shek and his Guomindang loyalists fled to Taiwan. In 1950, the Communists launched a wave of land reform, which coercively redistributed land titles to a more nearly equal basis. The redistribution was accompanied by carefully orchestrated 'struggle sessions' in which landlords were denounced, sometimes beaten and occasionally murdered by other farmers. Hardly had the land reform been completed, however, when the government began forcing farmers into collective units, culminating in the giant communes and state farms of the late 1950s.

In 1950, China entered the Korean War, which may have killed as many as a million Chinese. This reinforced the breach with the United States which originated in the earlier Civil War. The War brought China closer to the Soviet Union, which became a major source of material assistance and inspiration for the Chinese economic agenda until 1960, when the comrades split.

Many Western-trained economists left China during and after the war with Japan. My book *Jingji Xue* (Trescott, 2007) reported a post-war identification for 463 Western-educated Chinese economists. Of these 139 left China or failed to return. Forty per cent of those who studied in the US left China. Most of those who left China went to the US, but at least 49 went to Taiwan, helping to boost the academic level of National Taiwan University. A number of the émigré Chinese contributed significantly to economic research. Liu Dazhong became a distinguished econometrician at Cornell. Wu Yuanli and Li Zhuomin wrote extensively about China's economy. John Fei became a leading scholar of economic development. Alpha Chiang produced a path-breaking textbook on mathematical economics. Cheng Paolun even earned a place in Blaug and Sturges' (1999) *Who's Who in Economics*.

Transformation of Chinese universities proceeded gradually. In 1950, the China People's University ('Renda') opened in Beijing. Its activities were concentrated on social and political topics, and it became the principal venue for the few Chinese undertaking graduate study in Economics. Hardly any Chinese went abroad for study after 1950, except to Moscow. Beginning in 1953, there was concerted effort to incorporate Russian elements into the universities. Students and faculty were pressured to learn the Russian language. These professors also came to teach Marxist economics there and the odd Westerner, such as Joan Robinson (1903–1983) from Cambridge. Stalin's *Economic*

Problems of Socialism (1951) was used as a basic text in Chinese economics departments.

One of the most commendable actions of the Communist government was to enlarge the system of public education, bringing a radical reduction in illiteracy. However, higher education was shifted to emphasize science and technology. By the late 1950s, the number of graduates in Economics and Finance fell below pre-1949 levels. For Economics, it was assumed that an undergraduate degree plus political correctness was sufficient to qualify a person to teach in a university. Some Western Economics survived in the curriculum because Karl Marx (1818–1823) had acknowledged intellectual debt to Adam Smith (1723–1790) and David Ricardo (1772–1783). But in the period 1949–1956, there were no truly significant translations of Western economic works into Chinese (see the chapter by Fang later in this volume).

Mao Zedong launched a major attack on Western-oriented intellectuals in the Anti-Rightist campaign which began in 1957. Mao's invitation to express criticisms of the regime had elicited an impressive manifesto by several Western-trained economists. Of these, Chen Zhenhan, Wu Baosan and Luo Zhiru all had PhDs from Harvard, and Xu Yunan had a PhD from Cambridge. Most were outspoken Keynesians – Xu published a translation of Keynes's *General Theory* in 1957 – and the Anti-Rightist campaign focused intensively on attacking Keynesian ideas. A separate campaign was directed at Malthusian ideas, with Ma Yinchu the chief target. Although the targeted intellectuals were not physically abused, most were dismissed from their positions. The Anti-Rightist campaign was soon followed by the 'Great Leap Forward', which involved catastrophic mismanagement in industry and agriculture, with resulting mass starvation in 1959–1962. After a brief respite, Mao launched the 'Cultural Revolution' in 1966, bringing systematic persecution of intellectuals, especially those with Western connections. The universities were closed, some for as long as ten years.

Western Economics returns to China

Mao's fear of the Soviet Union inspired him to reopen relations with the United States. President Richard Nixon's visit to China in 1972 was a landmark in the restoration of civil order and decency. Mao's death in 1976 opened the way for Deng Xiaoping (1904–1997) to undertake more rational measures to promote economic growth. The universities were reopened, but Nobel Laureate James Tobin (1918–2012), who visited China in 1972, observed that 'academic economics is not in good shape.... The curriculum is largely ideological and certainly non-quantitative' (1975: 44).

Chinese students were once again permitted to study in the West. A directory was published in 1990 of about 17,000 full professors in Chinese universities as of 1987. Of the 646 Economics professors listed, 333 had received at least one degree by 1950 or earlier. Of these, 100 had studied abroad – 66 had studied in the US and 21 in Britain and Western Europe.

President Richard Nixon (1913–1994) whose visit to China in 1972 heralded a new era in US–China relations opened the door to Western economists. By 1971, China was inviting select American groups to tour China, working with the *Guardian* newspaper in the UK and the newly formed US–China Peoples Friendship Association (see Trescott, 2014). Full diplomatic relations were restored beginning in 1979. In August 1979, a Chinese delegation visiting the US included Pu Shan, who had received a doctorate in Economics from Harvard in 1950. He had been a part of the Chinese negotiating team which ended the fighting in Korea in 1953. Persecuted during the Cultural Revolution, he had been by 1979 restored to a high position in the Chinese Academy of Social Sciences. He taught for a year at Carleton College, in Los Angeles, California.

By 1979, Gao Hongye (Renmin University) had translated Paul Samuelson's popular elementary textbook which was published in that year. At the same time, a group of 17 Chinese scholars led by Chen Daisun formed the China Association for Research on Foreign Economics. Fuqian Fang (2013) described the Association's aims as follows:

> First, to study foreign economics and the contemporary history of foreign economics under the guidance of Marxism and Mao Zedong thought; second, to criticize the vulgar and revisionist economic theories; third, to absorb all the things from foreign economic theories that are useful for socialist construction.
>
> (Fang, 2013: 296)

More formal efforts began to develop US–China exchanges involving Economics. A delegation of American economists spent a month in China in late 1979, 'making contacts with Chinese economists from various circles and identifying Chinese and American research interests with an eye toward future exchanges'. This led to a conference on Alternative Strategies for Economic Development, in Racine, Wisconsin in November 1980. 'This effort involved the presentation of research papers, with Chinese economists analyzing empirical problems of development in the PRC and Western participants reviewing major theoretical themes' (Wilson, 1981: 1). Edwin Mansfield (1930–1997) and Nobel Laureate, Milton Friedman (1912–2006) came for a lecture tour in 1979–1980. Friedman's ideas, it is said, were quite popular among Chinese graduate students in the 1980s.

By 1980, Chinese students were again appearing in Western graduate programmes. In 1983, the US government revived the Fulbright one for Economics, providing financial support for Chinese studying in the US and sending Americans to teach in China. One of these, Professor Hu Teh-wei, prepared a useful survey of Economics in Chinese universities at that time (see Hu, 1984).

A crucial role in restoring China's connection with Western Economics was taken by Gregory Chow (1930–), who was at Princeton University. Born in China, Chow came to the US in 1948 to complete an undergraduate degree at Cornell. He received a doctorate from Chicago in 1955 and became a leading econometrician. In the 1960s, he partnered with S. C. Tsiang and T. C. Liu in advising the government of Taiwan. Taiwan's success impressed leaders of the People's Republic, and Chow was able to establish a personal relationship with Zhao Ziyang (1919–2005) who became Premier of the PRC in 1980. Chow visited China in 1980 to teach econometrics at the Chinese Academy of Social Sciences in Beijing. In 1981, he was responsible for creating a committee within the American Economic Association on US–China exchanges in Economics. In 1983, Chow composed a textbook which demonstrated the application of basic Western analytical tools to the Chinese economy. Entitled *The Chinese Economy*, it was published in the US soon after (see Chow, 1985) and translated into Chinese that same year, pursuant to a widely publicized meeting with Premier Zhao in July 1984.

In 1984–1986, Chow organized summer workshops dealing with micro-economics, macroeconomics and econometrics, sponsored by the Chinese Ministry of Education. The first, dealing with macroeconomics, was presented at Peking University by himself and Professors Sherwin Rosen, Marc Nerlove and Edwin Mills. Extending over six weeks in June–July 1984,

> the level of instruction was close to the first-year graduate level at a good American university. Approximately 60 graduate students, young teachers and researchers were selected nationally by the Ministry of Education to attend. The lectures were given in English without interpretation.
>
> (Chow, 1994: 40)

In 1985, the Chinese State Education Commission sponsored 62 young Chinese scholars to come to the US for graduate study in Economics. In September 1985, a year-round Training Centre began operating at People's University sponsored by the SEC and financed by the Ford Foundation. It offered a one-year course comparable to a Master's level in an American university. A second Centre, at Fudan University in Shanghai, began operating in 1987. These were open to students from all over China, chosen by competitive examination. Operating over the period 1985–1995, the programme brought in 47 Economics professors from several Western countries, including Nobel Laureates Leonid Hurwicz (1917–2008) and Robert Mundell (1932–). Twelve of the visitors were ethnic Chinese. Emphasis was on aiding Chinese universities to modernize their curriculum. A total of 417 students participated in the *Renda* programme and an additional 201 attended Fudan.[4]

The number of Chinese attending Western graduate schools expanded rapidly after the mid-1980s. Host universities steadily increased the availability of financial aid to Chinese students. Many of these chose to remain in the host countries. Returning to Chinese universities was unattractive to many. Those universities were still staffed by numerous holdovers from the 'Cultural Revolution', and Western-trained youngsters were often not welcomed. American immigration restrictions had been relaxed. Chinese graduate students welcomed the opportunity to enjoy improved living conditions and freedom from onerous restrictions, such as the 'one-child' policy.

As late as 1981, Chinese government pronouncements implicitly rejected Keynesian fiscal policies: 'China does not advocate deficit financing. Because China has a different social system from Western countries, she does not need to resort to deficit financing to stimulate economic growth as they do when there are over-production and insufficient investment' (Xu and Chen, 1984: 443). But demand management became a prominent feature of Chinese fiscal policy from that time (Trescott, 2012).

Again, Fuqian Fang's (2005) incisive article presents an admirable survey of the adaptation of Chinese universities to Western Economics since the 1980s (see his chapter later in this volume: further contributions will spell out more about this phenomenon, by Cohn, and others). The impact of economic policy-making may be noted too (see Webber and Zhu's chapter, also Zhang's contribution, on the influence on the economic reforms here).

Professional societies

The Chinese Economists Society was created in May 1985 in the US primarily by and for young economists from Mainland China. They established an English-language journal, *China Economic Review*, in 1989. In 1992, CES became part of the Allied Social Science Association, and has sponsored programmes at the annual ASSA meetings. According to CES online:

> In order to promote market-based economic reforms in China, [CES] has since 1993 organized its Annual Conference every year in China.... The CES has endeavored to make contributions to the advancement and dissemination of economics and management sciences in China. In the early 1990s, it mobilized its members to write a 14-volume Market Economics Book Series (1993), a three-volume Frontiers of Modern Economics (1989, 1993, 1998), and a 12-volume Modern Business Administration Book Series (1995) in Chinese.... Since 1990, the CES has run short-term teaching programs every year to support its overseas members to teach economic courses in Chinese universities.... So far, over 2,700 people have been or used to be CES individual members.
>
> (http://china-ces.org/AboutCES/Default.aspx?title=History
> (accessed 1 May 2015))

In 1986, ethnic Chinese economists from non-mainland locations formed the Chinese Economic Association in North America (CEANA). They do not have their own journal but do conduct annual meetings in conjunction with the ASSA. Cross-participation between the two organizations is evident in the papers of the CEJ and the CEANU initiatives.

With the new millennium, the flow of Mainland Chinese to study in the West continued to expand. Many of the Chinese with Western degrees remained in the West. Increasingly, some returned to teach in China, as Chinese universities approached the salaries and other benefits available in the West. The image now emerges of a cosmopolitan profession. Notable ethnic-Chinese economists (Justin Yifu Lin, Wang Jianye, Wang Yijiang, Cheryl Xiaoning Long and many others) move back and forth among locations in China, America and elsewhere with affiliations involving universities, think-tanks, international organizations and government agencies.

In the new millennium, a number of Chinese universities (and the Chinese Academy of Social Sciences) are authorized to grant doctoral degrees in Economics. Often, the doctoral students are not required to be fluent in a Western language. Many of the dissertations do not meet the standards which prevail in the West. The Summer 2013 issue of *US–China Review* reproduced several Chinese commentaries raising serious questions about quality in Chinese endeavours in this vein. These are endemic problems in a pluralistic system, with relatively easy entry, whether Chinese or American.

Conclusions

Although known earlier, Western Economic ideas truly came into China at a rapid pace after 1900. Figures such as Yan Fu, Liang Qichao and Sun Yat-sen published translations and interpretive works concerning Western Economics thinkers, such as Adam Smith, Henry George and Richard T. Ely and so on. Chinese students travelled abroad to learn new ideas, first in Japan, then in Western countries. The Protestant missionary colleges, notably Yanjing and Nanjing, taught courses modelled after American colleges, using textbooks such as that by Ely, and engaging numerous Western instructors, chiefly Americans, from Western countries. Those colleges, as well as *Qinghua*, channelled numerous Chinese Economics students into American graduate programmes, especially at Columbia and Harvard. Many of these returned to teach in Chinese universities. Those who studied in the United States received instruction heavily slanted toward Institutional Economics and were critical of free markets. There was very little attention paid to economic development at the time, but much given to international economics and monetary economics.

Significant numbers of Chinese Economics students attended universities in Britain (predominantly the LSE, as well as Cambridge), France (predominantly, Paris) and Germany (mainly, Berlin). German influence was strong at *Beida*, and British influence was strong at Wuhan. Returned students from Germany gave significant emphasis to public finance and to government management of the economy. Despite a late start, Nankai University became a leading bastion of Western Economics, especially in the work of He Lian and Fang Xianting.

It was thus a challenge for Chinese economists to adapt Western ideas to China's own needs. Keynesian economics, for example, although widely popular with Chinese students, has been said to be relatively inappropriate for China and distracted attention from the much-more-relevant quantity theory of money, some thought at the time. Even so, the diffusion of Western Economics notions still continued apace.

Notes

1 Much of this chapter is an update of points developed in my book, *Jingji Xue: The Introduction of Western Economic Ideas into China 1850–1950*. Citations, direct quotes and acknowledgements, as well as many full references to books and articles from that work, are available in that source (Trescott, 2007).
2 My comments on Yan Fu's translation were developed in collaboration with Professor Lai Cheng-chung, the leading Chinese scholar on Yan. I selected key passages from Smith and we tried to re-translate Yan – as it would have been perceived by Chinese readers. Smith's and Yan's perceptions of China's economy are quite consistent with those in Maddison (1998). On Smith's ideas in China, see Liu (2013).
3 On Ho, see Zhou *et al.* (2013); on Fang, see Trescott (2002).
4 The present author taught in both the Fulbright and Ford Foundation programmes described in the text. He was a Fulbright Professor at *Beida* 1983–1984. Other visiting American economists there and then were Bill Williams and Lu Chung-tai. Besides Hu Teh-wei (at Nankai), the other Fulbright economist was Wei Shih at Shandong University. Professor Willem (Wym) Houwink from University of Nevada at Reno had just arrived to begin a visiting professorship which lasted over 20 years at the Chinese University of International Business and Economics. Many of my *Beida* students came to the US for graduate work. The present author taught at Peoples University in the Ford programme in Spring 1992, with Alasdair MacBean. Only a few students showed interest in graduate work in the West. However, my teaching assistant, Mr Xiao Zhijie, received a full scholarship to Yale, completed a PhD there, and became a full professor at Boston College.

References

Blaug, M. and Sturges, R. P. [eds] (1999). *Who's Who in Economics*. Cheltenham: Elgar.

Buck, P. (1931). *The Good Earth*. New York, NY: Day.

[Burton, J. H.] Anon. (1852). *Political Economy for Use in Schools and for Private Instruction*. Edinburgh: Chambers.

Chinese Committee on Economics Education and Exchange with the US (2008). *Program of Economic Education Exchange with the US for 10 Years 1985–1995* (Chinese language). Beijing: The Committee.

Chow, G. (1985). *The Chinese Economy*. New York, NY: Harper & Row.

Chow, G. (1994). *Understanding China's Economy*. Singapore: World Scientific.

Ely, R. T. (1893). *Outlines of Economics*. New York, NY: Hunt and Eaton, translated into Chinese in 1910.

Fang, F. Q. (2005). 'Some Problems in the Western Economics Teaching'. *China University Teaching*, 9: 13–15.

Fang, F. (2013). 'The Changing Status of Western Economics in China.' In Y. Ma and H.-M. Trautwein [eds], *Thoughts on Economic Development in China*. London and New York, NY: Routledge, 295–305.

Farrer. T. (1883). *The State in Its Relation to Trade*. London: Macmillan.

Fawcett, H. (1863). *Manual of Political Economy*. London: Macmillan.

George, H. (1879). *Progress and Poverty*. New York, NY: Appleton.

Ho, F. L. (1967). 'Reminiscences of Ho Lien (Franklin L. Ho)' (typescript). Special Collections, Columbia University Library.

Hu, T. W. (1984). 'The State of American Economic Studies in the Peoples Republic of China' (mimeo). Washington, DC: US Information Agency.

Keynes, J. M. (1957) [1936]. *The General Theory of Employment, Interest and Money, (Jiu ye, li xi he huo bi tong lun)* was published in a Chinese translation by Y. Xu. Beijing: China SDX Joint Publishing Company.

Lai, C.-C. [ed.] (2000). *Adam Smith Across Nations: Translations and Receptions of the Wealth of Nations.* Oxford: Oxford University Press.

Liang, Q. (1903). *Concise History of Economic Thought* [Yin-ping-shih Wen-chi]. Beijing: n.p.

Liu, Q. (2013). 'The Reception of Adam Smith in East Asia; A Comparative Perspective.' In Y. Ma and H.-M. Trautwein [eds], *Thoughts on Economic Development in China.* London and New York, NY: Routledge, 35–55.

Lutz, J. G. (1971). *China and the Christian Colleges 1850–1950.* Ithaca, NY: Cornell University Press.

Maddison, A. (1998). *Chinese Economic Performance in the Long Run.* Paris: OECD.

Marx, K. (1938) [1867]. *Das Kapital/Capital,* translated into Chinese in a complete version by Y.-N. Wang and T.-L. Kuo. Beijing: Foreign Languages Publisher.

Marx, K. (1954) [1867]. *Capital.* Moscow: Progress Publishers.

Platt, J. (1880). *Money.* London: Simpkins and Marshall.

Reynolds, D. R. (1975). *The Chinese Industrial Cooperative Movement and the Political Polarization of Wartime China, 1938–1945.* Unpublished PhD dissertation, Columbia University.

Samuelson, P. A. (1979). *Economics.* Chinese version. 10th edition. Beijing: Commercial Press. Translated by H. Gao, Preface by H. Gao.

Smith, A. (1776). *An Inquiry into the Nature and Causes of the Wealth of Nations,* abbreviated as the *Wealth of Nations,* re-published in 1976. Oxford: Clarendon Press.

Smith, A. (1902) [1776]. *The Wealth of Nations [Origins of Wealth], (Yan fu),* translated by F. Yan. Shanghai: Nanyang Translation Institute.

Spence, J. (1990). *The Search for Modern China.* New York, NY: W. W. Norton.

Spurling, H. (2010). *Burying the Bones: Pearl Buck in China.* London: Profile.

Stalin, J. (1951). *Economic Problems of Socialism.* Beijing: Foreign Languages Press.

Sun, Y.-S. (1922). *The International Development of China.* London and New York: Putnam [originally published in Chinese in 1915].

Tobin, J. (1975). 'The Economy of China: A Tourist's View.' *Chinese Economic Studies,* 8: 25–46.

Trescott, P. B. (1992). 'Institutional Economics in China: Yenching University, 1917–1949.' *Journal of Economic Issues,* 26: 1221–1255.

Trescott, P. B. (2002). 'H. D. Fong and the Study of Chinese Economic Development.' *History of Political Economy,* 34: 789–809.

Trescott, P. B. (2007). *Jingji Xue: The History of the Introduction of Western Economic Ideas into China 1850–1950.* Hong Kong, SAR: Chinese University Press.

Trescott, P. B. (2010a). 'Western Economic Advisers in China, 1900–1949.' *Research in the History of Economic Thought and Methodology,* 28-A: 1–37.

Trescott, P. B. (2010b). 'Alfred Marshall's Ideas in China.' In T. Raffaelli, G. Becattini, K. Caldari and M. Dardi [eds], *The Impact of Alfred Marshall's Ideas.* Northampton, MA: Edward Elgar, 184–190.

Trescott, P. B. (2012). 'How Keynesian Economics Came to China.' *History of Political Economy,* 44: 341–364.

Trescott, P. B. (2014). 'American Radicals, the FBI, and the Formation of USCPFA 1970–74.' *US–China Review,* 38: 8–16.

Warner, M. (2015). 'Keynes and China: Keynesianism with Chinese Characteristics.' *Asia Pacific Business Review*, 21: 251–263.

Wilson, A. A. (1981). 'Scholarly Exchange Activities in Economics.' *China Exchange News*, 9: 1–5.

Wu, Y-L. (1956). *An Economic Survey of Communist China*. New York, NY: Bookman Associates.

Xu, Y. and Chen, B. (1984). 'Public Finance.' In *China's Socialist Modernization*. Beijing: Foreign Language Press, 440–455, no editor cited.

Zhou, H., Yang, L. and Feng, J. (2013). 'He Lian, a Founder and Practitioner of Chinazation [*sic*] of Western Economics.' In Y. Ma and H.-M. Trautwein [eds], *Thoughts on Economic Development in China*. London and New York, NY: Routledge, 158–174.

4 The diffusion of Western Economics in Japan

Kiichiro Yagi

Introduction

Since the Meiji Restoration in 1868, the influence of Western Economics over Japanese intellectual life has been cast in a history of over a century and a half. During this period, Japanese scholars have experienced several waves of Overseas Economics schools of thought, learned new approaches by reading Western books and journals and studying abroad, whilst at the same time attempting to create their own theories (see Sugiyama, 1994).

We can divide this period of influence into five phases:[1] *1. Encounter and enlightenment: from the 1850s to the 1880s; 2. Assimilation of German-style economics: from the 1890s to the 1910s; 3. Quest and disarray for Japanese economics: from the 1920s to the war years; 4. Rehabilitation after the war defeat: from 1945 to the 1970s; and 5. Age of globalization: from the 1980s to the present.* However, it is hopefully not necessary to delve too far into details of the fifth phase in which Japanese economics has become fully synchronized with that of the international level, as this is better known.

Encounter and enlightenment: from the 1850s to the 1880s

Nishi and Tsuda in Leiden

Probably, the first Japanese scholars to encounter Western Economics were Amane Nishi (1829–1897) and Mamichi Tsuda (1829–1903). They were sent to Leiden in the Netherlands, by the Tokugawa Shogunate from 1853 to 1857, in order to absorb Western knowledge.

Abandoning the seclusion policy under the pressure of the US fleet, the Shogunate followed the advice of Dutch diplomats to send young scholars to Europe in order to encounter Western knowledge and then bring it back to Japan. The curriculum that was arranged for them by their mentor, Simon Vissering (1818–1888), contained the subject of 'Political Economy'[2] (see also the chapter by Ohtsuki on business education in Japan later in this volume). After their return, they became influential academic advisors, despite the regime-change of the Meiji Restoration. However, they seem to have shown little interest in

Economics as a discipline. They studied it in Leiden as just part of the assigned curriculum.

Kanda and Fukuzawa

By contrast, Takahira Kanda (1830–1897) and Yukichi Fukuzawa (1835–1901) discovered Economics as a promising discipline that could guide Japan after its abandonment of its former seclusion policy (see Craig, 2009). Kanda published the first Japanese book on Western Economics, *Keizai Shogaku* (*Small Book of Economics*), in 1867. This book was the translation of British businessman and writer on Economics, William Ellis's (1800–1881) *Outlines of Social Economy* (1846) from its later Dutch edition.

In the following year, Fukuzawa introduced the basic ideas of Western Economics in the sequel to his best-seller, *Seiyo Jijo* (Situations of Western Nations) in 1868 (see Yagi, 2015). This was a free translation of an autodidact textbook in the series, *Chambers' Educational Course*. The author of this textbook, who was also known in China (see the chapters by Trescott in this volume) was identified first by A. M. Craig in 1984 as John Hill Burton (1809–1881), a Scottish advocate who was well-versed in Scottish Enlightenment thought, including the writings of David Hume (1711–1726) and Adam Smith (1723–1790).[3]

Prior to these translations, Kanda had vindicated, in his *Nosho-ben* (Arguments on Agriculture and Commerce, 1861), the Shogunate's decision to open ports, by attributing the wealth of Western nations to their pro-commerce policy. Fukuzawa followed Kanda by distributing a circular *Tojin Orai* (Transaction with Foreigners, 1865) written in a colloquial style – so as to persuade common people to reap the benefit of the 'open ports' policy. However, it is not clear if either of them had much knowledge of Western Economics in the early 1860s (see the chapter by Sakamoto later in this volume).

When Fukuzawa made his second visit to the US in 1867, he purchased an amount of textbooks to use in his private school (the origin of the present Keio University). Francis Wayland's *The Elements of Political Economy* (1st edn 1837) was one of them. It was this Economics textbook that was in Fukuzawa's hands at the time of the legendary class which he gave in the midst of tumult caused by the bombardment of the new government of the citadel defended by the remaining supporters of the old regime. It is said that Fukuzawa encouraged his students by stating that the future of Japan will stem from his 'small school'. The present Keio University still celebrates this day as a 'memorial day' of this lecture.

After the Meiji Restoration, Kanda proposed the new government permit the privatization of land and establish a taxation system based on its asset-value. Thus, Kanda may be said to have assimilated Western Economics in his vision of a *modernization* with the spirit of liberalism. Fukuzawa extended his research in Western Economics to 'Ethics under modern civil society' and endeavoured to establish the sense of independence among the 'emerging' middle class of the Japanese society (Yagi, 2015). Despite the fact that he rejected the invitation to join the new government and remained a private scholar until his death, his influence was felt in almost all intellectual spheres of the Meiji Japan. However, his liberalism was of a conditional nature, as was shown in his support of the restriction of residential freedom of foreign merchants, as well as his close relations with the Mitsubishi company that emerged as a conglomerate closely allied with the government. In this respect, he deviated from the doctrine of liberalism and stood close to protectionism. He declared that the criterion of judgment was solely to be the maintenance of Japan as an independent nation. Based on such a practical consideration, his recommendation of Economic Policy thus swung between liberalism and mercantilism.[4]

Three channels of introduction and diffusion

In the early years of the Meiji period, knowledge of Western Economics diffused by the routes of first, translations; second, economic journalism; and third, lectures in academia, which we will now discuss in turn.

Translations

Table 4.1 shows the list of Japanese translations of Western Economics in the early Meiji years. In this early stage, elementary textbooks for beginners occupied the centre of the stage. Most authors of original books were liberal British and American economists. However, it is noteworthy that the translation of the whole of John Stuart Mill's (1806–1873) *Principles of Political Economy*, which came out in English in 1848, had begun as early as in 1875. Such a brave attempt was succeeded by Eisaku Ishikawa (1858–1889) in the 1882 Japanese translation of Adam Smith's *Wealth of Nations* (first published in English in 1776), which was finally completed as early as 1888 by Shosaku Saga (1853–1890) – contrasting with *The Theory of Moral Sentiments* (1759) only being translated in the post-Second World War era (1948–1949) (see the chapter by Sakamoto on Smith and Japan later in this volume).

In the middle period, policy-oriented works of contemporary Economists such as H. C. Carey, H. D. Macleod, W. S. Jevons and Alfred and Mary Paley Marshall were translated. The appearance of the key work of Friedrich List (1789–1846), namely *National System of Political Economy* in the series of translations[5] intensified the controversy over free trade and protectionism in Japan. Its translator, Sadamasu Oshima (1845–1914) advocated protectionism and was called 'Japan's Friedrich List', whilst the translator of H. D. Macleod's *Principles*, Ukichi Taguchi (1855–1905), was dubbed 'Japan's Adam Smith' due to his liberal convictions.

Economic journalism

The Economics topics that appeared in journalism showed a similar tendency. It was the 'free trade vs protectionism' debate that first attracted journalists. First,

Table 4.1 Translated books of Western Economics in the early Meiji period (before 1880)

Keizai Shogaku, 2 vols. Tr. from Dutch edition by Takahira Kanda, 1867	William Ellis, *Outlines of Social Economy*, London, 1846
Seiyo Jijo Gaihen, 3 vols. Free translation by Yukichi Fukuzawa, 1868	William and Robert Chambers, eds, *Political Economy for Use in Schools, and for Private Instruction*, Edinburgh, 1853
Yowatari no Tsue, Ichimei Keizai Benmou, 2 +2 vols. Tr. by Noriyuki Ga, 1872–1874	Francis Wayland, *The Elements of Political Economy*, London, 1837
Hou-shi Keizaigaku, 5 vols. Tr. by Kensuke Nagata, 1877	Milicent Garret Fawcett, *Political Economy for Beginners*, 4th edn, London, 1876
Keizai Nyumon, Ichimei Seisan Michi-Annai. Abri. tr. by Tokujiro Obata, 1877	Richard Whately, *Easy Lessons on Money Matters: for the Use of Young People*, London, 1849
Keizai Yosetsu, 2 vols. 1877–1878. Tr. by Furusawa Shigeru from English translation by Alexander von Sieboldt	Henri Jouffroy, *Catechisme d'economie politique*, 1st ed., Leipzig and Paris, 1844
Taisei Keizai Shinron. Tr. by Tatsuo Takahashi Tatsuo, 1874	James E. Thorold Rogers, A *Manual of Political Economy for School and Colleges*, 2nd edn, Oxford, 1869
Kanban Keizai Genron. Abri. tr. by Masashi Ogata, 1869* (a full translation by Kawamoto Kiyokazu appeared as *Peri-shi Zoho Kaisei Rizai Genron*, 1880)	Arthur Latham Perry, *Elements of Political Economy*, 2nd edn, New York, 1867
Fukoku Ron. Abri. tr. by Hideki Nagamine, 1874	Amasa Walker, *The Science of Wealth: a Manual of Political Economy*, Philadelphia, 1872
Miru Keizairon. Tr. by Hayashi Kaoru and Shigetaka Suzuki, 1875–1885	J. S. Mill, *Principles of Political Economy*, London, 1848
Jiyu Koeki Ana-Sa,gashi. Tr. by Giichi Wakayama, 1877	John Barnard Byles, *Sophisms of Free-trade and Popular Political Economy Examined*, London, 1849
Fukoku Saku. Chinese translation by Fengzhao Wan, republished by Ginko Kishida with Japanese reading order, 1881	Henry Fawcett, *Manual of Political Economy*, London and Cambridge, 1863

Sources: miscellaneous.

Ukichi Taguchi (1855–1905) started the *Tokyo Keizai Zasshi* in 1879. This publication adopted economic liberalism and propagated it not only via itself, but also by printed lectures which were held at the local clubs of its readers. On the other hand, it was Tsuyoshi Inukai (1855–1932: later entering into politics) who translated H. C. Carey's *Principles* (1837), launched the short-lived *Tokai Keizai Shimpo* in 1880 and advocated the position of protectionism. As the economic treaties that Japan had concluded with Western countries in the 1850s did not admit Japan's autonomy to fix the rate of customs, the debate of the two journals focused on the pros and cons of the state-intervention in the construction of the railway network.

After the closure of Inukai's journal, several new ones appeared as rivals to Taguchi's *Tokyo Keizai Zasshi*. Among them, *Toyo Keizai Shimpo*, which was founded in 1895, was fortunate enough to have great economists as its successive Editor-in-Chief and became the leading business weekly journal of Japan around the years of the First World War (a list of journals then influential in Japan is included in the References section to this chapter).

Lectures in academia

The first Economics lecture at the newly established Imperial University (presently the University of Tokyo) was not delivered by a professional economist, but by a fresh graduate of Harvard University, Ernest Fenollosa (1853–1908). He taught the subject there from 1878 to 1885, along with philosophy and politics. It seems that he grounded his approach mainly in John Stuart Mill's *Principles of Political Economy* first published in 1848 as noted earlier and added the view of 'social evolution' under the prevailing influence of Herbert Spencer (1820–1903). From 1879, Inejiro Tajiri (1850–1923), an expert of the Ministry of Finance who had studied Economics and Public Finance in Yale, taught economics at the Imperial University.

At the professional school of the Ministry of Law, the invited French professor, Gustave E. Boissonard (1825–1910) taught Economics as a neighbour-discipline to law for a decade, since his arrival in 1873. His teachings were strictly as liberal as those of the mainstream academicians in France during that period.

At Keio, Fukuzawa's disciple, Tokujiro Obata (1841–1905), succeeded Fukuzawa in teaching economics using Wayland's textbook. Further, in 1889, the university invited American professor Garret Droppers (1860–1927) to head the economics faculty. His lecture was also based on Mill's *Principles*; however, he was in favour of the historical orientation of German economics from his previous study in Germany. Further, from 1878 to 1892, Dwight W. Learned (1848–1943) taught Economics at the Christian college, Doshisha in Kyoto.

The turning point in academia occurred in 1881, when Shigenobu Okuma (1838–1922) who was in favour of British-style constitutional government, was dismissed from the government. The leader of the new government, Hirobumi Ito (1841–1909), chose Prussian-style absolutism for the Constitution of Japan and changed the model country there, from Britain and France, to the new-born German Empire under Bismarck.

This political change accompanied a change of academic orientation of the Imperial University, in particular of its Law Faculty, and other schools under the government. The academic journal of the Law Faculty was named *Kokka Gakkai Zasshi* (Journal of State Science) and most of its future professors were sent to Germany to study the Prussian-style bureaucratic administration and state policies. The candidates of economics professors, who were at that time included in the Law Faculty, were not exceptional. They learned research methods and policies in the late nineteenth century school of German economics, that is, those of the German Historical School or Social Policy School, and applied them in Japan (Sugiyama and Mizuta, 1988).

Assimilation of German-style economics: from the 1890s to the 1910s

Shift to the German model

The shift of political as well as academic orientation in Japan to the German model brought about a change which continued up to the inter-war years (see Trescott's chapter on the influence of German Economics on China later in this volume). At the Imperial universities,[6] most professors had the experience of studying at German universities and were particularly sensitive to the topics and controversies in the German-speaking academic world. Even at the Colleges of Commerce,[7] 'Germanophilia' became prevalent albeit at a mitigated level, despite the fact that students had to learn business correspondence in English (see also the chapter by Ohtsuki on business education in Japan later in this volume).

A similar situation was also observed at private universities, whose graduates seldom entered the state-bureaucracy.[8] Professors would ground their teaching in social sciences and idealist philosophy derived from Germany, whilst English was the standard foreign language taught in the secondary education. At some private universities, the affinity to Anglo-Saxon learning was maintained. A typical case was Waseda University (then Tokyo Senmon Gakko), which was founded by Okuma in 1882. Here, the first chief of the department of commerce, Tameyuki Amano (1861–1938), learned Economics first from Fenollosa and published in 1889 his lecture, *Keizai Genron* (Principles of Economics), which was an improved version of the classical economy at the late stage of J. S. Mill.

In the world of business and journalism, the common international language was English. Thus, businessmen and journalists often had a more acute sense of the 'real-world' economy – than the afore-said Germanophile academicians. In other words, German remained as a language of academic elites in several areas of higher education (Economics, Law, Medicine and Philosophy).

The first outcome of the German turn of academicians in the field of economics was the introduction of methods, ideas and policies of the then prevalent German Economics. In the late nineteenth century, the historical school had criticized the abstract theory based on 'egoistic' economic man and proposed a historical and statistical approach that was regarded as the 'New Economics' in contrast to the old (classical) economics.

When Tajiri resigned from the Imperial University in 1887, Udo Eggert (1848–1893) was invited to teach Economics and Public Finance. Following his abrupt death in Japan, A. von Wenckstern, H. E. Wäntig, E. Foxwell, C. S. Griffin and M. W. Sprague were invited as foreign lecturers at the Imperial University, Tokyo. Apparently, Germans were to occupy the majority there.[9]

In the early 1890s, a group of academicians around Noburu Kanai (1865–1933), who had returned in 1890 after completing further studies from Germany, had monthly gatherings to study social policies, which developed into the first Japanese academic society in the area of Economics, *Shakai Seisaku Gakkai* (Society for Social Policies) in 1897. From 1907, this society held open annual assemblies, in which an annually chosen topic was discussed by its members that covered not only academicians but also businessmen and administrators.

Table 4.2 shows the topics of the society for its annual assembly.

Most members of this society were aware that the Japanese economy faced severe social problems that were not fully anticipated by their liberal seniors. Following the empirical approach based on statistical and historical studies, theoretical discussions were rather rare in this society. In policy orientations, however, they were as diversified as their German counterparts. Kanai followed Adolf Wagner's (1835–1917) authoritarian 'statism' and advocated social policies by state intervention. In contrast, Iwasaburo Takano (1871–1944) took a socio-liberal direction represented in Germany by Lujo Brentano (1838–1931) and expected the healthy growth of a labour movement in Japan.

Gustav Schmoller's (1838–1917) stress on detailed monograph research was also generally appreciated. Collaborating with the invited German lecturer, H. E. Wäntig, Takano opened a research office on Statistics and Economics at the Faculty of Law and introduced a seminar class that united research and

Table 4.2 Topics of assembly discussion of the Society for Social Policies

	Year	Topic
1	1907	Factory legislation
2	1908	Custom problems seen from the view point of social policy
3	1909	Immigration problems
4	1910	Municipal enterprise
5	1911	Workers' insurance
6	1912	Problems of living costs
7	1913	Labour disputes
8	1914	Protection of small farmers
9	1915	Taxation problems seen from the viewpoint of social policies
10	1916	Public enterprises and protected companies
11	1917	Problems of small scale manufacturers
12	1918	Problems of women workers
13	1919	Labour unions
14	1920	Problems of intermediate classes
15	1921	Institutions of wage and profit-sharing
16	1922	Tenant problems in Japan
17	1923	Not held due to the earthquake [?]
18	1924	Problems of labour union law

Sources: miscelleneous.

education. Training students using the statistical and historical approach in seminars was to become the standard model for economics students. With his students, Takano performed empirical research in the slums of the coastal area of Tokyo (in Tsukishima), where most workers of newly developed industries lived. From his seminars, many able students entered into the emerging union movement.

Fukuda and Kawakami[10]

It did not take long for the young generation of the society to be discontented over the lack of a consistent theory in Japanese Economics academia under the influence of the historical school. Tokuzo Fukuda (1874–1930) and Hajime Kawakami (1879–1946) were two representative figures of this frustrated generation. In Fukuda's view, Economics in Japan entered a new stage in which establishing its own theory was necessary after the introduction of first, Liberal Economics and then later, German Economics (see Morris-Suzuki, 1989: 65ff.).

Despite the fact that Fukuda himself acquired his doctoral degree under Lujo Brentano in the socio-economic history of Japan and in the style of the German historical school (Fukuda, 1900), he was to admit the superiority of British (and Cambridge) economists such as Alfred Marshall (1842–1924) and Arthur C. Pigou (1877–1959) in analytical theory. In his courses of General Economics, he used Marshall's *Principles of Economics* (1890) as its theoretical base. Fukuda further encouraged his students and friends to study almost all promising directions of Economic Theory, including Karl Marx (1818–1883) and Leon Walras (1834–1910). But when Marxism entered Japan, he became a staunch opponent of Marxian economics, based on his profound knowledge in the Western controversies around it. Fukuda taught at Hitotsubashi University (then the Tokyo College of Commerce) and Keio University (see the chapter by Ohtsuki later in this volume). It is said that almost all theoretical studies in modern economics in the first half of the twentieth century Japan had their origin in Fukuda's foresight.

However, what he wanted was to go beyond the quantitative analysis of prices and wages and to establish true Welfare Economics in which rights for the well-being of workers would be duly integrated. In 1918, when the democratic movement of the *Taisho era* was in its advent, Fukuda was engaged in it by establishing the *Reimei-kai* together with a political scientist, Sakuzo Yoshino. Despite his unexpected early death, his spirit of socio-liberal policies was followed by many of his disciples up to the post-1945 period.

Kawakami shared the wish to establish a new Economics discipline with Fukuda. His problem was how to conquer Adam Smith's premise of 'self-interest' in order to better ground the solution of social problems to which social policies were directed (see the chapter by Sakamoto later in this volume).

In Fukada's view, neither income redistribution nor state socialism could solve the social problems caused by the Capitalist Economy, in so far as they were not combined with a 'moral revolution' that conquers the 'egoistic' motivation of individuals. Divided by his desire to be altruistic and the economic doctrine based on self-love, Kawakami at last found the solution of his dilemma in Marxism that taught the unity of interest of individuals, with that of the working class as a whole. Kawakami launched his journal *Shakai Mondai Kenkyu* (*Inquiries into Social Problems*) in 1919 and supplied literature on Marxism together with his essays and articles in Marxism and Marxian Economics (see Yagi, 2007). Kawakami had to correct his 'moralistic' interpretation of Marxism through the criticism from Tamizo Kushida (1885–1934) and Kazuo Fukumoto (1894–1983).[11] Further, he had to answer the criticism of Marxian Economics of Fukuda and others.

Quest and disarray for Japanese Economics: from the 1920s to the war years

Boom of Marxism

Kawakami was not exceptional in this respect. In the 1920s, under the impact of increasing labour disputes in towns and the dissatisfaction of tenant farmers in the countryside, as well as the changing political atmosphere after the Russian revolution, Marxism attracted many of Japan's youth to its camp. In almost all universities and high schools, study-groups of Marxian literature were to be organized. When a commercial publisher began to publish the *Collected Works of Marx and Engels* (*Marukusu Engerusu Zenshu*) in 1928 with a non-expensive price, the 'Marx boom' reached its peak (see also the chapter by Metzler later in this volume).

However, in the same period, the Communist International strengthened its effort to control Communist Party movements in Japan.[12] The police took the preventive measure of arresting leaders of student clubs of Marxist study in March 1928 by applying the 'Peace Preservation Law'. Under the alleged charge of his support of leftist students, Kawakami had to leave the Kyoto Imperial University.

Academicians who took a research-sabbatical in Germany in the years of the Weimar Republic saw the competitive public propaganda of Communists and Socialists and their influence on academic publications. Some of them, in turn, came back to Japan as Marxist scholars. In these years, Marxism was an 'emerging science' that appeared to integrate natural science and social sciences in the united principle of Materialism. Marxian Economics represented in Marx's *Capital* (1867) began to occupy the 'centre-ground' of theoretical studies of Marxism. The translation of Marx's *Capital* into Japanese was completed in 1924 by Motoyuki Takabatake (1886–1928), a non-communist state socialist, whose work had been started under Fukuda's encouragement, although in a Chinese version until 1938. In the inter-war years, not only Marx's *Capital*, but also almost all the important literature of Marxian economics, such as Rudolf Hilferding's (1877–1941) *Financial Capital* (1910), Rosa Luxemburg's (1871–1919) *Capital Accumulation* (1913), as well as Vladimir I. Lenin's (1870–1924) *Imperialism* (1917) was available in Japanese translation.

Marxian economists in Japan had the will to establish their own analyses of Japanese capitalism and its crisis in the 1930s, so as to better understand the conditions of revolutionary change (see Yagi, 2007). One of the most controversial problems was the nature of 'landowner-tenant system' in the countryside. A group that gathered to publish the *Nihon Shihonshugi Hattatsushi Koza* (*Series of the Analysis of Japanese Capitalism*, publ. 1932–1933) regarded it as of a 'semi-feudal' nature on which the absolute power structure was built. This land-system in agriculture supplied the capitalist sector with both cheap labour and raw silk, by way of small manufacturers and the sideline output of farmers' family-members.

According to this so-called *Koza*-School view, the coming revolutionary change was a 'bourgeois-democratic' revolution based on the alliance of workers and farmers. Against this view, another group called *Rono-School* regarded the non-capitalist tenant system of a transitory nature in the process toward the capitalist development of the Japanese economy. In their view, the real power at least in the Economics-related area was already in the hand of monopoly capital. Thus, a 'socialist revolution' was to be accompanied by a goal of abolishing the semi-feudal system remnant in the country as the best strategy from the *Rono-School* viewpoint. The controversy of the two schools continued up to the late 1930s, when the controls over research and publication prohibited any activity of Marxist scholars, even if they were fortunate enough to avoid prison.[13]

In the third stage of Economics in Japan, when it quested for its own place as a contemporary of the world community, the activity of 'Economic Journalism' is worth mentioning. Grounded in the growth of industry and commerce in the early twentieth century, new Economics papers and journals such as the *Chugai Shimpo* (presently *Nippon Keizai Shimbun*) and *The Diamond* joined the rank of such journalism in which topics of business, finance and economic policies were discussed. In particular, when we consider the reception of Keynesian Economics in Japan, we cannot omit Tanzan Ishibashi (1884–1973) and *Toyo Keizai Shimpo*, on which he served as its fifth chief editor up to his entry in politics.

In the editorial of *Toyo Keizai Shimpo* on 27 March 1920 and following series-articles, Ishibashi introduced John Maynard Keynes' *The Economic Consequences of Peace* (1919) with utmost sympathy. Although Ishibashi welcomed the ideal of the League of Nations for the maintenance of peace, the 'selfish' demands of victors that would protect their vested interest not only in Europe but also in Asia was the target of Ishibashi's criticism. Before this introduction, Keynes' (1883–1946) name was not familiar, except perhaps in the expert circles of financial and monetary economists.[14]

Further, in 1932, Ishibashi advocated the policy of managed currency by citing Keynes' *Treatise on Money* (1930),[15] as well as the earlier *Monetary Reform* (1923). In the preceding years, Ishibashi and his fellow economist, Kamekichi Takahashi (1891–1974), had fought against the lifting of the gold embargo at the old par-rate, following Keynes' attitude in the case of Britain's return to the Gold Standard. Ishibashi tried to paraphrase the positive fiscal policy of the then Finance Minister, Takahashi Korekiyo, in Macroeconomic terms (see Smethurst's chapter later in this volume). When Keynes' *General Theory* appeared in 1936, Ishibashi promptly decided to publish its translation, which was realized in 1941 and was soon known in China (see the chapter on Keynes later in this volume).

Toyo Keizai Shimpo launched its English edition, *The Oriental Economist*, in 1934. It was highly appreciated by the international public as a precious medium to get information on the Economics of Japan. During the war years, Ishibashi made efforts to collect information on the post-war economic plans of the Allied Forces and organized study-groups privately. Thus, he could be optimistic for the future of post-war recovery of the Japanese economy, even after Japan's defeat in 1945.

Schumpeter's visit to Japan in 1931 and after

One of the most respected Western economists in the twentieth century among the Japanese was Joseph Alois Schumpeter (1883–1950). A general German orientation of Japanese academicians made him the best guide for them to step into contemporary economics. His first contact with the Japanese was the invitation of the Imperial University in Tokyo as its foreign lecturer in 1923, when he was in adversity after his involvement in the post-war Austrian politics. Though he cancelled his acceptance[16] due to the invitation from Bonn, he paid a visit to Japan in 1931 with lecture-tours in Tokyo and Kobe. When he was asked by a student at the lecture hall in Tokyo how to study Economics, his answer was 'Begin with Walras!' This advice to turn to 'general equilibrium analysis' was very influential, as Schumpeter was generally known as one of the best theoretical German economists (see the chapter by Metzler on Schumpeter later in this volume). The very student that asked the advice, Takuma Yasui (1909–1995), translated Schumpeter's first book (Schumpeter, 1908) that identified the essence of Economic Theory as the 'theory of general equilibrium'. Yasui became the leader of the advanced theoretical investigations into the Walrasian general equilibrium theory.

In Kyoto, Schumpeter met Yasuma Takata (1883–1972) and Kei Shibata (1902–1986), who were also interested in absorbing the general equilibrium analysis. Shibata, whose article on the relation between the Marxian reproduction scheme and general equilibrium theory was highly appreciated by Oskar Lange (1904–1965), later visited Schumpeter at Harvard in 1936. At that time, Shigeto Tsuru (1912–2006) was Schumpeter's assistant. Prior to his move to Harvard, Schumpeter hosted the research-stay of Ichiro Nakayama (1898–1980) and Seiichi Toubata (1899–1983) in Bonn. Both collaborated to publish the Japanese edition of Schumpeter's *Theory of Economic Development* (Schumpeter, 1926) in 1937. Schumpeter contributed a special preface to this Japanese edition. Together with Tsuru, the three who had close contact with Schumpeter became important figures in the policy-making, as well as academic researchers of post-1945 Japan.

Takashi Negishi (1933–) once called the series of theoretical economists in Kyoto after Takata, the 'Kyoto school of modern economic theory' (Negishi,

2004). Takata introduced the idea of general equilibrium in the theory of prices in his five volumes *Keizaigaku Shinko* (*New Lectures on Economics*) (Takata, 1929–1932). However, in the determination of wages and interest, he introduced the concept of power-relations to explain the equilibrium in causal terms. A mathematician at the Kyoto University, Shozo Sono (1886–1969), joined the group of economists to investigate the nature of economic equilibrium. Kei Shibata (1902–1986) introduced a mathematical analysis of Economic Equilibrium in his examination of capital and profit theory of Karl Marx (1818–1883) and Eugen von Böhm-Bawerk (1851–1915). His criticism against Marx's view of the fall in the rate of profit was confirmed later by Nobuo Okishio (1927–2003) and is now called the 'Shibata-Okishio theorem'. Shibata was followed further by Hideo Aoyama (1910–1992), who studied monopolistic competition and the theory of economic fluctuations. The last descendant of this school was Michio Morishima (1923–2004) who made efforts to rehabilitate Takata's 'sociological' interpretation of general equilibrium (power theory) in 1995 (Takata, 1995).

The Japanese Economic Association

Three years after Schumpeter's visit to Japan, a group of non-Marxian economists in Japan founded *Nihon Keizai Gakkai* (the 'Japanese Economic Association').[17] In contrast to the *Shakai Seisaku Gakkai*, this association focused on Theoretical Economics with a conscious orientation to the academic orthodoxy and exclusion of Marxism. In its early years, the main members of this academic society were oriented to Neoclassical Economics in the line of Leon Walras (1834–1910) and Alfred Marshall (1842–1924). Should this society develop on healthy lines, the pace of Japanese economists in catching up with the progress of contemporary Western Economics would be likely to be all the smoother.

Table 4.3 shows the titles of presentations of the annual Assembly of this association from 1934 to 1943. It is noteworthy that John R. Hicks (1904–1989) was already known to Japanese economists, whilst the name of Keynes did not appear in this list.

Investigations into the civil society in the war years

After the conflict with China developed into war in 1937, the pressure for conformism to the regime was too strong. Isolated from the international academic community, a considerable number of academic economists committed themselves consciously or unconsciously, to Japanese-style totalitarianism of the *Tenno State* and its spread to the whole of East Asia. Opposition to Anglo-Saxon dominance led to many Japanese scholars' quest for a genuine Japanese learning. Economics was no exception. Whilst some applied Gottle's philosophical ideas of life economics,[18] German ideas of *Geopolitik*, or *Gemeinshaft* in their concepts of Japanese economic regime, others directly relied on the ambiguous totalitarianism of the *Tenno State* and its extension to the whole of East Asia.

Table 4.3 Titles of presentations at annual meetings of the Japanese Economic Association

Year (place)	Titles of presentations
1. 1934 (Tokyo)	'Price theory and social power', 'Nature of the value of money', 'Significance of economic consideration', 'Form of price under duopoly', 'Ricardian value theory'
2. 1935 (Tokyo)	'Petty's value theory and Smith's compared', 'On capital interest', 'Relation of value theory and methodology', 'Agricultural protection and the theory of rent', 'Editions of A. Marshall's Principles', 'On economic value'
3. 1936 (Tokyo)	'Locality of economic life', 'Mind centered historical view', 'Solution of Cassel's equations', 'Rice price and economic fluctuation', 'Economy and power', 'On Sismondi'. 'Quesnay's value', 'Ground of Geldidealismus', 'Questions on the theory of general equilibrium'
4. 1937 (Tokyo)	'Money and economic fluctuation', 'Devaluation of money and fluctuation', 'Long term economic fluctuation', 'Controlled economy and reproduction process', 'Essence of money', 'Economic allocation and distribution problem', 'Competition and monopoly', 'Destination of the rent theory', 'Structure of economic ethics'
5. 1938 (Tokyo)	'Method of recognition of money', 'Mathematical formulation of economic theories', 'On power theory', 'Power theory', 'Value judgment in economics', 'On general rate of profit'
6. 1939 (Tokyo)	'Pareto's off-limit and indifference curve', 'Production and consumption', 'Parallel price and average production cost under free competition', 'Economy and religion', 'Examination of Wicksell's rate of normal interest', 'Reception of metalism and its criticism', 'Monetary theory of price policies', 'On Nazis' theory of finance'
7. 1940 (Tokyo)	'Unemployment problem', 'Demand of competitive goods', 'Economics and Statistics', 'Problems of economic philosophy', 'Greater East Asian Economic Zone and transportation policy of Japan', 'On Hicks' income effect and substitution effect'
8. 1941 (Kyoto)	'Agenda of economic calculation', 'Operation rate under planned economy', 'Essence of financial control', 'Measurement of economic power of nations', 'Pure economics and political economics', 'House economy and economy', 'Analysis of existence', 'Dynamic theory of firms', 'Pareto line of income', 'Controlled economy and control of demand and supply'
9. 1942 (Tokyo)	'Economy as power', 'Controlled economy and war economy', 'Competitive planning and forced planning', 'On the law of demand and supply', 'Hicks' theory of relational goods', 'Mathematical inquiry into monthly financial market of Tokyo'
10. 1943 (Nagoya)	'Steady state of the economy and the target of control', 'On the degree of control', 'Economy as responsibility', 'Theory of subjects and organization of national economy', 'Problems of modern national economy', 'System of state and system of industry', 'On controlled economy'

Source: see Nihon Keizai Gakkai (2010: 28–36).

Despite all these difficulties, it was in these dark years that a critical appreciation of Western literature of civil society began. Translation of classics of Western social sciences was a preferred job for scholars who were expelled from their academic chairs. Those who remained at universities published their critical studies of Adam Smith, Friedrich List, Max Weber and others, without mentioning their hidden references taken from Karl Marx. In the area of the history of economics, Zennya Takashima's (1904–1990) *Fundamental Problems of Economic Sociology* (Takashima, 1941) and Kazuo Okouchi's (1905–1984) *Smith and List* (see Okouchi, 1943) are worth mentioning. Hisao Otsuka's investigation into the Western Economic History started also in the war years. After 1945, these served for the investigation into economic aspects of modern civil society as a starting-point.

Rehabilitation after the war-defeat: from 1945 to the 1970s

Blanks left by war

In the period after 1941, when Japan had declared war against the US and Britain, Western books and journals became unavailable to ordinary Japanese scholars. However, a limited group of economists who had contact with the administrators involved in the Information-Services in ministries and military groups had some knowledge on the War-Economy of Western nations and the works of their fellow economists in the enemy-camp. They might have known of such ideas of 'national accounting', as well as 'input-output analysis'. However, they could not apply this knowledge to the economy in Japan. The War-Economy of Japan was characterized by the defective mobilization-plans of materials, personnel and funds, an approach which was influenced mainly from economic planning in Soviet Russia and Nazi Germany.

When Japan's prospective defeat had appeared on the road-map of the war, the US had organized an expert-team for its occupation and reconstruction. Thus, from its opening, the GHQ (General Headquarters of the Allied forces) in Tokyo had a group of able economists as its staff and a library for them, where the latest Economics journals were furnished. Many Japanese economists who wished to fill the gap between their knowledge and the international standards visited the library of GHQ and requested for the information that its economic experts could supply them.

At this stage, immediately after Japan's surrender, Tsuru was one of the rare Japanese who was familiar with the theory and practice of American policymakers in Economic Affairs particularly. Acquiring trust both from Japanese as well as American sides, he became the key person who was to intermediate between the GHQ and the Japanese government. As the chief of the Committee of the Board of Economic Stability, he wrote the first White Book on the Japanese economy in 1947. It was based on 'standard national accounting' to explain the current problems of the economy in simple words. After his leave from public service, he became the director of the Economic Research Institute of

Hitotsubashi University in 1965, and later assumed the Presidency of this University from 1972 to 1975. He translated the best-seller textbook of his former friend at Harvard, Nobel Laureate Paul Samuelson's (1915–2008) *Economics* (6th edition) in 1966, [1948] which became one of the most popular introductions for junior students in modern Economics for two decades after its publication and a later edition eventually became popular with young economists in China (see the chapter by Fang later in this volume).

Marxian Economics after 1945

Modern Economics, as it was known, had its rival in Marxian Economics. Since many of non-Marxian economists were discredited by their commitment to the war-regime, Marxian economists, who had been suppressed in the war years, returned to the centre of academic economics with the reflected glory of 'resistance'. In most universities, courses of Marxian Economics were held in parallel with those of non-Marxian modern Economics. Further, as in the case of land reform as well as the measures for concentrated production for recovery of the Japanese industry, the view of Marxian economists considerably influenced policies in the years immediately after 1945 (see Yagi, 2007).

In addition to the return of the elder generation, the younger generation of Marxian economists emerged. They were heavily influenced by the literature of Marx-Leninism, as formulated by Joseph Stalin (1878–1953) (which was also the case in China in the period after 1949). Most of them later had to regret their over-commitment to politics beyond scientific research – after Stalin's criticism in 1956. One of the results of such reflection was the foundation of the 'non-political' academic society, the 'Japan Society of Political Economy', in 1959.

Marxian Economics in Japan was not monolithic, however. A series of hot disputes emerged, such as on the nature of land-reform, the US dependency of Japanese capitalism vs its growth into independent imperialism, the nature of state monopoly capitalism in Japan and conditions of structural reform, and so on. Further, in the mid-1950s, a new theoretical school around Kozo Uno (1897–1977) emerged out of the camp of the *Rono-School*. Uno separated pure theory of capitalism, its stage theory and the contemporary analysis (see Itoh, 1980). However, noteworthy communications with Western Economics had been rare in Marxian Economics before the late 1960s when a 'Marx revival' occurred in Western nations.[19]

Progress with international academic community

It took several years after 1945 for Japanese economists to re-join the international community of modern Economics. The reconstruction of their academic associations began first in 1950, when the first Japanese meeting of the 'Econometrics Society' was held in Tokyo.

After 1951, Japanese economists began to contribute to international academic journals. Thanks to the GALIOA fund and later to the Fulbright Scholar

Program, a group of young scholars studied in the US and absorbed modern mathematical approaches and macroeconomic modelling. Some of them stayed in the US or in other Western countries, maintaining their contact with the Japanese academic world. By the late 1950s, Japan already had a series of internationally renowned economists such as Michio Hatanaka, Ken-ichi Inada, Takashi Negishi, Hukukane Nikaido, Miyohei Shinohara, Michio Morishima, Hirofumi Uzawa, and others.[20]

On the other hand, economic experts of the Japanese government, particularly those of the Economic Planning Agency, applied modern macroeconomics in their Economics. It is well known that the 'Income Doubling Plan' (1960) of Hayato Ikeda's cabinet was grounded on Roy Harrod's (1900–1978) growth equations. During this period, several groups of economists embarked on building econometric models as well as the input-output tables of the Japanese economy. Following the Economic Planning Agency, other ministries and large businesses wished to train their young staff in econometrics by sending them to American universities. Aspiring students in economics would find their way to enter graduate courses of American universities to acquire a PhD degree in economics.

In the early 1960s, advanced modern economics was becoming appreciated mainly for its practical value in policy-making. The so-called 'NeoClassical synthesis' advocated in the Preface of Samuelson's *Economics* ([1948] 1966) prevailed among non-Marxian economists and covered the flaws in the field – vis-à-vis the links between Macroeconomics and Microeconomics. With the belief that the government could control the economy by using financial and fiscal policies based on econometric models, the attraction of modern economics went on to surpass that of Marxian Economics.

Reconstruction of academic associations

Reconstruction of academic associations of non-Marxian Economics first began as the reorganization of the *Nihon Keizai Gakkai* ('Japanese Economic Association') to *Riron Keizai Gakkai* ('Theoretical Economics Association') in 1949, which issued the journal, *Kikan Riron Keizaigaku* ('Theoretical Economics Quarterly') in the next year. Besides, the foundation of the Japan branch of 'Econometrics Society' in 1950 developed into the 'Japanese Econometrics Association'. It organized the first Far Eastern Meeting of the 'Econometrics Society' in 1966 in Tokyo. As the two academic societies had considerable overlapping of members, after several years of close collaborations, they made a fusion in 1968 as *Riron-Keiryo Keizai Gakkai* ('Japan Association of Economics and Econometrics'). It was after 30 years that this association revived the old name of the 'Japanese Economic Association' that had discontinued its activity in the last years under the war. As this process of reconstruction suggests, international relations via the route of the 'Econometrics Society' played a significant role in the reconstruction of theoretical studies in non-Marxian Economics.

Criticism against the priority of economic growth

In 1956, the White Book on Economic Planning Agency declared the end of the post-war situation of the Japanese economy, even though economic growth remained as the main aim of Economic Policy in Japan. However, the rapid economic growth accompanied by drastic urbanization caused severe problems of environmental pollution. A conversion in economic thought in Japan occurred around 1970 by a questioning the value of economic growth. Tsuru was one of the opinion-leaders in this turn. Setting the priority as the standard of living of the people before economic growth, he organized an 'International symposium on environmental problems' in 1970 in Tokyo and published its result (Tsuru, 1970). His criticism of mainstream Economics that neglected the negative output of production process is comparable with Joan Robinson's (1903–1983) criticism at the plenary session of the American Economic Society in 1971.

Although the resurrected interest in Marxism since the late 1960s was mainly oriented to the criticism of civilization from a socio-philosophic viewpoint, it gave a chance to reconsider the basic presuppositions of established Marxian Economics, as well as that of mainstream Economics. Most productive collaborations of Marxian economists and non-Marxian heterodox streams in national, as well as international levels, begins in the 1970s.

The revival of classical value theory by Cambridge economist, Piero Sraffa (1898–1983) whose work had become influential (see Sraffa, 1960)[21] gave birth to a group of economists in Japan who were consciously oriented to an alternative economic theory to mainstream Neoclassical Economics. Together with Nobuo Okishio's mathematical Marxian Economics (Okishio, 1993), and Michio Morishima's Marx (Morishima, 1973) widened the perspective of Marxian economists, as well as mathematical economists.

Despite all these heterodox movements, in accordance with the return to the normalcy of the intellectual radicalism of the youth, the hegemony of the criticism to Keynesianism moved from the hands of Heterodox Economists – to those of Monetarists and followers of Nobel Laureate Robert E. Lucas Jnr (1937–). As time passed by, the weight of economists with an American PhD grew in academic positions as well as in economic journalism. In the end of the 1970s, the members of the *Riron Keiryou Keizaigakkai* ('Association of Economics and Econometrics') surpassed those of *Keizai Riron Gakkai* ('Society of Political Economy').[22]

Age of globalization: from the 1980s to the present

By the end of the 1980s, the synchronization of Japanese Economics with that of the international community seems to have been completed. In 1982, Takamitsu Sawa published a paperback with the title of *Keizai gaku to wa nandarou (What is Economics?)* in which he described the 'uniform' institutionalization of Economics in American universities in a rather satirical style. These scholars, who returned to Japan after acquiring an American PhD, made efforts to introduce in their universities the curriculum for graduate students according to the model they had known at American universities. In 1990, the 'Association of Economics and Econometrics' (renamed as the 'Japanese Economic Society' in 1997) decided to transform its journal *Kikan Riron Keizaigaku* (*Theoretical Economics Quarterly*) to a full English-language journal. It was renamed after five years as *The Japanese Economic Review* (from 1995). Today, most of the graduate courses in economics of Japanese universities follow their American antecedents.

However, this does not imply that Japanese economists as a whole became *a unified set*, as it is indeed not even the case for the international community of economists as a whole. After the belief in the 'Neoclassical synthesis' was lost in the 1970s, economists around the world, as well as in Japan, became divided between main streams and various heterodoxies. The share of heterodoxies is probably larger in Japan, where the heritage of Marxian economics is still alive. The 'Japan Society of Political Economy' comprised 880 members in 2014 and published *Kikan Keizai Riron* (the Political Economy Quarterly). In 2015, it launched the 'International Book Prize' for achievement in critical research in political economy. The first award was given to Samuel Bowles for his *Microeconomics: Behavior, Institutions, and Evolution* (2004) and *The New Economics of Inequality and Redistribution* (2012). The forum of Heterodox Economics in Japan is the 'Japan Association for Evolutionary Economics'. This association was founded in 1997 and has published a full English-language journal, *Evolutionary and Institutional Economics Review*, since 2003.

The introduction of the information and incentive paradigm, as well as the concept of 'bounded rationality', in the 1970s paved the way for the growth of institutional analysis. Along with the direction of comparative institutional analysis, which was established by Masahiko Aoki (1938–2015), a group of pro-Marxian economists were advocating their institutional analysis of Japanese and Asian capitalism in collaboration with the school of 'Regulationists' in France.[23]

The development and diffusion of 'Game Theory' as well as 'Computer Simulation' opened new areas for research. In recent years, 'Experimental Economics' also joined the new frontier.

Conclusions

We may thus conclude that Japan has had a rich tradition in the research of the history of Economic Theory and Economic Thought. Probably, this was a by-product of the reception of Western Economics in Japan. However, a critical study of the past and present classics in Economics in its background, formation-process and theoretical structure is, we may conclude, a source for the productive reappraisal of contemporary Economics. In every period of the diffusion of Western Economics in Japan, its adoption implied interpretation, examination, criticism, reconstruction and innovation. All of these are worth careful investigation.

Notes

1 Sugiyama and Mizuta (1988) is the pioneer work in this topic on the aspects of institutionalization of economics in higher education in the first and second periods in
particular.

2 See Vissering (1860–1865). His position in economics was a liberal close to the
French economist, J. B. Say (1767–1832). During the same period when Nishi and
Tsuda studied in Leiden, he published Vissering (1860–1865).

3 The textbook, *Political Economy, For Use in Schools, and for Private Instruction*,
Edinburgh: William and Robert Chambers, 1852, was published without the author's
name. See Craig (2009).

4 See Sugiyama (1994) and Yagi (2015) for further details.

5 *Rishi Keizairon* (List on Economics), 1889. Oshima translated it from its English
edition (1885).

6 After the foundation of the second Imperial University in Kyoto (1898), the number
of Imperial universities increased up to nine before 1945, in which two were located
outside of Japan itself.

7 Since the inception of the Training School of Commerce in 1975 by the initiative of
Arinori Mori (1847–1889), commercial education in Japan experienced difficult times
for its development in the Meiji years (1868–1911). However, in the early years of the
twentieth century, economists of commerce colleges acquired a competitive reputation against those in Imperial universities. In 1906, economists of three commerce
colleges of Tokyo, Osaka and Kobe collaborated to launch the first academic economics journal, *Kokumin Keizai Zasshi* (Journal of National Economy). The three
colleges acquired the rank of university in the 1920s, after the new University Decree
of 1919. Grounded in the economic expansion during and after the First World War,
the Japanese government turned to promote higher professional education and established numerous professional high schools and colleges in industry, agriculture and
commerce. Many staffs of these colleges, including economists, were sent abroad for
further studies. The 1920s were peak years for Japanese scholars in their direct communications before the closing of the door in the 1930s (see also the chapter by
Ohtsuki on business education in Japan later in this volume).

8 Before the new University Decree in 1919, commercial colleges as well as private
institutions were not ranked as universities. The year 1919 is memorable also for the
separation of the faculty of economics from that of law at the Imperial University of
Tokyo and Kyoto.

9 Karl Rathgen (1855–1921) came to Japan before Eggert and continued his teaching of
German state science and advisory activities for the government from 1882 to 1890.

10 See Inoue and Yagi (1998) on the relations and divisions of the two, who were generally known as the origins of modern economics and Marxian economics in Japan
respectively.

11 See Yagi (2007).

12 At the end of 1926, the Communist Party of Japan was reorganized under the theoretical leadership of Kazuo Fukumoto, who returned from his research in Germany.
Fukumoto revealed the revolutionary implications of Marx's system of the criticism
of political economy and advocated the Leninist principle of a vanguard party based
on theoretical class consciousness. However, Fukumoto was soon criticized by the
Communist International on the charge of a sectarian deviation. Since then, Moscow
became the final authority in the communist and pro-communist movement in Japan.

13 Cf. Itoh (1980), Hoston (1986) and Yagi (2016).

14 Kakujiro Yamazaki (1868–1945) discussed Keynes's *Indian Currency and Finance*
(1913) immediately after its publication. Cf. Ikeo (2014: 196f).

15 This was translated to Japanese by Nisaburo Kitoh (1900–1947) as *Kaheiron* (On
Money) in 1932.

16 After Schumpeter's cancellation, Emil Lederer came to Tokyo and taught economics there from 1923 to 1925. Alfred Amonn succeeded the job in 1926–1929. They were one of the sources of the current situation of European economics, that of Central Europe, including Austria in particular.

17 This society was not active in the communication with non-academicians. When it began to publish its *Nenpo* (Annual Bulletin) in 1941, Japan was about to declare war against the US and Britain.

18 Friedrich von Gottle-Ottlilienfeld (1868–1958) was regarded as a leading economic philosopher in the period of Nazi Germany.

19 See Yagi (2016).

20 Cf. Ikeo (2000, chap. 1).

21 The Japanese version of Sraffa (1960) was published by Izumi Hishiyama in 1962.

22 In chap. 2 of Ikeo (2000), the author offered the age structure of members of the two academic societies in a graph (Fig. 2–2, p. 71).

23 See Boyer and Yamada (2000), Aoki (2001).

References

* In Japanese

Amano, T. (1889). *Keizai Genron* (Principles of Economics). Tokyo: Tokyo Senmon Gakko.

Aoki, M. (2001). *Toward a Comparative Institutional Analysis*. Cambridge, MA: MIT Press.

Bowles, S. (2004). *Microeconomics: Behavior, Institutions, and Evolution*. Princeton, NJ: Princeton University Press.

Bowles, S. (2012). *The New Economics of Inequality and Redistribution*. Cambridge, MA: Cambridge University Press.

Boyer, R. and Yamada, T. (eds) (2000). *Japanese Capitalism in Crisis: A Regulationist Interpretation*. London and New York, NY: Routledge.

Burton, J. H. (anonym.) (1852). *Political Economy for Use in Schools, and for Private Instruction*. Edinburgh: William and Robert Chambers.

Byles, J. B. (1849). *Sophisms of Free-trade and Popular Political Economy Examined*. London: Seeleys. → *Jiyu Koeki Ana-Sagashi*. Tr. by G. Wakayama from the 1872 ed. Tokyo: G. Wakayama, 1877.

Carey, H. C. (1858). *Principles of Social Science*. Philadelphia: Lippincott. → *Kei-shi Keizaigaku*. Tr. by T. Inukai. Tokyo: Hakubundo, 1884.

Craig, A. M. (2009). *Civilization and Enlightenment: The Early Thought of Fukuzawa Yukichi*. Cambridge, MA: Harvard University Press.

Ellis, W. (1846). *Outlines of Social Economy*. London: Smith Elder.

Fawcett, H. (1863). *Manual of Political Economy*. London: Macmillan. → *Fukoku Saku*. Chinese translation by F. Wan, republished by G. Kishida with Japanese reading order. Tokyo: Rakuzendo, 1881.

Fawcett, M. G. (1876). *Political Economy for Beginners*, 4th edn London: Macmillan. → *Hou-shi Keizaigaku*, 5 vols. Tr. by K. Nagata. Tokyo: Nagata-shi, 1877.

Fukuda, T. (1900). *Die gesellschaftliche und wirtschaftliche Entwicklung in Japan*. Stuttgart: Cotta.

Fukuzawa, Y. (1865). *Tojin Orai (Transaction with Foreigners)*, (private circulation).

Hilferding, R. (1910). *Das Finanzkapital*, in *Marx Studien*, Bd.3, Wien: Wiener Volksbuchhandlung. → *Kinyu Shihonron*. Tr. by K. Hayashi. Kyoto: Kobundo, 1926–1927, Tokyo: Kaizo-sha, 1929.

Hoston, G. A. (1986). *Marxism and the Crisis of Development in Prewar Japan.* Princeton, NJ: Princeton University Press.

Inoue, T. and Yagi, K. (1998). 'Two Inquirers on the Divide: Tokuzo Fukuda and Hajime Kawakami', in Tanaka, T. and Sugihara, S. (eds), *Economic Thought and Modernization in Japan.* Aldershot: Edward Elgar.

Itoh, M. (1980). *Value and Crisis: Essays on Marxian Economics in Japan.* London: Pluto Press.

Ikeo, A. (ed.) (2000). *Japanese Economics and Economists since 1945.* London and New York, NY: Routledge.

Ikeo, A. (2014). *A History of Economic Science in Japan: The Internationalization of Economics in the Twentieth Century.* London and New York, NY: Routledge.

Ishibashi, T. (1920). **'Editorial', Toyo Keizai Shimpo* [newspaper], 27 March 1920, and subsequent issues.

Jouffroy, H. (1844). *Catéchisme d'économie politique.* Leipzig and Paris: Brockhaus and Avenariys. → **Keizai Yosetsu,* 2 vols. Tr. by S. Furusawa from the English translation by A. von Sieboldt. Tokyo: Okurasho, 1877–1878.

Kanda, T. (1861). **Nosho-ben* (Arguments on Agriculture and Commerce). Private.

Kanda, T. (1867). **Keizai Shogaku* (Small Book of Economics). Edo: Kinokuniya Genbee.

Keynes, J. M. (1913). *Indian Currency and Finance.* London: Macmillan.

Keynes, J. M. (1923). *A Tract on Monetary Reform.* London: Macmillan.

Keynes, J. M. (1930). *A Treatise on Money.* → **Kaheiron.* Tr. by N. Kito. Tokyo: Tokyo: Dojinsha, 1932.

Keynes, J. M. (1936). *The General Theory of Employment, Interest and Money.* London: Macmillan. → **Koyo, Rishi oyobi Kahei no Ippan Riron.* Tr. by T. Shionoya. Tokyo: Toyo Keizai Shimpo-sha, 1941.

Lenin, V. I. (1917). *Imperialism* (Russian). First published in mid-1917 in pamphlet form, Petrograd (St Petersburg). Source: *Lenin's Selected Works* (1963), Moscow: Progress Publishers, Vol. 1, p. 667. → **Teikoku Shugi-ron.* Tr. by S. Aono. Tokyo: Kibokaku, 1926.

List, Friedrich (1885). *The National System of Political Economy.* Tr. from German by S. S. Lloyd. London: Longmans. → **Rishi Keizairon.* Tr. from English by S. Oshima. Tokyo: Nihon Keizaikai, 1889.

Luxemburg, R. (1913). *Die Akkumulation des Kapitals.* Berlin: Vorwärts. → **Shihon Chikuseki-ron.* Tr. by T. Masuda and Y. Takayama. Tokyo: Dojinsha, 1927.

Macleod, H. D. (1972). *Principles of Economical Philosophy.* London: Longmans. → **Ma-shi Keizai Tetsugaku.* Tr. by U. Taguchi. Tokyo: Genroin, 1887.

Marshall, A. (1890). *Principles of Economics.* London: Macmillan. → **Keizaigaku Genri.* Tr. by K. Otsuka. Tokyo: Kaizo-sha, 1925–1926.

Marx, K. (1867–1894). *Das Kapital,* 3 vols. Hamburg: Otto Meisner. → **Shihon-ron.* Tr. by M. Takabatake. Tokyo: Daito-kaku and Jiritsu-sha, 1920–1924.

Marx, K. and Engels, F. (1928–1935). → **Marx = Engels Zenshu* (Collected Works of Marx and Engels). Tokyo: Kaizo-sha.

Mill, J. S. (1848). *Principles of Political Economy.* London: J. W. Parker. → **Miru Keizairon.* Tr. by K. Hayashi and S. Suzuki. Tokyo: Eirando, 1875–1885.

Morishima, M. (1973). *Marx's Economics: A Dual Theory of Value and Growth.* Cambridge: Cambridge University Press.

Morris-Suzuki, T. (1989). *A History of Japanese Economic Thought.* London and New York, NY: Routledge [and Nissan Institute for Japanese Studies, University of Oxford].

Negishi, T. (2004). 'Kyoto School of Modern Economic Theory', *Kyoto Economic Review* 73, 1–10.

Nihon Keizai Gakkai (ed.) (2010). *Nihon Keizai Gakkai 75 Nen-Shi* (75 Years of Japanese Economic Association). Tokyo: Yuhikaku.

Nihon Shihonshugi Hattatsushi Koza (Series of the Analysis of Japanese Capitalism) (1932–1933). Edited by E. Noro. Tokyo: Iwanami.

Okishio, N. (1993). *Essays on Political Economy: Collected Papers.* Frankfurt a. M: Peter Lang.

Okouchi, K. (1943). *Smith and List.* Tokyo: Nihon Hyoronsha.

Perry, A. L. (1867). *Elements of Political Economy*, 2nd edn. New York: Scribner → *Kanban Keizai Genron.* Abridged translation by M. Ogata. Tokyo: Daigakunanko: 1869 (A full translation by K. Kiyokazu appeared as *Peri-shi Zoho Kaisei Rizai Genron.* Tokyo: Suhara Ryohei, 1880).

Rogers, J. E. T. (1869). *A Manual of Political Economy for School and Colleges*, 2nd ed. Oxford: Clarendon Press. → *Taisei Keizai Shinron.* Tr. by T. Takahashi. Tokyo: Monbusho, 1874.

Samuelson, P. (1948). *Economics: An Introductory Analysis.* New York, NY: McGraw Hill. → *Keizaigaku.* Tr. from 6th edn by S. Tsuru. Tokyo: Iwanami, 1966.

Sawa, T. (1982). *Keizaigaku to wa nandarou ka* (What is Economics?). Tokyo: Iwanami.

Schumpeter, J. (1908). *Das Wesen und Hauptinhalt der theoretischen Nationalöknomie.* München u. Leipzig: Duncker u. Humblot. → *Riron Keizaigaku no Honshitsu to Shuyo Naiyo.* Tr. by T. Kimura and T. Yasui. Tokyo: Nihon Hyoron-sha, 1936.

Schumpeter, J. (1926). *Theorie der wirtschaftlichen Entwicklung*, 2. Aufl. München u. Leipzig: Duncker und Humblot. → *Keizai Hatten no Riron.* Tr. by I. Nakayama and S. Tohata. Tokyo: Iwanami, 1937.

Smith, A. (1948–1949). *The Theory of Moral Sentiments.* Tr. by T. Yonebayashi, 2 vols. Tokyo: Mirai-sha.

Smith, A. [1776]. *An Inquiry into the Nature and Causes of the Wealth of Nations.* 2 vols. London: W. Strahan and T. Cadell. → *Fukokuron.* Tr. by S. Saga. Tokyo: Keizaigaku Koshukai, 1882–1888.

Sraffa, P. (1960). *Production of Commodities by Means of Commodity* → *Shouhin niyoru Shohin no Seisan.* Tr. by H. Yamashita and I. Hishiyama. Tokyo: Yuhikaku, 1962.

Sugiyama, C. (1994). *The Origins of Economic Thought in Modern Japan.* London: Routledge.

Sugiyama, C. and Mizuta, H. (eds) (1988). *Enlightenment and Beyond: Political Economy Comes to Japan.* Tokyo: University of Tokyo Press.

Takashima, Z. (1941). *Keizai Shakaigaku no Kihonmondai* (Fundamental Problems of Economic Sociology). Tokyo: Nihon Hyoronsha.

Takata, Y. (1929–1932). *Keizaigaku Shinko* (New Lectures of Economics), 5 vols. Tokyo: Iwanami.

Takata, Yasuma (1995). *Power Theory of Economics*, edited and introduced by M. Morishima. London: Palgrave Macmillan.

Tsuru, S. (ed.) (1970). *Environmental Disruption: Proceedings of International Symposium, March 1970, Tokyo*, International Social Science Council.

Vissering, S. (1860–1865). *Handboek van Praktische Staathuishouldkunde*, 2 vols. Amsterdam: Van Kampen.

Walker, A. (1872). *The Science of Wealth: A Manual of Political Economy*, 5th edn Philadelphia: Lippincott. → *Fukoku Ron.* Abr. and tr. by H. Nagamine. Tokyo: Keishokaku, 1874.

Wayland, F. (1837). *The Elements of Political Economy*. Boston: Gould and Lincoln.→*Yowatari no Tsue, Ichimei Keizai Benmou*, 2+2 vols. Tr. by N. Ka. Tokyo: Eikasai, 1872–1887.

Whately, R. (1849). *Easy Lessons on Money Matters: For the Use of Young People*. London: J. W. Parker.→*Keizai Nyumon, Ichimei Seisan Michi-Annai*. Abr. and tr. by T. Obata. Tokyo: Tokujiro Obata, 1877.

Yagi, K. (2007). 'Emergence of Marxian Scholarship in Japan: Kawakami Hajime and His Two Critics', *Rekishi to Keizai* (The Journal of Political Economy and Economic Theory) 194, 34–45.

Yagi, K. (2015). 'The Reception of Western Economics by Fukuzawa Yukichi in the Context of the 19th Century Globalization', in Zachmann, U. M. and Uhl, C. (eds) *JAPAN und das Problem der Moderne*. München: Iudicium, pp. 254–270.

Yagi, K. (2016). 'Marxian Economics in Japan after 1945', in Yagi, K., Yokokawa, N., Uemura, H. and Westra, R. (eds), *Japanese Contribution to the Rejuvenation of Political Economy*. London and New York, NY: Routledge, pp. 11–29.

Journals

Evolutionary and Institutional Economics Review (2004–). Organ journal of the Japan Association for Evolutionary Economics.

*Kikan Keizai Riron (2014–). Organ journal of the Japan Society of Political Economy.

*Kikan Riron Keizaigaku (1949–1994). Organ journal of Riron:Keiryo Keizai Gakkai. From 1995 renamed *Japanese Economic Review*.

*Kokka Gakkai Zassi (Journal of State Sciences) (1887–). Founded by Kokka Gakkai in the Faculty of Law, Tokyo Imperial University.

*Kokumin Keizai Zassi (Journal of National Economy). Published by the Higher Commercial College of Kobe, later Economics Faculty of Kobe University.

Kyoto University Economic Review (1926–2003). Published by Faculty of Economics, Kyoto University. Renamed in 2004 *Kyoto Economic Review*.

Nihon Keizai Gakkai Nempo (1941–1944).

Oriental Economist (1936–1985). English economic and business journal published by Toyo Keizai Shimpo-sha.

Shakai Mondai Kenkyu (1919–1930). Published from Kyoto: Kobundo under Hajime Kawakami as the sole responsible editor.

*Tokai Keizai Shimpo (1880–1923).

*Tokyo Keizai Zassi (1879–1923).

*Toyo Keizai Shimpo (1895–present).

5   The diffusion of Western Economics in South Korea

Hoon Hong

Introduction

South Korea not only industrialized but also democratized during the last half a century or so. During the same period, it had been absorbing economic ideas from the Western world – as it had done earlier. This coincidence motivates us to suspect that there may have been significant interactions between its socio-economic development and its adoption of Western economic ideas.

New economic ideas, as have been the case with other socio-cultural things (bicycles) and thoughts (Christianity), go through a few stages until they are incorporated into everyday language: *introduction, rejection or acceptance, transformation, diffusion, final settlement and so on.* Given this background, the chapter examines how Western Economics has been reshaped and transformed in South Korea. This task starts with introducing a brief history of importing Western Economic Ideas (Lee, 1985; Cho, 2005).

A short history of imported economic thought in Korea

Western ideas started to land on the Korean peninsula from the end of the nine-teenth century onwards (see Chang, 2004). Initially most of them had been imported indirectly via Japan – during the colonial period. The same holds true of the initial spread of Economic ideas. At that time, Japanese scholars were more advanced in absorbing Western thought, primarily by means of translating Western socio-economic concepts and classics into Japanese (Morris-Suzuki, 1989) (see chapters by Das, as well as that of Yagi respectively in this volume). For this purpose, they relied heavily on Chinese classics and characters.[1] Western Economic ideas in particular were imparted by Japanese scholars resid-ing in Korea and Korean scholars who had studied in Japan.[2] Moreover, eco-nomic classics such as by Adam Smith (1723–1790), Karl Marx (1818–1883) and John Maynard Keynes (1883–1946) were read in Japanese editions.[3]

During this period, Western Economics, as interpreted by Japanese scholars and imported via Japan, was imbued with Historical and the Marxian perspec-tives. Thus, we can say that it was *holistic and interdisciplinary* in its approach. *It was not introduced as Economics in its narrow sense but as Political Economy or Social Economics embedded in philosophy and ethics.* Moreover, Korean intellectuals seemed to be sympathetic to this viewpoint. Given this, Political Economy was concerned not merely with commodity or goods, money, capital or market, but also with values of civil society and ultimate goals of human beings. For this reason, it placed equal weight on economic theory, economic history and history of economic thought. A real economist was required to be equipped with *balanced* knowledge about theory, history and thought.

Neither a specialization within Economics nor a division of labour among social sciences was appreciated. Every economist was supposed to be a social scientist, at least, to some extent. It is not analytical power or rigour – but broad and comprehensive knowledge that was taken as a primary virtue for scholars, including economists. Political Economy viewed in this way remained connected with laymen's common sense or intuition and its concepts shared many common aspects with their counterparts in everyday use. At that time, emphasis on common sense *à la Malthus* gained supremacy over Ricardian rigour (Malthus, 1827: 4–5).

All this underwent gradual changes after 1945, as Western Economic ideas began to be imported directly from the countries in the West (Hong, 2005). As a result, in 1993, foreign-trained economists already accounted for over half of all the Korean economists and for seven out of ten of all those teaching in Seoul (Choi, 1996: 97). Economists who were trained in foreign countries, especially in the US, began to concentrate on specific areas. Moreover they prioritized analytical power and rigour with the aid of mathematical and econometric tools, gaining ground in competition with the *holistic* viewpoint. *As a result, the hardcore of economics was reconceived as economic theory which was reformulated and redefined independently of economic history and history of economic thought. Economics, in this narrow sense, stood aloof from common sense and its definitions became alienated from their counterparts in everyday use. Now, analytical power became dominant over common sense.*

This account is not meant to suggest that Neoclassical Economics swept the academic circles – as soon as it arrived in South Korea. It was not until the end of the twentieth century that such a school of Economics prevailed over the other streams of thought. Up to this time, the holistic perspective of Political Economy had vied with the analytical perspective of the Neoclassical school. In particular, *Marxism* has survived underground among progressive intellectuals and antigovernment activists, although it was oppressed in the public after the Korean War (1950–1953). Moreover, it has been taught, albeit in its adulterated version, as part of the history of Economic Thought at most universities. Furthermore, after the restoration of democracy in 1987, it even enjoyed the short period of time to flourish in full bloom as an alleged alternative to Neoclassical economics (Lee, 1993; Hong, 2000, 2002; Jeong, 2007).

Amidst this rivalry, classics as well as textbooks, such as Samuelson's *Economics* ([1948] 1973) were to be held in high esteem. Among these classical economists were counted Smith, Ricardo, [J. S.] Mill, Marx and Keynes. As a result, they were translated into Korean, often with reference to their Japanese editions. Some of the first editions would be *The Wealth of Nations* (Choi and Cheung, 1960), *Principles of Political Economy and Taxation* (Choi, 1959), *On Liberty* (Sung, 1946), *Das Kapital* (Jeon and Choi, 1947), *Income* (Choi, 1954), *The General Theory* (Kim, 1955) and so on (see the References to this chapter).

Mercantilism (Mun, Petty), the German Historical School (List, Roscher, Schmoller) and the Austrian School (Menger, Böhm-Bawerk, Wieser) had been neither discussed nor considered very extensively, even though they have been mentioned from time to time in classes in the history of thought. Among others, lack of interest in the Historical School is noteworthy, even odd, since the 'Developmental State' of Korea which had pursued export-drive growth during the 1960s and 1970s was to bear a close resemblance to the position of the Historical School. One is tempted to suspect that there may be some scholars or bureaucrats who had read into the classics of the German Historical School, at least into the works of Friedrich List (1789–1846), in order to obtain insights about economic development (see chapter on List and China later in this volume). However, it comes as a surprise to find that few papers published in Korea at that time dealt with the Historical School (KEA, 1991: 26–27).

Other Western economists (such as Marshall, Veblen, Schumpeter, Hayek and Galbraith) were available as sources of economic thinking, even if some of them had *not* been translated into Korean. Nobel Laureate, Milton Friedman (1912–2006) was much less renowned as a preacher of market ideology than as a theorist. Unlike Friedrich Hayek's (1899–1992) *The Road to Serfdom* (1944), his *Capitalism and Freedom* ([1962] 1982) was not to be seen as a familiar item on the book-shelf of a serious Korean economist until recent decades.

Consequently, for more than half a century the two streams of economic thought have existed in conflict and often intermingled in the Korean intellectual circles. Moreover, although Korean economists recently educated in the US seem to be, in appearance, more attached to Economics in its 'narrow' sense, they seem to constantly fall into a conflict between the different perspectives of thought 'deep down' in their minds. The two streams do not correspond, on a one-to-one basis, to Market Ideology and Socialism. Rather their difference meshes more with the distinction between Dialectics and Holism, on the one hand, and Formal Logic and Individualism, on the other (Peng and Nisbett, 1999; Nisbett *et al.*, 2001). Needless to say, this conflict goes deeper than the typical 'micro-macro' divergence of economics.

Duality in the Korean academic community

In recent decades, most Western Economic ideas have been introduced into Korea through universities and colleges – by a large number of foreign-trained professors and from foreign sources. Once introduced, such ideas have, explicitly or implicitly, been interpreted in light of *domestic knowledge* available to lay-persons. Moreover, they have interacted with contemporary common sense and prevalent worldviews held by the public. *In general, Western ideas tend to be conceptual, abstract, explicit and global, whereas domestically held knowledge and common sense are likely to be practical, concrete, tacit and local* (Bellussi, 1999: 734; Gertler, 2003; Kleinknecht *et al.*, 2014: 1208–1209). For this reason, there have been discrepancies and conflicts between the two domains of knowledge. Moreover, the academic community has suffered from divergences between imported concepts/methods and real domestic issues.

The discrepancies and conflicts apparently have divided the Korean academic community into at least *two* groups. One group has laid more emphasis on imported concepts, methods and techniques, whereas the other has highlighted domestic empirical questions and issues. The former is more likely to have studied in the US, to hold jobs at major universities and to publish their papers in SSCI journals than the latter. The former has the merit of being more advanced in Economic theories and Econometric tools but at the same time the demerit of being less sensitive to specificities and peculiarities of the Korean socio-economic system. The opposite is true of the latter group. For instance, standard issues such as entry barriers have been handled by foreign-trained professors (Lee and Wang, 2007), whereas issues specific to the Korean economy such as *Chaebol* giant firms have been handled by domestically educated scholars (Kim, 2005).

In recent decades, however, the balance between the two groups has been decidedly shifting in favour of the foreign-trained scholars. The contributing factors can be enumerated as: a rapid increase in the number of foreign PhD holders; their contributions to SSCI journals: their landing jobs at some prestigious US universities and at major Korean universities; dominance of market ideology since the 1990s. For this reason, most Korean universities have been more dependent on US graduate programmes for the supply of professors and researchers. In parallel, education at Korean graduate schools has been on the decline. The Korean scientific community, as far as the field of Economics is concerned, has experienced difficulties in reproducing itself.

In line with the duality in scientific community and labour market for economists, some economic doctrines may lead a 'dual life' in that they are taught and learnt in the classroom but at the same time they are ill-suited for real issues and unwelcome in the real world. In a broader context, the role of applying economic doctrines to empirical issues and spreading them are frequently not assigned to university professors but to those intellectuals who have more practical interests. The latter includes policy-makers, especially government officials, economists affiliated with research institutes, journalists, businesspersons and intelligent lay-agents. Although these people share a common interest in current issues, rather than in academic cases, each of them has its own specific features.

As government officials are interested in coming up with policies in various fields, they interpret and apply economic theories in order to address current economic and social issues. Moreover, they are sensitive to government policies but also to the current and daily economic problems of the general public. For this reason, both government officials and journalists are conscious of the cases of other regions and countries. Researchers at government institutes address policy-issues with the budget provided by various branches of the government. They often assist government officials with designing policies. In more recent decades, private research institutes, founded or sponsored by major firms, have dealt with current social and economic issues in order to rationalize market ideology.

For this reason, in evaluating theories these people tend to prioritize relevance or simplicity to rigour or profundity. This is to be contrasted with the position of university scholars who would give priority to rigour and refinement. For instance, in the minds of journalists and lay persons, competition which punctuates the market system and the educational infrastructure of Korea is hardly understandable with the sophisticated notion of perfect competition. With another example, it is often said that going beyond the OLS method of regression would be a luxury for researchers at the institutes, not to mention for government officials.

By focusing on the relevance of theories, government officials, researchers and journalists, intentionally or unintentionally, contribute towards reducing the gap between *imported theories* and the real economy. Moreover, they mediate between academicians and the general public. Businessmen and lay-agents on their own play the role of reducing the discrepancy between theory and reality by means of their responses and (implicit) criticism. Needless to say, this process is very often accompanied with the cost of diluting or distorting the original meaning of theories and concepts.

This significant *duality* in the Scientific community and in Economics may account for intervention of the government into the scientific community in diverse ways. The most salient form of intervention was that the government organization called the *Korean Research Fund* initiated a general system of refereed journals. This system named KRI was designed to standardize academic papers and to enhance research capability of scholars. As is well-known, the Korean government has introduced institutional reforms in many fields of the society including economy and education over more than half a century. A typical example is found in structural reforms carried out after the outbreak of the economic crisis in 1997. In a similar vein, the 'referee system' was introduced by the government more than a decade ago and has now been taken as 'given' in the Scientific community. It goes without saying that the quality of the Korean journals within the system is yet to be improved – in order to be on an equal footing with journals indexed in SSCI or SCOPUS.

Given this background, it is not surprising to find that the spread of standard Economics has met difficulties. It may be useful to examine the ways in which new concepts are understood or misunderstood and how they are transformed and twisted. Clearly, the more an idea has affinity with the reality of the Korean society, the more chances it has to get disseminated. But in order to start with the task at hand, we have to find out the criteria which have functioned, in an explicit or implicit way, in the process of transformation of foreign ideas. *For this purpose, it is necessary to outline basic features of both Neoclassical Economics and Korean society.*

At some risk of oversimplification, it can be argued that Neoclassical Economics is built on two basic tenets: (1) rational choices on the part of individuals and (2) efficient market system based on price mechanism (Hong, 2007: 90–91). The first tenet can be analysed and operationalized as individualism. Individual-ism as a social philosophy is featured by the importance of choices, cool-headed calculation, pursuit of self-interest including maximization of utility and profits. Methodological individualism which postulates that a maximizing individual is the basic unit of analysis has been expanding its domains into law, voting, mar-riage, childbirth and crime by means of rational choice theory. It can be opera-tionalized by such terms as market, price, demand and supply, and efficiency.

Korean society, especially during the 1960s and the 1970s, has been charac-terized by the nationwide goal of economic development under the authoritarian rule of the Park regime (see Amsden, 1989; Wade, 2003). Contemporary Korea is associated with such slogans as: *modernization, better-life, economic growth, export target, new village movement, leadership and solidarity.*

Second, it has been punctuated by social relationships and collective thinking. Dependence on social relationships and on frequent group-activities constitutes a cultural dimension of East Asia. In fact many cultural psychologists endorse the view that East Asians rely heavily on 'human relations' (Markus and Kitayama, 1991, 2010; Markus and Schwartz, 2010). Other strands of thought go so far as to claim that social relationships are fundamental to human existence. These range from Aristotle and Marx to self-determination theory (Ryan and Deci, 2000; Ryan *et al.*, 2013) and economics of human relations (Sacco *et al.*, 2006). Dependence on informal social relationships has contributed towards formation of social capital and networks, despite its downsides such as corruption or collusion.

Third, it has been attached to context-specific and holistic ways of thinking. This can be considered as the Eastern socio-cognitive system as distinct from the Western system (Nisbett *et al.*, 2001). The system which depends heavily on teamwork and groupthink seems to have been *functional* in achieving export-targets and absorbing or innovating technologies (Nonaka and Konno, 1998; Nonaka and Toyama, 2002; Nonaka *et al.*, 2014). Physical-training at the top of a mountain at the dawn for developing the initial type of DRAM (dynamic random-access memory) is a striking example (Sohn and Kenney, 2007; Song, 2012).

Last, the Korean economy has been embedded in ethics and politics as was conceived by Karl Polanyi (1886–1964). Whenever Korean economic agents make decisions about 'purchase and sale', they are prone to take 'fairness and justice' into account (Fehr and Gächter, 2000; Cohn *et al.*, 2015). For this reason, heuristics involving reciprocity must be working along the lines of behavioural economics (Kahneman and Tversky, 1984).

The major obstacle to the spread of economic concepts

The most formidable obstacle to proper diffusion and education of Economic concepts in South Korea seems to be *Methodological Individualism*. Although individualism may go some way towards depicting the American society as it is, it is not realistic enough to account for diverse aspects of socio-economic phenomena in Korea. *Of paramount importance, for this argument, is the view that two or three kinds of self-construal, such as independent self and interdependent self (relational and collective) might coexist* (Brewer and Gardner, 1996; Howell and Shamir, 2005; Tabellini, 2008; Alesina and Giuliano, 2016: 13).

When an individual pursues his/her private goal or interests, the personal self is activated. By contrast, when he/she focuses on human relations or on the goals and interests of a collective where he/she belongs, the relational self or collective self is activated. During the period of Economic growth, the relational or collective self of Koreans as well as their personal self has been in operation. The relational self or collective self has been prompted by means of setting goals at the level of an organization or by means of offering slogans stimulating group-identity (Shin *et al.*, 2013).

Since different types of ego are activated in diverse social contexts, individuals as units of analysis are not as dominant in Korean society, as is assumed by Neoclassical Economics. Especially, standard economic theory assumes that the only thing an Economic agent does is to maximize her utility or profits. However, to the extent that social relationships and collectives compete with personal egos social preferences and social comparisons would prevail. Advocates of social preferences argue that people are interested in consumption and utility of their close others as well as their own consumption and utility (Fehr and Schmidt, 1999). Similarly, proponents of social comparison suggest that lay agents are accustomed to comparing themselves to their close others in terms of income or consumption and obtain utility from their relative position or ranking (Festinger, 1954; Frank, 1985; Frank *et al.*, 2014). This perspective originates from the idea of 'keeping up with the Joneses' which runs from Veblen through Galbraith to Duesenberry (see Veblen, 1899; Duesenberry, 1949; Galbraith, 1976).

Korean consumers, workers and students have very strong social preferences in that they are very conscious of their close others as regards their income, houses, cars, clothes, grade, school credentials, social status and so on. Various types of pro-social behaviours on the part of Koreans arise from the fact that the Korean socio-economic system is relational (see Kim, 1999). In particular, prevalence of positional goods in diverse domains of the Korean society lends support to the perspective of social comparison. It is obvious that social preference and social comparison are incompatible with Neoclassical Economics but cohere with Behavioural Economics.

Kinds of motivation and types of organization as well as types of 'ego' are relevant for the Korean society, although all of these are foreign to standard economics. As to kinds of motivation, one has to make distinction between intrinsic and extrinsic motivation, i.e. between work or study for its own sake and work or study for the sake of money or grades. Between two extreme forms may be posited two intermediate forms of motivation called 'introjective' and 'identified'. Introjection is a controlled form of regulation in which behaviours are performed to avoid guilt or anxiety but which is not fully accepted as one's own.

'Identification reflects a conscious valuing of a behavioral goal or regulation, such that the action is accepted or owned as personally important' (Ryan and Deci, 2000: 72; Gerhart and Fang, 2015). In Korea, the relational self or collective self has often been stimulated by intrinsic motivation and identified motivation (Brewer and Gardner, 1996; Kark and Shamir, 2002; Howell and Shamir, 2005). It is to be noted that Neoclassical Economics places a one-sided emphasis on extrinsic motivation (Iyengar and Lepper, 1999; Bénabou and Tirole, 2003).

As to types of organization, informal relationships and groups reinforce attachment of individuals with the formal organization by means of reducing impersonality. This also gives salience to their relational self and collective self and activates the intrinsic or identified forms of their motivation. Moreover, activation of their relational and collective self, unlike that of their personal self, is very often made into intrinsic motivation for them by social framing (Sunstein, 2003; Sunstein and Hastie, 2014). Goals or extrinsic incentives for a group might turn into intrinsic motivation for its group members and might inspire their devotion to their tasks. Social framing serves to internalize group goals into the minds of people and to identify themselves with their group. This framing and contextualization has taken place through a socio-political process rather than through a cognitive process on the part of individuals. At the outbreak of economic crisis in 1997, the nationwide sale of gold was framed as a patriotic action to save the country from the crisis rather than as a rational choice to compensate for a fall in one's income.

Examples of difficulties in the spread of concepts

Demand and supply

The concepts of price, demand and supply, and market seem to have been quickly absorbed into a daily set of words. By contrast, changes in quantities demanded and supplied in reaction to price changes and the subsequent equilibrium have not been fully understood. Especially, *tâtonnement* (meaning a process of 'search by trial and error') is very often misunderstood as taking place in real time, as this way of understanding it is more appealing to common sense. Moreover, supply and demand and prices have frequently been misconceived as being decoupled from rational choices on the part of individual agents. Consequently, individualism and market mechanism are often treated as two separate things. It is suspected that these aspects of twisted understanding could be attributed to the prevalence of relationships and collectives in South Korea. For lay-agents, market order, in distinction from equilibrium as economists conceive it, may well build on social structure or social relationships as well as on rational choices of individuals.

Substitutability and complementarity

The jargon of substitution (or complementarity) is often confused with substitution (or complementarity) in its everyday use. However, they are to be distinguished from each other. The former is inseparably linked with prices and income in contrast with the latter. According to the former, a house and a refrigerator could be substitutes or complements depending on their prices and the income of the consumer in question. By contrast, the latter highlights functional aspects of houses and refrigerators without taking into account (changes in) their prices and income. Coffee and milk could be substitutes or complements, if their prices and income of consumers are considered. However, if they are viewed in light of their functions, they may be complements all the time.

The point that the notions of substitutability and complementarity rest upon rational choices and the price mechanism is neither clearly stated nor conveyed in the classroom. This may be also the case in some US universities – since the concepts have flaws serious enough to be admitted by one of its major proponents in his later years (Samuelson, 1974: 1255). Still, part of the difficulty in understanding these concepts could be attributed to the divergence between Individualism assumed in Economic theory, on the one hand – and the significance of relationships and ethics/politics in the Korean economy, on the other.

Trade-off or conflict

Trade-offs between bundles of goods or between two different kinds of value in economics not only stand for conflicts in choices over alternatives – but also for quantitative exchange ratios between them. In this regard, trade-off entails 'trade' in the minds of economic agents which leads to the consequent substitution or combination at the margin. Simply put, a trade-off includes quantitative aspects whereas conflict remains purely qualitative. This distinction between trade-off and conflict in choices is made more explicit by behavioural economists (Shafir *et al.*, 1993; Dietrich and List, 2013). In Korean intellectual circles, the meaning of trade-off is often diluted and confused with conflict per se or misunderstood as an either/or question. This confusion stands in the way of application of trade-off and substitution to a wider range of socio-economic issues. This could be ascribed to the finding that social and political factors have impacted the Korean economy.

Utility function and production function

Utility function as used in Economics does not describe the activity of consumption, per se, as it goes on in a family. Instead, it serves to explain rational choices of consumers about consumption bundles, which are aggregated to constitute market demand curves. Moreover, consumption function which addresses the issue of the determinants of consumption levels in macroeconomics is much less concerned with consumption behaviour of a micro-unit. These aspects of utility function and consumption function are not easily conveyed to Korean students.

In parallel, production function as an academic term is designed to explain rational choices about quantities of outputs and inputs on the part of producers, which are aggregated to form market supply curves. It would be mistaken if one expects the function to say something substantial about what is actually taking place in a factory or in a firm. However, lay agents are prone to misidentify it with production-process which unfolds itself in real time.

Korean students very often fail to conceive utility function and production function in terms of rational choices and price mechanisms. They do not fully endorse general equilibrium system, which is built on utility function and production function. Instead, they implicitly feel more sympathetic to the classical view that the economy goes periodically through the stages of production, distribution, exchange and consumption.

Perfect competition

Perfect competition, roughly defined as price-taking behaviour on the part of a large number of small firms, is one of the hardest concepts to be taught due to its being static and unrealistic. Even apart from the age-old controversy over this notion, for many reasons it is less appealing to Koreans than to Americans. It is especially far-fetched in the eyes of Koreans who observe that their economy has been dominated by *Chaebol* conglomerates. The giant firms which have been fostered by the decade-long government policies for economic development appear obviously monopolistic in the domestic economy. This contradicts price-taking behaviour of atomic agents as defined by perfect competition. Moreover, this offers a critique of the traditional dichotomy between market and the state and suggests the existence of empire-type organizations as a third sector.

In a similar vein, the Berle and Means (1967) thesis of the separation of ownership and management which has been influential for nearly a century in the Anglo-Saxon academic community is highly misleading, when it is applied to Korean firms (Berle and Means, 1967; Cheffins and Bank, 2009). It is now widely known that a large number of Korean and Asian firms (as well as many Latin European firms) are either owned or managed by the families of their founders. This gap between the thesis and the reality has brought about confusions and distortions in the Korean academic circles. Sometimes, the tenet has been conveniently misunderstood as a normative rule for firms rather than as a description about the existing firms.

Koreans are more habituated to associating competition with entrance examination or with sports, than with firms in the market. Thus the notion of prefect competition is not comprehended fully, although it has been taught from generation to generation. 'Perfect competition' is irreconcilable with competition in Korean schools as well. Exams and entrance into universities constitute critical parts of the Korean society, as they lay the groundwork for social status and social networks (*Hakbol*). Fierce competition for participation in the higher education very often ends up with formation of rent-seeking associations of alumni in the labour market. In a word, competition in the educational system provides the basis for monopolies or monopolistic competition in the socio-economic system. Observance of procedural rules could be the only possible similarity between competition in Korean schools and perfect competition.

In order to account for competition in Korea, which spans from schools to markets and organizations, one needs a more dynamic and holistic concept of competition instead of the notion of perfect competition. This explains why perfect competition turns out to be one of the most inapplicable Neoclassical concepts in the Korean society.

Moral hazard

'Moral hazard' is concerned with an incentive system of insurance and is closely tied up with the market system. However, it is very often misunderstood as 'moral decay' which has neither to do with incentives nor with economic activity in the market per se. Rather this concept is often associated with corruption of government officials or with lack of filial piety or of marital faithfulness. One of the reasons for this association is that these ethical problems have been more familiar to Koreans. This misunderstanding may lend support to the view that the Korean economy is more seriously embedded in morality than is the US economy. In fact, presidents of Korean firms are more reticent about their profit-seeking goal and more vocal about the goal of employment or of national economic growth. This is a far cry from the fundamentalist market ideology which advocates that all that a firm is supposed to do is to maximize profits (Friedman, [1962] 1982).

Classification of goods

Economics textbooks tend to group goods into *four* distinct kinds by the two criteria of excludability and rivalry. This standard classification of economics is founded on its misleading dichotomy between the market and the government. According to this dichotomy, the market system which is composed of decentralized individuals allocates and distributes private goods, whereas the government as a central authority supplies public goods. This standard argument fudges distinctions among different levels of government. More important, it pays little attention to the role of human relationships. The prevalence of human relationships in Korean society motivates us to reconsider this traditional distinction, since facilitation and reproduction of relationships require relational-goods, club-goods or toll-goods instead of private-goods or public-goods (Ostrom, 2010). In parallel, the significance of human relationships and toll goods stands for community and civil society which lie between the market system and the government.

Criteria for evaluation

Belief in the market system that consumers are ultimate judges of goods and services is often accompanied with the idea that rules evolve spontaneously in the market (Hayek, 1979). However, this idea clashes with the perennial role of the Korean government in standardizing and certifying the quality of goods and services. Not only schools, lawyers, doctors and accountants but also hotels, restaurants, agricultural produce have been evaluated and qualified on the basis of criteria initially proposed by the government. The Korean government intervenes, to a stronger extent, into the educational system. It has imposed even on schools for tertiary education a set of strict regulations with respect to: establishment of institutes and departments; enrolment quotas; student admission procedures; tuitions; issuance of diplomas (Kim and Lee, 2006). All this may well place limits on, or replace, market valuation. This reality makes it difficult for the alleged efficiency of market mechanism and for the assumed validity of standard economic theory to gain ground.

The 45-degree line and the 'Keynesian cross'

The 45-degree line which represents the level of aggregate demand and determines the level of GNP in macroeconomics used to distinguish Keynesian Economics from Neoclassical tradition at most Korean Economics classes in the 1970s (Weber, 1974; Garrison, 1995). By contrast, the Korean economy during the same period was embroiled in the export drive propelled by the Park regime and suffered from obstacles on the supply side, not on the demand side. Nevertheless, this Keynesian line has been repeatedly drawn to emphasize the importance of demand gap and the need for macroeconomic policies. Moreover, Keynesian macroeconomic policies were not clearly distinguished from contemporary Korean government policies for export drive and economic growth. Keynesianism was taken for granted unconditionally. It was not made explicit that it specifically addressed the issue of unemployment in a deep depression with little possibility of inflation. Nor was it necessarily accompanied with the reservation that Keynes did not have in mind structural unemployment of underdeveloped countries but involuntary unemployment of the industrialized countries. These bear witness to the lag between Western Economic theory and the reality of the Korean economy and to the consequent difficulty of the theory in gaining currency in Korea, unlike as in China or Japan.

Rational expectations and perceived inflation

The 'rational expectations' hypothesis which lays the groundwork for neoclassical macroeconomics collides blatantly with the socio-economic phenomena of Korea. This hypothesis assumes an extreme level of rationality and predictive capability on the part of lay agents. On this basis, it declares Keynesian macroeconomic policy, especially monetary policy, as ineffective. Korean economic agents would not be persuaded of their own capability to forecast price levels or interest rates, comparable to econometricians or economic research institutes such as SERI. Moreover, since they have been accustomed to various government interventions under the regimes of state development, they would not come to believe in the alleged ineffectiveness of government policies. Among others, Korean government officials are devoted to discarding this hypothesis.

In spite of this hiatus, this hypothesis, along with natural rate of unemployment, is one of the most favourite concepts in the classrooms of Korean universities. It may even be the case that knowing the concept proves one's attendance at a macroeconomics class. A more reasonable way out of this pitfall could be not merely to revert to Keynesian economics, but also to consider behavioural economics which advocates bounded rationality and allows for nudges.

The divergence between the official rate of inflation and the rate of perceived inflation refutes the hypothesis of rational expectation in another way. The rate of perceived inflation denotes the rate of inflation that economic agents perceive to be prevalent in the economy. The divergence has been one of the major macroeconomic issues for decades in Korea. Moreover, controversy over this issue is still going on, as it was addressed in the most recent report of the Bank of Korea (July, 2015). A similar case came to the fore in the EU after its monetary unification (Brachinger, 2008).

Perception of inflation is backward looking, whereas expectation of inflation is forward looking (Ranyard *et al.*, 2008). Standard economic theory is forward looking in that it focuses on expectation about prices which may be either rational (monetarist) or adaptive (Keynesian). The issue of perceived inflation seems incompatible with the concept of expectation itself, be it rational or adaptive. In view of the Korean economic history it can be attributed to decades of distrust coming from frequent price freezes and discretionary monetary policies which the Korean government had exercised for the purpose of achieving economic growth. Or it can be ascribed to loss aversion on the part of consumers, following the perspective of behavioural economics (Brachinger, 2008; Dräger *et al.*, 2014). That is, they are allegedly prone to overestimate inflation rates, because they are more sensitive to price rises than to price falls.

Conclusions

To conclude, Korean social scientists including economists have been faced with the difficult task of reducing the chasm between theories and socio-economic reality. Given the fact that most theories are imported, tackling this task requires making it a rule to carry out critical reinterpretation and holistic contextualization of the Western theories on a constant basis.

Results of this interpretation would take the form of either a theoretical survey or a doctrinal history. It is only after the theories are reinterpreted and contextualized that they can be applied to domestic issues. Without this prior stage, application of a theory may degenerate into a mechanical imposition of Western theories on the Korean soil, as is currently very often the case. For the same purpose, it may be desirable for Economics teachers to prioritize reasoning via basic concepts on the basis of real world cases and data to training in mathematical or econometric techniques.

Clearly, the foregoing examination is not concerned with the entire Korean peninsula, but with its Southern half. It may be worthwhile to add a few words about its Northern one. The North Korean regime adopted Marx-Leninism as its ideological basis long ago (Hong, 2001: 138–143; Park, 2013: 23–27). A number of Communist scholars who chose to move to North Korea during the 1950s also contributed to establishing the North Korean system. Whilst the market economy and Neoclassical Economics advocate the price-mechanism and individualism, Marx-Leninism there is founded on planning and collectivism, as it was once so in the PRC. Along this line of thought, North Korea set up the goal of nurturing 'Communist' human beings who are accustomed to cooperating with others and to sacrificing their self-interests or desires for the collective will. This must have reinforced the *relational* or *interdependent* self of Koreans. This is to be contrasted with South Koreans who, due to their living in the capitalist economy, have a *hybrid* type of ego – which is made up of independent self and relational self.

Later, North Korea supplemented Marxist-Leninist ideology with its endogenous thought called *Ju-che Sa Sang* (meaning identity and autonomy). This pattern of thought was designed to protect people from Capitalist Ideology and from American Imperialism. Thus, it has laid strong stress on self-reliance and self-subsistence.

Given this thought, the North Korean economy, for decades, has struggled to minimize its dependence on foreign trade and to substitute domestically produced coal for imported oil. However, in the most recent decade, North Korea, owing to its serious economic difficulties, has slowly attempted to introduce 'deeper' reforms. Moreover, it has started to learn and teach the principles of 'market economy', at least in theory. Last but not least, it has made efforts to accommodate foreign capital, including joint ventures with the South, partly in imitation of the past Chinese reforms (Gray and Lee, 2015) but it is, as yet, too early to say where this may lead.

Notes

1 Some of the examples can be found in the respective sources translated.
2 To mention a few Korean scholars, Namwoon Baek, Soontak Lee and Hangjung Yoon were teaching at Yonhee College (Yonsei University) or Bosung College (Korea University) (KEA, 1991: 2).
3 Major classical works such as Smith's *Wealth of Nations*, Malthus' *Essay on the Principle of Population*, J. S. Mill's *Principles of Political Economy*, List's *Das Nationale System der Politischen Ökonomie* and so on were already translated into Japanese around the 1880s (Morris-Suzuki, 1989: 50, 60). But the Japanese edition of *Das Kapital* was completed only in 1924 (Hoston, 1984, see also Yagi's chapter in this volume).

References

Alesina, A. and P. Giuliano (2016) Culture and Institutions, *Journal of Economic Literature*, 53: 898–944.
Amsden, A. (1989) *Asia's Next Giant: South Korea and Late Industrialization*, Oxford: Oxford University Press.

Belussi, F. (1999) Policies for the Development of Knowledge-intensive Local Production Systems, *Cambridge Journal of Economics*, 23: 729–747.

Bénabou, R. and J. Tirole (2003) Intrinsic and Extrinsic Motivation, *Review of Economic Studies*, 70: 489–520.

Berle, A. and G. Means (1967) *The Modern Corporation and Private Property*, New York, NY: Harcourt, Brace and World.

Brachinger, H. W. (2008) A New Index of Perceived Inflation: Assumptions, Method and Application in Germany, *Journal of Economic Psychology*, 29: 433–457.

Brewer, M. B. and W. Gardner (1996) Who is This 'We'? Levels of Collective Identity and Self Representations, *Journal of Personality and Social Psychology*, 71: 83–93.

Chang, K. (2004) Experience in the West and the Understanding of Modernity of Korean Intellectuals in the Late 19th Century, *Studies in Modern Korean History*, 28: 7–37 (in Korean).

Cheffins, B. and S. Bank (2009) Is Berle and Means Really a Myth? *Business History Review*, 83: 443–474.

Cho, S. (2005) *History of Academic Research in Korea*, Economics, Chapter 1, Theory in General, Section I, 3–22 (*Hankook Eui Hak Sool Yoen Koo*), Seoul: The National Academy of Sciences, Republic of Korea (in Korean).

Choi, Y. B. (1996) The Americanization of Economics in Korea, *History of Political Economy*. Special Issue, 95–120.

Cohn, A., E. Fehr and L. Goette (2015) Fair Wages and Effort Provision: Combining Evidence from a Choice Experiment and a Field Experiment, *Management Science*, 61: 1777–1794.

Dietrich, F. and C. List (2013) A Reason-Based Theory of Rational Choice, *NOÛS* [sic], 47: 104–134.

Dräger, L., J.-O. Mentz and U. Fritsche (2014) Perceived Inflation Under Loss Aversion, *Applied Economics*, 26: 482–493.

Duesenberry, J. (1949) *Income, Savings and the Theory of Consumer Behavior*, Cambridge, MA: Harvard University Press.

Fehr, E. and S. Gächter (2000) Fairness and Retaliation: The Economics of Reciprocity, *Journal of Economic Perspectives*, 14: 159–181.

Fehr, E. and K. Schmidt (1999) A Theory of Fairness, Competition, and Cooperation, *Quarterly Journal of Economics*, 114: 817–868.

Festinger, L. (1954) A Theory of Social Comparison Processes, *Human Relations*, 7: 117–140.

Frank, R. (1985) The Demand for Unobservable and Other Nonpositional Goods, *American Economic Review*, 75: 101–116.

Frank, R., A. S. Levine and O. Dijk (2014) Expenditure Cascades, *Review of Behavioral Economics*, 1: 55–73.

Friedman, M. [1962] (1982) *Capitalism and Freedom*, Chicago, IL: The University of Chicago Press.

Galbraith, J. K. (1976) *The Affluent Society*, Boston, MA: Houghton Mifflin Company.

Garrison, R. (1995) Linking the Keynesian Cross and the Production Possibilities Frontier, *Journal of Economic Education*, 26: 122–130.

Gerhart, B. and M. Fang (2015) Pay, Intrinsic Motivation, Extrinsic Motivation, Performance, and Creativity in the Workplace: Revisiting Long-Held Beliefs, *Annual Review of Organizational Psychology and Organizational Behavior*, 2: 489–521.

Gertler, M. S. (2003) Tacit Knowledge and the Economic Geography of Context, or the Undefinable Tacitness of Being (There), *Journal of Economic Geography*, 3: 75–99.

Gray, K. and J. Lee (2015) Following in China's Footsteps: The Political Economy of North Korean Reform, *The Pacific Review*, www.tandfonline.com/action/showCitForm ats?doi=10.1080/09512748.2015.1100666 (accessed 21 October 2016).

Hayek, F. A. (1944) *The Road to Freedom*, London: Routledge.

Hayek, F. A. (1979) *Law, Legislation and Liberty*, Chicago, IL: The University of Chicago Press.

Hong, H. (2000) Marx and Menger on Value: As Many Similarities as Differences, *Cambridge Journal of Economics*, 24: 87–105.

Hong, H. (2001) Possible Ideological Conflicts upon the Reunification of the Korean Peninsula, *Korean Unification Studies*, 5: 119–155 (in Korean).

Hong, H. (2002) Marx's Value Forms and Hayek's Rules: A Reinterpretation in the Light of the Dichotomy between *Physis* and *Nomos*, *Cambridge Journal of Economics*, 26: 613–635.

Hong, H. (2005) *History of Academic Research in Korea*, Economics, Chapter 1, Theory in General, Section V, 188–204, The Seoul National Academy of Sciences, Republic of Korea (in Korean).

Hong, H. (2007) Recent Shifts in the Paradigm of Neoclassical Economics (1960–2006): Their Implications for Korean Mainstream Economics, *Review of Social and Economic Studies*, 29: 89–129 (in Korean).

Hoston, G. A. (1984) Marxism and National Socialism in Taisho Japan: The Thought of Takabatake Motoyuki, *Journal of Asian Studies*, 44: 43–64.

Howell, J. M. and B. Shamir (2005) The Role of Followers in the Charismatic Leadership Process: Relationships and their Consequences, *Academy of Management Review*, 30: 96–112.

Iyengar, S. S. and M. R. Lepper (1999) Rethinking the Value of Choice: A Cultural Perspective on Intrinsic Motivation, *Journal of Personality and Social Psychology*, 76: 349–366.

Jeong, S. J. (2007) Marxist Economics in South Korea since 1987, *Review of Social and Economic Studies*, 29: 49–88 (in Korean).

Kahneman, D. and A. Tversky (1984) Choices, Values, and Frames, *American Psychologist*, 39: 341–350.

Kark, R. and B. Shamir (2002) The Influence of Transformational Leadership on Followers' Relational versus Collective Self-Concept, *Academy of Management, Proceedings*, OB: D1–D6.

KEA (1991) *A Short History of Korean Economic Association (1953–1989)*, Seoul: Taejin [*sic*] (in Korean).

Kim, K. D. (1999) Toward Culturally 'Independent' Social Science: The Issue of Indigenization in East Asia, Chapter 5, *East Asia: Sociology in East Asia and Its Struggle for Creativity*, 63–72, Regional Volumes, 'Social Knowledge: Heritage, Challenges, Perspectives', Volume 2, International Sociological Association, Proceedings of the ISA Regional Conference for *Eastern Asia*. Seoul, Korea.

Kim, S. J. (2005) Changes of Corporate Governance and Financial System in Korea after the 1997 Crisis, *Journal of Asiatic Studies*, 121: 7–42 (in Korean).

Kim, S. and J. Lee (2006) Changing Facets of Korean Higher Education: Market Competition and the Role of the State, *Higher Education*, 52: 557–587.

Kleinknecht, A., F. N. van Schaik and H. Zhou (2014) Is Flexible Labour Good for Innovation? Evidence from Firm-level Data, *Cambridge Journal of Economics*, 38: 1207–1219.

Lee, C. (1993) Marx's Labour Theory of Value Revisited, *Cambridge Journal of Economics*, 17: 463–478.

Lee, J. and G. Wang (2007) The Comparison of Entry Deterrence between Bertrand and Cournot Competition, *Korean Economic Review*, 23: 33–48.

Lee, K. J. (1985) *Historical Research into the Adoption of Western Economics around the End of the Lee Dynasty (Suh Ku Gyoung Je Hak Do Ip Sa)*, Seoul: Il Jo Gak (in Korean).

Malthus, T. (1827) *Definitions in Political Economy*, London: John Murray.

Markus, H. R. and S. Kitayama (1991) Culture and the Self: Implications for Cognition, Emotion and Motivation. *Psychological Review*, 98: 224–253.

Markus, H. R. and S. Kitayama (2010) Cultures and Selves: A Cycle of Mutual Constitution. *Journal/Perspectives on Psychological Science*, 5: 420–430.

Markus, H. R. and B. Schwartz (2010) Does Choice Mean Freedom and Well-Being?, *Journal of Consumer Research*, 37: 344–355.

Morris-Suzuki, T. (1989) *A History of Japanese Economic Thought*, London and New York, NY: Routledge.

Nisbett, R., K. Peng, I. Choi and A. Norenzayan (2001) Culture and Systems of Thought: Holistic Versus Analytic Cognition, *Psychological Review*, 108: 291–310.

Nonaka, I. and N. Konno (1998) The Concept of 'Ba': Building a Foundation for Knowledge Creation, *California Management Review*, 40: 40–54.

Nonaka, I. and R. Toyama (2002) A Firm as a Dialectical Being: Towards a Dynamic Theory of a Firm, *Industrial and Corporate Change*, 11: 995–1009.

Nonaka, I., R. Chia, R. Holt and V. Peltokorpi (2014) Wisdom, Management and Organization, *Management Learning*, 45: 365–376.

Ostrom, E. (2010) Beyond Markets and States: Polycentric Governance of Complex Economic Systems, *American Economic Review*, 100: 1–33.

Park, C. (2013) *A Study on Education in North Korea*, Seoul: Hankook Haksul Jeongbowon (in Korean).

Peng, K. and R. Nisbett (1999) Culture, Dialectics, and Reasoning about Contradiction, *American Psychologist*, 54: 741–754.

Ranyard, R., F. Del Missier, N. Bonini, D. Duxbury and B. Summer (2008) Perceptions and Expectations of Price Changes and Inflation: A Review and Conceptual Framework, *Journal of Economic Psychology*, 29: 378–400.

Ryan, R. and E. Deci (2000) Self-Determination Theory and the Facilitation of Intrinsic Motivation, Social Development and Well-Being, *American Psychologist*, 55: 68–78.

Ryan, R. M., R. R. Curren and E. L. Deci (2013) What Humans Need: Flourishing in Aristotelian Philosophy and Self-determination Theory, in *The Best Within Us: Positive Psychology Perspectives on Eudaimonia*, edited by Alan S. Waterman, pp. 57–75, Washington, DC: American Psychological Association.

Sacco, P. L., P. Vanin and S. Zamagni (2006) The Economics of Human Relationships, Chapter 9, Vol. I, *Handbook of the Economics of Giving, Altruism and Reciprocity*, edited by S.-C. Kolm and J. M. Ythier [*sic*], London: Elsevier B.V.

Samuelson, P. A. ([1948] 1973) *Economics*, New York, NY: McGraw-Hill.

Samuelson, P. A. (1974) Complementarity: An Essay on the 40th Anniversary of the Hicks-Allen Revolution in Demand Theory, *Journal of Economic Literature*, 12: 1255–1289.

Shafir, E., I, Simonson and A. Tversky (1993) Reason-based Choice, *Cognition*, 49: 11–36.

Shin, T., J. Park, S. Lee and H. Hong (2013) Towards a Socioeconomic Model of Technical Change: A Comparative Analysis of Korea and the USA, presented at *25th Annual Conference, SASE:* Milan, Italy.

Sohn, D. and M. Kenney (2007) Universities, Clusters, and Innovation Systems: The Case of Seoul, Korea, *World Development*, 35: 991–1004.

Song, S. (2012) An Analysis on the Characteristics of Technological Development in Korea: Focusing on POSCO and Semiconductor in Samsung, *Korean Journal for the History of Science*, 34: 109–138 (in Korean).

Sunstein, C. (2003) What's Available? Social Influences and Behavioral Economics, *Northwestern University Law Review*, 97: 1295–1314.

Sunstein, C. and R. Hastie (2014) Making Dumb Groups Smarter, *Harvard Business Review*, 92: 90–98.

Tabellini, G. (2008) Institutions and Culture, *Journal of the European Economic Associations*, 6: 255–294.

Veblen, T. (1899) *The Theory of the Leisure Class*, New York, NY, London: Macmillan.

Wade, R. H. (2003) *Governing the Market: Economic Theory and the Role of Government in East Asia's Industrialization*, Princeton, NJ: Princeton University Press.

Weber, W. (1974) Government Spending in a Neo-Walrasian Economy: An Alternative to the Keynesian Cross Analysis, *Southern Economic Journal*, 41: 10–24.

Selected translations in Korean

Choi, H. (1954) *Income [1948]*, Arthur Cecil Pigou, Seoul: Jeongyeonsa.

Choi, H. (1959) *Principles of Political Economy and Taxation [1817]*, David Ricardo, Seoul: Bomoongak.

Choi, H. and H. Cheung (1960) *The Wealth of Nations [1776]*, Adam Smith, Seoul: Choonjosa.

Jeon, S. and Y. Choi (1947) *Das Capital [1867]*, Karl Marx, Seoul: Seoulchulpansa.

Kim, D. (1955) *The General Theory [1936]*, John Maynard Keynes, Seoul: Minjoongsuhkwan.

Sung, I. (1946) *On Liberty*, John Stuart Mill [1859], Seoul: Daesungchulpansa.

6 The diffusion of Western Economics in Malaysia

Rajah Rasiah

Introduction

This chapter attempts to examine the influence of Western Economics in the evolution of the Malaysian economy. After this introduction, the rest of the chapter is organized as follows. The second section discusses government efforts to restructure the economy through infrastructure build-up, ethnic restructuring and liberal policies to attract foreign direct investment to promote export manufacturing. The next section focuses on heavy industrialization by the government to develop national firms. Next, the return to export-orientation is analysed. I then trace the causes and consequences of the Asian financial crisis and evaluate the introduction of capital controls. The next section examines the return to liberal economic policies but also taking into account national ethnic considerations. I then finish with the conclusions.

From sedentary farming and petty commodity production largely for subsistence use, the Malaysian economy began to experience, over the years, commercial production of tin and rubber under British colonialism from the eighteenth century onwards in the age of Adam Smith (1723–1790), an author well-thumbed by Sir Stamford Raffles (1781–1826) the founder of Singapore. But International Trade had already begun well before, mainly to meet the growing demand for spices in India and Europe, particularly since the fifteenth century (see Reid, 1993).

Malaysia's integration as a raw material exporter into industrial capitalism had begun during British colonialism. As Malaysia grew as a major revenue-generator for Britain through tin and rubber exports (Madan, 1953), the colonial government took measures to build the infrastructure and security to support primarily migrant-labour brought from China and India, who toiled in the tin mines and rubber estates respectively.

British expenditure on both expanded sharply following the outburst of the Communist insurgency. Indeed, Malaysia became the jewel in the crown of Britain, from 1947 till its independence in 1957, as it was the largest generator of dollar-based revenue in the Sterling Area in the period following India's independence (on the early Economic History of the nation, see Lee and Wie, 2015). Whilst no Western economists were directly involved in defining monetary or fiscal policies in Malaya, the currency used in Malaya, British Borneo and Singapore since colonial rule until 1967 was the Malaya and British Borneo dollar with a *fixed-exchange rate* M\$8.57 to a British pound. Peter T. Bauer (1946), a Hungarian-born UK-based development economist (1915–2002), had worked on the impact of the 'Stevenson restriction-scheme', which was introduced by the British to check a sharp slide in rubber prices.

The fixed-exchange rate offered stability in the post-war world. In 1967, the independent government introduced the Malaysian dollar and the Ringgit in 1975. Whilst the pound was devalued by 14.3 per cent against the Malaysian dollar in 1967, exchange-rate fluctuations in Malaysia began in 1973 when Bank Negara Malaysia withdrew from the currency union with Brunei and Singapore. 'Keynesian-style' exchange-rate instruments were then largely abandoned, although fiscal and monetary policies were still used to reduce unemployment and poverty. One can say that such policies were applied eclectically until 1997, when the Asian financial crisis led the Malaysian government to impose capital controls between 1998 and 2004.

The first Malaysian university, that is, University of Malaya, was originally created in the Island of Singapore, which was part of British Malaya in 1949. The early origins can be traced to the takeover of Raffles College to train medical doctors. It was not until 1959, however, that an Economics Faculty was set up in the Malaysian branch of the university, in Kuala Lumpur. Ungku Abdul Aziz became the founding Dean, when the country's first Faculty of Economics and Administration was launched in 1966.

The pioneer economists in the field, that is, Silcock and Ungku Aziz (1953) analysed the Malaysian economy from an interdisciplinary perspective, as they screened the significance of nationalism in addressing developmental problems. Ungku Aziz (1964) subsequently undertook primary research to examine the causes of poverty in the country, although the emphasis was on Malay poverty. Ungku Aziz (1964) was concerned with 'middlemen' exploitation and abject poverty faced by the poor. Following this tradition, Salih (1982) later discussed the dangers over the impact of overdependence on primary commodities and its consequences over urban poverty in South-East Asia. Drawing on Neo-Marxist Economics, Salih and Young (1989) were even concerned about the eventual 'marginalization' of the Malaysian economy as a consequence of multinationals (MNCs) seeking to relocate in Malaysia, only to extend the exploitation of labour. Another local economist, Jomo (1996), then extended this argument using a 'class-analysis' framework. Ungku Aziz (1964, 1965) examined the causes of poverty in Malaysia in a radical way but without deploying such resorting to 'class'. Shari (1979) followed a similar methodology to examine poverty in Malaysia. Other Malaysian economists, such as Lim (1967) analysed the development of the Malaysian economy *without* any 'ideological anchor' until Lim (1973, 1983) took on a very Neoclassical approach to analyse production structure in the Malaysian manufacturing sector. Thorburn (1976) analysed the economic impact of primary commodity exports from Malaysia. Ariff and Hill (1985) and later Ariff (1991) presented a Neoclassical explication of

Malaysia's integration into the Pacific economy, arguing that liberalization had been the basis of rapid economic growth.

Unlike the early Malaysian economists, who demonstrated a keenness to tread a somewhat neutral line of ideological orientation, most Malaysian economists since the 1990s were trained in the standard 'Neoclassical' Western Economics framework, and hence, researched and published on several aspects of the Malaysian economy using such lenses (for example, Tham and Kam, 2014). The exceptions to the rule include the work of Rasiah (1995), Narayanan and Lai (2002) and Doraisami (1996) who let the economic evidence determine the analysis. Economic exponents at the Central Bank were a mix of professionals, with Lin and Chung (1995) driven by mainstream thinking and Sheng (2009) was to prefer to question Mainstream Economics using evidence typical of Heterodox Economists, in fact, he had worked with such economists, such as Joseph Stiglitz (1943–) and Ajit Singh (1940–2015), in the West.

First-round export-orientation

Departing from the fixed parity with the Singapore and Brunei dollars in 1975 offered Bank Negara Malaysia autonomy to regulate the Ringgit. However, the capital market was largely not promoted until 1985, though foreign ownership of land and buildings had already started since the Mukim Register and Torren System were introduced during colonial rule. Investment regulations were liberalized following the Investment Incentives Act of 1967, but its translation into massive inflows of FDI took off after the Free Trade Zones and Licensed Manufacturing warehouses were to open in 1972. Tariff-free operations in security guaranteed locations that were also equipped with excellent basic infrastructure and tax holidays attracted massive inflows of export-oriented firms (Rasiah, 1988, 1992).

However, whilst FDI was aggressively promoted, stock markets were not promoted heavily until 1985. Hence, whilst government policies to restructure the country and its economy ethnically and to alleviate poverty took an aggressive turn when the New Economic Policy (NEP) was launched through the second Malaysia Plan of 1971, and in contrast to Indonesia and Thailand, Malaysia enjoyed liberalization in the manufacturing sector, and especially sectors that largely exported. The Industrial Coordination Act of 1975 to enforce ethnic ownership conditions only affected nationals as foreigners engaged in export production were exempted from such restrictions. The principal customs area faced tariffs that were imposed following the Pioneer Industry Ordinance of 1958. However, the export-oriented sector began to dominate manufacturing since the early 1970s as the domestic market until the 1990s was too small to offer much currency to the import-substitution sector. Liberal FDI policies gave Malaysia an edge over Indonesia and Thailand and because of the communist insurgency also conveyed an advantage over the Philippines. Hence, in relative terms Malaysia enjoyed strong inflows of FDI in the 1970s. This development clearly was in sync with the Neoclassical arguments of the Western Liberal

Economics thinkers, Bhagwati and Krueger (1973) who even recommended sub-sidies as a means of supporting proscriptive intervention to undo the distortions created in the past.

Nevertheless, the government's forays into the economy to help the *Bumi-puteras* (those of the native Malaysian ethnic group) did not follow any 'Neolib-eral' tenets. Whilst the integration of the peasantry into the wage-based modern economy benefitted the poor, eclectic affirmative policies also undermined the development of a competent labour force to support industrial upgrading. Indeed, the civil service and public universities were dominated by *Bumiputera* employ-ment so much so that it undermined the second NEP prong, which was to remove the identification of occupations by ethnic groups.

Generous incentives to stimulate export-oriented manufacturing increasingly characterized investment promotion with Malaysia's Free Trade Zones (FTZs) in 1972. The Investment Incentives Act of 1968 gave export-oriented firms access to tax-holidays for periods of five to ten years, initially under pioneer status incentives and for subsequent five to ten years under investment tax allow-ances. It began offering financial incentives to attract export-oriented firms since the opening of the FTZs.

The Neoliberal orientation of industrialization that was promoted in the 1970s prevented the introduction of 'innovation-rents' to stimulate technological upgrading (see Schumpeter, 1934, 1943; see the chapter by Metzler on Schum-peter later in this volume). Neither were there grants for R&D nor was there the development of human capital and R&D labs like the industrial technical research institutes (ITRIs) of Taiwan. Hence, export-oriented industrialization in Malaysia in the 1970s was dominated by low wage and low value-added processing, testing and assembling operations (Rasiah, 1995). At the same time, a dual-economy emerged in which the principal customs-area (the primary, secondary and tertiary sectors) was subjected to the restrictions imposed by the NEP (Edwards and Jomo, 1993). Nevertheless, economic crises in the country were accompanied by 'soft landings' following government efforts to diversify primary commodity exports and the discovery of oil and gas off Kemaman in the late 1970s.

The main semblance of Keynesian policy use in the 1970s can be seen in the implicit efforts to use fiscal policies to create employment. Massive investments into infrastructure and agricultural development characterized the 1970s. This period faced Malaysia's highest inflation in 1973–1976 when oil-prices soared four times when Malaysia was a net oil-importer. The extensive focus on infra-structure helped transform the peasant economy into the emerging capitalist economy as in other parts of Asia (see the chapters by Das on East Asia in this volume).

Second-round import-substitution

The emphasis on FDI, however, fell in the first half of the 1980s when the gov-ernment assumed nationalistic efforts to bulwark local capital in heavy indus-tries. Impressed by the successes of Japan, and South Korea, Mahathir Mohamad launched the 'Look East Policy' in 1981 to spearhead national-ownership-based heavy industrialization. Since the examples used were Japan and Korea, one may claim that the influence came from Gershenkron (1952) but specifically Johnson (1982) and Amsden (1989). Protection and state ownership targeted at eventually leaving control to the *Bumiputeras* became the rallying call of the government to industrialize. High commodity prices enabled such a policy, which included massive highway and bridge construction across the Western corridor of Peninsular Malaysia. Whilst restrictions were not imposed on the export-oriented foreign capital incentives to these firms were gradually terminated. Such import-substitution policies resembled the type advocated by structural economists. However, these industries failed miserably because they not only lacked the introduction of the Schumpeterian innovation rents that Amsden (1989) had argued were critical in South Korea's catch-up, and also they lacked the use of the stick to ensure discipline and performance (see the chapter on Korea by Hong in this volume). Whereas the oil and steel company Perwaja has eventually scaled down its operations, the carmaker Proton is still functioning but without a significant presence in the national economy.

Some industries became successful from the second round import-substitution. Domestic rents helped boost development in klinker and cement production, and highway construction. Hence, YTL Corporation acquired Perak Hanjoong (a Korean firm) to become a successful cement manufacturer, whilst United Engineers Malaysia acquired the knowledge to build modern highways that enabled its successful forays abroad, including India. Where export markets and import competition was stiff as in steel and car manufacturing the firms have either failed or are merely surviving through the help of state-created rents.

By the mid-1980s, commodity prices had crashed to make debt-servicing difficult as the balance of payment deficit began to soar. If in Korea the government did not follow the Neoliberal prescription of floating the Won – when rising oil prices in 1973–1975 exacerbated the country's balance of payment deficit and yet successfully forced the chaebols to export so as to clear the deficit (Amsden, 1989), Malaysia promoted the stock market by removing capital gains on capital gains, renewed tax break incentives to FDI and devalued the Ringgit in 1986. Neoliberal policies as put forward by Bhagwati and Krueger (1973) and others came to dominate the Malaysian economy, although the heavy industries still enjoyed tariff- and quota-protection. Hence, whilst sales rents continued to buffer the heavy industries, their relative costs soared as the fallen Ringgit made payments for imported capital equipment and licensing fees extremely expensive. The lack of effective 'human capital' development-policies and pressure to upgrade left these firms remaining dependent on foreign technology. Indeed, the royalty deficit from licensing-fees has continued to grow in Malaysia.

Second-round export orientation

Initial losses and the mid-1980s recession changed the State's emphasis as export incentives were reintroduced through the Promotion of Investment Act of 1986 to attract FDI. Equity regulations under the Industrial Coordination Act of 1975 were amended to allow non-registration when involving paid-up capital of less than RM2.5 million. Foreign ownership conditions were also more clearly denned as firms exporting 80 per cent or more of output were to be allowed complete equity control. Exports were also stimulated through the use of export refinancing schemes, export abatement allowances and double deduction tax exemptions. Several industries began to experience export-surges primarily due to rising global demand and FDI redeployment. Electronics, textiles and garment production expanded manifold in Malaysia. Singapore and Malaysia had, since the early 1970s, become among the world's biggest production-platforms for electronics. Local sub-contractors expanded strongly into textile and garment export markets since the late 1980s as low wages and quota provisions dispersed operations in South-East Asia. Resource-based exports also grew as palm oil processing and wood products from Malaysia increased in importance. Growing domestic demand also stimulated domestic manufacturing, e.g. automobile assembly, cement, steel and garments.

Liberalization from 1986 was perceived by Western market-economists as the panacea that Malaysia required, as massive inflows of capital from Japan, South Korea, Taiwan and Singapore revived manufactured exports. In addition to the deregulation pursued by Malaysia the floating of the Yen, Won, New Taiwan dollar and the Singapore dollar following the Plaza Accord in 1985, and the withdrawal of the Generalized System of Preferences from the Asian newly industrialized countries in February 1988 attracted an avalanche of FDI from these countries (Rasiah, 1988).

Whilst the export-oriented foreign-led manufacturing sector grew rapidly so as to make Malaysia's economy look successful as the annual average GDP growth rate exceeded 8 per cent over the period 1988–1996, the inward-oriented IS sector performed dismally. Despite enjoying huge rents from protection, heavy industries in Malaysia did not enjoy massive profits because of escalating costs of imports and royalties. Snodgrass (1980) offered a balanced account of how growth with equity policies alongside export-orientation helped lower poverty and inequality in Malaysia. However, patronage derailed technological catch-up efforts by the heavy industries (Jomo, 1996).

Hence, the share of FDI in gross domestic investment in Malaysia rose from 10.7 per cent in 1980–1990 to 24.6 per cent in 1991–1993 (UNCTAD, 1996). Taiwan Province of China and the Republic of Korea emerged as major new investors, from the second half of the 1980s, as a consequence. The electronics industry whose foreign ownership share reached 91 per cent in 1993, became Malaysia's leading export-earner from 1987 accounting for 67.5 per cent of manufactured exports in 1995 (see Rasiah, 1995: ch. 5; 1998a). Indeed, the seeds for the 1997–1998 Malaysian financial crisis were sown in the period 1986–1996 as the Malaysian economy did not evolve the innovative faculties to compete in global markets in high value-added economic activities. Also, the Malaysian authorities did not observe the Keynesian dictum that leaving capital and cur-rency markets open could destabilize the currency market, as exchange rates appreciated in trend terms over the period 1986–1997.[1]

In addition, exchange rates depreciated in the second half of the 1980s until the early 1990s, cheapening exports and making imports more expensive. Malaysia's Ringgit had appreciated in the early 1980s due to a 'quasi-peg' basket of currencies, especially against the US dollar. The value of the Ringgit also fell in 1986, following the floating of the Yen and first-tier East Asian NIE currencies after the September 1985 Plaza Accord, putting pressure on Malaysia's nominal and real effective exchange-rates (NEER and REER respectively). The depreciating Ringgit cheapened production costs in Malaysia. The massive currency depreciations as well as domestic promotional efforts encouraged the relocation of producers from Japan and the first-tier NIEs. Singapore faced a relative increase in costs, which switched production emphasis to higher value-added activities, offering itself as the regional hub for production and marketing activities for the whole of South-East Asia. Indonesia and Malaysia in particular have since successfully integrated themselves into Singapore's regional production complex of Singapore-Johore-Rhiau (SIJORI). The falling REER helped reduce the adverse effects of tariff deregulation which characterized the Malaysian economy from the mid-1980s. Tariffs protecting IS industries began to fall, especially from the 1990s. Also, export producers enjoyed subsidies through double tax deductions, export credit refinancing and export-abatement allowances.

Aggressive promotion of stock markets using both direct state guarantees and implicit assurances boosted confidence in projects linked to plantation agriculture, infrastructural projects, manufacturing and telecommunication sectors. The result has been a dramatic rise in shareholder capital, including from foreign portfolio equity-purchasers. From a negligible share in 1980, foreign portfolio equity-investment reached 6.1 per cent of gross fixed capital formation in 1993 (see Rasiah, 1998b). Commercial banks began to expend loans, *inter alia*, using overvalued shares as collateral. Hence, although the expansion of stock markets took place without commensurate regulatory mechanisms to supervise and monitor against excesses, its growth along with FDI inflows pushed up the value of the Ringgit in the first half of the 1990s.

The captive domestic market, which grew substantially through growth in employment from export manufacturing and resource-based industries, helped generate demand for domestic ventures in the country. Hence, Proton and later Perodua, Kedah Cement, Perak Hanjoong, UEM, Renong, Sime Darby and PNB reaped enormous rents. A significant share of the rents was a mere transfer from domestic consumers whose options were sharply restricted by duties and opaque selection procedures. The domestic economy grew so much that even textile and garment firms began to move considerably into real sector speculation and property development. Whilst it can be argued a priori that contestation through open auction need not be the best allocative mechanism to establish maximization of efficiency *ex-post*, the alternative argued to explain the successful metamorphosis of rents in South Korea was achievable due to the effective use of the stick (Amsden, 1989; Khan, 1998; Rasiah, 1998c).

Export quotas were among the disciplinary mechanisms used to force firms to achieve efficiency-gains in South Korea. Little of such mechanisms (e.g. ineffective mechanisms such as management changes were a handful that have been used) were used in Malaysia. With the exception of a few obvious failures such as Perwaja, the microeconomic losses in consumer welfare were not evident during the boom of 1987–1995 as strong domestic demand masked such transfers in deadweight losses. Hence, a number of domestic ventures added to the snowballing effect of export manufacturing growth without tragically affecting the bubble. In short, Malaysia experienced massive upsurges in growth and structural change from 1986 due to a combination of external forces and local initiatives.[3]

The 1997–1998 financial crisis

Whilst falling exchange rates improved export-competitiveness in low value-added activities between 1986 and 1991, the reverse brought the opposite effect after that. Especially against the Chinese Renminbi devaluations of 1990 and 1994, the appreciation of the Ringgit from 1993 had a negative impact on the balance of payments and FDI inflows. The rising Ringgit alongside falling tariffs and other trade restrictions pushed up import-growth.

However, from 1992 imports of capital equipment and royalty payments of inward-oriented IS firms were cushioned from a rising Ringgit, which began as a consequence of massive expansion of the capital market following inflows of both FDI and portfolio equity capital from abroad. The development took place despite rising current account deficits over the period 1990–1996. A major argument that Keynes (1936) had advanced to prevent financial crises is that leaving currency and capital markets liberal at the same time will be destabilizing as any sharp depreciation in currencies will cheapen assets, thereby leading to a sharp increase in acquisitions in capital markets. Massive capital inflows through FDI and portfolio equity investment into stock markets raised exchange rates despite the presence of chronic trade imbalances (Rasiah, 1998b). Indeed, the economic bubble of the 1990s in the Malaysian economy was initiated in the late 1980s. The Malaysian economy was overheating in the 1990s as the massive FDI inflows saturated the labour market and infrastructure bottlenecks exploded into demand-supply deficits.

Also, intra-firm trade involving transnationals directly exporting assembled and processed items abroad accounted for a substantial amount of Malaysia's rigid manufacturing trade structure. The largely dollarized transnational-dominated manufacturing trade where demand is determined primarily in major markets prevented rising trade deficits from pushing the Ringgit down. The fallen Ringgit brought little change in investment demand in 1997. Unlike long-term currency depreciation that occurs gradually, which when faced with strong macroeconomic fundamentals can attract production from abroad, unstable currency movements have discouraged such inflows. The former is generally not possible as strong macroeconomic fundamentals will tend to improve currency values in the absence of government devaluation. In electronics, for example, foreign subsidiaries in Malaysia merely operate as assemblers and testers of manufactures whose key stages of production are located in developed economies. The 'currency crash' has helped lower production-costs in South-East Asia vis-à-vis North America and Europe but not against Japan and South Korea. Besides, because most major electronics firms have a major part of their lower value-added production stages in South-East Asia, the crisis has neither lowered import demand nor expanded export demand significantly. The recovery in the industry that emerged from 1997 is likely to attract further imports of intermediate items even though local currencies have fallen and Pacific Asia's demand has fallen. Since electronics is Malaysia's chief export, such sticky behaviour is likely to reduce the amount of additional foreign exchange earnings that can be gained from the devalued Ringgit.[2]

As FDI inflows began to slow down after 1996 and chronic current account deficits became unsustainable, news that loans and advances as a share of GNP at purchasers' value in Malaysia had risen from 133 per cent in 1992 to 185 per cent in 1995 aggravated market sentiments (computed from Bank Negara Malaysia, 1997). Although the Asian financial crisis began with the crash of the Bhat in 1997 its contagion became highly damaging only because Malaysia's economy had become vulnerable by then.

Whilst chronic current account deficits and an overvalued Ringgit had made the Malaysian economy vulnerable, the attack on the Baht in July 1997 provided the spark to ignite the crisis in Malaysia as the contagion spread through most of the regional economies. The Ringgit crashed from 2.45 to a dollar to exceed five Ringgit to a dollar by the end of 1997. The falling Ringgit dampened domestic demand, which seriously affected the property, automobile and the private healthcare market. The initial response by the government was to accept International Monetary Fund (IMF) structural adjustment prescriptions. Hence, interest rates and collateral for borrowing went up; due diligence exercise was introduced to evaluate the corporate governance fundamentals of large corporations facing serious cash flow problems. The conventional inter-bank interest rates for weekly deposits rose sharply from 6.4 per cent on 28 March 1997 to 25.5 per cent on 8 July 1997 just after the Baht crashed. The consequences were dire as the real economy contracted whilst several businesses went bust.

Capital controls

The Malaysian government took the bold step to depart from the recipe prescribed by the IMF to introduce capital controls on 2 September 1998. In doing so the government enjoyed the autonomy because its international reserves still exceeded its short-term debt service commitments and balance of payment deficits in foreign currencies. Unlike Indonesia, the Philippines, South Korea and Taiwan whose current account deficit and short-term debt service payments as a share of international reserves reached 138 per cent, 149 per cent, 251 per cent and 153 per cent respectively, Malaysia's was only 60 per cent at the end of 1996 (UNCTAD, 1997: Table 14).

The Keynesian package included the fixing of the Ringgit at MYR3.8 to a US$, and prohibition of external Ringgit accounts (Sheng, 2009). Once the easy flow of capital and fluctuations in the Ringgit was regulated, the government launched *Dana Modal* (Capital Fund) and *Dana Harta* (Asset Fund) to acquire non-performing loans, and lower interest rates in order to stimulate investment. The government intervened to lower interest rates, which fell to 6.3 per cent on 8 September 1998 following the introduction of capital controls and subsequently to 2.5 per cent on 13 August 1999. In addition, the government launched bank mergers to reduce their vulnerability to capital flights and lowered the collateral and forced banks to lend to small and medium size firms. Dana Modal and Dana Harta were also given the task by the government to restructure the loans and ownership portfolios of all firms facing NPL problems so as to prevent predatory acquisitions by others seeking to make quick financial gains from their vulnerable position.

A booming American economy and the lower exchange rates helped expand exports from Malaysia in 1997–1998 so that the Malaysian economy recovered by 1999. However, the Malaysian economy did not achieve high growth rates in early 2001 as it was already faced with de-industrialization owing to slow technological upgrading to compete in international markets. The share of manufacturing value added in GDP fell from 32 per cent in 2000 to 26 per cent in 2005 and 24 per cent in 2010 at a time when it was still dominated by low value-added activities, whilst it had not offered the structural fillip for upgrading in the primary and tertiary sectors. Hence, manufacturing did not achieve its full role as the engine of growth articulated by Young (1928) and Kaldor (1967).

Revival of deregulation

Liberalization returned from 2003 as the fixed exchange-rate was withdrawn and the government proceeded to liberalize the economy but without disturbing the special provisions targeted at the *Bumiputeras*. Emphasis was shifted from large firms to small and medium enterprises (SMEs) as the government targeted them for support through the Small and Medium Corporation (SME Corp) and the SME Bank following the launching of the Ninth Malaysian Plan in 2006. The Tenth Malaysian Plan of 2010 extended this further as a *Pemandu* ('Driver') minister was appointed in the Prime Minister's department to support the Corridor Development programmes. Typical of neoclassical prescriptions the government invested heavily in education and human capital development. Despite the forays of Khazanah Holdings into supporting high-technology companies, one of the government's sovereign wealth funds, none have yet to establish their competitiveness on the global stage.

The 2007–2008 global financial crisis attracted Keynesian-style policies again, as a huge fiscal stimulus was introduced to offset the crash in export demand but without capital controls. National infrastructure development support for SMEs was stepped up to expand domestic demand. Foreign workers from affected industries were retrenched.

Whilst ethnic policies returned as the government sought political support to remain in power, much of the economic policies targeted private-sector development, including through government-linked companies. Whilst Keynes (1936) had advocated intervention by governments to pursue full employment as a goal, he did not take the line of Schumpeter (1934) and Kalecki (1976) who called for intervention to be directed at stimulating the productive forces of the economies. Hence, whilst both John Maynard Keynes (1883–1946) and Joseph Alois Schumpeter (1883–1950) took the line that money and financial aggregates cannot be neutral and that they both highlight the crucial role of the credit market and the banks, it was the latter which went on to argue for the regulation of these aggregates to stimulate innovation. Hence, a major shortcoming of the Malaysian economy that slowed down government initiatives to stimulate structural change from low to high value-added activities was the lack of the Schumpeterian focus on the type of government intervention, although high-technology activities were promoted strongly from 1988, and especially from 1990 when the Action Plan for Industrial Technology Development (APITD) was launched. Tax deduction incentives for high-technology firms, double deduction benefits for approved R&D results, aggressive promotional efforts, technology prospecting and specially developed and subsidized infrastructure for high-tech firms have been created in Malaysia. Substantial investments were directed into the industrial and technological initiatives in the 1990s; e.g. MIMOS's wafer fabrication plants, Malaysian Industry-Government High Technology (MIGHT), the Malaysian Technology Development Corporation (MTDC), Second Industrial Master Plan (IMP2) and the Multi-media Super Corridor (MSC) activities.

Whilst such initiatives had important technological-deepening objectives serious coordination failures have restricted their viability. For example, the government's efforts to start several wafer-fabrication plants in the country have not succeeded because of a lack of a requisite policy to produce the human capital necessary and the basic research required in key semiconductor technologies.

Hence, Malaysia did not experience rapid structural transformation from low to high value-added activities as in South Korea and Taiwan. Given imperfections associated with labour markets – especially training and education involving long gestation-periods – and information asymmetries that typify underdeveloped markets, there is a strong need to stimulate state-business collaboration in creating and coordinating institutions to generate human resources for technological upgrading.

In Japan, Taiwan and South Korea, the share of engineers and R&D scientists and technicians rose quickly with the strong incentives offered for increasing their number. Malaysia lacked such human resource support to facilitate a rapid transition to higher-technology manufacturing. The share of technology-related human resources in Malaysia has been substantially lower than in the first-tier East Asian NIEs and developed economies (see the chapters by Das in this volume). Malaysia had four R&D scientists and technologists per thousand people in the period 1986–1990. Aggressive efforts in the 1990s to ameliorate the situation have come up against serious coordination problems (Malaysia, 1990, 1994; Rasiah, 1998d). By all measures, official technology transfer mechanisms have increased in Malaysia. The number of technology-transfer agreements in the manufacturing sector in Malaysia rose from 144 in 1975–1977 to 2,224 in 1993 (Rasiah, 1996b: Table 7).

The failure to upgrade has forced most of the manufacturing firms to hire cheap foreign labour to compete in low value-added operations. With such reserves exhausted, especially in the Western industrial corridor of Malaysia, firms began facing serious capacity expansion limits. In industries where changing production technologies have required more high-technology process tasks, as in microelectronics assembly and testing, demand for skilled workers grew even before labour shortages gripped the Malaysian economy (see Rasiah, 1996a, 2002). The premium for skilled workers has, thus, gone up in Malaysia, thereby accentuating a dual or segmented labour market. Especially cheap labour imports to Malaysia from neighbouring countries have held down unskilled workers' wages and slowed down labour-intensive firms' initiatives to upgrade their process technologies (see Edwards and Jomo, 1993; Rasiah, 1995). As a consequence, a dual-regime of multiskilled and casualized workforces coexists within and between firms (see Rasiah and Osman-Rani, 1997).

Conclusions

It can be seen that the Malaysian economy has been served by a rich vein of theories in Western Economics. However, government policy has been driven simultaneously by diverging economic arguments.

On the one hand, the government has largely followed a mixed monetary policy regime of keeping exchange rates largely flexible within a peg against a band of currencies since the link with the British pound was ended in the 1970s, though, the introduction of Keynesian-style capital controls in 1998–2006 saw the Ringgit pegged at MYR3.8 to the dollar. Whilst pursuing largely liberal macroeconomic policies, interest rates were also held down to support expansion of fiscal policies. On the other hand, industrial policies – both inward-oriented and outward-oriented – followed a mixed set of interventions for supporting domestic accumulation, as well as low tariffs to stimulate export-expansion.

Starting very much under free trade practices in the British Empire during colonialism, the independent government subsequently followed somewhat eclectic policies. On the one hand, the finance ministry followed Neoclassical policies that supported the market by offering tariff-free operations to export-oriented firms since the 1970s. However, the government intervened to keep inflation and exchange rate fluctuations low. The government also introduced incentives for exporting firms and those that participated in R&D activities, and regulated interest rates, as well as underwrote risks to spearhead recovery, and growth and structural change.

The small domestic market discouraged the introduction of blanket import-substitution policies across the country but selected heavy industries were aggressively promoted through such instruments from 1981. However, Malaysia's use of incentives, protective tariffs and grants only offered the carrots to the firms without the stick to enforce the discipline required for its translation into competitive exports. Hence, rent dissipation prevented government-supported national firms in the automotive and steel industries from reaching the technology frontier.

Liberal financial markets shortened the governments' reach in the economy by 1997. Whilst it helped reduce the undue and often destructive interventions by the government, it also opened the Malaysian economy to harmful predator roles by speculators. Against the advice of Keynesians, free capital and currency markets undermined the capacity of the Malaysian economy to stem large capital inflows and outflows over the period 1985–1997. Whilst the US monetarist guru and Nobel Laureate, Milton Friedman (1912–2006) had claimed (see Editorial, FEER, 1998) that the root cause of the Asian financial crisis was the government, the slow response of the government to stem volatile capital flight from private investors dragged the Malaysian economy into deflation. The IMF's call for squeezing credit without microeconomic scrutiny to shield efficient firms has worsened the situation. Fortunately, the introduction of capital controls in 1998–2006 helped stabilize the economy against volatile runs in the stock and currency markets.

The easing of capital controls and the focus on SMEs since 2006 was followed by a revival of liberal policies. However, such a policy framework, which is inevitable given Malaysia's integration into ASEAN and the global economy, did not attract significant FDI inflows and stimulate technological upgrading. This is a consequence of a lack of effective technological change, which is a consequence of an effective policy mechanism, which has not tied rents to performance. Hence, whilst Amsden (1989) argued that this 'carrot and stick' approach helped transform South Korea from a poor economy into a developed one in one generation, Malaysia has remained stuck among middle income countries. *Thus, any effort to revive structural change into high value-added economies would require an effective vetting, monitoring and appraisal mechanism to ensure that incentives and grants steer firms towards the technology frontier. On the one hand, this is important for macro-instruments to stimulate micro firm-level upgrading. On the other hand, macro-instruments should also produce the human capital through vocational and technical schools, and secondary and tertiary education to support upgrading in firms. Also, it is important to strengthen university-industry R&D linkages.*

Notes

1 See Amadeo (1996) for a lucid account of the management of exchange rates to restrict import explosion under conditions of liberalization.
2 Domestic demand for final electronics goods has fallen due to increased cost of imported items. Final domestic demand, however, constitutes a small share of overall electronics output in Malaysia and Thailand.
3 Nevertheless, considering the early stage of growth and rapid structural change, capital and total factor productivity measures should not be a major source of alarm, as they are generally associated with large initial outlays of lumpy investments.

References

Amadeo, E. J. (1996) 'The knife-edge of exchange rate-based stabilization: impact on growth, employment and wages', *UNCTAD Review*, 1–26.

Amsden, A. (1989) *Asia's Next Giant: South Korea and Late Industrialization*, New York, NY: Oxford University Press.

Ariff, M. (1991) *The Malaysian Economy: Pacific Connections*, Singapore: Oxford University Press.

Ariff, M. and Hill, H. (1985) *Export-oriented Industrialization: The ASEAN Experience*, New York, NY: HarperCollins, new edition published in 2010 by Routledge, London.

Bank Negara Malaysia (1997) *Quarterly Economic Bulletin*, Kuala Lumpur: Bank Negara.

Bauer, P. T. (1946) 'The working of rubber regulation', *Economic Journal*, 56: 391–414.

Bhagwati, J. and Krueger, A. (1973) 'Exchange control, liberalization and economic development', *American Economic Review*, 63: 419–427.

Doraisami, A. (1996) 'Export growth and economic growth: a reexamination of some time-series evidence of the Malaysian experience', *Journal of Developing Areas*, 30: 223–230.

Editorial, FEER (1998) 'Friedman: Asian miracle was real', *Far Eastern Economic Review*, 26 March: 1.

Edwards, C. B. and Jomo, K. S. (1993) 'Policy options for Malaysian industrialization', in K. S. Jomo (ed.), *Industrializing Malaysia: Policy, Performance and Prospects*, London: Routledge.

Gerschenkron, A. (1952) *Economic Backwardness in Historical Perspective: A Book of Essays*, Cambridge, MA: Belknap Press of Harvard University Press.

Johnson, C. (1982) *MITI and the Japanese Miracle*, Stanford, CA: Stanford University Press.

Jomo, K. S. (1996) *Southeast Asia's Misunderstood Miracle*, Boulder, CO: Westview Press.

Kaldor, N. (1967) 'Strategic factors in economic development', The Frank W. Pierce Memorial Lectures, Cornell University Press, Ithaca, NY.

Kalecki, M. (1976) *Essays on Developing Economies*, London: Harvester Press.

Keynes, J. M. (1936) *The General Theory of Employment, Interest and Money*, London: Macmillan.

Khan, M. (1998) 'An input-output framework of rents', mimeo.

Lee, C. and Wie, T. K. (2015) 'Indonesia and Malaysia', in V. Barnett (ed.), *Routledge Handbook of the History of Global Economic Thought*, London and New York, NY: Routledge, 316–314.

Lim, C. Y. (1967) *Economic Development of Modern Malaya*, Kuala Lumpur: Oxford University Press.

Lim, D. (1973) *Economic Growth and Development in West Malaysia 1947–1970*, Kuala Lumpur: Oxford University Press.

Lim, D. (ed.) (1983) *Further Readings on Malaysian Economic Development*, Kuala Lumpur: Oxford University Press.

Lin, S. Y. and Chung, T. F. (1995) 'Money markets in Malaysia', in D. C. Cole, H. S. Scott and P. A. Wellons (eds), *Asian Money Markets*, Cambridge, MA: Harvard Institute of International Development, 209–272.

Madan, B. K. (1953) *Economic Problems of Underdeveloped Countries in Asia*, Delhi: Indian Council of World Affairs.

Malaysia (1990) *Second Outline Perspective Plan*, Kuala Lumpur: Government Printers.

Malaysia (1994) *Mid-Term Review of the Sixth Malaysia Plan*, Kuala Lumpur: Government Printers.

Narayanan, S. and Lai, Y. W. (2002) 'Technological maturity and development without research: the challenge for Malaysian manufacturing', *Development and Change*, 31: 435–457.

Rasiah, R. (1988) 'The semiconductor industry in Penang: implications for NIDL theories', *Journal of Contemporary Asia*, 18: 24–46.

Rasiah, R. (1992) 'Foreign manufacturing investment', *Economic Bulletin for Asia Pacific*, 63: 63–77.

Rasiah, R. (1995) *Foreign Capital and Industrialization in Malaysia*, Basingstoke: Macmillan.

Rasiah, R. (1996a) 'Changing organisation of work in Malaysia's electronics industry', *Asia Pacific Viewpoint*, 37: 21–38.

Rasiah, R. (1996b) 'Institutions and innovations: moving towards the technology frontier in Malaysia's electronics industry', *Industry and Innovation*, 3: 79–102.

Rasiah, R. (1998a) 'Slowdown and bust: causes of the Southeast Asian financial crisis', *EIAS Briefing Paper* 98/01, European Institute of Asian Studies, Brussels.

Rasiah, R. (1998b) 'Export-manufacturing experience of Indonesia, Malaysia and Thailand: lessons for Africa', *UNCTAD Discussion Paper*, No. 137, Geneva.

Rasiah, R. (1998c) 'The Malaysian financial crisis: capital expansion, cronyism and contraction', *Journal of the Asia Pacific Economy*, 3: 358–378.

Rasiah, R. (1998d) 'Southeast Asia's ersatz capitalism: its dubious capacity to sustain growth', in K. S. Jomo (ed.), *Industrialising Southeast Asia*, London: Macmillan.

Rasiah, R. (2002) *Manufactured Exports, Employment, Skills, and Wages in Malaysia*, International Labour Organization: Geneva.

Rasiah, R. and Osman-Rani, R. H. (1997) 'Enterprise training and productivity in Malaysia's manufacturing sector', *IKMAS Working Paper*, No. 12, Bangi.

Reid, A. (1993) *Southeast Asia in the Age of Commerce, 1450–1680: Expansion and Crisis*, New Haven, CT: Yale University Press.

Salih, K. (1982) 'Urban dilemmas in Southeast Asia', *Singapore Journal of Tropical Geography*, 3: 147–161.

Salih, K. and Young, M. L. (1989) 'Changing conditions of labour in the semiconductor industry in Malaysia', *Labour and Society*, 14: 59–80.

Schumpeter, J. (1934) *Theory of Economic Development*, Cambridge, MA: MIT Press.

Schumpeter, J. A. (1943) *Capitalism, Socialism and Democracy*, New York: Harper.

Shari, I. (1979) 'Estimation of poverty lines and the incidence of poverty in Peninsular Malaysia, 1973', *The Philippine Economic Journal*, 18: 418–449.

Sheng, A. (2009) *From Asian to Global Financial Crisis: An Asian Regulator's View of Unfettered Finance in the 1990s and 2000s*, Cambridge: Cambridge University Press.

Silcock, T. H. and Ungku Aziz, A. (1953) 'Nationalism in Malaya', in W. L. Holland (ed.), *Asian Nationalism and the West*, New York, NY: Macmillan.

Snodgrass, D. (1980) *Inequality and Economic Development in Malaysia*, Kuala Lumpur: Oxford University Press.

Tham, S. Y and Kam, A. J. Y. (2014) 'Re-examining the impact of ACFTA on ASEAN's exports of manufactured goods to China', *Asian Economic Papers*, 2: 63–82.

Thorburn, J. T. (1976) 'Commodity prices and appropriate technology: some lessons from tin mining', *Journal of Development Studies*, 14, 35–52.

UNCTAD (1996) *World Investment Report*, Geneva: United Nations Conference for Trade and Development.

UNCTAD (1997) *Trade and Development Report*, Geneva: United Nations Conference for Trade and Development.

Ungku Aziz, A. (1964) 'Poverty and rural development in Malaysia', *Kajian Ekonomi Malaysia*, 1: 70–96.

Ungku Aziz, A. (1965) 'Poverty, proteins and disguised starvation', *Kajian Ekonomi Malaysia*, 2: 7–48.

Young, A. A. (1928) 'Increasing returns and economic progress', *The Economic Journal*, 38: 527–542.

7 The diffusion of Western Economics in the newly industrialized economies

Hong Kong, Singapore and Taiwan

Dilip K. Das

Introduction

The focus of this chapter is the three 'Newly Industrialized Economies' (NIEs) of East Asia, namely *Hong Kong SAR*, *Singapore* and *Taiwan*. In terms of size, the first two are island city-states, whilst the third one is a small island-economy. The Republic of Korea (hereinafter Korea) is the fourth Asian NIE, which has been excluded – because it is the focus of another contribution in this book (see the chapter by Hong in this volume). The four Asian NIEs and their business systems remained the most admired economies for rapid and sustained growth by theorists and policy-makers for many decades (see Nolan *et al.*, 2016). In terms of growth, 'Developing Economies' in Africa, Latin America, South Asia and West Asia were, however, no match for the NIEs. The NIEs, and other dynamic economies of Asia, have presently become the principal growth-drivers of the global economy, contributing *two-fifths* of total economic growth (World Bank (WB), 2015a).

Until 1960, all the four NIEs were desperately poor and low-income economies that displayed little promise of future rapid growth. They were often cited as examples of 'hopeless' economic cases. They had little in the name of natural resources and were believed to be condemned to perpetual poverty. This scenario soon underwent a dramatic transformation. During the 1970s and 1980s, before the *People's Republic of China* (hereinafter *China*) took off and became the most rapidly growing large economy globally (see Warner, 2014), the four Asian NIEs were the most lauded economies for their economic dynamism and textbook-perfect economic performance as well as measured and well-thought-out Macroeconomic policy frameworks. They are also extolled for stability in Social, Political and Macroeconomic environment. Adjectives like 'miracle' economies were freely used for them (see the earlier chapter by Das in this volume).

Their pragmatic use of the principles of *Neoclassical* Economics was noticed and appreciated by the academic community (see Wade, 1992; Hermes, 1997; Das, 2015). For the most part, these economies relied on market signals for resource-allocation. However, concomitantly governments went beyond the pure Neoclassical Economics prescriptions of providing public goods, like infrastructure, maintaining law and order and providing legislature. Government, or state, played a crucial role in economic growth process of these economies, which stood out as something of a contradiction to the principles of Neoclassical Economics. Hong Kong was, however, an exception in this regard.

Spectacularly rapid growth in the four NIEs focused the attention of analysts on the relevant lessons that could be learned for the other developing countries. The terminology devised for this group of high-growth performers – included terms like 'Neoclassical', 'Heterodox', 'New Interventionist', 'Revisionist' and 'Structuralist' Economics. Approbation of the economic success of the NIEs motivated a huge amount of research and spawned large literature, enough to fill a library. Several writings of this period became renowned in the academic literature and they are still widely alluded to in the corpus of work on 'Development Economics' (see Hughes, 1988; Amsden, 1989; Haggard, 1990; Krueger, 1995).

The NIEs defied all the early dismal prognostications about them and achieved high and sustained GDP growth-rates, as well as rapid industrialization. According to the statistics provided by the *World Development Indicators* (WB, 2015b), two of them are presently high-income economies. Gross national income per capita in Hong Kong SAR was US$40,320 in current dollars in 2014 and that in Singapore US$55,150. Rising from their egregiously impoverished social-economic levels, these economies became comparable to the advanced economies like Japan (US$42,200), Canada (US$51,690) and the United States (US$55,200) in terms of gross national income per capita. This remarkable economic achievement came about in an astonishing short time-span of two generations. According to the *World Economic Outlook Database* (IMF, 2015) gross national income per capita for Taiwan in 2014 was US$21,572. However, the National Statistics of the Republic of China, the same place, put the corresponding figure at US$23,298. These statistics indisputably reflect their unexcelled economic performance. Few developing economies of that period could match it.

The question, what kind of economic strategies did these economies peruse and where did they learn these Macroeconomic policies and Neoclassical Economics concepts?, has justly intrigued many academic scholars and policy mandarins. As Economics was not a 'native' science for this group of small countries, they arguably learned their Western concepts from the outside. The principal objective of this chapter is thus to determine the sources of these successful and efficacious ideas and policies in Economics.

Historical background

General

Now, there are abiding *historical similarities* between the two NIE city-states. *Hong Kong* comprises the islands of Hong Kong, Kowloon Peninsula and the New Territories. It is a coastal island located off the southern coast of China and used to be a natural port for the Guangdong province of Southern China. Until the beginning of the nineteenth century, these islands were sparsely populated.

They were fishing-villages, popular with travellers and pirates. During the infamous Opium Wars (1839–1842 and 1856–1860) in the middle of the nineteenth century, the British used Hong Kong as a naval-base. At the end of the first Opium War, the Treaty of Nanking as it was then called (1842) ceded the territory to Britain. In 1860–1861, Kowloon and Stonecutter islands were also added to Hong Kong. In 1898, Britain acquired Hong Kong on a 99-year lease from China. By this time, Hong Kong had become an important port for China's regional and global trade. It developed rapidly as a trading centre and as a burgeoning *entrepôt*.

The Second World War turned out to be a period of devastation. The Japanese bombed Kowloon and forced the British to lay down their weapons in 1941 but after the Japanese surrender in 1945 the British reclaimed the territory and Hong Kong once again began growing as a major trading-centre. At the time of the Communist Civil War (1946–1949) in China, thousands of people fled to Hong Kong from the Mainland. The colony was forced to develop domestic industries. In the 1950s and 1960s, this constant influx of people from China as well as Chinese capital led to development of light manufacturing industries. In 1984, the British reached an agreement with China that Hong Kong would revert to Chinese governance in 1997.

In 1961, Hong Kong's per capita income was a mere US$410. This is when the Hong Kong economy launched into robust and sustained growth (see Sung and Wang, 1998). Accumulation of physical and human capital and technological progress were among the sources of rapid growth. After it reverted and became a part of China in 1997, it began to be known as Hong Kong SAR, standing for 'Special Administrative Region' of China. This would be a *transformational* point and at this juncture Hong Kong had emerged as one of the world's premier trade, business, financial and education centres and a major transportation hub.

Singapore has had a similar history. The British East India Company (1600–1874) began turning it into a South-East Asian trading-perch in 1819. At that time, it was only a strategically located and sparsely populated island. The port-city of Singapore was taken over by the British after the British–Dutch treaty of 1824. It remained a British outpost from this point in time. It was declared an 'open' and 'free' port, free of duty. No taxation and little restriction over trade were its unique characteristics. Its status as a 'free port' provided Singapore a crucial advantage over other erstwhilst colonial ports like Jakarta and Manila. Like Hong Kong, it emerged as a busy trading-centre and as a flourishing *entrepôt*. European trading firms set up merchant-houses in Singapore. The British firms in particular had a large presence. Singapore became a cosmopolitan trading entity, with a host of active Arab, Armenian, Chinese, Indian, Jewish, American and European traders. A large number of Chinese traders were also well-established. They were prominent as middle-men between the Europeans and the Asians.

The Japanese army invaded Singapore in 1942 – this and the Second World War destroyed the economy. When it ended, Singapore reverted to British control, indeed it was granted more self-government than before the War. In 1959, Singapore became independent. Not sure of the new People's Action Party (PAP) Government, many British investors fled the city-state. At this time, Singapore was a large British naval-base. Its economy was limited to trade in commodities like rubber and palm oil brought from neighbouring Malaysia and Sumatra, processed and re-exported to Europe. For a short while, Singapore merged with the Federation of Malaysia (see the chapter by Rasiah in this volume). It separated from it in August 1965 and became an independent republic.

At the time of independence, per capita income of Singapore was close to US$300 and it suffered from inadequate infrastructure, limited capital, severe unemployment and widespread labour unrest and acute housing shortages. Small number of local industries produced low-end commerce for domestic consumption. Singapore was a poor but developing economy (Singapore Economic Development Board (SEDB), 2015). The first response of the government was to form the Jurong Industrial Estate, the first of many industrial estates, and establish the Economic Development Board (EDB) with a capital of US$100 million. The latter was set up to attract foreign capital. These were the first two steps to launch industrial development. Factories producing textiles and garments, toys, wood products and wigs were set up, along with those manufacturing, labour-intensive products. Realizing that the domestic entrepreneur class was small and inexperienced and capital scarce, the government regarded it important to attract foreign capital from the advanced countries to establish export-oriented industries. With that, creation of a modern service sector, based on banking and financial services, was also given a high priority. International trade was not only promoted as a preferred strategy but there also was a remarkable degree of continuity in Singaporean trade-policy over almost five decades (Peebles and Wilson, 2002).

The island of Taiwan was colonized by the Dutch in the seventeenth century. Han Chinese began immigrating into Taiwan from Fujian and Guangdong provinces of China. After the first Sino-Japanese War of 1885, it became a part of Japan. It served as a base for the Japanese colonial expansion into Asia during the Second World War. The Republic of China (ROC), led by Kuomintang (KMT), later referred to as the Guomindang, took control of Taiwan after the War. When the Communist Civil War (1946–1949) ended, the ROC Government under KMT withdrew to Taiwan. It was led by General Chiang Kai-shek (1887–1975) and was run as a single-party state for four decades, until democratic reforms began in the 1980s.

In the 1950s, the agrarian economy of Taiwan was in a shambles and it was heavily dependent on the American aid. With American help, a land reform agenda was implemented, which restricted the size of the land-holdings. It thus enhanced income equality among the rural population. Per capita income of Taiwan in 1952 was US$890 (see Lau, 2012). Rapid GDP growth and industrialization began in the late 1950s. At this point, small manufacturing enterprises began producing products for domestic consumption and export.

Hong Kong

Industrialization of Hong Kong began in the 1950s. Entrepreneurs fleeing from Shanghai brought with them both the skills to organize manufacturing, as well as capital. They took the initiative to establish cotton spinning-mills. Entrepreneurs from Shanghai utilized the refugees from China as their work-force and turned Hong Kong into a manufacturing centre (Krause, 1987). Textiles laid the foundation of Hong Kong's industrial development. Its diversification began in the 1960s into apparel, plastics, electrical appliances and other labour-intensive products for export (Schenk, 2008). Over the 1960s and 1970s, the Hong Kong economy expanded at a robust pace, averaging 9 per cent. During the 1980s, average growth rate slowed to 6.5 per cent (Goodstadt, 1995) and declined further to 3.5 per cent in the 1990s (see Sung and Wang, 1998).

At the initial stages, small- and medium-sized enterprises (SMEs) dominated industrialization. Low taxes, lax employment laws and promotion of free trade were among the principal support policies followed by the government. The textile and apparel industry became highly competitive and internationally successful. So much so that Hong Kong had to adopt voluntary export restraints. The manufacturing activity too was highly competitive, but it moved out to the mainland during the 1980s and 1990s. There was a *pari passu* surge in investment and growth of the services sector. This step led to a dramatic structural transformation of the economy.

Although the Hong Kong Government did not engage in active economic or industrial policy planning, it did not follow complete laissez-faire either. It provided strong support for infrastructure development, land reclamation and public housing. Industrial townships were built for housing hordes of immigrants from China. Government assistance was made available for industrial development and employment generation. Due to direct and indirect assistance from the government the Hong Kong manufacturing sector had the advantage of low cost (Schenk, 2008). In addition, since the 1950s, an ambitious public education programme had been launched. Primary and secondary schooling was made extensively available. By the early 1970s, education was made free for children up to the age of 15.

The principal economic strategies adopted by Hong Kong during this period were those based on Neoclassical Economics. They were essentially free-market economic concepts stressing that countries prosper through trade. Hong Kong – like Singapore and Taiwan – convincingly adopted an outward-oriented, or export-led, growth strategy and emerged a successful trading economy. Neighbouring Japan's successful post-War policies had a 'demonstration-effect' and the industrialists and entrepreneurs expected comparable outcome by adopting and promoting the same growth strategy (see Yagi's chapter later in this volume). Free flow of goods and capital was promoted as a major goal. Consequently, unlike the other developing economies Hong Kong did not suffer from the scarcity of foreign-exchange. Unlike other developing economies, Hong Kong was able to amass a good deal of it to import investment goods and make large productive investments.

A relevant important policy in Hong Kong was that as the price-system in Hong Kong – like in Singapore and Taiwan – worked fairly well, the direction of investment flows remained logical. Hong Kong was able to invest in the appropriate sectors. They reflected the 'comparative advantage' of the Hong Kong economy. The early investment went into low-technology, labour-intensive sectors. After an exhaustive survey of the developing economies, the *World Development Report* of 1987 had concluded that growth in income per capita was the highest in the developing economies that pursued outward-oriented policies – and low in those that followed inward-oriented policies. The same was found to be true for growth in total GDP and value-added in manufacturing, which reflected the efficiency of investment. These three countries also followed a relatively market-friendly approach to economic growth. Hong Kong's unique economic policy characteristics were its almost unrestricted free market and free trade. Hong Kong, like the other NIEs, did not have an interventionist government.

The manufacturing industries in Hong Kong – as in Singapore and Taiwan – paid a great deal of attention to technology-transfer and absorption and research and development (R&D). Consequently, they were able to move up the value-added ladder. Advance countries of the West and Japan were the principal sources of technology. To create a modern and competitive economy, as well as quicken GDP growth rate, the import of 'on-the-shelf' technology was methodologically done. This demarche was one of the important things that these economies learned from the rapid post-War economic achievements of Japan, as well as of the advanced economies of the West. Post-War success of Japan had a veritable 'demonstration effect' as noted earlier on Hong Kong and the other NIEs. The same applies for a 'business-friendly' government in Hong Kong, although State intervention is not one of the essential characteristics of Hong Kong's economic growth strategy.

Singapore

Singapore's status as a 'free port' and proximity to valuable natural resources and global shipping-lanes made Singapore a relatively prosperous city-state in the nineteenth century. Its economic success was halted by the Japanese invasion during the Second World War. The Japanese occupation was brutal and destroyed Singapore's economy. In 1945, the city-state of Singapore was war-ravaged and impoverished. When the British returned, they began rebuilding Singapore. Helped by new investment, Singapore became a regional focal point for airlines and telecommunications. It again began to emerge as the pivotal port between Asia and Europe.

Like the post-War Japan, Singapore's growth model was based on the export of initially low-technology, labour-intensive manufactured products to the world markets. This stage was followed by a gradual move up the technology and value-added ladder as comparative advantage shifted. High-technology manufacturing and services were the next to be developed. This model of growth was not only akin to that of Japan but also the other NIEs (see the chapter by Das earlier in this volume). Goods and capital were allowed a free flow. However, unlike Hong Kong, Singapore's economic development was substantially State-directed and also included a managed-float currency regime. Both of these were successful Japanese policy instruments (Peebles and Wilson, 2002). During the post-War period, the Ministry of International Trade and Industry (MITI) and the Ministry of Finance (MoF) played a uniquely proactive role in the rapid economic growth of Japan. Many of these economic strategies were learned by Singapore policy-makers.

Rapid industrialization gained momentum in the 1960s. By the end of the decade, manufacturing had become a lead sector, propelling economic growth. In the early 1970s, Singapore successfully developed the domestic financial market and offshore financial market. By this time it had also achieved full employment. Based on Neoclassical Economics, Singapore was known to have followed prudent fiscal and monetary policies. It resulted in budgetary surpluses. Singapore carefully managed growth of its exports despite real appreciation of its currency. It was also able to accumulate huge foreign exchange reserves (see Peebles and Wilson, 2002). Although Singapore's economy diversified out of manufacturing for exports and into high-value services, it continued to remain firmly State-directed. As in Japan, government institutions remained active in influencing the direction of the economy in Singapore. Over the past two decades, Taiwan has liberalized both economically and politically along many dimensions, which has reduced the State's role in the economic life. This did not happen in Singapore.

During the early phase of rapid economic growth, formulation and efficacious implementation of industrial policy, beyond market-friendly rules of property rights, was one of the important reasons behind rapid growth of Singapore and Taiwan. They followed the prescriptions of Friedrich List (1789–1846) who had been influential in both Japan and China emphasizing the role of the State (see the chapter by Liu later in this volume). Governments led a push to exports of manufactures. The popular wisdom of the so-called 'Washington Consensus' was not accepted by the policy-makers in these economies (see Wade, 2003). Their success is often cited as a reproach against the doctrine.

Modern Singapore is today respected as a leading Asian hub of technology-transfer, innovation and entrepreneurship. It has constantly refined its technology-transfer and innovation strategy, which resulted in tangible outcomes. Technology-transfer and absorption supported and sustained its robust GDP growth, a lesson learned from Japan. Like the other NIEs, it has a business-friendly government, which is another concept that these economies learned from Japan's post-War success. This included a pro-business tax regime and a wide range of flexible financial schemes. In terms of business and financial regulatory structures, Singapore is widely rated as the easiest place to do business. It is also known for having a skilled domestic labour-force and easy entry of foreign talent. Consequently, it was able to create an ever-expanding network of free trade. Its investment guarantee agreements gave Singapore-based businesses preferential and safe access to international markets. These innovative business strategies were developed by Singapore policy-makers and were subsequently imitated by others.

With the advent of the knowledge-based era in the twenty-first century, the government promoted a new business-model to make the industrial services sectors perform at a higher efficiency level and remain globally competitive. Based on its idiosyncratic circumstances, some of the modern policy concepts were developed by the Singapore Government policy-makers. Three of them are prominent: *First*, they devised their own state-directed immigration strategy. *Second*, they nurtured and supported dominance of multinational corporations (MNCs) and government-linked corporations in several important sectors of the economy. They developed an 'Entrepreneurial Economy' and promoted a strong private-sector. Whilst it is admired as an entrepreneurial hub, Singapore has not however developed large domestic private sector corporations like Acer, Hutchinson or Samsung. *Third*, Singapore's economy is less integrated into the Chinese economy than that of the other South-East Asian economies and the NIEs.

Taiwan

During the early stage of economic growth Taiwan was able to export agricultural products whether processed and unprocessed and earn foreign exchange for domestic investment. Rapid industrialization began in the late 1950s from humble origins. SMEs produced cheap manufactured products for export. In the 1960s, like the other NIEs, Taiwan adopted an outward-oriented economic strategy and started producing low-technology, labour-intensive, products and exporting them at competitive prices. The Classical principle of 'comparative advantage' was applied appropriately. The export drive over the 1960–1980 period fully opened the economy (Tsai, 1999). At this stage, the production technology was simple and rudimentary. However, by the 1990s Taiwan exported capital- and skill-intensive products, using high-technology. The government took a leaf out of the experience of Japan and encouraged private enterprises to import raw materials, semi-finished products and machinery to produce exportable products as well as consumer goods. The latter could replace imported goods in the domestic markets. This enabled Taiwan to establish a foundation for the development of industries producing domestic necessities. The government proactively encouraged selected industrial development by providing tax incentives to entrepreneurs (see Li, 1988).

At the next stage, during the 1970s and 1980s, it adopted the strategy of moving up the technology ladder in a concerted manner and creating an export processing economy. Again the principle of comparative advantage was put to profitable use by the policy-makers in Taiwan. As comparative advantage declined in the labour-intensive, low value-added products, industries moved up the capital- and technology-intensive sectors. These products were competitively produced and exported. This strategy led to Taiwan's rapid growth over the future years. As noted above, policy-makers in Taiwan learned many of their development strategies from Japan. They modified them to suit their distinctive requirements.

Taiwan also followed business-friendly policies and, like Hong Kong and Singapore, it is considered a country where it is easy to do business. Taiwan succeeded in developing its SME sector well. SMEs were bound together by flexible sub-contracting networks. They accounted for 90 per cent of all business enterprises in Taiwan. This was yet another beneficial lesson from Japan (see San, 2013). Taiwan's SMEs were competitive in international markets. Also, with the passage of time they moved up the value-added and technology ladder. Establishing Hsinchu [*sic*] Science-based Industrial Park facilitated the growth of technology-based industries. Like the other NIEs, the manufacturing sectors, both SMEs and large industries, continuously moved up and produced high-technology products and competitively sold in the world market place. Remaining competitive in the global markets was given high policy priority (see Li, 1988).

To further strengthen the SME sector, in the mid-1990s, the government promulgated the Statute for Small and Medium Enterprise Development to upgrade the SME sector. Assistance and encouragement was provided to import advance technology and upgrade industries. Likewise R&D and manpower training was supported under various government schemes. Government was market-friendly and continuously tried to improve investment environment. Like Singapore, a knowledge-based economy was promptly developed with the help of the government.

Discussion

Whilst the three NIEs discussed above followed comparable strategies of economic growth, there were differences based on their individual circumstances, policy preferences and domestic proclivities. What were their *commonalities*?

These resource-poor economies followed distinct export-led growth strategies and their monetary and fiscal policies were prudently conservative. Inflation-rates were cautiously restrained. Exchange rates were not allowed to be overvalued. Governments paid a lot of attention to infrastructure development as well as that of the educational system. In a short time the educational attainment of the labour-force improved markedly. Also, it rapidly shifted from agriculture to industrial employment. Saving and investment rates in these economies remained exceedingly high. The outward-oriented development strategy in these economies was squarely based on the principle of comparative advantage, a theory pioneered by the Classical economists like Adam Smith (1723–1790) and David Ricardo (1772–1823). The 'Heckscher–Ohlin' theory is, in its modern, or Neoclassical, version, one that focuses on 'factor-endowments' and is sometimes called the '$2 \times 2 \times 2$' model (see Das, 2015).

Many of their economies policies were based on Neoclassical Economics principles. Although as noted earlier in Singapore and Taiwan governments played a decisive role in economic policy-making and business life. They had formulated well-thought-out industrial development policies, which went counter to the grain of Neoclassical Economic Thought. Additionally, policy-makers in these three economies were highly influenced by the post-War economic achievements of Japan. Little wonder that a great deal of economic learning took place from the efficacious economic strategies adopted by Japan, in particular the export-led growth model. Many of the Japanese economic concepts were *adapted* before being adopted by planners in Hong Kong, Singapore and Taiwan. They were also improvised and refined in a pragmatic and effective manner.

That being said, the ingenuity of these societies, particularly the economic and business policy-makers, must not be underrated. Whilst they learned from the experiences of Japan, entire credit for their success cannot be justly given to Japan. These societies proved that they were enterprising, sensible, perspicacious, meticulous and goal-oriented in devising their own economic growth and macroeconomic frameworks and competitive business strategies. Whilst their initial learning process was assisted by what they observed the Japanese policy-makers do, they themselves were responsible in selecting which strategies to choose, adopt and how to refine and further develop them. First-rate education systems in these societies made refinement and implementation of economic strategies feasible.

Being essentially 'Sinic' societies, they were all influenced by 'Confucian' principles and therefore advancement and upgradation of education systems was constantly given a high priority by policy-makers in these countries. According to Confucius, no society can develop economically unless its population receives proper education (see Warner, 2014). Western education, including teaching of Economics, in Hong Kong and Singapore can be traced back to around 1900. This initiative was taken by the colonial governments in these city-states. In Taiwan, Western education was started during the Japanese colonial rule (1895–1945). The two city-states benefitted more from the efforts of the colonial governments' efforts than other countries like India and Malaysia, where the colonial governments had made similar endeavours. In the latter half of the last century, these countries sent a large number of their bright graduates for higher education to the best universities in Europe and North America. In particular, the doctoral programmes in these universities were heavily populated by students from the NIEs.

Accentuation on higher education naturally had a decisive and discernible impact on the economic policy-making and implementation in these countries. Governments in these countries consciously employed a great deal of their resources and efforts in creating an excellent education system, comparable to those in the advanced Western countries. Consequently, many of these countries have become high-scorers in the well-known OECD Program for International Student Assessment (PISA). The OECD began conducting this exercise in the mid-1990s. Under the PISA program, reliable data on knowledge and skills of students and performance of the educational systems are collected and compared. Higher growth rate leads to better educational system, in qualitative and quantitative terms and vice versa. This is a 'circular' relationship (see Bils and Klenow, 2000).

Both Hong Kong and Singapore have succeeded in developing world-class universities. They were modelled first on the British universities and then on the most prestigious universities in the US and followed their best traditions. They have now lost their 'British' character, more or less. The top two Asian universities in the global university ranking Quacquarelli Symonds (QS) for 2015/2016 are both from Singapore. They are Nanyang Technological University (13th) and the National University of Singapore (12th). The two major universities in the HKSAR, the University of Hong Kong and HKIST and University of Hong Kong, were 28th and 30th in the same global ranking.

The Economics Department of the National University of Singapore (NUS) is one of the largest in Asia. Qualitatively it is widely regarded as one of the finest. What was remarkable about it is that it is staffed by international scholars, both from other parts of Asia as well as Europe and North America. The same is true for the universities in Hong Kong. They built Economics departments of compelling quality with international scholars of high repute. Cambridge-based James A. Mirrlees, Nobel Laureate for 1995, was employed as a Visiting Professor by the Chinese University of Hong Kong. They offered high salaries and large research budgets to world famous economic professors and attracted them to their universities.

Economics became a highly popular subject among students in the latter half of the last century in the two city-states. As they had embarked on rapid industrialization and growth, Economics and business education was generally considered a practical and useful discipline by students. Lee Kuan Yew (1923–2015), the architect of rapid economic progress in Singapore, had endorsed and played up the direct relevance and usefulness of Economics and engineering education for the rapid development of the society. A clear and direct advantage of emphasis on Economics education was creation of a cadre of bureaucrats who were able to significantly contribute to industrialization drive and nation-building efforts in these economies. Many of the Economics graduates from these universities worked as top advisers to senior politicians and contributed significantly to the corporate world.

In the latter half of the last century Hong Kong and Singapore focused on creating business schools. Emphasis on business school education increased in the last three decades. Significant resources were deployed in establishing world-class business schools. Consequently both Hong Kong and Singapore now have high-quality AACSB-accredited business schools, ranked highly by *The Economist*. Singapore also has a modern and resourceful management university, called Singapore Management University (SMU) headed by a European Director.

Taiwan was a Japanese colony during 1895–1945 and the colonial government imposed the Western-style education system on Taiwan. It emphasized on learning modern skill in the same manner as in the West. With launching of four institutions, modern universities were started in the 1920s. Taihoku Imperial

University was the first university to be established in 1928. When the Japanese departed in 1945, Taiwan was the most educated society of Asia. In 1945, when Kuomintang (KMT) came, the Taihoku Imperial University was renamed as the National Taiwan University (NTU). Other institutions were also reorganized and renamed. In the 1960s, in response to the new global trends in higher education, Taiwan thoroughly reorganized its higher education institutions. Also, during the decade of 1960s, their number increased from 12 to 69. Educational reforms were made bearing in mind the targets of rapid economic growth in the island economy. The higher education in Taiwan was promoted to serve the economic developmental goals. Economics and engineering were considered areas of high priority and generally bright students opted for these disciplines. At this point the private sector entered the education sector and private sector institutions began competing with the government institutions. Curriculum standards were carefully watched by the government for quality (Chen, 2010; Chou and Ching, 2012; Chou, 2015).

NTU produced the important political and economic decision-makers in Taiwan. It has a large and prestigious Economics department. In response to changing trends and global competition, in 1995 higher education in Taiwan was reorganized again. Conscious attempt was made to incorporate the globalization processes into the educational system. Education was sensitized to cross-cultural interactions. International student exchanges were promoted. Economics and business education were the preferred disciplines because of intensifying international competition in business and economics arenas. The same was true for science and technology education. Universities were called on to play a role in knowledge-based economic development and were required to produce suitable human resources for running a modern globalized economy (see Chou, 2015).

When Hong Kong, Singapore and Taiwan started on their growth paths, not having modern technology was a serious and persistent bottleneck for them. Policy-makers were cognizant of technological backwardness of their respective economies and that pressing efforts were needed to make up for this lacuna. Building a technological foundation of their economies was one of the first important steps. At an early stage in their growth strategy, these economies became highly committed to technology-transfer and absorption of modern technology as well as constant upgradation of technology. They imported on-the-shelf technology in a methodical manner from the Western countries. Trade and foreign direct investment (FDI) were the other principal channels of technology-transfer. For the purpose of technology absorption and advancement, governments consciously promoted science, technology and engineering education. Sending students abroad for higher education in science and technology related disciplines and learning skills from abroad that cannot be learned locally was made a standard practice. Some scholars believe that steady technology-transfer and moving from producing low-technology manufactured products to high-technology products and services became the principal driver of growth for these economies (Lau, 2015). Significant investment in industrial R&D was another important policy concern, which these economies learned from Japan and the

Western economies. With the passage of time, all three of them went on increasing investment in R&D.

Globalization supported their endeavours to import and absorb advance foreign technologies in a cost-effective manner and develop a domestic skill base related to the newly absorbed technologies, so did the development of a Western technological education system and the practice of sending students abroad to prominent American and European engineering colleges for higher degrees as it made their growth productivity-based. They benefitted from the Neoclassical Economics concept of technological advancement contributing to total 'factor-productivity' (TFP). They successfully telescoped the technology-transfer process. Technologies that the Western countries took several decades to develop, these economies were able to do it in one. This track is known as the 'late-comer advantage'.

Hong Kong and Singapore adopted 'free trade' at an early stage. It was facilitated by the fact that they were city-states. Due to their *entrepôt status*, their trade volume is much larger than their GDP. However, Taiwan and the other dynamic economies of East Asia constrained their trade liberalization. Their trade strategy was influenced by the capacity of the domestic firms to compete with imports from the international markets, precisely on the lines suggested by List in the mid-1840s.

Many of the concepts from Neoclassical Economics successfully adopted by these NIEs also included getting the 'basics' right (WB, 1993). 'Free-market' economic thinkers, like Friedrich Hayek (1899–1992), were influential here, particularly in Taiwan but there was not much evidence of Marxist Economics in public policy (see the later chapter on Hayek and China in this volume). The 'basics' here implies keeping inflation low and stable, the exchange-rate competitive and not letting the budget deficit and trade deficit become chronic weaknesses of the economy – a common weakness in developing countries. It also includes keeping relative prices of traded goods closer to international prices. In the same vein, these economies also made heavy and sustained investment in social infrastructure which directly supported their rapid GDP growth.

Singapore and Taiwan are cited as the successful cases of Statist, or Listean, development strategy and formulation of industrial policy (Wade, 1990, 2015). Their success was essentially due to well-designed industrial policies involving strategies of industrial targeting by 'getting prices wrong', 'picking winners', even 'creating winners' (see Tsai, 1997). This is the oft-cited 'Revisionist' argument of rapid growth and industrialization in the NIEs. Both Wade (1990) and Lee (1994) documented extensive use of tariffs, quantitative restrictions, fiscal incentives and targeted credit policies by these governments. During the post-War period, after seeing the success of NIEs, several other economies made use of these strategies. Although once questionable and controversial, statist and interventionist policies achieved a new respectability after the Global Financial Crisis (GFC) of 2007–2009.

The economic policy learning-process for these economies was also influenced by the supranational institutions and US Treasury. In the first half of the

1990s, these economies began to be pushed towards liberalization by the US Treasury, the International Monetary Fund, the World Bank, the General Agreement on Tariffs and Trade (GATT) and the OECD. It was a part of these institutions' clear preference for the so-called 'Washington Consensus'. These economies did liberalize, particularly vis-à-vis financial flows. Many believe that this led to the over-indebtedness of several Asian economies and eventually to the Asian crisis in 1997–1998 (see Wade, 2003).

Conclusions

This chapter has dealt with three NIEs of Asia, Hong Kong, Singapore and Taiwan but excludes the fourth, Korea. From acute poverty and serious economic disarray in 1960, this sub-group of economies emerged as the fastest growing economies of the 1970s and 1980s. During that period, all three of them were regarded as the 'miracle' economies. They pursued well-thought-out and effectual macroeconomic policy frameworks. Their present per capita national incomes are comparable with those of many advanced economies. With the other dynamic economies of Asia, they emerged as the principal drivers of the global economy.

In this chapter, we focused on the question: What kind of economic strategies did these NIE economies peruse and where did they learn these macroeconomic policies and Neoclassical economic concepts? Many of their policies, as we have seen, were based on Neoclassical Economics principles. Although as noted earlier, in Singapore and Taiwan governments played a decisive role in economic policy-making and business life. They had formulated well-thought-out industrial development policies, which went counter to the grain of Neoclassical Economic thinking.

In short, Hong Kong was a sparsely populated island in the early nineteenth century. It had been a fishing-village, popular with travellers and pirates. In the mid-nineteenth century the British used it as a naval base and it was acquired by Britain for a 99-year lease. By this time, Hong Kong had become an important port for China's regional and global trade. It developed rapidly as a trading centre, as a burgeoning *entrepôt*. At the time of the Civil War in China, thousands of Chinese fled to Hong Kong. The colony was forced to develop domestic industries in the 1950s and 1960s. This was Hong Kong's launch into rapid and sustained export-oriented growth. Similarly, Singapore was a strategically located and sparsely populated island. It was taken over by the British in the mid-nineteenth century and declared an open and free port, free of duty. Like Hong Kong, it emerged as a busy trading-centre, with flourishing *entrepôt*. After the War, economic activity in Singapore was limited. It was a large British naval port and there was some low-end commerce. After independence Singapore began taking concerted measures to grow, attract foreign capital and develop labour-intensive manufacturing sector. Singapore also pursued outward-oriented growth strategy. Taiwan was originally colonized by the Dutch and became Japanese after the Sino-Japanese war of the late nineteenth century. The ROC took control of Taiwan after the War. When the Communist Civil War ended, the ROC Government under KMT withdrew to Taiwan. Initial economic reforms in Taiwan were the result of American initiative. Industrialization endeavours were started in the 1950s. At this point, small manufacturing enterprises began producing products for domestic consumption and export.

Industrialization of Hong Kong, as we saw, had begun with the advent of entrepreneurs and refugees from Shanghai in 1950. The textile industry laid its foundation. Diversified labour-intensive manufacturing for export caught momentum in the 1960s, which was the start of a robust growth period. SMEs dominated industrialization. They were supported by low taxes, lax employment laws and promotion of free trade. Consequently the textile industry became highly competitive. Whilst the government in Hong Kong was not directly interventionist, it was not completely Smithian laissez-faire either. Economic strategies adopted during this period were essentially based on neoclassical economic principles. There was a strong and undeniable commitment to an outward-oriented export-led growth. Technology-transfer, absorption and upgradation as well as R&D were paid a lot of attention. They were instrumental in the upward movement on the value-added ladder of the industrial sector as well as rapid GDP growth. This was one of the important lessons that Hong Kong, and the other NIEs, learned from the rapid post-War economic achievements of Japan as well as the advance economies of the West. Post-War success of Japan had a veritable 'demonstration-effect' on Hong Kong.

By 1960, Singapore had launched into swift and steady GDP growth, as described earlier. The outward-oriented growth model of Singapore was initially based on the low-technology, labour-intensive, manufactured exports to the world market. This was followed by gradual movement up the technology and value-added ladder, as the comparative advantage shifted, which in turn promoted robust GDP growth. This model was akin to that adopted by Japan, although Singapore adapted it to its own needs. Economic development in Singapore was state-directed, an antithesis of Hong Kong, but similar to that of Japan. Based on the neoclassical economic lines, Singapore was known to have followed prudent fiscal and monetary policies. It resulted in budgetary surpluses. Modern Singapore is today respected as a leading Asian hub of technology-transfer, innovation and entrepreneurship. Technology-transfer and upgradation supported and sustained its robust GDP growth. Technology-transfer and innovation strategy was continually refined, which paid rich dividend. This was a lesson learned from Japan. Singapore is widely rated as the easiest place to do business. It is also known for having skilled domestic labour-force and easy entry of foreign talent. Consequently it was able to create an ever-expanding network of free trade. As the knowledge-intensive industries grew in the twenty-first century, the government promoted a new business model to make the industrial services sectors perform at a higher efficiency level and remain globally competitive.

Rapid industrialization in Taiwan began in the late 1950s, when SMEs began producing low-technology, labour-intensive manufactured items for export and domestic markets, as we described earlier. They were able to export them at competitive prices. Taiwan also adopted an outward-oriented development strategy, as part and parcel of its adoption of Hayekian ideas on markets. In so doing, it took a leaf from the Japanese growth experience. Like the two city-states, constant attention was paid to technology import, absorption and upgradation. By the 1990s, Taiwan exported capital- and skill-intensive products, using high-technology. For technological transfer and development, the Taiwan Government had well-conceived policies of establishing technology parks. Likewise R&D and manpower training was supported under various government schemes.

To sum up, the main Western Economics ideas and writers who influenced the three dynamic Dragon economies in their post-War growth can be legitimately classified as 'Neoclassical'. To be sure, each individual economy adapted these economic principles to their domestic socio-economic circumstances. Thus, whilst these societies learned much from Japan, as well as the West, their own ingenuity must not be underrated. Being 'Sinic' societies, they have laid a great deal of emphasis on the development of knowledge. They in turn embraced outward-oriented export-led growth and developed their economic structures accordingly. Strategies for technology-transfer and R&D were assigned a high priority. This enabled them to climb the value-added ladder rapidly, which contributed to rapid and sustained GDP growth. All the three economies deployed a great deal of resources on the development of the domestic education systems, from primary to higher, on modern Western lines. Disciplines like Economics, Management, Science and Technology, as well as Engineering, were given extra emphasis, which also had in turn a direct constructive impact on their economies.

References

Amsden, A. H. (1989). *Asia's Next Giant.* New York, NY: Oxford University Press.

Bils, M. and P. J. Klenow. (2000). 'Does Schooling Cause Growth?' *American Economic Review.* 90, 1160–1183.

Chen, D. S. (2010). 'Higher Education in Taiwan'. Available at www.isa-sociology.org/universities-in-crisis/?p=417 (accessed 19 November 2015).

Chou, C. P. (2015). 'Education in Taiwan'. Washington, DC: Brookings Institution. Available at www.brookings.edu/research/opinions/2014/11/taiwan-colleges-universities-chou (accessed 19 November 2015).

Chou, C. P. and G. Ching. (2012). *Taiwan Education at the Crossroad: When Globalization Meets Localization.* Basingstoke: Palgrave Macmillan.

Das, D. K. (2015). *An Enquiry into the Asian Growth Model.* Basingstoke: Palgrave Macmillan.

Goodstadt, L. F. (1995). 'Government without Policies: Management of Economic and Social Development in Hong Kong'. Trinity College, University of Dublin. Unpublished paper. Available at www.hkimr.org/uploads/seminars/196/sem_paper_0_224_goodstadt-paper070419.pdf (accessed 19 November 2015).

Government of the Republic of China. (2015). *National Statistics: Statistical Tables: Principle Figures.* Taiwan.

Haggard, S. (1990). *Pathways from the Periphery: Politics of Growth in the Newly Industrializing Counties*. Ithaca, NY: Cornell University Press.

Hermes, N. (1997). 'New Explanations of the Economic Success of East Asia'. Groningen. The Netherlands. University of Groningen. Center for Development Studies. CDS Research Report No. 3. June.

Hughes, H. (1988). *Achieving Industrialization in East Asia*. Cambridge: Cambridge University Press.

International Monetary Fund (IMF). (2015). *World Economic Outlook Database*. Washington, DC: IMF, April.

Krause, L. J. (1987). 'Thinking about Singapore', in L. J. Kraus (ed.), *The Singapore Economy Reconsidered*. Singapore: Institute of Southeast Asian Studies, pp. 1–21.

Krueger, A. O. (1995). 'East Asian Experience and Endogenous Growth Theory', in T. Ito and A. O. Krueger (eds), *Growth Theories in the Light of the East Asian Experience*. Chicago, IL: University of Chicago Press, pp. 9–36.

Lau, L. J. (2012). 'Long-Term Economic Growth of Taiwan.' Hong Kong. The Chinese University of Hong Kong: Institute of Global Economics and Finance. Working Paper, No. 13. December.

Lau, L. J. (2015). 'Productivity Lessons for Asia's Tiger Cubs.' *East Asia Forum.* Canberra. Australian National University. Available at www.eastasiaforum.org/2015/11/24/productivity-lessons-for-asias-tiger-cubs/ (accessed 19 November 2015).

Lee, J. S. (1994). 'The Role of the State in Economic Restructuring and Development: The Case of Taiwan.' Taipei. Republic of China: Chung-Hua Institute for Economic Research. Occasional Paper, No. 9403, February.

Li, K. T. (1988). *The Evolution of Policy behind Taiwan's Development Success*. New Haven, CT: Yale University Press.

Nolan, J., C. Rowley and M. Warner. (eds) (2016). *Business Networks in East Asian Capitalisms: Enduring Trends, Emerging Patterns*. London: Elsevier.

Peebles, G. and P. Wilson. (2002). *Economic Growth and Development in Singapore*. Cheltenham: Edward Elgar.

San, G. (2013). 'Taiwan's Development Strategy for the Next Phase.' Paper presented at The Trans-Pacific Partnership meeting, Stanford University, Stanford, CA, USA, 11–12 October.

Schenk, C. (2008). 'Economic History of Hong Kong', in R. Whaples (ed.), *Net Encyclopedia*. 16 March. Available at http://eh.net/encyclopedia/economic-history-of-hong-kong/ (accessed 9 November 2015).

Singapore Economic Development Board (SEDB). (2015). *Economic History of Singapore*. Singapore. Available at www.edb.gov.sg/content/edb/en/why-singapore/about-singapore/our-history/1960s.html (accessed 19 November 2015).

Sung, Y. W. and K. Y. Wang. (1998). 'Growth of Hong Kong Before and After its Reversion to Chin'. Paper presented at the joint session of the American Economic Association and Chinese Economics Association in Chicago, IL, 28 April.

Tsai, P. L. (1997). 'Paradigm of Development: The East Asian Debate'. *Oxford Development Studies.* 25: 237–243.

Tsai, P. L. (1999). 'Explaining Taiwan's Economic Miracle'. *Agenda.* 6: 62–89.

Wade, R. H. (1990). *Governing the Markets: Economic Theory and Role of the Government in the East Asian Industrialization*. Princeton, NJ: Princeton University Press.

Wade, R. H. (1992). 'East Asia's Economic Success'. *World Politics.* 44: 270–320.

Wade, R. H. (2003). 'The Invisible Hand of the American Empire'. *Ethics and International Affairs.* 17: 77–88.

Wade, R. H. (2015). 'The Role of Industrial Policy in Developing Countries', in UNCTD, *Rethinking Development Strategies after the Financial Crisis.* Geneva: United Nations Conference for Trade and Development, pp. 67–81.

Warner, M. (2014). *Understanding Chinese Management: Past, Present and Future.* London and New York, NY: Routledge.

World Bank (WB). (1987). *World Development Report.* Washington, DC: WB.

World Bank (WB). (1993). *The East Asian Miracle: Economic Growth and Public Policy.* Washington, DC: WB.

World Bank (WB). (2015a). *East Asia and Pacific Economic Update.* Washington, DC: WB, October.

World Bank (WB). (2015b). *World Development Indicators.* Washington, DC: WB, September.

Part III
Economists

8 Adam Smith in China

From oblivion to half-hearted embrace?

Hongyi Lai

Introduction

No other scholar has exerted a greater influence on Economics than Adam Smith (1723–1790) who was a key figure in the now renowned eighteenth-century Scottish Enlightenment (see Rutherford, 2012) and who in time became an 'icon' of Western thinking in the field (see Schumpeter, 1954; Blaug, 1997; Haakonssen, 2006, for an overview). Whilst this observation may be true for most of the Western world for many years, this had not however been the case for China until the 1900s, well over a century after the original publication of his works.

In China, Adam Smith (Yadang Simi) and his theories were not known to many intellectuals until Yan Fu's (1854–1921) translations of Smith's work, *An Inquiry into the Nature and Causes of the Wealth of Nations*, (1776), (to be abbreviated hereafter as *The Wealth of Nations* (*WN*)) into Chinese in 1902 – as the *Origins of Wealth* (*Yuan fu*) (see Liu, 2013: 38). In the first few decades of the twentieth century that ensued after this original translation, Smith's works had attracted the attention of not many people there beyond the leading intellectuals of the time. In the 1920s and 1930s, with an increase in foreign-educated economists in China, Smith's theory became known more widely and respected by many such thinkers there. Nevertheless, noted economists and governments soon saw the need for firm governmental intervention in order to start the nation on its path to late industrialization and somewhat turned away from Smith's 'laissez faire' theory (see the chapters by Trescott earlier in this volume).

Under Mao Zedong (1893–1976), Smith was for the most part rather neglected. In the post-'Liberation' period after 1949, many of Smith's core-ideas, such as the 'market' as an 'invisible hand' (*kan bu jian de shou*), were rarely taught or mentioned due to their deviation from the official ideology. Arguably, it was after 1978 that mainland Chinese scholars and intellectuals started to more widely read and become more interested in Smith's works. This demarche was propelled by the practical need of policy analysts to understand a theoretical justification of the market economy and the need of the Chinese scholars to know about the 'fount' of Western Economics. Even so it was only after 1992, when the Chinese Communist Party officially dismissed criticisms of the market economy and sanctioned the market economy – did Smith gain official acceptance as a legitimate and mainstream theorist. Since the mid-1990s, however, Smith's works have become better known in China. Whilst before 1997, most Chinese mainly knew about his work *The Wealth of Nations* (1776), since then they started to heed closely his earlier other masterpiece *The Theory of Moral Sentiments* (1759). It is fitting to claim that Smith has gained a status as the 'founding father' of Western Economics deriving from his extensive writings and correspondence (see Tribe and Mizuta, 2002) which has dominated the curricula of the now many Economics departments in universities in China. Nevertheless, many economists and officials in charge of economic affairs in the PRC still appreciated the need for governmental intervention in the economy for the sake of economic growth and a response to economic crises (see the chapter later in this volume on Keynes and China).

In this chapter, I will survey the introduction and influence of the main works of Adam Smith in mainland China. The chapter starts with early translations and introduction of Smith's works in China prior to 1902, the translations of Adam Smith's main works (especially his two aforementioned works) in China during the years 1902–1937, and to the post-1978 period. It will then examine the impact of Smith's works in China, first in the respective periods of 1902–1949, 1949–1976, and then later in the post-1978 period. The last section is then devoted to issues related to how Smith's works were subsequently discussed in China.

This contribution thus mainly focuses on the period of 1902–1937 and on the post-1978 period, respectively. It argues that during 1902–1949 Smith's works became gradually more publicized. It also suggests that Smith's works were to begin to attract increasing attention in China since 1978 and that from the late 1990s onwards, Smith has been accepted as the 'founding-father' economist in China. During the 1930s and during the 1990s, up to the present day, both Smith's urge for minimal restrictions on the market, as well as others' voices for a strong role for the State in economic growth, were widely and concurrently circulated in China.

Translations of Smith's works in China

Prior to the translation of Smith's works, several books on Western Economics published in China in the 1880s and the 1890s provided only a brief summary of his theories. These included two books published by the customs service of the Government under the Qing Dynasty. The first was *A Treatise on Western Theories* (*xi xue lun shu*) authored by British missionary Joseph Edkin (1823–1905) and published in 1885. The other book was the 1896 Chinese translation entitled *Policies for Enriching Nations and Nurturing People* (*fuguo yangmin ce*) of a fellow-countryman, economist William Stanley Jevons's (1835–1882) *Primer on Political Economy*. In addition, Wang Tao (1828–1897), a noted Chinese nineteenth century scholar, mentioned Smith's theory in his work *An Examination of the Origin of Western Theories* (*xi xue yuanshi kao*). However, the full title of Smith's *Wealth of the Nations* was not mentioned (see Yang, 2003).

The first major effort to translate Smith's works was done by Yan Fu, a young Chinese reformer (1854–1921). He had studied in England at the Royal Naval College, which is located at Greenwich, in London and had ended his career as the distinguished President of Peking University. When in England, he soon became immersed in British economics, government, jurisprudence and sociology. He translated not only the publications of Adam Smith but also those of Thomas. H. Huxley (1825–1895), John Stuart Mill (1806–1873), Herbert Spencer (1820–1903) and others into Chinese throughout his rich life (see Table 8.1).

He was to spend six years (1897–1902) on translating Smith's *Wealth of Nations*. Entitled *The Origin of Wealth* (*Yuan fu*), Yan's version of Smith's work

Table 8.1 Chronology of Yan Fu's life

Date	Event
8 January 1854	Born in Fuzhou
1867	First admitted to the Fuzhou Naval Yard School
1877	Yan Fu was sent off to study at The Royal Naval College, London. His fellow students at the time included Sa Zhenbin, Liu Buchan, Lin Yongsheng and Ye Zugui
1879	He returned to Fuzhou Naval Yard School as a teacher and later transferred to Tianjin Beiyang Naval College as Head
1890	He was appointed as the Principal of the Tianjin Beiyang Naval College
1894	At this time, the first Sino-Japanese War broke out
1895	He published a series of articles in the *Zhi* newspaper in Tianjin to explain why China lost the war and to call for reform
1896	He began the translation of Thomas Henry Huxley's *Evolution and Ethics* into Chinese and published this in 1898. He first used the phrase 'survival of the fittest' in Chinese
1902	He published the translation of Adam Smith's *Wealth of Nations* (*Yuan fu*)
1903	Next, he brought out the translations of Herbert Spencer's *The Study of Sociology* and John Stuart Mill's *On Liberty*
1904	He met Sun Yat-sen in London and talked about the possibilities of a Chinese Revolution
1906	He was appointed the head of Anhui Teacher College and then took up the Presidency of Shanghai Fudan Public School (the predecessor of Fudan University)
1912	Yan was appointed as the first President of Peking University
1918	He went home to Fujian and settled in Fuzhou Langguan Xiang
1921	Yan finally passed away at the age of 67 in Fuzhou

Source: adapted from the Yan Fu Foundation website, www.yanfufoundation.org/who-is-yan-fu/ (accessed 28 March 2016).

contains eight volumes and had 450,000 Chinese characters. But Yan Fu was believed to have omitted a quarter of Smith's original writing and added over 300 comments totalling over 60,000 Chinese characters (see Yang, 2003; Borokh, 2012). During 1903–1930, Yan's translation of Smith's *Wealth of Nations* was reprinted by the Commercial Press (*shangwu yinshu guan*) founded in 1897, a pioneer in the diffusion of Western ideas in China, appearing in Shanghai three times, in 1903, 1929 and 1930, respectively. Yan's translation of Smith's work was not, however, reprinted by the Commercial Press again until 1981 (see Yang, 2003).

Nevertheless, a vernacular Chinese translation of Smith's *Wealth of Nations* by the Marxist economists, Guo Dali and Huang Yanan, was later published by August 1931 by Shenzhou Guoguang She in Shanghai which gained wider traction. Unlike Yan's translation, Guo and Huang's version did not omit Smith's original writing and in fact used modern Chinese expressions. It was reprinted three times in mainland China during 1931–1974, first by Zhonghua Shujiu in 1936, and then by the Commercial Press in Beijing in 1972 and 1974 (Yang, 2003). In 2001, a new vernacular Chinese translation of *Wealth of Nations* by Yang Jingnian, a Professor of Economics in Nankai University, was published by Shaanxi Renmin Chubanshe (see Yang, 2003).

Other than *Wealth of Nations*, Smith's further works were translated into Chinese after 1962. In December 1962, the Commercial Press (*shangwu yinshu guan*) published the Chinese version of *Lectures on Justice, Policy, Revenue and Arms Delivered by Adam Smith* published originally by Kelly & Millman in 1956; the translators were Chen Fusheng and Chen Zhenhua. Thirty years later, the Commercial Press in China published *The Correspondence of Adam Smith* as brought out by Clarendon Press back in 1977; it was translated by Lin Guofu. Other than *Wealth of Nations*, Smith's other best-known book is *The Theory of Moral Sentiments* (*TMS*, 1759). In 1997, the first Chinese translation (Smith, 1997) of this book was published in mainland China by again the Commercial Press. The translator was Jiang Ziqiang from the Department of Economics in Hangzhou University. This work by Smith has proved to be very popular among the publishing circles in China. During 1997–2012, nearly 30 Chinese versions of *The Theory of Moral Sentiments* were published in China, though the quality of translation varied (see Zhang, 2013).

Smith's influence in China: 1902–1971

Beyond the intellectuals, Yan's translation had little impact in business and policy-making circles for a number of reasons. First, Yan's use of traditional Chinese writing in his translation further limited the readability and popularity of his translation (see Wright, 2001). Second, Smith's ideas went against the prevalent Chinese tradition. Whilst Smith valued 'individual' pursuit of profit – and its unintended consequence of working to the benefit to society – in the Chinese tradition, 'societal' interests were given higher priority over individual benefits. In addition, due to the influence of Confucianism, merchants and pursuit of profits were held in contempt then. Thus, Smith's endorsement of a 'free market' as a critical institution for the society was not shared by many Chinese intellectuals. Third, the West imposed free trade on China by force and many Chinese intellectuals regarded 'free trade' as an obstacle to Chinese industrialization (Yang, 2003; Borokh, 2012). For example, Liang Qichao (1873–1929), one of the key Chinese intellectual leaders around the turn of the nineteenth and twentieth centuries, initially supported Smith's proposal of free trade prior to the 1898 failed reform in China. After witnessing the economic intrusion of the West into China, Liang abandoned his stance and embraced protective tariffs. He regarded free trade as a suitable policy not only for developed Western economies but also for China (see Cao, 1996).

Nevertheless, Yan actively promoted the following *three* important arguments by Smith – opposition to the governmental interference into the economy, a stand against monopoly and, last, promotion of free trade (see Li, 2004). Furthermore, Yan's translations were read by and attracted attention from a number of prominent and influential Chinese scholars, including Kang Youwei, Liang Qichao, Lu Xun and Hu Shi. In particular, Liang's writings helped Smith's ideas to gain more of an audience (see Trescott's chapter on China earlier in this volume). Liang, however, supported the 'Mercantilist' policies in China that Smith attacked in his book. Sun Yat-sen (1866–1925), on the other hand, supported socialist policies such as equalization of land-rights in an attempt to address inequality, which Liang rejected. The latter emphasized the importance of increasing production (ibid.). Liang agreed with Smith's argument that the government should allow individuals to engage in industrial and commercial activities that they were interested in in order to have a thriving economy (see Cao, 1996).

During the period 1902–1949, the Western Economic theories that attracted the most Chinese intellectual attention were probably the following: the Prussian Historical School, Marshallian economics, Keynesian economics, especially since the 1930s, American Monetary economics, Institutional economics and, among radical intellectuals, Marxism (see Trescott's chapters earlier in this volume). A great deal of scholarly attention in this period was devoted to economics related to the government and less on classical economics advocated by Smith. In policy terms, Sun Yat-sen supported government-driven industrialization and re-distribution of 'land-rights' – to reduce inequality and poverty in the countryside.

It is evident that these economic theories deviated from Smith's 'invisible hand' theory. The approach that was most seriously considered by the government and a number of leading scholars during the Republican era was probably of the Prussian Historical School (see Trescott's later chapter in this volume). They saw many more similarities between Prussia and China (both being backward and late industrializing nations) than between the developed Britain and the backward China. They found the phenomenal economic growth in Prussia after Bismarck's unification of the German nation in 1871 and economic policies based on the Prussian Historical School a very appealing example for a backward

China. Specifically, scholars found two elements in the Historical School of economics attractive – the strong role of the state in the developmental process and the tariffs to protect domestic industry at the earlier stage of development. Interestingly enough, some notable Chinese economists such as Ma Yinchu and Tang Qingzeng who were known for their liberal outlook, as well as Marxist scholars such as Qi Shufen, embraced the Prussian Historical School. Ma, for example, argued that the Chinese industrial base had not yet developed and that free trade would only allow domestic 'infant industries' to be destroyed by strong external competitors. Friedrich List (1789–1846) and Wilhelm Roscherl (1817–1894), in particular, attracted much attention among scholars in this school (see Liu's chapter later in this volume).

Yan (2011) thus noted a *paradoxical* mix of two conflicting trends among leading economists in the Republican era. On the one hand, noted scholars such as Ma regarded Smith's liberalism as rigorous and solid economic theory fundamental to Western Economics and accepted the free market as key to a thriving economy. On the other hand, in practice they regarded the Prussian Historical School as sound and practical policies more relevant for China's course of late industrialization, even though List's writing was far less rigorous and theoretically less elegant than Smith's. It is important to note that in the reform era (especially after 1992) such a 'dual embrace' of neoclassical theories and state-led developmental policies re-surfaced. This point will be taken up later.

During 1949–1976, Smith's influence was much eroded. In 1953, China started to introduce Marxist economics through translating the Soviet literature (in Russian) on the topic and the works of Stalin, in particular. The 'anti-rightist' campaign unleashed by Mao in 1957 aimed to attack liberal intellectuals. There were very few opportunities and little tolerance for the scholars to embrace Smith openly (see chapters by Trescott earlier in this volume). The only period when Western Economics was allowed to discuss was probably during 1962–1965, when the Chinese translations of Western economic works were published. The reason for this boom was probably due to Mao's proposal to offer classes a chance to criticize 'bourgeoisie idealism' as it was called. Thus, reading Western Economic works then was for the purpose of *rejecting* them, instead of accepting them (see Liu, 2010).

During the Cultural Revolution of 1966–1976, texts of Western economic and political liberalism were in turn banned. Chinese intellectuals, including the high-school students, who were sent down to the countryside to undergo 'education', had no access to writings of Adam Smith, for instance.

Smith as a 'mainstream' sage: 1972–present

The eased tension in China–US relations in the wake of the 1972 visit of US President Richard Nixon (1913–1994) in Beijing opened the door for the publications and readings of Western Economics (see the chapter by Cohn later in this volume). In 1972 and 1974, the Commercial Press in Beijing launched the third edition of the Chinese translation of *Wealth of Nations* by Guo and Wang.

The onset of the Chinese Economic Reforms (*jingji gaige*) in late 1978 paved the way for the scholarly exposure and introduction of Western Economics. This genre of economics only formally and openly returned to China in 1979 with the publication of the Chinese translation of a late edition of Paul Samuelson's (1979) popular economic textbook (see the chapters by Fang and Cohn respectively later in this volume). From then on, until most of the 1980s, Chinese scholars, college students (especially in the elite universities) and officials in charge of economic affairs eagerly sat down to learn Western Economics, especially macroeconomics and microeconomics. Nevertheless, the officially sanctioned stance was that Western Economics should neither be simplistically rejected nor mechanically accepted in China (Liu, 2010). In 1983, it was the Commercial Press again which published the Chinese translation of John Rae's *Life of Adam Smith* (1895), as well as Dugald Stewart's *Account of the Life and Writing of Adam Smith* (1793). The publication of the two biographies of Smith apparently signalled a renewed interest in this great economist in China.

The year of 1992 might well have re-defined the official and scholarly stance toward the market economy in China. In that year, the Paramount Leader, Deng Xiaoping (1904–1997), emerged from his semi-retirement and toured Southern China. He called for an acceptance of the market economy in China. In response, during 1992–1993 the Party amended its Constitution to support a 'socialist market economy' (SME) albeit 'with Chinese characteristics' and passed a resolution to build this. Since then the official stance toward the market economy has become far more positive, so has been the scholarly discussion on economics. As Smith is widely associated with the Classical economics and is regarded as one of the most authoritative proponents of the market economy, his theory has been accepted by an increasing number of intellectuals and people in China. Nevertheless, in the following years some Chinese scholars started to notice the excessive stress on private interests and a blatant neglect of norms and ethics in economic activities in China. They have started to pay closer attention to Smith's theory on *morality*. It was in this context that his second major work, *The Theory of Moral Sentiments* was first translated in 1997, a major publishing event in this field and in the following 15 years nearly 29 versions of the translations were published in China (see Zhang, 2013) (see the chapter by Sakamoto later in this volume).

In 2000, a national conference to commemorate the 100th anniversary of the publication of Yan Fu's translation of Smith's *Wealth of Nations* was held in Anhui Province. It was attended by over 80 scholars from over 40 higher education institutions in China. The participants duly recognized the *duality of individuals* in Smith's theory that has been widely coined in the term 'Smith Paradox'. According to Smith, even though individuals pursued 'self-interest' (*li ji*) and material benefit, they also have 'sympathy' (*tongqing*) for other human beings and 'altruism' (*litazhuyi*) is needed for them to be successful in economic transactions which in turn benefit the altruistic individuals (see the chapter by Sakamoto later in this volume on Japan). Scholars also recognized the virtue in the 'invisible hand' in Smith's theory to set up a competitive market, align individual interests with societal interests and to allow individual pursuit of selfish benefits to generate benefits for the society (Liu, 2003).

In particular, liberal economists in China still hold Smith in a very high regard and cite Smith in attacking the theories and policies in China that echo Keynesian economics. For example, Zhang Weiying (1959–), one of the best known Chinese economists in China and the former Dean of Guanghua Management School at Peking University, fiercely criticized several noticeable policies the government adopted, including excessive investment for the sake of creating demand instead of improving productivity as Smith called for, a shift toward consumption for stimulating economic growth and excessive attention to net exports (see Zhang, 2011).

One study (Zheng and Sun, 2006) might be representative of the Chinese scholars who responded positively to Smith's theory. It argued that the following elements in his theory are still profoundly relevant for today's China: (1) the pursuit of self-interest by rational individuals may serve as a basis for economics and for social progress; (2) free competition may motivate individuals to endeavour to produce goods and services that benefit society; (3) the 'invisible hand' of self-interest may best help regulate supplies and demand; (4) the government should not intervene in market activities, except for enforcement of laws, national defence and provision of public goods; (5) the government in China should pay greater attention to the protection of property rights, promotion of fair competition and intervene in the economy only in the case of reducing monopoly, market failures and supplies of public goods (see Zheng and Sun, 2006).

Despite the wide agreement with Smith's theory by many economists in China, there is also an apparent acceptance for an active and extensive role of the government in economic development in China, which continues to this day. This tendency is especially common among analysts for the government and economic officials. This seemingly *paradoxical* duality amongst economists and economic officials in fact possibly resembles that in the Republican era as noted earlier. Xu and Long (1994), for example, declared in their article published in a leading economic academic journal in China, that 'laissez-faire' and 'macro-management' by the government have been two key schools of theories in Western Economics. The former, they suggested, was represented by Smith's classical economics and Marshall's Neoclassical economics, and the latter by Mercantilism, the Prussian Historical School, US Institutionalism and Keynesianism. They argued that the 'visible hand' of the state should guide the 'invisible hand' of the market – and that both hands should be used together intelligently (see Xu and Long, 1994). Even Zhang Weiying's aforementioned poignant criticism demonstrated the often Chinese governmental deviation from Smith's preaching of the 'invisible hand' of the market in policies.

Two frequently discussed topics concerning Smith's theory

In the PRC, two topics were arguably among the most discussed ones other than the aforementioned ones concerning Smith's theories. One is the linkage between Smith's theory and the Marxist economic theory. The other is Smith's discussion of Imperial China, especially the state of China's economy and the causes for its stagnation.

It has been commonly held in the Chinese scholarly circles that Marxist economic theory drew from the 'labour theory of value' first developed by Adam Smith (1723–1790) and as then refined by his fellow British economist, David Ricardo (1772–1783). In particular, Karl Marx (1818–1893) had later inherited the view from Smith and Ricardo that the 'value' in goods was based primarily on the labour that their production consumed (see Baidubaike, 2016). One scholar in China boldly suggested that Marx pushed this view to the extreme and even thus concluded that the value of goods came *solely* from labour of workers, that capitalists played no role in the creation of the value in production and that they extracted what he called 'surplus value' from workers and hence 'exploited' them (see Cai, 2015). A Marxist scholar even maintained that Marx's value theory was still valid today, despite that its popularity was dwarfed by that of Western Economics in China. His article was re-posted on the People's Daily website (Zhao, 2014). Debates on these notions still continue up to the present (see the chapter by Cohn later in this volume).

The other topic was the discussion of 'China' in Smith's works. China's scholars took note of the following views of China in Smith's works: (1) China was more prosperous than Europe in Smith's time, but its economy remained stagnant; (2) despite the hard work of the Chinese labourers those at the low layer of the society were poorer than the poorest in Europe; (3) China's agriculture was advanced, but foreign trade was ignored; (4) Chinese institutions restricted economic growth through obstructing trade and discriminating against handicrafts and manufacturing. Despite that his view on the stagnation of the Chinese economy in the late eighteenth century was simplistic, Smith's analyses of the causes (especially the institutional causes) of slow progress in China's economy were largely fitting (see Du, 1996; Zhong, 2003).

Conclusions

This chapter has surveyed the introduction of the main works of Adam Smith and his influence in mainland China. The chapter starts with the translations of Adam Smith's works in China from the late nineteenth century to the early twentieth century, throughout the Republican period, then Mao's era and last, to the post-1978 days. The *main* thrust of the chapter is in fact on the period of 1902–1937 and on the post-1978 period when Western Economics were again taken up by Chinese scholars.

Specifically, analyses are made on the impact of the translated works on the intellectual and academic circles in China. It is suggested that in the first of the two aforementioned periods Smith's works translated by Yan Fu in 1902 had a profound impact on some of the leading scholars of the Intellectual Enlightenment movement in China, and that despite the growing number of Western Economics among leading universities during the 1930s and the 1940s, the 'free market' as championed by Adam Smith left little imprint on the governmental policies, as a number of scholars were to rather favour government-led industrialization and development. In Mao's China, Western Economics was largely ignored or even banned, and Smith was noted mainly for his 'labour theory of value', arguably a secondary element in his contribution to the economics.

In the post-Deng reform era, especially since the late 1990s, translated works of Smith have been increasingly accepted by mainstream economists in China. To an extent, similar to the period of 1928–1949, the governmental policies in the second period do not always favour a free market urged by Smith. The government does recognize, at least rhetorically, the significance of elements of the free market, such as 'efficiency' as associated with private ownership, 'performance-based' rewards for employees, and for more 'competition'. Moreover, Smith's 'invisible hand' as a key notion is very popular among economists and to a lesser extent, liberal scholars. Intellectuals and scholars, for example, use Smith's theories to criticize governmental intervention and distortions and to affirm pro-market governmental policies (see the chapter by Fang later in this volume).

Nevertheless, during the Republican and the reform eras a 'paradoxical' tendency in economics in China existed, as both Smith's classical theory on 'laissez faire' and the State's key role in economic growth and macro management, were in their respective ways both appreciated. Today, this fascinating tension between the two notions may still live on.

References*

*[Due to lack of space, we have kept the number of translations referred to the key ones]

Baidubaike (2016). 'Laodong jiazhi lun' (Labour Theory of Value), posted at http://wapbaike,baidu.com/view/118293.htm?adapt=1& (accessed 26 March 2016).

Blaug, M. (1997). *Economic Theory in Retrospect*, 5th edn, Cambridge: Cambridge University Press.

Borokh, O. (2012). 'Adam Smith in Imperial China: Translation and Cultural Adaptation', *Oeconomia*, 2: 411–441.

Cai J. (2015). 'Cong hunhe jingji xingcheng kan liangda jingji sixiang tixi ronghe' (Integration of Two Major Schools of Economic Thought in Light of the Formation of a Mixed Economy), *Xueshu yuekan (Academic Monthly)*, 47: 62–75.

Cao C. (1996). 'Jindai Zhongguo zichan jieji gailiangpai jingji ziyou sixiang zhi neirong jiqi tedian' (Contents and Features of the Liberal Economic Thoughts of the Bourgeoisie Reformists in Modern China), *Sichuan Shifan Daxue Xuebao (Journal of Sichuan Normal University)*, 23: (pages unknown).

Du J. (1996). 'Xiaoyi Guofulun yu Zhongguo jingji' (A Brief Comment on Implications of the Wealth of Nations for China's Economy), *Lilun yu gaige (Theory and Reform)*, No. 9, 46–48.

Edkin, J. (1885). *A Treatise on Western Theories (xi xue lun shu)*, Beijing: n.p.

Haakonssen, K. (ed.) (2006). *The Cambridge Companion to Adam Smith*, Cambridge: Cambridge University Press.

Jevons, W. S. (1896). *Primer on Political Economy*, Chinese translation entitled *Policies for Enriching Nations and Nurturing People (fuguo yangmin ce)*, n.p.

Li X. (2004). 'Cong Yadang Simi dao Yan Fu' (From Adam Smith to Yan Fu), *Caijing wenti yanjiu (Research on Financial and Economic Issues)*, No. 12 of the year and cumulative no. 253, 28–31.

Liu H. (2010). 'Kaijiang xifang jingjixue' (Teaching Western Economics), posted at http://reformdata.org/index.do?m=wap&a=show&catid=301&typeid=&id=2214 (accessed 4 March 2016).

Liu Q. (2013). 'The Reception of Adam Smith in East Asia: A Comparative Perspective', in *Thoughts on Economic Development in China*, edited by Y. Ma and H.-M. Trautwein, London and New York, NY: Routledge, 35–55.

Liu X. (2003). 'Jinian Yan Fu yiben "Yuan Fu" chuban 100 zhounian quanguo xueshu yantaohui zongsu' (A Summary of a National Academic Conference Commemorating the 100th Anniversary of the Publication of Yan Fu's Translation Work *Origin of Wealth*), *Jingji xue dongtai (Trends in Economics)*, No. 1, 40–42.

Rutherford, D. (2012). *In the Shadow of Adam Smith: Founders of Scottish Economics, 1700–1900*, New York, NY: Palgrave Macmillan.

Samuelson, P. A. (1979). *Economics*, Chinese version. 10th edn, Beijing: Commercial Press. Translated by H. Gao, Preface by H. Gao.

Schumpeter, J. A. (1954). *History of Economic Analysis*, London: Allen and Unwin.

Smith, A. [1776] (1880). *An Inquiry into the Nature and Causes of the Wealth of Nations*, edited by James E. Thorold Rogers, 2nd edn, Oxford: Clarendon Press, 2 vols.

Smith, A. [1776] (1902). *The Wealth of Nations [Origins of Wealth]*, Shanghai: Nanyang Translation Institute. Translated by F. Yan.

Smith, A. [1759] (1982). *The Theory of Moral Sentiments*, edited by D. D. Raphael and A. L. Macfie, Indianapolis, IN: Liberty Fund.

Smith, A. [1759] (1997). *Daode Qingcao Lun/The Theory of Moral Sentiments*, edited by D. D. Raphael and A. L. Macfie, translated into Chinese by Z. Jian. Beijing: Commercial Press.

Tribe, K. and Mizuta, H. (2002). *A Critical Bibliography of Adam Smith*, London: Pickering & Chatto.

Wang, T. (1890) *An Examination of the Origin of Western Theories (xi xue yuanshi kao)*, Beijing: n.p.

Wright, D. (2001). 'Yan Fu and the Tasks of the Translator: In New Terms for New Ideas', in *Western Knowledge and Lexical Change in Late Imperial China*, edited by M. Lackner, I. Amelung and J. Kurtz. Leiden: Brill, 235–256.

Xu Y. and Long W. (1994). 'Xifang jingjixue zhong shizhong chunzai zhe "ziyou fangren" yu "guojia hongguan tiaokong" liangzhong xueshuo' (Two Schools of Thought, i.e., Laissez Faire and Macro Management by the State in Western Economics), *Caijing yanjiu (Studies of Finance)*, No. 10, 55–60.

Yan P. (2011). 'Deguo lishi xuepai yu minguo shiqi Zhongguo jingjixue de fazhan' (The Prussian Historical School and the Development of Economics in China During the Republican Era), *Deguo yanjiu (Studies of Germany)*, No. 2, 40–45, posted at http://economy.guoxue.com/?p=6123 (accessed 18 March 2016).

Yang T. (2003). 'Yandang Simi zhuzuo zai Zhongguo de chuanbo' (The Spread of Adam Smith's Works in China), *Jingji xue dongtai (Trends in Economics)*, No. 1, 26–28.

Zhang W. (2011). 'Kaiensi zhuyi duhai Zhongguo jingji' (Keynesianism Poisons the Chinese Economy), *Shanxi qingnian (Youth in Shanxi)*, No. 7, 1–6.

Zhang Z. (2013). 'Daode Qingcao Lun zai Zhongguo' ('The Theory of Moral Sentiments' in China), *Zhongguo tushu pinglun (China Book Review)*, 8: 98–103.

Zhao Z. (2014). 'Zhao Zhenying: Sui shuo Makesi zhuyi laodong jiaji lun guoshi' (Zhao Z: Who Said Marxist Labour Value Theory Is Out-of-date), *Zhongguo shehui kexue bao (Chinese Social Sciences Paper)*, posted at http://theory.people.com.cn/n/ 2014/0121/c49157-24178458.html on 21 January 2014 (accessed on 26 March 2016).

Zheng S. and Sun X. (2006). 'Guofulun shichang tiaojie de jiben sixiang yu woguo shich-ang- zhengfu guanxi dingwei' (The Basic Ideas on the Regulation of the Market in *Origins of Wealth of Nations* and the Setting of the Government-Market Relationship in Our Country), *Luoyang shifan xueyuan xuebao (Journal of Luoyang Normal College)*, No. 3, 145–148.

Zhong W. (2003). 'Yadang Simi de guofulun yu Zhongguo' (China in Adam Smith's *Wealth of Nations*), *Hebei xuekan (Hebei Academic Journal)*, 23: 166–170.

9 German economics and China

List, Marx and others[1]

Paul B. Trescott

Introduction

The first known book devoted to Western Economics published in the Chinese language was prepared by a German missionary, Karl Friedrich Gutzlaff (1803–51). He was a colourful figure who was willing to travel on board opium-smuggling ships in order to distribute Christian literature. Around 1840, he published a text entitled *Outlines of Political Economy*; in it, he praised 'free-market' conditions but stressed the need for an appropriate system of law and justice (cited in Lutz, 1985: 82–83). Unfortunately, no copy of it has ever been found.

In 1871, a number of German principalities united to form a 'German Empire'. However, many ethnic Germans also lived in the neighbouring Habsburg Empire (Austria-Hungary), as did numerous other ethnic groups. The dynastic empires of the Hohenzollerns (Germany), the Habsburgs (Austria-Hungary) and the Romanoffs (Russia) were at that time experiencing internal agitations for greater political democracy, for ethnic self-determination, as well as for greater economic equality in face of early industrialization. The years following 1871 witnessed increasingly intense rivalries among the European nations which were fuelled in part by efforts of the ruling class to distract people from internal controversies. These rivalries extended to the competition for 'spheres of influence' in China around the turn of the century. Germany entered into competition with the United States, Britain and France in order to attract Chinese students to their universities (see Trescott, 2007).

Broadly speaking, Germany is generally credited with developing modern research-oriented universities in the nineteenth century. With this came the rise of Economics as a *specialized* subject, namely: *Wirtschaftswissenschaft*, which became the German terminology for the subject. Whilst British economic writing followed the lines of Adam Smith (1723–1790), Thomas Malthus (1776–1834) and David Ricardo (1772–1823), German economics tended to downplay abstract deductive theory. Such influential figures as Friedrich List (1789–1846), Gustav Schmoller (1838–1917) and Adolf Wagner (1835–1917) took a 'historical' approach, stressing the link between the economy and the broader dimensions of the society.[2] They favoured a strong, interventionist government, as epitomized by many of the policies of Bismarck and sought protective tariffs and other government interventions to promote industrialization. German economists tended to see international economic affairs as elements in the rivalry, in contrast to the cosmopolitanism which characterized British (but not American) attitudes. An extreme example was Werner Sombart's (1863–1941) 1915 book *Handler und Helden*, which could be translated as 'Hucksters and Heroes'. He poured scorn on the British (the Hucksters), whilst praising the noble, warlike spirit of the Germans (the Heroes).

Many Americans studied in the German universities in the late nineteenth century and returned to America to spread similar ideas. Notable was Richard T. Ely (1854–1943), an Institutionalist Economist, whose textbook was a best-seller in the US and was widely used in China, both in English and in its 1910 Chinese translation (Ely, 1893). Major writings of German economists were translated into Chinese in the 1920s and after (see the earlier chapter on China by the present writer in this volume).

In 1897–1898, the German government seized control of Qingdao and its environs in Shandong Province. They introduced some innovative ideas relating to land-value taxation, which caught the attention of soon to be leader of the new Republic of China, Sun Yat-sen (1866–1925). He was strongly influenced by the ideas of the American social reformer Henry George (1839–1897) who argued that land-owners benefitted unfairly from the rise in land-values which attended economic progress. He recommended that government tax the increments in land-values, a tax which would not harm productive incentives and would contribute to social justice. There was briefly a 'Sino-German University' founded in Qingdao. The Germans also set up a well-known brewery; it still operates, producing the world-famous 'Tsingtao Beer'.

China was just beginning to develop its modern universities around 1900. In 1898, the Chinese government created what eventually became its flagship university, *Peking University* – colloquially known as '*Beida*'. In 1907–1910, numerous Sino-German secondary schools were established in China. As universities developed, they often offered instruction in the German language. In 1907, Tongji University was established in Shanghai, emphasizing medical education and lecturing in the German language. By 1949, it had produced 2,251 graduates. It is still operating and is well regarded for instruction in science and technology. German influence was also significant in FuRen [*sic*] University, a Catholic university in the then Peking, which opened in 1925.

German influence on the educational system was enhanced by German-educated Tsai (Cai) Yuanpei (1868–1940). Tsai was Minister of Education in 1911–1912 and President of Peking University 1916–1926. An early chair of the Beida Economics Department was Ku (Gu) Mengyu, who had graduated from *Beida* in 1906 with a specialization in the German language. He studied in Leipzig 1906–1908 and Berlin 1908–1911. In the early 1920s, he was teaching socialist theory and systems in *Beida*. He left there in 1925 and became active in government and politics. By 1941–1948, he was Chancellor of National Central University in Nanjing. When the Communists took over, Ku left China, living at times in Hong Kong, the United States and Taiwan (Zhou, 1999: 329).

Two German nationals taught for the early *Beida* department. One was Friedrich Otte, who had received a doctorate from Jena with a dissertation on foreign control of China's finances. The other was E. Erde, of whom we know little. Li Tang, who had studied in Berlin, taught financial subjects at *Beida* 1914–1923; he later worked for the Ministry of Finance, serving as a director of the Customs Administration for five years (*Who's Who in Modern China*, 1954: 130). Ma Yinchu, who joined *Beida* in 1915, after completing a doctorate at Columbia, was a strong devotee of the ideas of the German, Friedrich List (1841–1927) and the Austrian, Othmar Spann (1878–1950).

Another noteworthy *Beida* faculty member was Chen Hansheng. He had studied in the United States; he then completed a doctoral thesis in history at Berlin. He joined the *Beida* faculty in 1924. He later acknowledged that 'he did not have the slightest idea about Marxism when he started teaching at Peking University' (Chiang, 2001: 162). *Beida* at the time had several prominent members of the newly formed Chinese Communist Party (CCP). Chen undertook to join the Party, but was persuaded to join the related 'Comintern' in 1926 instead. This began a long career as a 'spy'. In 1927–1928, he lived in Moscow, working at the International Agrarian Institute and developing an interest in the place of peasants in the Marxist theory of social classes and social *evolution. In 1929, he headed the Sociology department of the Academia Sinica*, of which Tsai Yuanpei was Head. This was a research organization created by the national government. Chen conducted a number of rural surveys, assembling vast amounts of information about poverty and inequality in rural China. His research was initially much influenced by the work of German Marxist, Karl Kautsky (1854–1938) (Chiang, 2001: 175). But Chen then found that Chinese conditions appeared to contradict Kautsky's analysis.

Karl Marx's (1818–1883) ideas were not widely known nor followed in China prior to the Russian revolution in 1917. By 1900, very few economists in the West then would have shown much interest in Marxian economics. Marx's *Das Kapital*, published as *Capital*, was published in 1867 but not translated into Japanese until 1924 and into Chinese until 1938. Marginal-utility economics was developed in part in the German language by Carl Menger (1902–1985) in Vienna and demonstrated the *fallacy* of Marx's labour theory of value and theory of surplus value. In Marx's view, societies passed through a series of stages, a process driven by 'class conflict'. Feudalism would give way to capitalism, which would set the stage for revolution and a 'dictatorship of the proletariat'. China seemed far from this stage, as did its neighbours (see the chapter by Yagi on Japan in this volume).

Maurice Meisner (1967) characterized Li Dazhao (1888–1927) as 'China's first Marxist' (1867: xiii). He had studied political economy at Waseda University in Japan and was appointed Professor of History and Economics at *Beida* by Tsai Yuanpei in 1918. He was also Head Librarian and recruited the young Mao Zedong (1893–1976) as a Library Assistant. Li was drawn to Marxism by the Russian Revolution:

> Unlike European and Russian Marxists, who had usually immersed them-selves in years of study of the fine points of Marxist theory, those who came into the Communist fold in China, were committed to a 'Marxist' revolution long before they had accepted even the basic assumptions of the Marxist world-view.
>
> (Meisner, 1967: 56)

Li recognized the fallacious nature of Marx's labour theory of value and favoured basing revolutionary strategy on the peasants. Before he was murdered by warlord thugs in 1927, Li was influential in enlisting Mao in the Communist cause.

In Sun Yat-sen's prolific writings after the First World War, he referred often to Marx and to developments in the Soviet Union under V. I. Lenin (1870–1924). Sun opposed violence and felt that, whilst Marx's theory of class conflict appeared to be valid for the West, he said it did not then apply to China and could be avoided by proper policies. His own vision for a state-dominated eco-nomic development programme owes much to Lenin's New Economic Policy. After Sun's death in 1925, Chiang Kai-shek (1887–1975) successfully led the Kuomintang/Guomindang in a military take-over of the Chinese government in 1927. From that point, overt Communist political activity would risk execution or imprisonment. However, many universities offered courses dealing with the history of economic thought or of socialist ideas. Marx's ideas were thus now widely disseminated.[3]

Chinese economics students in Germany

In *Jingji Xue* (*Economics*), my earlier book (Trescott, 2007), I identified 122 Chinese who studied the subject in Germany up to 1950. Subsequent research has added 12 more. Of these 134, 81 received doctorates. It is relatively easy to research these awards. The German Ministry of Education published an annual listing, *Jahresverzeichnis der Deutschen Hochschulschriften* (*Annual List of German University Publications*). My wife (Kathleen Trescott) and I scanned each issue for Chinese names. One source (Yuan, 1963) is a much more conven-ient tabulation, giving each student's name in Chinese (*hanzi*) as well as birth and death dates. However, it is not easy to identify which theses were really in Economics. I tried to examine each dissertation to determine if it was clearly Economics or some near-cognate. I have been able to examine 66 of them and continue to look for the rest. Before the Second World War, every thesis was published. Typically, the dissertation included a biographical sketch of the student and identified the faculty advisers.

The German-based students who did not receive doctorates were identified from a wide variety of sources. The records of Chinese university faculty often give their academic credentials. There are numerous 'Who's Who' publications. China has published several biographical directories of social scientists in general and economists in particular. Two recent and very valuable publications are a 'dictionary' of returned-students (Zhou, 1999) and a 'directory' of all the members of the Chinese Economics Association (Sun, 2006). Even so, our list is certainly incomplete.

Table 9.1 identifies the German universities attended by each student, where known. Many students attended more than one university, as it was very easy to transfer. Austria is also included since German was the predominant language and almost all Chinese students there studied after the 'Anschluss' (Annexation, or Connection) in 1938.

The largest number of Chinese students attended the University of Berlin, the *Friedrich-Wilhelm-Universitat*. Frankfurt and Leipzig also attracted double-digit enrolments. By far the largest number came in the 1930s after China and Germany reached an economic rapprochement involving trade and military assistance (see Kirby, 1984).

Why Germany?

From 1911 on, Chinese students could find financial support to study in the United States, Britain, and France – from 'Boxer Indemnity' funds. Chinese government units also provided support for study abroad. Germany was highly respected for the high quality of its public administration and for the policy emphasis on economic development, social justice and national strength. Chinese students who attended Tongji or *Beida* were alerted to these attractions. We have information on 'pre-Germany' study involving 68 students. Of these, eight attended Tongji and 15 *Beida*. The Japanese universities embodied great admiration for the German schools, and 12 of the Chinese who went to Germany had studied in Japan previously. A striking example was Chang Wu, born in 1886, whose early biography appears in his dissertation but we have little record of his

Table 9.1 Chinese Economics students in German universities, 1900–1950

University	Primary doctorate	Other	Secondary doctorate	Other	Total
Berlin	26	32	8	2	68
Frankfurt	12	3	0	0	15
Leipzig	10	0	1	2	13
Munich	4	1	2	1	8
Jena	4	1	2	0	7
Vienna	3	2	2	0	7
Freiburg	1	2	1	0	4
19 others*	21	4	9	1	35
Unidentified	0	9	0	0	9
Total	81	54	25	6	166
(–) Duplicates					–32
Total students					134

Sources: miscellaneous.

Note
* Including Technisches Hochschules.

demise. From age 17 to 20, he served in the Japanese military and was able to attend a military-geography institute for general staff. In 1910, he became a military official for Anwei Province, and in 1912 the provincial government financed his move to Germany for study. In 1917, he completed his doctorate with a dissertation on Chinese credit institutions – the only Chinese doctorate in Economics completed in Germany during the First World War.

His contemporary Chen Chieh (Jie) (1885–1951), had studied in Tokyo Imperial University for three years, then entered Berlin University in 1907 and studied law and political economy. He returned to China to a number of government positions and faculty appointments, becoming in 1938, the Ambassador to Germany (see below).

We have information on the birth year and year of completion of study in Germany for 73 students. Of these, 35 were 30 years of age or older when they finished their German study. Fifteen of the students going to Germany had significant employment before going, often with government and some of these employments brought support for study in Germany.

The financial burdens of study in Germany were greatly reduced by the monetary disequilibrium of the early 1920s. The foreign-exchange value of the mark fell much more than its internal purchasing power, making life in Germany very cheap for foreign students. Between the first Chinese student (in 1907) and 1921, there were nine doctorates by Chinese students. In 1923, there were three and in 1924, when hyperinflation ended, there were 11.

The German universities

Freiburg developed a distinguished programme in Economics; its most prominent figure was Walter Eucken (1891–1950) (see Grosekettler, 1989). Four Chinese attended the university in Freiburg. The only doctoral dissertation found was directed by Karl Diehl. This one was by Tchang Pi-kai (Zhang Pijie), on the fragmentation of land holdings (Bodensersplitterung) in China, completed in 1934.[4] Upon returning to China, he taught in several universities, most especially the Central Political Institute, which had a programme dealing with land management directed by Hsiao Cheng (below). He also translated a number of important German authors: Friedrich Damaschke (an authority on land policy), Werner Sombart, Friedrich List and Walter Eucken. In 1949, he moved to Hong Kong, where he established New Asia College, later to become part of the Chinese University of Hong Kong.

Another Freiburg student was Tschang Wen-hsi (Zhang Wenxi). He transferred to Munich and finally to Berlin, where he completed a 1934 dissertation on land rent and tenure in China. He became an official with the Bank of China dealing with farm loans. Tu Jen-chi (Du Renzhi) studied at Berlin, Freiburg and Frankfurt, but did not complete a doctorate. He then taught at several Chinese universities, including FuRen University in Peking, of which more later. He had attended the short-lived, red-tinged 'Shanghai Labour University' (Shanghai laodong daxue) which had international faculty and became a member of the

Chinese Communist Party in 1927 (Zhou, 1999: 127). Kao Hsin (Gao Xin) studied at Freiburg, then joined the faculty of National Chengchi University for the period 1931–1937. He became an official in the Guangdong provincial government, heading the Bureau of Land Utilization for several years. He moved to Taiwan and became an official in the Ministry of Education (Zhou, 1999: 345).

Many of the Chinese doctoral dissertations were undistinguished; they compare with a present-day Master's essay.[5] Most of them were written about Chinese topics. The German faculty often used their students to give them convenient information on conditions in China. We tabulated the names of the faculty advisers. In Berlin, we identified 23 in all. The largest number of dissertations was directed by younger scholars. These included Hans Weigman (5), Jens Jessen (8) and Horst Jecht (6). Jessen was part of a conspiracy against Adolf Hitler during the Second World War and was executed (see Schluter-Ahrens, 2002). Jessen directed one of the most unusual dissertations: *Mathematisch-statistische Untersuchung zur Chinesischen Industrie* (*A Mathematical-Statistical Examination of Chinese Industry*) (in Berlin, in 1937) by Wu Tao-kun.

After graduating from China's National Central University, Wu worked as an assistant in statistics and experimental psychology at Hunan University. Moving to Germany in 1935, he studied statistics at the *Berlin Technische Hochschule* (BTH) in addition to his Economics studies at Berlin University. Wu used Chinese data to illustrate various statistical and econometric procedures. The most interesting exercise generated parabolic cost and revenue functions for Chinese cotton-mills. Very few Chinese dissertations displayed this level of sophistication.

Another impressive dissertation from another Technische Hochschule was by Wu Dschi-han [*sic*] (Jihan): *A Scientific Investigation of Chinese Commerce* (in Stuttgart, in 1935). Wu had graduated from Tongji University and worked as an engineer before going to Stuttgart. The thesis gave detailed descriptions of China's resources, production and especially transport. There were 38 diagrams and 67 tables altogether.

Many prominent German professors appeared among the advisers to the Chinese students. Werner Sombart (1863–1941) at Berlin was widely known for his flamboyant and often outrageous positions. His work on *German Socialism* (published in 1934) supported much of the Nazi programme (Sombart, 1934). He denied the existence of universal 'laws' in economics and was sceptical of the moral value of capitalism.[6]

Herman Schumacher (1868–1952) was an older Berlin professor who advised on three Chinese dissertations. He had published a book on Chinese treaty ports (in 1898) and articles on foreign business in China. At Frankfurt, Chinese students were advised by Paul Arndt (1870–1942), a labour economist who used two Chinese dissertations as the core of a book on wages in China (see Arndt, 1937).

Students at Frankfurt were also exposed to Franz Oppenheimer (1864–1943). Joseph Schumpeter (1883–1950) characterized him as 'a powerful teacher who shaped many growing minds and did much to keep the flag of economic theory flying by spirited controversy' (Schumpeter, 1954: 854–855). Oppenheimer's books occupy five pages in the *National Union Catalog*. He opposed Marxism but was critical of private property in land. He directed a Chinese dissertation by Kuo Shien-yen (Guo Xianyan) entitled *Kapitalismus und Grundeigentum* (*Capitalism and Landed Property*) in China. Unfortunately, it is superficial and not very provocative. Heinrich Schmitthenner, who advised on four dissertations at Leipzig, was something of a 'China expert'. He was primarily a geographer who published two books on China as well as one dealing with 'living space and the conflict of civilizations'.[7]

We have identified 55 of our student sample of 134 who returned to China to teach in universities. At least 40 held government positions, including many who were also faculty.

Hsiao Cheng and land reform

Hsiao Cheng (Xiao Zheng) (1905–2002) completed his studies at Berlin in 1932. Hsiao had been very much influenced by the ideas of Sun Yat-sen on policies toward rural land. From his earliest writings (around 1900), Sun had dramatized the slogans of 'equalization of land rights' and 'all land to the tillers'. Although Sun died in 1925, his ideas continued to receive extensive attention, as the Guomindang regime tried to present themselves as his moral, intellectual and political heirs (see the earlier chapter by Das in this volume). Issues relating to rural land policy were widely addressed by German scholars, notably Friedrich Damaschke, with several of the Chinese students pursuing these topics, including Chang Pi-kai mentioned above. Chiang Kai-shek's regime had created the Central Political Institute (CPI) in Nanjing, closely linked to the national government and to the Guomindang political party. On his return to China, Hsiao Cheng became heavily involved in GMD politics and helped to establish a Research Institute of Land Economics within CPI (Zhou, 1999: 373). The subject of land policy generated a large literature in China – Chen Hansheng and his research staff were important contributors (see Fong, 1935). Inequality of land ownership was extreme in China before 1949. Despite 'lip-service', Chiang's regime took no significant action to alleviate rural poverty and inequality and those conditions helped fuel the Communist movement.

Hsiao Cheng moved, with many of the government leaders, to Taiwan as the communist take-over proceeded in 1949. He became Vice-Minister of Economic Affairs in Taiwan. He was an influential figure in Taiwan's non-violent land reform, which achieved much of what Sun Yat-sen had dreamed of. The government paid for the land it took to redistribute – although below market value. This land reform was an important element in Taiwan's rapid economic growth after 1949. On the Mainland, Mao Zedong had instituted his own land reform in 1950. But it was extremely violent: many landlords were murdered or physically abused. They were not paid for the land that was taken.

Although a large number of rural residents received additional land allotments, the whole system of private property and free markets was swept aside by a Stalinist regime of collectivization. Farm output expanded (resulting in large part from increased labour force participation rather than increased factor productivity) but rural residents derived little benefit from it. Residence restrictions forced most rural residents to remain where they were, and their incomes were far below those of the favoured urban workers. After Mao's death in 1976, farmers were once again permitted to engage in private farming, and the land allotments of the early 1950s finally became operative. This transformation helped achieve increased farm productivity and farm incomes. However, restrictive residence requirements still remain in effect in 2015, weakened but not fully revoked.

Tang Huisun studied agriculture in Japan, returned to teach in China at age 30 and moved to Germany, where he studied at Berlin Agricultural University. He returned to teach in several Chinese universities, including CPI. In 1946–1947, he was Deputy Director of the National Land Administration. He moved to Taiwan and served as a member of the Joint Commission on Rural Reconstruction, which played a major role in Taiwan's successful agricultural transformation (Zhou, 1999: 115–116; Sun, 2006: 483). Chu (Zhu) Ping had studied at the London School of Economics (LSE) in 1929–1930, then moved to Germany, first to Jena and then to Leipzig, where he wrote his 1933 doctoral thesis on land reform in China. He became the chief of the Jiangsu Province land bureau and a professor in the College of Land Administration. Huang Tung (Dung) studied in Japan, Britain and at the University of Bonn in Germany. He taught at several Chinese universities from 1928, including CPI College of Land Administration and National Chengchi University. He moved to Taiwan and became an official with the Land Bank of Taiwan.

Public finance

Returned students from Germany were also prominent in academic and government positions involving taxation and public finance. A distinguished example was Chu Chi (Zhu Qi) who completed a doctorate at Berlin in 1931, writing on problems of financial reform in China. He joined National Central University (Nanjing) in 1932 and became a Dean in 1939. He published several books on Chinese public finance. In 1942, he joined the Ministry of Finance, serving for a time as Deputy Director of the Customs Service. After 1949, he taught at Nanjing University (Zhou, 1999). Dschang [*sic*] Kowei (Zhang Guowei) completed a doctorate at Berlin in 1930 with a thesis on China's monetary situation. He taught at Amoy University and was an official in the Fujian Province finance bureau. In 1949, he moved to Taiwan and was on the faculty of National Taiwan University (Zhou Mian). Kwan Ge-yu (Guan Jiyu) studied at Berlin in 1930–1932 specializing in Public Finance. He held government positions in several provincial finance departments including Sichuan and Jiangsu. He published prolifically on tax matters; his biography lists ten titles. Like most former officials, he moved to Taiwan (see Sun, 2006).

Diplomatic developments

Many of the Chinese students who studied Economics in Germany entered China's diplomatic service, capitalizing on their language skills. Some Chinese embassy staff enrolled at Berlin University. During the 1930s, liaison between the KMT and Nazi leaderships was facilitated by Liang Ingwen, who had received an Economics doctorate from Greifswald in 1930. Liang had served as head of the Chinese Trade Bureau in Berlin, then becoming a secretary to Chiang (Kirby, 1984: 155). Oscar Hsu (Xu Ze) received a doctorate from Hamburg in 1934 with a thesis on China's international trade. He had been a member of the Hamburg consular staff from 1931 (*Who's Who in China*, 1940 Supplement: 19). Felix Wang (Wang Jiahung) wrote a Berlin doctoral dissertation on China's iron production and imports. Whilst a member of the embassy staff in Berlin, he brought out a work praising the Nazi regime – *The Third Reich*, published in Hankow, now part of Wuhan, in 1935 (cited in Liang, 1978).

The most noteworthy of China's German-educated diplomats was Ho (He) Feng-shan (1901–1997). Raised as a Christian, Ho graduated from American-sponsored Yale-in-China in 1926. He worked for the Bureau of Foreign Affairs of Hunan Province and that government financed his move to Germany to study in Munich. He completed a doctorate in 1932 and then entered China's Foreign Service. In 1937, he was sent to Vienna as First Secretary. By coincidence, the Chinese Ambassador to Germany was Chen Chieh, noted above.

The Germans seized control of Austria in March, 1938, and almost immediately instituted a large-scale, Anti-Semitic campaign. However, Jews were given the 'option' to emigrate – but it was almost impossible to find a country which would accept them. Ho Feng-shan, who was now Consul-General in Vienna, issued a large number of visas to Shanghai. The city was then under Japanese occupation and a visa was not required for entry. But the Nazi authorities required a visa before Jews could leave Germany. Quite a few of the emigrants did finally settle in Shanghai. But many more were able to use their visas as the starting-point to enter other countries, including Palestine, the Philippines, and even the United States. Eric Saul, who has been researching this episode, estimates that Ho Feng-shan probably saved as many as 10,000 Jews from persecution and death. Chen Chieh had become Ho's boss, and was very much opposed to the liberal issue of visas. He ordered Ho to stop, but Ho persisted, citing instructions from the Foreign Ministry. Chen sent a subordinate to Vienna to try to implicate Ho in selling visas, but the subordinate found nothing amiss. Ultimately, Ho left Vienna, and Europe, in 1940. He later moved to Taiwan, where he continued in diplomatic service, ultimately retiring to the United States. In 2001, the State of Israel posthumously conferred on Ho the title 'Righteous among the Nations' for his rescue contributions (Xu, 2008: 13) (see Appendix).

FuRen University

The FuRen ('Promotion of Righteousness') University was established in 1925 in Peking. It was one of three Roman Catholic universities created in China. Initially, it was sponsored by American Benedictines but financial difficulties led to its transfer in 1933 to the protective support of the Society of the Divine Word (SVD). The SVD was of German origin, dating from 1875. Created with a focus on overseas missions, it early on moved its headquarters to the Netherlands to escape Bismarck's '*Kulturkampf*' (*Cultural Struggle*) and then to the United States. Whilst SVD provided many teachers and administrators, the university relied increasingly on Chinese staff. Enrolment passed the 100 mark in 1929. In that year, they created a Department of Sociology and Economics.

Beginning in 1936, it was headed by Rudolph Rahmann (1902–1985), an SVD missionary, who was the top administrative officer of the university. German-born, Rahmann received advanced education in Holland and Austria, completing a PhD in Vienna in anthropology in 1935. In the 1938 FuRen catalogue, he was listed as teaching Social and Economic Origins, Principles of Sociology, Social Work and Social Encyclicals. By then, there were two other German nationals teaching Economics. Aloys Oberle taught A *General Introduction to Social and Economic Problems*. He was a sinologist and linguist by profession. Hans Conrad Ernest Zacharias, PhD, was teaching *Economic History of Modern Europe*. His doctorate from Giessen (1897) was in science. All three were still present in 1948, when they were joined by Ludwig Fabel. His doctorate in political economy was from Freiburg (1921), with a dissertation on small business in the textile industry.

By 1938, FuRen also had two German-educated Chinese teaching Economics. One was Tung Hsi-fan (Dong Xifan), who held a diploma in political economy from Berlin. He joined FuRen in 1937. In 1945, he transferred to Tongji University, of which he became President in 1946. The other was Liu Dse-ming (Liu Zeming), who completed a doctorate at Munster with a dissertation on the economic aspects of the Yellow River (1937). These were subsequently joined by Tu Jen-shi (Du Renzhi), who moved from Shanxi University, where he had headed the Law School. He subsequently returned to serve as Head of the School of Finance and Economics at Shanxi University and was a member of the Chinese People's Political Consultative Committee (Zhou, 1999: 127).

After the Japanese occupation in 1937, the major Chinese universities moved their operations to West China, followed in 1941 by 'Yenching', the chief Protestant missionary college. FuRen was able to continue its operations by trading on its German connection. Filling a vacuum left by the departure of the other schools, FuRen enrolments and staff expanded. Whilst in the mid-1930s there were about 600–700 students, the number expanded to over 1,200 in 1938 and reached a peak in 1947 when it was nearly 2,400. In that year, there were 441 Economics students (now a separate department), the largest in the university. From the 1930s, the majority of the Chinese teaching Economics were American-trained. We have identified 36 Chinese who taught Economics at

FuRen prior to 1950. Of these, 24 studied abroad, 18 of them in the US. Several American texts were used and English was frequently the medium of instruction. Several Economics faculty moved to FuRen from other Beijing universities when those schools migrated during the War.

FuRen was closed, along with the other missionary colleges, in 1952. Its social science programmes were transferred to Beijing Normal University but numerous economists moved to the newly formed Central Institute of Finance and Economics. A long-time faculty member and administrator, Chang Chong-yi (Zhang) was persecuted to death in 1952 in Jiang Qing's attack on Liu Shaochi.

Conclusions

To sum up, this chapter has identified about 1,600 Chinese who had studied Economics at the graduate level or equivalent in Western countries, as cited in my book *Jingji Xue* (Trescott, 2007). We are still adding to the list – but the proportions are not likely to change. *About three-fourths of the students studied in the United States.* But Germany (including Austria) accounted for 134, slightly below Britain (162), slightly above France (113). German universities were admired for their emphasis on state-dominated national economic development. Students were recruited to Germany from German-language schools in universities (such as Tongji, as well as *Beida*) and from study in Japan.

Many German-educated Chinese took positions in government, particularly in the diplomatic service (see Liang, 1978). Most of these left China after the Communists took over. *Intellectually, German-educated Chinese contributed especially to the study of land economics and public finance. However, the pathbreaking innovations in Economic Theory associated with Menger, Wieser and Bohm-Bawerk did not attract Chinese students.*

Appendix

a   Ho Feng-shan is profiled in *Who's Who in China* (1936: 80). The story of his rescue of the Jews appeared in *Spotlight on China*, the quarterly bulletin of the Lutheran Literature Society for the Chinese, March 2001. For further information, I contacted the editor, Dr Arne Sovik, who kindly sent me a typed detailed narrative prepared by family members.

b   FuRen University: unlike the Protestant missionary colleges, which are very well-documented, FuRen materials are not easy to find. I began with information provided by my colleague Lu Chung-tai, who was a FuRen student in the 1940s. There are several catalogues at the SVD headquarters in Techny, Illinois, as well as copies of the Yearbook and magazine. With the aid of Dr Wu Minchao of the Chinese Academy of Social Sciences, we located FuRen materials in the archives of Beijing Normal University and the Beijing Municipal Archives. FuRen published a historical memorial volume in 2008. Professor Lai Rongyuen obtained a copy for me. A short biography of Rudolf Rahmann is in *FuJen* (the old spelling) Studies, 1973.

c   There are two doctoral dissertations, as follows:

> Shih Li-lian (1999). 'Transformational Educational Leadership of the Founders and Educators of the Catholic University in Peking (1925–1944)', St Mary's University of Minnesota, 1999.

> Chen, Rev. John Shujie (2003). 'Catholic Higher Education in China: The Rise and Fall of FuRen University Beijing', Boston College, 2003.

Notes

1 An earlier version of this chapter was presented at a 2010 seminar at the Albert-Ludwigs-Universitat, Freiburg GE, through the generosity of Prof. Dr Sabine Dabringhaus. This chapter builds on material spelled out in great detail in Trescott, 2007. That is my excuse for leaving out a full list of references and a list of all the people who helped my research, especially my wife Kathleen Trescott. In recent preparation for this chapter, my helpers were Dr Gao Wei, Dr Li Quan, Dr Wu Minchao and Prof. Lai Rongyuen.

2 Liu Binglin, who studied at LSE and Berlin, published a book on List's life and ideas in 1925. Wang Kaihua wrote a 1929 German dissertation on the spread of List's ideas in China which was published in Shanghai as well as in Germany. He also translated List's *National Economics*. Wang taught at Zhongshan University, held numerous government positions, then moved to Taiwan.

3 However, Tschang (Zhang) Yen-yu wrote a 1935 dissertation in Vienna under Othmar Spann entitled *Sozial Frage und standische Sozialpolitik in Westen und in China* (*Social Questions and Social Policy in the West and in China*). It presented a history of attitudes and policy regarding labour in Germany and in China. There were references to prominent German economists: Schmoller, Brentano, Knapp and Spann, but with no reference to Marx.

4 German sources Westernized Chinese names in their own unique manner. I have reproduced the German Westernizations of Chinese names as they appear in the original documents.

5 German students who were serious about an academic career would typically go on to prepare a 'Habilitation', comparable to an American doctoral dissertation. I am not aware that any Chinese student prepared one of the former.

6 Sombart 'had never known any ambition other than to make money and attract attention to himself…' (von Mises, 2009: 87).

7 In contrast to Schumpeter, Ludwig von Mises (2009) spoke in very scornful terms of his contemporaries:

> Among the many hundreds of men who taught economics at German universities between 1870 and 1934, not one could be found who was acquainted with the works of the Austrian [Menger, Wieser, Bohm-Bawerk], Lausanne [Walras], or modern Anglo-Saxon [Jevons, Marshall] schools.
>
> (p. 30)

They were overwhelmingly critical of free market conditions. 'Private property and ownership should be formally retained, but business was to be managed according to government directives' (p. 12).

References

Arndt, P. (1937). *Der Arbeitslohn in China [Wages in China]*. Leipzig: Buske.

Chiang, Y.-C. (2001). *Social Engineering and the Social Sciences in China, 1919–1949*. New York, NY: Cambridge University Press.

Ely, R. T. (1893). *Outlines of Economics*. New York, NY: Hunt and Eaton, translated into Chinese in 1910.

Fong, H. D. (Fan, X.) (1935). 'Bibliography on the Land Problems of China', *Nankai Social and Economic Quarterly*, 8: 325–384.

Grossekettler, H. G. (1989). 'On Designing an Economic Order: The Contributions of the Freiburg School.' In *Perspectives on the History of Economic Thought* (D. A. Walker, ed.). Brookfield, VT: Edward Elgar, 38–84.

Kirby, W. C. (1984). *Germany and Republican China*. Stanford, CA: Stanford University Press.

Liang, H.-H. (1978). *The Sino-German Connection*. Amsterdam: van Gorcum.

List, F. [1841] (1927). *The National System of Political Economy [Guojia Jingjixue]*, translated into Chinese by K. Wang. Beijing: Commercial Press.

List, F. [1841] (1966). *The National System of Political Economy*. New York, NY: Kelly.

Lutz, J. G. (1985). 'Karl F. A. Gutzlaff: Missionary Entrepreneur', in *Christianity in China: Early Missionary Writings* (S. W. Barnett and J. K. Fairbank, eds). Cambridge, MA: Harvard University Press, 61–87.

Marx, K. [1867] (1938). *Capital*, translated into Chinese in a complete version by Y.-N. Wang and T.-L. Kuo. Beijing: Foreign Languages Publisher.

Marx, K. [1867] (1954). *Capital*. Moscow: Progress Publishers, in English, translators unknown.

Meisner, M. (1967). *Li Ta-chao and the Origins of Chinese Marxism*. Cambridge, MA: Harvard University Press.

Schluter-Ahrens, R. (2002). *Der Volkswirt Jens Jessen*. Marburg: Metropolis-Verlag.

Schumpeter, J. (1954). *History of Economic Analysis*. New York, NY: Oxford University Press.

Sombart, W. (1915). *Handler und Helden [Hucksters and Heroes]*. München: Duncker & Humblot.

Sombart, W. (1934): *Deutscher Sozialismus*. Charlottenburg: Buchholz & Weisswange. English translation (1937, 1969): *A New Social Philosophy*. New York, NY: Greenwood.

Sun, D.-Q. (2006). *The Development of Economics in China: The Chinese Economics Association (1923–1953)*. Shanghai: Sanlian Bookstore. (Chinese language: Gao Wei created for me a 57-page English digest of the 820 biographical sketches.)

Trescott, P. B. (2007). *Jingji Xue: The History of the Introduction of Western Economic Ideas into China, 1850–1950*. Hong Kong: Chinese University Press.

Von Mises, L. (2009). *Memoirs*. Auburn, AL: Ludwig von Mises Institute.

Who's Who in China (1936) in *Shanghai China Weekly Review Supplement*, annual, n.d., p. 80.

Who's Who in China (1940) in *Shanghai China Weekly Review Supplement*, annual, n.d., p. 19.

Who's Who in Modern China: From the Beginning of the Chinese Republic to the End of 1953 (1954), compiled by M. Perleberg, Hong Kong: Ye Old Printerie, p. 130.

Xu, Y. (2008). 'Chinese Goodwill Delegation Visits Jordan and Israel', *Voice of Friendship*, 149: 12–14.

Yuan, T.-L. (1963). *A Guide to Doctoral Dissertations by Chinese Students in Continental Europe, 1907–1962*. Reprinted from *Chinese Culture Quarterly*. Taipei.

Zhou, M. (1999). *Dictionary of Returned Students*. Nanjing University Press (Chinese language).

10 Friedrich List in China

The second face of Janus

Qunyi Liu

Introduction

The diffusion of ideas is also a process of intellectual creation. With the lack of domestic sources and with the urgent need for transformation, most of the Western concepts 'imported' into the country, such as Classical Economics and Marxism, had been re-created, diffused and then accepted in early modern China (see Trescott, 2007). However, the recreation and transmission of Friedrich List's (1789–1846) ideas in China at that time was not deemed successful. This chapter will examine the process of diffusion through the works of Kaihua Wang (1894–1976), in order to explore List's ideas for their 'Chinese characteristics' (see Warner, 2015 and in this volume).

A key author, Professor Yan (2011, 2015a, 2015b), discusses the transmission of List's theory into China in the early twentieth century, and argues that the reception was 'active' but not influential. Yet he distinguishes almost no difference between List's image in Germany and in China and demonstrates a strong tendency towards the development dimension. Another source, Wendler (2014: 105–114) summarizes several updated works of research on List and extends the time-span up to today's China. He finds that the PRC governments after 1949 have kept a positive attitude towards List, and even the 'Open Door' policy after 1978 was in turn in favour of self-reliance based on List's theories. Again, another view (see Trescott, 2007, as well as his chapters in this volume) depicts a comprehensive picture of the transmission of German Economics to China by returning students, at the turn of the twentieth century, including List's followers.

Key issues remain concerning the earlier ignorance and the then later complete absorption of List. We will try to answer the following questions vis-à-vis the exploration of List's image in the diffusion of his work. Has List been 're-created' through the transmission and reception of his works in China? Does the 'second face of Janus' in fact matter?

The chapter will begin with a brief illustration of Friedrich List's image in Germany and the United States as a reference-point; we will then introduce Wang's life in its historical context. Wang's description of List through his dissertation will also be analysed in detail. The fourth and fifth part will focus on

Wang's influence and the following reception of List in China. The chapter will end with a set of concluding remarks.

Friedrich List in Germany and in the United States

One scholar (Iggers, 1962: 17–40) has compared the different images of the German historian Leopold von Ranke (1795–1886) to disclose that what this writer himself had believed, was less important to the development of historiography than the image of Ranke in the historian's mind. Being in the same tradition, List distinguished himself not that differently.

List reminds the 'German People' of a *schlechtes Gewissen* (Heuss, 1956) which means a 'feeling of guilt', just because he is regarded as a symbol of Germany with his 'tragic fate'. However, List's ideas were relatively neglected after the Second World War in West Germany – and only referred to as a 'bourgeois' practice of capitalism (*bourgeoisen kapitalistischen Praktiker*) in East Germany (Wendler, 2013: 12). List is, additionally, more or less possibly 'dead' in today's Germany, one may argue, contrary to his surprising popularity from his death to the present century elsewhere.

It is said that List's *Das nationale System der politischen Ökonomie* (NSPO thereafter: List, 1841; Lloyd, 1885) proved to be a great success for a long time. The second edition and the third one were made only one year and three years after the first publication. Furthermore, in 1843 the book had been already translated into Hungarian as the first version in a foreign language, and it was followed in 1851 and 1857 by a French version, in 1856 an English one in Philadelphia, in 1860 in Melbourne and in 1885 in London. By 1904, there was a worldwide version which was printed in London, New York and Bombay at the same time. Other versions such as ones in Swedish and Russian had been released one by one (Wendler, 1976: 24). There are at least three Chinese versions, among which Kaihua Wang contributed the earliest one in 1927. One can argue that NSPO is the most read German work of economics – except for his opponent's, Karl Marx's *Capital* (1867). An international association Friedrich-List-Gesellschaft (The Friedrich List Society) was set up in the 1920s (Heuss, 1956; Wendler, 1976) but there was in a break during the Second World War and, in 1955, it was re-organized in List's hometown.

As a matter of fact, his fellow-countryman Karl Marx (1818–1883) and in turn his collaborator Friedrich Engels (1820–1895) also read List's works. According to Engels, 'Marx began his economic studies in Paris, in 1843, starting with the great Englishmen and Frenchmen. Of German economists he knew only Rau and List, and he did not want any more of them' (Engels, 1885: 9). But a *mixed* image of List exists in Germany. He is considered neither economist nor politician (Heuss, 1956) but as a coordinator of 'Theory' as well as 'Practice', especially in the field of domestic Commercial Policy.

Contrary to being a 'patriot' in Germany, List in the US has been looked upon as a 'cosmopolitan' (see Tribe, 2008), whose theory may even be seen as the basis of today's European Union. List's argument, such as 'Commercial union and political union are twins; the one cannot come to birth without the other' (List, 1846: 276) is referred to as an argument for his 'cosmopolitanism'. Despite the obvious tendency toward protectionism in NSPO, American economists prefer to stress the final goal of List's practice, that is, to realize a 'liberal free-trade system' around the world.

Nevertheless, the 'Post-Keynesians' in the US, such as Paul Samuelson, (1915–2009) went on to give an explanation of List from another perspective. Samuelson (1960) indicates that List is one of the most important 'American' economists, in that he emphasizes protectionism and nationalism, which is similar to most of the American economists in the past, and also acts as the originator of modern Development Economics. Compared with the positive evaluation of German people, Anglo-American academia notices the 'unsystematic' (Tribe, 2008), even 'confusing' theories, however (Krugman, 1994). Although the character of 'cosmopolitanism' in List's theory is singled out, he still stands as the opposite pole to Adam Smith (1723–1790) or the whole corpus of Classical Economics, at least in the eyes of many Americans.

Yet, List shows different faces in his two 'Motherlands', that is, the more 'practical' in Germany and the more 'theoretical' in the United States, demonstrating that 'indeed the world is ruled by little else. Practical men, who believe themselves to be quite exempt from any intellectual influence, are usually the slaves of some defunct economist' according to John Maynard Keynes (1883–1946) (Keynes, 2007: 383).

Wang's life and his book: between China and Germany

Kaihua Wang was also possibly attracted by the 'practical' values in Germany (see the chapters by Trescott in this volume) so that he finished his PhD Thesis on List and translated NSPO into Chinese as well. He reiterated his preference for the applied theory – in both of his publications.

Wang was born in Hubei Province, which is the hometown of the *xinjun* (the New Army led by Shikai Yuan 1859–1916 and later by Zhidong Zhang, 1837–1909, in Hubei Province) and the *ziqiangjun* (the Army of Self-strength led by Zhang). Both of the two armies symbolize the beginning of the modern Chinese military power with an armoury of a Western genre, mainly from Japan and Germany. The *Xinhai* Revolution in 1911 was launched by the *xinjun* in Wuhan, the biggest city of Hubei, which proved to be the decisive uprising to overthrow the Qing government of the time. Hubei is possibly also the 'cradle' of early Chinese industrialization. During the 'Self-Strengthening Movement' (*Zi qiang Yun doing*) (1861–1895) Zhidong Zhang founded one of the most successful Arsenals in Hubei. The Hanyang Ironworks in Wuhan was another main achievement from Zhang and laid the base of the steel-industry in the new China.

Wang was involved with the military all his life. He went to the Hubei Preliminary School of Army as a child. After his graduation in Germany in Tübingen, he then went back to Wuhan, at first as a professor in the National

University of Wuhan to teach German language and Economics and later he joined the army and became a lieutenant-general in the army of the then Kuomintang/Guomindang, led by Chiang Kai-shek (1887–1975). He was in charge of translation and further training in the Army for some time. Henceforth, he pursued his career between academia and the military, both of which supplied him with the chance to practice his learning gained in Germany.

Wang chose List and his works as the thesis' theme for the following possible reasons. He went to Germany in 1923, when there was an enthusiasm for that writer there, as mentioned before. Moreover, Tübingen University had a direct relation with List, who had taken his only academic position there and set up the first Economics faculty in Germany. As Wang's supervisor, Professor Carl J. Fuchs (1865–1934) would show, his strong standpoint was 'national' economics. But he himself was also interested in East Asia, and collected its art works to form the so-called *Sammlung Fuchs* (Fuch's Collection).

Wang finished his thesis and translated NSPO in only three years from 1923 to 1926. What he wrote was composed of 150 pages with seven chapters (see Appendix 10.1). Needless to say, his thesis contains little mathematical content, which was common not only for the Chinese students at the time but also for the economics professionals until the first half of the twentieth century. The data-work, mainly 16 groups of Tables, stems from an economic survey of China. He cited 27 items of literature (see Appendix 10.2), which can be divided into three groups, namely the six about List, including NSPO and other relative research materials; the 13 about China, e.g. the speeches of Yinchu Ma (1882–1982) and Sun Yat-sen (1866–1925); and the rest being basic textbooks. He then updated the references up to 1925 and data up to 1923, and almost all of the literature is in the German and Chinese languages, except the book of *The Foreign Trade of China*, the PhD thesis of Chongsu See (later known as Zongshu Shi), who had gained his PhD degree in Economics from Columbia University in 1919.

Wang demonstrated his inclination for the strong protectionism and active interference of economic policy in the works of Ma and Sun as noted above, which comprise mainly economic strategies for China's development. As for See (1919), despite his background of economic liberalism from the US, he considered the subject of free trade in China historically. The first part of the book is devoted to the history of trade from 1500 to 1860 and the second part from 1861 to 1918. He emphasized the independence of China's foreign trade vis-à-vis the turning point of the Convention of Peking (1860) in which many harbour-cities were forced to open or even be leased (such as Hong Kong) to foreign invaders. The book was selected possibly because of the author's standpoint of nationalism – as well as the rich sources of trade data.

The other two books by Chia Shei Yui (also known as Shiyi Jia, 1887–1965) and Tsien Chen Shou Sun (aka, Hidematsu Tsumura, 1876–1939) have *Japanese* origins, which was the most crucial channel of indirect transmission of the Listian school into China (see Yagi's chapter in this volume on Western Economics and Japan for an overview). Both of the books were considered 'bestsellers' and 'practice-oriented'. The book by Jia (1917) focuses on the history of public-finance management in China from the Qing dynasty to 1916, and the author was in charge of the consultant committee of China's financial policy when the book was published and later a member of the Tariff Commission. Tsumura's (1920) book was translated from its warmly welcomed version in Japanese, and the author stands in the group of the most famous economists in Japan. He graduated from the Hitotsubashi University, which was famous for its strong tradition of 'national' economics (see Yagi's chapter earlier in this volume). Nevertheless, his book tends to be 'liberal' within a framework of Classical Economics. Tsumara became the CEO of Osaka Iron Works (the present Hitachi Zosen Corporation) in 1904 and founded the former Tokyo Foreign Language University. The last but not least important reference in Wang's book is *dongfang zazhi* (The East Magazine). It was one of the famous magazines during early Republican China, which held up the flags of both nationalism as well as scientism.

The German literature in Wang's book is not so varied and typical compared with his selection of the above ones in China, but is more concentrated on List and on the Chinese context. Based on these descriptive materials, Wang insisted on List's status as economist (Wang, 1929, 1–4) and summarized the life of the German economist in 20 pages, which is partly similar to Friedrich Gold-schmidt's book *Friedrich List: Deutschlands großer Volkswirt* (published in Berlin, in 1878).

Contrary to the oversimplified contents of List's life, the explanation of List's theory was astonishingly clear, systematic and comprehensive. He explored the sources of List's theory and analysed the whole economy with a method of general equilibrium normatively and positively, such as the interaction among agriculture, industry and services. He did not refer to the sources of his analysis except for the NSPO, several relative research materials and textbooks. We browsed all of the referred works but found none with the same framework as Wang's. Yet concerning the popularity of List during Wang's stay in Tübingen, there is no reason to conclude that the whole system was created by Wang individually, as there are several quotations without further information on such authors (for example, the quotations from Einberg on page 73 and Brandt on page 74).

In the first part of the thesis, Wang verified List's image as economist and also systematized his theory but we are still not convinced that the process of the latter is *original*.

Understanding List in the Chinese context

Contrary to the comparatively ambiguous source of the German contents, Wang's second part is much more distinct, that is, on the application of List's method in China.

Wang delineated the whole structure of China's politics and economy at the beginning of the second part and then compared China with Germany as a basis for further analysis. He noticed the similarities between China and Germany not only in the 1920s but also in List's period, which shows his sense of the work of the Historical School. In his words, both China in his time and Germany in List's period have a *distinct* culture and philosophy. He called it the 'transitional period', namely, with a development demand but unstable environment both in political and economics perspectives. A few Chinese warlords were named as evidence for his argument. He takes them as an example to give reasons for so many customs posts in China as well. According to the table quoted from Yinchu Ma's speech on page 101, there were in total 665 domestic customs posts and 58 of them were located in Jiangsu Province at the most, ten in Shandong Province at the least.

Needless to say, the data are quoted to prove that China was similar to Germany almost 100 years ago and List's learning was suitable for China as a result. Wang, at the same time, pointed out the crucial difference between the two countries. Germany in List's period needed only to deal with the domestic barriers, whilst China in the early twentieth century was faced with foreign colonialists, even the Customs was out of the control from the Chinese government. Therefore, the mentioned bias for nationalism in his reference has a different background compared with List. For List and Germany, it means 'unification', and for Wang and China, similar to the US perspective, 'independence'.

The importance of List's theory for China, the main chapter of the second part, begins with the aim of its reception, that is, to contend with Marxism. It is well-known that Karl Marx, as a latecomer into German economics, was a strong opponent to List, not *vice versa*. In his often-cited work *Draft of an Article on Friedrich List's book: Das Nationale System der Politischen Ökonomie* (published in 1845), Marx spared no effort to criticize his peer for his idealism, his theory of productive forces, careless optimism, and even his plagiarism. Wang claimed that at that time China was dominated by Marxism, which was the first reason he introduced List's theory to his 'motherland'.

In the early 1920s, Marxism had been transmitted by the Chinese students in Japan, Russia and France to their home-country (see Trescott's chapters in this volume). Most of Marx's works were originally in Japanese versions, and Chinese students in Japan, such as Duxiu Chen (the Founder of the Chinese Communist Party, henceforth CPC, 1879–1942), Dazhao Li (a leader of CPC, 1889–1927) and Baoyin Chen (the first Chinese translator of Marx, 1886–1920) brought such popular Japanese translated books into China, no matter whether they believed them or not. The historic October Revolution (1917) in Russia led to the founding of *Chinese Communist Party* (CCP) in 1921. Before and after the founding of Party, some Chinese students led by Yuzhang Wu (1878–1966) went to France with a work-study programme, such as Zhou Enlai (1898–1976) and Deng Xiaoping (1904–1997), both of whom were forced to go abroad due to their political activities in the May Fourth Movement in 1919 (see Vogel, 2013). *The dominant Marxism thread, we may argue, then, stemmed from the above three origins interacting with each other.*

Wang's analysis corresponded to Yinchu Ma's, a protectionist as noted above, who had studied in the US. At the time, Ma gave a famous speech to a workshop of the *Zhongguo daxue shangxuehui* (Society for Business Research in Chinese Universities) in 1923. Wang was inspired by the speech and presented his arguments – mainly according to Ma's logic. In comparison with Ma, Wang was more familiar with List's theory and other German schools. Wang added more concrete materials to Ma's framework, for example, Marx's words from *A Contribution to the Critique of Political Economy* (1859: 1), 'the mode of production of material life conditions the general process of social, political and intellectual life'. Moreover, he listed two reasons that Marxism was not adapted to China. First, being still an agricultural country, there was no need to deal with the non-existing 'class conflict' between capitalists and workers. Second, 'internationalism' was not practical for China, as quite a few colonialists, including Germany, preyed on the former's coasts and riversides. Despite the two sufficient excuses, Wang did not refute Marxism completely. He adopted a historical attitude and stated that Communism, or a change of social institutions, would be realized in the 'future'. Meanwhile, he insisted the Soviet Union might be a 'good teacher' for China.

Although China was in a different international position compared with Germany, China possessed almost all of the necessary resources, productive agriculture and a plentiful labour force, which coincided with the prerequisites of List's stages of economic development. The following parts of the thesis supplies, with full data of the Chinese economy, enough to support Wang's argument. According to him, China's industrialization could follow the 'British way', that is, to build railway-networks and set up a steel and iron industry with the nations' rich natural resources. He cited data and arguments from Bertrand Russell's (1872–1970) work (1966) to indicate the importance of transportation system for China's industrialization.

With the target of industrialization and international independence, he suggested China take three steps of commercial policy, one by one (Wang, 1929, 131–132): a new tariff-system, a higher and discriminating tariff, and tariff autonomy. He discussed the political system in the last part, and through the German influence he considered that colonization had some advantage for a country with overpopulation, which shows his 'dual standards' for sovereign equity. He referred to *gelbe Gefahr* ('Yellow Peril'), a word originating from Germany, at the end of his thesis (page 150), to further warn China of the possible 'Anti-Sinicization' outcomes of development, which is a relevant comment even today.

Re-creating List in China

We can recognize certain contradictions in Wang's arguments, such as his attitude toward Marxism and colonialism, but with another perspective, we can find a relationship between his points with the Historical School. Therefore, Karl Marx is at least partly correct in his critique of List at least vis-à-vis his idealism. The Historical School states '*wie es eigentlich gewesen*' (simply to tell you how it was), but instead it does '*wie es eigentlich geworden*' (to describe how it evolved) (Iggers, 1962: 24).

Wang translated NSPO as he wrote his thesis and had it published when he went back to China in 1927 (see Lishite, 1927). The translation was warmly welcomed, as were other economic books in China at that time and reprinted in 1929, 1933 and 1935 (Yan, 2015a). Wang repeated his arguments in the preface and changed the book title to *guojia jingjixue* (National Economics) to emphasize the role that the Chinese government should play in the economic sector.

Although the translated book proved to be a success, List's theory was not totally accepted by the Chinese government, either by the left CPC or the right (Guomindang, henceforth GMD). List showed his 'Two Faces' to both these sides. The followers of List, including Wang and Ma, opposed Marxism in order to avoid radical change of social system. Meanwhile, List was introduced to hinder the economic liberalism – which was being promoted by quite a few of Chinese students coming back from the US (see Trescott's chapters in this volume).

Did List's theory matter in China?

Sun (2006) insists that indeed 'economic liberalism' was dominant in China before 1949, whilst Yan (2015b) holds a *different* opinion. The latter author divides the period into two phases, the first one is from 1927 to 1946, when the *zhongmei youhao tongshang hanghai tiaozue* (Sino-American Treaty of Friendship, Commerce and Navigation) was signed; the second one from 1946 to 1949, with the founding of the PRC. Also, the switch was considered to be the comprehensive agreement, as it includes almost all of the international factor mobility, with items like a common market agreement rather than a free trade agreement. Needless to say, it was the economic liberalist who pushed for the acceptance. Yan considers it a turning point from protectionism to liberalism and from economic development to military dropout for the GMD. The correlation between the agreement and GMD's destiny needs further research but one thing is certain that the agreement was a definite result of the open policy of the US and GMD agreeing to join in the free world system; due to its reliance on the military aid from the US. Being regarded as an inequitable agreement, it was cancelled as soon as the Party took over.

Boecking (2008) discusses the economic policy without considering whether it belongs to protectionism or free trade. His conclusion notes that having taken over the Maritime Customs Service, the GMD employed tariffs to manage its public debt. Comparing the average tariff rate with the calculation of the total tariff amount and the import value (see Figure 10.1), Boecking appears to be right. However, can the radical increase of the rate from 3.5 per cent to 27 per cent be attributed to the obvious intention of protectionism? Yet the problem is that GMD did not own the whole right of taxation. In this sense, Wang's argument works well. The threat that China faces is not from inside, but from outside.

The success of Marxism in China definitively symbolized the failure of List in 1949, but his opponent Adam Smith was also in the 'same boat'. Later, in

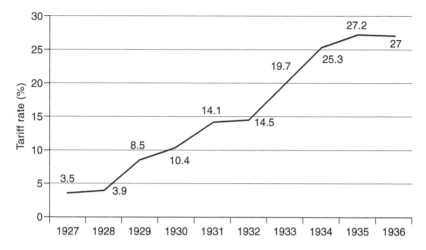

Figure 10.1 The average tariff rate of China (1927–1936, per cent).
Source: Liu and Wu, 2010: 1412.

1978, China opened its door again and began to adopt a mixture of List's and Smith's principles, and even with Marxism (see Lai's chapter on Smith in this volume). The seeming paradoxical coexistence of formerly rival theories is dubbed as *juyou zhongguo tese*, that is, with 'Chinese characteristics', implying an accommodating adaptation, as already noted.

The new followers of List celebrated the 90th anniversary of Wang's first translation at the beginning of 2015 and introduced a new theory to make more of his influence, that is, as *Neo-Listianism* (Jia, 2012; Yan, 2015c). The authors stress the industrialization process as an addition to List's theory of commercial policy and productive power, which reminds readers of the Japanese understanding of List during the two world wars (see Metzler, 2006). The new element of Neo-Listianism can be described as industrialization in a globalization era, similar to Wang's assertion of China's economic independence. Thus, the 'Re-creation' of List in China can be seen as an ongoing affair.

Concluding remarks

Few Chinese can access and read the Chinese economist, Kaihua Wang's dissertation in German but the transmission and reception of List's theory has been remarkably activated through his unread article. By reading his thesis, we can find the 'time-gap' between the former and later industrialization phases and various faces of the same List. Indeed: 'A thinker may be dead in some bits of the world and alive in others' (Skidelsky, 2007, 1; quoted in Warner, 2015 and in this volume), and in different periods. This has happened, we may conclude, to Friedrich List as well.

Appendix

Appendix 10.1 Contents of Kaihua Wang's dissertation

continued

Appendix 10.1 Continued

Pages	Literatur	References
91	Der Bergbau	e) Mining
92	Der Verkehr	f) Transportation
94	Die finanzielle Lage	g) The Financial Situation
97	Das Geldwesen	h) Monetary System
98	Das Bankwesen	i) Banking Industry
6. Kapitel	Vergleich zwischen dem List'schen Deutschland und dem heutigen China	Comparing Germany in List's Period and Today's China
99	Allgemeines	36. Introduction
101	Wirtschaftlicher Vergleich	37. Comparing the Economies
102	Unterschiede zwischen beiden Ländern	38. The Difference between the two Countries
7. Kapitel	Die Bedeutung der List'schen Lehre für China	The Importance of List's Theory for China
103	Der Marxismus und die chinesischen Verhältnisse	39. Marxism and China's Current Situation
107	Die Verbreitung der List'schen Lehre	40. The Transmission of List's Theory
110	China besitzt List's Voraussetzungen für eine Vollnation	41. China's Prerequisites for List's Whole Nation
113	Die Bedeutung der List'schen Lehre für die Industrie, Landwirtschaft und den Handel Chinas	42. The Importance of List's Theory for Industry, Agriculture and Services
120	Die Bedeutung der List'schen Lehre für die soziale Frage und Zollsystem Chinas	43. The Importance of List's Theory for the Social Problem und Tariff System in China
138	Die Bedeutung der List'schen Lehre für die soziale Frage und die Kolonisation Chinas	44. The Importance of List's Theory for the Social Problem and the Colonization in China
145	Die Bedeutung der List'schen Lehre für Chinas Politik	45. The Importance of List's Theory for China's Politics

Appendix 10.2 References in Kaihua Wang's dissertation with the original and the updated versions

1. Chia S. Y.: Die Finanzgeschichte der chinesischen Republik, 2. Aufl. Schanghai 1924.
   Chia, S. Y. 1924. *Die Finanzgeschichte der chinesischen Republik*, Shanghai: shangwu yinshuguan (Commercial Press).
2. Chong S. S.: *The Foreign Trade of China*, New York, NY n.p 1919.
   See, C. 1929. *The Foreign Trade of China*, New York, NY: Columbia University; London: P. S. King & Son. Ltd.
3. Commercial Press: Die östliche Zeitschrift.
   Commercial Press (1904–1948).
4. Damaschke, A.: n.d, Friedrich List, ein Prophet und Märtyrer deutscher Weltwirtschaft
   Damaschke, A. 1917. *Friedrich List: ein Prophet und Märtyrer deutscher Weltwirtschaft*, Jena: Fischer Verlag.
5. Das Ministerium für Landwirtschaft, Industrie und Handel in der Prov. Kiangsu: Die Spinnereien und Webereien in der Prov. Kiangsu.
   Das Ministerium für Landwirtschaft, Industrie und Handel in der Prov. Kiangsu. 1920. *Die Spinnereien und Webereien in der Prov. Kiangsu*.
6. Gide und Rist: Geschichte der volkswirtschaftlichen Lehrmeinungen (deutsch von R. W. Horn) dritte Aufl., Jena, 1923.
   Gide, C. und C. Rist. 1923. *Geschichte der volkswirtschaftlichen Lehrmeinungen*, R. Horn. (Trans.). Jena: Gustav Fischer.
7. Goldschmidt F.: Friedrich List, Deutschlands großer Volkswirt, 2. Aufl., Berlin 1878.
   Goldschmidt, F. 1878. *Friedrich List, Deutschlands großer Volkswirt*, Berlin: Verlag von Julius Springer.
8. Harms, B: Volkswirtschaft und Weltwirtschaft, Jena 1912.
   Harms, B. 1912. *Volkswirtschaft und Weltwirtschaft*, Jena: Fischer.
9. Hettner, A: Grundzüge der Länderkunde, II. Bd. 1. & 2. Aufl., Leipzig und Berlin 1924.
   Hettner, A. 1924. *Grundzüge der Länderkunde*, Leipzig und Berlin: Teubner.
10. Köhler, Y. C.: Problematisches zu Friedrich List, Leipzig 1908.
    Köhler, Y. C. 1908. *Problematisches zu Friedrich List*, Leipzig: C. L. Hirschfeld.
11. Kumpmann, K: Friedrich List als Prophet des neuen Deutschlands, 1915.
    Kumpmann, K. 1915. *Friedrich List als Prophet des neuen Deutschlands*, Tübingen: Mohr.
12. Liefmann, R: Geschichte und Kritik des Sozialismus, 2. Aufl., Leipzig 1923.
    Liefmann, R. 1923. *Geschichte und Kritik des Sozialismus*, Leipzig: Quelle & Meyer.
13. List, F: Das nationale System der politischen Ökonomie, 4. Aufl., Jena 1922.
    List, F. 1922. *Das nationale System der politischen Ökonomie*. Jena: G. Fischen Verlag.
14. Ma Y. C.: Vorträge über chinesische ökonomische Probleme, I. Bd. 1923, II. Bd. Schanghai 1925.
    Ma, Y. 1925. *Vorträge über chinesische ökonomische Probleme*, Beijing: Beijing Morgenzeitung Press.
15. Macay, V.: China, die Republik der Mitte, ihre Probleme und Aussichten, Stuttgart und Berlin 1914.
    Macay, V. 1914. *China, die Republik der Mitte, ihre Probleme und Aussichten*, Stuttgart und Berlin: Cotta.

continued

16. Mammen, Franz: Friedrich List, Dresden und Leipzig 1916.
    Mammen, F. 1916. *Friedrich List*, Dresden und Leipzig: Piersons Verlag.
17. Öhler, W.: Chinas Erwachen, Die Aue, Verlag in Wernigerode 1925.
    Öhler, W. 1925. *Chinas Erwachen*, Wernigerode: Die Aue, Verlag.
18. Derselbe: China und die christliche Mission in Geschichte und Gegenwart, Stuttgart
    1925.
    Öhler, W. 1925. *China und die christliche Mission in Geschichte und Gegenwart*,
    Stuttgart: Evangelischer Missionsverlag.
19. Russell, B.: China und die Probleme des fernen Ostens, München.
    Russell, B. 1925. *China und die Probleme des fernen Ostens*, Mit einer Einleitung
    von General Prof. Dr. Karl Haushofer, München: Drei-Masken-Verlag.
20. The China Year Book 1924.
    The Minister of Industry of Republic China. 1924. *The China Year Book*. Shanghai:
    Commercial Press.
21. Schulze, Ernst: Die Zerrüttung der Weltwirtschaft, 2. Aufl. Berlin-Stuttgart-Leipzig,
    Verlag von Kohlhammer 1923.
    Schulze, E. 1923. *Die Zerrüttung der Weltwirtschaft*, Berlin, Stuttgart und Leipzig:
    Verlag von Kohlhammer.
22. Shen Jui und Stadelmann, D.: China und sein Weltproblem. Dresden 1924.
    Shen, J. und D. Stadelmann. 1924. *China und sein Weltproblem*, Dresden.
23. Sun Yet Sen: Aufbau Chinas, 2. Aufl. Schanghai 1922.
    Sun, Y. 1922. *Aufbau Chinas*, Schanghai: Sanmin Press.
24. Tsien Chen Shou Sun: Der Grundriss der Volkswirtschaftslehre. (übersetzt von Ma
    Lin Eu), 4. Aufl. Schanghai 1924.
    Lingfu Ma (Tran.). 1920. *Jincun Xiusong, Der Grundriss der Volkswirtschaftslehre*,
    Shanghai: Qunyi Press.
25. Waltershausen, V.: Zeittafel zur Wirtschaftsgeschichte, Halberstadt 1924.
    Waltershausen, V. 1924. *Zeittafel zur Wirtschaftsgeschichte*, Halberstadt: H. Meyer.
26. Witte: Sommer-Sonnentage in Japan und China, Göttingen 1925.
    Witte, J. 1925. *Sommer-Sonnentage in Japan und China*, Göttingen: Vandenhoeck
    & Ruprecht.
27. Derselbe: Ostasien und Europa, 1914.
    Witte, J. 1914. *Ostasien und Europa*, Tübingen: Verlag von J. C. B. Mohr.

Sources: miscellaneous, publishing details listed where available.

References

Boecking, F. (2008). 'Tariffs, Power, Nationalism and Modernity: Fiscal Policy in
    Guomindang-controlled China 1927–1945', PhD dissertation, University of Cam-
    bridge, UK.
Engels, F. (1885). 'Preface to Capital II', in K. Marx, *Capital: Book II, the Process of
    Circulation of Capital*, www.marxists.org/archive/marx/works/1885-c2/ch00.htm (1 of
    13) [23/08/2000 16:09:05] (accessed 1 November 2015).
Goldschmidt, F. (1878). *Friedrich List, Deutschlands großer Volkswirt* (Friedrich List,
    the Great Economist in Germany), Berlin: Verlag von Julius Springer.
Heuss, T. (1956). *Friedrich List, 1789–1846*, Hermann Heimpel, Theodor Heuss
    und Benno Reifenberg (eds), *Die großen Deutschen* III, Berlin: Propyläen-Verl,
    201–213.
Iggers, G. G. (1962). 'The Image of Ranke in American and German Historical Thought',
    History and Theory 2, 17–40.

Jia, G. (2012). *xinlisitezhuyi: tidai xinziyouzhuyi quanqiuhua de xinxueshuo* (Neo-Listianism: an Alternative Theory of Neo-liberalism of Globalization), *xuexi yu tansuo* (*Study and Exploration*) 3, 95–103.

Jia, S. (1917). *minguo caizhengshi* (The Financial History of Republic China), Shanghai: *shangwu yinshuguan* (Beijing: Commercial Press).

Keynes, J. M. (2007). *The General Theory of Employment, Interest and Money*, Basingstoke and New York, NY: Palgrave Macmillan.

Krugman, P. (1994). 'Proving my Point', www.foreignaffairs.com/articles/1994-07-01/proving-my-point (accessed 1 November 2015).

List, F. (1841). *Das nationale System der politischen Ökonomie*, Stuttgart and Tübingen. J. G. Cotta and S. S. Lloyd (Transl.). 1885. *The National System of Political Economy*, London: Longmans & Co.

List, F. (1846). *Schriften, Reden, Briefe* (Essays, Speeches and Letters), Berlin: Robbing.

Lishite [*sic*] [List, F.] (1927). *Guojia Jingjixue*, Beijing: Commercial Press (translated into Chinese by K. Wang).

Liu, K. and Wu, T. (eds). (2010). *zhongguo jindai jingjishi* (1927–1937) (The Modern History of Chinese Economy (1927–1937), Beijing: People's Press.

Lloyd, S. S. (Transl.) (1885) of List (1841). *The National System of Political Economy*, London: Longmans & Co.

Ma, Y. (1923). *Makesi xueshu zu lishite xueshuo eryhe shu yiyu zhongguo* (Marxism and Listanism, Which One Is Better for China?), in Ma, Y. 2014. *mayinchu yanjiangji* (Speeches by Yinchu Ma), Taiyuan: *shanxi renmin chubanshe* (Shanxi: People's Press), 220–228.

Marx, K. (1845). 'Draft of an Article on Friedrich List's book: Das Nationale System der Politischen Oekonomie', https://marxists.anu.edu.au/archive/marx/works/1845/03/list.htm (accessed 1 November 2015).

Marx, K. (1859). *A Contribution to the Critique of Political Economy*, www.marxists.org/archive/marx/works/1859/critique-pol-economy/index.htm (accessed 1 November 2015).

Metzler, M. (2006). 'The Cosmopolitanism of National Economics: Friedrich List in a Japanese Mirror', in A. G. Hopkins (ed.), *Global History: Interactions between the Universal and the Local*, Basingstoke and New York, NY: Palgrave Macmillan, 98–130.

Russell, B. (1966). *The Problem of China*, London: George Allen & Unwin Ltd, www.gutenberg.org/files/13940/13940-h/13940-h.htm (accessed 1 December 2015).

Samuelson, P. A. (1960). 'American Economics', in Ralph E. Freeman (ed.), *Postwar Economic Trends in the United States*, New York, NY: Harper, 31–50.

See, C. (1919). *The Foreign Trade of China*, New York, NY: Columbia University.

Sun, D. (2006). *zhongguojingjixueshe de chengzhang: zhongguojingjixueshe yanjiu (1923–1953)* (The Development of Economics in China: The Chinese Economics Association (1923–1953)). Shanghai: Sanlian Bookstore.

Trescott, P. B. (2007). *Jingji Xue: The History of the Introduction of Western Economic Ideas into China 1850–1950*, Hong Kong: Chinese University Press.

Tribe, K. (2008). 'List, Friedrich (1789–1846)', in S. N. Durlauf and L. E. Blume (eds), *The New Palgrave Dictionary of Economics*, 2nd edn, London: Palgrave Macmillan. The New Palgrave Dictionary of Economics Online, www.dictionaryofeconomics.com/article?id=pde2008_L000118 (accessed 1 November 2015).

Tsumura, H. (1920). *Jincun Xiusong, Guominjingjixue yuanlun*, Shanghai: qunyi shushe (Qunyi Press), in Chinese.

Vogel, E. F. (2013). *Deng Xiaoping and Transformation of China*, Cambridge, MA: Harvard University Press.

Wang, K. (1929). *Die Bedeutung der List'schen Lehre für China*, Shanghai: The Lo-Chun Book Co.

Warner, M. (2015). 'Keynes and China: "Keynesianism with Chinese Characteristics"', *Asia Pacific Business Review* 21, 1–13.

Wendler, E. (1976). *Friedrich List: Leben und Wirken in Dokumenten*, Reutlingen: Örtel + Spörer.

Wendler, E. (2013). *Friedrich List (1789–1846): Ein Ökonom mit Weitblick und sozialer Verantwortung*, Wiesbaden: Springer Gabler.

Wendler, E. (2014). *Friedrich List im Zeitalter der Globalisierung: Eine Wiederentdeckung* (Friedrich List in a Globalization Era: a Reconsideration), Wiesbaden: Springer Gabler.

Yan, P. (2011). *zhongguo jingjixue xingcheng guocheng zhong de deguo chuantong* (The German Origin of China's Economics), *yanhua yu chuangxin jingjixue pinglun* (*Review of Evolutionary Economics and Economics of Innovation*) 2, 86–97.

Yan, P. (2015a). *minguo shiqi lisite jingji xueshuo de zaihua chuanbo* (The Transmission of List's Economic Theory in Republic China), *xuexi yu tansuo* (*Study and Exploration*) 1, 89–97.

Yan, P. (2015b). *guomin zhengfu you baohuzhuyi zhuanxiang ziyouzhuyi de xinlisitezhuyi jiedu* (The Interpretation of RC Government's Transformation from Liberalism to Protectionism), *jiaoxue yu yu yanjiu* (*Teaching and Research*) 3, 26–34.

Yan, P. (2015c). *zhanlvxing gongyehua: yige xinlisitezhuyi gongyehua lilun* (Strategic Industrialization: A Neo Listian Theory of Industrialization), *qinghuadaxue xuebao: zhexue shehuikexue ban* (*Journal of Tsinghua University: Philosophy and Social Sciences*) 5, 166–176.

11 The diffusion of F. A. Hayek's thoughts in Mainland China and Taiwan

Weisen Li, Xingyuan Feng and Liang Sun

Introduction

In course of the twentieth century, Friedrich August von Hayek (1899–1992) was to be recognized as a great thinker, as well as an economist, who would have a major influence on the understanding of modern societies. In his nearly 60 years of academic research life from the 1920s to 1980s, Hayek has left us with nearly 20 key works and a plethora of academic papers. In the 1920s and 1930s, F. A. Hayek and Ludwig von Mises (1881–1973) had debated with Oscar R. Lange (1904–1965) and Abba P. Lerner (1903–1982) on the possibility of what was known as 'socialist calculation', regarding the possibility of a rational economic calculation in a socialist economic system.

Hayek had already published his book on *Collective Economy Planning* in 1937, then *The Road to Serfdom* in 1944, and *Individualism and Economic Order* in 1948, in which he analysed the infeasibility of central planned economies in depth, interpreted the rational and functional efficiency of a market system as a 'spontaneous' order and discussed the general rules and principles of modern society, Democracy and the Rule of Law notwithstanding. In the 1930s and 1940s, Hayek went on to debate with John Maynard Keynes (1883–1946) (see the later chapter on Keynes and China in this volume), particularly on the issues of monetary theory and business cycles, for more than a decade, although remaining on most cordial terms.

In this period, such issues were discussed a great deal and business cycles theory, as marked by the 'Hayekian Triangle', in modern economics established. Then, in 'Economics and Knowledge' (in Hayek, 1948: 33–56), 'The Use of Knowledge in Society' (in Hayek, 1948: 77–91) and other papers that were published in the 1940s, Hayek discussed the function of *prices* in the process of resource-allocation, which has exerted a persistent impact on modern economics since the 1940s. In the 1950s, he published two significant works in psychology, *The Sensory Order: An Inquiry into the Foundation of Theoretical Psychology* (Hayek, 1952a) and *The Counter-Revolution of Science* (Hayek, 1952b). In the 1960s and after, he brought out *The Constitution of Liberty* (Hayek, 1960), *Studies in Philosophy, Politics and Economics* (Hayek, 1967), *Law, Legislation and Liberty* (Hayek, 3 volumes, 1973, 1976a, 1979), *Denationalization of Money*

(Hayek, 1976b) and *New Studies in Philosophy, Politics, Economics and the History of Ideas* (Hayek, 1978), amongst others.

In the late 1980s, the aged Hayek summed up the thoughts of his life and then finished his important work, *The Fatal Conceit* (Hayek, 1988). In 1974, the Swedish Nobel Committee had announced that the Nobel Prize for Economics was granted to Gunnar Myrdal (1898–1987), a Swedish economist, and to F. A. Hayek, an Austrian one, 'for their pioneering work in the theory of money and economic fluctuations and for their penetrating analysis of the interdependence of economic, social and institutional phenomena' (The Royal Swedish Academy of Sciences, 1974: 1). Hayek's analysis of the functional efficiency of different economic systems is now regarded as one of his most significant contributions to economic research in the broadest sense. His guiding principle for his analysis was 'to study how efficiently all the knowledge and all the information dispersed among individuals and enterprises is utilized' (ibid.).

Hayekian thought was introduced to China from the 1940s, onwards. However, he was regarded as particularly relevant to Marxism by the CCP's propaganda organ, after Mao Zedong (1893–1976) took power and indeed before the 'Cultural Revolution', because of the discussion about the impossibilities of 'socialist calculation' by Hayek and Mises in the 1940s, and Hayek's criticisms of the central planning economy in The Road to Serfdom. *Professor Weizao Teng (1917–2008), the late president of Nankai University from 1981 to 1986, as well as a well-known economist in China, went on to translate Hayek's* The Road to Serfdom *(1944) in 1962, as well as* Prices and Production *(1931) in 1958, into Chinese.*

As Hayek was regarded as a Western 'reactionary bourgeois ideologist', Teng pointed out in the prefaces of the two books that the aim of translation was just for critique and 'reference'. Consequently, the two books were published as 'internal readers' in this period and could not be read publicly by the lay intellectuals because of Hayek's 'reactionary position'. Even so, the two translated books had spread Hayek's thoughts in Mainland China. On the other side, after the complete withdrawal of the Nationalist Party of China (Kuomintang/Guomindang) from the Mainland to Taiwan, the regime of Chiang Kai-shek (1887–1975) controlled the spread of the Western liberal thought for a long period of time. Although some scholars translated Hayek's works into Chinese very early and wrote articles and books to recommend Hayek's thoughts in Taiwan, Hayek's thoughts were not truly accepted and put into practice by the Taiwan authorities until the 1990s. Seen from the chronological order, some liberal economists in Taiwan recommended Hayek's works much earlier than those in Mainland China, but the works published in Taiwan did not spread to Mainland China, mainly due to the tensions across the Taiwan Straits.

Nevertheless, the situation changed fundamentally from the late 1980s. With the reform and opening-up in China since 1978, a number of Hayek's works written after the 1940s on economics, laws, politics, social theory and so on were translated into Chinese, which was to have a significant impact on those fields in China.

Nowadays, in the social sciences community in China, especially among economists and students of economics, F. A. Hayek is widely known. A great number of young scholars of the new generation in economics and other fields of social science have read Hayek's works and papers, or are familiar with his thoughts, which make him somewhat of a popular thinker among many of the younger generation. His thoughts about the Market Economy and the Rule of Law, we will thus argue, have now begun to influence the process of China's reforms in practice.

In this chapter, the diffusion of Hayekian thought in Chinese-speaking areas will be comprehensively investigated. In the first section, the diffusion of the early thoughts of Hayek in Mainland China before 1949 and then in Taiwan will be examined; in the next section, the diffusion of Hayek's ideas in Mainland China after the 1980s will be discussed specifically; and in the third section, the publication status of Hayek's works in Mainland China and the statistics about the studies on Hayek will be summarized briefly.

The diffusion of Hayek's thought in Mainland China before 1949 and in Taiwan after 1949 by Taiwan scholars

In the history of Chinese contemporary thought, the first person to introduce Hayek's economics ideas to China was David Chow (1902–1986), who was Hayek's student at the London School of Economics and Political Sciences (LSE). Chow, born in 1902 in Changsha, Hunan Province, was an economist and one of the three pro-disciples of Hayek in China (the other two being Dr Sho-Chieh Tsiang (1918–1923) and Dr Yu-Sheng Lin (1934–), who will both be mentioned later. During the Anti-Japanese War, Chow had founded a semi-monthly journal, *China Road*. He served successively as the deputy director of Taiwan Foreign Exchange and Trade Reform Committee, the director of General Administration of Customs and Duties of Ministry of Finance of Taiwan and so on. He later died in Los Angeles in 1986.

Chow's Economics theory was integrated with the philosophy of law, sociology, politics and history. His combination of Chinese traditional culture and liberalism is emphasized both in his academic studies and practice. His antithetical couplet 'Do not believe your words can enlighten the world; do not achieve your successes based on people's sufferings' (Chow, 2011: 1) is widely known among scholars in both Mainland China and Taiwan. After Chow returned to China, as a scholar or as a government officer, his theoretical explanations, reform proposals, and his own extension on social economic ideas were all based on Hayek's ideas. According to his narration, his Western knowledge was influenced by Classical Economics, the ideas of David Hume (1711–1786) and Edmund Burke (1729–1797), as well as the Neoclassical School, the Swedish School, the Austrian School, as well as the work of Immanuel Kant (1724–1804). The Austrian School was to play a significant role in Chow's knowledge-development. Undoubtedly, it was he who became the first 'preacher' of Hayek's thought in China.

In 1920, Chow was admitted to the college preparatory department of Peking University. In this period, he read Hayek's latest monograph *Prices and Production* (1931), and got to know the neutrality of money and the 'Hayekian Triangle' theory which divided the production structure into a triangle that contains intertemporal production-stages from the final customer goods to many kinds of intermediate goods. In 1933, Chow was awarded funds to go to study in England by the Ministry of Railways of the Nationalist Government. At that time, Chow went to the London School of Economics and Political Science (LSE), where Hayek was teaching, so he came to England and became the sole Chinese student directly under Hayek's supervision before the Anti-Japanese War. When just acquainted with Chow, Hayek was quite impressed by Chow's knowledge of his academic thoughts. The student did not have a Bachelor degree when he arrived in London, and Lionel Robbins, the Chair of the Department of Economics at LSE, awarded him a degree by making an *exception* and enrolled him as a Doctoral candidate in Economics, with Hayek as his supervisor. When studying there, Chow attended the seminars organized by Robbins (1898–1984) and Hayek regularly and reported to the former every two weeks. Hayek once suggested Chow should select a topic as his Doctoral dissertation's title in order to do a PhD before going back to China. But Chow declined Hayek's offer and only hoped to read books under Hayek's guidance. At first, he advised him to study the Classical Enlightenment theories of David Hume (1711–1776) and John Locke (1632–1704) that were prior to Adam Smith's (1723–1790).

Meanwhile, Hayek reminded him to focus on the controversies on inflation and banking in the eighteenth and nineteenth centuries. Hayek told him that with this knowledge-preparation, he would understand that Keynes's works did not make as much a contribution as claimed and that his policies of inflation would lead to a worse economic crisis, even collapse. Throughout his study in this period, Chow's thoughts were so essentially influenced by Hayek that he reflected 'The distinction between my mind and materialism, as well as the rejection towards all forms of totalitarianism, took shape when I was studying abroad' (Chow, 2011: 1).

In 1936, Hayek wrote recommendation letters to Mises and Wilhelm Ropke (1899–1966) in order to help Chow leave LSE to go to the School of Philosophy at Berlin University in Germany for postgraduate study (see the chapters by Trescott on German Economics and China in this volume). In his nearly five years of study abroad Hayek had always been Chow's tutor, even when he was in Germany. At that time, Chow was the only disciple of Hayek in China, so that he had unparalleled knowledge and comprehension of Hayek's ideas. After the onset of the Anti-Japanese War in 1937, he ended his period abroad and returned to China. With a complete acceptance of liberalism, Chow spread Hayek's thoughts in the following ways.

First, Chow worked as a Professor in the School of Economics at Hunan University and started to diffuse the economics of liberalism. In 1938, Shouyong Li, the Dean of the School of Literature of Hunan University, founded a semi-monthly journal, called the *China Road*. Chow, as the editor-in-chief, published a good deal of political comment in this journal in which he labelled his ideas as the school of *subjectivity*, and here, *liberalism* and *individualism* were strongly recommended. According to the descriptions in Hunan University's annuals, Chow completed two important tasks in this period time whilst teaching. One was introducing and publicizing this economic liberalism in teaching. The other was co-founding the above journal, with Shouyong Li and working as the Editor-in-Chief, spreading classical liberalism via the journal. According to Chow, he was by now familiar with the controversies between Keynes and the Austrian School economists. Considering the situation at that time, he recommended the free-enterprise viewpoint of Mises and Hayek, and refuted any forms of planned economy, which was to have a possible influence on China before 1949.

Second, after getting involved in the political activities on the economic policy of the Nationalist Party, Chow started to put his economic thoughts on liberalism into *practice* as a participant in economic decision-making. In 1940, Chow was elected as a Senator of the National Council of the Nationalist Party, and became a Professor in the National University in Nanjing. He perceived that the senior staff of the Nationalist Party boasted of a controlled and even planned economy, so he argued with them and refuted the Act about the government sale of grains and price control, which was to be put into practice via the Parliament. This was his first public presentation of liberal economic ideas in front of the Nationalist Party government.

After the triumph of the Anti-Japanese War in 1946, the Central Committee of the National Party planned to levy a tax on real-estate and carry out compulsory acquisition on gold and US dollars, as well as to apply price-controls on them. Chow was shocked and warned Hung-Chun Yu (1898–1960) also well-known as O. K. Yui, the Minister of Finance, that the implementation of these policies would lead to economic disorder. He was to serve as Premier in the Taiwan regime between 1954 and 1958. Finally, Yu reported this crosscurrent to the Executive Yuan there, which postponed the plan for two years. Unfortunately, the senior staff of the Nationalist Party decided to put that plan into force in 1948, which caused the final collapse of China's currency system. Many think that Chow's advice based on liberal economic thought was right. After the Nationalist Party's retreat to Taiwan, the Western media gave a high evaluation to Chow's foresight and sagacity. But Chow did not get more opportunities in high level economic decision-making, mainly because the Tsiang family had a grudge against his knowledge and ability.

Third, Chow devoted himself to summarizing his own academic thoughts and translating Hayek's important academic works by himself or by other scholars recommended by him – after he retired in Taiwan in the late 1960s. This could be regarded as Chow's third contribution to diffusing Hayek's thoughts. Chow spent more than five years translating Hayek's *The Constitution of Liberty* with more than 800,000 words (see Hayek, 1981 edition). In 1965, he continued to write two essays, 'Introduction to F. A. Hayek for Chinese Intellectuals' (Chow, 2005: 185–195) and 'Studies on Social Philosophy of the School of Hayek' (Chow, 2005: 41–53). The former of these introduced the economic thoughts of Hayek, especially his theory of business cycles, to Chinese readers.

Although Hayek's theory of business cycles was considered difficult to understand in academic circles, Chow was able to introduce it to Chinese intellectuals most clearly. Nowadays, even though Chow was not the first one to study Hayek's academic thoughts, he can be considered as the one who spent the most time introducing Hayek's thought systematically. No one could compete with him in the study of Hayek. Besides the translation of *The Constitution of Liberty*, Chow also finished his own academic monograph, namely a *Summary on Contemporary Great Thinker F. A. Hayek*, with 26 articles covering the thoughts of social philosophy and the Rule of Law, economic principles and policies, theory of monetary neutrality, specific economic issues of Taiwan and so on (Chow, 1981). Hayek wrote the preface of this book specially, which reflected the importance of this academic monograph on the diffusion of Hayek's thoughts in China. In 2005, Peking University Press published this work, renamed *On Hayek by Chow Dewei* (Chow, 2005), in Mainland China. What is worth mentioning is that Hayek visited Taiwan three times in September 1965, September 1966 and November 1975 respectively, and Chow was Hayek's escorting interpreter. This could also be considered as Chow's contribution to accelerate the diffusion of Hayek's thoughts in the Taiwan region.

Another important economist who spread Hayek's thoughts in Mainland China before 1949 and in Taiwan after 1949 is Sho-chieh Tsiang (1918–1923). He was also one of Hayek's students. Tsiang was born in Shanghai, China in 1918. He is well-known as an economist who has influenced the track of Taiwan's economy with free-market thought. Tsiang went to study economics in England in 1937, and became a student of the Department of Economics at the LSE. At that time, this campus was really an outstanding platform, gathering many academic stars, including well-known economists such as Hayek, Arthur Cecil Pigou (1877–1959), Lionel Robbins (1898–1984) and so on. John Maynard Keynes who debated with Hayek was teaching economics in Cambridge at that time. The teaching and influence of these economic masters became the essential parts of Tsiang's knowledge of economic liberalism.

In his early days in England, Tsiang became a follower of Keynesian theory after reading his *General Theory of Employment, Interest and Money* (Keynes, 1936). However, he soon became an opponent of Keynes's ideas and turned into a defender of Hayek, after discovering many fundamental faults in Keynes's theory through his careful study. Tsiang was awarded his Bachelor degree in Economics at LSE in 1931. Then, he went on his postgraduate study at Cambridge University in the Second World War. Although Cambridge was an important research podium of Keynesian economics, Tsiang (1942, 1943) insisted on his own independent academic ideas and published two articles in *Economica* to critique the relationship between population growth and employment proposed by Keynes, and the 'stock speculation' theories by Nicholas Kaldor (1908–1986), respectively. Professor Hayek gave a high evaluation to his articles, and commented that they had made serious contributions to economics.

In 1945, 27-year-old Tsiang finished his doctoral dissertation entitled *Business Cycle and Fluctuation of Marginal Profits* under Hayek's supervision, which later on was published with the title of *The Variations of Real Wages and Profit Margins in Relation to the Trade Cycle* (Tsiang, 1947). He was awarded a doctoral degree of the LSE, and won the Hutchinson Silver Medal for the best dissertation. In the winter of 1945, he accepted a post as the head of Investigation and Research Division, Economic Committee of Northeast Bureau of China. Tsiang became a teacher in Peking University in 1946 at the invitation of President Hu Shih (1891–1962). Facing the disruptive situation of the Chinese Civil War, he had written articles to remind the authorities to regulate the financial system and to control inflation. In 1948, Tsiang fled to Taiwan with his family because of the Civil War and taught in the Economics Department of Taiwan University. In July 1949, he started to work with another Chinese economist Ta-Chung Liu in the research division of IMF in America. Deeply influenced by Hayek's thoughts, Tsiang had grown up as an excellent scholar that defended liberal economic thought. Although the field of economics was then occupied by Keynesianism, Tsiang pointed out the fallacies in its theory in his published articles. During this research period, he published many influential articles (Tsiang, 1944, 1947, 1949, 1956, 1969, 1973, 1977, 1980), which established his master-status in the fields of international finance and monetary theory.

While working at the IMF, fellow-economists Sho-Chieh Tsiang and Ta-Chung Liu often returned to Taiwan, and advised the authorities to carry out the reforms on building a free-market economy. Clearly, this was the adoption of Hayek's economic thought in Taiwan's economic practice. As one of the pro-disciples of Hayek, Sho-Chieh Tsiang was certainly both a 'preacher' and a 'defender' of liberal economic thought. As well as teaching in the university to spread these liberal notions among the college students, Tsiang also worked as a government official in Taiwan. This enabled him to turn Hayek's liberal social economic thoughts into the specific economic policies that led the positive economic growth of Taiwan. Meanwhile, he also left many economic works to the world. Tsiang at least got the Nobel Prize of Economics nomination in 1982 because of his excellent academic achievements and the outstanding contribution to Taiwan's economic reforms. He died in Taiwan in 1993.

The third important economist who spread Hayek's liberal economic ideas in Taiwan after 1949 was Daoping Xia, also one of David Chow's good friends. When Chow translated *The Constitution of Liberty*, he usually shared what he had learnt and discussed the optional translation of the terms he encountered with Xia. Although Xia had never learnt from Hayek personally, his thoughts were influenced by Chow's ideas, due to their close friendship. Xia was born into a rich merchant's family in Bao'an Town, Daye county of Hubei province in 1907. He was admitted to the preparatory department of Wuhan University in 1929. Two years later, he started his undergraduate study in the Department of Economics of the Law School at Wuhan University.

From 1929 to 1933, the capitalist world was experiencing the 'Great Depression'; whilst the socialist planned economic experiment of the Soviet Union appeared to have achieved its objectives and this led to the notion of a planned economy dominating teaching in economics. Not until the second and third year of his undergraduate study did Xia change his economic ideas in a liberal direction, for Kainan Ren, who had studied at the University of London, became his Professor in the field of economics. Xia recalled that he did not fully understand the connotation of Ren's saying that the notion of 'Institution' was merely the progeny of the German Historical School – until he began to study the history of economic thought. Moreover, as Ren supervised Xia's thesis-writing, they had many chances to meet each other. These frequent meetings with Ren led Xia's economic thinking to partially move in the liberal market direction.

After graduation, Xia worked as a teaching assistant in the School of Economics in Wuhan University. He planned to prepare for the government-sponsored overseas education scheme during the teaching period in that University. China was invaded by Japan two years later, so Xia had to give up his previous plan of studying economics in Europe or America sponsored by the government and moved to Leshan, Sichuan Province, with the university. Xia gave up his post as an academic and joined the army because of the frequent airstrikes by the Japanese and served as a civil military-officer at the Luoyang frontline. Then, he was delegated as the Director of the Research Department of the Economic Construction Promotion Committee of National Political Council in Chongqing. During this period, Xia became acquainted with Lei Chen, the Vice-Executive Secretary of the National Political Council, which seeded the later story that Xia became the Editor-in-chief for the semi-monthly journal *Free China*, after migrating to Taiwan. Xia was to move his residence there in 1949. When settled, he decided to work at the 'Huaguo Press', as he did not wish to be a governmental officer. Lei Chen who was preparing the semi-monthly journal noted above, thus invited Xia to be one of the Editors-in-chief.

Although the original intention of *Free China* was to resist Communism and Russia, all the Editors-in-chief were open-minded intellectuals who loved liberty and wished to pursue democracy. So, *Free China* turned to opposing and criticizing the Nationalist Party's governance. It gave Xia a platform to formulate his thoughts against totalitarian autarchy and a government-controlled market, based on his research on market economies. Xia published 116 articles in the journal as the Editor-in-chief, many of which criticized the government's dictatorship and the market intervention with the military departments, senior officials, as well as the official media of the National Party, as the targets. The most famous article written by Xia is 'Government Can't Lure Citizens to Crime' published in June 1951, which was regarded as the best article in *Free China*. This article irritated the military authorities who controlled its finance and almost led to the publication of *Free China* being suspended. Besides writing editorials, Xia also continued to study liberal theories and diffused these through the journal. For example, in 1957, he received a *USNWR* magazine from his friend, in which there was the abstract of Mises's book *The Anti-Capitalistic Mentality* (Mises, 1956). Although this was not the essence of Mises's thoughts, it clearly refuted all kinds of anti-liberalism theories in a popular way. Instantly, Xia thought that this was the best tool for spreading liberal economic thought and decided to translate the book and promote it in four volumes of *Free China*.

After the publication of *Free China* was stopped because of the Lei Chen case in 1960, liberalism faded in Taiwan. Xia returned to teach in Taiwan's National Chengchi University. Although Xia was in an adverse situation in this period, he did not give up pursuing democracy. He always exchanged ideas with the liberals, such as Hai-kuang Yin (Haiguang Yin) (1919–1969). They talked about liberty, democracy, Bertrand Russell (1872–1970), Hayek, liberal economy and so on. Xia also kept up his rapport with David Chow who had studied with Hayek directly at the LSE, until he passed away, as noted. Without any doubt, Xia was greatly influenced by Chow. He also maintained his eagerness for a lifetime study of liberal economic theories. Through translating and researching the thoughts of the established economists, such as Ludwig von Mises and Hayek, Xia became skilful in understanding the essentials of the liberal economic thought. Accordingly, Xia sufficiently realized that both experiential knowledge and transcendental ratiocination are necessary when analysing social problems deploying the viewpoint of rational liberalism.

When the socialist central planned economy had become popular globally and Keynes's theory had occupied the commanding heights of economic thought, Mises and Hayek could still keep their 'cool heads', and criticize the impossibility of a centrally planned economy. They even concluded that these practices that were opposed to the liberal market theories would completely fail finally. The predictions by these liberals, we can argue, have all turned out to be true. Thus, the studies by the liberal 'preachers', such as Xia, have become highly recognized academic achievements. Xia is regarded as a faithful advocate of liberal economic theory, because of his enormous achievements in the translation and recommendation of the classics of liberal economic theories (Xia, 2013). Xia translated the best one of the three Hayek collections *Individualism and Economic Order* (Hayek, 1948), Mises's *Human Action* (Mises, 1949), *Ultimate Foundation of Economic Science* (Mises, 1962) and Wilhelm Ropke's *Economics of the Free Society* (1963) into Chinese. With millions of words, the books translated by Xia may be considered as models for introducing Western economic thought from the perspective of their systematic nature, as well as their integrity, professionalism and excellence (see Xia, 1989a, 1989b, 2013).

Meanwhile, he also interpreted the liberal ideas in these classics in simple and understandable language in his own books, including articles on 'Fundamental Liberty', 'Democracy and Liberty', 'Hayek on Creativity of Freedom' and so on (see Yin, 2001, vol. I: 10–30, 164–228, 367–374). Although Xia was not the first one who translated the liberal economic theories of Austrian School of Economics, he translated these classic works innovatively in a fluent modern vernacular. Compared with David Chow's translation in classical Chinese, Xia's translation would be much easier to be understood and acceptable for readers of the theoretical works of Mises and Hayek. Chinese versions of these works as translated by Xia spread widely in Chinese-speaking areas. Moreover, he also persuaded the Taiwan authorities to give up the planned and government-controlled economy model and to promote economic marketization. The seeds of Hayek's liberal social economic theory were sown in China by both Chow and Xia. Their liberal economic theories became an effective weapon for criticizing politics in Taiwan. Meanwhile, the suggestion for the Taiwan authorities provided by some scholars of Austrian School of Economics, such as Sho-Chieh Tsiang and Ta-Chung Liu, were gradually accepted by Chung-jung Yin, the Minister of Economy of the Nationalist Party government. It means that the second round of liberalism then started, which went on to promote the 'miracle' of Taiwan's economy in the 1960s. Seen from the diffusion-map of Hayek's thoughts in China, the role of Xia's contribution is fundamental. His economic thoughts went on to reform Taiwan's economy indirectly but effectively.

Noting the background of the liberal ideologist who spread Hayek's thoughts in Taiwan, Hai-kuang Yin (Haiguang Yin) (1919–1969), we find that he was born in Hubei province, China. His father was a Christian priest in the countryside. His family arranged private tutoring education when he was a child. After his graduation from senior middle school in Wuchang, he started to study with the well-known scholars, Shili Xiong and Yuelin Jin, at Tsinghua University. Then he became a college student majoring in philosophy at Southwest Associated University. Later on, he went on to the Philosophy Research Institute of Tsinghua Research Academy, which was an independent academic organization at that time. Before his graduation from the research institute, he decided to give up the campus life and join the army. So, Yin had a short period of military experience. After retirement from the military, he received the attention of dignitaries of the Nationalist Party such as Hanchao Liang, Daofan Zhang, Xisheng Tao, because Yin had published many cogent comments on current politics. Yin moved to Taiwan as the editor-in-chief of the *Central Daily News* in 1949. In the early days, after moving to Taiwan, Yin expected the Nationalist Party to undertake some reforms. The reality was beyond his expectations, so he quit the job as a government officer and became a teacher in the Philosophy Department of Taiwan University. He also became one of the Editors-in-chief of the semimonthly journal *Free China*. He took it as a platform to carry forward the spirit of the May 4th Movement, thus Yin became one of the flagships diffusing liberal thought in Taiwan. After the publication of *Free China* was stopped in 1960, Yin was persecuted continuously and he died in serious poverty and sickness in 1969. Within two decades in Taiwan, Yin had however left a profound and abundant ideological heritage in accordance with his faith in idealism.

After the retreat of Nationalist Party to Taiwan, Yin begun to study liberal economic theories such as those of Hayek. These liberal thoughts gradually took the place of the 'Three People's Principles' (Nationalism, Democracy, People's Livelihood) he had recommended previously. He recognized that the democracy without human rights was just a kind of illusion. In 1953, Yin translated Hayek's famous book *The Road to Serfdom* into Chinese and serialized it in *Free China*. Actually, he was entrusted by David Chow to translate this book. Since 1951, Yin had been going to Chow's house, named 'Wisteria Cottage', for personally organized academic seminars. From then on, Yin became familiar with the work of Hayek and the Austrian School of Economics. Then, he knew more about Hayek's thoughts, mainly through communication with Yu-sheng Lin. Although the Chinese version of *The Road to Serfdom* translated by Yin could not restate Hayek's thoughts perfectly, it was a significant node in the process of the diffusion of these thoughts in China. His Chinese translation of *The Road to Serfdom* influenced many liberals at that time, including Yu-Sheng Lin, whom we will discuss later. In 1966, Yin published a book of *Hayek and His Thoughts* (Yin, 1966) in Taiwan to further introduce Hayek's life-story and theories to Chinese readers. He spent his whole life pursuing and exploring liberalism, and renewing his thoughts continuously. Among all the liberal ideologists, Yin identified with Hayek and Polanyi most, as we shall see later. He published many comments on current politics in order to advocate his thoughts about liberty and democracy through *Free China* and thus he became one of the 'star' editors of the journal. It is apparent that the achievement of Yin had a close relationship with Hayek's influence. He had, in fact, met Hayek once in October 1965.

The influences of Hayek's thought on Yin's mind-set would also be reflected in his attitudes towards Chinese traditional culture. Affected by the spirit of the May 4th Movement, he seriously resisted Chinese traditional culture at the time, which means he was anti-tradition, anti-idol, anti-past morality. Followed by a deep study of Hayek's thoughts, Yin realized that it is not proper to resist the traditional culture. As influenced by the Anglo-American empiricism, Hayek was opposed to French Rationalism all the time, so that his attitude to tradition was moderate. The aged Yin chose to compromise with the Chinese tradition, as he had accepted Hayek's thoughts by then. In 1969, he was stuck down with a serious illness and died in Taibei on 16 September 1969. Hai-kuang Yin was not an economist, but a pure liberal thinker. He had made a great contribution to the diffusion of liberal thought in China. His insistence on pursuing liberal thought was to be respected by posterity.

The last person to diffuse Hayek's thought in Taiwan, even in the global Chinese academic community, was Yu-Sheng Lin, a noted philosopher and the third pro-disciple of Hayek. Lin was born in Shenyang, Liaoning Province, China in 1934, and moved to Taiwan with his family in 1949. The liberal ideological trend of Lin's work was the result of Yin's thoughts and the theories of Bertrand Russell. In 1953, when he was studying in the Department of History of Taiwan University, Lin read the serial Chinese version of *The Road to Serfdom* in *Free China* by his teacher Hai-kuang Yin. He thought that the contents were profound, elaborated and systematic, so that he spent his first remuneration gained from writing, on buying an English version of *The Road to Serfdom*. He expected to study with Hayek directly in the future. His dream became true in the year of 1960. Lin got a chance to go abroad to the University of Chicago, where Hayek was a Professor in the Committee on Social Thought. Lin was looked after and advised by Hayek there. Five out of Lin's six years of overseas learning were funded by a foundation recommended by Hayek. With this help, Lin could learn Western social and political thought step-by-step, without any anxieties about tuition fees. He was awarded a PhD by the Committee on Social Thought, and then went on his postdoctoral study in the East Asian Research Center of Harvard University. Without Hayek's help, Lin could not

have performed so well in his studies. Lin had thus an immense degree of grati-
tude to Hayek all his life (Lin, 1988: 333–334).

During his study in Chicago, Lin read the works of Hayek and other scholars
of the Austrian School of Economics. Among them, Lin preferred Hayek's
theory most, and also recommended Edward Shils (1910–1995) and Michael
Polanyi (1891–1976), whose thoughts belonged to the same stream as Hayek's.
Lin had many chances to attend Hayek's classes, so he understood the late
Hayek's political and legal thoughts better than many others, especially the
theory of 'spontaneous order' proposed by this thinker at that time. In the
process of translating and introducing Hayek's chief works in China, many
translators and scholars including David Chow, Hai-kuang Yin, Dingding Wang,
Weisen Li, Qiu Feng, and others, visited him or wrote letters in order to guarantee the correct and systematic understanding of Hayek's thoughts. Although Yu-
sheng Lin was not the translator of Hayek's chief academic works, he assisted
other scholars to introduce Hayek's liberal socio-economic thoughts precisely
and systematically. It is also worthwhile to mention that Lin carried out innovative research on Chinese traditional culture based on Hayek's thoughts.

The diffusion of Hayek's thoughts in Mainland China after 1949

Seen from the chronological perspective, when Taiwan scholars were striving to
seed Hayek's liberal socio-economic thoughts, the diffusion of liberal ideas was
forbidden in Mainland China. Especially during the Cultural Revolution, any
comments against the socialist and revolutionary ideology would be forbidden,
including those based on Hayek's ideas. The occasional discussions on Hayek's
thoughts that took place were intended only for criticism (see the chapter by
Fang later in this volume).

After the opening-up of China in 1978, the reformist leadership represented
by Deng Xiaoping (1904–1997) proposed a degree of ideological emancipation,
which was followed by a phase of market-oriented reform in China. In accordance with this new trend, academic monographs of a number of typical liberal
theories, including Nobel Laureate Milton Friedman (1912–2006), Mises and
Hayek were translated and introduced in Mainland China. With this background,
scholars were responsible for introducing liberal economic thoughts to a Chinese
audience. With their efforts, generation by generation, more and more people
came to know about the main principles of market economies. For example that
'A Great Society' needs not only the market economy as the effective way for
resource allocation, but also the 'Rule of Law' as the guarantee of people's
action. The typical scholars involved were Weizao Teng, Zhenglai Deng, Weisen
Li, Keli Feng, Dingding Wang, Xingyuan Feng, Qiu Feng, and others. Hayek's
thoughts could not have drawn the attention of a number of ordinary citizens,
even government officials, without these scholars' efforts. The diffusion of
Hayek's thoughts in Mainland China by these scholars can now be summarized
as follows.

After the People's Republic of China was created in 1949, Weizao Teng (1917–2008) was probably the first economist to spread Hayek's thought in Mainland China. As mentioned above, he translated Hayek's two important works: *Prices and Production* in 1958 and *The Road to Serfdom* in 1962. Against the background of a planned economy, he certainly explained that the purpose for translating the works by Hayek, who was regarded as a Western 'reactionary' economist, was to criticize his works domestically. However, Teng's translation had sown a seed of liberalism vis-à-vis market economic development in China. Enlightened by *The Road to Serfdom* as translated by him, many scholars began to give up the illusion of the possibilities and priorities of the central planned economy, and to realize its inevitable results. Here, we argue Teng could be marked as the key milestone in the process of diffusing Hayek's liberal economic thought in Mainland China.

After the opening-up of China in 1978, the famous jurisprudential scholar Zhenglai Deng (1956–2013) was the top contributor in translating and introducing Hayek's thoughts. As is known, Hayek's polymathic research covers economics, politics, law, sociology, anthropology, psychology and so on. So, the diffusion of Hayek's thoughts is not limited to economics only, but extends to politics and law. Deng, with broad research interests, pursued research on Hayek on his own for 15 years, and had substantial academic achievements. Zhenglai Deng was born in Shanghai, China in February 1956. He was the Dean of the Institute for Advanced Study of Fudan University, Professor in the School of International Relations and Public Affairs before he passed away in 2013. In terms of academic achievements in the research of Hayek, the contributions of Deng could be listed as follows. First, he translated and published many of Hayek's important monographs, including *The Constitution of Liberty, Law, Legislation and Liberty* and *Individualism and Economic Order*. The total amount of the translation workload is nearly 2,200,000 Chinese characters. The enormous translation of Hayek's works made him the symbolic scholar on Hayek's thoughts. He was praised as the best scholar working on Hayek's thoughts in China. Deng innovatively added the translator's long introduction before the contents, which provided the Chinese readers with a shortcut to understand Hayek's thoughts systematically. As he started his academic career with the translation of Western academic theories with such a degree of achievement, Deng was honoured as one of the most important scholars who translated Western academic theory to China in the past two decades.

What's more, he was the author of many academic monographs on Hayek's thoughts, such as *Liberty and Order: A Study of Hayek's Social Theories* (Deng, 1998); *Hayek's Jurisprudential Theory* (Deng, 2009a); *Hayek's Social Theory* (Deng, 2009b), etc. Deng, both as a translator and a researcher, deeply excavated Hayek's thoughts and shared them with the scholars in Mainland China.

Keli Feng, a Professor of Political Science in the School of Politics and Public Administration of Shandong University, also went on to translate Hayek's works. Since 1990s, he has translated many important Western academic monographs. Thus, Feng's academic position in the public intellectual community is irreplaceable because of his breakthroughs and outstanding contributions to the diffusion of academic thought. Seen from the diffusion of Hayek's thought, he translated not only *Socialism: An Economic and Sociological Analysis* by Ludwig von Mises (1951), who had influenced Hayek deeply, but also many of Hayek's important academic works including: *The Fatal Conceit* (Hayek, 1988); *Studies in Philosophy, Politics and Economics* (Hayek, 1967); *New Studies in Philosophy, Politics, Economics and the History of Ideas* (Hayek, 1978); *The Counter-Revolution of Science: Studies on the Abuse of Reason* (Hayek, 1952b) and so on. He is also the Chinese translator of *Hayek's Challenge* written by Bruce Caldwell (2004). The main number of Feng's translation for Hayek's works are mostly in Mainland China. Feng, as a liberal theorist, published in both academic and media publications, such as *Frontier* and *Fortune Times* aiming at introducing Hayek's liberal economic thoughts to a wider public. The substantive translation of his monographs by Feng helped scholars and indeed many students in China to get to know the general theoretical framework and core concepts in Hayek's thought in a comprehensive way. Feng's efforts also brought Hayek's thought to the attention of governmental decision-makers.

Besides Zhenglai Deng and Keli Feng, Xingyuan Feng has also carried out a great deal of work in the translation of Hayek's works. He is a researcher in the Rural Development Research Institute of Chinese Academy of Social Science, a Professor in the Graduate School of Chinese Academy of Social Science, and a member of the Chinese Hayek Society. From 1982 to 1986, he studied at Tongji University majoring in German, and obtained a BA degree. He went on to post-graduate study in the Department of Finance and Trade of the Chinese Academy of Social Science, majoring in Finance from 1995 to 1999, and was awarded with a Master degree of economics. He was an academic visitor at Witten University of Germany in 1999 and received from there his PhD degree in economics in 2014. As is well known across the world, the rapid economic development and transformation of Chinese society over the past three decades has been called the 'Chinese Miracle'. His writings not only address the short-comings of existing interpretations but also develop a new multi-dimensional framework based on Nobel Laureate Douglass North's (1920–2015) theory of institutional change and Hayek's theory of institutional evolution to explain China's miraculous growth in the last 35 years (see also Cohn's chapter later in this volume). Its analysis shows that both the Hayekian spontaneous order and Karl Popper's (1902–1944) 'piecemeal social engineering' played a major role in promoting China's economic growth. Concretely, such a 'Miracle' may be traced back to a large degree to the unintended consequences and selective approximation to a competitive order as advocated by Walter Eucken (1891–1950), which includes a set of constitutive principles, including a functioning price-system, stability of monetary value (primacy of monetary policy), private property, open market, freedom of contract, liability, and constancy of economic policies (which means consistently enforcing all these principles).

The Press of the Chinese Academy of Social Science planned and published a *Modern Western Thought Series*, in order to let more scholars know and understand the works written by the influential Western scholars in the last century. Three of the 18 books in this series are Hayek's monographs, which could indicate that the editor paid much importance to Hayek. Xingyuan Feng, one of the editorial board members of the series, translated *The Constitution of Liberty* of Hayek and retranslated *The Road to Serfdom* based on Weizao Teng's version. In addition, Professor Weisen Li was invited to write a clear and logical brief introduction to Xingyuan Feng's 2013 refined version of the Chinese translation *The Road to Serfdom*, which was to help the reader understand exactly the elements of this book. Besides Hayek's works, he also translated the works on Hayek's thought written by some overseas scholars, such as *Wissen, Freicheit und Ordnung: Fried rich August von Hayek* by Gerhard Papke. As same as the other scholars, Xinyuan Feng also published papers in domestic academic journals to introduce Hayek's thoughts and make comments on the domestic economic issues in Hayek's theoretical framework, for example, 'Hayek's Thought on Efficiency and Equality of Taxation and its Practical Significance', 'Hayek and Eucken's View on Competition Order and its Connotation', 'Hayek is not a Flying Trapeze', 'Hayek's View on Competition', 'Understanding the Global Financial Crisis from the Perspective of Hayek's Business Cycle Theory', 'A Biography and Thoughts of an Intellectual Nobleman: Why to Discuss Hayek' and so on. Here, Xingyuan Feng focused on not only the theoretical evolution of Hayek but also his discussion on taxation, fairness, democracy and so on. What is more, he wrote about China's taxation and democratic political reforms within the framework of Hayekian theory.

Among the scholars who translated and introduced Hayek's thoughts to the readers in Mainland China, Zhongqiu Yao, whose penname is Qiu Feng, has also been a contributive translator. He planned and translated the *Austrian School of Economics Translation Series*, including Hayek's *Denationalization of Money: An Analysis of the Theory and Practice of Concurrent Currencies*, and the works of the chief economists of the Austrian School of Economics, for example, Menger, Mises, Wieser, Rothbard, Vaughn and so on. Besides translating Hayek's own books, Yao also translated *Friedrich Hayek: A Biography* written by Alan Ebenstein (2001) into Chinese. In recent years, Qiu Feng has deviated from his early research and spreading ideas of Western liberalism to concentrate on 'preaching' the notions of Confucianism in China.

As mentioned above, Zhenglai Deng and Keli Feng are the most important contributors in translating and diffusing Hayek's political and law thoughts after the economic reforms and opening-up in China. In fact, Dingding Wang, who is a Professor of Economics at Peking University, has been the one who introduced Hayek's economic thoughts first into Mainland China. He obtained a Doctoral degree in Economics at Hawaii University, and then went on to his postdoctoral study in the East-West Center of the same university. He has also been a Lecturer at the University of Hong Kong. He returned to China in 1997 and became a Professor of Economics in the National School of Development of Peking University in Beijing. The wide research interests of Wang cover economics, institutional economics, mathematical economics, behavioural economics, philosophy of economics, history of economic thought, new political economy, evolutionary social theory, philosophy of politics and so on.

As a liberal economist, Dingding Wang's wide research interests and the non-mainstream feature of his academic attitude draw much attention from domestic scholars and ordinary people. Seen from the few articles on the Internet and in other translator's publications, it is clear that most of Hayek's academic thought here is diffused in the vision of Professor Wang, and has even formed a part of his knowledge-framework. The introduction in the preface of the Chinese version *The Fatal Conceit* translated by Keli Feng was written by Professor Wang. In the introduction, he said: 'I borrowed this book from the library again in order to write the preface for its Chinese version....' It can be concluded that although he had read this book several years before. *The Fatal Conceit* was still expressive for him. He spent several months on re-reading this monograph, and finished an introduction with a sound critique. It really provides the readers with a comparably overall and accurate framework to study the work of Hayek from half a century ago. The introduction also includes the specific social background information when Hayek was writing it, which helps the readers understand the advocacies of this great thinker more easily.

Overall, Dingding Wang's contribution to the diffusion of Hayek's thought can be summarized briefly in two aspects: one is promoting *The Sensory Order* by Hayek that is still not published in China, in the form of an introduction; the other is the intangible diffusion of Hayek's thought about the 'Great Society' in China.

In the process of spreading Hayek's thought in China, Professor Weisen Li at Fudan University, whose pen-name is 'Weisen', one of the authors of this chapter, is regarded as influential in the academic community in this field. In the latter part of the Great Cultural Revolution, Weisen started to study Marxist Political Economy. In this context, he mainly focused on the topic of the central planning in the 1980s. In this period, he had accessed information about the debate on socialism between Ludwig von Mises, F. A Hayek, Oskar R. Lange and Abba P. Lerner but Weisen did not give up his academic views as to the possibilities of the central planned economy completely, and did not realize the infeasibility of the 'socialist calculation' either. He knew of the typical scholars of the Austrian School of Economics, such as Mises and Hayek in 1986, and had a chance to read one of Hayek's works *The Road to Serfdom* (1944) translated by Weizao Teng in 1962 (see Hayek, 1962). He even planned to re-translate the book with his good friend Keli Feng (see Hayek, 2013).

In 1987, Weisen was given a chance to study at the Australian National University for his Master's degree, and started his decade-long overseas research period. In Australia, his economic knowledge-framework then became obsolete, mainly due to the upheavals of the Soviet Union and Eastern European Communist regimes. It was difficult for him at this time to rebuild and update his knowledge of economic theories, but he did not give up the concerns over the economic situation of China and started to study the new 'Institutional Economics'. After getting a PhD degree from the University of Sydney, he returned to China and joined Fudan University, focusing his study on comparative institutional analysis, especially the economic theories represented by Hayek, North and so on. Henceforth, he was totally transformed from an advocate and interpreter for the central planned economy into a 'preacher' for this strand of liberal social and economic thought.

In more than a decade of reading and studying, Weisen Li never abandoned his concerns over the current economic issues of China, especially the economic 'transitional' issues. His studies focused on the language of economics at the beginning, and gradually moved to comparative institutional analysis, ethics of market economy, economic reforms, critiques and retrospection of macroeconomic policy and so on. China was to confront many economic and social practical problems after the financial crisis of 2008. At this turning-point, he endeavoured to recommend the liberal social economic theories of Hayek, aiming to solve the problems coming after high-speed economic growth, by persuading the national decision-makers to respect the rules of the market economy, and to reconstruct a free, democratic and well-ordered modern constitutional country with the Rule of Law. In the past decade, he published more than ten academic papers on Hayek's thought, as well as more than ten books which including some chapters on Hayek (Li, 2001, 2004, 2005, 2008, 2009, 2011, 2012, 2014a, 2014b). Particularly, in his recent book, *Re-Reading Hayek* (Li, 2014b), which won the award of the year's most popular book in Economics in China by the *New Beijing Daily*, Weisen gives a comprehensive introduction about Hayek's theories of economics, politics, law and democracy, particularly the debate with Keynes about monetary theory and business cycle in the 1930s. Weisen also participated in compiling the *Modern Western Thought Series* published by the China Social Sciences Publishing House.

With the efforts of Xingyuan Feng, Weisen Li and other academic colleagues, the three Chinese versions of Hayek's significant works, *The Road to Serfdom*, *The Constitution of Liberty* and *The Fatal Conceit: The Errors of Socialism*, were successfully published for readers in Mainland China. *Re-Reading Hayek* is a mentionable book here, in which Hayek's rather obscure theories are interpreted in simple and comprehensible Chinese by Weisen. The content of this book covers markets, role of government, the Rule of Law, democracy and liberty and includes one of Hayek's theoretical origins, Mises's thought and the debate between Hayek and Keynes. In *The Great Transformation: The Current Situation, Problems and Feasible Choices of China* (2012), Weisen interpreted the current social economic problems in China in a flexible use of Hayek's social and economic advocacies. *The Great Transformation*, whose content covers taxation legislation, budget democracy, 'the China Model' and other core economic issues, provides feasible suggestions on the choices facing China and what kind of society should be reconstructed in the future. Beside these academic papers and monographs, he tries his best to promote Hayek's liberal advocacies through the channels of *FT Chinese*, *The Wall Street Journal (Chinese)*, www.caijing.com.cn (a website about finance and economics) and all kinds of academic conferences, in order to enlighten the general public and central government decision-makers on the principle of market-operations that Hayek emphasized, and remind the central government of China to attach more importance to the Rule of Law and Democracy, in line with economic reconstruction.

The contribution made by Weisen to diffusing Hayek's thoughts in China may be summarized as follows. First, he promoted the publication of many of Hayek's works that were not published in China, through the *Modern Western Thought Series* and wrote prefaces for these Chinese versions with the purpose of helping the readers exactly grasp the essence of Hayek's thoughts. Second, he interpreted Hayek's huge corpus of work with understandable language in his monographs and enlarged the influential scope of Hayek's thoughts in Mainland China. Third, although Hayek's political, law and socio-economic thoughts have been spread widely in China through the efforts of Zhenglai Deng, Keli Feng, Xingyuan Feng, Zhongqiu Yao and Shoulong Mao and others, most of the scholars and students in Mainland China were not familiar with Hayek's economic theory, especially the theoretical clash between Hayek and Keynes in the 1930s. Since 2012, Weisen carefully re-read the works of Hayek and Keynes, and the debating papers on monetary theory and business cycles written by the two at that time, even going backwards to their thought-origins, to Knut Wicksell (1851–1926). He also published many articles on Hayek's economic thought in the *Chinese Journal of Social Sciences* (Li, 2004), the special column of *The Wall Street Journal* (Chinese), which not only has so much academic value domestically but also makes up many missing parts on Hayek and Keynes's economic thoughts internationally.

Publication of Hayek's academic monographs in Chinese versions and studies on Hayek's thoughts in the Chinese world

For years, thanks to the above-mentioned scholars' study, translation and introduction of Hayek's thoughts, principles and theories by F. A. Hayek have become more and more popular in Mainland China. This may be indicated by the Chinese version publications of Hayek's works, and by the spread of academic works and monographs on Hayek's thought. All of these may have helped make him a famous contemporary thinker in the academia of Mainland China.

According to our preliminary statistics, up to now, 23 of Hayek's main academic works have been translated into Chinese and published, except *Monetary Nationalization and International Stability* (Hayek, 1937), *Profits, Interest and Investment and Other Essays on the Theory of Industrial Fluctuations* (Hayek, 1939), *The Pure Theory of Capital* (Hayek, 1941), *John Stuart Mill and Harriet Taylor: Their Correspondence and Subsequent Marriage* (Hayek, 1951), *The Sensory Order: An Inquiry into the Foundations of Theoretical Psychology* (Hayek, 1952a) and some works in German such as *Freiburger Studien* (1969). Fortunately, the China Social Sciences Publishing House has been authorized to take the translation copyright of around 12 of Hayek's works which include a part of the above mentioned English works that remain untranslated. The translations (partly retranslations) were delayed, partly because of the change of the personnel in charge within the publishing house. Fortunately, the translation of *Freiburger Studien* has now been translated by Xingyuan Feng, Keli Feng and Shishi Wei recently and will be published in 2016.

Besides Hayek's books, more than seven *biographies of F. A. Hayek* written by overseas authors have been translated into Chinese, such as *Hayek's Challenge: An Intellectual Biography of F. A. Hayek* (2007) by Bruce Caldwell, *Friedrich Hayek: A Biography* (2001) by Alan Ebenstein, *Hayek: The Iron Cage of Liberty* (2005) by Andrew Gamble, *Keynes Hayek: The Clash that Defined Modern Economics* (2013) by Nicholas Wapshott and so on. Furthermore, over 25 academic monographs and more than 841 research papers were published in Mainland China; another 22 papers are also available in Taiwan.

Concluding remarks

In China, the diffusion of Hayek's thought follows two main lines: one in Taiwan, and the other in Mainland China, because of the specific historical and political circumstances. The introduction and study of Hayek's thought first originated with Taiwan scholars. What is more, its spread in the Mainland is based on the early work of these Taiwan scholars. The tide of studying Hayek's thoughts flowed from the 1950s, peaked in the 1960s, and then diminished after the achievement of a liberal regime and free market in Taiwan. However, in Mainland China, it began in earnest in the 1980s and rose further in the 1990s. A subsequent decline, as was the case in Taiwan, has not appeared. It is Hayek's thought that is said to have contributed to the 'economic miracle' of Taiwan in the late 1960s and affected the formation of its now more liberal regime and free market.

As for Mainland China, Hayek's thoughts have definitely affected the Open Door policy of the early 1980s. Furthermore, the influence of Hayek, we would argue, is now increasingly helping to shape the key direction of economic and political reforms of Mainland China, the world's second largest economy.

References (in Chinese and English)*

* Only the better-known key works and translations of Hayek, which are already so numerous, have been included in this bibliography, mainly due to restrictions of space; a number of less noted ones have thus been left out.

Caldwell, B. (2004). *Hayek's Challenge: An Intellectual Biography of F. A. Hayek*, Chicago, IL: University of Chicago Press.

Chow, D. (1981). *Summary on Contemporary Great Thinker F. A. Hayek*, Xinbei: Cheng Chung Books.

Chow, D. (2005). *On Hayek by Chow Dewei*, Beijing: Peking University Press.

Chow, D. (2011). *Writing Blows Storm Away: Anecdotes with National Party of China in My Life*, Taibei: Yuan-Liou Publishing Co.

Deng, Z. (1998). *Liberty and Order: A Study of Hayek's Social Theories*, Nanchang: Jiangxi Education Press.

Deng, Z. (2009a). *Hayek's Jurisprudential Theory*, Shanghai: Fudan University Press.

Deng, Z. (2009b). *Hayek's Social Theory*, Shanghai: Fudan University Press.

Ebenstein, A. O. (2001). *Friedrich Hayek: A Biography*, Basingstoke: Palgrave.

Gamble, A. (1996). *Hayek: The Iron Cage of Liberty*, Boulder, CO: Westview Press.

Hayek, F. A. (1931). *Price and Production*, 2nd edn, London: Routledge.

Hayek, F. A. (1931) [1958]. *Prices and Production* [*Wujia yu shengchan*], translated into Chinese by W. Teng and Z. Zhu, Shanghai: Shanghai Renmin Press.

Hayek, F. A. (ed.) (1935). *Collectivist Economic Planning*, London: Routledge.

Hayek, F. A. (1937). *Monetary Nationalism and International Stability*, London: Longmans.

Hayek, F. A. (1939). *Profits, Interests and Investment and Other Essays on the Theory of Industrial Fluctuations*, Clifton, NJ: Augustus M. Kelley Publishers.

Hayek, F. A. (1941). *The Pure Theory of Capital*, Norwich: Jarrold and Sons.

Hayek, F. A. (1944). *The Road to Serfdom*, London: Routledge.

Hayek, F. A. (1948). *Individualism and Economic Order*, London: Routledge & Kegan Paul.

Hayek, F. A. (1951). *John Stuart Mill and Harriet Taylor: Their Correspondence and Subsequent Marriage*, London: Routledge & Kegan Paul.

Hayek, F. A. (1952a). *The Sensory Order: An Inquiry into the Foundations of Theoretical Psychology*, London: Routledge.

Hayek, F. A. (1952b). *The Counter-Revolution of Science: Studies on the Abuse of Reason*, Indianapolis, IN: Liberty Press.

Hayek, F. A. (1960). *The Constitution of Liberty*, Chicago, IL: The University of Chicago Press.

Hayek, F. A. [1944] (1962). *The Road to Serfdom* [*Tongwang Nuyi Zhilu*], translated by W. Teng, and Z. Zhu, Beijing: Shangwu Yinshuguan.

Hayek, F. A. (1967). *Studies in Philosophy, Politics and Economics*, London: Routledge & Kegan Paul.

Hayek, F. A. (1969). *Freiburger Studien. Gesammelte Aufsätze von F. A. von Hayek*, Tübingen: J. C. B. Mohr-Paul Siebeck.

Hayek, F. A. (1973). *Law, Legislation and Liberty: Rules and Order (I)*, Chicago, IL: University of Chicago Press.

Hayek, F. A. (1976a). *Law, Legislation and Liberty: The Mirage of Social Justice (II)*, Chicago, IL: University of Chicago Press.

Hayek, F. A. (1976b). *Denationalization of Money*, London: Institute of Economic Affairs.

Hayek, F. A. (1978). *New Studies in Philosophy, Politics, Economics and the History of Ideas*, London: Routledge & Kegan Paul.

Hayek, F. A. (1979). *Law, Legislation and Liberty: The Political Order of a Free People (III)*, Chicago, IL: University of Chicago Press.

Hayek, F. A. [1960] (1981). *The Constitution of Liberty* [*Ziyou de xianzhang*], translated into Chinese by D. Chow, Taiwan: Taiwan Bank Economics Research Library.

Hayek, F. A. (1988). *The Fatal Conceit: The Errors of Socialism*, Chicago, IL: University of Chicago Press.

Hayek, F. A. [1944] (2013). *The Road to Serfdom* [*Tongwang Nuyi Zhilu*], translated by M. Wang and X. Feng, Beijing: Zhongguo Shehui Kexue Chushe, new edition.

Keynes, J. M. (1936). *The General Theory of Employment, Interest and Money*, London: Macmillan.

Li, W. (2001). *An Economic Analysis of Social Institutions*, Shanghai: Shanghai Sanlian Press.

Li, W. (2004). 'A Game-Theoretic Interpretation of Hayek's Concept of Spontaneous Order', *Chinese Journal of Social Sciences*, 6, 1–12.

Li, W. (2005). *Economics and Philosophy: The Philosophical Foundation of Institutional Analysis*, Beijing: Shanghai People's Publishing House in Beijing.

Li, W. (2008). *Market Economy, Rule of Law and Constitutional Democracy*, Shanghai: Shanghai People's Publishing House.

Li, W. (2009). *Economic Theory and Market Order: In Search of the Moral Foundation, Cultural Setting and Institutional Conditions of a Well-Functioned Market Economy*, Shanghai: Gezhi Press.

Li, W. (2011). 'China's Road to Rechtsstaat: Rule of Law, Constitutional Democracy and Institutional Change', in X. Huang (ed.), *The Institutional Dynamics of China's Great Transformation*, London: Routledge, 98–109.

Li, W. (2012). *The Great Transformation: The Current Situation, Problems and Feasible Choices of China*, Beijing: China CITIC Press.

Li, W. (2014a). *Language and Institutions: Language of Economics and Linguistic Dimension of Social Institutions*, Beijing: Commercial Press.

Li, W. (2014b). *Re-Reading Hayek*, Beijing: China CITIC Press.

Lin, Y.-S. (1988). *Creative Transformation of Chinese Tradition*, Beijing: Sanlian Press.

Mises, L., von (1949). *Human Action: A Treatise on Economics*, New Haven, CT: Yale University Press.

Mises, L., von (1951). *Socialism: An Economic and Sociological Analysis*, New Haven, CT: Yale University Press.

Mises, L., von (1956). *The Anti-Capitalist Mentality*, Toronto, Canada: D. Van Nostrand Company.

Mises, L., von (1962). *The Ultimate Foundation of Economic Science: An Essay on Method*, Princeton, NJ: Van Nostrand.

Papke, G. (ed.) (2001). *Wissen, Freiheit und Ordnung. Beiträge zu 'Werk und Wirkung Friedrich August von Hayek'* (The Modern Western Thought Series). Beijing: Zhong guo she hui ke xue Verlag, in Chinese.

Ropke, W. (1963). *Economics of the Free Society*, Chicago, IL: H. Regnery Co.

The Royal Swedish Academy of Sciences (1974). Economics Prize for Works in Economic Theory and Inter-Disciplinary Research: Press Release, 9 October. Available at: www.nobelprize.org/nobel_prizes/economic-sciences/laureates/1974/press.html (accessed 12 October 2015).

Tsiang, S.-C. (1942). 'The Effect of Population Growth on the General Level of Employment and Activity', *Economica*, New Series, 9, 325–332.

Tsiang, S.-C. (1943). 'A Note on Speculation and Income Stability', *Economica*, New Series, 10, 286–296.

Tsiang, S.-C. (1944). 'Prof. Pigou on the Relative Movements of Real Wages and Employment', *The Economic Journal*, 54, 352–365.

Tsiang, S.-C. (1947). *The Variations of Real Wages and Profit Margins in Relation to the Trade Cycle*, London: Pitman.

Tsiang, S.-C. (1949). 'Rehabilitation of Time Dimension of Investment in Macrodynamic Analysis', *Economica*, New Series, 16, 204–217.

Tsiang, S.-C. (1956). 'Liquidity Preference and Loanable Funds Theories, Multiplier and Velocity Analysis: A Synthesis', *American Economic Review*, 46, 539–564.

Tsiang, S.-C. (1969). 'A Critical Note on the Optimum Supply of Money', *Journal of Money, Credit and Banking*, 1, 266–280.

Tsiang, S.-C. (1973). 'The Rationale of the Mean-Standard Deviation Analysis, Skewness Preference, and the Demand for Money', *American Economic Review*, 62, 354–371.

Tsiang, S.-C. (1977). 'The Monetary Theoretic Foundation of the Modern Monetary Approach to the Balance of Payments', *Oxford Economic Papers*, New Series, 29, 319–338.

Tsiang, S.-C. (1980). 'Keynes's "Finance" Demand for Liquidity, Robertson's Loanable Funds Theory, and Friedman's Monetarism', *The Quarterly Journal of Economics*, 94, 467–491.

Wapshott, N. (2011). *Keynes Hayek: The Clash that Defined Modern Economics*, New York, NY: W. W. Norton & Company.

Xia, D. (1951). 'Government Can't Lure Citizens to Crime', *Free China*, semi-monthly journal, Taipei: Taiwan, 1–6.

Xia, D. (1989a). *Liberal Economic Thoughts*, Taibei: Yuan-Liou Publishing Co.

Xia, D. (1989b). *When I was in Free China*, Taibei: Yuan-Liou Publishing Co.

Xia, D. (2013). *Collective Essays of Xia Daoping*, Changchun: Changchun Press.

Yin, H.-K. (1966). *Hayek and His Thoughts*, Taibei: Biographical Literature Press.

Yin, H.-K. (2001). *Collective Works of Yin Hai-kuang*, in 4 vols, Wuhan: Hubei Peoples Publishing House.

12 On Keynes and China

Keynesianism 'with Chinese characteristics'

Malcolm Warner

Introduction

In order to shed light on this fascinating diffusion of economic ideas in the twentieth century and beyond, we look at the links between John Maynard (later Baron, known as Lord) Keynes (1883–1946) and China.[1]

The chapter is divided into three sections, respectively covering the early, interim and later periods of this connection. The early section deals with his initial interest in the 'Middle Kingdom'; the next one deals with the translation of his main works and the diffusion of his ideas in Republican China; and the last deals with the influence of his thinking in the People's Republic of China after 1978, up to the present time, vis-à-vis the notion of Keynesianism 'with Chinese characteristics'.

His surname may be represented in its Chinese form, in *pinyin* Mandarin, as '*Kai'ensi*'; his school of thought – namely 'Keynesianism' – as '*Kai'ensi li lun*'; and what has been called Keynesianism 'with Chinese characteristics' as '*juyou Zhongguo tese de Ka'iensi li lun*' (see Warner, 2001: 140; Alexandroff *et al.*, 2004: 114). *We then go on to discuss, in our analysis of the above, the apparent 'paradox' that, although Keynes' involvement in China may have been in a 'minor key', its interest in his ideas was decidedly in a 'major' one.*

Keynes, probably the most original economist of the twentieth century, has lately been named in a recent work on his life, as a 'Master', who is said to have now 'returned' (see Skidelsky, 2010: 1). The description is made by a scholar who had earlier come to prominence as his biographer, with a three-volume study of his life and times (Skidelsky, 1983, 1992, 2000) namely, Robert J. A. (later Baron) Skidelsky (1939–), who is Emeritus Professor of Political Economy at the *University of Warwick*. A number of this author's biographical works on Keynes have also been published in translation into Chinese, for example, a recent one entitled *Keynes: A Biography* (*Kai'ensi zhuan*), appeared in 2006 (Skidelsky, 2006; see WorldCat, 2016).

Keynes has also lately been compared by a number of contemporary Chinese commentators (see Skidelsky, 2007: 1), with another 'Master', this time one in antiquity, namely *Confucius* (551–479 BC), (*Kongzi*, literally 'Master Kong'). Skidelsky notes that:

A thinker may be dead in some bits of the world and alive in others. This has to some extent happened to Keynes. Keynes lives on in developing countries, even though his work was not about development at all. In some of these countries he is taken up as a critic of globalization, or apostle of a 'balanced' and 'harmonious' economy – strands which can readily be plucked out of his interwar writing, though they form no part of the General Theory model. In China he has been compared to Confucius. A thinker may be alive in a different sense to those so far discussed, because of the sheer fertility of his thought.

(Skidelsky, 2007: 1)

Other commentators, however, argue the case for Frederich A. Hayek (1899–1882), as being better known in contemporary China (see The Economist, 2011: 1). He was an economist of the so-called 'Austrian School' and later a Nobel Prize winner in Economics, who after 1931 held a Chair at the *London School of Economics* (LSE) and then after 1949 at the *University of Chicago* and who was a stringent critic of Keynes's work. Hayek had, in his time, taught many Chinese students at the LSE, who later went on to support his theories in China and *Taiwan* (Trescott, 2007: 83–84) (see the chapters by Trescott, as well as Li *et al.*, in this volume). One advocate of his thinking in China has been *Zhang Weiying* (1959–), formerly Dean of the *Guanghua School of Management*, a Professor at *Peking University* (known also as *Beijing Daxue*, or *Beida* for short); he has been described as the main Chinese 'anti-Keynesian' and has been dubbed the most cited economist in his country (see Bhattacharya, 2012: 1). But we argue, on the other hand, that Keynes has indubitably made his mark on Chinese economics as a subject and indeed more widely with respect to the economic policies adopted by the Chinese government in recent years.

Early period

Whilst we do not have much direct evidence regarding Keynes's knowledge of China (or Japan for that matter) in his formative years, it is clear that he read very widely across the disciplines and would have known as much about that country, if not more, as any well-educated person of his time and class. Public opinion in Britain had become increasingly concerned about the new challenge of Chinese nationalism in the first part of the twentieth century (see Chow, 2011: 3). Here, an early biographer of Keynes, Roy (later Sir Roy) Harrod (1900–1978) does not enlighten us much on this point (see Harrod, 1951). A later one, however, namely, Donald E. Moggridge (1943–) notes that the young Keynes was in favour of the 'Boxer Rebellion' in China early in 1900: 'I am pro-Boxer', he told his father (Moggridge, 1992: 43). In his recent short biography, Peter Clarke (1942–) adds little more about China in this context but not a great deal (see Clarke, 2009). Yet, in the same year, when he was 17 years old, it is claimed that Keynes had apparently penned a provocative essay, 'The Differences between East and West: Will They Ever Disappear?' (see Paulovicova, 2007).

In it, he looked at the examples of the Jews and the Chinese and offered some rather prejudiced opinions as far as most fair-minded people would perceive them, then and now but at the time not a few Western intellectuals shared his opinions. As far as the Chinese were concerned, he allegedly did not think much of them and any effort to turn them into a 'race of tigers' was futile, adding that 'Europeans could hope nothing less than a second flood that would exterminate them' (see Chandavarkar, 2000: 1619; Paulovicova, 2007: 43). Skidelsky describes a later Keynes's reaction to population expansion, as 'a typical Edwardian Yellow Peril coda' (1992: 430).

Between 1909 and 1911, Keynes had been preparing lecture-notes on Adam Smith (1723–1790) (see Keynes Papers, JMK/UA/6/15). He would have seen that the eighteenth century writer had noted China's historic economic achievements and its use of the 'division of labour', if with qualifications. Again, he would have undoubtedly have come across observations regarding that country in several economic sources much earlier, particularly in other works of the eighteenth century 'Enlightenment' economists (see Warner, 2014: 37). From his youth onwards, Keynes had collected antiquarian books and had acquired many first editions of classical economics works. There are indeed a number of references to China in Smith's works, including the following:

> [P]erhaps no country has ever yet arrived at this degree of opulence. China seems to have been long stationary, and had probably long ago acquired that full complement of riches which is consistent with the nature of its laws and institutions. But this complement may be much inferior to what, with other laws and institutions, the nature of its soil, climate, and situation might admit of.
>
> (Smith 1776, Book 1, Chapter 9, 15, cited in Warner, 2014: 37–38)

Chinese intellectuals had been much taken with the ideas of Adam Smith (*Yadang Simi*) and tried to promote his ideas of free markets. His key work, namely *The Wealth of Nations* (*Yuan fu*) (Smith, 1776) was first translated by Yan Fu (1854–1921), an intellectual who had earlier attended the *Royal Naval College* in Greenwich as a student in London. It was definitively published in 1902 in China in a Mandarin version (see Warner, 2014: 37), in a somewhat idiosyncratic translation, although it had been first published in Japan where a version had appeared in the early 1880s. It is quite possible that Keynes may have heard of these translations from the three undergraduates (*Zeng Zhongjian, Luo Zhongyi, Zhang Wei*) then studying in the Economics faculty at Cambridge, all hailing from China, the first ones to enrol in that subject there from 1906 onwards (Trescott, 2007: 85) (see the chapters by Trescott as well as by Lai on Smith in this volume). Even today, Smith still remains up-front on the reading-lists in the history of economic thought courses in the *People's Republic of China* (PRC), as now does Keynes, as we shall later see.

By 1912, Keynes's views on the Chinese seem to have softened. His lengthy review essay of *The Economic Principles of Confucius and his School* (*Kongmen licaixue*) (Chen, 1911), which had appeared at the time, in the *Economic Journal* of which he was Editor, is not however that well-known but is quite revealing (see Keynes, 1912: 584–588; see Moggridge, 1989: 239). The work's author, *Huan-Chang Chen* (1881–1931), was one of the early Chinese-born candidates to gain a PhD in Economics in the US and the first to do so at *Columbia University*, more than a century ago, having studied there with a number of well-known economists such as Edwin Seligman (1861–1939) and John Bates Clark (1847–1938). Chen, whose book still remains in print, believed that *Confucius* was 'a promoter of economic growth and prosperity' (Warner, 2014: 57). Here, Keynes thinks it is doubtful whether *Confucius* was in favour of private ownership of land but believes the latter was certainly a 'free-trader' and did not doubt it was 'wrong to charge interest', for 'capital is the mother and interest is her child' (Keynes, 1912: 584). The book review notes that *Chen* (1911) uses the methods of modern economists to deal with the economic history of China and praises the evocation of 'Gresham's Law' (Keynes, 1912: 585–586). Keynes goes on to view population growth as a major weakness: 'The Golden Age of China ... was not an age of teeming and overcrowded population' (Keynes, 1912: 588). The original copy of the book reviewed, remains in the 'Rare Books Collection' of the Marshall Library in Cambridge, '*ex libris* John Maynard Keynes'.

Keynes was, however, more aware of India, having served in the *India Office* in London at an early stage in his working career between 1906 and 1908 but was to resign to pursue his writings on probability theory in Cambridge. After a faltering first attempt, he soon became a Fellow of *King's College* and a member of the Economics Faculty at *Cambridge University* and continued to be associated with its circle throughout his lifetime. He published his first book *Indian Currency and Finance* (Keynes, 1913) soon after.

Interim period

Keynes's ideas had soon spread around the world, particularly after a book he published in 1919. It is said that as far as his 'best-seller' the *Economic Consequences of the Peace* (Keynes, 1919a) was concerned, a Chinese translation (see Keynes, 1919b) was soon undertaken by *Tao Meng*, also known as *L. K. Tao* (1887–1960), an early LSE graduate. The work was a trenchant critique of the Versailles Peace Conference, which Keynes had attended as an official advisor, just after the end of the First World War and it went on to sell over 100,000 copies across the world. However, there is only limited evidence in detail of translations into foreign languages of his works, other than in European ones such as French, Italian, Spanish, and so on and respectively, Japanese and Russian (see Keynes Papers, JMK/EC/5, EC/6). The Mandarin version, *Ouzhou he yi hou zhi jing ji* (Keynes, 1919b) and other translations which appeared (see Laurence, 2003: 225), nonetheless, would have clearly been of great interest to China, both generally on the making of the 1919 Peace Treaty, as well as specifically vis-à-vis the fate of former German and other enclaves there. A consequence of the resulting agreement, then granting territories in *Shandong* Province to the Japanese, was the 'May Fourth Movement' (*wusi yundong*), led by students in *Beijing*, in 1919, which set in motion many of the revolutionary changes in twentieth-century Chinese history, including the founding of the *Chinese Communist Party* (CCP) three years later (Schwarcz, 1986).

However, throughout his career, there are only limited references to China in the standard Keynes biographies (see for example, Harrod, 1951; Skidelsky, 1983, 1992, 2000). There is little more in his papers, with a few exceptions, such as a document concerning a currency system for China in 1910, a letter from Waley in 1915 and a report from the *Committee on the Chinese Situation* to boost trade between China and the UK to help recovery from the Depression in 1930 (see Keynes Papers, JMK/IC/3, JMK/PP/45/193 and JMK/EA/1 & 5; Howson and Winch, 1977; de Gruchy, 2008). Keynes had proposed building railways in China at that time, to help transport British exports into the country, funded by the *Boxer Compensation Fund*, to the *Economic Advisory Council* and its sub-Committee on which he sat (Laurence, 2003: 33, 132, 225). A little later, Skidelsky notes Keynes also thought China should concede territory to Japan in 1937 (Skidelsky, 2000: 33).

The central ideas of Keynes's *The General Theory of Employment, Interest and Money* (Keynes, 1936), which another famous economist of the day noted as 'the greatest literary success of our epoch' in macroeconomics (Schumpeter, 1954: 1170), soon diffused in China after the book's initial publication in the mid-1930 (see Trescott, 2012: 324ff.). A young Chinese economist, *Yao Qingsan*, who had previously studied in France, made the first-known presentation of Keynes's ideas in China soon after in the late 1930s. A number of scholars teaching there and/or who had studied in England also helped disseminate his work, particularly at *Yenching (Yanching) University*, at that time a Christian college located in *Beijing*, later disbanded by *Mao Zedong* (1893–1976). Amongst them was a Western Marxist academic, Michael (later Baron) Lindsay (1909–1994) and a group of Chinese economists. They had circulated an unofficial translation of Keynes's *General Theory* (*Kai'ensi tonglun*) there in the early 1940s based on Japanese notes (see Nakayama, 1939/1940). A Japanese translation was to appear in December 1941 with the first 7,000 copies being sold quickly and an additional 2,000 reissued (Keynes, 1941) (see the chapter by Yagi in this volume).

The *General Theory* was not formally published in China in a Mandarin translation until 1957, when *Xu Yunan* (1910–1958) of *Tsinghua (Qinghua) University* (with the aid of *Wang Chuan-lun*, then a post-graduate student on the same campus in *Beijing*) put it in the spot-light and it still remains in print (Keynes, 1957; Trescott, 2007: 253). A capable scholar, *Xu* was probably the first Chinese to be awarded a PhD in economics from Cambridge, who gained his degree in 1940, with a dissertation on the UK cotton industry in the Great Depression. But there is no evidence that the earlier *Tract on Monetary Reform* (Keynes, 1923) was ever translated into Chinese (and there is no reference in the Keynes Papers on this point, one way or the other). However, the *Treatise on*

Money (Keynes, 1930a) was eventually published in a Mandarin translation (as *Huobinlun*) in *Beijing* in 2008 (Keynes, 1930b).

Late period

The Chinese Nationalist Government had proposed asking Keynes to come over to be their Economic Advisor in 1932 (*Observer*, 3 January 1932: 13) but nothing ever came of this suggestion. He did, however, oppose a British loan to China in the early 1940s (see Treasury Papers of J. M. Keynes, Series 2, T/247/3 China: Stabilisation Fund, 1941–1945). Even so, Skidelsky notes his good relations with *T. V. Soong* (1891–1971), then Chinese Foreign Minister, with whom he had conducted a correspondence earlier in 1935 (see Keynes Papers, JMK/PP/45/306) and who gave him a birthday-dinner at the Nationalist Government's Embassy in Washington, DC in 1943 (Skidelsky, 2000: 120). The legendary *Soong* was a brother-in-law of both Generalissimo *Chiang Kai-shek* (1887–1975), the *Kuomintang (KMT)* (*Guomindang*) leader in charge of Nationalist China at the time, as well as of its 'founding father', *Sun Yat-sen* (1866–1925). Keynes, in any case, would have been unlikely to have taken a benign view of *Mao's* achievements, given his hostile view of Marxism, unlike a number of his contemporaries in the Economics Department in Cambridge and elsewhere. Even so, links between the faculty and China were very strong, partly because 33 Chinese students had studied there prior to 1949 and most took as 'received wisdom' Keynesian notions of 'market failure', although against this, 44 others had been students of the less enthusiastic LSE professors such as Hayek, mentioned above (see Trescott, 2007: 9, 85ff.).

The Maoist model had indeed been highly praised by many of those Western Marxists who took an interest in post-1949 China and went on to visit it at first-hand. One such pilgrim was the 'fellow-travelling' Cambridge economist Joan V. Robinson (1903–1983), originally a colleague of Keynes and a number of other scholars in the field (see Harcourt, 1995). The Archive of her documents and correspondence does not, however, reveal any evidence of an interest in China prior to the 1950s (see Robinson Papers). She later visited the PRC eight times over in the post-war years and penned a number of books on the Chinese economy, such as *China: An Economic Perspective* (Robinson and Adler, 1958), amongst others. If Robinson was a more or less 'apologist' for Maoism in its late phase and saw it as a guide for 'Third World' development (see Warner, 2014: 99) she appeared to have later recanted and go on to back the economic reforms (Harcourt and Kerr, 2009: 146).

Keynes, on the other hand, was never a Socialist, let alone a Marxist and viewed Soviet Communism in the final analysis as an intellectual *cul de sac* (Skidelsky, 1992: 235, 292, 488, 517). He was never influenced by Karl Marx (1818–1883) and he appeared to have no opinions on record relating *Mao* himself or to Chinese Marxism (indeed there is no evidence at all to be found in the Keynes Papers). He did, however, *pari passu* have an ongoing relationship with the Fabian Socialist stalwarts, Beatrice (later Baroness Passfield) Webb

(1858–1943) and Sidney (later Baron Passfield) Webb (1859–1947), as well as George Bernard Shaw (1856–1950) between 1915 and 1938 but remained critical of Soviet Russia (see Keynes Papers, JMK/45/340; Harrod, 1951; Warner, 1966; Skidelsky, 1992; Clarke, 2009). He had visited that country in 1925 for instance, with his wife, Lydia Lopokova (later Lady Keynes) (1892–1946), who was a ballet-dancer of Russian origin and later again in 1928 and 1936. He wrote critically about the key features of the Soviet economy in his collection of articles, *A Short View of Russia* (Keynes, 1925), anticipating later work on economic development (see Toye, 2006). Interestingly enough, however, some economists in Cambridge, like Maurice Dobb (1900–1976), or Joan V. Robinson (1903–1983) and Piero Sraffa (1898–1983), thought that Marx's and Keynes's ideas could be driven in tandem (see Harcourt, 1995: 1228–1243).

With the 'Liberation' in 1949, the Chinese Communist authorities soon expressed hostility to Keynes's ideas, and even more so, in the 'Anti-Rightist Movement' of 1957–1958. Strong efforts were made to import Soviet Stalinist-inspired economics in 1953 starting in *Beijing* at the newly launched 'flagship' *People's University* (*Renmin Daxue*, known as *Renda*) (Trescott, 2007: 297). Yet in the 1950s and 1960s, over 50 Western economic texts were translated into Mandarin, including ten chapters of Paul A. Samuelson's *Economics: An Introductory Analysis* (1948 and subsequent editions in 40 languages) and these works in Chinese were widely circulated. The latter US scholar (1915–2009) was a *Nobel Prize* winner and the text may be seen as building on the 'Keynesian' model (see Pearce and Hoover, 1995). Debates also continued on Malthus (1766–1834) and Keynes over the course of this period in the PRC (see MacFarquhar, 1960: 82). Symposia were, in addition, held on Smith, Ricardo (1772–1825), Marshall (1842–1924), as well as Keynes, amongst others (see Trescott, 2007: 361). However, during the 'Cultural Revolution' in the 1960s, discussion more or less ground to a halt and economists were harshly persecuted (Lin, 1981: 38). In 1975, the official English-language weekly, then-named *Peking Review*, stated that 'Keynes theory doesn't work' (Peking Review, 1975: 17). But after the Maoist era ended in 1976 and after the reforms of *Deng Xiaoping* (1904–1997) were launched in 1978, Keynesianism re-emerged as a legitimate topic of discussion (Trescott, 2007: 349, note 39) and, possibly unacknowledged, was said to have been incorporated in Chinese demand-management policy thereafter (see Alexandroff *et al.*, 2004; Trescott, 2012; Fang, 2013).

After 1978, Chinese economists took up Western notions again with renewed enthusiasm (see Ma and Trautwein, 2013: 2) in terms of what has been referred to as theories 'with Chinese characteristics' (*juyou Zhongguo tese*) (Hsu, 1991: 25). Amongst these, Keynesianism may be found, but with the latter being seemingly seen as more 'politically correct' there than the 'Chicago School' at the time. Western Economics, including translations of theorists such as Keynes and Schumpeter (1883–1950), were soon reinstated in the university curricula (Lin, 1981: 1–48). The following year, more reforms followed in economics teaching and research; a new complete version of Samuelson's textbook noted above was also published in Mandarin; and a *China Association for Research on Foreign*

Economics (CARFE) was in turn set up (Fang, 2013: 296). As noted earlier, Keynes's ideas were to influence the post-*Mao* thinking on running the economy and their influence grew in China in the late 1980s and the 1990s (see Trescott, 2007). A biography of Keynes (*Kai'ensi zhuan*) by *Ha Luo De* was published in Chinese by the *Commercial Press* in the early 1990s (see Ha, 1993) who had been the publishers of the earlier translation of the *General Theory*. Another biography, *John Maynard Keynes* (*Yuehan Meinade Kai'ensi*) was in print more recently (see Bao, 2009). Interest in 'Institutionalism', 'Neo-Keynesianism', 'Radical Economics', 'Regulation Theory' and so on, had spread across many of the economics faculties in the PRC (see Zhang and Xu, 2013: 309). Economists like Ronald Coase (1910–2013), Milton Friedman (1912–2006, Douglass C. North (1920–) and Oliver E. Williamson (1932–), all Nobel laureates, became familiar figures to interested Chinese students and faculty (see the chapters by Wang, as well as Cohn, later in this volume). Today, the so-called 'China model' is said to incorporate both Smith and Keynes as part of its core 'ideological arena' (Yip, 2012: 53).

As the early 2000s progressed, the Chinese economy was still on its 'Long March' of rapid economic growth, although it has been slowing down from the trend-rate of the last three decades (see Warner, 2013: 157). The annual rate of growth which had been sustained around 10 per cent per annum now struggled to rise above 7.5 per cent. Unemployment had risen, in fact coexisting with skilled labour-shortages and rising wages.

The Chinese Party/State's response to the 2008 global financial crisis, under the leadership of then Prime Minister *Wen Jiabao* (1953–) was to, in fact, boost 'aggregate demand' and the government took steps to stimulate the economy through a programme of 'quantitative easing', with extensive investments in nationwide infrastructure amongst other things, in a four trillion RMB (US\$586 billion) stimulus package, described as 'Dr Keynes' Chinese Patient' (see The Economist, 2008: 1). The question, however, was whether the 'structural imbalance' as between saving and consumption could be dealt with (Fang and Gang, 2009: 149). The 'multiplier effects' were possibly slow to work and boosting domestic demand might be easier said than done. There is a high degree of income inequality in the PRC, with a *Gini Coefficent* at officially 0.47, but in reality it may be much higher, perhaps over 0.60 (see Warner, 2013: 177).

A World Bank Working Paper has, however, concluded that the multiplier effects did in fact seem to have been effective and that:

> China's government economic stimulus package in 2008–09 appears to have worked well. It seems to have been about the right size, included a number of appropriate components, and was well timed. Its subnational component was designed to enhance the impact of the stimulus package on the economy and reduce the potential pro-cyclical elements that are usually built into subnational fiscal mechanisms in federal countries. Moreover, China's massive fiscal stimulus played an important role in the overall recovery of the global economy.
>
> (Fardousi *et al.*, 2012: 27)

A Western Marxist economist (John Ross) teaching in China, commented on the irony:

> Keynes explicitly put forward his theories to save capitalism. But the structure of the US and European economies has made it impossible to implement Keynes's policies even when confronted with the most severe recession since the Great Depression. The anti-crisis measures of China's 'socialist market economy' are far closer to those Keynes foresaw than in any capitalist economy.
>
> (Ross, 2012: 1)

In 2009, the Governor of the *People's Bank of China, Zhou Xiaochuan* (1948–), who had initially graduated with a top PhD in engineering (if not economics) from *Tsinghua (Qinghua) University* in 1975, recently resurrected Keynes's idea of 'an international reserve currency that is disconnected from individual nations and is able to remain stable in the long run' (see Zhou, 2009a: 1). This proposal, originally published by way of the *Bank for International Settlements*, in Basel, Switzerland, which set out a step-by-step process to resolving international imbalances, has been much discussed in the ensuing period (Zhou, 2009b). It received a good deal of publicity in the world's financial press at the time, however not a great deal has come of this proposal to date, but it has again kept Keynes's name alive both in China and globally in this regard (see Jaeger *et al.*, 2013).

In another exemplification, the Chinese have recently dubbed *Li Yining* (1930–), a Professor of Economics at the renowned *Peking University*, as 'the Keynes of China'. In 1955, he graduated from the Department of Economics at that seat of learning, classed today as the top Economics Department in the PRC (see CUCAS, 2012). Their website announced that:

> Few economists have steered China's development path like *Li Yining* since his idea of joint-stock reforms guided China to transform itself from a planned to a market economy, a transition captured in his theses published recently in English, entitled 'The Chinese Way of Economic Reform and Development', features 16 selected essays. These writings, collected between 1980 and 1998, were recently translated into English and published by the *Foreign Language Teaching and Research Press*.
>
> (see Li, 2010; Peking University, 2010)

Because of his advocacy of 'joint-shareholding' reform, it is said

> he is known to many Chinese as the 'Mr. Shareholding' and is sometimes called 'the Keynes of China' because the joint-share reform transformed China as much as the work of the British economist, John Maynard Keynes, transformed Western economic ideas.
>
> (Peking University, 2010: 1)

Another noted Chinese 'economics guru', indeed with a Keynesian penchant, is a former Chief Economist and Senior Vice-President of the *World Bank*, who became a Professor at *Peking University*, namely *Justin Yifu Lin* (1952–). He recently suggested a new *demarche* he called 'Beyond Keynesianism' (Lin, 2011), pointing out that:

> We are in a global crisis. And you have two paths. The traditional Keynesian focuses on the domestic economy and tries an approach that would, for example, dig a hole and pave the hole in order to create jobs. I suggest going beyond Keynesianism, which has two meanings. First, the fiscal stimulus should be used for investment to enhance future productivity growth; and second, the fiscal stimulus can go beyond national boundaries, since the global crisis needs a global solution. In high-income countries, there are some opportunities for productivity-enhancing types of fiscal stimulus...
>
> (Lin, 2011: 1)

He noted that in the high-income economies, many opportunities exist, but they are limited. They may not create enough jobs to help unemployment to go back to a normal level. Developing economies, including low-income countries, have many of these opportunities. However, there is a good deal of slack in the maturing sectors, even the tech sectors, in the high-income ones. He believes that we may see growth and investment in the developing examples as an opportunity both for both high-income and for developing examples. To do this, he suggests, 'we can create some kind of Keynesian-like optimism' (Lin, 2011: 1). His analysis of the fiscal stimulus in the Chinese economy in 2008–2009, referred to above, sets out how this might be achieved in practice (see Fardousi *et al.*, 2012).

Discussion

First, the influence of Keynes in China must be considered in the context of the spread of Western notions of 'modernity' to Asia and China, in particular over the last 150 years (see Woodside, 2006). Westernization spread with 'the flag' across Asia for good or for ill, depending on your point of view. A concept current at the time, both in general relevance and notwithstanding vis-à-vis economics, was *ti yong*, namely indigenous (Chinese) 'essence' (*ti*) versus exogenous (Western) 'usefulness' (*yong*) (see Warner, 2014: 93). These notions may today be also applied to, and are clearly of relevance for, 'Keynesianism' in its Chinese manifestation.

Second, a growing awareness of Western Economics over the period must be taken into account and specifically Keynes's theories in their diffusion in China and in a Chinese context (Trescott, 2007, 2012) over the last century and at the present time. Western theories are now in play in the PRC in what has been dubbed a synthesis of '*Confucius*, Lenin, Schumpeter and Keynes' called '*Guanxi* Economics' (see Nitsch and Diebel, 2008). The terms 'Neo-Keynesian' and 'Post-Keynesian' have also been employed here (Skidelsky, 2010). In another contemporary contribution, Marx's, Schumpeter's and Keynes's ideas have been seen as used to come to grips with the rapid nature of China's economic growth trajectory (see Lo and Zhang, 2011). Around 200 books in all, by, or on, 'Keynes' or 'Keynesianism', ranging from 1936 and 2016, appear in the *World Catalogue*, a major online international bibliographical site (see World-Cat, 2016). A recent search of Chinese economics journals found that 43 out of 111 papers published in Mandarin between 1977 and 2009 could be categorized as specifically 'Post-Keynesian' (see Zhang and Xu, 2013: 310).

Third, the last consideration is the degree to which contemporary Chinese economic theory or policy is dubbed 'Keynesian', with or without, this or that, set of characteristics. We have argued Keynesianism 'with Chinese characteristics' is a term which we argue may be useful in the debate but perhaps it is often used in a relatively broad sense, rather than a strict one (see Sheng, 2013). Policies adopted by the Chinese leadership may be given labels *post hoc*, whether they have read any one given Western economist or not, anyway. Great caution should be employed here, as it is often the case that economic commentators use adjectives an academic might be cautious to employ.

Concluding remarks

Whether the economic hegemony of the 'Washington Consensus' will still go on to last into the coming decades to be replaced by the 'Beijing' version (see Jacques, 2011: 427) and whether this will have a 'Keynesian' flavour is difficult to surmise. In any event, China's economic policies need to be much more open and transparent, as 'most of the world finds economic relations with China a complete puzzle' (Quah, 2013: 1). But we cannot take anything for granted, as we have stated in a previous contribution to the debate (see Warner, 2013: 157–161). As one commentator concluded:

> Deng Xiaoping famously said, on his death [he] was 'going to meet Marx'. But Deng may also be having an intense talk with John Maynard Keynes. And Keynes would be interested to discuss with Deng's two cats – who appear to have read the *General Theory* more closely and accurately than any administration in the West.
>
> (Ross, 2012: 1)

The debate on Keynesianism, albeit 'with Chinese characteristics', will no doubt continue for some years to come. We can, however, view the 'paradox' we mooted earlier – that although Keynes's involvement in 'the Middle Kingdom' was in a 'minor key', China's interest in his ideas was decidedly in a 'major key' – as a convincing one in the light of the evidence we have presented above.

Note

1 This is an abridged and amended version of an earlier published article presented here with permission, Warner, M. (2015). 'Keynes and China: Keynesianism with Chinese Characteristics', *Asia Pacific Business Review*, 21: 251–263. I am greatly indebted to the published scholarship of Robert Skidelsky in general, and Paul Trescott in particular, which was of great help in the writing of this commentary on Keynes and China, as cited, as well as to William Brown, Geoff Hodgson, Susan Howson, Riccardo Peccei, Rod Wye, Ying Zhu, amongst others, for their generous advice. The dates of births and deaths of economists and other figures mentioned above are only noted where available.

References

Alexandroff, A. S., Ostry, S. and Gomez, R. (2004). *China and the Long March to Global Trade: The Accession of China to the World Trade Organization*, London and New York, NY: Routledge.

Bao, L. D. (2009). *John Maynard Keynes (Yuehan Meinade Kai'ensi)*, Beijing: Huaxia Publishing House, in Chinese.

Bhattacharya, A. (2012). '*Zhang Weiying*: China's Anti-Keynesian Insurgent', *Wall Street Journal – Eastern Edition*, 12 October, 260(88): A11–A11, 1–1–2.

Chandavarkar, A. (2000). 'Was Keynes Anti-Semitic?', *Economic and Political Weekly*, 6 May, 1619–1624.

Chen, H. C. (1911). *The Economic Principles of Confucius and his School*, New York, NY and London: Columbia University Press and P. S. King & Son.

Chow, P. (2011). *British Opinion and Policy towards China, 1922–1927*, PhD thesis, London: London School of Economics and Political Science (LSE).

Clarke, P. (2009). *Keynes: The Twentieth Century's Most Influential Economist*, London: Bloomsbury.

CUCAS (2012). 'Top 50 Chinese Universities in Economics', China Academic Degrees & Graduate Education Development Centre, www.cucas.edu.cn/HomePage/2010-04-09/page_714.shtml (accessed 13 January 2013).

Economist, The (2008). 'China's Fiscal Stimulus: Dr Keynes's Chinese Patient', *The Economist*, 13 November, www.economist.com/node/12601956 (accessed 22 May 2013).

Economist, The (2011). 'Keynes-v-Hayek in China', *The Economist*, 17 November, www.economist.com/node/21537010 (accessed 22 May 2013).

Fang, F. (2013). 'The Changing Status of Western Economics in China', in [eds] Y. Ma and H.-M. Trautwein, *Thoughts on Economic Development in China*, London and New York, NY: Routledge, 295–305.

Fang, X. and Gang, F. (2009). 'Economic Crisis, Keynesianism and Structural Imbalance in China', in [eds] R. Garnaut, L. Song and W. T. Woo, *China's New Place in a World in Crisis*, Canberra: ANU Press, 137–154.

Fardousi, S., Lin, J. Y. and Luo, X. (2012). 'Demystifying China's Fiscal Stimulus', *World Bank Policy Research Working Paper*, 6221, October, 1–33.

Gruchy de, J. W. (2008). 'Towards a Study of Arthur Waley and China', University Bulletin, www.kjunshin.ac.jp/juntan/libhome/bulletin/No38/de_Gruchy.pdf (accessed 10 January 2014).

Ha, L. D. (1993). *Keynes: A Biography (Kai'ensi zhuan)*, Beijing: *Shangwu yinshu guan* (Commercial Press), in Chinese.

Harcourt, G. C. (1995). 'Obituary: Joan Robinson 1903–1983', *Economic Journal*, 15: 1228–1243.

Harcourt, G. C. and Kerr, P. (2009). *Joan Robinson*, London: Palgrave Macmillan.

Harrod, R. F. (1951). *The Life of John Maynard Keynes*, London: Macmillan.

Howson, S. and Winch, D. (1977). *The Economic Advisory Council, 1930–1939*, Cambridge: Cambridge University Press.

Hsu, R. C. (1991). *Economic Theories in China, 1979–1988*, Cambridge: Cambridge University Press.

Jacques, M. (2011). *When China Rules the World: The End of the Western World and the Birth of a New Global Order*, London: Penguin Books.

Jaeger, C. C., Haas, A. and Töpfer, K. (2013). 'Sustainability, Finance, and a Proposal from China', *Working Paper*, Institute for Advanced Sustainability Studies (IASS), Potsdam, December, 1–30.

Keynes Papers (1868–1951). Cambridge: King's College Archive Centre, 1868–1951.

Keynes, J. M. (1912). 'Book Review of H. C. Chen (1911) "The Economics of Confucius and his School"', *Economic Journal*, 22: 584–588, www.jstor.org/discover/10.2307/22 22270?uid=3738032&uid=2129&uid=2134&uid=2&uid=70&uid=4&si d=21103355576801 (accessed 12 June 2013).

Keynes, J. M. (1913). *Indian Currency and Finance*, London: Macmillan.

Keynes, J. M. (1919a). *Economic Consequences of the Peace*, London: Macmillan.

Keynes, J. M. (1919b). *Economic Consequences of the Peace (Ouzhou he yi hou zhi jing ji)*, Shanghai: *Xin qing nian she* (New Youth Society Press), Chinese translation in 1920 by *Menghe Tao*, with *Xingren Shen*.

Keynes, J. M. (1923). *A Tract on Monetary Reform*, London: Macmillan.

Keynes, J. M. (1925). *A Short View of the Soviet Union*, London: Hogarth Press.

Keynes, J. M. (1930a). *A Treatise on Money*, London: Macmillan.

Keynes, J. M. (1930b). *A Treatise on Money (Huobinlun)*, Xian: *Shanxi shifan daxue chubanshe* (Shanxi Normal University Press) in 2008, Chinese translation by *Z. Liu*.

Keynes, J. M. (1936). *The General Theory of Employment, Interest and Money*, London: Macmillan.

Keynes, J. M. [1936] (1941). *The General Theory of Employment, Interest and Money*, (*Koyo, Rishi oyobi Kahei no Ippan Riron*), translated into Japanese by T. Shionoya, Tokyo: Toyo Keizai Shimpo-sha.

Keynes, J. M. [1936] (1957). *The General Theory of Employment, Interest and Money*, (*Jiu ye, li xi he huo bi tong lun*), Beijing: *Shenghuo dushu xinzhi* (SDX Press) in 1957, then after 1963, Beijing: *Shangwu yinshu guan* (Commercial Press), Chinese translation by *Y. Xu*.

Laurence, P. (2003). *Lily Briscoe's Chinese Eyes: Bloomsbury, Modernism, and China*, Columbia, SC: University of South Carolina Press.

Li, Y. (2010). *The Chinese Way of Economic Reform and Development*, Beijing: Foreign Languages Teaching and Research Press.

Lin, C. (1981). 'The Reinstatement of Economics in China Today', *China Quarterly*, no. 85: 1–48.

Lin, J. Y. (2011). 'Beyond Keynes', *World Policy Journal*, May, www.worldpolicy.org/journal/spring2011/justin-yifu-lin-beyond-keynes (accessed 9 January 2014).

Lo, L. and Zhang, Y. (2011). 'Making Sense of China's Economic Transformation', *Review of Radical Political Economics*, 43: 33–55.

Ma, Y. and Trautwein, H.-M. [eds] (2013). *Thoughts on Economic Development in China*, London and New York, NY: Routledge.

MacFarquhar, R. [Ed.] (1960). *The Hundred Flowers*, London: Atlantic Books.

Moggridge, D. (1989). *The Collected Writings of John Maynard Keynes*, Volume XXX, Bibliography and Index, Cambridge: Cambridge University Press and the Royal Economic Society.

Moggridge, D. (1992). *Maynard Keynes: An Economist's Biography*, London and New York, NY: Routledge.

Nakayama, I. (1939/1940). *Keinzu ippan riron kaisetsu*, Tokyo: Nihon Hyoronsha, Showa (in Japanese editions).

Nitsch, M. and Diebel, F. (2008). 'Guanxi Economics: Confucius Meets Lenin, Keynes, and Schumpeter in Contemporary China', *European Journal of Economics and Economic Policies: Intervention*, 5: 77–104.

Observer (1932). News Report. *Observer*, [London] 3 January: 13.

Paulovicova, N. (2007). 'The Immoral Moral Scientist', *Past Imperfect*, 13: 24–55.

Pearce, K. A. and Hoover, K. D. (1995). 'After the Revolution: Paul Samuelson and the Textbook Keynesian Model', *History of Political Economy*, 27 (Supplement): 183–216.

Peking Review (1975). 'Worst Postwar Economic Crisis', *Peking Review*, 7 February, no. 6, 17–18.

Peking University (2010). 'Works of Keynes of China', http://english.pku.edu.cn/News_Events/News/Media/7574.htm (accessed 10 January 2012).

Quah, D. (2013). 'China's Journey to the West', *Global Policy*, 2 February, www.globalpolicyjournal.com/blog/02/02/2013/china%E2%80%99s-journey-west (accessed 10 January 2014).

Robinson Papers, Cambridge: King's College Archive Centre, 1920–1986.

Robinson, J. and Adler, S. (1958). *China: An Economic Perspective*, London: Fabian International Bureau.

Ross, J. (2012). 'Deng Xiaoping and John Maynard Keynes', *Marx, Keynes and China Today*, www.solidarityeconomy.net/2012/02/10/marx-keynes-and-china-today/ (accessed 7 January 2014).

Samuelson, P. (1948). *Economics: An Introductory Analysis*, New York, NY: McGraw-Hill.

Schumpeter, J. A. (1954). *History of Economic Analysis*, London: Allen and Unwin.

Schwarcz, V. (1986). *The Chinese Enlightenment: Intellectuals and the Legacy of the May Fourth Movement of 1919*, Berkeley, CA: University of California Press.

Sheng, A. (2013). 'In China, a New Era of "Likenomic" Begins with New Keynesian Reforms', *China Post (Taiwan)*, www.chinapost.com.tw/commentary/the-china-post/special-to-the-china-post/2013/11/10/393296/p2/In-China.htm (accessed 16 January 2014).

Skidelsky, R. (1983). *John Maynard Keynes: Hopes Betrayed, 1883–1920*, London: Macmillan.

Skidelsky, R. (1992). *John Maynard Keynes, The Economist as Saviour*, London: Macmillan.

Skidelsky, R. (2000). *John Maynard Keynes: Fighting for Britain, 1937–1946*, London: Macmillan.

Skidelsky, R. (2006). *Keynes: A Biography* (*Kai'ensi zhuan*), Beijing: *Shenghuo dushu xinzhi sanlian shudian* (SDX Press), Chinese translation by *Lanxin Xiang* and *Ying Chu*.

Skidelsky, R. (2007). 'Keynes in the Long Run', *World Economics*, 8(4), 1 October, www.skidelskyr.com/site/article/keynes-in-the-long-run/ (accessed 4 January 2014).

Skidelsky, R. (2010). *Keynes: The Return of the Master*, London: Penguin Books.

Smith, A. [1776] (1902). *An Inquiry into the Nature and Causes of the Wealth of Nations* (*Yuan fu*) translated by F. Yan into Chinese, Shanghai: Nanyang Translation Institute.

Toye, J. (2006). 'Keynes and Development Economics: A Sixty-year Perspective', *Journal of International Development*, 18: 983–995.

Treasury Papers of J. M. Keynes (1940–1946). London: Public Record Office, now the National Archives (TNA), 1940–1946.

Trescott, P. B (2007). *Jingji Xue: The History of the Introduction of Western Economic Ideas into China 1850–1950*, Hong Kong: Chinese University Press.

Trescott, P. B. (2012). 'How Keynesian Economics Came to China', *History of Political Economy*, 44(2): 341–364.

Warner, M. (1966). 'The Webbs, Keynes and the Economic Problem in the Interwar Years', *Political Studies*, 14: 81–86.

Warner, M. (2001). 'The New Chinese Worker and the Challenge of Globalization: An Overview', *International Journal of Human Resource Management*, 12: 134–141.

Warner, M. (2013). 'The Global Economy in Crisis: Towards a New Paradigm?' *Asia Pacific Business Review*, 19: 157–161.

Warner, M. (2014). *Understanding Management in China: Past, Present and Future*, London and New York, NY: Routledge.

Woodside, A. (2006). *Lost Modernities: China, Vietnam, Korea and the Hazards of World History*, Cambridge, MA: Harvard University Press.

WorldCat (2016). World Catalogue, www.worldcat.org/search?q=kw%3Akai%27ensi&q t=results_page (accessed 20 October 2016).

Yip, K. W. (2012). *The Uniqueness of China's Development Model: 1842–2049*, Singapore; Hackensack, NJ: World Scientific Publishing Co.

Zhang, L. and Xu, Y. (2013). 'The Transmission of Heterodox Economics in China, 1949–2009', in [eds] Y. Ma and H.-M. Trautwein, *Thoughts on Economic Development in China*, London and New York, NY: Routledge, 306–326.

Zhou, X. (2009a). '*Zhou Xiaochuan's* Statement on Reforming the International Monetary System', *Council on Foreign Relations*, www.cfr.org/china/zhou-xiaochuans-statement-reforming-international-monetary-system/p18916 (accessed 10 January 2014).

Zhou, X. (2009b). *Reform the International Monetary System*, Bank of International Settlements, Basel, www.bis.org/review/r090402c.pdf (accessed 10 January 2014).

13 Adam Smith's 'sympathy' in modern Japanese perspectives

Tatsuya Sakamoto

Introduction

Japan is the country where the name of Adam Smith (1723–1790) (Adamu Sumisu) has been widely known amongst the public for the past 150 years or so (see Mizuta, 2003). A complete Japanese translation of the *Wealth of Nations* (1776) (*Fukokuron*) was published for the first time in 1882–1888 by Eisaku Ishikawa (1858–1887), who was a student of Yukichi Fukuzawa (1835–1901), one of the greatest intellectuals of modern Japan.

Since then, more than 20 Japanese translations of the *Wealth of Nations* (WN) have been published, and Smith has become one of the most familiar Western thinkers known in the country (see Okochi, 2000). Fukuzawa's most scholarly work, *An Outline of a Theory of Civilization* (1875), made three references to Smith, *first* as the man who 'expounded' an economic theory, *second* as a great compatriot of James Watt (1736–1819) and *third* as the man who 'first formulated the laws of economics' (Fukuzawa, 2008: 14, 107, 117). Even his most own popular work, *An Encouragement of Learning* (1872–1876) mentioned the name in an important passage to discuss the vital role of the 'middle class' as the engine of modern civilization. In Western history, 'not one form of business or industry was creation of the government alone. Their foundations were always laid by the plans of scholars in the middle class'. Together with Watt and Stevenson, Smith was mentioned as the man who 'explained the principles of economics and completely changed the methods of business'. This was the 'power of intellect' of the 'middle class' who were 'neither government administrators nor the laboring masses' (Fukuzawa, 2012: 41).

Fukuzawa recollects an interesting episode in his classic *The Autobiography of Yukichi Fukuzawa* (1898). When requested by a 'certain high official' in the Treasury Bureau of the Tokugawa Shogunate to lecture on a recent English book on political economy, Fukuzawa translated the original word 'competition' into '*kyoso*' (literally 'race-fight'). Not finding any better Japanese expression, he actually invented the word. The official disliked it because the word contained '*so*' which meant 'fight'. Fukuzawa resisted by saying that that is 'nothing new' – and 'exactly what all Japanese merchants are doing'. He explained that if one merchant begins to sell things cheap, his neighbor will try to sell them even cheaper. Or if one merchant improves his merchandise to attract more buyers, another will try to take the trade from him by offering goods of still better quality. Thus, all merchants race and fight and this is the way money values are fixed.

(Fukuzawa, 2007, 190)

The official further responded that the business practice in the West was 'ruthless', and that 'the word *fight* is not conducive to peace. I could not take the paper with that word to the Chancellor'. Although Fukuzawa thought that the official 'would rather have seen some such phrase as "men being kind to each other" in a book on economics', he agreed to erase the word. In fact, Fukuzawa continued to use it elsewhere and the word had finally become an indispensable keyword in Japanese daily lives.

The English book that Fukuzawa was translating to the official was John Hill Burton's work on Economics (Burton, 1852). Burton (1809–1881) was a well-known Scottish polymath and the author of many books ranging from David Hume's (1711–1776) biography to a scholarly edition of Jeremy Bentham's (1748–1832) works. Fukuzawa had obtained a copy of the book during his visit to European countries in 1862, as an English interpreter in the Japanese government's embassy. In the small book, Burton emphasized the key role of 'competition' as the engine of capitalism for the purpose of attacking contemporary socialists. The above episode shows Fukuzawa's exceptional sensibility of the nature of advanced capitalism in the West (for profound influences of Scottish thinkers on Fukuzawa, see Craig, 2009). By contrast, the official's naïve resistance against the idea of free market competition represented the average sensibility of Japanese people of the time. A similar mentality still survives in the mind of many people in the country as best represented by a recent vigorous campaign against the proposed Trans-Pacific Partnership Trade-Pact (TPP) in 2015–2016. Since Fukuzawa's time, Japanese discourses on Western Economics have been divided between the pros and cons of 'free market' capitalism, respectively represented by Fukuzawa's confident endorsement of the 'ruthless' competition and the official's emotional and intuitive resistance against it.

Quite naturally, Adam Smith as an intellectual 'icon' in modern Japan has represented Fukuzawa's progressive position and the name of Smith as the 'founder' of modern economic science has dominated the country's public discourse to this day (see the earlier chapter by Yagi on Japan in this volume). However, Smith has been seen by many not merely as the *founder of economics*; he has been regarded as the founder of social science itself and as the inventor of everything relevant to modern civilization. He has been read and studied not only as a discoverer of the market mechanism and as the father of liberalist economics, but also as a powerful promoter of the fundamental values of modern civilization (see also the chapter by Lai on Smith and China earlier in this volume, as well as Liu (2013) on the translations in Chinese and Japanese respectively in the two countries). In particular, Smith has been regarded by

Japanese scholars as a typically 'democratic' thinker. Whilst there is no reason to believe that he was a 'democrat' in our sense of the term, Smith has certainly been designated as a great designer of the integrated system of market society and democratic government.

After 1945 in particular, Smith's name has been strongly associated with Karl Marx (1818–1883) as one of the most influential precursors here. No matter how anachronistic it was, in order to bridge the gap between Smith's capitalism and Marx's socialism by the idea of democracy, a convenient term 'civil society' was virtually *invented* by some Marxian Smith scholars in Japan during the Second World War (see also Metzler's chapter later in this volume). The term has been used until recently for indicating the ultimate ideal of human 'civiliza-tion', as a combined intellectual legacy of Smith and Marx. The present chapter however attempts *not* to provide a general survey of the historical complexities of the introduction of Smith's thought into modern Japan, as that task has been taken up to a certain extent by past studies (see Sugiyama and Mizuta, 1988, Okochi, 2000, Mizuta, 2003, and Sakamoto's forthcoming paper on Yoshihiko Uchida).

This chapter rather seeks to analyse the various contexts in which Smith's theory of 'sympathy' has been translated and interpreted by Japanese scholars, and to argue for the fundamental similarity in the way in which Smith and Fuku-zawa had respectively discussed the nature and function of 'sympathy' in rela-tion to such principles as 'justice' and 'prudence'. By so doing, I wish to discuss the important sense in which both Smith and Fukuzawa established the moral centrality of 'sympathy' and of the relevant moral concepts such as the 'impar-tial spectator' (Smith) and the 'spirit of independence' (Fukuzawa) for the making of Western and Japanese civilizations.

Smith's 'sympathy' in the history of Japanese translations

At the opening passage of *The Theory of Moral Sentiments* (TMS) in 1759, Smith announces the fundamental outlook of the masterpiece as a whole.

> How selfish soever man may be supposed, there are evidently some prin-ciples in his nature, which interest him in the fortune of others, and render their happiness necessary to him, though he derives nothing from it except the pleasure of seeing it. Of this kind is pity or compassion, the emotion which we feel for the misery of others, when we either see it, or are made to conceive it in a very lively manner.

> (TMS, 60)

In discussing the empirical process in which pity or compassion arises in the breast of a spectator at the sight of misery and pain of others, Smith introduces 'sympathy' as the core principle of human nature to explain a variety of appar-ently non-egoistic sentiments and behaviour. Contrary to what was felt by the above-mentioned Japanese official against the 'ruthless' Western Economics, the father of the science had actually started his ethical inquiry by emphasizing the far-from egoistic nature of human sentiments. In fact, the apparent contradiction between the self-love of the *Wealth of Nations* (1776) and the sympathy of the *Theory of Moral Sentiments* (1759) has long been discussed as a famous academic issue, 'the Adam Smith Problem'.

The debate first started by nineteenth-century German scholars once appeared to have been settled completely. The editors of the Glasgow edition of Smith's works confidently claimed that the 'so-called Adam Smith Problem' was 'a pseudo-problem based on ignorance and misunderstanding' (TMS, 29). However, the debate is still continuing, and a variety of non-egoistic (that is, Kantian, republican or virtue-ethics) readings of TMS is gaining increasing popularity and support (for an updated survey of the problem, see Otteson, 2000; for the recent trends in Smith studies in the West, see Sakamoto, 2015).

Apart from the ongoing debate, a similar sense of contradiction between egoistic and altruistic interpretations of 'sympathy' has long existed in the traditional moral discourses in Japan. There is a well-known Confucian saying to teach that 'an act of pity is not for the sake of others'. A national survey conducted by the Agency for Cultural Affairs of Japan in 2001 showed that the majority made an 'altruistic' interpretation of the saying to think that a pitiful caring for others would not result in the true benefit of the others. However, the correct meaning of the saying was an egoistic one and an even Hobbesian lesson that people help others for the sake of themselves by expecting a similar return in the future. Needless to say, the egoistic interpretation is counter-balanced by the existence of an altruistic strand in the same Confucian moral teaching. The Confucian ideals of '*jin*' and '*renbin*' are the equivalents of benevolence, compassion and pity. Inazo Nitobe (1862–1933), the author of *Bushido: The Soul of Japan* (1899), originally published in 1900 by the Leeds and Biddle Company in Philadelphia, characterizes them as 'the highest of all the attributes of the human soul' (Nitobe, 2008, 25), as best instanced by the soul of the Samurai warrior.

Thus, the interpretive divide over the egoistic or altruistic nature of 'sympathy' is clearly traceable in Western and Japanese moral traditions. It has also been reflected in the history of Japanese translation of Smith's 'sympathy' (see Nakajima, 2006). So far, there have been four Japanese translations of TMS. The translators are Tomio Yonebayashi, Hiroshi Mizuta, Tetsuo Taka and Akiko Murai=Tomoko Kitagawa. Yonebayashi translated the 'sympathy' into '*dojo*', and Mizuta into '*dokan*', Taka and Murai–Kitagawa into '*kyokan*' respectively. A modern Japanese–English dictionary gives at the different entries of '*dojo*' and '*kyokan*', the same translation of 'sympathy'. By contrast, the same dictionary gives at the entry of '*dokan*' two separate translations; 'sympathy' and 'agreement'. Between the prewar '*dojo*' and the recent '*kyoka*', Mizuta's '*dokan*' dominated the country's Smithian scholarship for decades. In fact, the word was already used before the war, and the word itself was not Mizuta's invention. However, it was Mizuta that had clear purpose of infusing a new meaning into the word.

Smith's original 'sympathy' has two distinct meanings. The first is a broader sense of a spectator's imagination of placing oneself in the circumstances of another (agent) and sharing the agent's sentiments and feelings. The second is a more restricted sense of moral approval and disapproval as the result of the spectator's imaginary sharing of the agent's situation and sentiments. It has a more *individualistic* and self-distancing character than the first sense. Given the distinction, Smith argues that a complete sympathy in the first sense between agent and spectator produces the second sympathy of moral approval. Without the first sense of sympathy, the second sense of moral agreement and approval does not take place in Smith's account. Therefore, Smith's 'sympathy' operates through dual functions of imagination in contrary directions. Whilst a spectator shares the situation and sentiments of an agent by the first function of sympathy, the second function enables the spectator to distance himself from the immediate situation and sentiments of the agent. As will be discussed shortly, through the dual processes of imagination, what Smith called the 'impartial spectator' is gradually formed in the mind of the actual spectator.

To place a particular emphasis on the rational and individualistic sense of Smith's sympathy meant for Mizuta a democratic and egalitarian interpretation of Smith's theory. This was the result of his fundamental understanding of Smith's theory of 'civil society' (Mizuta, 1975). While the original Japanese word '*dokan*' has two different meanings in ordinary use, that is, 'sympathy' and 'agreement', Mizuta placed a particular emphasis on the sense of 'agreement'. Mizuta focused on the rational, cool and individualistic aspect of Smith's sympathy. Mizuta did this in order to replace the '*dojo*' – because the word was becoming synonymous with sympathy with sorrow and pain only and therefore more altruistic. Mizuta's '*dokan*' was intended to be true to Smith's original meaning by being more neutral than the '*dojo*' and to cover both kinds of sentiments; pleasure and pain. This means also that Mizuta's '*dokan*' necessarily weakened the sense of emotional, irrational and altruistic aspect of Smith's original 'sympathy'.

Mizuta chose to focus on the self-distancing and self-regulating role of Smith's sympathy as the moral foundation of the 'civil society' of free and independent citizens. Smith's 'civil society' in Mizuta's version has a prominently individualistic and even egoistic character. His translation was intended to be fitting in this context because the second sense of the '*dokan*' as 'agreement' sounds cool and detached, and even self-centred and egoistic. By contrast, the '*dojo*' which was prevalent before the war sounded for Mizuta as excessively emotional and warm, and as such involved a danger of endorsing the feudal nature of the pre-war Japanese mentality. By replacing it with the new '*dokan*', he highlighted the aspect of rational moral judgement to cool down the warmth of the old '*dojo*' and to provide a more appropriate moral foundation of a new democratic and individualistic society of Japan. Mizuta's translation was not merely the result of his creative interpretation, but also an intellectual exercise of a democratic thinker living in the critical age of Japan's post-war democratic reconstruction (for an intellectual history of Mizuta himself, see Sakamoto, 2014).

Justice and independence in the *Bushido*

When a person sympathizes with any others by maintaining a sense of distance, it is not easy to maintain an appropriate balance between the two opposite and simultaneous operations of sympathy. Smith famously called the person who is by nature or training capable of realizing the proper balance an 'impartial spectator'. The nature of Smith's 'impartiality' has been the subject of academic controversy for a long time. I do not delve into the complex issue here, but the idea of impartial spectator presents intellectual and moral challenges for the Japanese people because the Western tradition of moral discourses relevant to Smith's 'impartial spectator' was inseparable from the Christian ideals of moral rectitude, honesty and independence.

Smith discussed the issue at great length in several parts of TMS. He does so in the context of establishing the logical consistency between the 'impartial spectator' and the 'conscience' as a sublimation of moral autonomy and independence. Smith defines and redefines the concept of 'conscience', and attempted to show in the final analysis that the moral 'propriety' of the impartial spectator is identical with a familiar quasi-religious embodiment of 'conscience' or 'demigod'. These theoretical framework and device provide the ultimate guarantee for the conceptual unity or identity between the above-discussed two opposite operations of 'sympathy'. No matter how difficult it may be to bridge the gap in practical situations between the assimilating-altruistic function of sympathy and its distancing-egoistic function, Smith believes in principle at least that the innermost 'conscience' or 'demigod' as the sublimated form of 'impartial spectator' would effectively function as the pivotal role of realizing the unity of the two counteracting operations of sympathy.

In the Japanese ethical tradition as well, the subject of the right balance between the altruistic and egoistic sides of sympathy has been at the centre of moral discourses. According to Nitobe's classic *Bushido, the central virtues of the Samurai are 1. Rectitude or Justice, 2. Courage, 3. Benevolence, 4. Politeness, 5. Veracity or Sincerity, 6. Honour and 7. Loyalty.* The list curiously overlaps and contrasts with the traditional catalogues of virtues in the West. From the classical Four Cardinal Virtues of Prudence, Justice, Temperance and Courage to Smith's Prudence, Justice, Beneficence and Self-Command in the new Part VI of the 1790 edition of TMS, the Western tradition largely emphasizes the importance of the self-centred and individualistic virtues. All of the Cardinal Virtues are self-regarding. Two of Smith's virtues, prudence and self-command, are self-regarding and the other two, justice and beneficence, are other-regarding. However, Smith's sense of justice and beneficence are other-regarding only in highly limited senses of the words. Justice for Smith is 'a negative virtue, and only hinders us from hurting our neighbour', and people 'may often fulfil all the rules of justice by sitting still and doing nothing' (TMS, 124–125). As to 'beneficence', Smith is clear about its ethical limitation by saying that a human society 'may subsist, though not in the most comfortable state, without beneficence; but the prevalence of injustice must utterly destroy it' (TMS, 129). For Smith, no matter how indispensable, justice is a negative virtue, while no matter how laudable, beneficence is not indispensable. Smith's other-regarding virtues are either negative or dispensable.

Bushido or the Samurai ethics presents a clear contrast with Smith's account. Only two of the seven virtues of Samurai, rectitude or justice and courage, are self-regarding and all the other five virtues are other-regarding. This never means that the virtue of justice was not essential for Samurai. Nitobe traces the virtue of justice back to Confucianism, and refers to Mencius calling 'Benevolence man's mind, and Rectitude or Righteousness his path'. Even in the latter days of feudalism, 'when the long continuance of peace brought leisure into the life of the warrior class, the epithet Gishi (a man of rectitude) was considered superior to any name that signified mastery of learning or art' (Nitobe, 2008: 19). He illustrates the shining quality of the Samurai virtue of justice by a historical event of 1702. This was the case of 47 Samurai in which a band of leaderless Samurai avenged the death of their master, who was ordered to kill himself by being convicted of high treason which the 47 believed to be the result of an unfounded accusation. They avenged the death by killing a high-ranking Samurai official responsible for the master's death, were charged of high treason as the result, and killed themselves in a tragic manner. The event soon became a national legend and popularized in Japanese culture as a glorious symbol of Samurai virtues. The popularity grew rapidly during the Meiji era (1868–1912) – when Japan was undergoing its Modernization and Westernization.

However, the virtues of justice and courage as essential part of the Samurai ethics were the other side of the feudal morality, no matter how individualistic and self-centred they might appear. They functioned as the moral and spiritual pillars of Japan's feudal system, and never served, as in modern Western morals, as the historical cause of the moral collapse of feudalism. Needless to say, the other-regarding Samurai virtues of benevolence, politeness, veracity, honour and loyalty were part and parcel of the Japanese feudal system. In fact, the country's traditional ethics as a whole had been saturated with anti-individualistic collectivism or alter-egoism ever since the ancient maxim of Prince Shotoku (572–622) that 'harmony is the greatest of virtues'. The spirit still lies at the heart of the Japanese moral mentality in the form of a more secularized popular truism, as in Chinese, that 'the nail that sticks out gets hammered in'.

As a member of the lower Samurai caste himself, Fukuzawa once confessed that

> although the samurai of this time seemed fiercely independent, their spirit sprang neither from a personal, chauvinistic attitude nor from a strong individuality that exulted in the self's freedom from all outside influences. It was always motivated by something outside the person or at least aided by it.
>
> (Fukuzawa, 2008, 200)

It was not by accident that Fukuzawa was an isolated intellectual who had made an open criticism of the feudal nature of the 47 Samurai case. In Chapter Six of the *Encouragement of Learning* entitled the 'Importance of National Laws', he developed a wholesale attack against the case of the 47 Samurai by saying that their childish behaviour was a criminal act of private judgement and vengeance even within the limitation of the rule of law in the Shogunate government (for a more positive assessment of the Samurai spirit, see Ikegami, 1995).

This stands in sharp contrast with Smith's ethical individualism that was developed as the foundation of modern market society. In particular, the virtues of prudence and self-command were clearly conceived by Smith as the moral engine of the rising bourgeois' saving and investment. This was, one may argue, a secularized version of Max Weber's (1864–1920) renowned thesis on the 'Protestant Ethic and the Spirit of Capitalism'. The ethics of the Samurai caste embodied Japanese feudal society itself and was antithetical and even hostile to any form of commercial civilization. Nitobe made a convincing observation on the anti-commercial nature of the Samurai ethics.

> Of all the great occupations of life, none was farther removed from the profession of arms than commerce.... The samurai derived his income from land and could even indulge, if he had a mind to, in amateur farming; but the counter and abacus were abhorred.

He further pointed out the degraded and immoral manners of the common people's economic behaviour before the Meiji Restoration. 'The obloquy attached to the calling [commerce] naturally brought within its pale such as cared little for social repute' (Nitobe, 2008: 36–37). This once again presents a fundamental difference from Smith's account of modern commercial classes. As he confidently said,

> [I]n the middling and inferior stations of life, the road to virtue and that to fortune ... are, happily in most cases, very nearly the same. In all the middling and inferior professions, real and solid professional abilities, joined to prudent, just, firm, and temperate conduct, can very seldom fail of success.
>
> (TMS, 108)

Smith's careful wording in the above quotation reveals his clear awareness that it was from the 'middling and inferior stations of life' only that he could expect an ultimate unity of the road to virtue and that to fortune. In other words, Smith was not entirely complacent about the moral and economic reality of his times. He certainly had the realistic understanding that the 'middling and inferior stations of life' were, though rising in number and strength, still far from the majority among many other classes, and that in the higher and lower extremes of social classes, the road to virtue and that to fortune were not necessarily united. In Smith's economic theory, the exceptionally wealthy were a small number of elites, and they were largely supporters and beneficiary of the mercantile system. As he observed, they accumulated a tremendous wealth by morally corrupt means such as regulation, control and monopolistic privilege. The opposite extreme of the labouring poor could not make their ends meet merely by 'prudent, just, firm, and temperate conduct'. They had to earn their living by far from laudable means, and their extreme poverty might sometimes force them to turn to criminal means for mere survival.

Indeed, Smith's description of the social divide between 'rich and poor' in Book Five of WN is striking. For one very rich man,

> there must be at least five hundred poor, and the affluence of the few sup-
> poses the indigence of the many. The affluence of the rich excites the indig-
> nation of the poor, who are often both driven by want, and prompted by
> envy, to invade his possessions.
>
> (WN, Vol. 2, 122)

Nevertheless, Smith was optimistic about a future growth of the middling classes. His optimistic vision of civilization derived less from the social reality of his time than from the social and historical viability of the prominently middle-class virtues of justice, prudence and self-command. As the moral foundation of an emerging civilized society, the virtues were praiseworthy as a modern version of the classical cardinal virtues, and the roads to virtue and fortune were practically unified in the vision of modern commercial civilization. Therefore, the feudal nature of the Samurai ethics was diametrically opposite to the modern nature of Smith's system of morality. After discussing the historical causes of 'the fate of many a noble and honest samurai who signally and irrevoc-ably failed in his new and unfamiliar field of trade and industry, through sheer lack of shrewdness in coping with his artful plebeian rival', Nitobe summarizes the issue in a strikingly anti-Smithian phrase.

> It will be long before it will be recognized how many fortunes were wrecked
> in the attempt to apply Bushido ethics to business methods; but it was soon
> patent to every observing mind that *the ways of wealth were not the ways of
> honor*.
>
> (my italics, Nitobe, 2008: 37; for a non-Samurai origin of the
> commercial spirit in Japan, see Bellah's classic work, 1970)

Smith's 'superior prudence' and Fukuzawa's 'spirit of independence'

A question of vital significance arises in this context. Given Nitobe's contrast between the anti-commercial mentality of the Samurai and the pro-commercial character of the 'artful plebeian rival', *when and how* was the former gradually replaced and finally prevailed over by the latter? No doubt, it was around the time of Meiji Restoration of 1868, and by Yukichi Fukuzawa in particular, that the issue was seriously addressed for the first time in Japanese history. The impressive dialogue between Fukuzawa and a government official introduced at the outset of the present chapter was a sure manifestation of the issue at the vital transitional period. The official who resisted the translated word of 'competition' as 'ruthless' represented the anti-commercial mentality of the passing Samurai caste, and Fukuzawa who took the word for granted as if it had already become the name of the game was a reflection of the steady rise of the commercial mentality among the middle class. His classic works were strategically directed to the rising and expanding body of people as the ideal audience of his works. They were neither the simple-minded populace blinded by traditional Confucian morality, nor the immoral 'plebs' who sought for economic gains by any disgraceful means.

The audience of Fukuzawa was an enlightened body of ordinary people with a high level of intellectual enthusiasm and aspiration. They were not just seeking for mere economic success, but striving for bettering their cultural lives through reading and learning. The *Encouragement of Learning* made an unprecedented bestseller of 3.4 million copies. Given the total population of 35 million in Japan, the number is truly amazing, and demonstrates the existence of a growing and vigorous reading public. Indeed, Fukuzawa was far from one-sidedly optimistic about the moral and intellectual quality of the Japanese populace at large. He wrote quite a few critical comments about the deeply feudal mentality still persisting among the general public. As he wrote, '[T]he independence of a nation springs from the independent spirit of its citizens. Our nation cannot hold its own if the old slavish spirit is so manifest among the people' (Fukuzawa, 2007, 314). His criticism and pessimism was such that he even thought that, 'the government is as despotic as before, and Japanese subjects continue to be stupid, spiritless, and powerless' (Fukuzawa, 2012: 29).

Nevertheless, read against the more extensive and long-term historical background of Japan's Modernization and Westernization after the Meiji Restoration, Smith's modern cardinal virtues acquire a new interpretive dimension for understanding Fukuzawa's own moral principles. Smith's individualistic virtues of justice, prudence and self-command read as if overlapping with Fukuzawa's version of pro-commercial morality. His autobiography is a great historical evidence of the man who had made deliberate and strenuous efforts to transform himself from a man of impoverished low-ranking Samurai family to a Western type of modern intellectual. As he recollects, throughout his life, 'my general determination was to be independent, to earn my own way and not to beg, borrow or covet other men's property' (Fukuzawa, 2007: 265). His life-long motto of 'Independence and Self-respect (*dokuritsu-jison*)' was a classic Japanese version of Smith's individualistic virtues. Whilst there is no doubt about the parallel relationship between Fukuzawa's spirit of 'independence' and Smith's 'justice' and 'self-command', a further profound similarity between Fukuzawa's 'independence' and Smith's 'prudence' is unquestionable.

Both of Smith's and Fukuzawa's moral principles were conceived as something more than a mere 'egoism'. Indeed, as to the ordinary kind of prudence 'when directed merely to the care of the health, of the fortune, and of the rank and reputation of the individual', Smith gave a negative assessment of its moral quality as commanding 'a certain cold esteem' and not 'entitled to any very ardent love or admiration'. However, Smith went on to discuss the 'superior prudence' as 'wise and judicious conduct, when directed to greater and nobler purposes'.

> We talk of the prudence of the great general, of the great statesman, of the great legislator. Prudence is, in all these cases, *combined with many greater and more splendid virtues, with valour, with extensive and strong benevolence*, with a sacred regard to the rules of justice, and all these supported by a proper degree of self-command. This superior prudence, when carried to the highest degree of perfection, necessarily supposes the art, the talent, and the habit or disposition of acting with the most perfect propriety in every possible circumstance and situation. It necessarily supposes the utmost perfection of all the intellectual and of all the moral virtues. *It is the best head joined to the best heart. It is the most perfect wisdom combined with the most perfect virtue.*
>
> (my italics, TMS, 229)

While Smith's 'superior prudence' originally derives from selfish motivations, it transforms itself into an even more non-egoistic, not to say altruistic, character than a mere privately beneficent man by being 'combined with many greater and more splendid virtues'. Fukuzawa's spirit of independence was also something more than an ordinary prudence, and quite close to Smith's 'superior prudence'. It is true, as Alan Macfarlane pointed out, that, to many of his contemporaries, this individualism and 'all this hard work, financial and political independence, planning and ambition makes Fukuzawa sound a dry, two-dimensional person' (Macfarlane, 2014: 23). He himself was conscious of the need to avoid a possible misunderstanding in this respect, and explained the reason why his independent and individualistic style of life in the Japan of the day appeared as something egoistic to his fellow citizens. 'It may thus appear that I am a queer bigoted person, but in reality I am quite sociable with all people. Rich or poor, noble or commoner, scholar or illiterate – all are my friends' (Fukuzawa, 2007: 292). Fukuzawa was certainly aware of himself being a man of independence and self-respect even to the degree that he might appear as egoistic, greedy and vain in the eyes of the ordinary people of his time, but he was even more convinced that he was a man of uncommon sympathy, affection and sociability.

The non-egoistic character of Fukuzawa's spirit of 'independence and self-respect' was best demonstrated by the simple fact that he was not a mere brilliant scholar. He carried out a number of entirely new and even adventurous enterprises that had never been even heard of before in Japan. Apart from the noteworthy business organizations and companies that he helped others found, such as Maruzen (1869–) and Yokohama Specie Bank (1880–, later the Bank of Tokyo), the list of non-profit organizations that he himself founded and organized includes Keio Gijuku (now Keio University, 1858–) as the first higher education institution in the country, the Institute for Study of Infectious Diseases (1873–, now the Faculty of Medicine, Keio University) and the newspaper

Jiji-Shinpo (literally, *The Times*, 1883–1955). As Norio Tamaki and Helen M. Hopper amply demonstrated, Fukuzawa was an unprecedented, and still rarely heard of, type of scholar/entrepreneur (see Tamaki, 2001; Hopper, 2005; see also Nishikawa 1998). He was highly motivated to envision and achieve a variety of social projects for building a new Japanese civilization by bottom-up approaches. The inner principle that produced his life-long achievements properly deserves the name of 'superior prudence'. His projects were strategically carried out in a direct opposition to the Meiji government's top-down policy of systematic industrialization and militarization.

The national policy of the 'Rich Country, Strong Army' was, for Fukuzawa, not the correct way of modernization and civilization of Japan. He firmly believed that the government's policy critically lacked a dimension of the *human* civilization, and devoted itself to mechanical kinds of modernization. In a famous passage in the *Encouragement of Learning*, Fukuzawa wrote as follows.

> Civilization of a country should not be evaluated in terms of its external forms. Schools, industry, army and navy, are merely external forms of civilization. It is not difficult to create these forms, which can all be purchased with money. But there is additionally *a spiritual component, which cannot be seen or heard, bought or sold, lent or borrowed.* Yet its influence on the nation is very great. Without it, the schools, industries, and military capabilities lose their meaning. It is indeed the *all-important value, i.e. the spirit of civilization*, which in turn is *the spirit of independence of a people.*
>
> (my italics, Fukuzawa, 2012: 38)

Smith's reference in the previous citation to 'the best head joined to the best heart' and to 'the most perfect wisdom combined with the most perfect virtue' sounds as if it echoes in the distant background of the above quote from Fukuzawa. Both thinkers believed that the modern virtue of prudence derives its profound driving force of civilization not merely from selfish passions and interests, but more decisively from what Smith called 'superior' prudence. The Japanese nation was facing a formidable challenge of civilization by overcoming the feudalistic mentality by adopting a policy of scientific and technological Westernization. For a national as well as individual success in this challenge, Fukuzawa pointed out the vital need of the 'spirit of civilization' as the 'spirit of independence of a people'. Moreover, he clearly defined the nature of the spirit of independence in general, and the relationship between national and individual independence. As he says in a critical passage of *An Outline of a Theory of Civilization*, the only reason for making the people in our country today advance toward civilization is to preserve our country's independence. Therefore, '*national independence is the goal, and our people's civilization is the way to that goal*' (my italics, Fukuzawa, 2008: 256). He made it abundantly clear that his ideal of civilization was inseparable from a national spirit of independence and, as such, was something more than individualistic or negative virtue of private prudence or justice.

Concluding remarks: revival of sympathy and public spirit in Japan?

As Smith discussed 'superior prudence' as an exceptional moral quality of the 'great general, of the great statesman, of the great legislator', Fukuzawa defined his 'spirit of independence' as the spirit of a people. The apparent difference comes from the different context in which each discussed his subject. Smith's argument was mainly directed to general readers on the special moral quality of great figures in history. Fukuzawa's interest was to arouse the nation's critical awareness of the danger they were facing under the increasing pressures and threats generated by the colonial expansions of the Western powers in Asia. As a matter of fact, Fukuzawa was issuing a desperate caution to the enlightened part of the public about a possible loss of independence of their country. He warned against committing a national 'error' of following the tragic paths of China, Korea and other Asian countries. Fukuzawa's universalistic ideal of civilization was ultimately driven by the nationalistic, or more appropriately, *republican* dimension of his public discourse. Smith's 'superior prudence' was highly appraised as the exceptional moral quality of great leaders and politicians at any time in the past and most typically as that of 'republican virtues' in ancient Greece and Rome. He discussed the exceptional quality in sharp contrast with modern private virtues of prudence, justice, beneficence and self-command to be expected from the ordinary people.

The difference, however, is minimized when it is recalled that Smith's private virtues themselves were developed as more than mere selfish and private virtues. The highest guiding principle for Smithian elites, as well as ordinary people alike, was the 'impartial spectator', and 'the man within'. In critical cases of the rupture between the majority's opinion and an agent's internalized impartial spectator's voice, it should definitely be the latter that the agent ought to follow. Smith illustrated this by the historic case of the 'unfortunate Calas, a man of much more than ordinary constancy, broke upon the wheel and burnt at Toulouse for the supposed murder of his own son, of which he was perfectly innocent' (TMS, 156). As Donald Winch rightly claims, Smith 'has addressed the problem of reconciling republican ideas of liberty with non-interventionist conceptions of individual freedom by maintaining that negative liberty cannot be achieved without the positive versions associated with republicanism' (Winch, 2002: 299). *Smith and Fukuzawa almost completely agreed about the paramount importance of moral autonomy and independence, and they both made great efforts to appeal to their respective audience on the highest moral requirement in the form of a just and proper combination of the non-egoistic and socializing function of 'sympathy' and the individualistic and autonomous function of the 'impartial spectator'.*

If Mizuta's translation of Smith's sympathy into '*doka*' was a historical product of the post-war democratic reconstruction of Japan, what was the social background that encouraged the recent translators to adopt the '*kyokan*' to emphasize the non-egoistic and even altruistic character of sympathetic assimilation with other's sentiments? One might answer that Mizuta's democratizing strategy of translating Smith's 'sympathy' into '*dokan*' has become historically irrelevant by the profound changes in the country since the 1990s. Japan was to become a full-fledged democratic country, with the second biggest economy in the world until recently.

Japan has long been struggling through the difficult times of the so-called 'Lost Twenty Years', ever since the sudden burst of the 'bubble' economy in the early 1990s. A high level of economic equality, once the country's national pride, has been gradually but decidedly undermined. As the result of the neo-liberalist economic policy of the Koizumi administration (2001–2006), the social and economic divide between 'rich and poor' in present-day Japan is expanding at an unprecedented level in post-war history. Mizuta's one-sided emphasis on the individualistic aspect of Smith's idea of 'sympathy', once received by the reading public positively as a symbol of a democratizing project of post-1945 Japan, is now facing a critical danger of being misunderstood as a symbol of the egoistic individualism of neo-liberalist 'greedy' capitalism.

In addition to drastic economic changes, Japan has been experiencing an equally unprecedented rise of political tension and geopolitical instability in the East Asian region. The negative political factors are undoubtedly encouraging Japanese people to turn in a nationalist and protectionist direction. Under the increasing pressures, the recent translations of Smith's 'sympathy' into the '*kyokan*' might possibly have a positive moral implication. The emphasis on the non-egoistic – and even altruistic character of the sympathetic sharing of the sorrows and pains of other people – might be taken as an indication of the awakening of the Japanese people's 'sympathetic imagination'. Be it nationalism or humanitarianism, the recent arrival of the new translations, with the emphasis on Smith's altruistic aspect of 'sympathy', might indicate a sure sign of the rise of non-egoistic and non-individualistic desire for a 'public spirit' and 'superior prudence' among the Japanese people in the twenty-first century.

References

Japanese sources

Fukuzawa, Y. (2007) *The Autobiography of Yukichi Fukuzawa*. Revised translation by E. Kiyooka, with a Foreword by A. Craig. New York, NY: Columbia University Press.

Fukuzawa, Y. (2008) *An Outline of a Theory of Civilization*. Revised translation by D. A. Dilworth and G. Cameron Hurst III, with an Introduction by T. Inoki. New York, NY: Columbia University Press.

Fukuzawa, Y. (2012) *An Encouragement of Learning*. Translation by D. A. Dilworth with an introduction by S. Nishikawa. New York, NY: Columbia University Press.

Nakajima, Y. (2006) *An Intellectual History of Sympathy* (in Japanese). Tokyo: Tofusha.

Okochi, K. (2000) 'A Short History of Translations of the Wealth of Nations', translated by T. Sakamoto. In: Lai, C. ed. *Adam Smith Across Nations: Translations and Receptions of The Wealth of Nations*. Oxford: Clarendon Press.

Smith, A. (1883–1888) *An Inquiry into the Nature and Causes of the Wealth of Nations.* Translation by E. Ishikawa, 12 vols. Tokyo: Keizai-Zasshi-Sha (Economic Journals Company).

Smith, A. (1948–1949) *The Theory of Moral Sentiments.* Translation by T. Yonebayashi, 2 vols. Tokyo: Mirai-sha.

Smith, A. (1973) *The Theory of Moral Sentiments.* Translation by H. Mizuta. Tokyo: Chikuma Shobo.

Smith, A. (2003) *The Theory of Moral Sentiments.* Translation by H. Mizuta, 2 vols. Tokyo: Iwanami Shoten.

Smith, A. (2013) *The Theory of Moral Sentiments.* Translation by T. Taka. Tokyo: Kodansha.

Smith, A. (2014) *The Theory of Moral Sentiments.* Translation by A. Murai and T. Kitagawa. Tokyo: Nikkei BP.

English sources

Bellah, R. N. (1970) *Tokugawa Religion: The Values of Pre-industrial Japan.* Boston, MA: Beacon Press.

Burton, J. H. (1852) *Chambers' Educational Course: Political Economy for Use in Schools and Private Instruction.* London: William and Robert Chambers.

Craig, A. M. (2009) *Civilization and Enlightenment: The Early Thought of Fukuzawa Yukichi.* Cambridge, MA: Harvard University Press.

Hopper, H. M. (2005) *Fukuzawa Yûkichi: from Samurai to Capitalist.* New York: Pearson/Longman.

Ikegami, E. (1995) *The Taming of the Samurai: Honorific Individualism and the Making of Modern Japan.* Cambridge, MA: Harvard University Press.

Liu, Q. (2013) 'The Reception of Adam Smith in East Asia: A Comparative Perspective'. In Ma, Y. and Trautwein, H.-M. eds. *Thoughts on Economic Development in China.* London and New York, NY: Routledge, 35–55.

Macfarlane, A. (2014) *Yukichi Fukuzawa and the Making of the Modern World.* Published in part-works by Amazon Digital Services LLC.

Mizuta, H. (1975) 'Moral Philosophy and Civil Society'. In: Skinner, A.S. and Wilson, T. eds. *Essays on Adam Smith.* Oxford: Clarendon Press.

Mizuta, H. (2003) 'Adam Smith in Japan'. In: Sakamoto, T. and Tanaka, H. eds. *The Rise of Political Economy in the Scottish Enlightenment.* London: Routledge.

Nishikawa, S. (1998) 'Fukuzawa, Yukichi'. In: Warner, M. ed. *The IEBM Handbook of Management Thinking.* London: Thomson, 233–237.

Nitobe, I. (2008) *Bushido: The Soul of Japan.* Radford, VA: Wilder Publications.

Otteson, J.R. (2000) 'The Recurring "Adam Smith Problem"', *History of Philosophy Quarterly*, 17, pp. 51–74.

Sakamoto, T. (2014) Foreword to *The Mizuta Library of Rare Books in the History of European Social Thought: A Catalogue of the Collection Held at Nagoya University Library.* Tokyo: Edition Synapse and London: Routledge.

Sakamoto, T. (2015) 'Review of *The Oxford Handbook of Adam Smith*', *Eighteenth-Century Scotland*, 29, pp. 15–16.

Sakamoto, T. (forthcoming) 'Adam Smith's Dialogue with Rousseau and Hume: Yoshihiko Uchida and the Birth of the *Wealth of Nations*', *Adam Smith Review.*

Smith, A. (1981) *An Inquiry into the Nature and Causes of the Wealth of Nations*, Campbell, R. and Skinner, A. eds. Indianapolis, IN: Liberty Press. Abbreviated in the text as WN.

Smith, A. (1982) *The Theory of Moral Sentiments*, Macfie, A.L. and Raphael, D.D. eds. Indianapolis: Liberty Press. Abbreviated in the text as TMS.

Sugiyama, C. and Mizuta, H. eds. (1988) *Enlightenment and Beyond: Political Economy Comes to Japan*. Tokyo: University of Tokyo Press.

Tamaki, N. (2001) *Yukichi Fukuzawa, 1835–1901: The Spirit of Enterprise in Modern Japan*. Basingstoke and New York, NY: Palgrave.

Winch, D. (2002) 'Commercial Realities, Republican Principles'. In: Gelderen, M. van and Skinner, Q. eds. *Republicanism: A Shared European Heritage* (*Vol. 2, The Values of Republicanism in Early Modern Europe*). Cambridge: Cambridge University Press.

14 Japan's Keynes

Takahashi Korekiyo (1854–1936)

Richard J. Smethurst

Introduction

This chapter has been written as a study in economic policy, not in economic theory as such (see Smethurst, 2007). The subject, Takahashi Korekiyo (1854–1936), served seven times as Japan's Finance Minister between 1913 and 1936, and is most famous as 'Japan's Keynes', or 'Keynes before Keynes'. John Maynard (later Lord) Keynes (1883–1946) was born later than Takahashi and died even later.

Takahashi had introduced expanded fiscal spending using borrowed money to stimulate the economic recovery in the summer of 1932, three-and-a-half years before the first publication of John Maynard Keynes' *The General Theory of Employment, Interest and Money* in February 1936 and not much after Keynes' former student and later collaborator, Richard (later Lord) Kahn (1905–1989), had introduced the 'multiplier' to economic parlance. In fact, Takahashi had already written about fiscal spending working 'twenty or thirty times over' in a pre-Kahn 1929 essay, in which he invited the nation to go to a 'geisha-house' and spend wastefully (morally) *and* productively (economically). Barry Eichengreen (2015) has dubbed his actions 'Takahashi's Revenge', since he reversed the actions of his 'contractionist' predecessor as finance minister and challenged the fiscal orthodoxy of the times (Eichengreen, 2015: 253–258).

The point of this contribution will be that – although we cannot find a 'smoking gun', that is, a direct connection between Keynes' idea of a spending policy to bring economic recovery during the depression and Takahashi's policies – it is clear that Takahashi was a 'modern' economic statesman who spoke and read English fluently and could easily have learned Keynesian, or more to the point, proto-Keynesian ideas during his long policy apprenticeship and acted as if he had done so.[1]

Background

On New Year's Day 1935, two months before the publication of his *magnum opus* mentioned above, John Maynard Keynes wrote to his friend the playwright George Bernard Shaw,

I believe myself to be writing a book on economic theory which will largely 'revolutionize' – not I suppose, at once but in the course of the next ten years – the way the world thinks about its economic problems. I can't expect you, or anyone else, to believe this at the present stage. But for my mind I don't merely hope what I say – in my own mind I am quite sure.

(Cassidy, 2011: 1)

Takahashi Korekiyo became Finance Minister of Japan for the fifth of seven times on 13 December 1931, and on his first day in office prohibited the export of gold, that is, took Japan off the Gold Standard, to devalue the yen and stimulate exports. Before the end of his first few months in office, Takahashi lowered the 'prime-rate' sharply, introduced the 'Diet' (Parliamentary) legislation to increase sharply the amount of money in circulation, and then in the summer of 1932 launched a fiscal stimulus through increased government spending. The money for the fiscal stimulus came through the issuance and sale of Treasury bonds. He came up with the innovative idea of selling the bonds to the Bank of Japan and not on the open market. The bank's job was to choose the right time for open-market operations. Thus, in the interim between the bank purchase of the bonds from the Treasury and its sale of them on the bond-market, usually 4–6 months, money in circulation increased sharply and 'crowding out' was avoided. This gave people more money to spend, which increased demand and further stimulated economic growth – the 'multiplier effect'. Between 1931 and 1936, the year Takahashi was murdered by army officers, the Japanese economy grew in real terms by 33 per cent and the Tokyo stock-index by 235 per cent; this followed a small, 2.1 per cent growth of the real economy and a 50 per cent fall in the stock index as the Hamaguchi Cabinet sharply cut government spending and raised the value of the yen to return to the Gold Standard at the pre-First World War exchange-rate in 1929–1931 (Bank of Japan, 1966: 253; Ohkawa and Shinohara, 1979: 258–259).

Economic historians are divided over which part of Takahashi's policies – exchange rate, monetary or fiscal policy – was the most important. Some scholars emphasize that devaluing the yen brought about an increase in exports, especially to British colonies in South and South-East Asia; others that fiscal spending was more central (Nanto and Takagi, 1985: 369–374; Cha, 2003: 127–144; Shibamoto and Shizume, 2014). But whichever was most important, the concomitant increase in employment, wages and thus demand returned Japan to full employment by 1935, six years before America's defence spending in preparation for the Second World War brought about its recovery. Before returning to the question of the economic atmosphere in Japan at the time of Takahashi's return to the Ministry of Finance, which followed the ideas of orthodox European and North American financial leaders, and of Takahashi's ability to introduce 'Keynesian' policies four years before the publication of Keynes' *General Theory*, I would like to introduce briefly the development of economic policy in Japan from the Meiji Restoration in 1868 to the Great Depression of the 1930s (see Das's chapter on East Asia, as well as Yagi's chapter on Japan earlier in this volume).

As is well-known, Japan entered the modern world in 1853, when Commodore Matthew Perry and his 'Black Ships' visited Edo/Tokyo Bay. Between the expulsion of the Portuguese in the early seventeenth century and the arrival of Perry over 200 years later, the most important revolution in the history of the world had taken place: 'The Industrial Revolution', that is, use of non-animal energy to run machines. When Perry and then the British, French, Russians and Germans came to Japan in the 1850s, they came with steam-ships and modern weapons, and products like cotton-textiles, produced on steam-driven looms, that flooded Japan's markets. The Europeans and North Americans also came with a new attitude, one that did not just ask for the 'opening' of Japan but even demanded it. So, the West came to Japan in the age of 'Imperialism'. These countries were indeed building empires in Africa, Siberia and South and South-East Asia, and knocking forcibly on the doors of China, Korea and Japan.

After the Meiji government came to power in 1868, Japan's leaders had to decide how best to deal with the military, economic and financial pressure of the 'post-Industrial Revolution' West. Everyone agreed that Japan had to *learn from the West* to *protect Japan against the West*, but not on how best to do it. Two overlapping approaches appeared: one was to learn from the foreigners about how to grow Japan's economy in order to develop a modern military able to defend Japan. This approach emphasized government-funded heavy transplant industry through the building of 'model factories' with imported equipment and advisers to produce iron, chemicals, steel and other goods essential for producing warships and other weapons (and also factories to make the weapons themselves): namely, 'Rich country, Strong army' (*fukoku kyohei*). The other approach emphasized learning from the foreigners about how to modernize and grow Japan's existing economy to make its people richer: 'Rich country, Prosperous people' (*fukoku yumin*) as Takahashi wrote in an 1885 memorandum decrying the finance ministry's high tax policy during the Matsukata deflation period (Shinagawa, 1999: 24–29). But a national defence that went beyond the people's ability to pay for it was not a solid one. Takahashi from early in his career enlisted in the second group. The government's job is to help raise everyone's standards of living by helping private companies expand production and markets. The government provides infrastructure, both physical like railroads, ports for steamships, and telegraphs, and institutional like modern banking and educational systems, and inexpensive capital – the purpose of the infrastructure is economic growth, and only secondarily national defence as the army proposed. Private entrepreneurs must decide how best to use this infrastructure and capital. Takahashi was a member of a group headed by Maeda Masana (1850–1921), an up-and-coming official in the new Ministry of Commerce and Agriculture that advocated, in the 1880s, the establishment of loosely integrated regional industrial banks to which the finance ministry provides half the funds but delegated allocation of its monies to regional officials and entrepreneurs. In other words, the government could use fiscal policy to help a modernized, regional, 'traditional' economy grow. Takahashi believed it had to be done together with businessmen – bureaucrats could not make decisions about what industries to support or what companies to help. They did not have the intimate knowledge of markets, methods of production, necessary raw materials, and the like that the company owners and managers did. Even in the depths of the 1930s depression, Finance Minister Takahashi opposed government-directed aid to the depressed agricultural sector because to him, 'every community has its own unique problems'. Give local people money and let them decide how to use it, but don't tell them how to use it. Takahashi has often been called 'Japan's Keynes', but he might equally also be called 'Japan's Hayek' or Japan's 'Adam Smith', in this respect. As Takahashi wrote, in his 1885 memorandum, not listening to *markets* leads directly to failure.

The Maeda/Takahashi group supported the development of export industries, particularly raw silk and later cotton-textiles. From the Meiji period to the Great Depression, raw silk, exported largely to the US for making silk-stockings, provided one third of the value of all Japanese exports (raw silk exports by weight grew by 47 times between 1870 and 1930, as Japan replaced China as the world's largest raw silk producer). This market shrank in value in the 1930s, but cotton textiles stepped in to replace it (Li, 1982: 196–197). In other words, the key to paying for Japan's pre-war economic development was light, not heavy, industrial exports. We should point out here that the Maeda/Takahashi group did not carry the day in the 1880s. Leading officials such as General Yamagata Aritomo (1838–1922) emphasized heavy industry because as Japan developed a modern army and navy, it needed steel, coal, chemicals, and the other products of large-scale, Western-style mines and factories to build its weapons. If Admiral Heihachiro Togo's (1848–1934) battleships in Japan's 1904–1905 war with Russia were built in Scotland and England, its Second World War ships like the Yamato and Musashi were produced in Japanese shipyards. Finance Minister Matsukata Masayoshi (1835–1924), a realist, understood that to nurture heavy industry Japan had to pay for it. Although he played a central role in defeating Maeda's decentralized plan in 1885–1886, he supported the use of light export-industries to pay for the steel-mills and ship-yards thereafter. Thus, Japan's pre-1937 industrial development combined both light and heavy industry. The exports, raw silk and tea, paid for the imports, petroleum, iron ore, scrap iron, technology (the shipbuilders who built the two gigantic battleships above used American machine tools for much of the metal work and the Japanese steel industry relied on imported American technology for producing rolling equipment right up until the US government froze Japanese assets in the US in the summer of 1941) and other needs of the heavy industrial sector. But the emphasis for most of Japan's pre-Second World War modern history was on 'Strong army', not on traditional industry and its producers, who would have become the 'Prosperous people'.

Within both groups, that is, within the light industry, export-oriented group, and within the heavy industry military-power-oriented group, different sub-groups came to have different views of the best exchange-rate, monetary and fiscal policies for Japan. One group emphasized keeping the value of the yen low vis-à-vis silver, and then after Japan joined the Gold Standard in 1897, low vis-à-vis gold to stimulate exports, and the use of fiscal stimulus to expand demand. The key figure in this group was the entrepreneur Shibusawa Eiichi (1840–1931). The other group emphasized the importance of a strong, sound currency on the Gold Standard and a rigorous, balanced budget to maintain economic and financial probity. The key figure in this group was Matsukata, who also founded the Bank of Japan and as Finance Minister led Japan onto the Gold Standard in 1897.

What we have here are two sets of actors, what one can call the 'expansionists' and the 'contractionists'. Takahashi was what I would call a 'modified expansionist'. Although Hamaguchi Osachi (1870–1931), Finance Minister and Prime Minister in the 1920s and a hardcore gold-standard 'contractionist', called Takahashi a 'reckless spender' (*homan shugisha*), Takahashi actually went both ways. While he supported using government policy to stimulate growth, he also understood that there were times when the government had to raise the value the yen vis-à-vis gold and silver and when government spending had to be reined in. He actively supported Finance Minister Matsukata when Japan took the contractionary step of joining the Gold Standard in 1895–1897, but Takahashi advocated doing so at half the value of the yen proposed by Matsukata. And, most famously, he called for reducing government spending, much of it to the military, after Japan had returned to 'full employment' in 1935, leading to his assassination by young army officers on 26 February 1936 (Matsumoto, 2013: 226–227).

Japan was thus on the Gold Standard from 1897 to 1917. This helped it borrow heavily from the United States and European countries during its war with Russia in 1904–1905. British, American, French and German investment houses provided over half of Japan's war-time and immediate post-war costs, allowing it to defeat the Russians and maintain fiscal probity even after Japanese government leaders realistically withdrew their demand for reparations when the Russians hinted they might restart the war if Japan did not back down. Although the post-war army and navy demanded larger budgets to guard Japan's enlarged empire, the Gold Standard and the burden of repaying the war-time borrowing required Japan to maintain a contractionist fiscal policy. The First World War changed this. Japanese goods flooded into British and French export markets during the First World War, and the Japanese economy, on the verge of meltdown, boomed: 'divine providence'. But the boom brought inflation and in 1917 Japan, along with all of the major combatants, was forced to prohibit the export of gold and thus to leave the Gold Standard (Metzler, 2006: 115–137).

In the 1920s, the powers returned to the Gold Standard, one by one. This required them to balance budgets and keep interest rates high. Men like United States Treasury Secretary Andrew Mellon (1855–1937), who has been called not just a 'contractionist', but actually a 'liquidationist', because he believed that recession forced weak companies into bankruptcy and thus strengthened the economy, not to mention Takahashi's bête noire, Hamaguchi Osachi, in Japan, thought that the constraints of the Gold Standard were morally good and that excess consumption was morally bad: frugality not luxury. In Mellon's words,

Liquidate labor, liquidate stocks, liquidate the farmers, liquidate real estate.... That will purge the rottenness out of the system. High costs of living and high living will come down. People will work harder, live a more moral life. Values will be adjusted, and enterprising people will pick up the pieces from less competent people.

Or as Hamaguchi put it, Japan needed to 'wring out' the economy (Hoover, 1951; Nakamura, 1993: 114).

Even preparing to go back on the Gold Standard in Japan led to a severe deflation of wholesale and consumer prices. Consumer prices in Japan from 1920 to 1929 fell by 15.3 per cent. Yet unlike the other countries, Japan did not go back to gold. The 'Great Kanto Earthquake' of 1923 and the 'Financial Crisis' of 1927 intervened. Not until the Hamaguchi government, with former Bank of Japan Governor Inoue Junnosuke (1869–1932) as Finance Minister, came to power in July 1929, did Japan finally undertake to return to the Gold Standard.

Japan's move was ill-timed. It returned to the Gold Standard in January 1930 just as the world was going into one of the greatest depressions in its history. To go back on the standard at the pre-First World War value of the yen versus gold, the yen had to be revalued upward by 15 per cent. This made exports more expensive and intensified the deflationary impact of the imported, world depression. In other words, Japan was hit by a double-depression. Consumer prices 1929–1931 fell by 19.3 per cent, a greater drop in two years than that of the whole decade of 1920–1929, already deflationary, thus reducing Japan's nominal GNP sharply.[2]

The Hamaguchi-Inoue decision to return to the Gold Standard at the pre-First World War value of the yen did not go uncontested. Ishibashi Tanzan (1884–1973) and his group at the *Far Eastern Economic Review* (*Toyo Keizai Shinpo*) argued that Japan should follow Italy and France – and return to gold at the current exchange rate rather than follow the US and UK and return at the pre-1914 exchange rate. They understood that economically Japan in 1929–1930 was not even Italy, and certainly not the US, UK or France. If the Japanese government had followed Ishibashi's suggestion, the 'double-depression' would have been avoided.

Takahashi Korekiyo, at the time out of office between his fourth and fifth terms as Japan's Finance Minister, argued that returning to gold at some point was desirable, but that the timing was bad in deflationary 1929. His idea was that what Japan needed at the time was 'expansion' through devaluation of the yen and expanded fiscal spending, not the 'contraction' of the Gold Standard. He made his point in a 1929 article in which he used his famous 'geisha-house' analogy:

To put it in plain language, if a person goes to a geisha-house and calls a geisha, eats luxurious food, and spends 2,000 yen, we disapprove morally. But if we analyze how that money is used, we find that the part for food helps support the chef's salary, and the part used to buy fish, meat, vegetables, and seasoning, and the part for transporting it is paid to the supplying merchants. This part then wets the pockets of farmers and fishermen. The farmers, fishermen, and merchants who receive the money then buy clothes, food, and shelter. And the geisha uses the money to buy food, clothes, and cosmetics, and to pay taxes. If this hypothetical man does not go to a geisha-house and saves his 2,000 yen, bank deposits will grow, but the efficacy of his money will be lessened. But he does go to a *geisha*-house, and the money is transferred to the hands of farmers, artisans, and fishermen. It goes in turn to other producers and works twenty or thirty times over.

(see Metzler, 2006: 211, and Smethurst, 2007: 245–246 for slightly different translations of Takahashi's statement)

In other words, if the nation goes to a '*geisha*-house' and lives luxuriously (the reverse of the Mellon/Hamaguchi prescription) the '*multiplier effect*' will stimulate demand and bring economic recovery. But from 1929 to early 1930, the public was caught up in the return to gold. Great nations like the US and UK went back on the Gold Standard at the pre-First World War parity; lesser nations like France and Italy went back at the current exchange rate. The public thought Japan stood with the US and UK as a top-level world power, not with its actual economic equals. Thus, it must follow the US and UK and revalue the yen upward by 15 per cent. National pride led to a double-dip depression. (Japanese GDP in 1929 was at the same level as Italy; the US economy was seven times, the UK economy two times, the French economy 1.5 times and the German economy 1.3 times Japan. Japan had the lowest per capita GDP of the five. Japan's per capita income in 1929 was two thirds of Italy's, the next lowest.) By the time the Hamaguchi government fell in December 1931, 25 per cent of the urban workforce was unemployed, the stock-market index had halved and factories were operating well below capacity – there was no market incentive to invest in new productive facilities, much less fully use the existing ones (Bank of Japan, 1966: 252–253; Maddison, 1995: 180–200) This economic crisis enabled Takahashi as Finance Minister in the new Inukai cabinet, to leave gold, devalue the yen, lower interest rates and expand government spending. In the economic crisis of 1930–1931, the pendulum of public opinion swung from deflation to reflation.

Takahashi had supporters as he began his reflationary policies in December 1931. Let me mention four: First, the economic journalist Ishibashi Tanzan (1884–1973), publisher of a Japanese translation of *The Economic Consequences of Mr. Churchill*, John Maynard Keynes' critique of the British return to the Gold Standard in 1925 published in that year, which pointed out the economic costs in the UK, no longer the world's greatest economic power, of the treasury's contractionist policies. Second, Fukai Eigo (1871–1945), Vice Governor of the Bank of Japan. Although a central banker who was committed to fighting inflation, Fukai realized in December 1931 that Japan needed to leave gold to reflate the economy, and he met with his long-time mentor, Takahashi, the day he was appointed Finance Minister, to encourage him to abandon the Gold

Standard. To Fukai, a central bank must fear deflation as much as it fears inflation; many central bankers focus more on inflation without thinking about the equally invidious effects of deflation, but Fukai understood the dangers of both. Third, Kubo Hisaharu (1891–1961), an economic journalist who in October 1929 published a book critical of the decision to return to the Gold Standard entitled *Ending the Embargo on the Export of Gold Will Destroy The Nation* (*Kinkaikin bokoku ron*), with a recommending introduction by none other than Takahashi Korekiyo (Kubo, 1929, reprinted 1998). And finally, Muto Sanji (1867–1934), president of the Kanebo Spinning Company, who had written also in 1929 that Inoue's contractionist policies to go on the Gold Standard were like 'opening the window in the middle of a typhoon' (Nakamura, 1986: 46).

These men were in a minority of officials and business leaders in 1929–1931. What Keynes proposed and Takahashi actually did was considered radically unorthodox in 1929–1932. Even FDR, in recent years perhaps incorrectly criticized as Keynesian, only undertook full fiscal stimulus *at the earliest in 1937–1938*. The 'New Deal', again, did *not* include a fiscal stimulus through government borrowing. In fact, according to Robert Skidelsky (1992: 288), Japan and Sweden were the only two countries in the world that carried out what later came to be called 'Keynesian' stimuli in that period.

On 21 January 1932, a little more than a month after taking over as Finance Minister, Takahashi spoke to the House of Peers, and his 'contractionist' predecessor, Inoue Junnosuke, responded. Takahashi began his speech by blaming Hamaguchi and Inoue and their government's 'extreme frugality budget' as the primary cause of the recession Japan was entering. Takahashi concluded his speech by saying:

> To sum up, the previous government's policy of returning to the gold standard and of a tight fiscal policy ran counter to the needs of the times and threw the people's economic situation into extreme disarray. When the present government came to power, Japan's future looked bleak. The former government oppressed the financial world, killed industrial production, and recklessly forced our economy into depression. We have left the gold standard to save most of the population from dire straits, to promote industry, and to raise the people's standards of living. We are reducing the exchange rate and consumer prices, and stimulating production.
>
> (see Smethurst, 2007: 254–258)

At this point, Inoue replied just as strongly. He began by hinting that Takahashi had colluded with major Japanese banks in buying dollars before Japan left the Gold Standard, when two yen equalled one dollar, and then rebuying yen when the exchange rate had moved to three yen to the dollar. As Inoue slyly stated, 'Isn't it interesting that people who sold a great deal of gold to buy dollars preached that Japan should leave the gold standard.' Because of Takahashi's leaving the gold standard these speculators made a great deal of money. Inoue also accused Takahashi of inviting retaliation from Japan's trading partners by devaluing the yen, and of breaching international morality in the process. Inoue concluded by stating:

> In today's world, when political thinking has taken a turn for the worse, I am anxious. No announcement has been made yet about fiscal policy, but I fear we can expect a large increase in government spending before too long. Not just I, but the whole nation worries about this.
>
> (see Smethurst, 2007: 254–258)

But apparently the whole nation didn't worry too much. Members of the Parliament began to drift out of the chamber as Inoue spoke, and Takahashi's political party, which had won only 174 seats to Inoue's party's 273 in the February 1930 election, won the February 1932 election by a land-slide, 303 to 146 seats. As the journalist Imamura Takeo, a Takahashi biographer and a listener to the January 21 debate put it, 'The sails were already set. Takahashi had caught a good wind, and Inoue a reverse one' (see Smethurst, 2007: 254–258). Takahashi was able to carry out his exchange rate, monetary and fiscal policies because he had a strong legislative majority to work with.

One final point to make about Takahashi and exchange rate, monetary and fiscal policy in the 1930s: it was all *in the timing*. One has to know when to carry out a stimulus policy and when to end it. By 1935, Takahashi understood that Japan's recovery from the depression was nearly complete, and began to cut spending to bring the budget back into balance. He called for sharp reductions in the army's and navy's budgets. On 26 February 1936, young army officers, incensed by Takahashi's efforts to cut military spending, brutally murdered him. I would argue that the 26 February terrorist attack on key civilian government leaders eliminated all meaningful opposition to Japan's road to war.

Takahashi's education

How did Takahashi Korekiyo develop these 'Keynesian' ideas for bringing about Japan's recovery from the Great Depression in the 1930s? How did he develop economic ideas in Japan, that were so unorthodox even in Europe and North America, at the time? The answer, I think, has to do with his unorthodox upbringing and education. Takahashi had an unpromising beginning for a man who rose to become Prime Minister, seven times Finance Minister and Governor of the Bank of Japan later in his life. He was born July 1854, an illegitimate child, the son of an artist who worked in the Shogun's palace in Edo and a 15-year-old scullery-maid, and adopted as an infant into a family of hereditary foot-soldiers, that is, the very lowest rung of the *samurai* class. If the feudal order had continued Takahashi would have served and then retired from samurai service at the end of his career as a private in the army. He would have had no chance of any upward mobility, even to the rank of private first class. He was not only too low ranking in the warrior-order to receive a good Confucian education in a school for samurai but also too old to have the chance of a Western-style education when modern schools were established after the Meiji Restoration in 1868. Takahashi's flexible and open-minded views, as we shall see, came from the luck of timing, that is, from being 'educated' at the right time, and thus *because* he did not have either an orthodox samurai or university education. Younger men like Hamaguchi and Inoue went to Tokyo Imperial University and learned classical economics from Western or Western-trained professors. Takahashi learned 'on the job' and by reading and talking to people, and by reading and talking to people in both Japanese and English.

The good timing: in 1864, the leaders of Sendai domain, in which Takahashi's adoptive family served, decided that they needed to learn about Western military technology. To do so, they decided to send a group of young samurai to Yokohama to learn English, the primary imperialist language of the 1860s. Because Takahashi and a few of his fellow 'foot soldiers' lived in Edo, not Sendai, and were closer to foreign teachers of English, he was chosen, at the age of 10, to study with Clara Hepburn (1818–1906), wife of American medical missionary, Dr James Hepburn (1815–1911), in the newly opened treaty port. After a year and a half of daily tutorials with Mrs Hepburn, Takahashi at age 11 took a job as a 'boy' for Alexander Allan Shand (1844–1930), British banker in Yokohama. In August 1867, at 13, Sendai domain sent Takahashi to San Francisco, to continue his language studies. While there, he worked as a household servant and unwittingly sold himself into bonded servitude. In his 'adopted' home he spoke regularly with the mistress, her children, the Irish and Chinese cooks and the girl on the next ranch and her family. In the summer of 1868, Takahashi bravely ran away from his servitude, and in December, just after the Meiji Restoration, Takahashi returned to Japan, but he came home with two skills few Japanese at the time had: an ability to speak and read colloquial English.

Unlike Hamaguchi, Inoue and most Japanese leaders of their generation, who learned their English in the classroom, Takahashi learned by speaking to 'real' English-speakers and those of different classes and nationalities. Takahashi even knew 'obscene' English – one doubts that Hamaguchi and Inoue did. Takahashi's second skill was that he could talk with foreigners completely unselfconsciously. He moved when in foreign circles, not as an exotic outsider who spoke 'broken' English but as an equal member of the group in which he was involved.

Takahashi returned to Japan as an 'outlaw', because his domain, Sendai, had resisted the efforts of warriors from Satsuma and Choshu to establish the new Meiji regime. Takahashi was protected by Mori Arinori (1847–1889), a leading member of the new government, because Mori recognized Takahashi's important language skills. In March 1869, on Mori's recommendation, Takahashi became a teacher at Daigaku Nanko, the top school of Western studies at the time and a forerunner of Tokyo Imperial University. He was still only 14, and had little education except for English. At Daigaku Nanko, he taught older ex-samurai with higher ranks and better educations than his – but Takahashi spoke fluent English and they did not.

Although this was an important turning point in Takahashi's life, we should not think Takahashi's career was now on the 'fast track', nor his success assured, in spite of his English. And, I should add, his life was not dull either. Takahashi had a 'drinking problem' before he left Yokohoma for San Francisco. Between becoming an English teacher in 1869 and joining the Bank of Japan in 1892, Takahashi held 16 jobs, eight in government, eight in the private sector. He lived for a while with a '*geisha*', and worked as her *hakomochi*, that is, he carried her musical instrument from assignation to assignation. He ran an English-language school in Karatsu whilst still a teenager and went temporarily blind from excess alcohol consumption. He worked, by his own account, as an unscrupulous stock-broker. He sold cattle at a cattle-market in Nagano. He served as a translator – in this capacity, he helped translate Alfred Marshall's *The Pure Theory of Modern Trade* (which was published in English in 1879) soon after. He also interpreted for foreign advisors to the Japanese government such as David Murray, an American professor brought to Tokyo in the 1870s to help Japan establish a uni-versal education system. All the while, he was a 'free spirit' – a young man who disliked being ordered around, which caused him to fall out of jobs. But his English-language skills got him back in.

In the 1880s, Takahashi made a major contribution to modern Japan when he penned Japan's first and second sets of copyright and patent laws. He was chosen for the job because he had the ability to read the American and British laws. To prepare for writing the second set of laws, Takahashi studied copyright and patent law in New York, Washington, London, Berlin and Paris (while in the United States, he saw the first American productions of the *Mikado* in New York, Washington and Chicago, and wrote a scathing review, entitled, 'Yum Yum Kisses', in a Chicago newspaper.[3] He also studied ballroom-dancing so he could ingratiate himself with the patent office secretaries.) After returning home, Takahashi served as Japan's first Patent and Copyright Commissioner, and is mentioned in the official history of the US Patent Office. But even this did not guarantee his success.

Takahashi also ran a silver-mine high in the Andes in Peru in 1889–1890 and this was his greatest failure – through no fault of his own. The mine turned out to be barren – the Japanese investors, who put their money into the mine in the hopes that Japan could develop an independent source of silver and not have to depend on foreign banks for its supply, had been duped and Takahashi had to come home and tell them that they had lost all of their investment. Takahashi paid to bring the mineworkers back to Japan with his own money and was forced to sell his home and move with his wife and children into a tenement smaller than his childhood one. Takahashi's career finally got on track in 1892, when at the age of 38, he joined the Bank of Japan, first to oversee the construction of the Bank of Japan Building in downtown Tokyo, and then as first Manager of the Western Japan office of the bank in Shimonoseki in 1893–1895. He became Vice-Governor in 1899, Governor in 1911 and Finance Minister for the first time in the Yamamoto Cabinet in 1913.

Along the way he had no teachers (except maybe Mrs Hepburn), but he had many mentors. The list of his mentors, that is, the people he talked to and corres-ponded with, reads like a 'Who's Who' of Meiji Japan (and the world): James and Clara Hepburn and Alexander Allan Shand in Yokohama in the 1860s and Shand again in London 40 years later; Mori Arinori, Guido Verbeck, David Murray, William Eliot Griffis and Ito Hirobumi in Tokyo in the 1870s; Maeda Masana, Hara Takashi and Schuyler Duryee of the US Patent Office in the 1880s; Matsukata Masayoshi, Jacob Schiff, Lord Revelstoke (John Baring), Lord Rothschild and his Paris cousin Edmond deRothschild, Fukai Eigo and Ishibashi Tanzan in 1890–1920. The list of Takahashi's English-language correspondents, in addition to the above, includes Nicholas Murray Butler, president of Columbia University; Ernest Cassell, aka 'Windsor Cassell'; Lillian Wald, the socialist founder of the Henry Street Settlement House in the Lower East Side of Manhattan; Herbert Croly the founder of *The New Republic*; G. K. Menzies; W. M. Koch of Panmure Gordon; Cecil F. Parr of Parr's Bank; J. W. Robertson-Scott; Benjamin Strong of the New York Federal Reserve; and Paul M. Warburg of the Hamburg Warburgs, amongst many others. Takahashi recounts in his memoirs a 1904 shipboard conversation with Lillie Langtry – one assumes he did not mention this to King Edward VII when they met in 1905. All are fascinating characters: one of them, Guido Fridolin Verbeck (1830–1898) alone deserves serious study because of his importance both in Nagasaki in the 1860s and Tokyo in the 1870s as a teacher and advisor to many of Japan's most important modernizers. Verbeck gave Takahashi a Christian Bible, which Takahashi told us he read daily for the rest of his life. Two of these mentors, Maeda Masana (1850–1921), a Satsuma samurai who spent the 1870s studying in France, and Jacob Schiff (1847–1920), in 1904 when he met Takahashi in London one of the richest men in the world, stand out as most important. In the 1880s, Maeda taught Takahashi the importance of economic development, of raising people's standards of living in the process, of the need for inexpensive capital, of controlling unproductive government spending (that is, military spending), of basing economic development on an understanding of existing local conditions, not theory, and of letting local officials and entrepreneurs, not Tokyo bureaucrats, make decisions about how best to use the inexpensive capital. Maeda called for the establishment of local industrial banks, which would receive half of their funding from the central government but would make all lending decisions locally – even when using central government funds. In other words, Takahashi learned from Maeda the importance of listening to 'market' signals (see Sakamoto's earlier chapter in this volume on Adam Smith and Japan).

To my mind, Maeda's 1884–1885 original development proposal, 'Opinions on Developing Industry' (*Kgyo iken*), before it was rewritten by Matsukata Masayoshi's (1835–1924) subordinates in the Finance Ministry in 1884, is one of the most important proposals of modern Japanese history.

If Maeda's plan to develop Japan economically based on the modernization of traditional industries such as raw silk and tea production, and to do so from the bottom up rather than from Tokyo, that is, by listening to local officials and entrepreneurs, had been put into practice, pre-war Japan might well have developed in a more democratic and less centralized and militaristic way. Takahashi's lifelong views about an economic development that raised people's standards of livings and did not just make the state rich were deeply influenced by lessons he learned from Maeda in the 1880s.

Takahashi's second key mentor was Jacob Schiff, senior partner of the New York investment house, 'Kuhn, Loeb'. Takahashi first met Schiff at a dinner party in London on 3 May 1904. Takahashi was sent to sell Japanese war bonds after the war with Russia began. He was very successful in this task. Half of the total cost of the war, as we have seen, was raised abroad, and Kuhn, Loeb and M. M. Warburg, the Hamburg house of Schiff's son in-law, underwrote half of that half. So Schiff and his son-in-law's family alone underwrote one quarter of the total cost of Japan's victory in 1905. Between 1906 and Schiff's death in 1920, Takahashi and Schiff corresponded regularly. I have copies of 52 letters they exchanged over the period. Although neither was a native English-writer, both wrote in beautiful, Edwardian English.[4] Schiff's lessons to Takahashi were: First, the need for financial probity when borrowing abroad. You have to open your books to your creditors – your dealings must be transparent. Second, the importance of playing by the international rules when dealing with important financiers in the City of London, Wall Street, Paris and Hamburg. Schiff told Takahashi to tell Tokyo in the summer of 1905 to forget about demanding an indemnity from Russia – and he also told him that if Japan did not back down, Schiff and the London bankers would cut Japan off, but if it took the prudent course, Japan could count on London and New York help. Third, Takahashi learned here that even if the Americans and British did not always treat Japan as an equal, it was in Japan's interest to stay firmly within the Anglo-American framework, which in 1905 did not preclude 'empire-building'. After all, Schiff, the Rothschilds, Parr's Bank, Baring Brothers, The Hong Kong Shanghai Bank headed by Sir Ewen Cameron, Edward VII, William Howard Taft and Theodore Roosevelt all preapproved in 1904–1907 Japan's annexation of Korea – it was just part of the imperialist game of the time. Fourth, Schiff reinforced Taka-hashi's ideas about the importance of sharing the benefits of economic growth with the working class. While Schiff seems an unlikely social democrat, he told Takahashi in a 25 June 1916 letter that it was incumbent on the Europeans to reward the working class after the war. The workers were the 'actual' producers of wealth and deserved to be rewarded for their efforts. And fifth, Takahashi learned at this time that Japan was not a world power in the same way the US and UK were. Whilst many Japanese, elated by their victory over a European country, thought Japan had become one of the powers, Takahashi understood that there were powers and there were powers. He understood that foreign policy must be made on the basis of reality, on real power, harsh as that may be, not on the basis of what one wanted or hoped for.

Takahashi became Finance Minister for the second time in 1918 in the gov-ernment of Hara Takashi (1856–1921), Japan's first Cabinet in which the Prime Minister was selected because he was simultaneously the head of the majority political party in the Parliament, and this experience continued his education. Japan had gone through a boom during the First World War, Gross National Expenditure for 1914–1920 more than tripled, but at the same time consumer prices had doubled. The years 1918 to 1920 were a good time for fiscal contraction. But Takahashi, under pressure from his Prime Minister, who used fiscal spending to win grassroots support for his party, and the army, which carried out a feckless adventure in Siberia during Takahashi's years in office, allowed the economy to overheat. In Mark Metzler's pithy words, 'Bubbles had risen on top of bubbles in 1919, and most of them burst in 1920' (Metzler, 2006: 135). The Tokyo stock-index had reached its pre-war apex in 1919 and had fallen by over half by 1919–1922. The government's current account's budget grew by one-third 1918–1922, the Takahashi years. It was in 1920 that Hamaguchi Osachi, probably legitimately, had called Takahashi a 'reckless spender'. Takahashi walked away from this experience with the understanding that there were times to stimulate the economy but also times to cut spending and avoid runaway inflation.

Between 1918 and 1927, Takahashi served three times as Minister of Finance, once as Prime Minister, and once as Minister of Agriculture and Commerce. During this time, Takahashi wrote a series of memoranda, speeches and magazine articles, which, whilst in some ways politically unrealistic, marked him as one of the most progressive politicians in the pre-war mainstream. It also showed the direction of his thinking as Japan went into its 'democratic' decade, the depression and the beginnings of the road to war. He called for putting 'new wine in new wine skins', in biblical terms (Mark 2:22), by replacing the militaristic German model with the democratic Anglo-American one; abolishing the military's general staffs; making 40–50 per cent reductions in military budgets; appointing civilians as army and navy ministers; establishing parliamentary government through universal suffrage; doing away with the Ministry of Education because different regions have different educational needs; privatizing national universities because academic research should be free from bureaucratic influence; decentralizing government power through the election of provincial governors and the delegation to towns and villages of the power to collect land taxes and run their own schools (and select their own textbooks); giving the Prime and Foreign Ministers complete control over foreign policy (he did this during the Siberian Intervention when the army told Prime Ministers Hara and Takahashi and their Foreign Ministers that only the army had the authority to withdraw Japanese troops from the Russian territory); and growing the economy through indirect government policy.[5]

As Prime Minister, then head of the Seiyukai Party when it was out of power 1922–1924, and member of the cabinet in a coalition government 1924–1925, Takahashi advocated a graduated income-tax because he believed that rich people were more likely to save their money, whilst middle-class and poor people were more likely to spend it – thus, a graduated income tax would create demand and grow the economy more quickly than a flat-tax system would. In the same period, as Japanese industry began to increase productivity through the use of electricity as the motive force of its machines and through other labour-saving technology, Takashashi wrote that the companies with increased productivity should share the savings with their workers by raising wages and by creating new jobs for the workers who were no longer needed. *To Takahashi, increased productivity should lead to higher wages for more and more workers – which in turn should create demand, grow production, and raise wages and employment even more – the 'multiplier effect' before Richard Kahn had proposed the idea to Keynes in 1930.*

As Japan went into recession and the military began a series of provocative and aggressive steps on the Asian mainland, which opened with the dispatch of Japanese troops to north China in 1927, the assassination of the Chinese general Chang Tso-lin in 1928 and the invasion of Manchuria in 1931, a coterie of bureaucrats such as Kishi Nobusuke (1896–1987) began to call for the introduction of a 'command economy' modelled after the Soviet Five-Year Plan into Manchuria and then later into Japan. Takahashi resisted their efforts, going to far as to say, 'What that gang will do to Japan is beyond my comprehension… Manchuria is part of China; it is not Japan' (Matsumoto, 2007: 56).

Takahashi, as we have seen, was neither a top-down industrial planner nor a free-market ideologue – he opted, as Keynes did, for the 'middle way'. In the 1930s, Takahashi established a coalition that historians, like Matsuura Masataka for example, has called the 'Takahashi Line', a group committed to 'The Politics of Productivity', that is, to growing the economy and to controlling military spending (see Matsuura, 2002: 127–133, 150–161; Smethurst, 2007: 284–285).

Takahashi's coalition consisted of both large- and small-scale producers (Matsumoto Takashi has written that unlike Hamaguchi and Inoue, Takahashi saw the economy from the point of view of producers, not of financiers), some government officials, some members of both bourgeois and social democratic parties, and Japan's largest pre-war labour union, the Greater Japan Federation of Labor. He also advocated the establishment of union-run factory committees in all Japanese work-places, including military arsenals.

In January 1936, only a few weeks before his murder, Takahashi, a sitting Finance Minister in a country on the road to war, had a leading newspaper publish a photograph of him reading Sidney and Beatrice Webb's *Soviet Communism: A New Civilisation?* (1935), the Webb's paean to the USSR, which had been published only a few months earlier and was a book which the Home Ministry censors had banned from importation into Japan. At about the same time, Takahashi met with the Soviet Ambassador to Japan and told him: 'Those who brandish the sword perish, while those who show morality flourish, is something I believe. If the Japanese military continues doing what it is doing, in the end it will probably perish' (see Smethurst, 2007: 254–258). I think we can safely say that Takahashi was not a typical mainstream Japanese cabinet minister in the increasingly militaristic 1930s. A few months later, army officers, with the tacit approval of some of their superiors, brutally murdered Takahashi.

Conclusions

*Thus, Takahashi does not give us a 'smoking gun' answer to the question, 'How did Takahashi Korekiyo become "Japan's Keynes"?' The answer offered by some economic historians is that he was not really 'Japan's Keynes'. But their reason for saying this is that Takahashi was not a 'theorist' as Keynes was, but a government leader carrying out a set of policies similar to those that later came to be called Keynesian. In other words, Takahashi was a Finance Minister, not an economist. So, maybe, I should re-state the question and ask, how did Takahashi Korekiyo learn the exchange rate, monetary and especially the fiscal policies he introduced in Japan in 1931–1936? And in developing these policies, what were his sources? Were they 'Western' economic ideas or were they Japanese?

The answer to this question is that his sources were largely 'Western', but that we cannot footnote them – no 'I read Keynes on fiscal stimulus today and was impressed' here. Although Keynes' major works, *The Economic Consequences of the Peace* (1919), *A Tract on Monetary Reform* (1923), *The Economic Consequences of Mr. Churchill* (1925), *A Treatise on Money* (1930) and *The General Theory* (1936) all appeared in Japanese translation within a few years of their publication, finding an audience among some bureaucrats, businessmen, economists, journalists and other educated people, I have found only one explicit reference to Keynes in Takahashi's writings: in an April 1933 speech, Takahashi used Keynes' opinion to back up his view that the Gold Standard was the cause of the world depression. In the same paragraph, Takahashi 'quotes' William Jennings Bryan by writing, 'the gold standard is crucifying mankind upon a cross of gold' (Takahashi, 1936: 567–568). *But even if Takahashi read Keynes or about him,* The General Theory *was published the same month as Takahashi's death and 'Keynesianism' not created in his lifetime (see Yagi's chapter on Japan earlier in this volume); it soon came out in 1941 in Japanese. Rather, I think he learned the ideas for his policies from reading widely and talking with many people interested in such new ideas and from thinking about solutions to problems that he faced as a financial bureaucrat and leader.*

During Takahashi's 81-year life, many men and women influenced his thinking in one way or another. The basis for his 'Politics of Productivity' came primarily from the influence of Maeda Masana, the bureaucrat who advocated market-driven, but government-assisted industrial growth in the 1880s. Maeda, as we have seen, was a disciple of Eugene Tisserand (1884–1972), a French bureaucrat in the French Agriculture and Finance Ministry. The basis for Takahashi's commitment to the Gold Standard came from Matsukata Masayoshi, who studied with Leon Say (1826–1896) in Paris, and his occasional switch to supporting 'Bi-metalism' came from a number of sources.

Takahashi also read on a daily basis many foreign-language newspapers, including the *Times* of London and the *Japan Advertiser*, the primary English-language newspaper in Japan before the Second World War – he told his son-in-law that he preferred the English-language papers to the Japanese ones because the reporters were less likely to trim their sails to the prevailing winds. He regularly read the *Far Eastern Economic Review*, Ishibashi Tanzan's magazine that was the *donjon* in pre-war Japan of what would later become 'Keynesian economics', although Ishibashi told us that he did not think he had any influence on Takahashi's decision to carry out a programme of fiscal stimulus based on government borrowing – *he only reinforced what Takahashi had already decided.* The point here is that while Takahashi did not have a formal education in economics, he learned a great deal about finance and economics over the years because at the age of ten, Sendai Domain sent him to study English with Clara Hepburn. Whether he read about Keynes and his ideas deeply or not, we do not know. But we know he had the language skills to do so. And since he read the *Times* regularly, it is most likely he knew something of Keynes' ideas.

Later, I. I. Rabi (1898–1988), one of the leading physicists in the Manhattan Project (a US Nobel laureate), wrote that, 'We had on one side this crazy nation and this demon in Germany … and these funny people who didn't know what the Western world was about, who tackled the United States' (Interview in Else, 1981). The point of this chapter is that this kind of thinking, which is not unique to Rabi, is wrong. Japan had many, many educated people in the 1930s who knew what the Western world was about, and Takahashi Korekiyo and Ishibashi Tanzan were among the best of the group. Takahashi, with Ishibashi cheering him on, used Western economic ideas to bring Japan out of the depression in 1931–1936, and died for his efforts. The story of why the man who by 1935 had succeeded in bringing about Japan's unique economic recovery from the Depression was murdered for allegedly not doing what he had done remains to be told another day.

Epilogue

In 1884, Takahashi's mentor Maeda Masana wrote in the introduction to his *Opinions on Industrial Development*,

> In discussing the industry of our country the theorists run after theory and ignore our country's reality. They say 'protection', they say 'laissez faire'. There are a hundred ideas and each meets the standards of development theory. All are exceedingly wrong because they ignore the special national conditions of our industry.
>
> (Smethurst, 2007: 83)

On 15 December 1931, three days after Takahashi became Finance Minister for the fifth time and took Japan off the Gold Standard, his son-in-law, Oka Chisato, a recent Economics graduate of Keio University, asked him, 'Do you intend to go back on the Gold Standard at a new parity?' Takahashi replied, *'How can I know that now. It is best for people who stand in the real world to adopt the best solution to each problem. Theory is for scholars, but not the rest of us' (cited in Oka, 2002: 265).*

Notes

1 Most of the material for this contribution is drawn from Smethurst's previous research (1998: 226–238; 2000: 1–24; 2006: 20–25; 2007; 2008: 1–15; 2010) then re-interpreted and re-written by the author.
2 There are many evaluations of the 'debate over ending the embargo on the export and import of gold', that is, the debate on returning to the Gold Standard before and whilst the Hamaguchi government was in power. In English, I recommend Metzler (2006) and Wakatabe (2014), In Japanese, I recommend Nakamura's classic (1982).
3 The Chicago *Daily News*, 1886, n.d.
4 Forty-nine of the letters can be found either in the Constitutional History Room of the National Diet Library in Tokyo or the Jewish-American Archive in Cincinnati, Ohio. The other three are quoted in Adler (1929).
5 The 'new wine in new wine skins' remark comes from one of the essays, entitled 'Zen sekai no monko kaiho' (An Open Door for the Whole World) published in 'Gaiko jiho' (Foreign Policy Report), 436, 1 January 1923. In the essay, Takahashi calls for an end to imperialism, militarism, protectionism and 'the rule of power', so that resource-poor, economically weaker countries like Japan can have the opportunity to develop their own sources of raw materials in countries outside of Japan. He argues that the 'new wine' is the 'richness of life' of the citizens of each country of the world. Each government's job is to ensure economically secure lives for its citizens.

References

Adler, C. (1929). *Jacob Schiff: His Life and Letters*, London, William Heinemann, Ltd.

Bank of Japan (1966). *Hundred-Year Statistics of the Japanese Economy*, Tokyo, Statistical Department, Bank of Japan.

Cassidy, J. (2011). 'The Demand Doctor', *The New Yorker*, 10 October. www.newyorker.com/magazine/2011/10/10/the-demand-doctor, accessed 30 September 2015.

Cha, M. S. (2003). 'Did Takahashi Korekiyo Rescue Japan from the Great Depression', *Journal of Economic History*, 63: 127–144.

Eichengreen, B. (2015). *Hall of Mirrors: The Great Depression, The Great Recession, and the Uses – and Misuses – of History*, Oxford and New York, NY, Oxford University Press.

Else, J. (1981). *The Day After Trinity*, documentary film, in association with KTEH public television in San Jose, California.

Hoover, H. (1951). *The Memoirs of Herbert Hoover: The Great Depression*, Vol. 3, New York, NY: Macmillan.

Kubo, H. (1929, reprinted 1998). *Kinkaikin bokokuron* (Ending the Embargo on the Export of Gold Will Destroy the Nation), Tokyo, Kubo Economic Research Centre.

Li, L. (1982). 'Silk by Sea: Trade, Technology, and Trade in China and Japan', *The Harvard Business Review*, LVI-2: 1–10.

Maddison, A. (1995). *Monitoring the World Economy, 1820–1992*, Paris: OECD, Development Centre of the Organisation for Economic Co-operation and Development.

Matsumoto, T. (2007). 'Meiji kenpoka no zaisei seido' (The Financial System under the Meiji Constitution), *Fainansu* (Finance), 19: 56.

Matsumoto, T. (2013). *Motozaru kuni e no michi* (The Road to Becoming an Economically Weak Country), Tokyo: Chuo bunko.

Matsuura, M. (2002). *Zaikai no seiji keizaishi* (A Political and Social History of Financial Leaders), Tokyo: Tokyo University Press.

Metzler, M. (2006). *Lever of Empire: The International Gold Standard and the Crisis of Liberalism in Prewar Japan*, Berkeley, Los Angeles, CA and London: University of California Press.

Nakamura, T. (1982). *Showa kyoko to keizai seisaku* (The Showa Crisis and Economic Policy), Tokyo: Nikkei shinbunsha.

Nakamura, T. (1986). *Showa keizaishi* (An Economic History of the Showa Era), Tokyo: Iwanami Seminar Books.

Nakamura, T. (1993). *Showashi* (A History of the Showa Era), Vol. 1, Tokyo: Toyo keizai shinposha.

Nanto, D. K. and Takagi, S. (1985). 'Takahashi Korekiyo and Japan's Recovery from the Great Depression', *American Economic Review*, 75: 369–374.

Oka, C. (2002). 'Showa kyoko: Takahashi Korekiyo kaku katariki' (The Showa Depression: Conversations with Takahashi Korekiyo), *Bungei shunju*, 265.

Ohkawa, K. and Shinohara, M. (1979). *Patterns of Japanese Economic Development: A Quantitative Appraisal*, New Haven, CT and London: Yale University Press.

Shibamoto, M. and Shizume, M. (2014). 'How Did Takahashi Korekiyo Rescue Japan from the Great Depression?' Institute for Monetary and Economic Research, Bank of Japan, Working paper.

Shinagawa Yajirô kankei monjo (1999). (The Shinagawa Yajiro papers), Vol. 5, Tokyo: Yamakawa Shuppansha.

Skidelsky, R. (1992). *John Maynard Keynes: The Economist as Saviour, 1920–1937*, Vol. 2, London: Macmillan.

Smethurst, R. J. (1998). 'The Self-Taught Bureaucrat: Takahashi Korekiyo and Economic Policy in the Great Depression', in Singleton, J. (ed.), *Learning in Likely Places: Varieties of Apprenticeship in Japan*, Cambridge, New York, NY and Melbourne: Cambridge University Press, 226–238.

Smethurst, R. J. (2000). 'Takahashi Korekiyo's Economic Policies in the Great Depression and their Meiji Roots', *Politics and the Economy in Prewar Japan*, London: The Suntory Centre, London School of Economics and Political Science, 1–24.

Smethurst, R. J. (2006). 'Takahashi Korekiyo, the Rothschilds, and the Russo-Japanese War, 1904–1907', *The Rothschild Archive Review of the Year*, London: The Rothschild Archive, 20–25.

Smethurst, R. J. (2007). *From Foot Soldier to Finance Minister: Takahashi Korekiyo, Japan's Keynes*, Cambridge, MA and London: Harvard University Press.

Smethurst, R. J. (2008). 'The Historical Legacy of Takahashi Korekiyo: A Liberal Visionary in the Early Twentieth Century', *The International House of Japan Bulletin*, 1–15.

Smethurst, R. J. (2010). *Takahashi Korekiyo: Nihon no Keinzu – sono shōgai to shisō*, Tokyo: Tōyō Keizai Shinpōsha.

Takahashi, K. (1923). 'Zen sekai no monko kaiho' (An Open Door for the Whole World), *Gaiko jiho*.

Takahashi, K. (1936). *Takahashi Korekiyo Keizairon* (Takahashi Korekiyo's Ideas on Economics), Tokyo: Chikura shobo.

Wakatabe, M. (2014). 'The Lost Thirteen Years', in Asada, T. (ed.), *The Development of Economics in Japan*, Abingdon and New York, NY: Routledge, 13–38.

Webb, S. and Webb, B. (1935). *Soviet Communism: A New Civilisation?*, London: Longmans.

15 Schumpeter and Japan
Development through cycles

Mark Metzler[*]

Introduction

In any country, the production and dissemination of Economic Ideas is a *teleological practice*. Economists may pretend to work in a world of pure theory but we do not comprehend the social actualities of Economic Work – until we know the ends it is aiming for. This aspect of teleological practice is especially visible in Japan (see the chapter by Yagi on Japan earlier in this volume).

Western-influenced Economic thinking began in Japan with the realization of a dangerous developmental gap between Japan and the advanced Western countries. The sense of threat was paired with an awareness of the enormous potential gains offered by Western-style techniques and institutional arrangements. From the beginning of Japan's modern era, thinkers in Economics were thus concerned to direct their own national historical development and to speed it up. This teleological practice has gone together with a close attention to questions of historical stages and transitions, institutions and structures, all understood as immediate practical problems.

Liberal Economics thinking, as it came to Japan in the late 1860s and 1870s, was apprehended in this *developmental* sense. The liberal social and political vision was taken in as an ideal by Japanese reformers but liberal political economy was understood also as a powerful statecraft technology, which Japan could either emulate or be subject to as a victim. In the second and third decades of the twentieth century, Marxism was apprehended in a similar 'dual' sense, first as a social critique and vision for social transformation but then also as a technique of power. This 'catch-up, over-take' aspect became significant especially after the inauguration of the First Five Year Plan in the USSR. In the middle decades of the twentieth century, the theoretical system put together by Joseph Schumpeter (1883–1950) fitted easily into this developmental context.

This chapter surveys some moments of the reception of Schumpeter's ideas in Japan, taking his developmental schema as a point of reference and as an object for constructive criticism. For historians, Schumpeter's dynamic and dramatic vision of Economic Development has the advantage of helping bring into a single focus the whole span of Japan's modern history.

In this, it is like the unifying historicized vision of Karl Marx (1818–1883), whose first volume of *Das Kapital* (originally published in German in 1867) was translated into Japanese in 1924 (see Yagi's chapter earlier in this volume). Schumpeter's work was in many ways a response to Marx, and this aspect of it was in people's minds in Japan.

Unlike Marx, Schumpeter tried to exclude 'non-economic' factors including imperialism, militarism and war from his model, but nonetheless he ended up including a wide sweep of history. Unlike the crisis-focused approaches of many of Marx's later interpreters, Schumpeter's approach engages the 'boom' side of economic life as fully as the side of 'depression' and crisis. Schumpeter died before Japan's long post-war boom began, but his vision may fit the actualities of Japanese history most closely of all in regard to the 'Era of High-Speed Growth' (*kodo seicho jidai*) of 1955–1973. This connection opens a still wider field of questions, for Japan's growth was the 'opening act' in a new style of intensive capitalist development now set in Asian, rather than Western countries (see Das's overview chapter earlier in this volume).

The opening phase of the new era was also the one when Schumpeter's ideas had their greatest practical influence in Japan. Two ideas deserve special consideration here. The first is Schumpeter's analysis of the role of capital-creation by banks. The second is his idea of 'long waves' (Kondratiev cycles) in economic development, particularly as developed and extended by the economist Shinohara Miyohei (1919–2012). In the spirit of this style of analysis, the chapter concludes by offering an outline of successive leading paradigms in the history of Japanese Economic Thought.[1]

Stage setting

Schumpeter's ideas came to Japan at a time when liberalism, German-style historicism and Marxism were all simultaneously active. The developmental profile of liberalism has already been mentioned: this was the first wave of Western-influenced Economic Thought in Japan.[2] The second wave began in the 1880s, with the introduction of German Historicism; this movement was consciously antithetical to 'laissez-faire' doctrines (see Yagi's chapter on Japan in this volume). It was in this context, in 1889, that Friedrich List's developmental manifesto, *The National System of Political Economy* (1841), was published (see List, 1889) in Japanese translation, although his ideas were as much American as German (Metzler, 2006b) (see Liu's chapter earlier in this volume). Subsequently, reformist 'social policy' thought ran strong in the early decades of the twentieth century, also in a primarily German mode (Pyle, 1974; Ishida, 1984). This German intellectual orientation helped create the context for the intellectual shock of Marxism, which likewise came to Japan mainly in a German mode. This third, Marxist wave of thought emerged in the 1920s and ran into the 1930s, when it was violently suppressed. Marxism would re-emerge after 1945, gaining a position of intellectual predominance in the 1950s and 1960s.

Schumpeter's thought was received in the context of this Marxist wave. In a 1959 memoir, the Tokyo University Marxist economist Ouchi Hyoe (1888–1980), who was by then a great senior figure in the world of Economics there, noted the 'mysterious influence' that Schumpeter already had in Japan in the era after the First World War. However, he said, it was especially in the dark period of reaction during the Second World War that Schumpeter's Economics, with its 'external aspect of neutrality', 'had a vogue especially in Japan' (Ouchi, 1959: 266–267; Metzler, 2013: 21–22).[3] 'Schumpeter's translation and dissemination', Ouchi noted, 'was mainly carried out by Mr. Nakayama Ichiro and Mr. Tōbata Seiichi' (1959: 266). Nakayama Ichiro (1898–1980), the leading economist of his generation, was a professor at Tokyo Commercial University (which was renamed Hitotsubashi University in 1949, when Nakayama himself became University President). Tobata (or Tohata) Seiichi (1899–1983) was a Professor of Agricultural Economics at Tokyo Imperial University. Nakayama and Tobata had studied together with Schumpeter in Bonn in 1927–1929, in a decade when many young Japanese Marxists also studied in Germany. Nakayama's 1933 book *Pure Economics* (*Junsui keizaigaku*) was Japan's first textbook of Neoclassical Economics. As such, it helped found the school of thought that would largely displace Marxist Economics by the 1980s, including in Marxist strongholds, like Tokyo University. (As noted below, this version of Economics was 'pure' because of what it left out.)

Nakayama's *Pure Economics* also presented the basic schema of Schumpeter's *Theory of Economic Development* (hereafter, *Theory*), as introduced below. In 1937, Nakayama and Tobata published their full translation of Schumpeter's *Theory*. Schumpeter wrote a new preface for that edition, stating provocatively that his picture of statics was inspired by Leon Walras (1834–1910) and his picture of dynamics by Marx. Indeed this reflected the dualities of Schumpeter's system: on one side, he presented a self-contained world of Neoclassical equilibrium; on the other side, he presented a conflictual, equilibrium-breaking dynamic – which was ultimately derivable from a basic entrepreneurial impulsive process.

Schumpeter published his two-volume opus *Business Cycles* in English, in America, in 1939. Japan's full-scale military onslaught in China had begun two years before this, and in this dark moment, in 1937 and 1938, a group of non-Communist Marxist professors, including Ouchi Hyoe and Arisawa Hiromi, were arrested and accused of membership in a putative 'People's Front' (Hein, 2004: 64–68). This event was a situation on which Schumpeter appeared to have an 'aspect of neutrality'. Japanese economists read *Business Cycles* in the original English, and many of them read it avidly.[4]

As for the fact that those big two volumes of Schumpeter were so widely read, while it may have been unconscious, after all it met the demands of an age that wanted to take refuge somewhere from the storm of Marxism,

as Ouchi saw it (Ouchi, 1959: 266).

Joseph Schumpeter himself was born in 1883, the year that Marx died (as Schumpeter liked to point out). He was accordingly part of a remarkable generational cohort that included John Maynard Keynes (1883–1946) and, in Japan, the Keynesian-minded Ishibashi Tanzan (1884–1973).[5] This 'Keynes-Schumpeter' generation was also of the 'fascist' generation of Benito Mussolini (1883–1945), Kita Ikki (1883–1937) and Tojo Hideki (1884–1948). For their part, Nakayama Ichiro and Tobata Seiichi (born 1898 and 1899) were non-Marxist members of a 'Marx generation' in economics, whose members included Arisawa Hiromi (1896–1988), Yamada Moritaro (1897–1980) and Uno Kozo (1897–1977), among many others (Oshima, 2001). This generation also included senior political leaders during the 'Era of High-Speed Growth', including prime ministers Ikeda Hayato (1899–1965, p.m. 1960–1964) and Sato Eisaku (1901–1975, p.m. 1964–1972). Notably also, the above era was a time when numerous Marxist-trained economists held prominent public and private leadership positions in capitalist Japan. They included Arisawa and many other students of Ouchi's.[6]

This, then, was Schumpeter's historical stage. His theoretical stage had an equally mediating or dualistic character. As Ouchi put it, Schumpeter set up a 'dual stage' of static equilibrium (Walras-style) and dynamic development (Marx-style) and on this stage he set the various factors of production in motion; 'people who were watching this dual stage from a distance thought, yes, indeed, this is economics!... This economics, as against the classical school and as against Marxism, has the external shape of a third empire' (1959: 266). In fact, Ouchi said, it was 'a converted use of the results of Marxism. But that is hidden' (1959: 266). One might say as much for many aspects of mid twentieth-century Japanese development.

The basic cyclic schema: inflationary 'forced savings' ® 'automatic deflation'

Nakayama Ichiro was professionally active and prolific right through the waves of war and intellectual suppression. Then, from the day following Japan's unconditional surrender, 16 August 1945, he was almost ceaselessly active on various important government commissions until 1965. Nakayama is famous, among other things, for his 1959 proposal for a 'Wage-Doubling Economy'; the discussion this stimulated was current when Ouchi Hyoe completed the memoir quoted above. In November 1960, Nakayama's 'wage-doubling' slogan was realized in policy as Prime Minister Ikeda's 'Income-Doubling Plan', which became a symbol of Japan's 'Era of High-Speed Growth'. Almost incredibly, the plan's investment target was achieved within its first year rather than the ten years projected (see Shinohara, 1964). In fact, Japan's national rate of industrial investment, year after year, was probably the highest in the world and certainly the highest in the non-Communist world. It is therefore all the more interesting to listen to Nakayama addressing the question of these high investment rates in 1960. *What was the source of these massive investment funds? Specifically, did they result from prior savings?* Nakayama's answer was *no*:

After all, *it was funding that came first*, and growth that came first. And so savings was the result.... Or to consider it the other way around, it's completely impossible to think that such high investment happened because of [prior] savings.... [This is] the key to explaining various questions that come out of Japan's economic growth.

(Metzler, 2013: 53, 61, original italics)

Although the logic may not be immediately obvious, Nakayama's point goes to the basic nature of capitalist *money* – of which more, in a moment.

Another statement on this point comes from Okita Saburo (1914–1993), the Japanese State's Chief Economic Planner in the 1950s and later a prominent development advisor to other Asian countries. Okita collaborated with Nakayama on numerous planning commissions; in fact they were together, joined by Arisawa Hiromi and Ouchi Hyoe, at the first historic post-war planning meeting on 16 August 1945.[7]

In 1957, Okita explained, 'in the early state of Japan's modernization [i.e. from the 1870s], *government and banks first created money and credit*, which stimulated the establishment of various enterprises, and then later collected private savings in money form [original italics]'. That is, credit-creation came first, and investment came next. Indeed, a distinctive feature of Japanese development after 1868 was the early establishment of Western-style banks, which largely preceded the development of modern industry. Okita also thought that 'if the amount of new investment [were] to be confined strictly to the amount of savings collected by the financial institutions or by the government, not much could be done' (Okita, 1957: 36–37).

A third statement comes from Shinohara Miyohei, a Hitotsubashi University econometrician and sometime government economist who was himself a student of Nakayama Ichiro. As Shinohara saw it in 1964,

The typically Schumpeter-type development, that is, *credit creation → carrying out of new combinations*, represents the financial aspect of Japanese economic development since the latter part of the 1800's more definitely than in the case of the other advanced nations.

(Shinohara, 1964: 32, original italics)

This aspect may indeed appear *more* definitely in Japan – but we might consider also this 1925 statement of Friedrich von Hayek (1899–1992) concerning industrialization in the Western countries: 'There can be no doubt at all that the development of the capitalistic economy over the last hundred years would not have been possible without the *'forced saving'* effected by the extension of additional bank credit' (quoted in Festre, 2002: 464, original italics).

The connection between these various statements is to be found in Schumpeter's original *Theory of Economic Development* in 1912 (see Schumpeter, [1912] 1954). In Schumpeter's basic schema, capitalist development is driven by entrepreneurial *'new combinations'*.[8] These system-changing innovations involve the mobilization (rechannelling) of productive resources by new enterprises; the specifically *capitalist* method of mobilizing productive resources is to hire or purchase them using credit-capital created by *banks*. In Schumpeter's sense, *capital*, meaning the creation of credit and investment, is thus an active relational process rather than a substantial thing that has somehow been stored up and only then put to use. Banks create capital directly when they create new credits (=purchasing power) for entrepreneurs, or they create capital more indirectly when they create credit for investment in company shares. Schumpeter thus brought banks integrally into his theory of capitalism and placed them at the organizing centre of the capitalist process.

This type of new credit creation is intrinsically inflationary. Entrepreneurs are enabled by newly created purchasing-power to bid for existing goods and labour services. Banks, thanks to the magic of 'lending' based on fractional reserves, do not create new credits on the basis of prior savings, except to a fractional, practically token extent. Rather, the newly created credits are based on a promise of future repayment. In this way, 'from the viewpoint of banks as a whole, something is created from nothing', in the rather Schumpeterian phrasing of the Japanese government's 1957 Economic White Paper (*Economic Survey of Japan*, 1956–1957: 199).

Schumpeter called this process 'credit inflation' and originally described its effect as a de facto *'forced savings'* (*erzwungenes Sparen*). One might say, very abstractly, that at the level of the whole society, all investment indeed comes out of social savings, as in the economics textbooks. But these 'savings' are forced from the wider society via a private inflation tax. Nakayama and Tobata thus translated the term, more precisely, as *'forced economizing'* (*kyosei sareta setsuyaku*). Schumpeter did not quite state openly that the creation of new credit by banks was an appropriation of social resources, but that is the idea. Here we meet an open question, for Schumpeter failed to incorporate a theory of expropriation or exploitation into his framework. Marx himself, who was so keen to analyse the production and extraction of 'surplus value' *within* the production process, never truly integrated an analysis of surplus extraction by monetary (credit) means. Some later Japanese Marxists did perceive this process as an aspect of contemporary bank-centred capitalism.

In Schumpeter's vision, these innovatory 'new combinations' should lead to greater and more efficient production; more and cheaper production would lead in turn to a *decline* in the price of products. (Here, Schumpeter had an industrial economy rather than a service economy in view.) The back-and-forth movement of credit inflation followed by 'automatic deflation' is thus intrinsic to the capitalist developmental process, which has an essentially *business-cyclic* nature (see also Hagemann, 2003). The bunching in time of innovation and investment give this process a wavelike character, not only at the level of the individual firm but also at the level of the whole economy. Thus, in general and at least in the short run, waves of investment are inflationary; when new productive capacity comes on line, it should be deflationary. Schumpeter attempted to connect this abstracted cyclical model to actual historical development in his 1939 book *Business Cycles*.

Long cycles

'Analyzing business cycles means neither more nor less than analyzing the economic process of the capitalist era' – this is the opening sentence of 'those big two volumes' of Schumpeter (see Schumpeter, 1939: v). The history of business cycles – *conjunctural* history in the most basic and original sense of the word – is exceptionally well developed in Japan. It was already established before Schumpeter visited Japan in 1931 and it was stimulated further by *Business Cycles*, which got a much warmer reception in wartime Japan than it did in America. This reception reflected a consciousness that was already present in Japan, and Schumpeter's work helped to sharpen that consciousness.[9]

The framework of the book is a three-cycle schema of multiple, additive cycles. Here, Schumpeter's central and most innovatory contribution was to introduce 'long waves', or 'Kondratieff cycles' in Economics. (It was Schumpeter who coined this name after N. D. Kondratiev (1892–1938); on this point, see Kondratiev, 1926; Barnett, 1998; Ohtsuki, 2007.) Each of these long cycles is composed of an inflationary trend period, running for 20-some years, followed by a comparably long deflationary trend period, as seen in the statistical records of Britain, France and the United States in the nineteenth and early twentieth centuries. He dated them as follows (from price trough, to price peak, to price trough):

1787–1815–1842
1843–1873–1897
1898–1920–[1930s]

In Schumpeter's vision, these movements are more than 'mega-' business cycles; rather, they are successive industrial revolutions. Schumpeter here adapted Marx's vision of revolutionary and indeed dialectical change, but he shifted the timescale from Marx's macro-level 'feudal' and 'bourgeois' stages, happening on a scale of centuries, to a meso-level multi-decadal timescale. He also substituted his own capitalist-developmental mechanism, as described above, for Marx's succession of modes of production. Each long cycle is thus characterized by the deployment and development of a distinctive package of new technologies built around certain backbone sectors (first, coal and iron; then railroads, steamships, and steel; then electrical, chemical and automotive industries). With each new technological package come shifts in characteristic institutions and styles of thought. Schumpeter unpacked this whole schema in around 1,000 pages of dense text.

Many writers have extended the picture into the late twentieth century; especially interesting in the present context is the work of Shinohara Miyohei. Like his teacher Nakayama Ichiro, Shinohara took as much from Keynes as from Schumpeter; he then added Hayek to the mix (Amsden and Suzumura, 2001; Nakamura, 1999).[10] Over the course of a long career, Shinohara (1989, 1991, 1994) extended the Schumpeter-Kondratiev schema into the early twenty-first century, analysing a post-war long wave formed of 'three conjunctures' (*san kyokumen*) as follows:

> 1950s–1973: A 'Keynes–Schumpeter conjuncture', meaning strongly rising demand (credit creation) accompanied by strongly rising supply (technical upgrading). This was a 'plus-sum' situation.

> 1970s: A 'Hayekian' or 'non-Keynesian' conjuncture, in conditions of monetary inflation and supply shocks; this was a 'zero-sum' situation.

> 1980s–early 2000s: A 'global adjustment conjuncture' characterized by disinflation, falling raw material prices, technological revolution and long-term slowdown.

Whilst Schumpeter gave primacy to technological innovation and tried consciously to exclude both wars and financial bubbles from his model, Shinohara rejected the idealized and unrealistic aspects of Schumpeter's approach, returning to Kondratiev's original suggestion of a multi-factor process. By the 1980s, Shinohara was giving special emphasis to the effects of dramatic shifts in the relative price structure at the world level, as exemplified in the great rise of oil prices in the 1970s and their great fall in the 1980s; to systemic debt crises, as experienced by commodity-exporting countries in the 1980s; and to shifts in the international monetary system, as seen in the transformation of the Bretton Woods system and the emergence of Japan as the largest international creditor. From the 1990s, in the wake of Japan's great 'bubble' and 'post-bubble' slowdown, he also understood great speculative 'bubbles' as fundamental to the long-wave process, not epiphenomenal as Schumpeter had suggested.

'Alternating situations' in the history of economic thought

In the terminology of several German economists including Schumpeter's close friend Arthur Spiethoff (1873–1957), business cycles are *Wechsellagen*, or 'alternating situations' (see also Shinohara, 1999: 96–108). Such alternating situations present themselves also in the history of economic thought. This section concludes the discussion by applying such an idea to Japan. For this purpose, three excellent starting-points are the periodizations offered by Yagi (see the chapter on Japan earlier in this volume) for economic thought, as well as others (see Barshay, 2004, ch. 2) for social science thought more broadly, and the discussion by Oshima (2001) of generational cohorts in Economics. I have freely adapted these frameworks in constructing the following chronology.

Each phase here is characterized by one or more *leading styles*. These leading styles were not necessarily politically dominant, as seen particularly in the case of Marxism, which was radically oppositional. At the same time, changes in the dominating political structure could be decisive also, as in the exclusion of the Okuma-Fukuzawa group from politics in 1881, or the suppression of Marxism in the 1930s. Contending positions within Japan's internal intellectual field have frequently been defined in terms of foreign models, and we see that here as well.[11]

1867–1881. The biennium 1867–1868 was not only the time of the Meiji revolution but was also when the first real statements of Western Economics were published in Japanese. In this age of both '*Encounter and Enlightenment*', the Western ideas on offer were those of British-style Liberalism. The tone was cosmopolitan, optimistic and politically reformist. Economic thinking in this period was the work of generalists; the first phase of translation work was almost entirely of textbooks and almost entirely from English. Fukuzawa Yukichi (1835–1901), the representative figure of this movement, belonged to the same generation as the Meiji Restoration leaders (see the chapters by Yagi and Sakamoto respectively in this volume), including economic statesmen Okubo Toshimichi (1830–1878), Matsukata Masayoshi (1835–1924) and capitalist founding-father Shibusawa Eiichi (1840–1931). In terms of the international economic conjuncture, this original 'liberal' age included the final few years of the 'Great Victorian boom' and the beginning of the long deflation in the gold-standard countries. In Japan, however, the economic conjuncture was different, as an inflationary boom developed in the 1870s and peaked at the beginning of the 1880s; the 'Matsukata deflation' policy enforced in 1881 was integral to the political change of that year (Ericson, 2014, 2016).

1880s–1900s. This *neo-traditional moment* (see Barshay, 2004) was a phase of conservative consolidation of the new political structure. British-style liberalists, as represented within the government by Okuma Shigenobu and outside of it by Fukuzawa Yukichi, were abruptly distanced from power in 1881 in a kind of soft coup. The upsurge of the rebellious liberal movement (the 'Movement for Liberty and People's Rights') in the early 1880s was violently suppressed. A thorough-going liberal like Taguchi Ukichi (1855–1905) now stood as an oppositional figure (Oshima, 2001). At the new Imperial University in Tokyo, the German academic model came into ascendancy, whilst British-style liberalism retreated to private colleges.[12] This was also the period of the *assimilation of German Economics* (see Yagi's chapter on Japan, as well as Trescott's on China earlier in this volume), continuing into the 1910s. In the 1880s and 1890s, the German studies group in Japan also consciously excluded more liberal (not to mention radical) German-language material (Ishida, 1984: 40). Representative figures in the 'new generation' of this period were conspicuous for their turn from liberalism to nationalism (Pyle, 1969; Oshima, 2001). In the Kondratiev/Schumpeter long-wave schema, this was a period of economic downturn succeeded after about 1896 by a major global upturn.

1900s–1920s. In this new *liberal moment*, there was an ongoing assimilation of German Economics in a more progressive and universalizing spirit of social and political reformism (see also the chapters by Trescott on China earlier in this volume). This movement can be dated from the establishment in 1897 of the *Shakai Seisaku Gakkai*, modelled on the German *Verein für Sozialpolitik*, which exercised a key influence on the emerging field of academic Economics continuing into the 1910s (Pyle, 1974; Ishida, 1984: 45–71). Fukuda Tokuzo (1874–1930), who studied with the pioneering welfare-economist, Lujo Brentano (1844–1931) in Munich, was a representative figure and is considered a founder of the modernist tradition in Economics (Tamotsu, 2002). Significantly for the present story, Fukuda was also Nakayama Ichiro's teacher. Fukuda was part of a 'new liberal' generation born in the 1870s, which also included Kawakami Hajime (1879–1946), a founder of the Marxist tradition in Economics. In the Kondratiev/Schumpeter long-wave schema, this was a phase of upturn, giving way to an incipient downturn after 1920.

1920s–1945. Yagi sees in this era *a quest for Japanese Economics and disarray*; Barshay (2004) identifies it as the first phase of a *Marxist moment.*[13] Marxism (in a German vein) radically polarized the intellectual field (Hoston, 1986; Oshima, 1991; Barshay, 1996, 2004; Hein, 2004). There was an extraordinary but quickly suppressed 'red boom' in high schools and universities especially around 1930, coinciding with a comprehensive economic and political crisis of the liberal order in 1930–1931 (Metzler, 2006a). There followed a 'one-country' economic recovery under the 'Keynesian' policy of Takahashi Korekiyo (Smethurst, 2007) (see Smethurst's chapter in this volume). The *nationalist-fascist reaction* thereafter included a turn to radical nationalist economics. Not only Marxism but liberalism too was violently suppressed. In the long-wave schema, this was a long downturn period.

1945–1970s. With the end of the war came the sudden re-emergence of *Marxism* (and less dramatically of *liberalism*). The early phase of this period was when the Schumpeterian economists introduced here were most active in policy circles. Marxism was intellectually predominant and was quickly institutionalized in universities. This was the era, simultaneously, of a radical leftist student movement and of state-corporate 'growthism' (Barshay, 2004: 67–68; O'Bryan, 2009). Growthism existed in a kind of synergy with a specifically Marxist-derived kind of 'national developmentalism' exemplified by Arisawa Hiromi (Gao, 1994, 1997; also Arisawa *et al.*, 1960a, 1960b; Hein, 1994, 2004). This was also the age of emergence of 'post-war modernism' on the US model. In the long-wave schema, a long upturn began after about 1950, with an initial downturn coming after 1973.

1980s–present. This is the era of '*globalization*' (see the chapter by Yagi earlier in this volume) and of Shinohara's 'global adjustment' conjuncture. It points to a new culturalism, plurality and confusion. There was a radical fading away of Marxism as an intellectual force, whilst politically conservative US-style 'modernist' economics made increasing claims to be the only possible economics (Ikeo, 2000). In turn, US-style economics also took on an increasingly neo-liberal valence. In the long-wave schema (e.g. as analysed by Shinohara), this was a long downturn. In the early 1980s, Japan itself largely escaped the international economic crises affecting old industrial regions and commodity exporting regions around the world. Japan then fell into a chronic slump after the great bubble of 1989 and began a long but extremely slow recovery after about 2003.

Conclusions

The foregoing sketch meshes with the Schumpeter-Shinohara model described above and suggests that these global economic movements interact strongly with generational processes of intellectual and policy change. It also suggests some unexpected resonances, if not continuities with the succession of economic-policy paradigms in the late Tokugawa era (see Metzler, 2010; Metzler and Smits, 2010). Obviously, there is much more at work in the history of economic thought than simply 'alternating situations' – this schema represents merely one quasi-coherent aspect of a multifaceted total situation that is always new. Thinking with such a framework, however, may sharpen the sense of just what is new and distinct in each historical situation.

In the spirit of this discussion, a final observation is that the prospective economic upswing of the early twenty-first century – if it is that – offers no outlook for a return to the very high rates of industrial growth experienced in the past, which now seem neither possible nor desirable. Schumpeter's schema in Economics, as noted already, applies to an industrial system, and it is not at all clear how his model of inflationary investment automatically balanced by deflationary production increases might work under conditions of a low-growth (or no-growth), heavily service-oriented economic structure. The needs of our own times seem more to be met by a new human-centred and ecologically oriented Economics, and indeed work in this spirit seems now to be emerging.[14]

Notes

* Japanese names are given in this chapter in the Japanese order, family name first.
1 Many themes in this chapter are developed in detail in Metzler (2013); here, going beyond that book, I pull together some specifically *conjunctural* threads of the argument. Bassino (1998) was the first to introduce Schumpeter's significance in Japan to a non-Japanese audience. There is a relatively extensive body of writing in English on the history of economic thought in Japan. Morris-Suzuki (1989) offers an excellent all-around starting point, whilst Yagi (in this volume) provides a fine overview. Economic thought during the Tokugawa period (1600–1867) has been deeply researched in Japanese but relatively little studied in English: for a recent foray into the field see Gramlich-Oka and Smits (2010) and the bibliography given there; Najita (1987) is especially interesting in this connection.
2 For the reception of liberalism in Japan, see among others Blacker, 1964; Havens, 1970; Tamaki, 2001.
3 Laura Hein (2004) presents a prosopography of Ouchi and his group, which included Arisawa Hiromi.
4 *Business Cycles* was published in Japanese translation in five volumes in 1958–1964, under the title *Shunpeta keiki junkan ron*. It was only published in German in 1961, entitled *Konjunkturzyklen*.
5 The economic journalist/publisher and post-war political leader, Ishibashi Tanzan, was remarkable for remaining a 'liberal' in an 'illiberal' age. He also had a remarkable role in Japan's post-war recovery and boom; see Nolte, 1987; Metzler, 2006a and Metzler, 2013.
6 Gao, 1994, 1996 provides the closest approach to the tricky subject of Marxist-inspired capitalist development. A full social and cultural version of this story would

also explain how the Japan Communist Party became an advocate for the interests of small businesspeople.

7   This was the famous Special Survey Committee, whose report is a fascinating statement of purposeful 'Japanese economics'; see Ministry of Foreign Affairs, Special Survey Committee, [1946] 1992; O'Bryan, 2009: 21–28, 32–36; Metzler, 2013: 66–69.

8   'New combinations': *neue Kombinationen*; in Japanese, *shin ketsugo*. In the 1934 English translation of *Theory* and again in *Business Cycles* (1939), Schumpeter replaced this term with the Latinate English word 'innovation' (rendered in Japanese as a new loan word, *inobeshon*, or too narrowly, as *gijutsu kakushin*, meaning technological renovation).

9   Especially notable is the work of Tsuru Shigeto, a heterodox Marxist-Institutionalist who had studied with Schumpeter at Harvard in the 1930s and wrote his PhD thesis on the history of business cycles in Japan (summarized in Tsuru, 1941; see also Tsuru, 1993). Tsuru authored the Japanese government's first post-war Economic White Paper in 1947.

10 Reminding one also of Richard Smethurst's point (Smethurst, 2007 and in this volume) that Takahashi Korekiyo was 'Japan's Hayek' as well as 'Japan's Keynes'.

11 Bourdieu's idea of the *intellectual field* is useful here; for discussion in similar terms of the alternation of policy situations in eighteenth- and early nineteenth-century Japan, see Metzler (2010). The field of economic thought in modern Japan was not a bipolar field, though external forces during the Cold War era especially tended to construct it as such.

12 From 1867 to 1889, 186 books on Economics were translated into Japanese: 71 from England, 30 from America, 30 from France and 30 from Germany and Austria. Of the German-language books, only seven were translated before 1880. However, by the end of the 1880s, more than half of the Economics books being translated were German (Ishida, 1984: 37).

13 The eclectic developmentalist 'Japanese' style economists such as Takahashi Kamekichi (1891–1977) and Akamatsu Kaname (1897–1974) were in many ways closest to our image of a twentieth-century 'Japanese model' (Nishikawa, 1996: 182–183; Ikeo, 2008; Ohtsuki, 2011). Here especially we can see 'a converted use of the results of Marxism'. We might also categorize Arisawa Hiromi and Tsuru Shigeto in this way.

14 One significant indication of this new spirit is the radically interdisciplinary 'Humanosphere' project directed by Sugihara Kaoru (Sugihara *et al.*, 2012).

References

Amsden, A. H. and Suzumura, K. (2001). 'An Interview with Miyohei Shinohara: Nonconformism in Japanese Economic Thought'. *Journal of the Japanese and International Economies*, 15: 341–360.

Arisawa, H., Tōbata, S., Nakayama, I., Wakimura, Y. and Okita, S. (1960a). 'Keizai shutai kara mita Nihon shihonshugi' [Japanese capitalism seen from the standpoint of economic selfhood]. In H. Arisawa, S. Tōbata and I. Nakayama (eds), *Keizai shutaisei koza* [Lectures on economic selfhood]. 7 vols. Tokyo: Chuo Koronsha, 245–315.

Arisawa, H., Tōbata, S. and Nakayama, I., eds. (1960b). *Keizai shutaisei koza* [Lectures on economic selfhood]. 7 vols. Tokyo: Chuo Koronsha.

Barnett, V. (1998). *Kondratiev and the Dynamics of Economic Development: Long Cycles and Industrial Growth in Historical Context*. Basingstoke: Macmillan.

Barshay, A. E. (1996). 'Toward a History of the Social Sciences in Japan'. *Positions*, 4: 217–251.

Barshay, A. E. (2004). *The Social Sciences in Modern Japan: The Marxian and Modernist Traditions*. Berkeley, CA: University of California Press.

Bassino, J.-P. (1998). 'The Diffusion and Appropriation of Schumpeter's Economic Thought in Japan'. *History of Economic Ideas*, 6: 79–106.

Blacker, C. (1964). *The Japanese Enlightenment: A Study of the Writings of Fukuzawa Yukichi*. Cambridge: Cambridge University Press.

Economic Survey (1956–1957). *Economic Survey of Japan*, Tokyo: Economic Planning Agency.

Ericson, S. (2014). 'The Matsukata Deflation Reconsidered: Financial Stabilization and Japanese Exports in a Global Depression, 1881–85'. *Journal of Japanese Studies*, 40: 1–28.

Ericson, S. (2016). 'Intellectual Origins of Financial Stabilization in Meiji Japan: Rethinking Influences on the Matsukata Reform, 1881–1885'. *Monumenta Nipponica* (forthcoming).

Festre, A. (2002). 'Money, Banking and Dynamics: Two Wicksellian Routes from Mises to Hayek and Schumpeter'. *American Journal of Economics and Sociology*, 61: 439–480.

Gao, B. (1994). 'Arisawa Hiromi and His Theory for a Managed Economy'. *Journal of Japanese Studies*, 20: 115–153.

Gao, B. (1997). *Economic Ideology and Japanese Industrial Policy: Developmentalism from 1931 to 1965*. Cambridge: Cambridge University Press.

Gramlich-Oka, B. and Smits, G., eds. (2010). *Economic Thought in Early Modern Japan*. Leiden: Brill.

Hagemann, H. (2003). 'Schumpeter's Early Contributions on Crisis Theory and Business-Cycle Theory'. *History of Economic Ideas*, 11: 47–67.

Havens, T. R. H. (1970). *Nishi Amane and Modern Japanese Thought*. Princeton, NJ: Princeton University Press.

Hein, L. E. (1994). 'In Search of Peace and Democracy: Japanese Economic Debate in Political Context'. *Journal of Asian Studies*, 53: 752–778.

Hein, L. E. (2004). *Reasonable Men, Powerful Words: Political Culture and Expertise in Twentieth-Century Japan*. Washington, DC: Woodrow Wilson Center and Berkeley, CA: University of California Press.

Hoston, G. A. (1986). *Marxism and the Crisis of Development in Prewar Japan*. Princeton, NJ: Princeton University Press.

Ikeo, A. (2000). 'Economists and Economic Policies'. In A. Ikeo (ed.), *Japanese Economics and Economists since 1945*. London and New York, NY: Routledge.

Ikeo, A. (2008). *Akamatsu Kaname: Waga taikei o norikoete yuke*. Tokyo: Nihon Keizai Hyoronsha.

Ishida, T. (1984). *Nihon no shakai kagaku* [Japanese social science]. Tokyo: Tokyo Daigaku Shuppankai.

Kondratiev, N. D. (1926). 'Die Langen Wellen der Konjunktur'. *Archiv für Sozialwissenschaft und Sozialpolitik*, 56: 3, 573–609. Partially translated by W. F. Stolper (1935) as 'The Long Waves in Economic Life'. *Review of Economics and Statistics*, 17: 105–115.

List, F. [1841] (1885). *National System of Political Economy*, transl. S. S. Lloyd (London, 1885 [1922 reprint]).

List, F. (1889). [Furiidorihhi Risuto], *Ri-shi keizairon*, 2 vols, edited and translated by Tomita T. and Oshima S. (Tokyo: Nihon Keizaikai, 1889).

Metzler, M. (2006a). *Lever of Empire: The International Gold Standard and the Crisis of Liberalism in Prewar Japan*. Berkeley, CA: University of California Press.

Metzler, M. (2006b). 'The Cosmopolitanism of National Economics: Friedrich List in a Japanese Mirror'. In A. G. Hopkins (ed.), *Global History: Interactions between the Universal and the Local*. London: Palgrave Macmillan, 98–130.

Metzler, M. (2010). 'Policy Space, Polarities, and Regimes'. In B. Gramlich-Oka and G. Smits (eds), *Economic Thought in Early Modern Japan*. Leiden: Brill, 217–250.

Metzler, M. (2013). *Capital as Will and Imagination: Schumpeter's Guide to the Postwar Japanese Miracle*. Ithaca, NY: Cornell University Press.

Metzler, M. and Smits, G. (2010). 'Introduction: The Autonomy of Market Activity and the Emergence of *Keizai* Thought'. In B. Gramlich-Oka and G. Smits (eds), *Economic Thought in Early Modern Japan*. Leiden: Brill, 3–21.

Ministry of Foreign Affairs, Special Survey Committee, ed. [1946] (1992). *Postwar Reconstruction of the Japanese Economy*, compiler, (ed.). Tokyo: University of Tokyo Press.

Mirowski, P. (1989). *More Heat than Light, Economics as Social Physics: Physics as Nature's Economics*. Cambridge: Cambridge University Press.

Morris-Suzuki, T. (1989). *A History of Japanese Economic Thought*. London: Routledge and Oxford: Nissan Institute for Japanese Studies.

Najita, T. (1987). *Visions of Virtue in Tokugawa Japan: The Kaitokudo Merchant Academy of Osaka*. Chicago, IL: University of Chicago Press.

Nakamura, T. [1987] (1999). 'Shinohara Miyohei kyoju no gyoseki ni tsuite' [On the achievements of Prof. Shinohara Miyohei]. In M. Shinohara, *Choki fukyo no nazo o saguru* [Investigating the riddle of long-term recession]. Tokyo: Keiso S, 307–318.

Nakayama, I. (1933). *Junsui keizaigaku* [Pure economics]. Reprinted in *Nakayama Ichirō zenshū*, Vol. 1 (Tokyo: Kodansha, 1972), 1–195.

Nishikawa, J., ed. (1996). *Ekonomisuto o shiru jiten* [Dictionary for knowing economists]. Tokyo: Nihon Jitsugyō Shuppansha.

Nolte, S. H. (1987). *Liberalism in Modern Japan, Ishibashi Tanzan and His Teachers, 1905–1960*. Berkeley, CA: University of California Press.

O'Bryan, S. (2009). *The Growth Idea: Purpose and Prosperity in Postwar Japan*. Honolulu, Hawaii: University of Hawaii Press.

Ohtsuki, T. (2007). 'N. D. Kondratiev to S. de Wolff no Daijyunkan Kenkyu: The History of Economic Thought', *The Society for the History of Economic Thought*, 49: 35–51.

Ohtsuki, T. (2011). 'The Background of K. Akamatsu's *Genkou Keitai Ron* and Its Development: Early Empirical Analysis at Nagoya'. In Heinz D. Kurz, Tamotsu Nishizawa and Keith Tribe (eds), *The Dissemination of Economic Ideas*. Cheltenham: Edward Elgar, 292–313.

Okita, S. (1957). 'Savings and Economic Growth in Japan'. *Economic Development and Cultural Change*, 6: 32–41.

Oshima, M. (1991). 'A Distant View of the Debate on Japanese Capitalism'. *Osaka City University Economic Review*, 26: 23–34.

Oshima, M. (2001). 'Nihon keizaishigaku no seiritsu – tenkai to Kokusho Iwao' [Kokusho Iwao and the establishment and development of the study of Japanese economic history]. In T. Yamada and M. Tokunaga (eds), *Shakai keizai shigaku no tanjo to Kokusho Iwao*. Kyoto: Shibunkaku Shuppan, 42–68.

Ouchi, H. (1959). *Keizaigaku gojunen* [50 years of economics], 2 vols. Tokyo: Tokyo Daigaku Shuppankai.

Pyle, K. (1969). *The New Generation in Meiji Japan: Problems of Cultural Identity, 1885–1895*. Stanford, CA: Stanford University Press.

Pyle, K. (1974). 'Advantages of Followership: German Economics and Japanese Bureaucrats, 1890–1925'. *Journal of Japanese Studies*, 1: 127–164.

Schumpeter, J. A. [1926] (1934). *The Theory of Economic Development: An Inquiry into Profits, Capital, Credit, Interest, and the Business Cycle*. Translated by Redvers Opie. Cambridge, MA: Harvard University Press. (Translation of the second [1926] edition of *Theorie der wirtschaftlichen Entwicklung. Eine Untersuchung über Unternehmergewinn, Kapital, Kredit, Zins und den Konjunkturzyklus.*) Translated into Japanese in 1937 by I. Nakayama and S. Tobata.

Schumpeter, J. A. (1937). Preface to the Japanese edition. In Nakayama Ichiro and Tobata Seiichi, trans., *Keizai hatten no riron* (translation of Schumpeter 1926/1934). Tokyo: Iwanami Shoten.

Schumpeter, J. A. (1939). *Business Cycles, A Theoretical, Historical, and Statistical Analysis of the Capitalist Process* (2 vols). New York, NY: McGraw-Hill. Translated into Japanese as *Shunpeta Keikijunkan ron – shihonshugi katei no rironteki – rekishiteki – tokeiteki bunseki—*. 5 vols, trans. Kin'yu Keizai Kenkyujo. Tokyo: Yuhikaku, 1958–1964.

Schumpeter, J. A. [1912] (1954). *Economic Doctrine and Method: An Historical Sketch*. Trans. Redvers Opie. New York, NY: Oxford University Press. (Translation of *Epochen der Dogmen- und Methodengeschichte.*)

Shinohara, M. (1964). 'Factors in Japan's Economic Growth'. *Hitotsubashi Journal of Economics*, 4: 21–36.

Shinohara, M., ed. (1989). *Kokusai tsuka – gijustu kakushin – choki hado. Sekai keizai no 21seikizo o saguru* [International currency, technological innovation, long waves: imaging the 21st century world economy]. Tokyo: Toyo Keizai Shinposha.

Shinohara, M. (1991). *Seikai keizai no choki dainamikusu, choki hado to taikoku kobo* [Long-term dynamics of the world economy: Long waves and the rise and fall of great powers]. Tokyo: TBS-Britannica.

Shinohara, M. (1994). *Sengo 50-nen no keiki junkan, Nihon keizai no dainamizumu o saguru* [Fifty years of postwar economic cycles: exploring the dynamism of the Japanese economy]. Tokyo: Nihon Keizai Shinbun Sha.

Shinohara, M. (1999). *Choki fukyo no nazo o saguru* [Investigating the riddle of long-term recession]. Tokyo: Keiso Shobo.

Smethurst, R. J. (2007). *From Foot Soldier to Finance Minister: Takahashi Korekiyo, Japan's Keynes*. Cambridge, MA: Harvard University Press.

Sugihara, K., Wakimura, K., Fujita, K. and Tanabe, A., eds. (2012). *Rekishi no naka no nettai seizonken – ontai paradaimu o koete—*. Kōza seizon kiban ron, vol. 1. Kyoto: Kyōto Daigaku Gakujutsu Shuppankai.

Tamaki, N. (2001). *Yukichi Fukuzawa, 1835–1901: The Spirit of Enterprise in Modern Japan*. Houndmills: Palgrave.

Tamotsu, N. (2002). 'The Impact of German Economic Thought on Japanese Economists before World War One'. In Y. Shionoya (ed.), *The German Historical School: The Historical and Ethical Approach to Economics*. London: Routledge.

Tsuru, S. (1941). 'Economic Fluctuations in Japan, 1868–1893'. *Review of Economic Statistics*, 23: 176–189.

Tsuru, S. (1993). *Japan's Capitalism: Creative Defeat and Beyond*. Cambridge: Cambridge University Press.

Yagi, K. (n.d.). 'Japanese Theory of Modernization/Industrialization between Liberalism and Developmentalism'. Asia International Forum (online at www.siue.edu/EASTASIA/); accessed 22 October 2015.

16 The legacy of Belgium and the Netherlands, *'L'Institut Supérieur de Commerce d'Anvers'* and business education in Japan

From the 1880s to the 1940s

Tadashi Ohtsuki

Introduction

With the end of its long period of national seclusion under the Tokugawa Shogunate, lasting from 1639 to 1854, Japan was to see the onset of the 'Meiji Restoration' in 1868. The newly organized Meiji government soon set up a new educational system, adopting academic subjects, including Economics and Commercial Studies, from 'Western' countries.[1] Until the Tokugawa era (or Edo period), the higher education of commerce was not regarded as significant, however. But in 1862, the Japanese government was to send two scholars, Nishi Amane (1829–1897) and Tsuda Mamichi (1829–1903), to the Netherlands. They took private lessons on 'economics', 'international law', 'national law', 'natural law' and 'statistics' from Simon Vissering (1818–1888), who was the Professor of Political Economy at Leiden University at the time (see Morris-Suzuki, 1989: 49). Vissering, the most eminent Dutch economist of his day, was a keen advocate of laissez-faire (see Morris-Suzuki, 1989: 49–50).

After their return to Japan, they introduced the first 'Western Economics' in Japan – via *Grondtrekken der Staatshuishoudkunde* written in Dutch – the original version of which was *Outlines of Social Economy* (1846) by William Ellis (1800–1881), a British businessman and writer on Economics. This Dutch version was translated into Japanese by Kanda Takahira (1830–1898) in 1867 (see the chapter by Yagi on Japan in this volume, and Yagi, 1999). The significance of Dutch as the medium of the importation of Economics from the West, however, decreased over time. Instead, thereafter, Economics from the UK, the US, Germany and France was directly introduced into Japan (Tamanoi, 1971: 2–20).

The notion of Economics, Commercial Studies and Management imported from the West was, however, almost alien to most Japanese people at that time. In such a situation and after the Restoration, the Japanese government, which was to send many lecturers to the 'West' and also employ foreign ones at home, attempted to establish educational institutions in order to teach these subjects and also to develop those who would be later engaged in business with the outside world.

Looking back on the development of Economics and related studies in Japan, two higher educational institutions were of significance: one, the *Imperial universities*, the other being the *National higher commercial schools*.[2] Already in 1878, Tokyo (later Imperial) University had begun to give lectures on Economics – before the establishment of the first national higher commercial school in 1884. This was followed by Kyoto Imperial University in 1899. But both these universities had started to give their lectures on the subject in the Faculty of Law.

In contrast, the roles of what were to be called the 'higher commercial schools' were quite different. In Japan, the first national higher commercial school was attached to the 'Tokyo School of Foreign Languages' in 1884, which was modelled on 'L'Institut Supérieur de Commerce d'Anvers', namely the Institute of Higher Studies in Commerce (henceforth to be referred to 'L'Institut'), located in *Antwerp, Belgium*, which was a pioneer of business education in Europe. The Institute has since flourished over the years and is now, as of 2003, part of the University of Antwerp. But the Belgians did not emerge as a nation and become independent from the Netherlands until 1831, so establishing a new identity.

The number of higher commercial schools in Japan soon rose to 15 in the first half of the 1920s, which played important roles in the introduction and development of Economics and Commercial Studies in Japan. After the educational reforms in 1949, they were reorganized as the faculty of Economics or the school of Economics of many universities.

Despite such significance, neither the details of higher commercial schools themselves nor the influence of Belgium and the Netherlands has been studied sufficiently in the mainstream of history of Japanese Economic Thought, although that of Germany has been well cited. This study will examine this unrecognized part of the narrative of the development of Economics and related subjects in Japan.

'L'Institut' and the beginnings of HCSs in Japan

After its opening of the country to the outside world in 1854, Japan had only lower- and middle-level educational institutions for its commercial education. With the industrial development of Japan, however, 'for the purpose of cultivating the future lecturers of commercial schools and those who would engage in business' (Tokyo Gaikokugo Gakko, 1885: 31), at the beginning of March 1884, the Ministry of Education planned to establish the higher ones modelled on the Anvers model.

This 'Institut' was founded in Anvers/Antwerp in Belgium in 1852, the main city in Flanders and historically long linked to the Netherlands, and was regarded as one of the most influential higher commercial schools in the world at the time, as noted, around or just after the turn of the century, long before US 'business schools' opened their doors.

At the end of March 1884, this plan was accepted by the Japanese government and the institution was established. It was named the '*Tokyo Gaikokugo*

Gakko shozoku Koto Shogyo Gakko' and was attached to the 'Tokyo School of Foreign Languages' (presently known as *'Tokyo Gaikokugo Daigaku'* or 'Tokyo University of Foreign Studies'). It became the first national higher commercial school in Japan.

The curriculum of this school shows its dependence on 'L'Institut' which provided a two-year course of study in Europe. The first-year class included Commercial Administration, History of Commercial Products, Commercial and Industrial Geography, Political Economy, Statistics, Principles of Law, as well as languages such as English French, Dutch, German, Italian and Spanish. The second one provided Commercial Administration, History of Commercial Products, General History of Commerce and Industry, Commercial and Maritime Law, Customs Legislation, Construction and Armaments, as well as English, French, Dutch, German, Italian and Spanish (Hooper and Graham, 1901: 112–114).

Japan's first higher commercial school provided a four-year course of study. In the first-year course, only one subject (Bookkeeping) related to Commercial Studies was taught, and others were the general subjects such as Ethics, Japanese, Arithmetic, Algebra, Geometry, Physics, Geography, Calligraphy, English and Physical Education. But the second year did not include these general subjects, except for Ethics and Japanese, as well as Arithmetic, Bookkeeping, Commercial Practices, History of Commerce, Chemistry, as well as Geography. In the third grade, Business Correspondence, Commercial Law, Statistics and so on were included. The fourth grade included the higher level of these technical subjects, except for Industrial Geography (Tokyo Gaikokugo Gakko, 1885).

Furthermore in March 1885, the Japanese government employed Julian van Stappen (1852–1915), who had graduated from 'L'Institut', on a two-year contract for the substantive implementation of the curriculum (National Archives of Japan, 1885). At first, he taught bookkeeping and geography. Regarding the former, he used the textbooks, *The Art of Single Entry Book-keeping* and *The Science of Double-Entry Book-keeping*, written by Christopher Columbus Marsh (cited in Tokyo Gaikokugo Gakko, 1885: 174). These textbooks had already been translated into Japanese by Kobayashi Gisyu and published by the Ministry of Education before van Stappen's arrival. During the Summer holidays – when he carried out research on the specialty in various areas in Japan with a translator, Naoyuki Nagai (Ministry of Education, 1914: 394) – he used the original English version. During his stay in Japan, not only did he engage in the class-teaching but also a wide range of research. But the latter was not however completed and was continued by the next foreign lecturer, from Belgium, Arthur Marischal.

In September 1885, however, only six months after his arrival, this first national 'Tokyo Gaikokugo Gakko shozoku Koto Shogyo Gakko' was merged with the private school 'Tokyo Syogo Gakko (Tokyo School of Commerce)'.[3] It had been originally established as a private school 'Shoho Koshujo (the Commercial Training School)' in 1875 by Mori Arinori (1847–1889) a British-educated reformer, who was later the first Minister of the Ministry of Education, amongst other senior roles.

One can point out two important differences between these schools. First, the education in this school was duly dependent on a chain of Commercial Colleges (the Bryant & Stratton Chain of Business Schools) in the US, but not on 'L'Institut'. In fact, William Cogswell Whitney (1825–1882) of this chain came to Japan to teach the American-style book-keeping – from the opening of the school in 1875 to 1878. Second, this private school did not award a higher but only an elementary-level education under the direct supervision of the Ministry of Agriculture and Commerce. When the 'Tokyo Gaikokugo Gakko shozoku Koto Shogyo Gakko' was merged, it was renamed as the 'Tokyo Syogo Gakko (Tokyo School of Commerce)'. The word 'Higher' was completely removed from this newly organized school. This demotion of the school made Van Stappen angry, although the subjects on commerce did not change so much (Tokyo Gaikokugo Gakko, 1885; Tokyo Shougyou Gakko, 1886). He left Japan in November 1885. Two years later, after his return home, the school again was raised to a *higher* class as the 'Tokyo Higher Commercial School'.

Instead, a number of teachers who also graduated from 'L'Institut' arrived at the school as lecturers: Arthur Marischal (as noted earlier) taught middle-level commercial studies and engaged in arrangement of displays of commercial products from 1886 to 1892, and then Edward Joseph Blockhuys taught the practice of Foreign Trade, Commercial and Industrial Geography, and Commercial Arithmetic from 1892 to 1930 (see Itani, 1974: 24; Hitotsubashi Daigaku Gakuenshi Kankou-iinkai, 1991, 1995; Nishizawa, 2007: 229).

In selecting the lecturer to come after van Stappen, the school planned to employ a graduate from one of several possible colleges, namely 'L'Institut' as well as the 'Gremial Handels-Fachshule der Wiener Kaufmanschaft' in Wien/ Vienna, the 'Handelshochschule' in Frankfurt or the 'École des Hautes Etudes Commerciales' in Paris. The graduate from the first one in this list, making up the qualification demanded from Japan, was finally invited to take up the post (Ministry of Education, 1914: 387). Both Marischal and Blockhuys were the graduates of 'L'Institut', which meant the continuity of the Antwerp curriculum was thus maintained in Japan.

According to the archives, one can find the following eight textbooks used in the class of Economics: *Political Economy for Beginners* by Millicent Garrett Fawcett (1847–1929), *Money and the Mechanism of Exchange* by William Stanley Jevons (1835–1882), *The History, Principles, and Practice of Banking* by James William Gilbart (1794–1863), *Principles of Political Economy* by J. S. Mill (1806–1873), *Free Trade and Protection* by Henry Fawcett (1833–1884), *The Theory of Foreign Exchange* by George Joachim Goschen (1831–1907), *Traité de la science des finances* by Paul Leroy Beaulieu (1843–1916) and *The Principles of Political Economy* by Henry Sidgwick (1838–1900). Except for the seventh book, the original non-translated books were used (Tokyo Shougyou Gakko, 1886: 17–18). These titles show that the Economics taught was not just confined to Belgium, or specifically Antwerp but was chosen from a wider set.

The 1900s saw the rapid development of higher commercial education in Japan. With the industrial growth after the end of the first Sino-Japanese war in

1894–1895, this created the demand for workers with a higher knowledge of commerce and foreign languages, especially English. But in this period, higher commercial education in Japan was still in its early stages, so not only the curriculum of the newly established HCS was inevitably almost the same as that of Tokyo HCS, but also the Principal, Professors or Lecturers of commercial studies were basically graduates from Tokyo HCS.

In 1902, the second national higher commercial school was established in Kobe,[4] which had a customs post and was the key city vis-à-vis transportation connecting the Western and the Eastern parts of Japan. In addition, here one found many foreigners who worked as trading-company employees. This school was in most cases also modelled on 'L'Institut'. This was because of its first Principal, Mizushima Tetsuya (1864–1928). He had entered as a student of 'Tokyo Gaikokugo Gakko shozoku Koto Shogyo Gakko',[5] and was then a Professor of Tokyo HCS. Mizushima adopted the curriculum of Tokyo HCS, which meant that Kobe HCS was also modelled on 'L'Institut'. In fact, the textbook for Economics was *Political Economy for Beginners* by M. G. Fawcett, the same as in the case of Tokyo (Kobe Koto Shogyou Gakko Gakuyukai-nai Toudai-shi Hensyukai, 1928: 16).

But we can point out one important difference between Tokyo HCS and Kobe which was the *school emblem* it adopted. The emblem of 'L'Institut' was in fact 'Mercury', which represents the 'god of commerce'. Tokyo HCS also adopted this as its emblem. Most HCSs established in Japan in the 1900s to 1920s also took up this as the symbol of the schools. But the Principal of Kobe HCS chose 'Chrysanthemum' as the emblem. This was because Kobe has a historical connection with a Samurai in the fourteenth century – whose family crest was the Chrysanthemum (Kobe Koto Shogyou Gakko Gakuyukai-nai Toudai-shi Hensyukai, 1928: 12).

Turning the attention to the economics in Belgium in this period, it was not flourishing as productively as it had before, especially after the death of Emile Louis Victor de Laveleye (1822–1892), an economist at the faculty of the nearby Université de Liège (University of Liege).

Instead, Economics, Commercial and Technical Studies in Germany, especially the German model including the 'German Historical School', were rapidly being taken up in Japan (see Metzler's chapter in this volume on Schumpeter and Japan).

From around the end of the nineteenth century to the beginning of the twentieth century, the interest of Tokyo and Kobe HCSs clearly moved from 'L'Institut' to Economics and Commercial Studies in the German style, or to commercial universities. Fukuda Tokuzo (1874–1930) of Tokyo HCS, who was studying under Lujo Brentano (1844–1931) and was a leading economist in Japan (see Morris-Suzuki, 1989: 68), noted that at the time 'from the viewpoint of the level, "L'Institut" was no more than that of commercial junior high school' (Fukuda, 1928: 1791–1792).

As for the other scholars in Japan in the same period, Ishikawa Bungo (1877–1946), who was an assistant professor of Tokyo HCS, had also arrived at

Belgium in 1899 to study commerce but moved to Berlin in 1900 on the advice from Fukuda.

Academic research began to be strongly influenced by the German Historical School in Economics from this period, especially in Tokyo HCS, criticizing or just not accepting the work of Karl Marx (1818–1883). Curiously enough, the educational system in Japan, however, did not change, as is explained below.

In 1905, following Kobe HCS, two HCSs were established in Nagasaki and Yamaguchi. As previous HCSs, the curricula of both new schools were also the same as that of 'L'Institut' (see Yamaguchi Koto Shogyou Gakko, 1905: 24–25; Nagasaki Koto Shogyou Gakko, 1935: 12–13). In Nagasaki HCS, Kumamoto Aritaka, who worked at Tokyo HCS as a Professor and School Inspector of the Ministry of Education, was invited as Principal, and prepared its educational system depending on that of Tokyo and Kobe HCSs (Nagasaki Koto Shogyou Gakko, 1935: 4).

Such a situation was the same in Yamaguchi HCS. According to Sakudo and Eto (1970: 206–207), it also employed the graduates of Tokyo HCS as Professors: Gamou Yasusato (Economics, Commercial Studies, Industrial Geography), Tadami Toru (Commercial Studies, Commercial Arithmetic, Bookkeeping), Sakamoto Touichi (Industrial Geography, Commercial Studies), as well as Katano Jitsunosuke (Commercial Studies, Bookkeeping).

With regard to another important point, these two HCSs were also reflecting the influence of 'L'Institut', which was not found in the establishment of Tokyo and Kobe HCSs. That was in the now developing field of 'colonial studies' in Economics. In 1901, 'L'Institut' began to provide lectures on 'colonies' for the third-grade students – with the nationalization of Congo, formerly owned by Leopold II of Belgium (presently known as Democratic Republic of the Congo). Such a situation was of keen interest to Japan then. Both Yamaguchi and Nagasaki HCSs were located near the continental part of Asia, so they aimed to produce those graduates who would be useful to the business there (Nagasaki Koto Shogyou Gakko, 1935: 3). For this purpose, students of Nagasaki HCS could choose as the second foreign language from Chinese, Korean, German or Russian, in addition to the ordinary commercial education (ibid., 12). In the case of Yamaguchi HCS students could choose Chinese or Korean (Yamaguchi Koto Shogyou Gakko, 1905: 24). In addition, these schools opened a one-year special course on foreign trade – for those who graduated from HCS: Yamaguchi HCS in 1915 and Nagasaki HCS in 1917. The former specialized in studies of trade with China.

The national HCSs in Japan continued to be largely influenced by it – from the beginning to the middle of 1900s even though the impact of 'L'Institut' in the Western countries was becoming less prominent, especially after the appearance of competing higher-level educational institutions, commercial colleges, or universities of commerce in France, Germany, the UK and the US from around the beginning of the twentieth century. In fact, the academic interest of the Japanese lecturers moved on to these studies in such countries.

However, as Ishikawa (1910) notes, their interest in the commercial education did not change. The beginning of the colonial studies courses modelled on those of 'L'Institut' also increased the interest in studies in continental parts of Asia, and created the basis of the wider development of such studies from the end of the 1920s. At the same time, from around this period, as will be explained in the next section, some changes in the 'Antwerp-style' educational systems were also to be found at the new HCSs established in the 1910s.

Watanabe Ryusei and the new educational style from the US: Otaru and Nagoya HCSs

In 1910, the fifth HCS was built in Otaru, Hokkaido. With regards to this school, one can find some significant points in the introduction of Economics and/or Commercial Studies into Japan. It is worth mentioning Takashima Saichiro (1884–1959), who was on the faculty. He was regarded as one of the scholars that introduced Keynesian ideas for the first time in Japan as early as 1915 and had translated three chapters of Keynes' (first) book, which was on Indian currency (see Kamikubo, 2003: 120–121: Ikeo, 2014: 50–52, 196).

The most outstanding point of this school that was different from previous HCSs was that the ideas of education and research there were newly introduced by the Principal, Watanabe Ryusei, based on his experience in the US. He majored in ethics and received the Doctor of Philosophy from the Graduate School of Cornell University in upstate New York in 1894. After returning to Japan, from 1895, he became Lecturer of the 'Tokyo Higher Normal School' presently known as Tsukuba University, and then from 1901, Principal of the 'Tokyo Music School', presently the faculty of Music of Tokyo Geijutsu University ('Tokyo University of Arts'). From 1902, he was also invited as the Education Advisor of Yuan Shikai for seven years. After these jobs, when studying in Humboldt University in Berlin, he was appointed as the Principal of the new HCS in Otaru (Otaru Syouka Daigaku, 1961: 8; Hotta, 2005: 24–25).

Watanabe himself visited 'L'Institut' – before his arrival at Otaru as its Principal. Indeed, at first he also tried to employ a foreign lecturer from this school – as Tokyo HCS did – but his request was not realized (Otaru Syouka Daigaku Hyakunen-shi Hensan-shitsu, 2011: 120). With regard to the Japanese lecturers in Economics and Commercial Studies, he adopted the graduates from Tokyo HCS as had previous HCSs: Kunimatsu Yutaka (Commerce, Bookkeeping and Computation), Sakamoto Touichi (Commercial Studies; previously Professor of Yamaguchi HCS), Iura Sentarou (Economics and Commerce; previously Professor of Kobe HCS) and Ohnishi Inosuke (Economics and Finance) and so on (Otaru Syouka Daigaku, 1961: 13–18).

The curriculum of Otaru HCS, 'largely dependent on that of the existing one there' (Watanabe, 1929: 6) had some differences. Instead of general subjects, Watanabe newly arranged three kinds of practical subjects, including 'practical commerce', 'practical business' and 'product experiment', all of which had not been taught before in HCSs in Japan (Watanabe, 1929: 6). Watanabe regarded 'commercial studies in the existing HCSs as just a means' (Otaru Syouka Daigaku, 1961: 11), and emphasized the importance of practice as:

John Dewey says that a school is not a place to prepare for social life, but a society itself. Considering that our school is not a place for preparing for commercial society but a commercial society itself, we have put the emphasis on the practical subjects.

(Watanabe, 1929: 6–7)

In fact, on the basis of *pragmatism*, he constructed a special room for 'practical commerce', where simulation-classes of commercial systems, banks, warehouses, insurance and transportation were given.

Watanabe also regarded it necessary for students to acquire detailed knowledge on natural sciences for the better understanding of products (Watanabe, 1929: 58–59), and prepared laboratories for both chemistry and physics. The second-year students could choose the basic class for experiments in quantitative and qualitative analyses of organic and inorganic compounds, and physical experiments and so on. Depending on the basic knowledge, the third-year student carried out experiments in analysing the manufacturing processes and the quality of important products (Otaru Koto Shogyou Gakko, 1926: 36; Otaru Syouka Daigaku Hyakunen-shi Hensan-shitsu, 2011: 68).

Regarding 'Practical Business', it was planned around 1919 to build a soapworks – to thus start a further practical business education stream based on Frederick Winslow Taylor's (1856–1915) management theories (see Warner, 1994). This idea had originated with Professor Kunimatsu, who had studied Taylor's management system in the US – from H. K Hathaway of Tabor Manufacture Co. in Philadelphia, Pennsylvania for half a year. Another Professor, Ohara Kametaro, who majored in product-experiments, also played an important role because he had a wide experience of the business world in Tokyo. In February 1920, the soap-works began to operate and students actually made the products and sold them publicly, being known as 'Kosho Sekken' or 'Higher Commercial Soap'. They studied cost-accounting, factory management, production and improvement of efficiency (Otaru Syouka Daigaku, 1961: 30–31; Watanabe, 1929: 7).

This new educational method started in Otaru was also continued at the sixth HCS built in Nagoya in 1920, ten years after the establishment of Otaru HCS. With the establishment of the Nagoya HCS at the end of November 1920, the Principal, Watanabe, was transferred from Otaru HCS to Nagoya HCS as the Director there, with a number of Professors of Otaru HCS, including Kunimatsu. The curriculum of Nagoya HCS, the basic part of which was the same as that of previous HCSs, also adopted 'practical commerce' and 'product experiments', as begun at Otaru HCS. At Nagoya HCS, studies on 'commercial efficiency' were added, instead of the 'practical business' ones that were adopted at Otaru HCS.

For these practical subjects at Nagoya HCS, instead of soap-works in Otaru, Watanabe decided to establish a printing-factory for studies on 'commercial efficiency' (Watanabe, 1929: 60). This construction was started in 1924, and was completed in October 1926. In the factory, students actually put what they learned in the classroom into practice. In this factory, for example, the journal of

Nagoya HCS, entitled *Shougyo Keizai Ronso* (*Journal of Commercial Studies and Economics*) began publication from July 1926 onwards.

Watanabe also adopted 'psychology in commerce and industry' in the curriculum. According to him, 'economists have studied only capital and depended on studies on human beings by philosophers.... Experimental psychology has appeared now with Fechner's work on the subject' (Watanabe, 1929: 59). This trial was the first one to take place in Japan.

Watanabe furthermore became interested in 'the Case-Method education system' at the Harvard Business School launched in 1908. So, he instructed two young professors – Akamatsu Kaname and Miyata Kiyozou, both of whom had just graduated from the two-year specialized course of Tokyo HCS in 1921 – to attend the classes there using this educational system.

During his two-month stay in the US in 1926, the first named, later to become a well-known economist, Akamatsu Kaname (1896–1974) attended Copeland's classes, and was 'surprised at the atmosphere of the discussion' (Akamatsu, 1975: 33). At the same time, he was also attracted to the works on business administration and the empirical analysis of business conditions run by the Committee on Economic Research of the Graduate School of Harvard University.

On his return to Japan in July 1926, he suggested to Watanabe that 'a Bureau of Business Research should be established' (Akamatsu, 1975: 34). In the same year, *Sangyou Cyousashitsu* (the Bureau of Business Research, Nagoya Commercial College) attached to Nagoya HCS was founded, and the educational and research methods introduced from Harvard were substantively introduced.

The Harvard 'Case-Method' was for the first time accepted in Japan as a part of the curriculum of the one-year business administration course. It was opened in 1924 for those who graduated from the three-year course of HCS. In 1927, in order to have the knowledge of the 'Harvard system', two articles written by Wallace Brett Donham (1877–1954), the second Dean of the Harvard Business School, were translated into Japanese, and were published as the second issue of the journal published by the Bureau mentioned above. This educational system was continued till the end of the 1930s at Nagoya HCS, although 'collecting the cases took much time and effort' in Japan then (Akamatsu, 1975: 41).

As to empirical analysis, the following three kinds of research were included: an investigation into business administration in the Japanese spinning industry, quantitative indexes of products made in Japan, and creating a business barometer mainly for the textile industry. The first one enabled Akamatsu to develop his '*Wild Geese Flying Pattern Theory*' in the field of Economics in the 1930s, which explains the variations in the development of an industry in a developing country[6] (see Ohtsuki, 2010, 2011) and anticipates post-war thinking in Development Economics. This model of Economic Development (*sangyo hatten no ganko keitairon*) is widely known in Japan and is still regarded as the key economic theory underlying Japan's economic aid to developing countries (see Das's chapters on East Asia, as well as on NIEs, earlier in this volume).

The '*Wild Geese Flying Pattern Theory*' was further advanced in the latter half of the 1930s, within the framework of the major Economic cycle-theory of Soviet economist Nikolai D. Kondratiev (1892–1938). After the Great Depression in 1929, Kondratiev's theory came to be studied in Japan, mainly through his German article 'Die langen Wellen der Konjunktur' printed in *Archiv für Sozialwissenschaft und Sozialpolitik*, in 1926.[7] In Akamatsu (1937, 1939), the advanced version of his own theory was presented, explaining the structural changes of the world economy, with an approximately 60-year cycle. The second research in this area was started by Ernest Francis Penrose (1895–1984), an economist nicknamed 'Pen' who worked as a Lecturer in Economics at Nagoya HCS from 1925 to 1930[8] not long after his graduation from Cambridge University (eventually marrying Edith Penrose, 1914–1996, later another noted figure in International Economics), and was later taken up by Koide Yasuji, a graduate of this HCS. Koide completed the quantitative index of all products in Japan from 1894 to 1931. Afterwards this index was introduced in Penrose's publication (Penrose, 1940), and widely known as 'Meikosho Shisu' (the Index of Nagoya HCS) or 'Koide Index'. The third one was started in Nagoya HCS by Warren Milton Persons (1878–1937) who later taught Economics at Dartmouth and later Harvard.

From around the period when Watanabe moved from Otaru to Nagoya, changes in the lectures on Economics came to be found at Otaru HCS, whilst keeping Watanabe's education policy. That was the increase in the role of Theoretical Economics (Otaru Syouka Daigaku, 1961: 40). Teduka Jyurou (1896–1943), for example, arrived at Otaru in 1919, after his graduation from Tokyo HCS, writing his thesis on Arthur C. Pigou (1877–1959) and Heinrich H. Gossen (1810–1858). At Otaru, Teduka especially engaged in the study on Léon Walras (1834–1910) after his study in France for about five years. Another important example was Minami Ryozaburo (1896–1985), who became a lecturer in Economics at Otaru HCS in 1923 and studied the work of the British economist, Thomas Robert Malthus (1766–1834). According to the recollections of the students at that time, he often mentioned Malthus in the classes on Economics (see Otaru Kosho-shi Kenkyu-kai, 2002: 85–117). From the 1910s to 1920s, Watanabe introduced new educational and research methods from the US to Otaru and Nagoya HCSs.

Colonial studies to war-time investigations

The First World War brought economic prosperity to Japan, which enabled the then Prime Minister Hara Takashi (1856–1921) to implement what was called the 'Positive Policy', such as the enhancement of national defence, the expansion of higher education, the promotion of industry and the development of transportation. Following the foundation of Nagoya HCS, seven HCSs were also established in the first half of the 1920s: Fukushima and Oita in 1921, Hikone and Wakayama in 1922, Yokohama and Takamatsu in 1923, and Takaoka in 1924.[9] But the innovations in education found at Otaru and Nagoya HCSs were not fully completed.

Among them, only one, Yokohama HCS, had adopted new courses such as 'practical commerce', 'product experiments' and 'psychology in commerce and industry' in the curriculum (Yokohama Koto Shogyou Gakko, 1943: 22–24). The other six schools partly included these subjects but as a whole were dependent on the older curriculum of 'L'Institut', as before.

What was most noticeable among these schools was that from the beginning, they had classes related to colonial studies and specific geographical areas of Japan. Students in all the seven schools could choose Chinese or Russian as a second foreign language. This was for the convenience of students who would engage in industry and commerce related to these areas after the graduation. In addition, six schools excluding Takamatsu HCS offered a class on colonial policy in the third grade (Hikone Koto Shogyou Gakko, 1922: 5–7; Oita Koto Shogyou Gakko, 1922: 12–13; Fukushima Koto Shogyou Gakko, 1926: 42–43; Takamatsu Koto Shogyou Gakko, 1926: 17–8; Takaoka Koto Shogyou Gakko, 1926: 5–6; Wakayama Koto Shogyou Gakko, 1935: 5–7; Yokohama Koto Shogyou Gakko, 1943: 22–24).

From the end of the 1920s to 1940, the Japanese government planned the 'emigration' of surplus population, a policy which arose from the Depression. To groom the Instructors necessary in the destinations, with the exceptions of Wakayama and Takamatsu HCSs, the five HCSs additionally opened a new course specialized in trade, this time mainly with South America – as well as East Asia.

In 1929, Yokohama HCS established the one-year short-term trade course for those who graduated from junior high schools. It provided the knowledge necessary for the migration to South America and the trade with this area. South America was then attractive to Japan because it was full of developing areas and natural resources and could be a promising export-market. For this purpose, students were taught Spanish or Portuguese as a first foreign language, the outlines of agriculture and its practice. Fifteen out of 34 of the first graduates actually migrated to Brazil and engaged in farming or commerce, even though their teachers did not actually investigate South America. It was seven years after the establishment of the one-year course that the professor responsible actually visited this area (Yokohama Koto Shogyou Gakko, 1943: 67–70). This kind of a short-term trade course was also established in Yamaguchi and Nagasaki HCSs in 1929, and Fukushima HCS in 1938.

The other three HCSs opened the three-year special course on East Asia, partly including Russia after the 'Marco Polo Bridge Incident' in Peking, in July 1937, seen as initiating the Second Sino-Japanese War. In 1939, Hikone HCS opened the 'China course', and in 1940, Oita and Takaoka HCSs established the 'East Asia course'. As reflecting the situation of Japan in this period, they offered lectures on Economics, Economic History, Economic Geography, Finance, Law and National Character regarding the colonial areas of Japan's orbit. Takaoka HCS, which was located near not only China but also Russia, included studies on the latter's affairs. Besides these schools, Otaru HCS also established the three-year course specializing in the East Asia area.

In the beginning of the 1940s, the worsening of the war-effort made the controls by the Ministry of Education over the higher-level education much stricter than those in the 1930s. From April 1941, the Ministry of Education, in order to meet the demands of the business world, decided to change the curricula of HCSs. This forced students to study and investigate the situation related to the 'controlled economy' of Japan and the East Asian economy (Sakudo and Eto, 1974: 176–177). In October 1943, the Japanese cabinet approved the mobilization of students. In 1944, national HCSs were changed into the following three types: 'technical junior colleges', 'industrial management junior colleges' and 'junior colleges of Economics'. This institutional change meant that the words 'commerce' or 'commercial' were to be regarded as if acting *against* the national policy.

The first group included Hikone, Wakayama and Takaoka, the second one included Nagasaki, Nagoya and Yokohama, and the third was Yamaguchi, Otaru, Fukushima, Oita and Takamatsu. The reorganized educational system in war-time Japan started in Spring, 1944. Tokyo and Kobe, both of which had been already raised to commercial university status from HCS, were also changed into 'Tokyo University of Industry' and 'Kobe University of Economics' in 1944.

In the 'technical junior colleges' and 'industrial management junior colleges', lectures on natural science were beginning to be taught instead of commercial studies and foreign languages. In 'junior colleges of economics', by contrast, such a significant change in the education system was not made. At Otaru HCS, for example, only one class on factory-management was added (Otaru Kosho-shi Kenkyu-kai, 2002: 66). Even in 1944, lectures on the renowned British Classical Economists noted earlier – such as Smith, Malthus and others – as well as the theory of 'marginal utility' of Marshall – were given (ibid.: 235–236). Additionally, the journal of this HCS, '*Shogaku Tokyu*' (*Investigations on Commercial Studies*) also continued to be published till 1945, although the frequency and the quantity of publication were becoming less. But at the same time from 1941 to 1944, ten academics were forced to go to the war-front, some of whom died (Otaru Syouka Daigaku, 1961: 77–78).

In the case of Tokyo University of Commerce, more than 40 people, retaining their status as professors, students and so on, directly cooperated on the 'research' investigations by the Japanese Army in East and South-East Asia – from the end of 1943 to the end of the Second World War. This request was made from Takase Keiji (1905–1982), who was then Lieutenant-Colonel of the Imperial Military Headquarters and the younger brother of the then President of Tokyo UC, Takase Sotaro (1892–1966). At first, this group headed by Akamatsu, who moved from Nagoya HCS in 1939, planned academic research work in Economics, as he had done so in Nagoya. The Japanese military administration, however, demanded not academic investigations but practical research in the development of natural resources urgently needed to advance the war-needs. By March 1945, secondary or higher-level education was completely at a standstill. After the end of the Second World War, however, the educational system which had been changed in war-time was restored to its former state.

Conclusions

With the beginning of the reform of education system in May 1949, 'new universities' were reorganized, consisting not only the former Imperial universities but also the previous higher-level schools which taught Humanities, Social Sciences and Natural Sciences or Technology. All the previous HCSs but one became a faculty of Economics of these universities. Only Otaru HCS, joining or being joined with no other schools, became, independently, the 'Otaru University of Commerce'.

With a few exceptions of practical studies from the US, the educational system of the HCSs which had been set up in Japan in 1884 *was not*, and/or *could not be institutionally free* from the influence of the Belgian and Netherlands' legacy of 'L'Institut' until the end of the Second World War. This was especially the case vis-à-vis the following two points: the curriculum taught and the role of colonial studies, both being regarded as significant characteristics of higher-level commercial education in Japan.

Considering that the *institutional maturity* of higher-level commercial education in Japan was still limited after its importation at the time of the opening-up of Japan, this was probably inevitable.

Notes

1 In this case, 'West' basically means Europe and the US.
2 Higher education was almost exclusively orientated towards men in this period. Japan's national first institution of higher education for women was the 'Tokyo Women's Normal School' founded in 1875. In 1890, this was reorganized as the 'Women's Higher Normal School', now known as 'Ochanomizu University'. Regarding private schools, the 'Nihon Joshi Daigakko' established in 1901 was the first one. This held the departments of 'Home Economics', 'Japanese', 'English', 'Preparatory Course of English Literature', and is now known as 'Japan Women's University'.
3 In this merger, the 'Tokyo Gaikokugo Gakko' ('Tokyo School of Foreign Languages') disappeared. But in 1897, the 'Gaikokugo Gakko' ('School of Foreign Languages') was formed again as an organization affiliated with 'Koto Shogyo Gakko' (Higher Commercial School). In 1899 the 'Gaikokugo Gakko' was renamed the 'Tokyo Gaikokugo Gakko' (Tokyo School of Foreign Languages), and was separated from the 'Higher Commercial School'. The 'Tokyo Gaikokugo Gakko' (Tokyo School of Foreign Languages), now known as ''Tokyo University of Foreign Studies', does not have any faculty or school of economics or commerce (www.tufs.ac.jp/english/abouttufs/history.html, accessed on 1 March 2016).
4 In 1901, Osaka City had established 'Osaka Higher Commercial School' (formally 'Osaka City Commercial College') before Kobe HCS. Osaka was not selected for the establishment of the second national HCS. For the details, see Kobe Koto Shogyou Gakko Gakuyukai-nai Toudai-shi Hensyukai (1928: 3–7). In 1904, Waseda University (a private school) established the school of commerce. This was also regarded as modelled on 'L'Institut'.
5 Among the students of the first national higher commercial school was Hirao Hachisaburo (1866–1945) known as the founder of the private school 'Konan Gakuen' in Kobe. This includes the present Konan University.
6 He presented this theory in the book by Akamatsu (1935) for the first time.
7 Some Japanese economists, including Akamatsu (1896–1974), also studied the major cycle theory by Dutch economist, Sam de Wolff (1878–1960). But both his works, the

Dutch version (De Wolff, 1921) and the German version (De Wolff, 1924), were not examined directly at first. In comparison to the Meiji period, the influence of De Wolff on Japanese economists was quite limited.

8 With regard to his memoirs at Nagoya, see Penrose (1895–1984); see 1975, 1987. Another well-known foreign lecturer at Nagoya HCS was G.C. Allen; see Allen (1900–1982) (see 1983).

9 In addition to these HCSs, the Japanese government also established four HCSs in the colonial part of Japan then: Taipei and Tainan in 1919, Pyongyang in 1922 and Dalian (Dairen) in 1936. All of them went out of Japan's control after the war.

References*

* Titles in [ ] are abridged English translations of the Japanese title by the author of this chapter.

Primary

Akamatsu K. (1935). Wagakuni Youmou Kougyouhin no Boueki Susei. *Syougyou Keizai Ronsou*, Nagoya: Nagoya HCS, 13(1): 129–212 [Trend of the trade of wool products of Japan].

Akamatsu K. (1937). *Sangyoutousei Ron*. Tokyo: Chikura Syobou [*Theory of Industrial Control*].

Akamatsu K. (1939). Cyouki Hadou nitsuite. In *Keizaigaku Keizaishi no Syomondai*, edited by Y. Sakanishi *et al*. Tokyo: Iwanami Syoten: 1–29 [On Long Waves].

Akamatsu K. (1975). Gakumon Henro. In *Gakumon Henro*, edited by K. Kojima. Tokyo: Sekai Keizai Kenkyukai: 9–68 [*Akamatsu: His Life and Works*].

Allen, G. C. (1983). *Appointment in Japan: memories of sixty years*. London: Athlone Press.

de Wolff, S. (1921). Prosperiteits- en Depressie- Perioden. *De Socialistische Gids. Maandschrift der Sociaal- Democratische Arbeiderspartij*, Amsterdam, VI: 19–40.

de Wolff, S. (1924). Prosperitäts-und Depressionsperioden. In *Der lebendige Marxismus. Festgabe zum 70. Geburtstage von Karl Kautsky*, edited by O. Jensen. Jena: Thüringer Verlagsanstalt und Druckerei: 13–43.

Fukuda T. (1928). *Keizai-gaku Zensyu*, Vol. 4. Tokyo: Dobun-kan [Complete Works on Economics by Fukuda Tokuzo, Vol. 4].

Fukushima Koto Shogyou Gakko ed. (1926). *Fukushima Koto Shogyou Gakko Ichiran Taisho 11–12*. Fukushima: Fukushima HCS [*The Curriculum of Fukushima HCS, 1921–1922*].

Hikone Koto Shogyou Gakko ed. (1922). *Hikone Koto Shogyou Gakko Ichiran Taisho 12–13*. Hikone: Hikone HCS [*The Curriculum of Hikone HCS, 1922–1923*].

Hitotsubashi Daigaku Gakuenshi Kankou-iinkai (1991). *Hitotsubashi Daigaku Gakusei-shi Shiryou*, Vol. 12. Tokyo: Hitotsubashi Daigaku [*Historical Archives of Hitotsubashi University*, Vol. 12].

Hitotsubashi Daigaku Gakuenshi Kankou-iinkai (1995). *Hitotsubashi Daigaku Hyaku-nijyu nenshi*. Tokyo: Hitotsubashi Daigaku [*120 Years History of Hitotsubashi University*].

Hooper, F. and J. Graham (1901). *Commercial Education at Home and Abroad*. London: Macmillan.

Hotta S. (2005). *Nagoya Koutou Syogyo Gakko*. Nagoya: Nagoya Daigaku Daigaku Daigaku Bunsyo Shiryou-shitsu [*History of Nagoya HCS*].

Ikeo, A. (2014). *A History of Economic Science in Japan: the internationalization of Economics in the twentieth century.* London and New York, NY: Routledge.

Ishikawa B. (1910). Antwerp Koto Shogyou Gakko no Kinjyou. *Keizaigaku Syougyougaku Kokumin Keizai Zattushi.* Kobe: Kobe HCS, 8(4): 92–104 [Recent Education at 'L'Institut Supérieur de Commerce d'Anvers'].

Itani Z-I. (1974). Belgium Anvers Syouka-daigaku to Nihon. *Waseda Syogaku*, 241: 3–29 [L'Institut Supérieur de Commerce d'Anvers and Japan].

Kamikubo S. (2003). *Nihon no Keizaigaku wo Kizuita Gojyu-nin.* Tokyo: Nihon Hyouron-Sya [*50 Japanese Economists who Contributed to the Development of Economics in Japan*].

Kobe Koto Shogyou Gakko Gakuyukai-nai Toudai-shi Hensyukai ed. (1928). *Toudai Nijyu-gonen-shi.* Kobe: Kobe HCS, Toudai-shi Hensyukai [*25 Years History of Kobe HCS*].

Ministry of Education (1914). *Nihon Teikoku Monbusyou Nenpou 13, Meiji 18.* Tokyo: Ministry of Education [*Annual Report of Ministry of Education, 1885*].

Morris-Suzuki, T. (1989). *A History of Japanese Economic Thought.* London and New York: Routledge and Nissan Institute for Japanese Studies, University of Oxford.

Nagasaki Koto Shogyou Gakko ed. (1935). *Nagasaki Koto Shogyou Gakko Sanjyunen-shi.* Nagasaki: Nagasaki HCS [*30 Years History of Nagasaki HCS*].

National Archives of Japan (1885). Berugi-kokujin Stappen Yatoiire-no-ken. *Kobunroku, Meiji 18, 142.* Tokyo: National Archives of Japan, available by microfilm Reel No. 056300 [The Employment of Van Stappen].

Nishizawa T. (2007). *Marshall to Rekishigakuha no Keizai Shisou.* Tokyo: Iwanami Shoten [*Economic Thought of A. Marshall and Historical School*].

Ohtsuki T. (2010). *Akamatsu Kaname no Gankou-Keitai-Ron to Sono Tenkai.* PhD Theses of Tokyo University of Foreign Studies [Akamatsu Kaname's '*Gankou Keitai Ron*' and its Development – His Nagoya Period and the Perspectives of a Stage Theory of Economic Development].

Ohtsuki T. (2011). The Background of K. Akamatsu's '*Gankou Keitai Ron*' and its Development: Early Empirical Analysis at Nagoya. In *The Dissemination of Economic Ideas*, edited by H. Kurz, T. Nishizawa and K. Tribe. Cheltenham: Edward Elgar: 292–314.

Oita Koto Shogyou Gakko ed. (1922). *Oita Koto Shogyou Gakko Ichiran Taisho 12–13.* Oita: Oita HCS [*The Curriculum of Oita HCS, 1922–1923*].

Otaru Kosho-shi Kenkyu-kai ed. (2002). *Otaru Kosho no Hitobito.* Otaru: Otaru Syouka Daigaku [*Peoples of Otaru Higher Commercial School*].

Otaru Koto Shogyou Gakko ed. (1926). *Otaru Koto Shogyou Gakko Ichiran, Taisho 6–7.* Otaru: Otaru HCS [*The Curriculum of Otaru HCS, 1917–1918*].

Otaru Syouka Daigaku (1961). *Ryotuu-kyu Gojyunen-shi.* Otaru: Otaru University of Commerce [*50 Years History of Otaru University of Commerce*].

Otaru Syouka Daigaku Hyakunen-shi Hensan-shitsu ed. (2011). *Otaru Syouka Daigaku Hyakunen-shi: Tsu-shi Hen.* Otaru: Otaru University of Commerce Press [*100 Years History of Otaru University of Commerce: Overview Volume*].

Penrose, E. F. (1940). Japan, 1920–1936. In *The Industrialization of Japan and Manchukuo 1930–1940. Population, Raw Materials and Industry*, edited by E. B. Schumpeter. New York, NY: Macmillan: 80–270.

Penrose, E. F. (1975). My Nagoya Era and Professor Akamatsu. In *Gakumon Henro*, edited by K. Kojima. Tokyo: Sekai Keizai Kenkyukai Kojima ed.: 323–327.

Penrose, E. F. (1987). Memoirs of Japan, 1925–1930. In *Japan and World Depression*, edited by R. Dore and R. Sinha. New York, NY: St Martin's Press: 6–13.

Sakudo Y. and Eto T. ed. (1970). *Hana Naki Yama no Yamakage no*. Tokyo: Zaikai Hyouron Shinsya [*65 Years History of Yamaguchi HCS*].

Sakudo Y. and Eto T. ed. (1974). *Oita Daigaku Keizai-gakubu Gojyunen-shi*. Tokyo: Zaikai Hyouron Shinsya [*50 Years History of the Faculty of Economics, Oita University*].

Takamatsu Koto Shogyou Gakko ed. (1926). *Takamatsu Koto Shogyou Gakko Ichiran Taisho 14–15*. Takamatsu: Takamatsu HCS [*The Curriculum of Takamatsu HCS, 1925–1926*].

Takaoka Koto Shogyou Gakko ed. (1926). *Takaoka Koto Shogyou Gakko Ichiran Taisho 14–15*. Takaoka: Takaoka HCS [*The Curriculum of Takaoka HCS, 1924–1925*].

Tamanoi Y. (1971) *Nihon no Keizaigaku*. Tokyo: Cyuou kouron-sya [*Economics in Japan*].

Tokyo Gaikokugo Gakko (1885). *Tokyo Gaikokugo Gakko Ichiran-Ryaku. Honko Syozoku Koutou Shougyou Kisoku Meiji 17–8*. Tokyo: Tokyo Gaikokugo Gakko [*The Curriculum of the Tokyo School of Foreign Languages and the Higher Commercial School Attached to it, 1884–1885*].

Tokyo Shougyou Gakko (1886). *Tokyo Shougyou Gakko Ichiran Meiji 19*. Tokyo: Tokyo Shougyou Gakko [*The Curriculum of the Tokyo School of Commerce, 1886*].

Wakayama Koto Shogyou Gakko ed. (1935). *Wakayama Koto Shogyou Gakko Ichiran Taisho 12–13*. Wakayama: Wakayama HCS [*The Curriculum of Wakayama HCS, 1923–1924*].

Warner, M. (1994). Japanese culture, Western management: Taylorism and human resources in Japan. *Organization Studies*, 15: 509–535.

Watanabe, R. (1929). *Kanpo shiki Jisyu*. Nagoya: Nagoya HCS [*Selected Speeches by R. Watanabe*].

Yagi, K. (1999). *Kindai Nihon no Syakai Keizai-gaku*. Tokyo: Chikuma Syobou [*Social Economics in Modern Japan*].

Yamaguchi Koto Shogyou Gakko (1905). *Yamaguchi Koto Shougyou Gakko Ichiran Meiji 38–39*. Yamaguchi: Yamaguchi HCS [*The Curriculum of Yamaguchi HCS, 1905–1906*].

Yokohama Koto Shogyou Gakko (1943). *Yokohama Koto Shougyou Gakko Nijyunen-shi*. Yokohama: Yokohama HCS [*20 Years History of Yokohama HCS*].

Secondary

Beaulieu, P. L. (1877). *Traité de la science des finances*. Paris: Guillaumin.

Ellis, W. (1846). *Outlines of Social Economy*. London: Smith, Elder and Co. Dutch translation by H. H. Graafland (1852) *Grondtrekken der Staathuishoudkunde*. Utrecht: Dekema.

Fawcett, H. (1878). *Free Trade and Protection*. London: Macmillan.

Fawcett, M. G. (1870). *Political Economy for Beginners*. London: Macmillan.

Gilbart, J. W. (1882). *The History, Principles, and Practice of Banking*. London: Bell.

Goschen, G. J. (1861). *The Theory of Foreign Exchange*. London: Effingham Wilson.

Jevons, W. S. (1875). *Money and the Mechanism of Exchange*. New York: D. Appleton and Co.

Kondratiev, N. D. (1926). Die langen Wellen der Konjunktur. *Archiv für Sozialwissenschaft und Sozialpolitik*, 56: 573–609.

Marsh, C. C. (1836). *The Art of Single Entry Book-keeping*. New York: J. C. Riker.

Marsh, C. C. (1841). *The Science of Double-Entry Book-keeping*. Philadelphia: Hogan & Thompson.

Mill, J. S. (1848). *Principles of Political Economy*. London: John W. Parker and Son.

Sidgwick, H. (1883). *The Principles of Political Economy*. London: Macmillan.

Part IV

Themes

17 Western Economics in China since 1979

Four views in Chinese academia

Fuqian Fang

Introduction

The People's Republic of China (henceforth the 'PRC') is today known as a social-ist country under the central leadership of the Communist Party of China (CPC) – with Marxism as its leading inspiration. From 1 October 1949, when it was first established, up to 1979 when it began to implement the Economic Reforms and Open Door policy, Western Economics[1] in China had long been *criticized* and *rejected* as an 'anti-Marxist' economic theory and a 'Western capitalist' ideology.

During this 30 years, apart from the *Principles of Economics* (1890) of Alfred Marshall (1842–1924), *The General Theory of Employment, Interest and Money* (1936; abbreviated as the *General Theory* throughout this chapter) of John Maynard Keynes (1883–1946) and a few other famous Western writings that had been translated and published to date, *almost no Western Economics textbooks were imported into China* (see the chapters by Trescott in this volume).

In the teaching-plan of most Chinese universities at that time, the basic theory of Economics taught was called '*Marxist Political Economy*', with no courses on Western Economics to speak of. Only a few top seats of learning, like Fudan University, Nankai University, Peking University, Renmin University and Wuhan University offered lectures on what they called 'Western Bourgeois Economics Criticism' [*sic*], which were mainly to introduce and critique the various schools of Western thought. At that time, the unanimous view of the Chinese academics and the Party propaganda departments was that Western Economics was a kind of 'bourgeoisie vulgar economics' [*sic*] aimed at defending the capitalist system, the contradictions of capitalism and an ideology contrary to Marxist Political Economy.

Therefore, scholars could not positively teach and introduce Western Economics in the classroom – but only *criticize* it or *deny* it. Even the small number of Western Economics classics already translated into Chinese was also set up as an object of criticism. The versions of famous works on Western Economics were generally accompanied with book-reviews written by famous Chinese scholars, the contents of which were mainly to point out how the book was a 'defence' of the rationality of the capitalist system and was 'in opposition' to 'Marxism'. As a result, the readers had to read it with a critical eye.

The first translation of Alfred Marshall's *Principles of Economics* (1890) was published in China in 1964, at the beginning of which there was an introduction written by a Chinese scholar, Zai Shi, entitled 'An Assessment of Marshall's Principles of Economics'. The author of this review wrote that Alfred Marshall, the most famous economist at the end of the nineteenth century and at the beginning of the twentieth century, absorbed the old and the new 'Vulgar Economics' theories at that time and that 'the book, the *Principles of Economics*' established an economics system with 'eclecticism' as its main characteristic. At that time, it noted: 'The British ruling classes urgently needed a new economic theory to justify the strengthening exploitation on the working class. Marshall's economics text thus fitted this need' (Marshall, 1964, preface: 2).

The earliest Chinese full translation (the first Chinese edition) of John Maynard Keynes's *General Theory* (1936) was published in 1957 by China SDX Joint Publishing Company translated by Y. Xu (Keynes, 1957) and in 1963 it was re-published by the Commercial Press (Keynes, 1963). When the latter reprinted the book in 1977 (Keynes, 1977), it increased the length of the Chinese version's preface. The preface author, Y. N. Li, wrote: 'John Maynard Keynes is a famous British bourgeois vulgar economist.... All of Keynes's life is to maintain the monopoly bourgeoisie, to oppose revolution, oppose communism, and oppose Marxist theory' (Keynes, 1977, preface: 1).

It concluded after summarizing the basic viewpoints of the *General Theory* as follows: 'it is clear that this theory "Keynes-trafficking" is completely vulgar and anti-science' (Keynes, 1977, preface: 5). He finally wrote: 'reprinting the Chinese version of the *General Theory* is to make it negative teaching material, in order to carry out criticism of the Keynesian Theory and develop Marxism in the struggle' (Keynes, 1977, preface: 32). The comments over the period of these two Chinese scholars on Marshall's *Principles of Economics* (1890) and Keynes's *General Theory* (1936) typically represented the mainstream attitudes and evaluations of Chinese academia vis-à-vis Western Economics at that time (see the chapter on Keynes in this volume).

The situation of Western Economics in China since 1979

In 1979, Deng Xiaoping (1904–1997) was to launch his 'Economic Reforms' (*gaige kaifang*) and 'Open Door' (*kaifang*) policies. After this opening-up to the outside world, China not only introduced foreign capital, technology and so on, but also went on to import the natural and social science knowledge needed for these reforms. After 1979, the fate of Western Economics in China was thus changed – from being completely denied – to be *partially* affirmed – and then to *mostly* affirmed.

After Deng's economic reforms, the first Western Economics textbook (translated by Hongye Gao) to appear in China was the tenth English edition of *Economics* by Nobel Prize Laureate, Paul A. Samuelson (1915–2009) which had originally come out in the West in 1948; in November 1979, the Chinese version of its first half was published by the Commercial Press.[2] From the translators' preface to the book, we can see the subtle changes in the attitude of Chinese academia towards Western Economics. The translator offered a basic evaluation of the new ideas in the preface, which were still the same as those before the reforms, and believed that this textbook represented the inheritance and development of traditional 'vulgar' economics having no scientific value. However, he also thought that perhaps some individual concepts, arguments and methods had *practical* relevance to China and believed that it might be a useful reference-book for Chinese academia.

In the preface, the translator wrote:

> Although from the point of the whole system, the Post-Keynesian Mainstream Economics, namely Neoclassical synthesis, basically has no scientific value, the book has practical significance only in some individual concepts, arguments and methods, and this book is to be regarded as a useful reference work, which can make us get the information and knowledge that we should master.
>
> (Samuelson, 1979, preface: xvi)

Although this text was still mainly the target of criticism, after being published in China in the year 1979, the translator of the book also presented a commentary, 'Ten Reviews on Samuelson's Economics', elsewhere to systematically criticize him as the representative of the Neoclassical synthesis theory. But Chinese academia was to become a rather different place with the onset of the reforms. More and more scholars, as well as college students and graduate students, read the textbooks carefully. They found that the contents, methods, concepts and systems of this textbook were totally different from the familiar 'Political Economy' taught by Chinese economists, and which offered a completely new kind of knowledge. It was not only easy to understand, with high readability, but also seemed to be very useful – it, for example, explained daily economic phenomena, and could help them understand ongoing issues.

Thus, this particular textbook soon became known on many Chinese campuses. From 1979 to 1991, Samuelson's *Economics* (tenth edition) had been reprinted ten times, with a total 103,900 copies sold in China, with its author subsequently becoming the most familiar and popular Western economist in Chinese academic circles.[3] In the 1980s, the economists who were active in Chinese academia, including the enrolled undergraduate and graduate students in the Economics majors, received their knowledge in both Microeconomics and Macroeconomics mainly from the Chinese version of Samuelson.

In 1983, the Commercial Press published the next Chinese edition of Keynes's *General Theory* (1936) (the translator was the same as with the first edition, Y. N. Li); the preface of the Chinese version (written in 1980) still came from the same author, but its contents underwent a major change (Keynes, 1983). The author wrote in this new preface that 'John Maynard Keynes is a famous British bourgeois economist' but deleted the word 'vulgar' in front of his mention of the economist in the first edition of the Chinese version. Although when talking about 'how should we view the Keynesian economic theory', the author of the preface still thought: 'the same with the vulgar economics theory in the history, Keynesian theory is very closely contacted with the bourgeoisie politics and serving for the dictatorship of the bourgeoisie' (Keynes, 1983, preface: xxxii). Also, 'Keynes argues against socialism and communism, and defends capitalism' (Keynes, 1983, preface: xxxiii). However, 'for some certain specific issues, we can refer to some of Keynes's analysis'.

The author of the preface gave a number of examples to verify the statement, such as Keynes's discussion on increasing the employment-rate by expanding investment in incomplete employment conditions, the multiplier theory, the discussion on inflation caused by expanding aggregate demand after achieving full employment, the analysis of the regulation scope, degree and time of fiscal and monetary policy and, as the author concluded, 'these analyses reflect the actual situation' (Keynes, 1983, preface: xxxiv). From the comparison between the prefaces in the two *General Theory* editions, we can also see the attitude of Chinese economists on Western Economics changed before and after the reform and opening up – *from complete negation – to partial affirmation.*

With the further development of the reforms, Chinese academia's attitude towards Western Economics became more and more tolerant and pragmatic, and the negation and affirmation parts changed. They gradually realized that Western Economics had something useful to offer to China and had scientific components, and these useful things or scientific components were not limited to individual concepts, arguments or methods. By the late 1980s, the content of this kind of Economics was developed from being partially affirmed – into a required course for the students with Economics major in Chinese universities. In 1987, the Chinese Ministry of Education officially assigned Western Economics, including both Microeconomics and Macroeconomics, as one of the 12 core-courses for the Finance and Economics majors in Chinese universities (see the chapter by Cohn later in this volume).

This change of opinion implied that the Chinese government had recognized the need to grasp the knowledge of Western Economics in China's reform and opening up and in its economic and social development. Since then, the methods and theories of Western Economics have been gradually applied to China's economic research, economic practice and policy-making. Although around 1987, 1994 and 2005, Chinese academia had had intensive discussions and debates on the problems of 'how to correctly treat the Western Economics' and 'how to deal with the relationship of Marxist Political Economy and Western Economics' (which are still ongoing), the general trend was that Western versions were receiving more and more attention in academic circles in China, and that Western Economics theory and method was applied much more than before.

In this context, scholars further put forward ideas to 'localize' Western Economics in China to make Chinese economics 'standardized' and 'internationalized' (see Lin, 1995). Some scholars even published articles and stated that the Political Economy theory – the 'old' or 'traditional' paradigm of economics – should be criticized and abandoned (see Fan, 1995). These views and ideas could not be delivered before the reform-era and at that time, discussing such thoughts or opinions in class or conference, even without publishing them, might well be punished.

Four attitudes of Chinese academia towards Western Economics

From about the mid and late 1980s, the attitudes of Chinese economists to Western Economics soon became *differentiated*, from being almost unanimously negative to a new position: the *first* attitude was the completely negative attitude; the *second* attitude was completely positive, taking Western Economics as a universal truth that applied to China; again, economists with the *third* attitude believed that at least some schools of Western Economics theories and policies were suitable for China; whilst economists with the *fourth* attitude believed that learning and applying Western Economics required a combination of it and Chinese actual practice.

The first attitude

The scholars holding this attitude still insisted on denying and criticizing Western Economics, and believed that it was not only useless, but also harmful to China. They at most admitted that some individual concepts, arguments and methods in Western Economics had 'reference-value' for China. The scholars holding this view generally came from two age-groups: over the age of 70 and under the age of 45. The former was called the 'Old Left' in the academic circles of China, who formed their attitude to the Western Economics before the reform and opening up and still insist on this attitude today. The latter was known as the 'New Left' in academia of China, who were born during the Cultural Revolution in China (1966–1976) but agreed with the attitude of the former and even denied Western Economics more thoroughly. For example, a scholar over 70 years old, namely Professor Bing Din, wrote in an article in 2006 about 'how to correctly understand and deal with the Western Economics' as follows: 'Western Economics reflects bourgeois interests and protects the ruling of the capitalist private ownership, which is a defensive and unscientific theoretical system' (Din, 2006: 17).

Why was Western Economics not scientific?

The scholar discussed the issue from three angles regarding research methods, research objects and research purposes. In research methods, Western Economics did not study the nature behind economic phenomena he noted, and 'it tends to stay on the surface of economic relationship'; in research objects,

> Western Economics only studies the relationship between human and material issues related to the allocation of resources, instead of the human

relations involved. Although it also sometimes involves the interest-relationships between people, it avoids talking about the 'capitalistic exploitation' between people which is the most essential issue as well as avoiding talking about 'class relations'.

(Din, 2006: 17)

In research purposes, 'Western Economics tries to explain that the capitalist system was the most reasonable and eternal system' (Din, 2006: 17). A young scholar had also published a book in 2002 (see Han, 2002) to specifically criticize Samuelson's *Economics*, by mainly denying the two basic principles of Western mainstream thinking, that is, Adam Smith's (1776) 'invisible hand' and that 'competition' was able to lead to the efficient allocation of resources.

The second attitude

The second attitude is completely contrary to the first one. These scholars thought that economics was the same as mathematics and physics as applied to the entire world, so that economics had no borders, no 'Eastern' or 'Western', no 'class nature', and that Western Economics had general applicability in China. Unlike the first attitude, the second kind of attitude believed that Western Economics was useful to China not only in individual concepts and methods, but also in the basic theory. Although the basic theory was put forward by the Western scholars, it was *universal* – as well as the scientific knowledge that people of different countries were required to master.

Another critic, Gang Fan (2005) was one of the representatives of scholars supporting the second kind of attitude. He believed that like any other fields that could be called 'science', Economics also had differences between the basic theory and the applied theory. *Also, like the basic theory in other scientific fields, the basic one in Economics itself had universal and general scientific significance, and it had no national boundaries, no periodicity and no class nature.* In Economics theory, he continued, there were many contents belonging to the category of the basic Economics theory, such as the behavioural theory, the basic theory on the relationship between consumption preference and material resource allocation, the theory of production function, the theory on the role and interrelations of various factors in the process of economic growth, the theory on the balance between the aggregate demand and aggregate supply, as well as the theory on the formation and evolution of the economic system. These Economic theories could be considered as a common heritage. He concluded that Chinese scholars should seriously learn and master these, even though they were developed by foreigners with different social, historical and cultural backgrounds (see Fan and Liu, 1999).

Here, it was pointed out that for a long time, we had been arguing about how to use Western Economics and how to develop our own economics. In the past, there was a common view that the basic content of Western Economics was not acceptable and what we could refer to and make of use were the specific tools of analysis and other approaches for solving practical problems, such as the various schools of policies due to different policy opinions. From this contributor's point of view, this is just a kind of 'upside down' argument. Regarding the modern Economics developed by Westerners in the recent one or 200 years, the most useful and important part includes the basic theories that belong to the *common heritage* and the related basic contents and methods (see Fan and Liu, 1999).

The third attitude

The scholars holding this attitude neither completely affirmed nor completely denied Western Economics; they affirmed and accepted some certain Western economists or schools of economics theory, and rejected others at the same time. Scholars who held this attitude generally had the experience of overseas study in the United States or United Kingdom after the reform and opening up. Weiying Zhang (2009, 2010) was representative of scholars supporting this kind of attitude. He had already received a Master's degree and a PhD in economics from University of Oxford respectively, in 1992 and 1994. After the 2008 American Sub-prime Mortgage Crisis was evolving into the International Financial Crisis, China's economy was also to suffer and fall into recession. In 2009, when the Chinese government embarked on the *proactive* fiscal policy to expand aggregate demand and restore economic growth, Zhang put forward an appeal to 'completely bury the Keynesian' (see the chapter on Keynes in this volume). He said:

> It is wrong that some people attribute the reasons for this economic crisis to market failure, especially to economic liberalization. This crisis is not the result of market failure, but the failure of government policy. It is the result of government intervention and excessive intervention. Therefore, it is necessary to return to the position of Austrian school represented by Mises and Hayek that have a firm belief in the market. We should seek the explanations of the cause of economic crisis and the solution to the crisis from the economic theory of Mises and Hayek, and completely bury Keynesian view that advocates government intervention.
>
> (www.sina.com.cn, 17 February 2009)

Zhang also wrote:

> The factual and logical analysis show that rather than market failure, the crisis is the failure of government policy; rather than business people being too greedy, it is the failure of the government officials in charge of the currency. In my opinion, this crisis may offer the opportunity to revive the Austrian School of Economics and to complete bury Keynesian Economics.
>
> (Zhang, 2009)

In 2010, when China's economy entered a new round of downward cycle, he also proposed that it was 'back to Adam Smith, farewell to Keynes'.

He thought that according to Adam Smith's view (1776), a country's economic growth and development came from the 'division of labour' and then there was 'specialization'. This was followed by improved skill-levels and concentrated R&D, and finally there was invention and creation. The depth of the division of labour was determined by the scale of market transactions. The expansion of market scale would thus lead to the development of the division of labour, technological progress and economic development, and further expand the market by increasing the level of income, which formed a 'virtuous cycle'.

Therefore,

> from the perspective of Adam Smith's (1776) theory, China's economic growth needs further opening up and developing the domestic market, to create new products to meet market demand, which is the duty of the entrepreneurs. From the point of view of Keynesian theory (1936), economic growth depends on the increasing of domestic demand, especially through monetary policy and fiscal policy to stimulate aggregate demand, which becomes the function of the government. From Smith's point of view, the increase in demand means to develop the market, which must rely on the innovation of the entrepreneur. Whilst from Keynes's point of view, the increase in demand does not rely on innovation, but rely on the economic stimulus policies by the government.... Due to the influence of Keynes's theory, we have formed some misunderstandings.
>
> (Zhang, 2010)

Among the scholars holding the third attitude, some people believed in the 'New Institutional Economics' represented by Nobel Prize winners, Ronald Coase (1910–2013) and Douglass North (1920–2015), whilst others appreciated another Laureate, Milton Friedman (1912–2006) as the representative of 'Monetarism'; last, further others took up 'Evolutionary Economics' or 'Supply-Side Economics'.

The fourth attitude

These scholars believed that Western Economics was the theory and experience of Western developed market economies. Compared to such countries, China had on the other hand different national conditions present in its system, culture, as well as in its economic and social development level. Hence, we should study and use Western Economics according to the actual situation in China, neither totally denying Western Economics, nor ignoring its conditions and indiscriminately imitating Western versions.

In 2005, Chinese academics set off on a new round of discussions on 'how to deal with Marxist Economics and Western Economics'. When talking about 'what kind of road should China's economics follow', Hongye Gao (2005) wrote:

China's economics should go in the lead with Marxism as the guide, and combine Marxist Economics with Western Economics. The reasons are as follows: first, our country is in the socialist market economy, and the Western countries are the capitalist market economy. Although there are crucial differences between the two economic systems, they have a lot in common as the market economy. Second, one of Deng Xiaoping's contributions was to point out that market economy was just a means or method in managing the economy. Since it is a method, socialism can also use it, and our country is doing so at present. Third, as a method, it must be subject to the guidance of certain kind of theory in use in order to obtain the benefit for the people. That is to say that the management methods of the market economy must be guided by Marxism. Fourth, Western Economics has dual nature; it is not only the component of Western ideology, but also the experience of Western market management. We certainly should abandon the former, but for the latter methods summarized, we can use for reference and absorption. Of course, the reference and absorption of the management method must also take account of the differences in national conditions. Experience cannot be completely separated from the theoretical guidance, which is another reason why it must be under the guidance of Marxism. Fifth, as a method, Western Economics may not always be logically correct. Many examples show that there are inappropriate places in the theoretical basis of Western Economics. Sixth, at present, the vast majority of people in the world either believes in Marxist Economics or believes in Western Economics. Even from the surface phenomenon, the two have their vitality and value. Hence, it is necessary to combine the two economics theories.

(Gao, 2005: 1)

Ten years ago or so, this contributor (Fang, 2005) had pointed out that even apart from the contents of the system, ideology and values, Western Economics was written based on the practice and experience of the developed market economy countries, as well as generated and developed vis-à-vis the background of the economic conditions and issues in the those countries. There were, it was noted, at least three aspects of differences between China's national conditions and that of the Western developed countries:

First, China is now in the primary stage of socialism. This means that China's social systems are different from those of the developed countries and the development stages and development levels of China's economy are different from those in the developed countries. It is a critical time for China to catch up with the developed ones vis-à-vis the development level. Second, China is in the transition to the socialist market economy. It means that both the old and the new systems will play a role in the economic operation of China. Third, China is a large developing country with a population of over 1.3 billion. This means that the huge population pressure, the contradiction between population and resources and environment, the contradiction between population growth and economic growth and the improvement of living standards are the unique and important economic and social problems that we are facing. Therefore, we cannot simply apply Western Economics to China, but should combine it with China's national conditions, carry on a kind of '*Chinization*' transformation of Western Economics and then use it to study economic issues.

(Fang, 2005: 13)

He continued:

To learn and study Western Economics, we not only need to systematically study the assumption premise, logic structure, and analysis methods of Western Economics, but also need to carry on analysis and reflection on the following questions: What's the contents of Western Economics we can use directly? What's the contents that need to be transformed? What's the contents that should be abandoned? What's the contents that China does not have and not mature in the current economic conditions, and temporarily not suitable for use?

(Fang, 2005: 14)

In this way, writers could best carry on the '*Chinization*' of Western Economics, whilst combining it with 'Chinese realities' (Fang, 2005: 15).

We can now see from the mainstream trends and policy practice in Chinese economists' circles, that there are more and more currently holding the fourth kind of attitude. Now, in their research and publications, Chinese economists generally take a *pragmatic* attitude towards the Western Economics: if a certain theory, model or method is useful in analysing the economic problems in China, they just take and use it directly. But sometimes, they need to slightly adjust these theories, models and methods to use them according to the actual local situation; they have no comments or ignore the theories, models and methods that are not suitable for the analysis of its economic problems.

Discussion

Since the onset of Deng's reforms in 1979, the position and influence of Western Economics in China has decidedly changed. Before and at the beginning of the reform and opening up, Western Economics in China was criticized, denied and rejected, whilst it is nowadays applied much more than before in Chinese academia and government policy-making. Many people even think that the Western model has become China's mainstream economics, whilst 'Marxist Economics' has become *marginalized* and public discussion continues on this point (see the chapter by Cohn in this volume).

The *Economics Research Journal* sponsored by the Economic Research Institute of the Chinese Academy of Social Sciences is the *most influential journal* in the field of Chinese Economics. According to the statistics of articles published annually in this very journal, at the beginning of the reform era, the proportions of the papers written on the basis of Marxist economic theory, Western Economics theory and other theories respectively were 54.5 per cent, 40.9 per cent and 4.5 per cent; since the mid-1990s, the proportions of these three respectively are less than 1.0 per cent, close to 100 per cent and almost zero. *In other words, papers published in the journal are almost swamped by Western Economics, as shown in Figure 17.1.* This also indicates that the turning point of Marxist Economics and Western Economics in Chinese economics appears in the mid-1980s.

In 1998 and then in 2008, in order to cope with the impact of the Asian financial crisis and the international financial crisis on China's economy, the Chinese government conducted a massive intervention to expand domestic demand and stable economic growth, which was regarded as an application of Keynesian economics in China. Since November 2015, the Chinese government has, in turn, begun to implement the 'Supply-Side Structural Reform', which is considered as the most recent key change in the Chinese economic policy guidance. However, the debate still continues.

Conclusions

Why has the fate of Western Economics in China thus seen such a dramatic change? This contributor believes the main reasons include: (1) the transition of the Chinese economic system from a highly centralized planned economic system to a socialist market economic system needing Western Economics. For Chinese academia and the government, how to build China's socialist market economy and how to run and manage the market economy are new issues.

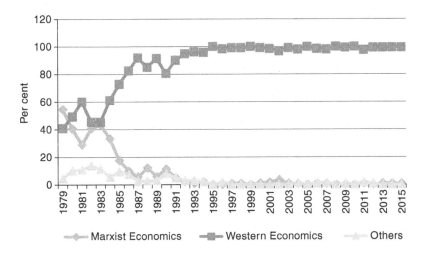

Figure 17.1 The influence of Western Economics on Chinese Economics.

Source: papers published in *Economic Research Journal*, 1979–2015.

Western Economics is the theoretical summary of the operation and practice of the market economy in the Western developed countries. The contents include general analysis and principles of the market economy. (2) China continues to deepen reform and opening up and is becoming more and more inclusive of the technology, knowledge, culture and even religion from abroad, and it has more confidence in the absorption of foreign knowledge and culture. (3) Due to the continuous reform policies experienced, more and more Chinese economists recognize that it is time to make a distinction between Economics and Ideology: Western Economics contains Western culture and the values of Western World, but it is not the equivalent to being the ideology of the Western countries.

Notes

1 The 'Western Economics' in the chapter refers to the popular mainstream economics in Western developed countries after the end of the Second World War, including micro-economics, macroeconomics and other economics schools. Chinese economists divide these before the Second World War into two different stages according to Marx's view: first it was called 'bourgeois classical economics', later called 'bourgeois vulgar economics'. The economics evaluations of the two stages are also very different: classical economics is seen as the coexistence of science and 'vulgar' ingredients, but with the main component of science, whilst 'vulgar' economics is 'unscientific'.
2 The book was translated by Professor Hongye Gao, Renmin University of China, Beijing and the Chinese version was in three volumes and published respectively in 1979, 1981 and 1982 by the Commercial Press.
3 The eleventh to the nineteenth Chinese versions of Samuelson's *Economics* were published later in China and translated by Hongye Gao and other Chinese scholars.

References

Din, B. (2006). 'Correctly understanding and treating Marx's economics and Western Economics', *Journal of Nanjing University of Finance and Economics*, 1: 16–17.
Fan, G. (1995). 'Soviet style criticism', *Economic Research Journal*, 10: 70–80.
Fan, G. and S. D. Liu (1999). *Study on the Development of Economic Theory in Economic Reform*. Changsha: Hunan People's Press.
Fang, F. Q. (2005). 'Some problems in the Western Economics teaching', *China University Teaching*, 9: 13–15.
Gao, H. (2005). Comment, *Guangming Daily*, 27 December: 1.
Han, D. Q. (2002). *Critique of Samuelson's Economics: Competitive Economics*. Beijing: Economic Science Press.
Keynes, J. M. [1936] (1957). *The General Theory of Employment, Interest and Money*. Chinese version. Beijing: Commercial Press. Translated by Y. Xu.
Keynes, J.M. [1936] (1963). *The General Theory of Employment, Interest and Money*. Chinese version. Beijing: Commercial Press. Translated by Y. Xu, reprint of 1957 edition.
Keynes, J. M. [1936] (1977). *The General Theory of Employment, Interest and Money*. Chinese version. Beijing: Commercial Press. Translated by Y. Xu.
Keynes, J. M. [1936] (1983). *The General Theory of Employment, Interest and Money*. Chinese version. Beijing: Commercial Press. Translated by Y. Xu.

Lin, J. Y. (1995). 'Localization, standardization and internationalization', Beijing: *Economic Research Journal*, 10: 13–17.

Marshall, A. [1890] (1964). *Principles of Economics*. Beijing: Commercial Press. Translated by Z. Zhu.

Samuelson, P. A. [1948] (1979). *Economics.* Chinese version. 10th edition, Beijing: Commercial Press. Translated by H. Gao.

Smith, A. [1776] (1880). *An Inquiry into the Nature and Causes of the Wealth of Nations*, edited by James E. Thorold Rogers. 2nd edition, Oxford: Clarendon Press, 2 vols [translated into Chinese by F. Yan in 1902].

Zhang, W. Y. (2009). 'Completely bury the Keynesian.' An address in Yabuli China Entrepreneurs Forum, *Sina Finance and Economics* (www.sina.com.cn, accessed 2 February 2009).

Zhang, W. Y. (2010). 'The return to Adam Smith, farewell to Keynes.' *Sina Finance and Economics* (www.sina.com.cn, accessed 20 November 2010).

18 Western Neoclassical vs Marxist Economics in the PRC after Mao

Another kind of revolution?

Steve Cohn[1]

Introduction

The most important development in the first decade of the twenty-first century in the People's Republic of China (PRC, hereafter to be referred to as 'China'), at least from the focal point of this chapter, has arguably been the return of a sufficient number of Western-trained economists to create a critical mass of Neoclassical economists. In 1998, China had significantly increased the 'perks' offered to returning Economics PhDs, such as salaries *four times* the normal scale at its universities (Chow, 2000: 57) and approval of joint positions that permitted professors to continue to teach at Western ones for significant portions of the year. This initiative is part of a broader continuing Chinese project to repatriate scientific and technical experts living abroad.[2]

Interestingly, a Chinese economist, Cong Cao (2008) cites one other unusual factor that had formerly discouraged the return of Western educated PhDs. This is the attenuation of their social networks (*guanxi*) after they had spent long time-periods overseas (Cao, 2008: 331, 340). *Guanxi* (a Chinese version of 'who you know') has traditionally played a significant role in Chinese political, economic and social life for centuries, perhaps casting a bigger shadow than in the West. Until many foreign-educated economists returned to China, Western educated economists lacked the strong social networks necessary for professional advancement in China. The recent assemblage of a critical mass of Neoclassical adherents holding official positions in Chinese universities, think-tanks and government offices has enabled networks like those of the Chinese Economists Society to offer social linkages to returning students. Indeed, more economics degree holders have returned to China than other advanced degree-holders (see Trescott's chapters in this volume).

Current profile of Chinese economic thinking

The current structure organizing Chinese Economics education and research has, in my opinion, several key characteristics:

1   *It has become significantly 'Neoclassical' since 1979.*
2   *It has been influenced by the eminent 'Chicago School'.*[3]

3   *It has favoured mathematical argument in both research and Economics instruction and appears to encourage a somewhat narrow technocratic approach to analysis.*
4   *It privileges the 'New Institutionalist' Economics, in the tradition of Nobel Laureates Douglass North (1920–2015) and Ronald Coase (1910–2013), when addressing historical and institutional issues.*
5   *Its subtexts may be interpreted to strongly endorse the transition to capitalism in China.*
6   *It now gives relatively little attention to Marxist and non-Marxist Heterodox Economics paradigms.*
7   *Its major critics are most likely to come from outside rather than inside the economics profession.*
8   *It has recently opened up at least modestly to 'Heterodox' Economics thinking.*

The discussion below goes on to elaborate many of these points.

Current status of Neoclassical Economics

A 1987 review of Chinese Economics education by the *World Bank* played an important role in reorganizing Chinese economic education along Neoclassical lines. By 2010, most introductory Economics textbooks in China were probably similar to those used in the United States.[4] Today, the institutional signature of Neoclassical Economics is visible everywhere: from an airport bill-board picture of top 'guru', Professor Justin Yifu Lin (1952–), advertising Peking University's economic expertise, to the study-guides for admission to graduate study; from the editorial policies of leading Chinese Economics journals to the requirements for securing a university teaching position and academic promotion. Since the turn of the century, there has been a flood of academic conferences largely elaborating Neoclassical theory, both in China and among Chinese economists overseas. Illustrative of these meetings are the annual conferences of the Chinese Economists Society, the Chinese Economic Association of North America, and the China Center for Economic Research. Neoclassical models also provide the back-drop for many business-oriented conferences in China. In this regard, Hong Kong's Universities have also contributed actively to the Neoclassical menu, as well as Taiwan's (see Das's chapters in this volume).

Most Chinese economics discussions give little attention to Heterodox Economics. A bibliometric study of the articles published in the *China Economic Review (CER)* (the journal of the Chinese Economists Society) *1989–2010*, for example, found that less than 1 per cent of the papers addressed Heterodox Economics or methodological issues as defined by JEL subject codes (Du, 2011: 24). From 1977 to 1990, only 3.5 Heterodox articles were published per year in 11 leading Chinese journals (Zhang and Xu, 2013: 311).

The evolution of Chinese Economics continues to follow the path taken by the US profession. Three-quarters of the top 30 researchers referenced in *CER* articles (1989–2010) were affiliated with US institutions. Only about one-sixth were affiliated with Chinese institutions, despite the focus of the journal on Chinese economic issues. Furthermore, a foreign PhD (usually American) is required to teach at most prestigious Chinese universities. This still ongoing 'Americanization' of Chinese Economics education has had predictable consequences.

There has been a tendency in such education to concentrate on training students to use relatively complicated mathematical techniques. This habit has tended to 'crowd out' extended reflection on the social theory embodied in Economics models as well as in Economic Theory itself. Many key assumptions are accepted uncritically, as students struggle simply to master the quantitative techniques. This habit of mind seems to have migrated to Chinese Economics education, creating problems that are acknowledged even by Neoclassical economists such as Harvard's Dwight Perkins (1934–):

> [M]uch work on developing economies involves finding a data set and then seeing what kinds of statistically significant relationships one can find using one's econometric skills.... One does not learn much about the problems that dominate the economies in which these studies are carried out or the solutions to those problems.
>
> (Perkins, 2002: 413–414)

Ever since the entrance exams used for admission to Princeton's Gregory *Chow's* (1930–) prestigious Summer Workshops in the mid-1980s, a project that launched the renewal of Neoclassical Economic education in China, the recruitment of students with strong math and science backgrounds has characterized the 'Westernizing' of these departments. Today, the presence of mathematical requirements appears to be taken as a proxy for 'rigour' in assessing such Chinese programmes. Expertise in 'Political Economy' (the term often used to represent Marxist orientations) is devalued. For example, at the *Shanghai University for Finance and Economics* (SUFE), one of the most 'pluralist' Economics institutions in China, all PhD students in Economics and Political Economy (that is, Marxist Economics) have to pass three qualifying exams: one in largely Neoclassical microeconomics, one in largely Neoclassical macroeconomics, and one in econometrics. When suggestions were made that students have the option of substituting an exam in Political Economy for one of the three qualifying exams, administrators worried about 'diluting the rigour' and reputation of SUFE.

Since the late 1990s, the leading Chinese Economics journal *Economic Research* (*Jingji Yanjiu*) has tended to emphasize econometrics-oriented articles similar to those published in American Neoclassical journals. A bibliometric study of the methodology of *CER* articles found them becoming more formalistic (that is, 'formal plus empirical' data) from 2000 to 2010 (Du, 2011: 28–30).

Another commentator, *Zhou Yi*, an especially thoughtful Professor at Shanghai's *Fudan* University, has described the typical Chinese Economics article as follows:

The standard assembly line for 'manufacturing' an economics paper ... intended to be published in such a leading Chinese mainstream economics journal should be like this: Literature overview→Copy an econometric model from a Western mainstream economics source→Put data and statistics from Chinese 'reality' into the model→Use of standard econometric technique....→If the result is satisfactory, the author will eulogize the Western mainstream model.... If the result seems all too aberrant, then he will write that ... improvement for the paper will depend on further research in the future.[5]

Neoclassical subtexts

In many ways, the mathematics of Neoclassical Economics and general equilibrium theory has served as a *Trojan Horse* for the popularization of 'free-market' subtexts in China. This outcome was more a sociological result of Neoclassical training than a logical result of human reason. The implicit and explicit assumptions of Neoclassical theory concerning matters such as human nature (methodological individualism and *homo economicus*), market efficiency (perfect information) and the purposes of economic activity (to maximize GDP per capita) have been internalized in contemporary Chinese theory. The pre-1978 focus of Chinese Economics on understanding the 'laws of motion' of capitalism as a social system and the implications of different public policies for building socialism in China has largely been abandoned.

Epistemologically, recent Chinese Economics has tended to de-politicize China's market reforms by portraying them as a form of technical rationality. Longxiang Song's doctoral dissertation, completed in the US, provides a striking example of the internalization of this stance. Song (1995) characterizes Neoclassical theory as a science that should command belief in the same fashion as modern physics. This claim allows the subtexts of this genre of Economics to similarly enjoy scientific status. He writes:

Economics has gained the status of a science.... [M]odern mathematical tools have been widely used.... [E]conomics is widely recognized as an *experimental* discipline much like the physical and biological sciences.... [E]conomic research has been highly *professionalized and technically* oriented.... There is significant *consensus* on the fundamental principles of the discipline among mainstream economists.... [P]rominent philosophers of science ... hold mainstream economics in almost as great esteem as they hold physics.... Undoubtedly, economics in the Western World is a science.

(Song, 1995: 1–4, emphases in original)

The above uncritical transformation of a paradigmatic view of Economics into universal truths reflects the self-image of the Neoclassical school. This self-portrait has been most eloquently challenged by the University of Chicago-trained economist, D. McCloskey (1942–). In many scholarly articles, and most comprehensively in her book, *The Rhetoric of Economics* (1985), McCloskey convincingly argues that Neoclassical Economics cannot be treated in 'positivist' terms as a universal, objective, science. It is best understood as a plausible set of metaphors and stories that aim to make useful inferences about topics for which it is generally impossible to do experiments. The recent blindsiding of most Neoclassical economists by the financial crisis of 2008, illustrates the misreading of modern Economics embodied in Song's bold claim that such conclusions can be afforded the status of the predictions, laws and other claims of modern physics.

Another source, *Wang Hui*, like McCloskey, treats Neoclassical Economics as a system of 'metaphors' but, unlike this latter work, he rejects these metaphors as adequate depictions of economic reality. He portrays such Economics as a kind of technical ideology that has increasingly oriented Chinese economic practice towards Neoliberalism. He writes,

> Today ... the dominant discipline in China is neo-classical economics. This is a development of the nineties.... [A]fter 1990, Hayekian ideas gained real ascendancy.... So currently economics is not just a technical discipline, anymore than its predecessors: it too is an imperative worldview.
>
> (Wang, 2003: 77–78)

Counter tendencies challenging neoclassical and neoliberal paradigms

Over the past 20 years, several events have encouraged the Chinese to reassess Western models. These include: the 1997 Asian financial crisis and heavy-handed IMF response, a major critical study of Neoliberalism undertaken by the Chinese Academy of Social Sciences in 2003–2004, public outrage over corrupt privatizations in 2004–2005, resentment over US Congressional denunciation of Chinese efforts to purchase Unocal (a US oil company) in 2005, continuing US–China acrimony over exchange rates, and, probably most importantly, the weakness of the US and other Western economies during the global financial crisis of 2008 and the subsequent recession. Popular concerns in China about growing income and wealth inequality, unemployment and economic insecurity, corruption, environmental degradation, and the crowding-out of both Chinese firms by large foreign corporations and traditional Chinese culture by consumerism have also contributed to potential interest in reviewing current Economic theory.[6]

Another factor suggesting the potential for rethinking Economic policies (as well as theories) in China has been the rising level of social protest and labour protest in China.[7] Many of these incidents were about unpaid wages and pensions and the expropriation of rural peasant land for non-agricultural use without fair compensation. It is not yet clear what the ideological spillover of these protests will be, but some echoes have surfaced in what has become known as the Chinese New Left. A New Left website, *Utopia*, had 47 million hits between 2003 and 2008 (Li, 2008: 2). Attacks on neoliberal policies have also emerged from the New Rural Reconstruction Movement. Almost all of my interviewees in 2014, however, found little influence of the 'New Left' within university economics departments at either the student or faculty level.

I am not sure what the impact of these protests has been on economic theorists within the Chinese Communist Party (CCP). In 2004, Cheng Enfu, a leading Marxist economist, challenged the Communist Party's retreat from Marxist theory. In particular, he attacked the teaching of Neoclassical Economics as the core of the subject by some instructors from the Central University of the Communist party, at an educational retreat for Ministers and 'leaders of promise'. His attack was apparently well received by some audiences (Interview, 28 May 2011, notes).

Current status of Marxist Economics

Marxist Economics continues to enjoy the costs and benefits of official state support. All students in Chinese universities, regardless of their major, are still required to study some Marxist theory, which includes discussion of Marxist Political Economy. The amount of required study has been reduced significantly however since 1978, as measured in terms of required courses and/or credit hours. The amount of Marxist Economics required of non-economics majors has almost disappeared, having been condensed into a short section or two of a single required course. Co-curricular Marxist oriented requirements, such as required Saturday political-study groups, also seem to have been discontinued.

One of the factors that may have contributed to the weakening of Marxist Economics for non-majors was the difficulty of covering in one or two courses both traditional Marxist themes and the ideas of theorists allied with Deng Xiaoping's (1904–1997) marketization demarche. One of my interviewees in 2011 implied that the authorities sometimes pushed the new ideas at the expense of traditional Marxist Economics analysis, leading to a loss of depth and perhaps overall coherence in the traditional segments of the course. The redesign of the curriculum appears to have been directed by the Ministry of Education.[8]

Another criticism some students have made about university Marxist Economics courses is that they repeat material covered in high school without raising the level of difficulty or subtlety to a college-level. Sometimes, this criticism points to the relatively low level of 'math' used in Marxist, as compared to Neoclassical, university classes. The publication of a new textbook series in Marxist Political Economy including many more mathematical models has tried to respond to this criticism (Zhou, 2016).

The near unanimous ridicule of the required Marxist course among students was particularly striking. Descriptions like 'mind numbing and useless' abounded among both proponents and critics of orthodox Neoclassical Economics. By student accounts, most required Marxist theory courses concentrate on memorization of key passages of Marxist literature and identification of dates and important Party pronouncements. They appear to repeat material covered in high school in a similarly routinized and unappealing way. As one student memorably put it, they 'taught us everything we don't believe' (Interview). His remark elicited confirmatory laughter among a group of fellow graduate students at a meeting I attended of students interested in exploring alternatives to Neo-classical Economics. On the other hand, when taught by thoughtful and motivated instructors, it appears that required Marxist courses can still retain student interest. This seems to be the case at *Renmin (People's) University* in the capital, where the President and traditional campus culture have been more supportive of Marxist Economics (Interview, 2011). At *Peking University*, nearby, one thoughtful professor of Marxist Economics estimated that only 10–20 per cent of his students get excited by his Marxist class.

Whilst there appear to be many dedicated professors of Marxist Economics in China (especially among the older faculty), the institutional presence of Marxist Economics is often more heavy-handed and less subtle than the work of these scholars and teachers. Rather than treating Marxist Economics and Marxist theory as an intellectual framework open to challenge, creative evolution and contested applications, the theory has been simply treated by the State as a matter of faith. This is probably due to the theory's ongoing role in legitimizing the monopoly of political power held by the Communist Party in China. Theoretical discussions among some leading Chinese Marxist economists about the status of the 'labour theory of value', for example, have been heavily influenced by the politics of 'legitimation'. Rather than debate the empirical or conceptual validity of the labour theory of value, it appears the theory's status in Chinese Marxism is still a function of its perceived political usefulness.

As might be expected, the Chinese Communist Party's attempt to protect Marxist theory from criticism appears to have backfired in academia. It has rendered Marxism a 'dead theory' among many college students, and it has undermined the ability of Marxist theory to compete with other theories. But times may be changing.

Marxist Economics for undergraduate students in economics schools

Students enrolled in Economics schools (which may include academic concentrations such as accounting majors as well as pure Economics majors) are required to take more Marxist Economics than students in other schools. Here too, however, the presence of Marxist Economics has been greatly reduced.

Administratively, some Marxist economists are housed in separate 'groups' (frequently termed political-economy groups) or in separate institutes for the study of Marxism, distinct from Economics groups or departments. The latter are heavily dominated by professors trained in the Neoclassical school. There does not appear to be significant collaboration or interaction between the Marxist and Neoclassical groups. Undergraduate majors take mainly Neoclassical economics courses, with an emphasis on mathematics. There remain, however, more residual Marxist classes offered (especially as 'electives'), and a greater presence of the history of Economic Thought and Economic History in Chinese programmes than in the United States.

For example, whilst the Economics major at Peking University emphasizes Neoclassical ideas, the major still includes a two-year, four-course history-requirement. This appears to be a legacy of tradition and the reputation of Peking's department for strength in this area. The focus exceeds the attention to historical issues in many other university curricula.[9] Even here, however, the substantive impact of history on Economics education seems to be declining. The methodology used in Economic History classes also seems to have shifted towards Neoclassical models of rational, optimizing individuals. As one professor put it, some of the history courses are actually 'anti-history', taught in the methodologically individualistic tradition of the rest of Neoclassical Economics. Professors at other Chinese universities report pressures to replace the historical components of Chinese economics education – with more technique-oriented courses on the above lines.

My impression is that most Chinese Economics majors are studying the subject because they believe it will help them 'find a good job'. Seeking employment with foreign firms in the financial sector seems to be especially popular. These students are not likely to regard Marxist Economics as something that will be helpful in achieving their career-goals in the business or academic world.

Marxist Economics, graduate school and academic employment

Even more than undergraduate study, graduate programmes in Economics departments are dominated by Neoclassical ideas. Getting a teaching position at an elite university, and increasingly even at a moderately good Chinese university, almost requires a foreign PhD with a Neoclassical stamp. Often, the best undergraduate Economics majors do not enrol in China's leading universities' graduate programmes; they go abroad (Interviews, 2014).

If they are able to get a university teaching position after they graduate, the pressures to maintain a Neoclassical research agenda continue. Chinese Economics departments appear to have a relatively formal set of publishing requirements for promotion. Journals are divided into several quality-levels, as in the West. Candidates have to publish in a predetermined number of these journals at particular levels to be promoted to associate and full professor. The journal rankings generally privilege the above cited Neoclassical Economics. At some universities, professors also get significant monetary bonuses (as much as 50,000–100,000 Yuan/RMB) for a publication in one of the designated elite journals (Interview, 2011).

As noted earlier, beginning around 1992 and accelerating in the mid-1990s to the present, the proportion of Marxist articles in the leading Chinese Economics journal, *Economic Research* (*Jingji Yanjiu*), declined significantly (see the chapter by Fang in this volume). By the early 2000s, the journal accepted few Marxist papers.[10] A publication in a leading Western Neoclassical journal, such as the *American Economic Review*, is treated as equivalent, or perhaps even superior, to the leading Chinese journals. It appears that much less 'credit' is given for publications in Western Heterodox Economics journals, especially journals not indexed in the SSCI.

Self-criticism by Marxist economists

Some of the Marxist economists I interviewed criticized their Marxist colleagues for failing to innovate or update Marxist thinking. They lamented the lack of attention to mathematical techniques and the continued use of old textbooks. They implied that this gave students the impression that Marxism was dated and had been superseded by more modern theories. The administrative separation of Marxist economists from economics departments in China may have contributed to a similar shift of emphases in Chinese Marxism.

There also appears to be a tendency among some disingenuous or poorly trained Marxist economists to abandon the substance of the theory and use Marxist language to convey Neoclassical ideas. This charade sometimes leads to statements reminiscent of Orwellian 'doublespeak'. David Kotz, an American Marxist economist who co-directs the Political Economy programme at the Shanghai University of Finance and Economics (SUFE), has collected some memorable quotes from a conference in Beijing on property rights in 2006. Here are two brief oxymoronic examples:

> When an SOE [State Owned Enterprise] is turned into a joint stock corporation with many shareholders, it represents socialization of ownership as Marx and Engels described it.
> [and]
> The nature of ownership of the enterprise has no bearing on whether a country is capitalist.... Enterprises should always be privately owned and operated for a profit.
>
> (Kotz, 2007: 60)

Reviving Marxist Economics

One promising avenue for reviving Chinese Marxism is the growing popularity of 'Ecological Marxism' in China. Interest in Ecological Marxism has been spurred by China's serious environmental problems, the global impact of green movements, and residual elements in the Communist Party still interested in Marxist critiques of capitalism (Wang, 2012).

Ecological Marxism links inherent aspects of capitalism, such as what are dubbed commodification, capitalist competition, and consumerism, to current global environmental crises. From a Marxist perspective, capitalism's great success has been enabling and imposing pressures for capital accumulation and market expansion on host societies. This has produced, they go on, impressive economic growth and enormous power for leading capitalist states. But this process contains within itself no limiting principle and, left unchecked, threatens to destroy the environmental support system surrounding the economy. Thus, what has been a positive strength of capitalism has turned into a potentially serious liability. Ecological Marxism explores the nature of this contradiction and the design of alternative socialist principles for regulating humanity's interaction with the environment.

Prior to 1990, there had been only four articles on Ecological Marxism published in Chinese academic journals. However, by 2010, an astounding 598 articles had been published, along with nine books, 15 dissertations and 69 Masters theses (see Wang, 2012: 36–37; Wang *et al.*, 2013, 2014). Based on the pattern of citations I have seen, it appears that many important initiatives are coming from platforms outside of economics departments, such as from philosophy and sociology departments, and researchers associated with *Wen Tiejun's* 'New Rural Reconstruction Movement'. Attention to environmental issues accelerated especially quickly after the Party's commitment to an 'ecological civilization' in 2007.

There are, however, serious constraints on Ecological Marxism's expansion within China. This is partly due to the subtexts of primary stage theories of socialism that call for maximizing economic growth and the advancement of the forces of production. The *Dengist* statist project of maximizing Chinese national power also undermines pursuit of ecological Marxist projects.

Professor Cheng Enfu is an important scholar who has undertaken several institutional initiatives to re-energize Chinese Marxism. He is the head of the Academy of Marxism of the Chinese Academy of Social Sciences (CASS), one of the founders of the Shanghai School of Marxism and the World Association for Political Economy (WAPE), as well as the chief editor of WAPE's journal, the *World Review of Political Economy*. Whilst retaining a fairly orthodox Marxist viewpoint, he has tried to open Marxist discourse in China to interactions with other Heterodox paradigms, such as Post-Keynesian, Ecological, Neo-Ricardian-Sraffan and, to some extent, Feminist economics. He has also tried to welcome more mathematical analysis alongside qualitative analysis. These projects are reflected in a new three-volume set of Marxist political-economy textbooks co-edited by Cheng in 2012. Their attention to mathematical models is especially distinctive (Zhou, 2016).

WAPE has sought to build intellectual bridges between Chinese Marxists, Marxist theorists around the globe, and other interested left-oriented economists. The *World Review of Political Economy* (established in 2010) combines a focus on traditional topics of Marxist Political Economy, such as value theory, crisis theory and analysis of the labour process, with an openness to issues highlighted in other Heterodox paradigms, such as environmental issues. David Kotz is one of WAPE's five Vice Chairpersons. In collaboration with Terrence McDonough (a member of WAPE's standing council), he has helped develop the theory of Social Structures of Accumulation – an approach that combines ideas from Marxist theory, institutionalist theory and Post-Keynesian theory to help explain the behaviour of different macroeconomic periods. This kind of analysis illustrates the spirit of the *World Review of Political Economy*.

The *China Review of Political Economy* (CRPE) is another recently established Marxist journal that seeks to re-energize Chinese Marxist theory and link Marxism to broader intellectual currents. Founded in 2002 as a book publisher, CRPE began journal publication in 2010. The journal's editorial board reflects a variety of Marxist perspectives and includes economists Robert Brenner, Makoto Itoh, Dic Lo and John Roemer.

As these brief descriptions indicate, both the CRPE and WAPE combine academic goals with the political project of rebuilding a basis for socialism within China. This subtext distinguishes Marxist analyses from many other Heterodox paradigms, whose projects more often involve reform or regulation of capitalism, rather than its transcendence.

Political sensitivities make it difficult to investigate how the Chinese Communist Party thinks about Economics education. Chinese universities still have a dual administrative structure. The formal academic line of authority flows from university presidents through deans to department chairs. It is shadowed by a parallel Communist Party line of authority with its own equivalent of department representatives, deans and university leaders. It seems likely that this bureaucracy endorsed or at least tolerated the shift in economics education, but I have little direct information about this. No one I interviewed identified the Party structure as a major force shaping university economic discourse.

Future prospects of Marxist Economics

Whilst Marxist Economics retains official endorsement and some financial support from the Chinese government, as well as a latent familiarity among many people (critics often refer to this as 'nostalgia'), Marxist Economics has suffered a loss of credibility among the general public and total rejection by Western trained economists in China. Whilst all university students are still required to take a college course on Marxism, the class does not appear to be taken seriously by most students. Marxist economic research is not valued highly by many leading Chinese Economics journals and a PhD from a Western or Japanese university (usually geared towards Neoclassical Economics) is required for most elite teaching positions. It seems likely that attention to Marxist theory in Economics will lag behind attention to Marxist ideas in other disciplines.

Current status of Heterodox Economics

Heterodox Economics, interestingly enough, was well represented in China during the first half of the twentieth century (Trescott, 2007). Many Chinese students studied economics in the West and brought home American Institutionalist economics, a forerunner of Post-Keynesian, Neo-Ricardian and neo-Marxian economics and the ideas of Henry George (1839–1897).

After 1949, the status of all variants of Western Economics collapsed. Very few Heterodox articles, books or translated works were published in China from 1949 through the late 1970s. When Western Economics returned to China, circa

1978, it came back chiefly in modern Neoclassical form (see the chapters by Trescott, as well as Wang respectively in this volume).

My interviews with Chinese professors and students in 2011 and 2014 suggest that attention to Heterodox Economics is increasing modestly. This impression is reinforced by the level of attendance at Heterodox Economics conferences and lectures by touring Heterodox Economists, invitations to Western Heterodox economists for Visiting Professorships, Chinese student and faculty participation in Heterodox workshops and study groups, Chinese translations (authorized and unauthorized) of associated books and articles, and the vitality of such blogs and We-Chat (*Weixin*) groups.

Four factors seem most responsible for the modest increase of interest in Heterodox Economics:

1 *A continuing reaction to the policy failures that led to the global financial crisis of 2008 and the recession that followed.*
2 *The Chinese government's interest in Economic Theories that legitimize and enable a larger state role in the economy than frequently emerges from orthodox theory.*
3 *The accumulation of social costs, such as large social inequalities and environmental degradation, from over 30 years of neoliberal-oriented economic policies.*
4 *A perception among some students that the assumptions behind Neoclassical models are old-fashioned and unconnected to the 'real world'.*

Accordingly, several important Institutionalist Economics conferences were held in Shandong and Beijing between 2012 and 2014. Works by old Institutionalist Economists were slated to be the first materials translated by the Commercial Press's new 'Western Heterodox Economics' initiative (Zhang and Xum 2013: 323).

Post-Keynesian (PK) Economics, it may be argued, is now the most active Heterodox paradigm in China, as interest in Keynesian theory has flowered again (see the chapter on Keynes in this volume). Its practitioners include participants from disciplinary homes beside economics departments, such as physicists and system theorists Ping Chen and Wang Yougui, and management and finance professionals, such as Michael Pettis and Henry C. K. Liu. Again, Hyman Minsky's (1919–1996) work on the financial sector seems to be especially well-known in China.[11]

In May 2014, I attended the first three meetings of the newly formed Beijing Heterodox Economics Study Group. Many of the attendees were already familiar with Post-Keynesian (PK) theory, though much less knowledgeable about other Heterodox paradigms. I suspect that the more realistic assumptions of PK theory are especially appealing to students. In explaining their interest in Heterodox Economics, the students criticized Neoclassical theory for elevating mathematical beauty over realism. *They also faulted the Neoclassical paradigm for being a-historical, methodologically narrow, disconnected from other social sciences, insufficiently attentive to dynamic (rather than static) modelling, and insufficiently attentive to disequilibrium (rather than equilibrium) moments.*

On a different occasion, I spoke with a PK economist from Peking University about his students' responses to PK ideas. He reported that about 10–20 per cent of his students got engaged and excited by PK ideas, and noted that they were usually his best students. Interestingly, this is the same percentage of students who were energized by the aforementioned introductory Marxist Economics class.

There have been a number of global initiatives in recent years that have given institutional support to Heterodox economic activities in China. Two of the most important of these are the formation of the World Economics Association (WEA)[12] in 2011 and the Institute for New Economic Thinking (INET) in 2009. The birth of the Rethinking Economics movement in 2013 may also prove to be significant. The WEA enables potentially isolated critics of and sceptics about Neoclassical Economics from around the world to participate in international discussions of Heterodox ideas. Ten Chinese economists were among the original 150 or so founding members of the WEA.[13]

The INET has been able to leverage the resources available for local Heterodox initiatives in China, such as the Beijing Heterodox Economics Study Group.[14] The Internet has created the potential for Heterodox economists and Heterodox ideas to circumvent some of the gatekeepers of Neoclassical Economics that are ensconced in editorial boards, admissions committees and promotion committees. Lectures by leading theorists at INET and other economics conferences, for example, are now available to students and professors around the globe, even if they cannot attend the conferences in person. 'We-Chat' and micro blogs have also emerged as another medium for shared economics discourse.

There remain, however, serious obstacles to the expansion of Heterodox Economics in China, due to Neoclassical theory's strong-hold on most of the formal institutions of the Chinese economics profession. To offset this, Zhang and Xu have called for efforts to find more clearly defined common ground among Heterodox theories. They recommend that Heterodox economists: (1) ally with Marxist economists in a broad community of Heterodoxy; (2) hold ecumenical meetings of the 'Heterodox tendency' at annual conferences of Chinese economists; (3) push for continued translations of Heterodox ideas under the Commercial Press project; (4) put together textbooks on Heterodox economics; and (5) increase ties with foreign Heterodox economists (Zhang and Xu, 2013: 322–323).

Conclusions

Economic reform has brought with it a deep rooting of Neoclassical Economic Theory (with a well-developed branch of Chicago School economics) in Chinese Economics departments. Polemical government attacks on 'Western ideas', at official level, such as those made by for example, Yuan Guiren, the PRC's

Minister of Education and others in the last year or two, are unlikely to mobilize widespread academic support but one cannot be sure. *Far more effective in expanding the realm of economic discourse in China would be freeing-up Marxist theory from political oversight and expanding support for Heterodox Economics research and course offerings. Cross-pollination among Marxist and Heterodox economists might produce a genuine alternative ('with Chinese characteristics') to the 'Washington Consensus' so-called (light and strong versions) emerging from Neoclassical Economics.*

Notes

1 This chapter is based on material drawn from a longer manuscript on the coevolution of the Chinese Economy and Chinese Economic Theory. I would like to acknowledge financial support for this research from Knox College. I also thank the China Studies Institute in Beijing, for inviting me to teach in their programme in the Winter Term, 2014. Many of the people listed below hold very different views. Nothing in acknowledgements below should be mistaken for an endorsement of the positions expressed in the chapter. I alone am responsible for any errors. Among the people I would like to thank for helping me do this this research are: Mark Blecher; Cheng Enfu; Fang Min; James Galbraith; Gu Limei; Guo Fei; He Yin; David Kotz; Li Minqi; Keith Maskus; Mike Schneider; Shuyan Shipplett; Song Jianmin; Sun Youli; Wang Fang; Wang Yougui; Malcolm Warner; Norton Wheeler; Xie Fusheng; Xiong Wanting; Yang Yuan; Yao Jie; Yao Xianguo; Zhou Yi; and Zhu Andong. Special thanks must be offered to Nancy Eberhardt.

2 See for example 'A matter of honours', *The Economist*, 22 November 2014 (www. economist.com/news/china/21633865-china-trying-reverse-its-brain-drain-matter-honours; accessed 3 September 2015) and materials from the Center for China and Globalization (en.ccg.org.cn) at this time.

3 The Chicago School theorists most important in China are Milton Friedman, Ronald Coase and Gregory Chow, as well as the New Institutionalist economic historians, like Douglass North. Well-known Chinese offspring include Zhang Wuchang (Steven Cheung), Tian Guoqiang and Zhang Weiying. After the mid-1990s, the influence of Chicago's free market models weakened a bit (Ma and Trautwein, 2013: 268). Even when not in the majority, Chicago economists tend to define a realm of discourse by encouraging 'mainstream' Neoclassical economics to appear as the 'left' option.

4 Personal interviews 2011, 2014; see also Chow, 2000: 53; Fang, 2013: 302–303 and Zhao, 2010: 309.

5 Personal correspondence with *Zhou Yi*, 27 December 2011.

6 Public discontent over environmental degradation may have replaced corrupt land grabs as the most explosive public policy issue in China (Bloomberg News, 6 March, 2013, 'Chinese Anger Over Pollution Becomes Main Cause of Social Unrest'. Chai Jing's film (*Under the Dome*), calling for increased public pressure in China to protect the environment, enjoyed 200 million views within a week of being posted on the web in 2015. It was subsequently removed by Chinese censors ('China's "Silent Spring" Moment?' by Daniel Gardner, *New York Times*, 18 March 2015).

7 There are have been many as 180,000 public protests in China officially noted annually (Lagerkvist, 2015: 137). For recent information on growing labour unrest, see numerous reports published by the Hong Kong-based China Labour Bulletin, such as News: 3 December 2015, News: 5 January 2015, Newsletter: 15 November 2014 and News: 11 September 2013. The increase in reported incidents seems to reflect both a rise in incidents and an increase in reporting.

8 Recently, some in official circles including the Ministry of Education have followed a different tack, criticizing the influence of Western thinking and Western textbooks in Chinese universities. The criticisms seem heavy-handed and unlikely to effectively question the paradigmatic nature of Chinese Neoclassical Economics. The attacks have found little support among students or faculty. Whilst the attacks do seem polemical, the underlying reality of paradigmatic discourse is too facilely dismissed by *New York Times* reporters (Dan Levin, 'China Tells Schools to Suppress Western Ideas With One Big Exception', *New York Times* (NYT) (Sinosphere), 9 February 2015; Chris Buckley, 'China Warns Against "Western Values" in Imported Textbooks', NYT, 30 January 2015; David Bandurski, 'The "Cancer" of All Things Western', China Media Project, 24 March 2015; Chris Buckley and Andrew Jacobs, 'Maoists in China', NYT, 4 April 2015; Javier Hernandez, 'China Turns to Online Course', NYT, 21 October 2015; 'Chinese Students "Brainwashed" by Western Theories, Say Scholars', *Financial Times*, 2 June 2016, all print editions).

9 Discussion with an Economics Professor in Peking University, Economics department (May 2014).

10 One of my interviewees (2011) indicated that around 2010 it became possible again for Marxist articles to be published in *Economic Research*. Zhang and Xu (2010) similarly suggest that there had been an increase in interest in Heterodox Economics ~2008–2010 (p. 12).

11 The Levy Institute held a successful two-day conference in China in 2012 on Minsky's ideas. Randy Wray and Paul Davidson, two important Post-Keynesian economists, have had a number of speaking engagements in China. Michael Hudson (honorary Professor of Economics, Huazhong University of Science and Technology) is also well known. Post-Keynesian work by Marc Lavoie, Steven Keen and Sheila Dow has been translated into Chinese. Economists such as David Kotz (Shanghai University of Finance and Economics and the University of Massachusetts), Dic Lo (Renmin University and the University of London) and John Ross (Jiao Tong University and Renmin University) have offered Chinese economists creative ways of combing Marxist and Post-Keynesian analysis. In May 2015, more than 70 students from ten different Chinese Universities met at Beijing Normal University for the 1st Forum on Rethinking Economics and New Economic Thinking in China. Among the Heterodox paradigms explored were Post-Keynesian economics, Austrian economics, behavioural finance and econo-physics.

12 The World Economics Association is an online association of people interested in expanding economic discussion beyond orthodox Neoclassical boundaries. It already has over 12,000 members and publishes three online journals (the *World Economic Review*, *Economic Thought* and the *Real World Economic Review*), a newsletter and books. It also oversees online conferences and blogs. From 5 May to 14 June 2013, it organized an online conference about reforming the economics curriculum.

13 The ten individuals are: Ping Chen, Peking University and Fudan University; Xiaoqin Ding, Chinese Academy of Social Science; Shulin Gu, Tsinghua University; Kainan Huang, Shandong University; Yanli Huo, Chiba Institute of Technology; Henry C.K. Liu; Dic Lo, Renmin University of China and University of London; Ying Ma, Wuhan University; Yougui Wang, Beijing Normal University; and Dapei Zuo, Institute of Economics, Chinese Academy of Social Sciences.

14 Two members of the Beijing study group attended a 2014 INET conference in Toronto with INET financial assistance. An INET staffer helped the study group make 'Skype' contacts with other Heterodox study groups and well-known Post- Keynesian theorists.

References

Cao, C. (2008). 'The Teaching of Modern Economics in China: Why Government Policies Have Failed to Attract First-rate Academics to Return', *Asian Population Studies*, 4: 331–345.

Chow, G. (2000). 'The Teaching of Modern Economics in China', *Comparative Economic Studies*, 42: 51–60.

Du, Y. (2011). *A Bibliometric Portrait of Chinese Research through the Lens of China Economic Review*, Faculdade de Economia, Universidade do Porto, Portugal.

Fang, F. (2013). 'The Changing Status of Western Economics in China' in *Thoughts on Economic Development in China*, in eds. Y. Ma and H-M. Trautwein, London and New York, NY: Routledge, 295–305.

Kotz, D. (2007). 'The State of Official Marxism in China Today', *Monthly Review*, 59: 58–63.

Lagerkvist, J. (2015). 'The Unknown Terrain of Social Protests in China: "Exit", "Voice", "Loyalty", and "Shadow"', *Journal of Civil Society*, 11: 137–153.

Li, H. (2008). *China's New Left and Its Impact on Political Liberalization. EAI Background Brief No. 401*, East Asian Institute [EAI]: Singapore.

Ma, Y. and H.-M. Trautwein (eds) (2013). *Thoughts on Economic Development in China*, London and New York, NY: Routledge.

McCloskey, D.M. (1985). *The Rhetoric of Economics*, Madison, WI: The University of Madison Press.

Perkins, D. (2002). 'The Challenges China's Economy Poses for Chinese Economists', *China Economic Review*, 13: 412–418.

Song, L. (1995). *The Methodology of Mainstream Economics and Its Implications for China's Economic Research*, PhD dissertation, Washington University of Saint Louis, Ann Arbor, MI.

Trescott, P.B. (2007). *Jingji Xue: The History of the Introduction of Western Economic Ideas into China 1850–1950*, Hong Kong, SAR: Chinese University Press.

Wang, H. (2003). 'The New Criticism' in *One China, Many Paths*, ed. C. Wang, New York, NY: Verso.

Wang, Y., Fang, N., Wang, B. and Liu, R. (2014). *A Study on Contemporary Chinese Intelligentsia and Media Elite – Survey II of Contemporary China's New Social Structural Changes*, Beijing: Institute of Political Science, CASS.

Wang, Z. (2012). 'Ecological Marxism in China', *Monthly Review*, 63: 36–44.

Wang, Z., Fan, M., Dong, H., Sun, D. and Li, L. (2013). 'What Does Ecological Marxism Mean for China? Questions and Challenges for John Bellamy Foster', *Monthly Review*, 64: 47–53.

Zhang, L. and Xu, Y. (2013). 'The Transmission of Heterodox Economics in China, 1949–2009 (originally a conference paper given at the "Thoughts on Economic Development, China and the West" conference at Wuhan University in 2010)' in *Thoughts on Economic Development in China*, eds. Y. Ma and H.-M. Trautwein, London and New York, NY: Routledge.

Zhao, H. (2010). 'Economics Education in China', *International Journal of Pluralism and Economics Education*, 1: 303–316.

Zhou, Y. (2016). 'The Tragedy of the Anticommons in Knowledge', *Review of Radical Political Economics*, 48: 158–175.

19 The impact of Western Economics on China's reforms from the late 1970s to the present

An overview

Ying Zhu and Michael Webber

Introduction

The People's Republic of China (PRC, hereafter 'China') has been significantly involved in implementing 'Economic Reforms' for nearly four decades now. During this period of transformation, its overall policies have shifted from time to time. These shifts have been associated with ideological debates, national and international conditions, Western Economic theoretical discussions and pressures from domestic interests groups and citizens, including 'capitalist-*versus*-workers' issues. This chapter specifically focuses on the impact of Western Economic theories on the Chinese Economic Reforms (*gaige kaifeng*) as introduced by Deng Xiaoping (1904–1997) from the late 1970s – and up to the present.

Generally speaking, Western Economic ideas began to circulate in China with the emergence of Classical Economic Theory in the eighteenth and nineteenth centuries. In the last two centuries, following the introduction of the ideas of Smith, Ricardo and Marx – amongst others – into China, Economics gradually became a major area for research, teaching and in turn of policy-formation for central and provincial governments (Zhang, 2015) (see the chapters by Trescott in this volume). As elsewhere, the emergence of 'Economics' as an independent object of study and of policy formation in the 1930s, distinct from the classical views of 'Political Economy', in which the focus was not distinct from broader considerations of social policy (Mitchell, 2008), set the stage for the development of Economics in China. Despite some beginnings before and anti-Japanese War and the Second World War, the establishment of the PRC in 1949 and particularly its adoption of Economic Reform in the late 1970s led to the rapid development of Economics as a 'study-major' at universities. Subsequently, research in the field developed rapidly and became more and more influential on the policy front. One might say that a new period of 'Let a Hundred Flowers Bloom' (*baihua qifang*) – as in the mid-1950s – has appeared in history once again.

By the end of 1978, the Chinese Communist Party (CCP) policy started to shift towards 'Economic Reform and Openness' (*jingji gaige kaifang*) as the central goals for national development. This new policy was sharply different from the former emphases on 'class-struggle' and independent economic development – through cutting links with the major Western capitalist economies that characterized the Mao era (Zhu *et al.*, 2010). With its prioritization of economic change over social relations and environmental stewardship, 'Developing a Socialist Market Economy with Chinese Characteristics' (*zhongguo tese shehuizhuyi shichang jingji*) became the new 'slogan' for achieving what has been dubbed 'industrialization, informationalization, urbanization, marketization and internationalization/globalization' (Zhang, 2015). By the year 2010, China had become the second largest economy in the world, with average GDP per capita of more than $4,000 (Li, 2013) and its size has since expanded further.

The experience of China's transformation since 1949 provided a good lesson. As Zhang has noted:

> The journey of China's revolution, reform and economic construction demonstrate that we could neither entirely copy the Soviet Planning Economic Model nor implement Western Economic Models. What we can do is to develop our own Economic model 'with Chinese Characteristics…'
>
> (Zhang, 2015: 13)

Thus, this chapter will focus on tackling some key questions: What are those Economic models, languages and systems 'with Chinese characteristics'? How were these models, languages and systems influenced by Western Economic theories and other social, political and associated factors?

The chapter first identifies the different stages of 'Economic Development' in China from the late 1970s to nowadays, and then analyses the impact of Western Economic ideas on the formation of government's reform policy and agenda, as well as the debates among different Political and Economic interest groups within Chinese society regarding the development of a 'Socialist Market Economy with Chinese Characteristics'. Whereas earlier chapters (see for example those by Trescott, then Fang and later Cohn respectively in this volume) trace the movement of people bringing ideas from the US, as well as Europe, Japan and the USSR into Chinese universities and financial institutions, this contribution focuses on the effects (if any) that those ideas had on *debates* and *policies* within China.

Early stages of economic reform and the influence of Western economic theory in the 1980s

After 30 years of the post-1949 Central Planning Economic System and particularly the ten years of 'Cultural Revolution' (*wenhua da geming*) between 1966 and 1976, the Chinese leadership started to think about adopting a new way of Economic Development, in order to achieve what the then Premier Zhou Enlai (1898–1976) dubbed the 'Four Modernizations' (*sige xiandaihuain*) in 1963 (that is, of industry, agriculture, science and technology, and defence) (Zhu *et al.*, 2010). Which policy should guide future development had been debated and struggled over by political leaders as well as policy-advisors, such as Economics professors at universities and Political Economists at various social science academies. The struggle pitted the inheritors of the 'Cultural Revolution' ('Get the social relations right and production will look after itself' type of argument) against the more moderate faction ('It's the economy, stupid' line), all entangled with the threat of military intervention (see MacFarquhar, 1993).

After Mao Zedong (1893–1976) died, the new interim Chairman Hua Guofeng (1921–2008) led a campaign in 1976 with the slogan of 'the two all' (*liangge fanshi*), namely 'we must safeguard firmly all of the decisions made by Chairman Mao, and we must follow consistently all of the instructions made by Chairman Mao', whilst at the same time rejecting the extremism of the 'Gang of Four'. On the other hand, Deng Xiaoping, the then recently returned to power third-ranking CCP leader, emphasized that the principle guiding the party direction should follow the concepts of 'seeking truth from facts' (*shishi qiu shi*) and 'liberating the thought' (*jiefang sixiang*). The ideological debate between these two lines appeared publicly through party-controlled media and brief: many people inside and outside the CCP strongly supported Deng's idea (MacFarquhar, 1993). By 1978, the debate broke the constraint of 'the two all' principle and promoted the movement of ideological liberation nationwide (Zhu *et al.*, 2010). Such ideological debate also constituted an important theoretical platform for adopting the Economic Reform and Open Door policies at the Third Plenary Session of the Eleventh Central Committee of the CCP in 1978 (see Zhang, 2015).

This was a *turning-point* in China both ideologically and practically with a sense of new direction which allowed Economics thinkers to think more freely and borrow ideas from established Western economies vis-à-vis both theory and practice (Warner, 2014). Deng (and other leaders) vacillated between more openness, as at the 'Democracy Wall' in Beijing in 1978 and increasingly through the 1980s (until the 'Tiananmen Square' events in 1989), and on the other hand the need for stability to permit continued pursuit of the Four Modernizations (Baum, 1993; MacFarquhar, 1993) but other changes were soon to open up Chinese intellectual spaces.

By the late 1970s, American and Chinese economists were engaging in joint conferences and the influx of Chinese graduate students into Western universities had begun (see the chapters by Trescott, Fang and Cohn respectively in this volume). Furthermore, as the CCP tried to abandon 'Mao Zedong Thought' as the guiding ideological principle, it also needed new principles by which to guide the new reform programme.

Therefore, the early years of reform period in the first half of the 1980s had the effect of allowing 'Hundred Schools of Thought' to debate (*baijia zhengming*). The first period of debate on Economic Policy was at that time between the 'partially planning and partially market' principle whose market orientation was rooted in fundamental Western Economic theory (that is, Classical and Neoclassical Economics) and supported by the so-called 'reformists' (*gaige pai*) on the one hand, and the traditional Socialist Planning principle that was wholeheartedly believed by the so-called 'conservatives' (*baoshou pai*) on the other hand (see the chapter by Cohn in this volume).

A number of economists in the early 1980s were involved in drafting the State Council's 'Preliminary Opinions about the Economic System Reform' (Xue, 1982, 1983), which clearly indicated a mixed Economic reform direction towards a 'planned commodity economy' (Guo and Zhang, 2013). Their rationale was that the division of labour was an important condition of commodity production, in which different agents would have different interests. Hence, the new Economic Policy should reflect the reality of commodity production and exchange activities through *markets*. But given that China had many years of a planned economy, a radical shift towards a full 'free-market system' would not be possible. The parallel development of a partially market- and partially planned-system could be a way of moving forward at the early stage of Economic Reform.

On the other hand, the 'conservatives' took a negative attitude towards such a market-oriented reform agenda. Several papers were published by the CCP official peak magazine, namely the *Red Flag* (*hong qi*) in 1983, which identified the major objections (Guo and Zhang, 2013). They believed that, although 'Commodity Production and Exchange' existed in China, this did not justify a general characterization of the country as a 'Commodity Economy' because the State-Owned Enterprise (SOE) sector, a leading part of the economy, was not dominated by the 'Law of Value'. The planned economy was the most essential feature of socialism, otherwise, there would be blurred boundaries between socialism and capitalism, and eventually the future direction could lead to a fully 'anarchical' capitalism in China. Therefore, the suggestion for government Economic Policy should be to stick to the principle of taking the planned economy as the *core* – with some market regulations as a supplement.

In the early years of the Economic Reform period, not only were fundamental market-oriented Western Economic theories (that is, Classical and Neoclassical theories represented by the so-called 'Chicago School') introduced into China through university education and policy debates but also different Economic theories were also brought into China, predominantly Keynesianism (*Kai'ensi li lun*) and neo-Keynesianism on the role of State and Economic policy, Northian neo-institutional theory, as well as others such as 'Radical Economics', 'Regulation Theory' and so on (see chapters by Trescott, Warner, Fang and Cohn respectively in this volume).

Given the timing of early reform, 'path-dependent' upon a history of strong government intervention, a mixed Planning and Market Economic System required theoretical underpinning. Keynesianism ideas fit such an environment better than the free-market principle approached by the 'Chicago School' (see the earlier chapter on Keynes and China in this volume). As Zhang (2015) indicated, in 1985, a group of economists and policy-makers gathered on the *Bashan Lun*, a cruise-ship on the Yangzi River run, to discuss Keynes' theory on using financial policy to adjust the relationship between total social demand and supply, and policies to reduce unemployment. As it was recorded, such a theoretical workshop enabled policy-makers to be informed about these ideas and subsequently to act with some theoretical guidance. In the meantime, some basic concepts of Western theories, such as using laws to regulate and manage market Economic activities, scarcity, opportunity cost, marginal effects, equilibrium price, GDP and GNP, production consumption indices, Gini coefficients and the like, were also introduced into Chinese parlance (Zhang, 2015). These early efforts at introducing fundamental Economics concepts and tools enabled policy-makers and economists to carry out relevant analysis and work out evidence-based policy initiatives which were very different from the intuitive decision-making processes of the planning system.

However, in 1989, after ten years of Economic Reform, the partially market and partially planned Economic System had created a number of serious problems. These included misuse of power for allocating wealth to the new 'ruling class' (officials and new capitalists), corruption among officials, lack of political transparency and citizens' participation, unfair competition and monopolies of certain Economic sectors, and increasing inequality among different social groups in the society. These problems led to massive students and citizens' demonstrations all over the country and eventually the post-1989 'Tiananmen Square crackdown' occurred (see Baum, 1993) which created a great deal of uncertainty for future development in China. These triggered further ideological debates, including about which Economic theory and policy could be the guiding principles for further Economic Reform in China.

The second stage of Economic Reform and debates on economic principles in the 1990s

After the 1989 events, those who supported the traditional planning system began to criticize the market-oriented reform agenda more openly. Their position was strengthened by the perceived need within the Party to reinstate social discipline, to rein in the openness of debate in the years leading up to this point. The traditionalists implied that the Reform Programme was associated with the social conflicts that had led to Tiananmen and argued that the transition to a market economy meant abolishing public ownership, denying Socialism and the leadership of CCP (Guo and Zhang, 2013). They argued that as a consequence of the market-oriented reforms, the inflation rate reached the historical high of 1988 and most likely led to the political disturbances of 1989. The pro-market reformists were here on the defensive and there was a risk that the reforms would be rolled back.

After two years of no further reform action, the political climate changed due to Deng Xiaoping's dissatisfaction with stagnation and the anti-reform views. After his trip, the 'Inspection Tour', to a number of southern China cities and Special Economic Zones in 1992, he defined a Socialist Market Economy as combining both planning and market elements; these, he argued, were simply methods for Economic development, and did not carry particular ideology, whether socialism or capitalism. The goal of China's Economic System Reform should therefore be to set up a 'socialist market economy' (*shehuizhuyi shichang jingji*). This new direction was adopted at the 14th National Congress of the CCP as its guiding-principle in October 1992 (Zhu *et al.*, 2010).

Hence, the 1990s' reform agenda became focused on establishing such a Socialist Market Economy that in practice was less oriented towards planning and more towards the market. Under the influence of such an agenda, reforming the traditionally dominant sector, namely the SOEs, became one of the first priorities, and this move provided opportunities for several Western Economics theories to influence the reform process. Two groups of economists influenced the policies adopted to reform SOEs: free-market oriented economists pushing for full privatization of all SOEs on the one side (in English, see for example Wong, 1986; Chen 1998), and on the other a group of 'moderate' economists who proposed a reform model that combined denationalization, pluralization of SOEs and privatization (in English, see Naughton, 1995; Qian, 1996).

As for the 'true believers', the Neoclassical economists, SOEs could be seen as the most inefficient entities. They claimed that 'privatization is the only way to solve the SOE conundrum' (Zhang, 1995). The underpinning rationale generally referred to government interference in the 'proper' operation of firms. Government officials on behalf of the public determined the degree of autonomy of the SOE. Autonomy could provide positive incentives to the manager, but also open the door for discretionary activities that ran counter to the principal's interests (Klaes and Zhang, 2013).

Therefore, the origin of the inefficient performance of SOEs was attributed to 'rent-seeking' behaviour on the part of the principal – for example, seeking high levels of employment within a firm rather than more efficient staffing levels. The optimal degree of autonomy could be determined as a trade-off between the sale of decision rights and the imposition of constraints on managers' discretionary power. The policy recommendation for reforming SOEs, hence, was to restrain such 'rent-seeking' by shifting ownership of the firm to private owners; otherwise, vested interests on the part of the 'principal' of the SOE would lead to a deadweight loss (Klaes and Zhang, 2013).

On the other hand, another group of economists tried to work out a 'compromise' model. The underpinning thinking was that SOEs and private firms shared a common problem, namely failures of 'corporate governance' due to the separation of ownership and control (Lin *et al.*, 1998) (see the chapter by Zhang later in this volume). Under the planning system, the State was unable to rely on relative performance in its evaluation of SOEs, for their profitability was largely attributable to the set levels of imposed input and output prices, rather than the competence and performance of managers. However, under the market economy, market competition would establish a level playing-field between firms and reveal sufficient information on the actual performance of managers. Hence, improved performance could be achieved without changes in the underlying structure of property rights (ownership changes). *Privatization could be one option, but more important in this argument was market competition among SOEs.*

To move SOE reform forward, the compromisers suggested a combination of denationalization as well as privatization, and pluralization. Denationalization would shift public assets to more local levels of government. The involvement of local governments would, it was hoped, provide more local control of public assets and increasing competition in capital and managerial labour markets within the public sector as well as between the public and private sectors. Consequently, it was hoped that the political costs of public ownership could be kept in check and incentives to local governments for efficient asset management could also be enhanced (Lin *et al.*, 1998). In addition, they also suggested 'pluralization' of SOEs. In this scheme, the government would hold a majority of shares in a firm and other institutional and individual investors could also hold shares, thus forming a new joint stock company. By doing so, private investors could become members of the board of directors thus becoming involved in decision-making and monitoring managers' performance. Pluralization also provided opportunities for further reform of the ownership system in the future (see Jin and Qian, 1998).

The then-CCP leadership, under the President Jiang Zemin (1926–) and Premier Zhu Rongji (1928–), pushed for further SOEs reform along the lines of the compromise model, under the slogan 'Holding the bigger one and letting the small go' (*zhuada fangxiao*) (Zhu *et al.*, 2010). This meant that the central government would control only a number of large SOEs and those with strategic significance, while small and medium sized SOEs would be privatized, localized and pluralized. Many small and medium sized SOEs were privatized in this process; this created severe criticism in the following years (see the following section). Nowadays, there are only about 110 larger SOEs under the control of the central government (SASAC, 2015).

The third stage of Economic Reform and Economic Policy debate in the 2000s

In the 2000s, two major issues dominated Economic Policy debate. These were the 2004–2006 'dispute' about how to evaluate the effect of the reform policy of the past decades, and China's Economic policy responses to the 2008–2009 Global Financial Crisis (GFC).

In the mid-2000s, the debate was not about whether reform was needed or what kind of reform was needed, but about how to evaluate the reform policy. A number of economists worried that the SOEs' reform had gone too far; in particular, they criticized the administrative staff of SOEs who had stolen public assets through the system reform (i.e. privatization) (Lang, 2004). Such criticism stirred up public outcry about other social and Economic problems, including healthcare reform, educational reform, regional, urban-rural and income disparities, and social insurance reform (Zhou, 2004; Liu, 2005). This group of economists argued that the 'property rights' issue was a small part of SOE management, that privatization could not solve the entire problem of SOEs. By selling public assets into private hands at very low prices, in particular selling to former managers of SOEs, the entire nation and ordinary people lost greatly (Ding, 2000; Huang, 2003). These economists believed that the direction of privatization of property rights among SOEs was wrong and they called urgently to stop such activities.

On the other hand, the pro-market economists objected to this argument and claimed that the assets of SOE did not suffer losses through this reform, but increased their total value even faster. These economists believed that as long as the total national wealth increased as an outcome of increasing profit and taxation contribution, the reform could be seen as successful and should be continued. In addition, they argued that the income gap, social inequality and environmental deterioration were mainly due to the incompleteness of the marketization reforms. In order to achieve better outcomes, those with vested interests in the old system should be constrained (Duckett, 2002), monopolistic industries paying higher wages should be controlled (Zheng and Chen, 2007), the distortions on prices on resources should be eliminated to achieve better environmental outcomes (World Bank, 2008) and education, job opportunities and healthcare should be made more widely accessible (Zhang and Kanbur, 2005).

Responding to these debates in the last decade, the CCP Central Committee, under the then leadership of President Hu Jintao (1942–) and Premier Wen Jiabao (1942–), expressed its firm wish and determination to move the reform forward. A new slogan of adopting scientific development concepts (*kexui fazhan guan*), promoting a harmonious society (*hexie shehui*), and establishing a moderately prosperous society (*xiaokang shehui*) was adopted at the 17th National Congress of the CCP in 2007. This slogan reveals an attempt by the CCP leadership to formulate a compromised approach to this debate, mixing its signals.

However, the GFC suddenly occurred at the end of 2007; its negative impact on China's economy became obvious in 2008. A strong government push for easy financial and monetary policies based on neo-Keynesianism came to dominate the centre stage of Economic policy responses toward GFC (see the chapter by Warner in this volume). The central government released more than RMB40 trillion into the economy with the goal of preventing recession. Such action may have saved the economy temporarily and has left a legacy of transport infrastructure, but has also created problems that appear to impede further reform. These problems include over-developed production capacity, excess supply of energy, materials and consumption goods, stagnation of market demand, and the accumulation of huge bad debts among firms, local governments and central government organs (such as banks) and so on.

The current Economic Policy debate under the notion of developing a 'new norm'

Since 2013, Chinese Economic Reform has been under a new direction labelled as 'Chinese economy in dual transition' led by a new CCP leadership team under President Xi Jinping (1953–) and Premier Li Keqiang (1955–) (see Li, 2013).

The 'dual' transition refers to a transition of the Economic System and a transition of the development model, with more emphasis on Economic and Social 'Sustainable Development' (Li, 2013). Given that President Xi had been formally awarded a PhD in Law from Qinghua University and that Premier Li has a bachelor degree in Law and formally gained a PhD in Economics from Peking University, both are said to be familiar with many leading Western theories in the areas of Law and Economics. This familiarity might have an impact on the principles of a new Economic Reform agenda along the lines of 'developing new social and economic norms by following the rule of law' (Wang, 2013: 1). The goal of further Economic Reform under the new leadership has been said to realize the so-called 'China Dream' (*Zhongguo meng*).

According to Khun (2013), the 'Chinese Dream' has four parts: *Strong China* (Economically, politically, diplomatically, scientifically, and militarily); *Civilized China* (equity and fairness, rich culture, high morals); *Harmonious China* (amity among social classes); *Beautiful China* (healthy environment, low pollution). Khun states that 'a moderately well-off society' (another term referring to *xiaokang shihui*) is one in which all citizens, rural and urban, enjoy high standards of living. This includes a doubling of the 2010 GDP per capita (approaching $10,000 per person) by about 2020 and completing urbanization (to roughly one billion people, 70 per cent of China's population) by about 2030. 'Modernization' means China regaining its position as a world leader in science and technology as well as in Economics and Business; the resurgence of Chinese civilization, culture and military might; and China participating actively in all areas of human endeavour (Khun, 2013).

Based on the new principles of Economic Reform and new directions for the nation to move forward, the new leadership team seems to have responded to the criticisms of the mid-2000s by setting up a new agenda to address the negative consequences of the previous stages of reform. These include: serious official corruption and misuses of power (for example, not respecting property rights by using force to evacuate citizens from their home or land for so-called 'development'); social and economic inequality at individual and spatial levels; environmental and moral degradation. The new leadership team is said to believe that one of the important causes for serious corruption and misuse of power has been the lack of a comprehensive institutional environment, particularly the lack of the 'rule of law' and 'legal enforcement' (see Yang, 2015).

A 'Northian' approach to the 'New Institutional Economics' here has had a quite strong influence on Chinese economists and policy-makers (see Li and Trautwein, 2013). Nobel Laureate, Douglass North's (1920–2015) definition of institutions appear to people as useful for addressing the current challenges in its Economic system: 'institutions are a set of rules, compliance procedures, and moral and ethical behavioural norms designed to constrain the behaviour of individuals in the interests of maximizing the wealth or utility of principals' (North, 1981: 201). In later years, North (1990) added that institutions consist of a set of constraints in the form of rules and regulations; a set of procedures to detect deviations from the rule and regulations; and a set of moral and ethical behavioural norms which define the contours that constrain the way in which the rules and regulations are specified and enforcement is carried out. These statements seem to imply to people in China that Economic Reform has reached a crucial moment: that China needs to develop frameworks for interaction that limit the choice sets of agents in the interests of principals (see Li and Trautwein, 2013) – assuming that people are the principals and governments their agents.

Under the influence of North's approach, both the Chinese leadership and a number of leading scholars in the field (including Lin, 2009; Xu, 2011) have paid particular attention to the criticism made by new institutional scholars regarding 'the Chinese puzzles' – the 'poor institutions, poor legal protection of property rights, poor corporate governance, lack of democratic accountability, and an absence of the rule of law' (Xu, 2011: 1080). We might posit that the concept of the so-called 'new norm' (*xin changtai*), as proposed by the new President Xi, may reflect the influence of North's institutionalism.

Conclusions

Nearly 40 years of Economic Reform has thus made China a very different country from that of 1978. Its economic size, weight and influence nowadays cannot compare with its status 30 or 40 years ago. We can see that China has adopted some unique aspects to its development trajectory, which many identify as 'with Chinese characteristics'. However, there exist many influences of Western Philosophical and Economic thinking, though some of these could lead to significant outcomes at certain key periods but not at other times.

Yet, there is a strong controlled selection of which Western Economic ideas may be adopted. The reform policies selection process reflects a strong CCP leadership involvement through judgement of the arguments made by different interest groups, including owners/companies (thinking about making profits, like capitalists) and workers/ordinary citizens (thinking about fairness and social justice).

Economists within China are, in turn, divided into different groups representing different voices from the different classes/social groups and selectively using different Economic Schools of Thought as the underpinning of policy debates. We can see that an Economic Agenda had dominated the earlier years of reform, creating many social and environmental problems for Chinese society. The questions posed by the new institutional scholars (Xu, 2011) – how far can China's Economic Reform move forward without addressing fundamental issues such as lack of comprehensive institutional frameworks and 'the rule of law' – challenge the current Chinese leadership to correct wrongdoing in the past, as well as to develop 'a new norm' in order to achieve the new goal of realizing 'the China Dream'. It could well take a number of years to see the ultimate results.

References

Baum, R. (1993). 'The road to Tiananmen: Chinese politics in the 1980s', in R. MacFarquhar (ed.), *The Politics of China: The Eras of Mao and Deng* (2nd edn), Cambridge: Cambridge University Press: 340–471.

Chen, A. M. (1998). 'Inertia in reforming China's State-owned enterprises: the case of Chongqing', *World Development*, 26: 479–495.

Ding, X. L. (2000). 'The illicit asset stripping of Chinese State firms', *The China Journal*, 43: 1–28.

Duckett, J. (2002). 'Political interests and the implementation of China's urban health insurance reform', *Social Policy and Administration*, 35: 290–306.

Guo, X. B. and Zhang, P. (2013). 'Thirty years of disputes on China's economic reform', in Y. Ma and H.-M. Trautwein (eds), *Thoughts on Economic Development in China*, London and New York, NY: Routledge: 217–234.

Huang, Q. H. (2003). 'The private enterprises: a main engine to the sustaining growth of China's economy', in Yao S. J. and Liu X. M. (eds), *Sustaining China's Economic Growth in the Twenty-First Century*, London: Routledge-Curzon.

Jin, H. and Qian, Y. (1998). 'Public vs. private ownership of firms: evidence from rural China', *Quarterly Journal of Economics*, 113: 773–808.

Khun, R. L. (2013). 'How China's leaders think: the inside story of China's reform and what this means for the future', *China Daily*, 19 July: http://usa.chinadaily.com.cn/opinion/2013-07/19/content_16814756.htm (accessed 12 October 2016).

Klaes, M. and Zhang, Y. (2013). 'Chinese reform and schools of thought in Western Economics: Chicago school versus principal-agent theory', in Y. Ma and H.-M. Trautwein (eds), *Thoughts on Economic Development in China*, London and New York, NY: Routledge: 255–273.

Lang, L. (2004). 'Greencool: revel in the grand banquet of privatization', Speech at Fudan University, Shanghai.

Li, W. S. and Trautwein, H.-M. (2013). 'Northian perspectives on China's economic reform', in Y. Ma and H.-M. Trautwein (eds), *Thoughts on Economic Development in China*, London and New York, NY: Routledge: 235–254.

Li, Y. N. (2013). *Chinese Economy in Dual Transition*, Beijing: China People's University Press.

Lin, J. Y. (2009). *Economic Development and Transition: Thought, Strategy, and Viability*, Cambridge: Cambridge University Press.

Lin, J. Y., Cai, F. and Li, Z. (1998). 'Competition, policy burdens, and State-owned enterprise reform', *American Economic Review*, 88: 422–427.

Liu, G. G. (2005). 'Some problems in research and teaching of economics', *Economic Research Journal*, 10: 7–12.

MacFarquhar, R. (1993). 'The succession to Mao and the end of Maoism, 1969–82', in R. MacFarquhar (ed.), *The Politics of China: The Eras of Mao and Deng* (2nd edn), Cambridge: Cambridge University Press: 248–339.

Mitchell, T. (2008). 'Rethinking economy', *Geoforum*, 39: 1116–1121.

Naughton, B. (1995). *Growing out of the Plan: Chinese Economic Reform, 1978–1993*, Cambridge: Cambridge University Press.

North, D. C. (1981). *Structure and Change in Economic History*, New York, NY: Norton.

North, D. C. (1990). *Institutions, Institutional Change and Economic Performance*, Cambridge: Cambridge University Press.

Qian, Y. Y. (1996). 'Enterprise reform in China: agency problems and political control', *Economics of Transition*, 4: 427–447.

SASAC (2015). 'The list of the SOEs under the control of the central government 28/9/2015', Beijing, The State-owned Assets Supervision and Administration Commission (SASAC) of the State Council.

Wang, Y. Q. (2013). 'The east Asia development model reconsidered', in Y. Ma and H.-M. Trautwein (eds), *Thoughts on Economic Development in China*, London and New York, NY: Routledge: 274–294.

Warner, M. (2014). *Understanding Management in China: Past Present and Future*, London and New York, NY: Routledge.

Wong, C. P. W. (1986). 'The economics of shortage and problems of reform in Chinese industry', *Journal of Comparative Economics*, 10: 363–387.

World Bank (2008). *Addressing China's Water Scarcity: Recommendations for Selected Water Resource Management Issues*, Washington, DC: World Bank.

Xu, C. (2011). 'The fundamental institutions of China's reforms and development', *Journal of Economic Literature*, 49: 1076–1151.

Xue, M. Q. (1982). 'Several problems that the economic management system reform needs solving', *Economic Research Journal*, 1: 1–5.

Xue, M. Q. (1983). 'About several questions concerning the theory of economic system reform, which are in need of continued deep discussion', *Economic Research Journal*, 1: 1–6.

Yang, J. (2015). 'Building a law-based government in China', *Qiushi Journal* (English edition) 7, http://english.qstheory.cn/2015-05/20/c_1115271839.htm (accessed 15 March 2016).

Zhang, W. (1995). *The Entrepreneur of the Firm: Contract Theory*, Shanghai: People's Publishing House (in Chinese).

Zhang, X. B. and Kanbur, R. (2005). 'Spatial inequality in education and health care in China', *China Economic Review*, 16: 189–204.

Zhang, Z. Y. (ed.) (2015). *The Development of Chinese Economics Research to Start with 'Historical Perspectives on Chinese Economics'*, Beijing: China Academy of Social Sciences Press/CASS (in Chinese).

Zheng, Y. N. and Chen, M. J. (2007). 'China's recent State-owned enterprise reform and its social consequences', Nottingham, UK: University of Nottingham China Policy Institute.

Zhou, Q. R. (2004). 'Why I do reply to Professor Lang', *The Economic Observer*, 12 September.

Zhu, Y., Webber, M. and Benson, J. (2010). *The Everyday Impact of Economic Reform in China: Management Change, Enterprise Performance and Daily Life*, London and New York, NY: Routledge.

20 Western ideas of corporate governance

China's reform of large state-owned enterprises

Jin Zhang

Introduction

The historical development of 'Corporate Governance' (*gongsi zhili*) in China has gone through four stages over recent decades. In the *first* stage, from 1949 to 1983, state-owned enterprises (SOEs) dominated the Chinese economy and the state commanded and controlled almost every aspect of its activities. Corporate governance, as understood in the West, did not exist in China. The *second* stage, from 1984 to 1993, involved the beginning of the separation of government and enterprise in China, under reforms launched by Deng Xiaoping (1904–1997). During this period, China formally established the Shanghai Stock Exchange and the Shenzhen Stock Exchange, and a new government body, the China Securities Regulatory Commission, was created to be the country's main regulator of the newly born stock market. The *third* stage, from 1994 to 2005, marked the beginning of experimentation in modern enterprise structure, including passage of the first Company Law – the first comprehensive law that fully delineated the rights and responsibilities for modern companies in China. The Company Law has since had a great impact on corporate governance and the economy as a whole in China. However, state shareholders enjoyed overwhelming favouritism over individual investors. The *last* stage, from 2006 onward, has witnessed the continuing growth of corporate governance in China, including legislation aimed at balancing the power asymmetry between state shareholders and individual shareholders in companies. As China enters into a new stage of SOE reform marked by the policy of promoting mixed-ownership (*hun he suoyou zhi*) in 2016, corporate governance continues to be, in our view, the key aspect of the reform.

This contribution examines the dissemination of the Western Economic ideas of corporate governance among Chinese economists and policy-makers and their influence on China's gradualist reform of its largest SOEs.

It is divided into four sections. The *first* discusses the dissemination of the theories of corporate governance since the 1980s, focusing on the 'principal-agent problem' and mechanisms of board of directors; the *second* examines the influence of Western ideas on the policy measures of restructuring of the China's largest SOEs, in the strategic economic sectors in the late 1990s and the establishment of the 'modern industrial enterprise' in the 2000s; the *third* looks into the key issues involved in the current reform of ownership of the central SOEs (CSOEs), namely the 'principal-agent' problem; and *fourth*, the role of the Chinese Communist Party (CPC) pertinent to the further reform of China's largest SOEs.

Research

The research of corporate governance in China originates from the necessity of reforming SOEs in the early 1990s (Zheng, 1998). Academic research in the 1990s was marked by introducing Western literature on corporate governance and in the 2000s by numerous empirical studies applying Western analytical frameworks. In the meantime, policy research on corporate governance focused on comparative studies of corporate governance approaches in the West and reflected on the challenges of SOE reform. Today, such research in China is a well-established subject in universities, research institutions and government think-tanks. Research centres dedicated to corporate governance research have been established in universities, the most prominent of which is the *Corporate Governance Research Institute* of Nankai University in Nanjing, led by Professor Li Weian. The institute has published an annual corporate governance index since 2003. In 2015, the index included 2,590 listed companies in China's stock markets, accounting for 99.96 per cent of the total listed companies.

The Western concept of corporate governance was first introduced into the theoretical analysis of China's enterprise reform at the *International Conference on the Next Reform of China's Economic System* in Beijing in 1994. The paper presented by the late Professor Masahiko Aoki (1938–2015) of Stanford University, an eminent Japanese-born economist, on 'insider dealing' in SOEs and Professor Qian Yingyi, Dean, School of Economics and Management, Tsinghua University another (Chinese) expert on the topic, on corporate governance reform and financing reform introduced Western theoretical concepts of corporate governance and greatly influenced the discourse and discussion on the topic in China (Aoki and Qian, 1995; Zheng and Wang, 2000).

In 1995, three international conferences focused on governance and the reform of SOEs. In June, the *Economic Research Journal*, a prominent journal on economic theories and policy, edited by the Economic Research Institute of the China Academy of Social Sciences, organized a seminar on the principal and agent problem in SOE reform; in July, at the conference on SOE reform organized by the *Chinese Economists Society* founded in New York in 1985, Nobel Prize winner the late Professor Merton H. Miller (1923–2000) of the University of Chicago analysed the two strategic choices of corporate governance (Miller, 1996) – the *Anglo-Saxon* model dominated by the stock market and the *German-Japanese* one dominated by the banking-sector. Chinese economists responded enthusiastically on the implications on the definition and nature of corporate governance and policy implications for governance in China (Xu and Wen, 1996; Lin *et al.*, 1997a, 1997b). At an international seminar on enterprise supervision in China in October, the translation of the term of 'corporate governance' into Chinese was brought into question by Professor On Kit Tam of Monash University in Sydney. He proposed using '*qiye dudao zhiheng jizhi*' – instead of '*gongsi zhili jiegou*'. However, both terms were used in the published collection of papers edited by him (1997). Today, the adopted Chinese translation of corporate governance is, as noted, '*gongsi zhili*'.

In addition to the scholarly effort made by Chinese scholars and their Western counterparts, another important channel of disseminating Western ideas of corporate governance involves international organizations, such as the World Bank and OECD. Both organizations produce literature on governance and China (Xu and Wang, 1997; Tenec *et al.*, 2002) through collaboration with Chinese researchers at the *Development Research Centre of the State Council* and engagement with government officials at SASAC and SOE executives. For example, the *China-OECD Corporate Governance Policy Dialogue*, set up in 2004, promotes 'use of the OECD Principals of Corporate Governance and OECD Guidelines on Corporate Governance of State-Owned Enterprises, adapting them to national priorities' (OECD, n.d.).

Chinese scholars' introduction of Western Economics and in particular ideas on corporate governance and their empirical research is extensive, including topics on the definition, the principal-agent problem, the composition and function of board of directors, the control-mechanisms and the different approaches to corporate governance by different countries (Lu, 1994; Wu, 1994; Aoki and Qian, 1995; Zhang, 1996, 1999; Lin *et al.*, 1997a, 1997b; Zheng, 1998, 2011; CIRD, 1999; Li, 1999, 2001; Zheng and Wang, 2000). *This chapter will focus on two key issues of the principal-agent problem and the function of board of directors in the following discussion. These two issues are at the core of the reform of corporate governance of the SOEs in China.*

Principal-agent problem

The principal-agent problem was first identified as a useful conceptual tool to analyse the problems of SOE governance. Chinese scholars attribute to Adam Smith's (1732–1790) book on *The Wealth of Nations* (1776) the intellectual origin of identifying the problem of the separation of ownership and control and the associated problems it brings (Zheng, 1998; Lin *et al.*, 2001) (see Lai's chapter earlier in this volume). This also introduces Berle and Mean's argument from their book *The Modern Corporation and Private Property* (1932) that the increasing power of the managers is detrimental to the interests of the shareholders of American corporations, which is to say interests of managers and shareholders are divergent. Their work has generated rich research on how shareholders control and monitor the behaviour of managers. However, Stigler and Friedland (1983) have pointed out there is no clear empirical evidence in support of Berle and Means' thesis. Lin *et al.* (2001) further argue that this thesis overlooks the adaptability of corporate governance systems – corporations adapt their governance systems to the control and monitoring mechanisms internal and external to the corporations. Jensen and Mackling (1976) identified the incentives for managers not to align their objectives to those of the shareholders.

Furthermore, comparative studies on corporate governance show that shareholding in British and American companies is more *diversified* than their counterparts in Germany and Japan. The principal-agent problem in the Anglo-Saxon approach demonstrates itself as the conflict between professional managers and diversified shareholders, whilst the same problem in the German and Japanese approach shows itself as the conflict between large and small shareholders (Yang and Lu, 2015).

However, the principal-agent problem is even more complicated in the reform of SOE corporate governance in China. Zheng (1998, 2011) pointed out the dilemma of corporate governance reform in Chinese SOEs. Business autonomy in SOEs would enable them to improve efficiency but could also result in insider-dealing and control, which leads to damage of the interest of the state as shareholder. The monitoring and control of SOEs by the state as the dominant shareholder is necessary but could lead to excessive and bureaucratic 'meddling' in governance.

Board of directors

Chinese researchers have studied the system of *board of directors* in different countries (Zheng, 2011). They summarize three typologies: the British and American model, the German and Dutch model and the French and Japanese model. The British and American model does not have supervisory boards. The majority of the board of directors are independent non-executive directors. The German and Dutch model consists of a supervisory board and management board with the former supervising the latter. The French and Japanese model has no legal requirement on setting up a supervisory board or introducing independent non-executive directors. Chinese scholars note that these models are deeply rooted in the political and social circumstances of different countries and hence the call for finding a model that would work in a Chinese context (see the chapters by Das earlier in this volume).

The most contentious issue regarding board of directors among Chinese researchers is the introduction of independent non-executive directors (Zheng, 2011). Some argue that the introduction of independent non-executive directors originates from different legal and corporate governance system and question its merit in the Chinese political and legal system. Others argue that the introduction of independent non-executive directors could strengthen the monitoring function of the supervisory committee and deter insider dealing and control.

SOE reform in practice

Chinese economists acknowledge the influence of the introduction of Western concepts and ideas of corporate governance on the policy of SOE reforms (Zheng, 1998). As discussed earlier, Chinese economists' reflections on the applicability of Western theory of corporate governance in SOE reform are grounded in their understanding of the Chinese circumstances. Nevertheless, they find Western concepts and ideas helpful to identify the key problems in corporate governance in SOEs. The policy implications drawn from their research such as separating business from government (*zhengqi fenli*), establishing boards of directors, appointment of non-executive directors, executive incentives and so on are well demonstrated in actual policy-measures in CSOE reform.

Who are they? Central state-owned enterprises

The central state-owned enterprises (CSOEs) are a set of 113 large SOEs (SASAC, 2014) directly under the administration of the central government, hence the name of 'central SOEs' (*zhongyan qiye*, or *yang qi*). They operate in industrial sectors that are considered to be *strategic* for the development of the national economy – aerospace, airliners, automobile, chemicals, coal, defence, electronics technology, high-speed trains, nuclear power, oil and gas, power generation and distribution, ship-building, steel and telecommunications. The fact that these CSOEs are mostly evolved from various government ministries in the command economy provides a unique perspective to examine the evolution of corporate governance in China.

The CSOEs are an important contributor to China's economy (see Warner, 2014). By 2014, the CSOEs held 53 per cent of the country's SOE assets at RMB53,707 billion, the rest of which is in the hands of the SOEs under the administration of provincial and municipal governments (*di fang guoqi*). In the same year, the revenue from the SOE sector stands at RMB48,064 billion, equivalent to 7.6 per cent of China's GDP, 61 per cent of which is contributed by the CSOEs. The tax collected from the CSOEs accounts for 77 per cent of the whole SOE sector.

By 2013, China had 93 firms in the *Fortune Global 500* ranked by revenue[1] and 43 firms are CSOEs. China had 32 firms in the *FT 500* ranked by market capitalization[2] and only 4 are CSOEs.[3] The market capitalization of Chinese firms in the *FT 500* was third, behind only the US and the UK, and Chinese banks have occupied four positions (3rd, 6th, 8th and 9th) among the top ten in the banking sector. Amongst the top 100 Chinese multinational companies ranked by foreign assets (CEC/CEDA, 2014), 43 are CSOEs and 40 CSOEs are among the top 50 in the list.

However, the Chinese companies that have entered into these global ranking-lists are by no means as 'multinational' or 'global' as those from the US, Europe and Japan in terms of geographic distribution of assets, revenue, profits and employees. They are predominantly oriented towards the *domestic* market, operating in highly protected sectors such as energy, power generation and distribution, telecommunications and financial services. The United Nations Conference on Trade and Development (UNCTAD) provides an annual list of the top 100 non-financial transnational corporations ranked by foreign assets for the world as well as for firms from developing and transition economies.[4] In 2013, only four

Chinese companies, Hutchison Whampoa, CITIC, COSCO, CNOOC, have entered the list for the world. A comparison with the annual ranking of the top 100 largest Chinese MNEs by the CEC/CEDA (China Enterprise Confederation and China Enterprise Directors Association) shows CNPC and Sinopec are qualified to be included into the UNCTAD list. But even with their inclusion, China would have only six companies among the world's top 100 TNCs.

Who is who? Principal and agent

The CSOEs today have come a long way from their previous existence as government ministries. China's situation is in many ways different from that of other East Asian countries,[5] which has been closely examined in literature (Whitley *et al.*, 2013). China has long been reforming a comprehensively state-administered industrial system (Nolan and Wang, 1999). To understand today's Chinese CSOEs and their governance, it is essential to understand in the context of the systemic reform of the Chinese 'Political Economy' (see the chapter by Zhu and Webber in this volume).

Identifying principal and creating agents

Starting from the early 1980s, the goal to reform the state-owned sector was to 'separate businesses from government'. Meanwhile, China in the late 1970s looked completely different from what it is today. The state devised economic plans and implemented the production and distribution of goods and services through a bureaucratic system from central government ministries to provincial plants and distribution bureaux – and right down to the county-level production and distribution units. In this schema, there are no economic 'firms'. The reform of the state-owned sector is never about to liberalize the system per se. It has also involved, throughout three and half decades, reforming the state governance system. Since 1978, China has implemented innovative institutional reforms to achieve this goal (Nolan and Wang, 1999). From the very start of the reform and opening up, the state has had the function of first creating and then gradually reforming businesses, whilst transforming itself into a modern system to serve the function of governing businesses. During this process, one formidable task was to transform the government ministries of industrial sectors into large state-owned corporations.

The idea of reforming the SOEs through *corporatization* – restructuring the economic ministries into corporations – started in the early 1980s and immediately caused intense debate (Wei, 2002). *The debate centres here on where the locality of corporate power should reside, at the corporate level or with the individual plants* (Nolan, 2001; Zhang, 2004; Li, 2014).

In a multi-plant firm, the plants are operating units while the corporate headquarters has the authority of strategic decisions such as research and development, capital investment, mergers and acquisitions. The struggle was between those who advocated 'enterprise autonomy' at the level of individual plants across the country and those who tried to consolidate these plants and centralize managerial power at the level of the corporate headquarters. Despite the debate, a group of industry-wide corporations were established during the 1980s: China Nuclear Industrial Corporation (CNIC), China National Offshore Oil Corporation (CNOOC), China Petrochemical Corporation (Sinopec), China National Petroleum Corporation (CNPC), China General Coal Mining Corporation (CGCMC) and China Weaponry Industrial Corporation (CWIC). They respectively took over most existing productive assets from the Ministry of Nuclear Industry, the Ministry of Petroleum Industry, the Ministry of Coal Industry and the Ministry of Weaponry Industry, which were abolished correspondingly.[6]

The next major step to further separate the business from government is to further restructure the government departments and turn the corporations into modern enterprises by establishing corporate boards and getting them listed in international markets. This reform agenda was launched in 1998. The model was to group together the core-assets of the corporations and float them onto the international stock market. This process typically involved the professional services from international investment banks, accounting and auditing firms. It also involved equity investment from global industrial and/or financial giants as strategic investors. For example, each of the three Chinese oil-majors were listed on the New York Stock Exchanges as well as London Stock Exchanges between 1999 and 2001 and global oil-majors such as BP and Shell and financial giants such as Goldman Sachs were strategic investors.

The corporatization and overseas listing of SOEs is a process of transforming government ministries involved in economic activity into joint stock corporations. However, who is the 'principal' who represents the state as the 'owner' of these assets? On the part of the state, the creation of the State-owned Assets Supervision and Administration Commission in 2003 represents a breakthrough in the attempt to achieve separation of government and enterprises. Under SASAC, the SOEs are grouped into two categories. The CSOEs are those that are directly supervised by SASAC at the state ministry level while local SOEs are those that are supervised by SASAC at the provincial and municipal level.

The function of SASAC as principal

The function of SASAC is two-fold. It acts as the shareholder of the state assets while leading reforms on corporate governance and restructuring the state-owned assets across industrial sectors.

Asset reorganization

During the tenure of Li Rongrong (1944–), SASAC launched a series of programmes to reform the CSOEs with the objective to turn them into commercially competitive enterprises that can increase the value of state-owned assets. The first was in the area of asset reorganization, as to define 'core businesses' for each CSOE. Each of the CSOEs was required to define their core businesses and focus on the growth of these businesses. The objective of this programme was to turn these SOEs into enterprises that have the discipline to focus on developing capabilities in a range of core businesses. SASAC issued directives that each CSOE should devise a recurring three-year plan for core businesses as well as annual growth plan, both of which would be commented and evaluated by a team of experts organized by SASAC. By 2007, SASAC approved the scope of core businesses of all the CSOEs (154 in total) in seven lists that were published on the website of SASAC. The most difficult issue for SASAC to tackle was the lucrative real estate business that many of the CSOEs had in their portfolio. It would need special approval from SASAC to retain the real estate businesses for industrial companies. After a lengthy process of negotiation between enterprises and SASAC, 78 out of 154 enterprises that had unfinished real estate projects managed to retain real estate in their business portfolio. However, they were required to exit the market as soon as the projects were finished. In addition, SASAC approved 16 enterprises that defined their core business as real estate. By 2009, these 16 enterprises accounted for 85 per cent of the total assets of real estate businesses of all the CSOEs, 86 per cent of the total revenues and 94 per cent of the total net profits.

Furthermore, SASAC has been engaged in asset reorganization among the CSOEs. There were over 190 CSOEs when SASAC was established in 2003. By 2007, the number of SOEs was reduced to 153. By 2013, there were 113 CSOEs. Within ten years, the number of CSOEs was reduced by 40 per cent. This demonstrates a consolidation process of core businesses in strategic sectors and the formation of oligopolistic competitive structure among the CSOEs. For example, the 53 largest CSOEs are from around 15 industrial sectors including aerospace, automobile, aircraft manufacturing, airliners, defence, electronics, nuclear industry, power generation and distribution, ship-building, steel and telecommunications.

Performance evaluation

In the meantime, SASAC evaluates the performance of the CSOEs on the basis of financial performance and management performance (SASAC, 2006). For example, the quantitative financial performance criteria that carry a weight of 70 per cent include profit, quality of assets, debt risks and business growth. Management performance criteria that carry a weight of 30 per cent include risk control, human resources practices and corporate social responsibilities. They are measured qualitatively by a panel of experts. Each of the sub-criteria is also weighted. Each CSOE is benchmarked against a set of industrial standards that are determined by evaluation institutions approved by SASAC. SASAC is responsible for the overall performance of the corporation while the corporations are responsible for the evaluation of their subsidiaries. The performance evaluation covers the enterprises as well as the top executives of the enterprises. The performance measurements are highly technical and procedural. In 2013, 46 CSOEs scored 'A', accounting for 41 per cent of the total CSOEs. Acting as the shareholder of the state assets, SASAC believes it is performing its duty to make sure the value of state assets under its supervision would be maintained and even increased. The meticulous performance evaluation is an important mechanism to fulfil this duty.

Regulation of overseas investment

As discussed earlier, the CSOEs are an important force of domestic and international business from China. In order to monitor the management and performance of the overseas investment and asset transactions, SASAC issued two special directives on the management of state-owned assets in foreign countries. The 2011 directive focuses on monitoring overseas state-owned assets. It stipulates that CSOEs should report to SASAC and register property rights if they and their subsidiaries set up new overseas enterprises through 'greenfield' investments, mergers and acquisitions or equity investment and if their overseas enterprises change their names, location of registration, share of equity or core businesses. The CSOEs have the power to decide and approve transactions of overseas state-owned assets. However, SASAC has the power to examine and verify the asset transactions if they would lead to the change from a 100 per cent state-owned overseas enterprise into a majority SOE or a majority state-owned overseas enterprise into a minority SOE.

Furthermore, the 2012 directive focuses on the management of overseas investment. In principal, CSOEs should not engage in businesses overseas that are not within the scope of their core business portfolio. If there is a special need to engage in non-core businesses overseas, SASAC must examine the businesses and verify the necessity. The directive stipulates that CSOEs should report to SASAC their overseas investment management system that should include guiding 'principals', accountability, decision-making process, risk control system, and internal auditing and monitoring system. They also should submit to SASAC for examination their annual overseas investment plan that should include the scale of the investment, the sources of capital and capital structure. The CSOEs must submit filings to SASAC for their 'major investment projects' that are within the remit of their overseas investment decision processes. In addition, SASAC will monitor the risks of the overseas investment as well as guide the CSOEs to cooperate in overseas investment so as to avoid vicious competition among themselves.

Board of directors

SASAC regards corporate governance mechanisms as crucial for SOEs to establish a modern enterprise management system. Since 2004, it has been guiding the process of establishing company boards in CSOEs. SASAC stipulates the principals and compositions of boards in these enterprises. The model includes board of directors and supervisory committee. The supervisory committee is above the board of directors as those in the German and Dutch model. However, in reality the head of supervisory board administratively ranks below the

Chairman and CEO in CSOEs. To strengthen the supervision of the company boards, independent non-executive directors are introduced onto such boards.

The company boards have a three-year term and should have no less than nine board members, one of which must be elected by the employees as their representative on the board. The Chairmen and Vice Chairmen as well as independent directors are appointed by SASAC approved by the Central Organization Department of the Communist Party of China (see below). The remuneration of board members including independent directors is determined by SASAC. By 2013, all of the 53 largest CSOEs have established company boards.

The executive appointment and remuneration are two important managerial rights for company boards. The remuneration of CSOE employees are significantly higher than those working for other SOEs in China but significantly lower than those from international companies of similar scale in the same industrial sector. These are very sensitive issues for SASAC to tackle.

Issues

As embodied in the SASAC functions, the state governance mechanisms are indeed intervening at the micro level of managerial practices. It is understandable that SASAC's mandate is to maintain and increase the value of state-assets. However, micro-level intervention may cast serious doubts over the commercial nature of these CSOEs. On the other hand, the abolishing of the previous economic ministries left a void in the system to carry out policy coordination, as well as regulation for industrial sectors.

Problems have also been identified with the *agents* – the SOEs, of which inside dealing is the most prominent one (Zheng and Wang, 2000). It has been argued that the dominant position of the state-ownership and the unclear nature of the entity representing the state shareholder are the main causes of inside dealing, corruption, anti-mergers and acquisitions, and loss of state assets. The recent anti-corruption campaign in CSOEs, such as CNPC, Sinopec, Huarun and so on, reveals the lack of monitoring of these large firms.

Mixed ownership reform

The previous round of SOE reform in the late 1990s produced 'mixed ownership' of many CSOEs when they listed a minority of their shares on stock exchanges to attract private capital. The recent SOE reform centres on the further diversification of shareholders by increasing interest from private investors and allowing employees to hold shares. In July 2014, SASAC published a reform plan in line with the spirit of the Third Plenum of the 18th CPC Congress on SOE reform. The plan selected six CSOEs as pilot-projects for reform, focusing on bringing in shareholders from the non-state sector and improving SOE corporate governance, for example, giving company boards more power to appoint executives and decide executive remuneration (Wen and Ma, 2014). Corporate governance scholars suggest the key issues include determining who represents the ownership of the state-owned assets (the principal), to what extent CSOEs can be privately owned (the categorization of CSOEs), and the corporate governance mechanisms in relation to the appointment and incentives for executive managers (Yang and Lu, 2015).

Principal and agents

So, the SASAC is now at the crossroads. As previously discussed, SASAC has acted as a shareholder and a regulator. The governance structure of SASAC–CSOEs is open to questioning of the nature of CSOEs as commercial entities. This is particularly fraught *in the process of internationalization of CSOEs*. Scholars and policy researchers (Yang and Lu, 2015) suggest the desirability of: (1) establishing a few state capital investment companies as the shareholders of the state-owned assets in the CSOEs concerned; (2) retaining the regulator function of SASAC and transforming SASAC into a government regulator for the CSOEs. This structure of SASAC–state capital investment companies–CSOEs is regarded as a remedy to the lack of autonomy of the board of directors and the dominant position of the state shareholding to the detriment of the minority shareholders. It is further suggested that the board of directors have the decision-making power for strategic investment, executive appointment and evaluation. The CEO would have the mandate from the board of directors and is responsible for the operation of the CSOEs.

However, most of the CSOEs are operating in industrial sectors that are considered to be *strategic*. To what extent these CSOEs could be privately owned is a highly contentious issue. Scholars and policy-researchers argue that it is no longer desirable to consider SOEs in sectoral categories in mixed ownership reform, rather SOEs industries should be categorized based on the nature of business they are in. Three categories have been suggested by researchers: public-goods SOEs, functional SOEs and competitive SOEs (Yang and Lu, 2015). For public-goods SOEs in public transportation, public health and education, national defence and environmental sanitation, they should retain dominant state-shareholding and operational control; for competitive SOEs in manufacturing and service industries, private capital should have the dominant shareholding position; for functional SOEs, the state-shareholding should be higher than the private shareholding and the operational control should be with the private capital. Furthermore, it has been suggested that SOEs in each category should have different composition and supervision of the board of directors. However, it still remains to be seen if these research results and policy proposals would become government policies to be implemented.

The role of Communist Party of China (CPC)

Studies on the role of the Communist Party of China in China's political economy shows that the CPC encourages the increasing enterprise autonomy and commercial success of its CSOEs, whilst retaining control of the appointment of the

Chairmen and Presidents of the largest CSOEs and manages a cadre transfer system that enabled the rotation and transfer of these business leaders to senior state and CPC positions (Brodsgaard, 2012; Li, 2014). The Central Organization Department (COD) of the CPC is at the heart of this process more than ever (see Warner, 2014).

The COD of the CPC is responsible for the appointment, administration and training of cadres and high-level government officials including those Chairmen and Presidents of the 53 largest CSOEs. The mechanism of appointment of the business leaders was described as a process of consultations, suggestions, recommendations and deliberations among company employees as the first step. It is followed by SASAC, approved by COD, selecting the top ten candidates for the top position from which the company employees elect, by vote, their nominees. The list will be ranked by the number of votes. If SASAC and COD disagree with the result, the second round of voting will take place. Finally, the number of candidates will be reduced to two. Once the incumbent top executive steps down, SASAC, in consultation with the company board, makes its recommendation for which of the two candidates should be the new leader. All is subject to the approval of the COD (Brodsgaard, 2012). In addition, most of the top executives of the 53 central SOEs are CPC members, of which 12 of the leaders of these companies were elected to the 17th CPC Central Committee in 2007. Some of them have been transferred to ministerial and provincial leadership positions. The current 18th CPC Central Committee, 205 of full members and 171 alternate members, has 14 members from CSOEs, four full members and ten alternate members.

Downs and Meidan (2011: 1) provides insights from the national oil companies (NOCs) on CPC's control of the careers of the executives in state-owned enterprises:

> [The NOCs] are bound to the CCP through deeply entrenched structural ties and must therefore remain subject to the CCP's goals. But when the NOCs prioritize corporate objectives over CCP goals –as they have in the past – and are seen to be steeping out of line, the CCP has several levers to rein them in.... Indeed, the establishment of boards of directors and the appointment of two different individuals to occupy the positions of chairman of the board/ party secretary and general manager does not diminish the CCP's authority over the NOCs because the CCP determines who holds all three posts.

Scholars pointed out the relationship between CPC committee and board of directors, supervisory board and executive management committee is critical for effective corporate governance (Lu, 1994; Zheng and Wang, 2000). The latest 2015 reform directive of the CPC Central Committee and the State Council calls for the upholding of party leadership and for the provision of political, organizational and human resources to support the development of SOEs. However, senior SOE executives are aware that there are no examples available to learn from and much work is needed to find a constructive way forward.

Conclusions

Research on corporate governance in China arises out of the necessity of reforming its SOEs. Chinese researchers look to academic literature in the West for ideas, study the corporate governance system in different countries and analyse the issues of corporate governance reform in China attempting to use the same terminology as their overseas counterparts. They also reflect on the applicability of Western corporate governance systems to the reform of corporate governance in SOEs. The dissemination of such ideas of corporate governance in China is mainly through Chinese scholars' research efforts to know more, as well as the numerous exchanges of knowledge and understanding between them and international organizations, such as the World Bank and OECD. The key issues we have identified in this chapter are the principal-agent problem and the board of directors.

This chapter clearly shows, we argue, that the diffusion of Western Economic ideas on corporate governance has produced a profound impact on the reform of corporate governance in China's CSOEs. The PRC has come a long way in corporate governance reform regarding identifying principal and agent and the function of board of directors. The current round of mixed ownership reform will continue to tackle the core-issues of the principal-agent problem and the board of directors. It is yet to be seen, however, to what extent these issues will be resolved. But one can be sure that it will involve a great deal of experimentation and evolution based on what has already been achieved. China will keep learning from the Western Economic theory and practice on corporate governance and continue to find a way that is suitable for China on corporate governance.

Notes

1 Excluding Hong Kong, SAR.
2 Including Hong Kong, SAR.
3 Of the 32 Chinese firms, 12 are from the banking sector, four from the life insurance sector.
4 Data are from company annual reports. However, it is interesting to note that the UNCTAD lists South Korea and Taiwan as 'developing economies'.
5 Amsden (1985) provides a similar account of Taiwan's transformation process. However, Taiwan had a military government commanded by the Nationalist Party (Kuomintang/Guomingdang) and the scale of transformation has been much smaller.
6 Li (2014) gives a fascinating account of the intense debate on the fate of the China Automobile Industry Corporation (CAIC) in the 1980s.

References

Amsden, A. A. (1985). 'The state and Taiwan's economic development', *Bringing the State Back In*, P. B. Evans, D. Rueschemeyer and T. Skocpol (eds), Cambridge: Cambridge University Press, 78–106.

Aoki, M. and Qian, Y. (1995). *Corporate Governance Structure in Economies in Transition: Insider Control and Role of Banks*, Beijing: China Economic Press.

Berle, A. A. and Means, G. C. (1932). *The Modern Corporation and Private Property*, New York, NY: Macmillan.

Brodsgaard, K. E. (2012). 'Politics and business group formation in China: the Party in control?', *China Quarterly*, 211: 624–648.

CEC/CEDA (China Enterprise Confederation and China Enterprise Directors Association) (2014). *Top 100 Chinese Multinational Enterprises 2013*, www.cec1979.org.cn/c500/chinese/content.php?id=146&t_id=1 (accessed 1 August 2014).

CIRD (China Institute for Reform and Development) (ed.) (1999). *Corporate Governance in Chinese Firms*, Beijing: Foreign Languages Press.

CPC Central Committee (2013). *Communiqué of the Third Plenary Session of the 18th Central Committee of the Communist Party of China*, www.china.org.cn/china/third_plenary_session/2014-01/15/content_31203056.htm (accessed 1 August 2014).

CPC Central Committee and the State Council (2015). *Directives on Deeping the Reform of State-owned Enterprises*, www.gov.cn/zhengce/2015-09/13/content_2930440.htm (accessed 15 September 2015).

Downs, E. and Meidan, M. (2011). 'Business and politics in China: the oil executive reshuffle of 2011', *China Security*, 19: 1–10.

Jensen, M. C. and Mackling, W. H. (1976). 'Theory of the firm: managerial behaviour, agency costs and ownership structure', *Journal of Financial Economics*, 3: 305–360.

Li, C. (2014). *China's Centralized Industrial Order: Industrial Reform and the Rise of Centrally Controlled Big Business*, London and New York, NY: Routledge.

Li, J. (1999). *On Corporate Governance*, Beijing: Economic Science Press.

Li, W. (2001). *Corporate Governance*, Nanjing: Nankai University Press.

Lin, J. Y., Fang, C. and Zhou, L. (1997a). 'The nature of modern enterprise system and the direction of state-owned enterprise reform', *Economic Research Journal*, 3: 3–11.

Lin, J. Y., Fang, C. and Zhou, L. (1997b). *Complete Information and State-owned Enterprise Reform*, Shanghai: Shanghai People's Publishing House.

Lin, J. Y, Fang, C. and Zhou, L. (2001). *State-owned Enterprise Reform in China*, Hong Kong, SAR: Chinese University of Hong Kong.

Lu, C. (1994). 'Corporate governance institutions and the relationship between the new and old three committees', *Economic Research Journal*, 11: 10–17.

Miller, M. H. (1996). 'Alternative strategies of corporate governance', in *The Reformability of China's State Sector*, G. J. Wen and D. Xu (eds), Singapore: World Scientific, 3–16.

Nolan, P. (2001). *China and the Global Business Revolution*, New York, NY: Palgrave.

Nolan, P. and Wang, X. (1999). 'Beyond privatization: institutional innovation and growth in China's large state-owned enterprises', *World Development*, 27: 169–200.

OECD (n.d.). China–OECD Corporate Governance Policy Dialogue, www.oecd.org/china/china-oecdcorporategovernancepolicydialogue.htm (accessed 20 October 2015).

SASAC (State Asset Supervision and Administration Commission) (2006). 'Detailed criteria of performance evaluation of central SOEs', www.sasac.gov.cn/n1180/n1211/n2695/n4592/12349041.html (accessed 7 August 2014).

SASAC (State Asset Supervision and Administration Commission) (2014). 'List of the central state-owned enterprises', www.sasac.gov.cn/n1180/n1226/n2425/index.html (accessed 24 June 2014).

Smith, Adam [1776] (1976). *An Inquiry into the Nature and Causes of the Wealth of Nations*, R. H. Campbell and A. S. Skinner (eds), Indianapolis, IN: Liberty Fund.

Stigler, G. L. and Friedland, C. (1983). 'The literature of economics: the case of Berle and Means', *Journal of Law & Economics*, 26: 237–268.

Tam, O. K. (ed.) (1997). *Enterprise Supervision Mechanisms in Reform*, Beijing: Economic Press China.

Tenev, S., Zhang, C. and Brefort, L. (2002). *Corporate Governance and Enterprise Reform in China: Building the Institutions of Modern Markets*, Washington, DC: World Bank and the International Finance Corporation.

UNCTAD (United Nations Conference on Trade and Development) (2014). *World Investment Report*, New York, NY and Geneva: United Nations.

Warner, M. (2014). *Understanding Chinese Management: Past, Present and Future*, London and New York, NY: Routledge.

Wei, Y. (2002). 'Corporatization and privatization: a Chinese perspective'. *Northwestern Journal of International Law and Business*, 22: 219–234.

Wen, Y. and Ma, C. (2014). 'Guoqi gaige yi shijian bojie maodun' (SOE reform: solving problems through practice), *Guangming Daily*, 18 July, www.sasac.gov.cn/n1180/n1271/n20515/n2697175/15968596.html (accessed 1 August 2014).

Whitley, R., Witt, M. and Redding, G. (2013). 'Change and continuity in East Asian business systems', in *Oxford Handbook of Asian Business Systems*, M. A. Witt and G. Redding (eds), Oxford: Oxford University Press, 626–657.

Wu, J. (1994). *Modern Corporation and Enterprise Reform*, Tianjin: Tianjin People's Publishing House.

Xu, D. and Wen, G. (eds) (1996). *Reform of State-owned Enterprises in China*, Beijing: Economic Press China.

Xu, X. and Wang, Y. (1997). 'Ownership structure, corporate governance, and corporate performance: the case of Chinese stock companies', *World Bank Policy, Research Working Paper*, No. WPS 1794.

Yang, H. and Lu, T. (2015). 'SOE corporate governance under mixed ownership reform', *Macroeconomic Research*, 1: 42–51.

Zhang, J. (2004). *Catch-up and Competitiveness in China: The Case of Large Firms in the Oil Industry*, London: RoutledgeCurzon [*sic*].

Zhang, W. (1996). 'Ownership, governance structure and principal-agent relationship', *Economic Research Journal*, 9: 3–15.

Zhang, W. (1999). *Theory of the Firm and Enterprise Reform in China*, Beijing: Peking University Press.

Zheng, H. (1998). 'Theory of corporate governance and reform of state-owned enterprises', *Economic Research Journal*, 10: 20–27.

Zheng, H. (2011). 'Review on corporate governance research in China', *Review of Economic Research*, 42: 32–50.

Zheng, H. and Wang, F. (2000). 'Research on corporate governance reform in China: a theoretical review', *Management World*, 3: 119–125.

Part V

Comparisons

21 Economic policy-making in Asia

The Western vs Eastern legacy of philosophical and economic thought

Bernadette Andreosso-O'Callaghan

Introduction

When studying the philosophical basis of contemporary Economics in Asia and Europe, we need to take as a point of departure the impact of a number of well-known philosophers on the concept of 'Man', as they then referred to humanity, as in the universe, society, or group of individuals. All these thinkers in the East and the West were born at around the same time: Laozi and Confucius, on the one hand (both born in China in 571 BC and 551 BC respectively), and Plato and Aristotle, on the other (both born in Greece in 427 BC and 384 BC respectively).

We will argue in this chapter that whilst Asian and European philosophy schools have impregnated the Chinese (Asian) and European (Western) mind-sets, as well as their political and economic systems respectively, the contemporary literature on the conceptual and philosophical roots of Economic thought and policy-making is filled with references to Confucianism and to a lesser extent to Daoism (or Taoism) in the case of Asia,[1] whereas the Platonic and Aristotelian heritages seem to have been forgotten by both Economic thinkers and policy-makers in Europe and the West.

Asia's opening to the rest of the world since the nineteenth century has facilitated the historic infiltration of the dominant Western-born 'Neoclassical' paradigm into economic policy-making and teaching in Asian countries, including a recalcitrant China. As will be discussed, this is the new 'scientific' paradigm imposing itself in the area of Economics and Economic policy-making, in a similar way as other scientific paradigms may have won out in other fields, albeit after a period of hesitation and controversy, such as for example the theory of 'Relativity' in Physics (see Kuhn, 1962: 102).

These preliminary remarks lead to the enquiry into how Economic ideas going back to Greek philosophy have been overshadowed by other schools of thought emerging all along Europe's history in the case of Europe – and how contemporary policy-making in Asia, despite its strong classical philosophical tradition, could increasingly 'accommodate' the dominant paradigm. In order to do so, this chapter has two main objectives: first, to explain how and why the legacy of Plato and Aristotle has been overshadowed in Europe, and second, to analyse the mutual interaction between the Asian and European philosophical bases, in particular the increasing influence of the dominant Western Economics paradigm on economic policy-making in Asia noted above, in spite of a strong philosophical tradition in East Asia. This second objective will be met by referring to the 'role of the State' in the analysis.

In the first section, we will first explain how contemporary Economic policy-making in Europe, and in the West in general, has gradually been shaped by theories that have increasingly aspired at being seen as 'scientific', or devoid of any references to ethics or moral judgements. A second section will first use some core elements of Asian philosophy, in order to explain the philosophical foundations of the Asian economic 'specificity'. The second will also try to highlight the similarities and differences existing between the early European and Asian philosophical schools, when we appraise them in shaping Economics in both cases. This section will then succinctly discuss the growing convergence of Economics in East Asia towards the Western dominant paradigm. With this step, the analysis will be framed by the focus on the role of the State and it will highlight what is so specific about the type of policy-making shaping the capitalist systems in East Asia. Finally, some conclusive avenues to make sense of the above will be suggested in a final section.

From Plato to the triumph of physics, or the 'scientification' of economic theory in Europe

The *Neoclassical paradigm in Economics*, shaped in Europe during the second half of the nineteenth century (see Johnson, 1937), has been and still is the dominant one in economic policy-making there and in the US, with only a limited interruption represented by John Maynard Keynes (1883–1946) and the associated 'Keynesianism' so-called between the Great Depression of the 1930s and the better times of the post-war decades, if one refers to the 'role of the State' in economic affairs over the period (see the chapter on Keynes earlier in this volume).

With Asia's increasing integration in the world economic system since the late nineteenth century, this paradigm has tended to impose itself as the *dominant* one in that part of the world too. The most distinctive feature of this paradigm, when appraised in a continuum of philosophical ideas and economic thought, is that it sees the field of Economics *at par* with other sciences such as Physics. This is a culminating point in an intellectual debate that was rife in Europe during the Age of Enlightenment relating to the works of Adam Smith (1723–1790) and others. It is important to note that both the '*scientification*' of economics (in the seventeenth century) and then its emancipation from other sciences (two centuries later), happened after a quasi-uninterrupted two millennia of fertile ideas in Europe that had been sowing the seeds of the organization of cities, of human societies, of economic systems and of economic policy-making. Elevating the field of *Political Economy* to the level of a science can therefore be seen as a relatively modern 'construct' in European Economics thought and the legacy of European early philosophers should therefore not be dismissed

In particular, the work of Plato (427–348 or 347 BC), that has been credited for being the main inspirer of the Christian concept of 'Man', so-called, is regarded as the point of departure of economic and social philosophy in the Western civilization (see Denis, 1983). Plato developed his famous concept of the 'ideal city' in his book *The Republic* published around 380 BC. This refers to a *synthetic* conception of the world where the individual is at the service of the *city* and where man must learn what order and justice are by contemplating the order of the *cosmos*. A disciple of Socrates (470/469–399 BC), who invented ethics (at least according to the German philosopher, Georg Wilhelm Friedrich Hegel, 1770–1831), Plato was fundamentally a moralist who posited that happiness can only be found in the practice of virtue. In *The Republic*, the 'ideal' city is one where injustice is a factor of division between individuals and is contrary to the essence of wisdom. Consequently, the aim of rulers (and of politics) is to allow good to triumph over evil, and the objective of the philosopher is to determine the laws/rules that render the ideal city compatible with justice.

Plato's vision of the State is one in which it has a crucial role to play in terms of wealth-distribution and trade-policy. The personal interest is subsumed to the ultimate good functioning of the city – where private property is therefore discouraged.[2] The 'division of labour', as in Adam Smith, is here an important organizational feature in the ideal city and the different aptitudes of the different individuals can here only be detected through an adequate educational system (*The Republic*, Book II and Book III). The only knowledge that allows the discovery of the good, in particular of the political good associated with justice, is the knowledge acquired through reasoning, discussion and dialectics (*dialectike*).

Aristotle entered Plato's *Academy* at the age of 18 and agreed with Plato on several points, namely that: *first*, the unlimited search of wealth is a vice; *second*, the world is composed of strictly hierarchical elements from minerals to God, through vegetation, animals and human beings; *third*, the State, although less dominant, still has an important role to play; it should own some of the land, and the use of private property should be exercised in common. Many of the teachings of both Plato and Aristotle were to be echoed by the 'founders' of Christianity and by the representatives of the early Christian church up to the fourth century AD (see Walter, 1975) and they were revived further down in history by theologians such as St Thomas Aquinas (1235–1274). The latter, like Aristotle, claimed that society is *superior* to the individual – in the same way as the whole is superior to the parts – in developing his idea of the 'common good'. According to his vision, the State should be confined to having a *marginal* role and it should intervene *only* when the interests of a social class are jeopardized.

Yet, what follows is a general movement of *distancing* between the State on one side and the increasingly contested Catholic Church on the other, leading to anti-clerical movements that facilitated the advent of the Protestant Reformation. During the period of the Renaissance in Europe (fourteenth to seventeenth century AD), the State is increasingly seen as an *autonomous* force rather than as being subordinate to the Church (see Denis, 1983). With the schism in the

Church, the Christian attitude vis-à-vis the concept of wealth changes radically and the field of political economy is gradually fine-tuned and conceptually organized with the advent of the 'Mercantilist' school in the sixteenth century. According to this view, the *State* can increase its strength, whilst at the same time allowing the enrichment of all its citizens, and wealth becomes a supreme value. Understandably, the thesis gained support among the merchants, financiers and manufacturers, and it was echoed in the writings of John Hales's (1584–1656) book (1581), Antoine de Montchrétien's (1575–1621) work (1615) and Thomas Mun's (1571–1641) study (1621), and for whom wealth is the warrant of social order. It is perhaps easy to see that, with this new *zeitgeist*, the conditions for wealth accumulation are to conquer new markets and to increase the quantity of money in circulation. The discovery and mastery of gold-mines and of other precious metals reserves in the New World, as well as the conquest of new markets, were facilitated by what was to become widespread European colonialism.

The gradual divergence of the State from the Church was greatly enhanced by a radical 'shake-up' occurring in the field of scientific knowledge during the sixteenth and seventeenth centuries AD. The dominant Aristotelian vision of the world became undermined by a number of scientific discoveries by Nicolaus Copernicus (1473–1543) who opposed Aristotle's geocentric model, Galileo Galilei (1564–1642) and Johannes Kepler (1571–1630). In particular, with Galileo's law of 'free fall', it becomes clear that mathematical formulae are now essential to understand physics since these formulae and laws enable causes and effects to be connected and further certain phenomena to be forecast. In the domain of what is now known as the 'social sciences', the role of René Descartes' (1596–1650) work (1644: 566) is central. Descartes' 'scientific method' permeates all fields of knowledge, including moral, and it puts therefore in question the moral tradition of the Church (see Denis, 1983).

Since all fields of knowledge can be understood through the 'scientific method' and since most scientists and intellectuals concur to show that Physics govern the entire life-system – including the economic system – religion (and the Church) loses its prominent role here as a possible driving economic policy-making authority.[3] Consequently, with the growing opposition to 'Mercantilism' in the seventeenth and eighteenth centuries, one more step is to argue against the unnecessary involvement of the State in economic affairs; this is epitomized by the famous saying of Vincent de Gournay (1712–1759) a prominent intellectual and political figure in the French eighteenth century 'Physiocratic' school in Economics and in French politics: '*laissez faire et laissez passer*'. A connecting thread between the (vanishing) ethical vision of human societies and the new (increasing) vision of a Political Economy based on 'freedom' is encapsulated in Adam Smith's *The Theory of Moral Sentiments* (1759), published earlier than the *Wealth of Nations* (1776). In this first work, Adam Smith envisages the aim of human activity as being both the 'pursuit of wealth' and the 'search of wisdom', two apparently conflicting objectives (see the chapters by Lai and Sakamoto respectively earlier in this volume).

The *scientification* of the field of Political Economy was further made possible with the delineation of key Economics concepts and theories, such as 'Utility theory', as developed by Jeremy Bentham's (1747–1832) work (1789) – under the influence of David Hume's (1711–1776) earlier writings (1751), for whom human sciences had to be founded on *experimental* methodologies, based on the observation of facts (rather than, as previously, on prescriptive Christian values) and on the derivation of laws (see Harris, 2015). Both the 1789 French Revolution, as well as the ongoing British-born Industrial Revolution at the time, created an opportune environment for the wider acceptance of the 'measurable' – and therefore scientific and objective – concept of utility and for other mathematically grounded economic concepts and theories.[4] The Industrial Revolution gave rise to an unprecedented number of technological innovations, supported by the spread of scientific discoveries in physics, chemistry and other domains. Not surprisingly, the nascent Neoclassical Economics school of the second half of the nineteenth century borrowed many of its new concepts from the fields of Physics and Chemistry, such as *elasticity, fluidity* (of information) and *atomicity* (of economic agents).

For Neoclassical economists, such as Léon Walras (1834–1910), raising the new Economics (1874) to the level of a 'science' would allow him to win an ideological battle against the socialists. In an earlier publication, Walras (1860) had clearly stated his intention to demonstrate, with the systematic use of mathematical modelling, that his theory would totally invalidate the arguments of the socialists, such as Pierre-Joseph Proudhon (1809–1865) whose key work (1846) highlighted a number of contradictions inherent in the then existing economic capitalist system that explained poverty and social injustice. Walras' resulting 'general equilibrium' model is indeed a mathematically sound model – although it uses simple tools such as linear algebra and differentiation – a model that made the field of Economics look 'respectable' and widely accepted as being superior, and therefore incontestable.[5] This is a model where 'market forces', orchestrated through the 'auctioneer', are the most efficient framework for resource-allocation, and where government intervention and the role of the State can therefore be reduced to nil.

The increasingly widespread acceptance of Neoclassical Economic theory in Europe and in the West in general went undisturbed – apart from the short Keynesian parenthesis which placed more emphasis on the role of the State, as noted above – in spite of the many limits embodied in the very content of Neo-Liberal theory, limits going beyond the restrictive assumptions upon which the theory rests.[6] In particular, according to Nobel Prize Laureate, Amartya Sen (1933–) who pointed out (1987) that these weaknesses explain the inability of the '*homo oeconomicus*' concept to help us understand ethical norms. As noted elsewhere (Andreosso-O'Callaghan, 2011), the question of the origin of *individual endowments* – as the basis of the exchange in Walras' model – still remains entirely open and the utility concept is intrinsically arbitrary, a limitation that had already been noted by Irving Fisher (1867–1947) in 1892 said to be the first 'Mathematical' Economist in the US. Since rather arbitrary measures are placed on individuals' utilities and on endowments, and since decision-making results from hedonistic economic agents acting independently and for their own sake (individual utility-maximization) in a 'free' market, conflict and/or major disequilibria are bound to arise.

Yet, in the 1970s, the various 'oil shocks' and the ensuing declining profit-rates in industry led the Chicago School of Economists (or 'New Economists') to argue further for less State-interference in economic affairs as a way to revive the Western economies at the time. This followed a Keynesian episode which became increasingly undermined as unable to solve the economic problem of 'stagflation' in Europe and in the US. Consequently, the Neoclassical Economics paradigm was revived at a timely moment – indeed when frequent economic crises occurring between the 1860s and the Great Depression had become but a distant memory – when it was given an additional impetus with the fall of the 'Berlin Wall' in 1989 and the eventual demise of the Soviet model, leading in part to the hegemony of so-called current 'Washington Consensus' (see the chapters by Das, Trescott, Yagi, Cohn and others respectively earlier in this volume).

This paradigm therefore imposed itself as the *only possible paradigm* in Western countries and it was being given further credibility through various attempts at including *equity* and *justice* considerations in mathematical modelling. This was done, for example, by introducing a social 'welfare function' with due recourse to the utility concept and to weighting coefficients of given individual utilities (see Samuelson, 1977). As is the case in such models, weighing coefficients remain grossly arbitrary, implying that these attempts at introducing an ethical dimension in Economics thinking have been 'more a formally elegant way to suppose that a problem is solved rather than a contribution to its solution' (Wolfelsperger, 1999: 181).

Although these contributions do open up a new interesting vista and should not therefore be entirely dismissed, the different attempts at fine-tuning the above paradigm look more like an exercise of clinging to a theoretical model – whatever the economic circumstances; this amounts to fitting a (fragile) theoretical framework to economic reality rather than to using the evolving economic reality, so as to develop a new, more adequate and pertinent, economic paradigm.[7] As argued by Leroux (1999) and by Leroux and Marciano (1999), the work of some prominent scholars writing in the Neoclassical tradition, such as Nobel Laureate Friedrich von Hayek (1899–1992), fits more in the category of 'ideologies', as opposed to that of 'sciences' (see the chapter on Hayek and China earlier in this volume). Karl Marx (1818–1883) and Friedrich Engels (1820–1899) in their work, *The German Ideology* (1932) show how 'ideology' is the direct expression of class interest and how its ultimate objective is to serve the interests of a specific group, namely the *ruling class*. In the end, ideology allows a given economic and political system that serves the interests of a ruling class, to *reproduce* itself.

In summary, it can be inferred that, in spite of all, the Neoclassical Economics paradigm has been quite successful in driving the course of economic policy-making in Europe, in North America as well as in other parts of the world over almost 150 years. It has survived, and perhaps even been reinforced by, the limited Keynesian post-Second World War episode as noted earlier. It has gradually imposed itself, we may argue, as a guiding Economics paradigm in crises-stricken Asian economies and particularly in Japan since the 1990s and other East Asian economies after the 1997 Asian crisis (see the chapters by Das earlier in this volume).

An obvious important question arises at this juncture: to what extent has this paradigm been sweeping away the fundamental principles derived from classical philosophy in Asian countries? Another corollary question would be: will this paradigm survive long after other Western-born global financial crises, such as the 2008 recession? The ensuing sections will try to bring some elements of an answer to these questions.

The philosophical basis of economic thought in East Asia

This section will start by succinctly identifying some key philosophical roots of Economics thinking and policy-making in East Asia, focusing on China and by highlighting the similarities and differences existing between the early European and Asian philosophical schools in terms of shaping Economics therein. The impact of Western ideas since East Asia's opening and modern industrialization during the mid-nineteenth century and the convergence towards the dominant Western Economics paradigm also will be alluded to. The interdependency between Western and East Asian Economic thought will be analysed more comprehensively with a discussion on policy-making in three selected East Asian economies, namely *China*, *Japan* and *South Korea*; this discussion on the extent to which the dominant paradigm has infiltrated itself into policy-making in these economies will revolve around the role of the State. This is because the State is still regarded as an important differentiating factor vis-à-vis the three Asian economies vis-à-vis their Western counterparts.

Philosophical foundations of economic thought in East Asia

This sub-section draws partly from the work of Zhang Dainian (1909–2004), (see Zhang, 2002), but first published in Chinese in the late 1980s and subsequently translated into English some ten years after that. Zhang's very comprehensive work presents a listing of classical philosophical concepts and categories (*zi*) over a long period of time which stretches from Laozi (571–480 BC) to the scholars of the Ming–Qing dynasties (1363–1911), such as Guo Qingfan (1844–1896). It should be noted that since the well-known term of 'relationship' (*guanxi*) did not appear in Chinese philosophical work before 1368, it is therefore not regarded as a 'fundamental concept in classical Chinese philosophy' (Zhang, 2002: xx). Consequently, this term is discarded from Zhang's work and from our analysis here.

For the Economist, the task consists in selecting – in the most possible objective manner – those classical philosophical concepts that help explain the formation of a certain conception of an Economic system in general and of policy-making in particular. In doing so, we will keep in mind the role of the State in policy-making in East Asia (see the chapters by Das earlier in this volume). Zhang's division of these concepts and categories into three main groups, namely metaphysics, anthropology and epistemology, is a useful point of departure (Zhang, 2002). It is from this typology that one can select some fundamental and relevant concepts and categories that still explain today the specificity of the 'Asian State'.

One such important term is *li* (principle) which originally meant the lines visible through a piece of jade. According to Mencius (372–289 BC), 'principle' was meant to refer to the standard of moral conduct. In subsequent extensions, the concept became understood to be both 'that by which x is x' and 'that by which x ought to be x', although no distinction is made between these natural (that is, positive) and normative approaches. Connected to this concept is the term *ze* (rule) which is what is naturally so as opposed to what emanates from the law (Zhang, 2002).

Undoubtedly, a fundamental philosophical concept that has been permeating Chinese culture all along is the *qi* which is listed in Zhang's work under the broad heading 'Metaphysics'. In the eyes of the Western scholar, the word '*qi*' is better explained by the word 'energy' (see Rochat de la Vallée, 2005).[8]

By being at the same time the air that one breathes and any gaseous substance (in its popular understanding) as well as the movement (according to its philosophical interpretation), *qi* is what exists as well as what has the ability to become (Zhang, 2002); it is the principle of life and the life that animates the human body. Each individual is bestowed with the task of keeping the *qi* intact, and since conflict is an obstacle to the good flow of energy or indeed is a waste of energy, conflict must be avoided. This can be done by seizing more opportune circumstances, by displaying flexibility and/or by adapting to the changes facing the individual (see Chaigne, 2008).

As noted by Zhang (2002), *yin* and *yang* (darkness/light) are the two aspects of *qi*, as for example the *qi* of heaven and earth refer to the harmony of cold and heat. According to Kim (1996), the binary concept of the universe in terms of *yin-yang* is indeed another key influential idea in East Asia that has been used to explain change, including historical and socio-economic change. The interaction between the two opposite forces that form a closed system of the universe promotes change and development, with a moving equilibrium which requires a maximum degree of flexibility within the system.

Still listed by Zhang (2002) under the broad heading of 'Metaphysics' but referenced in a sub-category of 'coordinating concepts', the expression *yi ti* (the whole) is another crucial concept for the understanding of the organization of 'bodies', such as the political body and its various components. The concept of *yi ti* implies that all things can be considered as one unit and the concept mirrors the idea of harmony between the parts and the whole (the body). Used in the context of the political body, it implies that the wise ruler is entrusted with the task of securing first the welfare of its people. Although, as mentioned by Kim

(1996), the term 'society' does not have a direct equivalent in Chinese, Japanese or Korean classical thought, groups of individuals can easily be identified such as the family, kin group or clan, village community and so on and, finally, the State (or national family) (see the chapters by Trescott, Yagi and Hong respectively earlier in this volume).

In the same vein, the Chinese ethical concept of *gong* (public interest) is listed under the broad heading of 'Anthropology' (and under the sub-heading 'moral philosophy') and it denotes the idea of transcending the self. This term first appeared in the *Record of Rites* (475 BC to 220 AD) where it is stated that the 'great commonwealth' means that all under heaven is for the general public (Zhang, 2002: 311).[9] For Cheng Yi (1033–1107), the public interest becomes the first principle of morality. Consequently, wealth is despised and its storing for oneself is derisory. In other elaborations of this crucial concept, a clear distinction is made between private and public interests, such as in the Book of Lord Shang (*Shang Jun Shu*, around the third century BC). The sustainability of a State depends on the relationship between *private* and *public* interests. Private interests have to work for the benefit of the State and the public interest consists in governing all under heaven, all rejoicing in the way the State is administered (see the chapters by Lai on China and Sakamoto on Japan respectively in this volume).

High ethical standards by the ruler to the benefit of all, who themselves behave in the manner of 'gentle folk', imply other ethical guiding concepts such as *zhong yong* (moderation and harmony), listed in Zhang's book under 'Anthropology and moral philosophy'. The first Chinese character *zhong* (centre) is a basic concept in Confucian philosophy, and it implies acting in moderation, at the centre, or not falling into extremes. Together, the two characters mean that all things have a norm or a limit, a principle that ought to be applied to daily life.

This brief overview, appraised in the background of the first section, leads to the following conclusions:

i   There is a remarkable continuity in terms of Chinese philosophical thought over two and half millennia in that the concepts of classical philosophy have impregnated human action and that they still shape Asian culture today, despite their evolution in philosophical discourse and an increasing pressure to conform to the dominant Western paradigm since the latter part of the nineteenth century. This explains the plethora of references to Confucianism in academic work on business organization in East Asia (see Nolan *et al.*, 2016), as well as well-known official contemporary slogans such relating to Capitalism 'with Chinese characteristics' (*juyou Zhongguo tese*).

ii   This continuity in China and East Asia is in contrast with a paradigmatic change taking place in Europe up to the nineteenth century, as discussed earlier.

iii The *scientificity* of contemporary economic thinking in Europe in particular and in the West in general is in stark contrast with a still very much value-laden approach in East Asia, an approach which was the norm in Europe before the field of Economics became *elevated* to the status of 'science'.

iv   Many of the Chinese concepts of classical philosophy find an *equivalence* (or are common to) Western classical philosophical/theologian thought; this is the case for example of the *yi ti* concept (the whole) which can also be found in Christian thinking, as in St Thomas Aquinas' work.

v   This implies that with this 'scientification' of Economics, the distance between Asian and European philosophical schools has increased. Here, the distance is best epitomized by the Chinese concept of *gong* (public interest); the view of this by Plato and St Thomas Aquinas is close to the Chinese view – but it is very different from that defended by the so-called Welfare Economics, which sees the public interest simply as an aggregation of private interests, with a collective welfare function being determined on the basis of a mathematical aggregation of different individual welfare functions. However, what the concept of *gong* tells us is that the welfare of 'all under heaven' is more than the sum of the welfare of all individuals. The classical view of this term obviously explains a great deal in terms of the role of the State in China and in other East Asian countries.

Before we venture into this latter part of our study, a summary of all reviewed classical Chinese philosophy concepts and their implications in terms of economic policy-making is suggested in Table 21.1.

The inflow of Neoclassical Economics thinking in East Asia

Unsurprisingly, the exposure of East Asian countries to the West – including the US – since the signing of the 'unequal treaties' from 1842 onwards has resulted in a *one-way flow* of Economic thought: from the technologically and economically 'superior' West to East Asia.[10] Consequently, the opening of East Asia from the mid-nineteenth century nurtured the circulation of foreign ideas and the Neoclassical paradigm could gradually encroach on policy-making in East Asia, including China. In the case of Japan, Sugiyama's work (1994) shows how Western ideas represented an impetus for modernization in the country (see the chapter by Yagi on Japan earlier in this volume).

The selective approach exercised by the Meiji administration from 1868 onwards implied importing concepts of economic laissez-faire from England, combined with notions of popular rights from France, as well as Statist and technological-military ideas from Germany, particularly after its victory over France in 1871. This pragmatic approach contributed to rapid industrialization and to the emergence of a successful capitalist model, if by 'successful' one means the ability of Japan to become a military and economic superpower in the Asian region in the space of only a few decades (see the chapters by Yagi, Smethurst and Ohtsuki and others respectively in this volume).

In China, as argued by Gaulard (2014), the then well-established Western capitalist mode of production characterized by the 'commodification of labour' starts making an inroad in the nineteenth century, and it is given an impetus with the victory of Sun Yat-sen (1866–1915), the first and short-lived President of the

Table 21.1 Implications of Chinese classical philosophical concepts for economic policy-making in East Asia

Concept	Category	Meaning	Economic implication
li (principle)	Metaphysics	Standard of moral conduct	Normative versus positive approach
qi (energy)	Metaphysics	Gaseous substance and movement	Optimum allocation of resources
			Shifting equilibrium (flexibility, adaptability, ability to manage change, pragmatism)
ying yang	Metaphysics (Cosmology)	Opposite forces	Moving equilibrium
			Change, flexibility
yi ti (the whole)	Metaphysics (coordinating concepts)		Sustainable social order
			Individual utility maximization to be in harmony with that of the society/group as a whole
			Social welfare > sum of individual welfares
gong (public interest)	Anthropology (moral philosophy)	1st principle of morality (*cheng yi*)	Strong and enlightened State, acting in the interest of all
zhong yong (moderation, harmony)	Anthropology (moral philosophy)	Sets ethical standard	Importance of the 'centre' as opposed to the extremes
			'Happy medium', pragmatism

Sources: miscellaneous.

new Chinese Republic in 1911. It continues to dominate in the inter-war years. Later, the coming to power of the Chinese Communist Party (CCP) in Beijing, with the so-called 'Liberation' in 1949, by Mao Zedong (1893–1976), does not provoke a *radical break* in terms of economic organization, we may argue, since it did in fact coincide with a remarkable degree of *organizational continuity* compared with pre-Mao times; this is best shown by the fact that Kuomintang/ Guomindang's civil servants of the Republican era massively joined the ranks of China's Communist Party after 1949, and that many factory chief executives became top managers in the now State-owned companies – after receiving a substantial financial compensation against their expropriation (see Bergère, 2007).

Pragmatism continues with the post-1978 economic reforms under Deng Xiaoping (1904–1997), which initiated yet another 'opening-up' of China to the West and to countries further afield. Deng's selective approach towards embracing some specific concepts and elements of Western Economics thinking are summarized by his characterization of 'Developing a Socialist Market Economy with Chinese Characteristics' (*zhongguo tese shehuizhuyi shichang jingji*) (see the chapter by Zhu and Webber on Chinese economic reforms in this volume). Consequently, and in spite of it being labelled 'Communist', Mao's and post-Mao China has, one may argue, been all along characterized in effect by a 'Capitalist' system of production.

This system has been successful in absorbing and blending different economic ideas from different schools (showing its Pragmatism), namely: neo-Marxism under Mao (centralized organization of production); Keynesianism (role of the State in stimulating growth, see the chapter on Keynes in this volume) and the Neoclassical school (commodification of labour during Mao's time; gradual and partial economic liberalization since Deng). Obviously, with China's greater inclusion in the world economy since 1978, the Neoclassical paradigm has tended to become increasingly dominant in China (see chapters by Trescott, Cohn, Zhu and Webber respectively earlier in this volume). According to Gaulard (2014), such a capitalist system is fraught with many *contradictions*, which might only eventually be resolved in a financial and economic crisis.

Besides opening, crises have been another reason why dominant ideas have been diffused to Asia in recent decades. To many (Singh, 2006; Ha and Lee, 2007), Japan's 'lost decade(s)', as well as the 1997 Asian financial crisis, have been interpreted as a proof that some of the Asian economic systems were *under-performing* compared with Western economic systems (see the chapter by Metzler on Japan earlier in this volume).

Crony capitalism, nepotism (see Kim, 1996: 69), low industrial performance, too dominant a State and so on were all seen as reasons for the 1997 crisis (Singh, 2006), which was viewed as signalling the end of the Asian economic miracle. Liberal recipes were brought in, which strengthened the view that Neoclassical based policy-making was the only possible way forward (see Ha and Lee, 2007). This belief subsisted almost unchallenged up until the 2008 crisis.

Implications for policy-making in contemporary East Asia: the role of the State

As can easily be inferred from the above analysis, the harmonious functioning of socio-economic relations – with moderation, pragmatism and inclusiveness – is a core guiding principle of the organization of Asian socio-economic systems. The type of 'production mode' dictates the nature of social relations between individuals as well as between individuals and the State. *The tradition of a strong State is one major element that distinguishes the three East Asian countries from their Western counterparts.* This is not to say that the classical philosophical concepts have been perfectly applied throughout the course of economic development in these three countries over the past centuries. Indeed, from the sixteenth century an inefficient and controversial State inhibited technological, economic and social progress in China (see Gaulard, 2014), whereas a foreign affairs crisis, nurtured by weak leadership and insufficient unity to allow a modern and stable State to emerge may have been 'core-factors' explaining the fall of the Tokugawa period in Japan in the last century but one (see Inkster, 2001). These examples show that the State has not always succeeded in its mission of guaranteeing *harmonious* development, but, despite its crises, the Asian State remains nevertheless today a central actor in economic policy-making in these countries.

In Japan, one important legacy of the Tokugawa period (1603–1868) was a 'weak' bourgeoisie unable to nurture modern industrialization in the country. The newly created Meiji Government in 1868 instilled a number of State-led reforms focusing on infrastructural and industrial development with, for example, the establishment of a nation-wide postal/telegraph network and the foundation of government-owned factories in several industries such as ship-building, steel, chemicals and paper (see Inkster, 2001). The Ministry of Industry was in charge of these new State-led investments, which, for a large part, were sold to the private sector after the financial crisis of the 1870s. This was followed by the formation of strong conglomerates of highly diversified multi-divisional firms, including banking and trading corporations, the *zaibatsu* conglomerate groups, which enjoyed high profits through preferential government support. Although these *zaibatsu* firms were actually smaller than their European (German) counterparts at the time (Miyajima *et al.*, 2003), they allowed Japan to become an economic and military power at the beginning of the twentieth century. Because of their involvement in warfare, the 15 *zaibatsus* were dissolved after the Second World War and their assets redistributed, leading to the formation of what were to be called *keiretsu* groups.

The newly established Ministry of International Trade and Industry (MITI) became the main actor in post-war Japanese industrial policy, acting as a *monopsony* and driving down the cost of foreign imported technology (OECD, 1972). Although the average growth rate of 9.2 per cent per annum between 1951 and 1973 might be explained by the convergence of a few favourable conditions, among which a long 'Kondratiev' wave of technological change driven by the US features (see the chapter by Metzler in this volume), the global dollar-spending power, a cheap and docile labour force and a dynamic demand at home, as well as the role of the State and its relationship to private firms may also have been key drivers in this regard (see Itoh, 1990). This State is neither dominant or coercive nor submissive to private firms and, as time passed, Japanese industrial development became more independent from 'political protection and control' (Itoh, 1990: 162); this demonstrates a large degree of Pragmatism (see the chapters by Yagi and Metzler on Japan respectively in this volume).

In the case of South Korea, the policy of rapid industrialization-through-invitation under President Park Chung Hee (1961–1979) stirred what is known as the 'Korean economic miracle' with growth-rates soaring to 8.9 per cent in 1967, and culminating at 16.9 per cent in 1973 (see Sunoo, 1994). Known as a 'democracy by movement' with reference to the June 1987 Democratic Uprising that put an end to the authoritarian regime, the country enjoyed rapid sustained growth during several decades under a State-led development strategy. State intervention has indeed been pervasive in all domains: capital markets, labour markets, product markets, as well as international trade and finance. For example, in 1964, the South Korean government selected new target-industries, such as textiles and consumer electronics, and the 1973 industrial restructuring programme launched by the Korean government put the emphasis on the development of new priority sectors such as steel and non-ferrous metals, chemicals and petrochemicals, machinery, shipbuilding and electronic industrial equipment. These choices show the ability to adapt to changing economic circumstances. In its 'bigger is better' approach to industrialization, the government used the *chaebol* conglomerate notion as an engine of industrialization. These family-dominated conglomerates – many of them originating from business-government relations during the Rhee regime of the 1950s – consist of tightly linked large and small multiproduct firms (such as Hyundai and Samsung). These firms have benefitted from systematic government policies providing cheap loans, government contracts, and so on (see the chapter by Hong on Korea earlier in this volume).

In China, the strong grip of the State on a more market-oriented economy today is attributed to the long historical tradition of centralization by past emperors. Deng Xiaoping's China transformation from a central planning system to a more market-oriented system has not, nevertheless, diminished the importance of the State. It still continues today to be a 'key actor' in the productive and 'developmental' process of the country. Even though the 1978 economic reforms have allowed the private sector to hold a larger share of industrial assets, value-added and output, the State – that is, China's Communist Party (CCP) – is still very much in control (see Fabre, 2013). What matters is indeed less the size of the State in the economy than its control over key areas, such as finance, for example (see Andreosso-O'Callaghan and Gottwald, 2013). Although not all the newly emerged 100 or so national champions are owned by the State, they fall under the scrutiny of the Party and even though many SOEs have been privatized, the CCP still heavily controls them (see the earlier chapter by Zhang in this volume). Today, Sovereign Wealth Funds, county-owned enterprises (COEs) and SOEs are now major investors abroad.

To sum up thus far, the example of the three East Asian countries denotes:

i   *The existence of a 'Pragmatic' State, shown by an ability to change (from import substitution towards export-led growth), by different evolving priorities (from labour-intensive to capital-intensive and to R&D or high skill-intensive industries) (see Chowdhury and Islam, 1993).*

ii *That State involvement in the early stages of industrial development was a necessary condition for economic growth.*

iii *The existence of a State promotes long-term perspectives, which to say that is a developmental State or a State that has tended to promote a high level of social equality (Low, 2004).*

Yet, several economic and geo-political circumstances have challenged both the supremacy of the State in economic affairs and the application of Chinese philosophical concepts to economic policy-making over the years. *This all suggests that the East Asian States have changed under the influence of their being connected to both Western Economic systems and (modern) thought.*

Conclusions

Economic policy-making in Europe and Asia, we may thus conclude, is intimately delineated by dominant economic schools that have been deeply shaped by philosophers, and by theologians in the case of Europe. We have seen that European (i.e. Greek) and Asian (mostly Chinese) classical philosophies share a number of common features and concepts between them, notably their ethical basis and the concept of a 'virtuous' human-being who acts for the ultimate objective of the common good. In Europe, the 'scientification' of the field of political economy since the seventeenth century eradicated any references to an ethical dimension in economic policy-making, and it led gradually to the triumph of the Neoclassical paradigm maybe in the same way as other scientific paradigms won in other fields (Kuhn, 1962).

By contrast, East Asian countries have witnessed some continuity in terms of economic thinking despite two major disruptive forces: on the one hand, the forced opening of the three countries from the nineteenth century and on the other, the Asian-born and Asian-confined economic crises at the end of the twentieth century. At the time of the 'unequal treaties', two opposing philosophy-based economic systems were indeed visible, when appraised with the eyes of the nineteenth century scholar: a supposedly 'scientific' economic system in the West and a still very much value-laden system in the Far East. The technological superiority of the West was another factor that convinced the three East Asian countries to encourage the diffusion of Western Economic ideas – and to accommodate gradually many elements of this genre of Economics thinking into their policy-making (pragmatically) – and this resulted in *sui generis* East Asian Economic systems, with for example the existence of a strong State. The examination of the role of the State in the three countries we cited (particularly in contemporary China) shows how economic policy-making, impregnated by a certain philosophical tradition, is still rather different from what exists in the West.

However, under the pretence of being 'scientific' and therefore uncontestable, the Neoclassical paradigm appears as being no more than a mere ideology. This is best shown by the fact that this paradigm has been consolidated and fine-tuned for the ultimate purpose of allowing the ruling class (drawn from the spheres of finance and politics) to perpetuate itself. Also, the recurring economic crises of ever increasing amplitudes, culminating so far with the Western-born 'Great Recession' of 2008, signal that the supremacy of the Western Economics paradigm has severely been put to the test, and that the benefits arising from an uninterrupted 'convergence' of East Asian policy systems to the Western system are now being called into question.

To sum up, it might be that the one-way flow of Economics thinking (from the West to Asia) may be coming to an end and that ways forward imply the following: first, in the case of Western countries, the imperative necessity of an exit from ideology and of a more pragmatic approach; second and relatedly, in both cases, a return to respectively the East Asian philosophical tradition and also to the Western classical philosophical one.

Notes

1 Many social scientists writing on the influence of culture on management and on economic growth and policy identify Confucianism as an important explanatory variable, in line with Geert Hofstede's work (Hofstede, 1980). For example, Green and Mendis (2008) see Confucianism as an institution in the case of China, whereas Chaigne (2008) discusses the forces of tradition shaped by both Daoism and Confucianism. Although discredited by Mao Zedong who saw them as being part of feudal traditions, as did Max Weber (1864–1920), Daoism and Confucianism continued to permeate Chinese culture after the proclamation of the People's Republic of China in 1949. Note the recent official revival of Confucianism through the educational sphere since 2007 and through the introduction of a number of very selective teachings by Confucius in current Chinese propaganda (Dotson, 2011).

2 This view has been credited for sowing the seeds of communism in Europe (see Walter, 1975). On Plato's views with regard to the issue of property, see Plato (1950 edition of *The Republic*, Book V, 2).

3 It should be noted that Descartes' thinking is able to reconcile faith and science, since his metaphysics is grounded on the proof of the existence of God and of the human soul (summarized in his famous 'cogito ergo sum') (see Descartes, 1637: 147–153).

4 It is interesting to note that the nascent Neoclassical school exercises a very selective approach to the choice of the economic concepts born in the eighteenth and early nineteenth centuries. Whereas Bentham's utility theory is paramount in Neoclassical economic thinking, Neoclassical economists refute at the same time other concepts and laws developed by the same classical school, such as for example Ricardian 'labour theory of value' which was to become central in Karl Marx's (1818–1883) life and writings.

5 Antoine Augustin Cournot (1801–1877) was actually the first economist to make extensive use of mathematical tools in the field of political economy; his 1838 publication was totally overshadowed by the free-trade dogma prevailing at the time in France.

6 For more on these limitations, one can refer to Deraniyagala and Fine (2001), in the case of trade theories.

7 Inputs from neo-Marxist schools such as the regulationist school are very much marginalized in this debate.

8 To simplify, Zhang (2002) suggests that Einstein's famous formula $e = mc^2$ is the best Western translation of this term.

9 See the *Record of Rites* 9, Evolution of Rites; credited to Confucius, the original text of the *Record of Rites* was subsequently re-worked by several scholars during the Han Dynasty (206 BC–AD 220). Note that the legalists were the major protagonists of the public interest in the sense of reducing a person to a 'mere cipher' (Zhang, 2002: 311). This view conflicts with Confucian philosophy which stresses the moral person in a family setting.

10 This is not to infer that Western scholars remained hermetic to Asian classical thought. However, the supremacy of the Neoclassical paradigm was such that no challenging new idea could displace it at the time. It is interesting to note how, as shown by Joseph Needham's (1900–1885) work (1954), China's influence on the world's knowledge started to decline at about the time when modern science and technology were developing in Europe.

References

Andreosso-O'Callaghan, B. (2011). 'Economic Crises, Neoclassical Theory and Paradigmatic Change'. In *The Transformation of Europe and Asia*, edited by B. Andreosso-O'Callaghan and P. Herrmann, Chapter 2, 23–41, Hauppauge, NY: Nova Science Publishers.

Andreosso-O'Callaghan, B. and J. Gottwald. (2013). 'How Red is China's Red Capitalism? Continuity and Change in China's Financial Services Sector During the Global Crisis'. *Asia Pacific Business Review* [Special Issue 'Demystifying Chinese Management: Issues and Challenges], 19: 444–460.

Bentham, J. (1789). *The Principles of Morals and Legislation* (2005 Edition). Boston, MA: Adamant Media Corporation.

Bergère, M.-C. (2007). *Capitalismes et capitalistes en Chine*. Paris: Perrin.

Chaigne, C. (2008). 'What Do Law, Conflict and Trial Mean for Chinese Firms?' In *Asia and Europe: Connections and Contrasts*, edited by B. Andreosso-O'Callaghan and B. Zolin, 347–357, Venice: Libreria Editrice Ca' Foscarina.

Chowdhury, A. and I. Islam. (1993). *The Newly Industrializing Economies of East Asia*. Routledge: London.

Cournot, A. (1838). *Recherches sur les Principes Mathématiques de la Théorie des Richesses* (Œuvres Complètes, Tome VIII, 1980 Edition). Paris: Librairie J. Vrin.

De Montchrétien, Antoine. (1615). *Traité de l'Economie Politique* (1889 Edition). Paris: Plon, Nourrit.

Denis, H. (1983). *Histoire de la Pensée Economique* (7th Edition). Paris: Presses Universitaires de France.

Deraniyagala, S. and B. Fine. (2001). 'New Trade versus Old Trade Policy: A Continuing Enigma'. *Cambridge Journal of Economics*, 25: 809–825.

Descartes, R. (1637). *Discours de la Méthode*, in: *Oeuvres et Lettres* (1953 Edition), Bibliothèque de la Pléiade, Part IV, 147–153, Paris: Editions Gallimard.

Descartes, R. (1644). *Les Principes de la Philosophie*, in: *Oeuvres et Lettres* (1953 Edition), Bibliothèque de la Pléiade. Paris: Editions Gallimard.

Dotson, J. (2011). 'The Confucian Revival in the Propaganda Narratives of the Chinese Government'. US–China Economic and Security Review Commission Staff Research Report, 21 July, Washington, DC.

Fabre, G. (2013). 'The Lion's Share: What's Behind China's Economic Slowdown?' Fondation Maison des Sciences de l'Homme, Paris, Working Paper, No. 53, October.

Fisher, I. (1892). *Mathematical Investigations in the Theory of Value and Prices* (1961 Edition). New Haven, CT: Yale University Press.

Gaulard, M. (2014). *Karl Marx à Pékin – Les racines de la crise en Chine capitaliste*. Paris: Editions Demopolis.

Green, L. and P. Mendis. (2008). 'Does Culture Matter in Hindu and Confucian Economies?' *Global Economic Review*, 37: 429–445.

Ha, Y.-C. and W.-H. Lee. (2007). 'The Politics of Economic Reform in South Korea – Crony Capitalism after Ten Years'. *Asian Survey*, 47: 894–914.

Hales, John. (1581). *A Discourse of the Commonweal of this Realm of England* (first printed in 1581 and commonly attributed to William Stafford; 1954 edition). Cambridge: Cambridge University Press.

Harris, J. A. (2015). *Hume: An Intellectual Biography*. Cambridge: Cambridge University Press.

Hofstede, G. (1980). *Culture's Consequences: International Differences in Work-Related Values*. Beverly Hills, CA: Sage Publications.

Hume, D. (1751). *An Enquiry Concerning the Principles of Morals* (1998 Edition, ed., T. L. Beauchamp). Oxford/New York, NY: Oxford University Press.

Inkster, I. (2001). *The Japanese Industrial Economy: Late Development and Cultural Causation.* London: Routledge.

Itoh, M. (1990). *The World Economic Crisis and Japanese Capitalism.* London: Macmillan.

Johnson, E. A. J. (1937). *Predecessors of Adam Smith: The Growth of British Economic Thought.* New York, NY: Prentice Hall.

Kim K.-D. (1996). 'Towards Culturally "Independent" Social Science: The Issue of Indigenization in East Asia'. In *Sociology in East Asia and its Struggle for Creativity,* edited by S.-H. Lee (Proceedings of the ISA Regional Conference for Eastern Asia, Seoul, 22–23 November, Chapter 5, 63–72).

Kuhn, T. S. (1962). *The Structure of Scientific Revolutions.* Chicago, IL: Chicago University Press.

Leroux, A. (1999). 'Idéologie et science'. In *Traité de philosophie économique,* edited by A. Leroux and A. Marciano, 17–43, Bruxelles: De Boeck and Larcier.

Leroux, A. and A. Marciano. (1999) (eds). *Traité de philosophie économique.* Bruxelles: De Boeck and Larcier.

Low, L. (2004) (ed.). *Developmental States: Relevancy, Redundancy or Reconfiguration.* Hauppauge, NY: Nova Science Publishers.

Marx, K. and F. Engels. ([1845] 1932). *The German Ideology.* New York: International Publishers; Moscow: Marx-Engels Institute.

Miyajima H., Y. Omi and N. Saito. (2003). 'Corporate Governance and Performance in Twentieth-Century Japan'. *Business and Economic History On-line,* 1: 1–36.

Mun, Thomas. (1621). *A Discourse of Trade from England unto the East Indies* (1930 edition). New York: The Facsimile Text Society.

Needham J. (1954). *Science and Civilization in China.* Cambridge: Cambridge University Press [volumes cover 1954–2008].

Nolan, J., C. Rowley and M. Warner. (2016) (eds). *Business Networks in East Asian Capitalisms: Enduring Trends, Emerging Patterns.* London: Elsevier.

OECD (1972). *Industrial Policy in Japan.* Paris: OECD.

Plato [Platon]. [1950 edition]. *La République.* In *Oeuvres Complètes,* Bibliothèque de la Pléiade, Paris: Editions Gallimard, Volume 1.

Proudhon, J. (1846). *Système des Contradictions Economiques ou Philosophie de la Misère* (1850 Edition). Paris: Garnier Frères.

Rochat de la Vallée, E. (2005). *A Study of Qi.* London: Monkey Press.

Samuelson, P. A. (1977). 'Reaffirming the Existence of "Reasonable" Bergson-Samuelson Social Welfare Functions'. *Economica,* 44: 81–88.

Sen, A. (1987). *On Ethics and Economics.* Oxford: Blackwell Publishing Company.

Singh, A. (2006). 'Corporate Governance, Crony Capitalism and Economic Crises: Should the US Business Model Replace the Asian Way of "Doing Business"?' Centre for Business Research, University of Cambridge, Working Paper, No. 329.

Smith, A. [1759] (1790). *The Theory of Moral Sentiments* (1790 Edition). London: A. Millar.

Smith, A. [1776] (1880). *An Inquiry into the Nature and Causes of the Wealth of Nations,* edited by James E. Thorold Rogers (2nd edition, 1880). Oxford: Clarendon Press, 2 vols.

Sugiyama, C. (1994). *The Origins of Economic Thought in Modern Japan.* New York, NY: Routledge.

Sunoo H. H. (1994). *20th Century Korea*. Seoul: NAMAM Publishing House.

Walras, L. (1860). *L'économie politique et la justice: Examen critique et réfutation des doctrines économiques de M.P.J. Proudhon*. Paris: Guillaumin.

Walras, L. (1874). *Eléments d'Economie Politique Pure ou Théorie de la Richesse Sociale* (1976 Edition). Paris: Librairie Générale de Droit et de Jurisprudence.

Walter, G. (1975). *Les origines du communisme: judaïques, chrétiennes, grecques, latines*. Paris: Petite Bibliothèque Payot.

Wolfelsperger, A. (1999). 'L'économie normative comme éthique minimaliste'. In *Traité de philosophie économique*, edited by A. Leroux and A. Marciano, 171–196, Bruxelles: De Boeck and Larcier.

Zhang, D. (2002). *Key Concepts in Chinese Philosophy*. New Haven, CT: Yale University Press.

22 Concluding remarks

Culture, ideas and Western Economics in East Asia

Malcolm Warner

Introduction

We have, throughout this edited volume, focussed on the *primacy of ideas*, perforce those which have consequences in the 'real world' on both events and people. The most famous economist of all time, Adam Smith (1723–1790) refers to 'theories of *political oeconomy*' [*sic*],[1] in *The Wealth of Nations* (1776), but only in passing and only three times; he notes that 'different theories ... have had a considerable influence, not only upon the opinions of men of learning, but upon the public conduct of princes and statesmen' (1776: Book I, 12). A philosopher's 'duty', speaking broadly, wrote Karl Marx (1818–1883) is not just to use ideas to 'interpret' the world but to 'change' it, words also carved on his tomb in Highgate Cemetery in London (Marx, [1854] 1969: 15). In more recent times, another well-known economist, John Maynard Keynes (1883–1946) in turn noted 'The ideas of economists and political philosophers, both when they are right and when they are wrong, are more powerful than is commonly understood' (Keynes, 1936: 383).

Ideas had flowed in both directions between 'East' and 'West' for millennia, ranging from ancient religious beliefs to modern scientific concepts, just as material goods were shipped in their train across the 'Silk Roads'[2] linking the land-mass continents. Joseph Needham (1900–1995), the Cambridge historian of science, has shown in extraordinary detail how a *two-way* traffic evolved across the centuries between China and the West (see Needham, 1954). But 'China's influence on the world's knowledge started to decline at about the time when modern science and technology were developing in Europe' (see Andreosso-O'Callaghan's chapter in this volume, note 11).

Initially, East Asian (mainly Chinese) ideas had been taken up by European Enlightenment thinkers in the eighteenth century (see Clarke, 1997) and these are said to have shaped Western Economics thinking at that time, taking the case of the French Physiocrat economist, Francois Quesnay (1694–1774) a physician to the Royal Court at the time, as an example. He proposed a philosophy of 'natural order' which would bring prosperity to France, as he thought it had done so in China (see Jacobsen, 2013). He argued in his *Le Despotisme de la Chine*, written in 1767, that 'Oriental Despotism' might be a model for the West. It is even said that the notion of 'laissez-faire', or 'laissez passer' associated with his line of thought – but coined by his colleague, Vincent de Gournay (1712–1759) – had 'Daoist' origins – in terms of the philosophy of 'wu-wei' meaning namely 'to do nothing' – but this remains a moot point (see Gerlach, 2005). In turn, we can note that Adam Smith in fact wrote about China long before the 'Middle Kingdom' knew anything about him (see Warner, 2014: 38). In fact, he mentions China 63 times in *The Wealth of Nations* (1776), and the East Indies on 56 occasions but only refers to Japan in eight instances.

It is ironic that Karl Marx (*Makesi*) (1818–1883) who only knew of the 'Middle Kingdom' tangentially over a century and a half ago, wrote about it quite often – as a commentator on international affairs in the *New York Daily Tribune* from 1852 to 1861 – as well as at other times with his lifelong collaborator Friedrich Engels (*Engesi*) (1820–1895) acting as 'ghost-writer' (see Marx, 1853). This was some years before he published the first volume of *Das Kapital/ Capital* in 1867 and 'well before the Chinese knew anything at all about the said Dr Marx' (Warner, 2014: 4). In the first volume, he only refers to China four times however, to Japan just three and the East Indies a mere two.

In due course, Western ideas became known outside the countries in which they originated and eventually were passed on to East Asia (see the chapters by Das, Trescott, Yagi, Hong and Rasiah and others respectively, in this volume). New Economic notions spread very quickly during the age of the Enlightenment across the Atlantic and to Europe, even to Russia. Smith's two major works, *The Theory of Moral Sentiments [TMS]* (1759) and particularly *The Wealth of Nations [WN]* (1776) in time found their respective readerships.[3] As there were close links between Britain and France, Smith had visited Voltaire, (François-Marie Arouet, 1674–1778), at his home in Ferney. The latter *philosophe* was one of the early European thinkers to interpret history in terms of Economics, although his views were mainly expressed piecemeal. As well as the aforementioned Quesnay (see Vignery, 1960), Smith kept in touch with other economists on the Continent but went on to criticize their notions of 'Mercantilism' and 'Physiocracy'.

The influence of Smith thus spread across Europe; his books were well-received in Germany, for example, at first – if later superseded by the works of Friedrich List (1789–1846), who emphasized the role of the State in national development (see Tribe, 2007), as well as those of Marx whose critique of the capitalist system was to attract attention from its radical intellectuals (see Kurz et al., 2011). As Joan Robinson (1903–1983) notes, such views 'bear the stamp of the period when it was conceived' – comparing Marx, Marshall and Keynes (Robinson, 1960: 1). After a few decades, these new notions spread to the 'East', many thousands of miles away, by land and by sea, to the region we have focussed on, to initially Japan and then China (see the chapters by Liu, Trescott as well as Metzler and others respectively in this volume).

It was shown earlier in this edited collection how Japan was the first to encounter Western 'modernity' in a significant way in the mid-nineteenth century but it had earlier learned a good deal from the Netherlands by way of what was known as 'Ranguku' in the seventeenth century (meaning literally 'Dutch study' from the early visitors who occupied the trading-post of Dejima quarter of Nagasaki in Japan and by extension 'Western learning'). New scientific knowledge and technologies from the West had significantly passed through this portal (see Jansen, 1984). But the movement became obsolete after the British and American incursions occurred after the last decades of the Tokugawa regime (1853–1867). Later, Japanese students were sent to the Netherlands and they soon brought home Western Economics[4] (see the chapter by Ohtsuki in this volume) with 'a disproportionate significance for the development of economics in the Meiji period' (Morris-Suzuki, 1989: 49). Other European influences were to prevail. Japanese scholars were acquiring a working knowledge of English, French or German (1989: 50).

Indeed, Japan was to be ahead of most of East Asia by a long-ish chalk in embracing the 'new'. In order to stand up to the West, it had to have the 'right' tools, indeed 'Western' ones in order to do this. It was thus to institutionalize the 'Rich State and Strong Army Policy' (*fukoku kyohei*) of the Meiji regime over the period 1868–1912, which was originally taken from an ancient Chinese text of the Warring States period of the Zhou Dynasty from 475 BC onwards.

Similarly, Western economic ideas were translated into Japanese somewhat more quickly than in the Chinese case (see the chapter by Yagi in this volume). Japan also had a literacy-rate of 40 per cent, possibly comparable to Western Europe in 1868, whereas China achieved only around 5 per cent. Smith's *The Wealth of Nations* was substantively translated into Japanese by 1882 (see the chapter by Sakamoto in this volume) but a comparable rendering in China did come somewhat later, in 1902 (see the chapter by Lai in this volume). Both of these renderings were treated with much intellectual enthusiasm at the time but were only intelligible to an elite audience (Borokh, 2012).

Western Management ideas also spread alongside Economics, first to Japan, then to China, as in the case of the work of US theorist and practitioner, Frederick Winslow Taylor (1856–1915) (see Warner, 1994). His main book was entitled *Principles of Scientific Management*, published in 1911 (Taylor, 1911) and initially translated into Japanese by Yukinori Hoshino in 1912 and later into Chinese by Mu Xiangyuin in 1916 (see Morgan, 2003). Sun Yat-sen's Industrial Plan (*shiye jihua*), a form of Taylorism on a macroeconomic scale, came out originally in Chinese in 1921 and in English a year later (Sun, 1922), as *The International Development of China*, as an early step in articulating an integrated economic development plan for a unified nation (see Warner, 2014).

Culture and diffusion

Some observers take *the nation-state* (or national culture) as the focal point for the study of the diffusion of Economic Ideas. As one writer points out, 'the idea of national traditions and economic understanding has a notable if controversial history' (see Barnett, 2015: 3). In this context, a country's *culture*[5] may be regarded as a significant intervening variable in determining how economic ideas are adapted to national settings (see Rogers, 1962; Hofstede, 1980; Hodgson and Knudsen, 2010; Warner, 2014). In the international transmission of ideas in the nineteenth and twentieth centuries largely flowing from West to East, there was almost always an almost Darwinian adaptation of Economics notions to local circumstances, as these new notions were *selectively* taken up and implemented (see Ma and Trautwein, 2013: 2). Writings on Western Economics were enthusiastically welcomed, particularly when the host-culture was receptive and foreign ideas are soon 'incorporated' into the corpus of 'tradition' (Morris-Suzuki, 1989: 3).

Translations were sometimes only approximate rendering of the original. The literary polymath, George Steiner (1929–) notes that:

> [T]he complete translation, the definitive insight and generalization of the way in which the translated language relates word to object would require a complete access to it from the translator. The latter would have to experience a total mental change.
>
> (1975: 309)

As has been observed by scholars recently the process of diffusion, whether in the original or in translation, was rather a 'flux' of economic ideas making any generalization 'difficult, even impossible' (Kurz *et al.*, 2011: 3). Such works had to be easily understood by their readership in this process of popular dissemination, as well as by the scholars of the elites. As English did not become the world language until the twentieth century, Smith and others were sometimes read in French, German, or other European language versions (Morris-Suzuki, 1989: 43) but it is hard to estimate actual numbers here (Kurz *et al.*, 2011: 4).

We may indeed speak of linguistic 'Silk Roads', with *translation* a key mechanism in the transfer of ideas. The earliest renderings from the original languages, first in Japan (later in China), were frequently of *glosses* of these major publications, although sometimes of minor authors.[6] *Substantive* translations of original works into Japanese did not appear until the 1880s, with Adam Smith's *The Wealth of Nations* in 1882 and its selective rendering into Chinese in 1902, as noted above (Xie, 2009). But no extensive translations of David Ricardo (1772–1823) or Karl Marx appeared in the Meiji period. The first of these authors was known in Japan at that time only indirectly or through commentaries, although John Stuart Mill (1806–1873) and Thomas R. Malthus (1766–1834) had already been translated (see Takenaga, 2016).

An appropriate *terminology* appeared to be a problem. The importation of the new science required coining an ideogram for 'Economics'. In ancient China, the economic focus had been on '*Fu guo xue*' or 'country-enrichment study' (Zhao, 2014: 68). There was then a tension for centuries between the notions of 'state enrichment' and 'people enrichment', with a further complication in terms of the Confucian one of 'family enrichment'. The Japanese used the term '*keizai*' to refer to the economy for a long time, derived from '*keikoku saimin*' meaning 'administering the nation and alleviating the suffering of the people' mainly in the Tokugawa period; but its meaning was far from modern definitions and usage (Morris-Suzuki, 1989: 13). They also invented the term *jingji xue* using Chinese characters for what we now call 'Economics'. The first character had meant 'governing the world' or 'national governance' during the Ming and Qing periods and the second, 'study'. Words like 'supply' and 'demand' did not exist in Japanese, or other Oriental languages, so new terms were invented, '*kyoshu*' (provide) for the first of these and '*bejuyo*' (take) for the second (Morris-Suzuki, 1989: 43).

After its introduction in academic curricula in Japan with the introduction of modern universities after 1870 and then with their equivalents in China, it was eventually to mean Western Economics exclusively in its usage, based on *abstraction, individuals* and *laws*, 'all three approaches distinct from the past' (Campagnolo, 2013: 108). After 1911, Sun Yat-sen proclaimed that Economics should indeed be referred to as '*Jingji*' and so it has been ever since (Cheng *et al.*, 2014: 3). Qingzeng Tang (1902–1972) in his seminal *History of Chinese Economic Thought* (1936) went so far as to state 'that it was not just the name that came from China but also very origin of the subject itself' (cited in Cheng *et al.*, 2014: 5), as Sun himself had insisted earlier.

A cultural explanation

Looking to an explanatory mechanism, one might argue that 'Culture', whether societal or national (see Hofstede, 1980) may act here as an *intervening* variable (as noted earlier) in the diffusion of Western Economics and in turn may work as a *filter*. The 'nation' defined by 'language, culture, customs and ways of life' was a key idea put forward by the German Enlightenment thinker, Johann Gottfried (after 1802: von) Herder (1744–1803), a predecessor of Friedrich List (1789–1846) an economist who emphasized the 'nation-state' in Economic theory (see Szporluk [*sic*], 1991: 92). In 1772, Herder published his influential work, *Treatise on the Origin of Language*; his view of History consisted on nations learning from each other and that self-realization came from identifying with the nation (1991: 93).

In a suggestive essay, a Japanese scholar, Wakatabe (2014) refers to the 'cultural context of economics' (2014: 137). He notes Hall's model which focusses on *relationships to existing theories, nature of the national economy, associations with similar theories and exponents* and *administrative biases* (1989: 371). But we must also look not only in terms of conventional characteristics, as well as ideas, theory and analysis and so on but also place them in their historical and institutional contexts (see Coats, 2000: 1). National cultures still do continue to have a major influence on diffusion, although such influence may now be somewhat weakened by globalization (see Barnett, 2015: 3–6).

We may also point to a *dual* transmission of ideas within a region, as in the case of translations of Western books by one country – *and re-translation* – to another as noted earlier, say, from English to Japanese and later being rendered into Chinese or another local language (see Lai, 2000). In this regard, Japan may be said to have acted as an intellectual 'middle-man' in this process. This was also true in the Korean case where many works were translated from the Japanese versions (see the chapter by Hong in this volume). However, later, the spread of English as a *lingua franca* of economics meant books could be published and read almost simultaneously in East Asia with North America and Europe. Places where university teaching was in English, such as Hong Kong, Singapore and Taiwan mostly in the second part of the last century, facilitated this process, as opposed to the early days in China and Japan.

A five-stage model

The specific model of the diffusion of ideas we would like to put forward here, is a *five-stage* (possibly linear) one. In Stage 1, there is a *'finder'* who goes abroad to study and brings back what he believes are 'interesting' foreign-language works, or someone interacting with traders and missionaries locally and comes across imported books and tracts; in Stage 2, we find a *'popularizer'* who starts to translate such works incorporating these ideas; in Stage 3, there is an *'ideas-champion'* who produces definitive translations of the major works and promotes them; in Stage 4, we may see a *'guru'* who begins to systematically teach students locally about these new theories and practices; and last, in Stage 5, there is a *'policy-maker'*, who takes the knowledge in the above four stages and applies it to public policy.

There are sometimes instances of where more than one of these roles may be performed by the same person but by and large only a few people come to mind who encompass all five of them. In the case of Japan, Yukichi Fukuzawa (1835–1901) encompasses most of them. His student, Eisaku Ishikawa (1858–1887) produces a Japanese translation of the *Wealth of Nations* (1776) for the first time in 1882–1888. A journalist, Oshima Sadamasu (1854–1914) also translated a number of the key works of Malthus, Jevons and List around this time (see Morris-Suzuki, 1989: 50).

In China, a young aspirant scholar, Yan Fu (1854–1921), who was studying in London at the Royal Naval College on the River Thames at Greenwich, has a comparable role, plus or minus (see Wang, 2009), when he translates the same Smith work into Chinese in 1902, as noted above, which was to become known as the *Origin of Wealth (Yuan fu)*, as well as introducing the ideas of Darwinian 'natural selection' around the same time by way of a version of Thomas Huxley's (1825–1895) *Evolution and Ethics (Tianyan lun)* in 1898 (see the chapters by Lai as well as Sakamoto respectively in this volume). As we shall note later, the translation of Darwin's *Origin* (1859) attracted much attention in both China and Japan.

During his years in London, he became acquainted with China's first ambassador, Guo Songtao (1818–1891), and despite their age and status differences became close friends. An eminent American sinologist, Benjamin Schwartz (1916–1999) mentions in his biography of Yan (he calls him 'Yen') that 'they often spent whole days and nights discussing differences and similarities in

Chinese and Western thought and political institutions' (Schwartz, 1964: 29). Zhang Yuanji (1867–1959), an eminent Chinese reformer of the period, was an ardent promoter of Western works in translation (see Reed, 2004: 169ff.) at first in the Nanyang Institute which published the translation of Smith's book and then the Commercial Press, soon to be the largest publishing house in modern China in Shanghai and later in Beijing which published a host of others. For example, Charles Darwin's *On the Origin of Species* (1859) was translated by Ma Junwu (1881–1940) as *Wu zhong qi yuan* into Chinese in 1920 (see Darwin, 1920), although a few decades earlier by Senzaburo Tachibana as *Seibutsu shigen* into Japanese in 1896 (Darwin, 1896).

Dates of translations

At this point in our discussion, we need to look at the specific *dates* of the original publication of particularly well-known works in the field of Economics, as well as those of their translation into East Asian languages. In some cases, there may well be a significant gap in time between the first and the second of these. In other cases, the work may be found in its original language but the translation may be much quicker. Many works were first translated into Japanese and then into Chinese from that source, particularly around 1900. Half the modern loanwords in Chinese are 'said' to be of Japanese origin and many Chinese are apparently unaware of this origin (Wong, 1979: 5). There may well even be a *lag* of a century or more in some cases, as we noted earlier but later this narrows, as in the case of Japan in the interwar years (see Morris-Suzuki, 1989: 93). Scholars have also concerned themselves about the very *nature* and *quality* of the translations, whether literal or with explications and so on (see Clements, 2015, on early translations of Western works in early modern Japan; Luo and He, 2009 on the Chinese equivalents).

Translations of Western Economics works into Chinese by foreign-trained economists, who were recent 'returnees', were at full-speed ahead in the 1920s according to a well-known authority (see Trescott, 2007). This source lists 30 major works for the period 1920–1949 but excludes textbooks (2007: 5, table 1–3). Apparently, over 500 translations took place over the years 1919–1948, the bulk Western, a number Japanese and a few Russian (2007: 317, note 6).

If we take a number of 'key' cases, Adam Smith (1723–1790), Friedrich List (1789–1846), Karl Marx (1818–1883), John Maynard Keynes (1883–1946) and Friedrich Hayek (1899–1992), amongst others respectively, the *date of first publication* of their best-known work in the original language and that of the translation narrows considerably in the case of East Asia, particularly as we approach the present (see Table 22.1). It originally took quite a long time, almost a century, for Smith's *Wealth of Nations*) (1776) to be first translated into Japanese in 1870 as a gloss and then later as a complete version in 1882 in many volumes, as well as substantively in Chinese in 1902, indeed over a century. List's work (1841) is translated into Japanese in 1889 but not into Chinese in 1927. A shorter period ensued for Marx's *Das Kapital* (1867) to be translated

Table 22.1 Timeline of key translations of selected Western Economics classics in East Asia

1776	Publication of Adam Smith's *Wealth of Nations*.
1841	Publication of Friedrich List's *National System*.
1867	Publication of Karl Marx's *Capital, volume 1*.
1882	Translation of Adam Smith (1776) into Japanese.
1889	Translation of Friedrich List (1841) into Japanese.
1902	Translation of Adam Smith (1776) into Chinese.
1924	Translation of Karl Marx (1867) into Japanese.
1927	Translation of Friedrich List (1841) into Chinese.
1936	Publication of John Maynard Keynes' *General Theory*.
1938	Translation of Karl Marx (1867) into Chinese.
1941	Translation of John Maynard Keynes (1936) into Japanese.
1944	Publication of Friedrich Hayek's *Road to Serfdom*.
1947	Translation of Karl Marx (1867) into Korean.
1954	Translation of Friedrich Hayek (1944) into Japanese.
1955	Translation of John Maynard Keynes (1936) into Korean.
1957	Translation of John Maynard Keynes (1936) into Chinese.
1962	Translation of Friedrich Hayek (1944) into Chinese.
1960	Translation of Adam Smith (1776) into Korean.

Sources: miscellaneous.

sketchily into Japanese in 1920 (and fully in 1924) and Chinese substantively in 1938, around a half-century later at first, although the *Communist Manifesto* (1848) written with Engels, was converted fully into these tongues much earlier, in 1904 for the one and 1908 (possibly earlier) for the other respectively (see Ishikawa, 2013). As far as Keynes' *General Theory* (1936) was concerned, it was rendered by Tsukumo Shionoya (1905–1983) into Japanese in 1941, just as the Second World War broke out in the Pacific selling over 7,000 copies initially and another 2,000 copies reprinted (see King, 2012: 325) – and into Chinese officially in 1957 during the 'Let a Thousand Flowers Bloom' (*baihua yundong*) demarche in that period, say, a half-decade or so after in the first instance – and one and a half decades later for the second (Trescott, 2007: 303). Hayek (1944) was translated into Japanese in 1954 and in 1962 into Chinese (see Machlup, 1976). Today, Western Economics and Management books may be published in English the very same day in Tokyo, as in New York and translated within months into the local language.

How rapidly their contribution of a seminal work or a School of Western Economics was to have an impact on the world of affairs is another matter. The influence of particular economists and their work may be seen analytically as either *direct* or *indirect*, or both. It may also be seen as *ex ante*, as well as *ex post*, that is to say that there may be an influence *prior* to the actual publication of a major work as ideas spread around the world through word of mouth or the written press – or *after* their publication later in time in one or more translations. Those who are *policy-makers*, as noted earlier, may hear about a set of ideas which are 'in the air' and translate these into action. Such influences may be seen as 'proto-phenomena'. A good example was 'proto-Keynesianism', as in some countries in the West and Japan (see Hall, 1989) (see the chapters by Smethurst in this volume on the Japanese 'Mr Keynes', Korekiyo Takahashi 1854–1936). The most likely channel of diffusion is possibly both *indirect* and *ex post*. It may be by way of an *ideas-champion* like Yukichi Fukuzawa or Zhang Yuanji, as mentioned earlier, who produces or publishes a translation of a key Economic work, may teach it and help apply it in the policy domain, *ex-post*.

Next, we must point out that the development of an 'Economics profession' in East Asia proceeds *pari passu* with the diffusion of Western Economics, albeit with possible time-lags. We see in the respective chapters in this volume on China, Japan, Korea and so on, who had studied Economics, what was taught and how it influenced thought and policy (see the chapters by Das, Trescott, Yagi and Hong respectively in this volume). Whilst Smith was an overarching influence, the work of List soon takes off, as seemingly appropriate to the Statist requirements of the modernizing trajectory of the new economic regimes (see the chapter by Liu). As for Marx, his influence in departments of Economics has remained strong even today in many places and during the post-1945 period was as strong in both China and Japan for a long period, in spite of the latter being a 'liberal' economy (see the chapters by Yagi, Li *et al.*, Cohn and Metzler respectively). The role of Keynes waxed and waned and his opponents rose to prominence, whether Institutionalist, Neoclassical or Monetarist (see the chapters by Trescott, Yagi and Warner respectively). 'Academic pluralism' was, in time, to take root in post-1978 China (see the chapters by Fang, Cohn, Zhu and Webber, as well as Zhang, respectively).

On the other hand, the diffusion of Economics from East to West in recent times has been somewhat imbalanced. Many Japanese-authored books and a lesser number of Chinese ones on the subject have been published in English or in translation. A number of Chinese and Japanese economists have enjoyed an international reputation (see Chow and Perkins, 2014; Ikeo, 2014), as well as a few from Korea and the NIEs. A notable example has been Masahiko Aoki (1938–2015), who was Professor of Economics jointly at Kyoto and Stanford Universities who wrote about the theory of the Japanese firm (see Aoki, 1988). No Chinese or Japanese economists have, however, yet achieved Nobel Prize status in Economics (although one Indian has, Amartya Sen, 1933–, for his work in Welfare Economics) compared with the set who have gained this in Literature or Science in either country. One Chinese scholar did become the Chief Economist at the World Bank, Justin Yifu Lin (1952–) and is now back as a Professor at *Beida*. He is known for his theory of *New Structural Economics* (Lin, 2012).

But the transmission of knowledge to the West has been possibly as great in the field of Management. In the case of China, books from classical times, such as the work by Sun Tzu or Sunzi (544–496 BC) 'The Art of War' (*Bing Fa*), for example, have become part of Western military academy and even business school curricula. The 'Analects' of Confucius, Kongzi (551–479 BC) has also become applied to both Economics and Management as well as modern works on Confucian Management so-called. In the case of Japan, traditional Samurai and Zen texts such as those of Teu Shwai (To Sotsu San Kwan), who lived in the eleventh century AD (see Phillips, 2009), and those on more recent pre-Meiji practices, such as the 'ringi seido' have been circulated, as well as many works on modern Production Management practices like '*Kaizen*', Quality Circles and the like, which have become de rigueur (see McMillan, 1985).

Conclusions

To sum up, we started with a panoramic look at the spread of ideas from West to East diffused in Asia as a new 'paradigm' in Economics, similar to that in the physical sciences (see Kuhn, 1962). As part of this drive to 'modernity, Western Economic ideas were introduced into and then diffused across East Asia, first to Japan, then later to China, Korea and other countries in the region. However, this process was not entirely one-way or indeed neatly symmetrical.

One scholar (Gong, 2014) sees the diffusion of Western Economics ideas had both a *supply* and *demand* component. He notes that: 'the two words "push" and "pull" indicate, [that] the introduction of western economic ideas into China could be filled with competition between the Western and the indigenous' (2014: 24). It could also be a process 'where Chinese indigenous economic thoughts, instead of being a passive receiver, actively participated in the process' (2014: 25). As a consequence, he continues, 'the introduction of Western knowledge should be in the light of specific social and historical conditions. Translation of economics should integrate classical signification with modern one' (2014: 28).

Whilst *major* works were as yet to be translated – such as those by Adam Smith and such classic thinkers – the process was *first* sparked by the transmission of knowledge by what we dubbed the '*finder*' via minor literature, such as textbooks and manuals. Later, more serious translations took place, often with the help of an '*ideas-champion*'.

In Table 22.1, a timeline of translations lays out the path across *time* – as far as the main writings translated were diffused. Many ideas were also to spread across *space*, spanning the oceans as part and parcel of what we may call early *globalization*, which was set on its course by the economic, political and social momentum of the emerging capitalism of the West. Smith emphasized here that the 'wealth of a nation' was dependent on foreign commerce; Ricardo went to further argue the case for the reciprocal benefits of trade across borders; yet others such as J. S. Mill carried this message on laissez-faire to a wider audience (see Takenaga, 2016).

New ideas were first introduced by missionaries and traders, amongst others, via works in their original languages, starting with Dutch, then English, French and German principally, but translations were needed to impart the new knowledge to the young in the new educational institutions set up at the time, by what we called 'professional academics', such as American polymath, Ernest Fenolossa (1853–1908) who was one of the first to teach Western Economics and Philosophy at Tokyo Imperial University but who was in fact primarily an art historian (Morris-Suzuki, 1989: 47). Few Japanese spoke and/or read Western languages, such as English, in those early days, even fewer Chinese at the time. The chapters in this volume indeed bear witness to the *dialectic* of the intellectual challenge of the exogenous facing up to the adaptation/translation to the indigenous.

As new paradigms or schools of Western Economic Thought were introduced, in the East they were to soon influence the way people thought about the world and to thus change the 'zeitgeist'. They could, in turn, mould new institutions to help modernize the recipient Society and State. They could also shape the way Economics was thought of and taught locally. Last, they could then significantly affect economic policies and policy-making, such as the evolution of the 'developmental state' in their own countries.

Notes

1 Smith uses both spellings, namely the archaic one and the newer one.
2 We use the plural here, as there were many 'Silk Roads' (see Needham, 1954; Warner, 2014: 27; Frankopan, 2015). One may say that it was no single entity but rather a set of veins and arteries of routes leading from China to the Mediterranean, with 'relays' rather than direct trade.
3 The WN was probably better known but it is hard to know what its precise readership figures were.
4 These were mainly from Simon Vissering (1818–1888) who taught law and economics at Leiden University.
5 Sometimes, the term 'societal culture' is used which may differ from a 'national' one. Indeed, a 'nation' may have more than one culture. The Han culture in China is both a societal as well as a national example.
6 Such as the work of the British businessman and writer on Economics, William Ellis, (1800–1881) (see the chapters by Trescott and Yagi respectively in this volume).

References

Aoki, M. (1988). *Information, Incentives, and Bargaining in the Japanese Economy*, Cambridge: Cambridge University Press.

Barnett, V. (ed.) (2015). *The Routledge Handbook of the History of Global Economic Thought*, London and New York, NY: Routledge.

Borokh, O. (2012). 'Adam Smith in Imperial China: translation and cultural adaptation', *Oeconomia*, 2: 411–441.

Campagnolo, G. (2013). 'Three influential thinkers during the "break-up" period in China: Euken, Bergson and Dewey', in Ma, Y. and Trautwein, H.-M. (eds), *Thoughts on Economic Development in China*, London and New York, NY: Routledge, 108–109.

Cheng, L., Peach, T. and Wang, F. (2014). 'Introduction', in Cheng, L., Peach, T. and Wang, F. (eds), *The History of Ancient Chinese Economic Thought*, London and New York, NY: Routledge, 1–32.

Chow, G. and Perkins, D. H. (eds) (2014). *Routledge Handbook of the Chinese Economy*, London and New York, NY: Routledge.

Clarke, J. J. (1997). *Oriental Enlightenment: The Encounter between Asian and Western Thought*, London: Routledge.

Clements, R. (2015). *A Cultural History of Translation in Early Modern Japan*, Cambridge: Cambridge University Press.

Coats, A. W. (ed.) (2000). *The Development of Economics in Western Europe since 1945*, London and New York, NY: Routledge.

Darwin, C. R. (1859). *On the Origin of Species by Means of Natural Selection, or the Preservation of Favoured Races in the Struggle for Life*, London: John Murray.

Darwin, C. R. [1859] (1896). *The Origin of Species [sic] (Semei shigen)*, translated into Japanese by S. Tachibana. Tokyo: Keizai Zasshisha.

Darwin, C. R. [1859] (1920). *Origin of Species [sic] (Wu zhong qi yuan)*, translated into Chinese in 1920 by M. Junwu. Shanghai: Zhonghua Books.

Frankopan, P. (2015). *The Silk Roads: A New History of the World*, London: Bloomsbury.

Gerlach, C. (2005). '*Wu-Wei* in Europe. A study of Eurasian economic thought', *Working Papers of the Global Economic History Network* (GEHN) 12/05, Department of Economic History, London: LSE/London School of Economics and Political Science.

Gong, Q. (2014). '"Jixue" and modernization of Chinese economic thoughts', *International Multilingual Journal of Contemporary Research*, 2: 23–35.

Hall, P. A. (1989). *The Political Power of Economic Ideas: Keynesianism across Nations*, Princeton, NJ: Princeton University Press.

Hayek, F. (1944). *The Road to Serfdom*, London: Routledge.

Hayek, F. [1944] (1954). *The Road to Serfdom [Reijyu he no Michi]*, translated into Japanese by T. Ichitani. Tokyo: Sogensha.

Hayek, F. A. [1944] (1962). *The Road to Serfdom [Tongwang nuyi zhilu]*, translated into Chinese by W. Teng and Z. Zhu. Beijing: Shangwu Yinshuguan.

Herder, J. G. (1772). *Treatise on the Origin of Language [Abhandlung über den Ursprung der Sprache]*, Berlin, n.p.

Hodgson, G. M. and Knudsen, T. (2010). *Darwin's Conjecture: The Search for General Principles of Social and Economic Evolution*, Chicago, IL and London: University of Chicago Press.

Hofstede, G. (1980). *Culture's Consequences: International Differences in Work-Related Values*, Beverly Hills, CA: Sage Publications.

Huxley, T. H. [1893–1894] (1898). *Evolution and Ethics [Tianyan lun]*, translated by F. Yan. Shanghai: Datong Translation Bureau.

Ikeo, A. (2014). *A History of Economic Science in Japan: The Internationalization of Economics in the Twentieth Century*, London and New York, NY: Routledge.

Ishikawa, Y. (2013). *The Formation of the Chinese Communist Party*, New York, NY: Columbia University Press.

Jacobsen, S. G. (2013). 'Physiocracy and the Chinese model', in Ma, Y. and Trautwein, H.-M. (eds), *Thoughts on Economic Development in China*, London and New York, NY: Routledge, 12–34.

Jansen, M. B. (1984). 'Rangaku and Westernization', *Modern Asian Studies*, 18: 541–553.

Keynes, J. M. (1936). *The General Theory of Employment, Interest and Money*, London: Macmillan.

Keynes, J. M. [1936] (1941). *The General Theory of Employment, Interest and Money [Koyo, Rishi oyobi Kahei no Ippan Riron]*, translated into Japanese by T. Shionoya. Tokyo: Toyo Keizai Shimpo-sha.

Keynes, J. M. [1936] (1957). *The General Theory of Employment, Interest and Money [Jiu ye, li xi he huo bi tong lun]*, published in a Chinese translation by Y. Xu. Beijing: China SDX Joint Publishing Company.

King, J. E. (ed.) (2012). *The Elgar Companion to Post Keynesian Economics*, Cheltenham: Edward Elgar.

Kuhn, T. S. (1962). *The Structure of Scientific Revolutions*, Chicago, IL: University of Chicago Press.

Kurz, H.-D., Nishizawa, T. and Tribe, K. (eds) (2011). *The Dissemination of Economic Ideas*, Cheltenham: Elgar.

Lai, C.-C. (ed.) (2000). *Adam Smith Across Nations: Translations and Receptions of the Wealth of Nations*, Oxford: Oxford University Press.

Lin, J. Y. (2012). *The Quest for Prosperity: How Developing Economies Can Take Off*, Princeton, NJ: Princeton University Press.

List, F. [1841] (1889). [Furiidorihhi Risuto], *Ri-shi keizairon*, 2 vols, edited and translated into Japanese by T. Tomita and S. Oshima. Tokyo: Nihon Keizaikai.

List, F. [1841] (1927). *The National System of Political Economy* [*Guojia Jingjixue*], translated into Chinese by K. Wang. Beijing: Commercial Press.

List, F. [1841] (1966). *The National System of Political Economy*, New York, NY: Kelly.

Luo, X. and He, Y. (eds) (2009). *Translating China*, Bristol, Buffalo, NY and Toronto: Multilingual Matters.

Ma, Y. and Trautwein, H.-M. (2013). 'Introduction', in Ma, Y. and Trautwein, H.-M. (eds), *Thoughts on Economic Development in China*, London and New York, NY: Routledge, 1–11.

Machlup, F. (ed.) (1976). *Essays on Hayek*, New York, NY: New York University Press.

McMillan, C. J. (1985). *The Japanese Industrial System*, New York, NY: Walter de Gruyter.

Marx, K. (1853). Articles on China, 1853–1860, Revolution in China and in Europe: 14 June 1853, Marxists.Org website, www.marxists.org/archive/marx/works/1853/06/14.htm (accessed 19 May 2016).

Marx, K. [1867] (1924). *Das Kapital*, 3 vols, Hamburg: Otto Meisner [*Shihon-ron*], translated into Japanese by M. Takabatake. Tokyo: Daito-kaku and Jiritsu-sha.

Marx, K. [1867] (1938). *Das Kapital/Capital*, translated into Chinese in a complete version by Y-N. Wang and T-L. Kuo. Beijing: Foreign Languages Publisher.

Marx, K. [1867, volume 1] (1954). *Capital*, Moscow: Progress Publishers.

Marx, K. [1854, volume 1] (1969). 'Theses on Feuerbach' (1845), Thesis 11, Marx Engels Selected Works, (MESW), Moscow: Progress Publishers, p. 15.

Morgan, S. L. (2003). 'China's encounter with scientific management in the 1920–30s', *The Business History Conference, Business and Economic History On-Line*, www.hnet.org/~business/bhcweb/publications/BEHonline/2003/Morgan.pdf (accessed 12 April 2016).

Morris-Suzuki, T. (1989). *A History of Japanese Economic Thought*, London and New York, NY: Routledge [and Nissan Institute for Japanese Studies, University of Oxford].

Needham J. (1954). *Science and Civilisation in China*, Cambridge: Cambridge University Press [volumes cover the period 1954–2008].

Phillips, F. Y. (2009). 'Zen and management education', *Journal of Centrum Cathedra*, 2: 10–21.

Quesnay, F. (1767). *Le Despotisme de la Chine*, Paris, n.p.

Reed, C. A. (2004). *Gutenberg in Shanghai: Chinese Print Capitalism, 1876–1937*, Vancouver, BC: University of British Columbia Press.

Robinson, J. (1960). *Marx, Marshall and Keynes*, New Delhi: Delhi School of Economics.

Rogers, E. M. (1962). *The Diffusion of Innovations*, New York, NY: Free Press.

Schwartz, B. I. (1964). *In Search of Wealth and Power: Yen [sic] Fu and the West*, Cambridge, MA: Belknap Press of Harvard University Press.

Smith, A. [1776] (1880). *An Inquiry into the Nature and Causes of the Wealth of Nations*, edited by James E. Thorold Rogers, Second Edition, Oxford: Clarendon Press, 2 vols.

Smith, A. [1759] (1882). D. D. Raphael and A. L. Macfie (eds), *The Theory of Moral Sentiments*, New York: Liberty Fund.

Smith, A. [1776] (1902). *An Inquiry into the Nature and Causes of the Wealth of Nations* [*Yuan fu*], translated into Chinese by F. Yan. Shanghai: Nanyang Translation Institute.

Steiner, G. (1975). *After Babel*, Oxford: Oxford University Press.

Sun, Y-S. (1922). *The International Development of China*, London and New York: Putnam, original in Chinese (1921), n.p.

Szporluk, R. (1991). *Communism and Nationalism: Karl Marx versus Friedrich List*, New York, NY: Oxford University Press.

Takenaga, S. (ed.) (2016). *Ricardo and the History of Japanese Economic Thought: A Selection of Ricardo Studies in Japan During the Interwar Period*, London and New York, NY: Routledge.

Tang, Q. (1936). *History of Chinese Economic Thought* [*Zhongguo jingji sixiang shi*], Shanghai: The Commercial Press.

Taylor, F. W. (1911) *Principles of Scientific Management*, New York, NY: Norton.

Trescott, P. B. (2007). *Jingjie Xue: The History of the Introduction of Western Economics into China, 1850–1950*, Hong Kong SAR: Chinese University Press.

Tribe, K. (2007). *Strategies of Economic Order: German Economic Discourse, 1750–1950*, Cambridge: Cambridge University Press.

Vignery, R. (1960). 'Voltaire's economic ideas as revealed in the "Romans" and "Contes" ', *The French Review*, 33: 257–263.

Wakatabe, M. (2014). 'Is there any cultural difference in economics? Keynesian and monetarism in Japan', in Asada, T. (ed.), *The Development of Economics in Japan: From the Inter-war Period to the 2000s*, London and New York, NY: Routledge.

Wang, F. (2009). 'The relationship between Chinese learning and Western learning according to Yan Fu (1854–1921)', *Knowledge and Society Today*, Lyon: Multiple Modernity Project.

Warner, M. (1994). 'Japanese culture, Western management: Taylorism and human resources in Japan', *Organization Studies*, 15: 509–535.

Warner, M. (2014). *Understanding Chinese Management: Past, Present and Future*, London and New York, NY: Routledge.

Wong, S.-L. (1979). *Sociology and Socialism in Contemporary China*, London: Routledge & Kegan Paul.

Xie, S. (2009). 'Translating modernity towards translating China', in Luo, X. and He, Y. (eds), *Translating China*, Bristol, Buffalo, NY and Toronto: Multilingual Matters, 135–156.

Zhao, J. (2014). 'Fu Guo Xue and the "economics" of ancient China', in Cheng, L., Peach, T. and Wang, F. (eds), *The History of Ancient Chinese Economic Thought*, London and New York, NY: Routledge, 66–81.

Index